¿Entiendes?

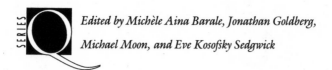

SERIES Q

Edited by Michèle Aina Barale, Jonathan Goldberg,

Michael Moon, and Eve Kosofsky Sedgwick

¡Entiendes?

Queer Readings, Hispanic Writings

Edited by Emilie L. Bergmann and Paul Julian Smith

DUKE UNIVERSITY PRESS

Durham and London 1995

© 1995 Duke University Press

All rights reserved

Printed in the United States of America on acid-free paper ∞

Typeset in Galliard by Tseng Information Systems, Inc.

Library of Congress Cataloging-in-Publication

Data appear on the last printed page of this book.

To Spanish-speaking lesbians,
gay men, and bisexuals

Contents

Acknowledgments

This collection would not have been possible without the enthusiastic collaboration and encouragement of the contributors and Duke University Press. We would like to express our gratitude to Eve Sedgwick, who encouraged us to submit the collection to Series Q. From his warm response to our initial inquiry, Ken Wissoker supported the project and he and Jean Brady shepherded it through the technical details of production. Jean, Ken, and Ken's assistant Richard Morrison have earned our gratitude for making this collection a reality. We would also like to thank George Yúdice and Benigno Sánchez-Eppler for their detailed critical readings of each essay.

We are grateful to the Committee on Research, the Department of Spanish and Portuguese, the Center for Latin American Studies, the Graduate Division, and the Center for German and European Studies at the University of California, Berkeley, for providing funding to defray some of the production expenses of the book. The editors wish to thank Eleta Trejo-Cantwell for her excellent organization of the index. At a crucial deadline during final preparation of the manuscript, Charlotte Rubens was generous with her time and technical expertise; we are deeply grateful for her unfailing humor and friendship.

Through the efforts of Billy Bussell Thompson, we are able to include John K. Walsh's essay "A Logic in Lorca's *Ode to Walt Whitman*" which was written four years before his death in 1990. We thank the University of Chicago Press for permission to include Jorge Salessi's essay, "The Argentine Dissemination of Homosexuality: 1890–1914," previously published in the *Journal of the History of Sexuality*. The Frumkin/Adams Gallery granted permission to reproduce Arnaldo Roche Rabell's painting "For the Record: The Eleventh Commandment" to accompany Arnaldo Cruz-

Malavé's essay. For the illustrations to Yvonne Yarbro-Bejarano's essay, we thank Marcia Ochoa for permission to reproduce her photographs from the series "(sometimes it's the little things that give you away)" and from the triptych "La Ofrenda"; and Esther Hernandez for her serigraph, "La ofrenda," from the cover of *Chicana Lesbians: The Girls Our Mothers Warned Us About*. We also thank Selma Margaretten and Tomás Rodríguez Rapún for locating and providing a reproduction of Rodríguez Lozano's drawing to illustrate John K. Walsh's essay. Finally, we would like to thank all the students and colleagues who expressed unqualified enthusiasm for the volume. Their response shows how much has changed within the few years since lesbian and gay studies have come into existence.

¡Entiendes?

Paul Julian Smith and Emilie L. Bergmann
Introduction

Questions of Homosexuality—Questions of Identity and Community

¿Entiendes?: literally "Do you understand?"; figuratively "Are you queer?"
By giving this collection of critical essays, the first of its kind, a question for
a title, we are not only making a gesture of respect toward those Spanish-
speaking lesbians and gays who use the term themselves (including the
Comunidad Gay de Madrid, who named their newsletter *¿Entiendes?*); we
are also alluding to the radically open nature of a field which is only just
emerging into visibility and whose very existence poses a number of questions (see Foster). One such question is the relation between homosexualities in Spain and in Spanish America. Here it is important to note and
to regret that there are no historical studies for Spanish-speaking nations
comparable to those which exist for Britain and the United States. It is
for this reason that we include, later in the introduction, brief accounts
of some aspects of lesbian and gay history in the Spanish-speaking world.
What is more, the very concept of nationality is called into question by
the prevalence of exile, whether forced or voluntary, among those writers
who have identified as lesbian or gay. Representative of these are Cuban
Reinaldo Arenas, living and dying in the United States; Spanish novelist
Juan Goytisolo leaving Franco's Spain for Paris and North Africa; Mexican Sara Levi-Calderón pressured to leave Mexico City for San Francisco
by her scandalized family; and Cristina Peri Rossi forced to leave Uruguay
for Barcelona. If the writers and performance artists treated in this volume
have a home or a nation it is not a geographical territory but rather the
multiple and varied forms of the Spanish language itself.

If the "field" of Hispanic literatures is necessarily and productively fragmented, then that field's relation to British, U.S., and French queer theory will clearly be problematic also. Some scholars and activists believe that to import U.S. or European concepts and debates into Hispanism is inevitably to compromise the latter and to place it in a subordinate position. However, the question of drawing the line between the native and foreign, proper and alien, is always a complex one. For if certain emphases of English-language discussion of homosexuality (such as the continuing stress on the closet) seem inappropriate to some Spanish speakers, then historically it remains the case that Hispanic queers have not always resisted foreign concepts. For example, as we shall see later, there was in Spain in the 1970s an early engagement with a certain French queer theory derived from Deleuzian antipsychiatry. It is thus inevitable that the contributors to this volume, trained in different intellectual traditions and active in varied institutional contexts, should display a rich diversity of approaches to material that is equally disparate, irreducible to any simple or single approach. Any appropriation of European or North American theory will therefore always also be an incorporation: a process in which the alien is drawn into and absorbed by the body of Hispanic texts and interpreters.

It thus follows that lesbian and gay studies in Hispanism share a number of interests with Anglophone queer theory, but those interests are always inflected by the very particular position of Spanish-speaking cultures and their underrepresentation in countries with English-speaking majorities. Those interests include: the problem of the canon and the rereading of authoritative authors who are frequently the object of uncritical obeisance; the question of history and the retrieval of subject positions and identities throughout a multiplicity of Spanish-speaking cultures and countries; the related theme of ethnicity, and its implications for a Spain composed of autonomous regions and a Spanish America in which national identity has always been the object of debate and has never been assumed, simply, to exist; the problem of biography and the attempt to rewrite a personal history while paying proper respect to the desire of writers (especially lesbian writers) to protect themselves from the dubious benefits of visibility; the questions of the queer reader, and her/his own implication in the text that is read; and finally, the relation between theory and practice, and a call to action by those of us whose work within the academy has sometimes brought us into conflict with the demands of activists. If much queer theory tends (like many of the essays in this volume) to question the continuity and integrity of identity and community, it has troubling implications for the political agency of Spanish-speaking lesbians and gays, often doubly disadvantaged by culture and sexuality, implications which we cannot afford to ignore.

We shall return later to the relation between theory and Hispanic practice, arguing that the social formations of Spain and Spanish America may have anticipated some of the social constructionist tendencies which now dominate queer theory. But let us first look in more detail at the various questions sketched briefly above. Firstly, the canon. In its respect for hierarchy, in its genuflection to the notion of successive "generations" of writers, much criticism of Spanish-language literature shows itself deeply wedded to a gallery of canonic authors. While the celebration of such figures may serve as a focus for cultural pride, it can also tend to silence divergent or dissident readings. One question asked by Mary Gossy in her reading of Cervantes is thus how to account for a canonic text as both a Hispanist and a critical theorist. Her reading of *Don Quijote* in the light of the butch/femme paradigm is thus not merely iconoclastic, though clearly it is in the context of mainstream Cervantine studies (particularly in Spain); it is also scrupulously attentive to and respectful of the letter of Cervantes's text and the integrity of the early modern context in which that text was produced. Likewise, Dan Balderston's analysis of the "fecal dialectic" in Borges may well prove shocking to more traditionalist admirers of a writer who, like Cervantes, has come to a large extent to embody the figure of a nation. Yet his retrieval of Borges's silence, self-censorship, and homosexual panic displays an irreproachable respect for scholarly proprieties, which is clearly Borgesian, most notably in its juxtaposition and examination of textual variants.

But if canonic authors are to be reread within the discursive context which frames their production, then that context remains in many cases to be established. Thus Jorge Salessi and Oscar Montero examine queer lives in turn-of-the-century Buenos Aires and Havana, respectively. Salessi shows how Spanish American experiences did not necessarily shadow North American. For example, the triumph of homosexuality as a discrete identity proclaimed by many U.S. scholars for this period is not borne out by the continuing obsession in Argentine disciplinary literature with the "passive pederast." Moreover, the surveillance and punishment of such individuals are inseparable from a very particular historical moment in which the incorporation of women into the work force, mass migration, and the growth of the metropolis become fused with fantasies of a "homosexual invasion." In his attempt to rebuild queer Havana in the same period, Montero also focuses on the geography of the city and on those public spaces which at once facilitated and problematized same-sex relations. The "centers of clerks," created once more by mass immigration, form a focus for medical, legal, and even literary discourse on the perils and pleasures of pederasty. Cruising with decadent poet and journalist Julián del Casal, Montero retrieves a historical moment in which attention began to shift from the visible forms of "degeneracy" (the queenly conduct of "passive" youths; the morbid bloom of syphilitic sores) to the invisible vice of respectable and manly Cuban citizens, patrons of homosexual prostitution. Respectful, once more of historical specificity, Montero refuses to "out" Casal, but rather examines with sympathy and attention that sentimentalism and stylization of his work which has so often been dismissed without further analysis as "decadent."

Essays which examine the conjunction of nationalism and colonialism in dependent cultures also vindicate once despised forms of expression. This is most clearly the case with José Piedra's espousal of the sissy as hero/ine of the colonial experience. Drawing attention (like the authors of other essays in the collection) to a founding distinction which is not that of hetero and homo but rather insertive and receptive ("bugarrón" and "maricón"), Piedra suggests that national and colonial identities are at once fluid and material, subject to historical change but also brutally physical in their effects. By adopting a willfully playful tone, Piedra also reveals that humor is not to be equated with a lack of seriousness, a lesson that queens and sissies have always known better than their more sober sisters and brothers. In a rather similar way Arnaldo Cruz-Malavé argues that, far from being marginal, transvestism and a certain homosexuality are central to the self-representation of Puerto Ricans as colonial subjects. Moving beyond the stale dialectic of identity and repression, Cruz-Malavé charts an unacknowledged generalization of homosexual desire in diverse examples of contemporary literature. Focusing on a single and disturbing narrative of Puerto Rican homophobia, Agnes I. Lugo-Ortiz shows how the relationships between orality and literacy and between blackness and masculinity take on a particular view in the context of the sense of pervasive loss of authority in the Puerto Rico of the 1960s. Expelled from and finally murdered by the very vocal community to which he had belonged, the silent, effeminate youth of Luis Rafael Sánchez's "¡Jum!" crystallizes questions of desire and nationality, identity and ethnicity. Treating the very different context of Latina cultural production in California, Yvonne Yarbro-Bejarano also charts the complex interaction between nationalities which informs a lesbian body. Yarbro-Bejarano shows how performers such as Mónica Palacios negotiate the bilingualism and biculturalism which is such a rich source of both insight and comedy. More particularly, she pays close attention to the context in which such performances are made and the conditions under which they take on meaning for diverse audiences.

If theatrical performance is always and necessarily communal, then the social articulation of biography is less transparently, but no less pervasively, so. Thus John K. Walsh in his rereading of García Lorca's *Poeta en Nueva York* not only contrasts the standard text with an original version privately printed for the poet's intimates; he also places that text within the communal space of a sexual geography of New York City in the 1920s, showing how a poem often read as the expression of personal anguish is transformed by an awareness of a public space, which was itself subsequently lost. Sylvia Molloy and Licia Fiol-Matta address the interaction of public and private spheres in the figures of Teresa de la Parra and Gabriela Mistral, respectively. Scrupulously erudite, Molloy documents the erasure of de la Parra's relationship with Cuban writer and folklorist Lydia Cabrera from published versions of her life story. But she also argues for the historical specificity of de la Parra's cultural ideology: her reception of Colette and *Mädchen in Uniform* and her nostalgia for a colonial period which was determined by both an undeniable class bias and a quest for lesbian autonomy. Likewise Fiol-Matta seeks neither, disrespectfully, to reveal the supposed "truth" of Mistral's private life nor to disavow her conservative politics. Rather she shows how Mistral's acceptance of the role of pious pedagogue lent her unaccustomed access to the public sphere and a measure of autonomy denied other women. The project of biography in these essays is thus not only to speak the silences of previous accounts, but to reveal the significance of those silences, both the costs they entailed and the possibilities they afforded.

Some contributors make explicit their own voices as queer readers of queer texts. Suzanne Silverman thus addresses Alejandra Pizarnik from a bisexual position, demanding a personal response from a disturbingly complex and violent text. Likewise, Luz María Umpierre (herself a distinguished poet) makes explicit her demand as a Puerto Rican lesbian for a Puerto Rican literature which will fully engage her as reader. Alternately attracted and distanced by Carmen Lugo Filippi's text, Umpierre charts the "tantalizing" process through which a lesbian reader can take her pleasure in a work which may not appear to address her directly.

Choosing to take up an overtly bisexual, lesbian, or gay position clearly engages questions that are at once theoretical and political. And the conjunction of theory and practice is clear in both Brad Epps's and David Román's contributions. Epps not only documents the complex relationship between language and lesbianism in Catalan novelist Carme Riera; he also raises the problematic question of sexual relations between teacher and pupil, one also found in Esther Tusquets's novel *El mismo mar de todos los veranos* [The Same Sea as Every Summer]. Román addresses both the exclusion of lesbians and gay men from some Latino performance platforms in Los Angeles, and those contributions made by them to AIDS activism in other contexts. In its stress on urban geography (from Pico to Downtown) Román's article provides a contemporary update on the historical versions of the queer metropolis elsewhere in the volume and a reminder that scholarship and activism are not mutually exclusive; indeed that scholars can intervene in activism not only as activists, but also as scholars.

From this account of the essays in the collection it is clear that there is a significant community of interest between lesbians and gay men. It remains the case, however, that each group has specific interests to explore. What follows are thus two short historical sketches concentrating on women and men, respectively. Our purpose here is at once to provide concrete examples of some of those general issues raised above and to offer provisional pointers to a social context for some of the texts (both Spanish American and Spanish) treated in the essays.

Questions of Lesbianism—Questions of Feminism

While much of queer theorizing has focused on gay male sexuality (de Lauretis 1991, vi–vii), in the essay, "Chicano Men: A Cartography of Homosexual Identity and Behavior," Tomás Almaguer acknowledges a discursive debt to lesbian writing and gender studies by Chicana feminists, the "first to shatter the silence on the homosexual experience of the Chicano population" and to "candidly [document] the perplexing issues Chicanos confront in negotiating the conflicting gender and sexual messages imparted by the coexisting Chicano and European-American cultures" (90). Almaguer notes a significant distinction observed in Cherríe Moraga's writing: "Male homosexuality has always been a 'tolerated' aspect of Mexican/Chicano society, as long as it remains 'fringe'. . . . But lesbianism, in any form, and male homosexuality which openly avows both the sexual and the emotional elements of the bond, challenge the very foundation of la familia" (91, citing Moraga 11). Any extension of Almaguer's and Moraga's arguments to Latin American contexts requires careful attention to cultural specificities; however, the sexual system Almaguer describes in Mexican society, which precludes the formation of "gay" or "lesbian" sexual identities, in combination with the traditional homophobia of nationalist projects, has a similar effect in other areas of Latin America.

The agenda of repressive political regimes includes gender conformity and, specifically, persecution of homosexuals, as is made obvious in the recent murders of gay men and transvestites in Chiapas (López García 1992, 32). In addition to the violence that threatens gays and lesbians, it would be difficult to overestimate the effects of the confining circumstances of everyday life and family expectations (Almaguer 82). The lesbian threat to "la familia" described by Moraga is met by political reaction to perceived threats against the social order in countries where feminist and lesbian feminist *Encuentros* are convened. The risk of writing and organizing conferences involving all aspects of women's sexuality is obvious in reports of right-wing threats against the sixth feminist *Encuentro,* held in El Salvador from 30 October to 5 November 1993. Despite media campaigns by the right claiming that the *Encuentro* was controlled by the FMLN and international solidarity groups, and associating it with lesbianism and "destruction of moral values," the Organizing Committee reaffirmed its autonomy from political parties as well as its support of freedom of sexual preference (Bouger 1993, 8). The *Encuentros* resist the long tradition of marginalizing lesbians to keep heterosexual women under control. In October 1987, immediately preceding the fourth feminist *Encuentro* held in Taxco, Latin American and Caribbean lesbians organized their first *Encuentro* in Cuernavaca, followed by a meeting in Costa Rica in 1990. Lesbians traveling to these gatherings, confronting the complex security measures, networks of answering machines deferring identities and concealing meeting places and dates, participate in the practice of encoding gay and lesbian texts deciphered in the essays by Licia Fiol-Matta, Sylvia Molloy, Oscar Montero, and John K. Walsh.

Considering the social structures that preclude formation of gay and lesbian identities in Latin American society, and the sexual politics that separate men and women, the appearance of self-identified gay men as well as lesbian feminists organizing, speaking publicly, and publishing on homosexual issues in feminist journals calls for some analysis. A self-defined lesbian feminist who came out in San Francisco, Sandinista Rita Arauz envisions a Nicaraguan lesbian and gay movement that resists U.S. gay cultural imperialism, but bringing about such changes in the present historical reality involves complex theoretical and practical questions (Randall 1994, 278). Under more repressive regimes, where living one's sexuality openly is perceived as a political threat warranting suppression by state violence, the mere questioning of the sex/gender system can be punishable by death: the feminist founder of *fem,* Alaïde Foppa, was assassinated by Guatemalan death squads in 1980. One of the central concerns of Latin American feminist journalism is violence against women as a human rights issue; thus, a legitimizing strategy for articles on lesbianism is to discuss the persistence of physical violence and other forms of repression (López García 1990, 31; Hiriart).

The titles of articles on lesbianism and homosexuality in the Mexican feminist journal *fem* are often encoded. An article by the poet Juan Carlos Bautista, read at the first Forum on Lesbian Human Rights, is deceptively titled "La sonrisa de sor Juana" [Sor Juana's smile]. His topic is not the seventeenth-century nun, whose name, *pace* Octavio Paz, has become a code word for lesbian poetry. The article is, in fact, a survey of contemporary Mexican lesbian poets: Silvia Tomasa Rivera, Rosa María Roffiel (author of the novel *Amora*), Anabel Rodrigo, Nancy Cárdenas, and Sabina Berman. As Cristina Peri Rossi's exiled character Equis in *La nave de los locos* [The Ship of Fools] points out, "Hay que saber mirar" [One has to know how to look] (Vaughn 259). Two articles on lesbian writing in *fem* published in 1993, "Las 'otras' voces de mujeres: narrativa y poesía" [The "Other" Voices of Women: Narrative and Poetry] and "Conversación con Magali Alabau," are by Elena M. Martínez, who writes from what is likely to be a more secure teaching position in New York. Alabau, a Cuban poet, also lives in New York. Despite the obvious risks, Claudia Hinojosa, writing in Mexico, published "Una perspectiva lesbiana del lesbianismo" in 1980 and "Confesiones de una mujer de 'costumbres raras'" in 1983. In her 1990 article on Gay Pride Month, Argentine poet Diana Bellessi contrasts the embattled circumstances of the Comunidad Homosexual Argentina [Argentine Homosexual Community] with the massive U.S. feminist support for gay pride marches.

Everyday, often invisible, lives and struggles, visible and publicized organizing efforts, and the representation of lesbian and gay relationships respond to different circumstances and cultural contexts. In an interview published in 1989, Ana Maria Moix contrasts the "episodes of lesbianism" in writing by Spanish women, with the typical North American "coming out" story or lesbian *Bildungsroman*. Moix explains that these incidents in Spanish fiction present lesbianism as "an option" but never the only option (Nichols 114). While her discussion of lesbianism privileges a bisexual perspective, psychological paralysis resulting from the repression of lesbian desire is at the center of her novel *Julia* (1970). In contrast, Moix addresses male homosexuality in her writing, perhaps reflecting in a Spanish context the distinction between gay men and lesbians that Cherríe Moraga observed about Chicano culture. Moix notes that her brother Terenci publicizes his homosexuality, but she balks at discussing her own sexuality (Nichols 114). As Brad Epps points out in his essay, some Spanish women writers who have published novels and short stories about lesbian relationships make great efforts to distance themselves from their fictional characters. Rosa Montero's article in the Sunday supplement to *El País* (31 October 1993) claims to tell what lesbians are and how they live in Madrid in the 1990s, but Montero writes as an outside observer. While she does not explain how she met the lesbians she interviewed, she depicts the diversity of attitudes and experiences among self-identified lesbians. The history of Catalan and Spanish lesbians, and of women who dissociate themselves from their homoerotic writing, is quite different from that of their Latin American counterparts. If we are fully to understand their position, we should reexamine the historical expressions of homosexuality in Spain.

Questions of Homosexuality—Questions of Hispanism

While there has been much talk of respecting cultural difference in queer theory, there has as yet been little acknowledgment that the process of addressing national and linguistic borderlines requires a slow and patient labor of translation. Ironically, the social-constructionist bias now dominant in English-language queer theory has done little to right that wrong. It is worth considering at this point some widely accepted commonplaces of that social constructionism and contrasting it with the history of homosexualities in Spain.

Sexual preference, once felt to be the essence or "kernel" of personal identity, is now held to be a cultural or historical category, called into being by the medical and legal discourses of the late nineteenth century. Scholars may debate the exact moment of the appearance of "the modern homosexual," but they agree that in this disciplinary model (adapted from Foucault) homosexuality is not repressed but is rather called into being by those social structures which cause it to be ever on the margins of visibility: neither completely hidden (and therefore impossible to control) nor wholly apparent (and thus socially sanctioned). With the shift from essence to construct, then, comes a shift from being to knowing, ontology to epistemology. And with the now familiar stress on gender as performance has come a parallel move from identity to activity: from butch/femme relations to drag queens and voguing, performance has lost its negative associations of "inauthenticity" and been revalued as a parodic redirection of heterosexual norms. In this critique or subversion of identity, modern western homosexuality is often contrasted with forms of desire in antiquity, in early modern Britain, or in African or Asian cultures in which the use of such terms as "homosexual" or "gay" might seem anachronistic or Eurocentric (Halperin). But of what value is this recent Anglo-American critique of identity (also visible in the explosion of categories of self-proclaimed deviants embracing the label "queer") for those cultures in which sexual preference has never been the basis for identity, in which no political or social community has been constructed around same-sex desire? We would argue that this is the case of Spain, and perhaps (though this remains to be established), of parts of Spanish America.

It may be no accident that the history of male homosexuality in Spain has followed a reverse movement to that of the United States and the United Kingdom. Under the Napoleonic Code of the nineteenth century, homosexuality was not a crime. It was, ironically, under the Penal Code of the Republic that male homosexuality was made illegal, when combined with "public scandal" or "corruption of minors" (Smith 7). Under the Franco regime legal repression became progressively harsher. Revisions to the notorious Ley de Vagos [Law of Idlers] of 1953 rendered known gay men and lesbians subject to "security measures." Justification for the supposed increase in vice in the period was based on the "recruitment" of young men to the queer cause by "foreigners and artistic celebrities," the effeminacy of male clothing, and the "virilization" of urban women incorporated into the work force: right thinking males were advised to be suspicious of female shop assistants who showed insufficient deference to them (Sabater 183, 209). By the 1960s, as gay liberation began to flourish in Britain and the United States, "homosexual centers" were established in Madrid: penal camps in which deviants were subjected to solitary confinement and minute medical examination (Chamarro Gundin). The "Ley de peligrosidad social" [Law of Social Dangerousness] of 1970 raised penalties to a maximum of three years for a single offense (previously conviction was dependent on proof of "repeated genital acts").

With the transition to democracy in the late 1970s, however, and the historic "change" of the handover to the Socialists in 1982, lesbians and gay men were (theoretically, at least) given equal rights with their straight counterparts. Impeccable antidiscrimination clauses were written into the constitutions of the new autonomous regions. A paradox remained, however. In the eighties it was not tolerant Spain but the repressive U.K. and the United States with their hostile rightist governments which continued to provide the example of a visible lesbian and gay community and a viable public sphere in which it could write and speak. Why was it that Spain failed to produce that public sphere, even under the most propitious of circumstances?

It seems likely that the answer is partly that, in a naive and quite untheorized way, repression tends to produce resistance. When Britons protested to Spaniards or Catalans that the latter were apolitical, they tended to respond that they had nothing to be political about and did not suffer under the burden of governmental hostility. Visibility is often in proportion to a perceived threat to the social structure; and while a British filmmaker such as Derek Jarman was perceived in a harsher climate to be fiercely critical of the establishment, a Spaniard such as Pedro Almodóvar could be wholly integrated into an official ideology of libertarianism, one which contained and neutralized the diverse menu of libidinal options celebrated in his films.

Moreover, the tiny groups of Catalan and Spanish activists had held from the very beginning that sexual identities were social constructs: a text of 1975 argues that the first task of lesbian and gay liberation is to attack the category of homosexuality (Guílver and de Gaimon 12). Such tendencies not only testified to an engagement with French theory which preceded Anglophones by a decade; it also corresponded to the lived experience of lesbians and gay men in Spain, who had tended to be less likely to stick to a rigorously segregated social life, who sometimes preferred to socialize in "mixed" bars and nightclubs.

A glance at a recent Spanish study of homosexuality shows the pluses and minuses of this tendency. Oscar Guasch's *La sociedad rosa* [The Pink Society] presents itself as a sociological study of the male gay world. Earnestly progressive, Guasch fails, however, to address the problem of his own place in relation to the subculture he dissects. While the North American Laud Humphreys had taken up the role of "watch queen" in his observance of public sex in the United States (Humphreys 26–30), Guasch (writing some twenty years later) remains obdurately disembodied, whether describing practices in the bath houses or modes of dancing in nightclubs. With pseudo-scientific dispassion Guasch divides the men he studies into a bizarre taxonomy: *locas* [female identified], *machos* [male identified], and *blandos* [literally, "softies," stranded between the two extremes] (Guasch 98).

It would be easy to make fun of Guasch's aspiration to objectivity, of his love of categorization, so reminiscent of medical specialists a hundred years ago. But more important is his rejection of "homosexual" or "gay" as words alien and irrelevant to Spanish-speaking cultures. Guasch proposes the use of the verb *entender* [to understand], a slang term also used beyond

Spain in some parts of Spanish America. "Understanding" is clearly a cultural, not a natural category: it cannot take place outside of defined social structures. It is also a matter of knowing, rather than being: a woman or man can be married and straight identified, but still be "wise" to same-sex desire. Finally, it is not an identity but an activity, requiring at least two partners in order to take place.

Hence, both in the written texts of queer activism and in the oral tradition of lesbian and gay slang, Spanish speakers may have anticipated that critique of identity and community implicit in much recent Anglo-American queer theory. This is not, of course, to deny that there have been in many Spanish-speaking countries lesbian and gay movements of different kinds, nor is it to infer that any attempt at organization around sexual preference must be along Anglo-American lines. Rather it is to suggest that many Spanish speakers retain a certain skepticism about what they see as the willingness of English speakers to "pigeon hole" themselves, to fragment the libidinal flow into discrete territories. The lack of a sense of common purpose amongst men who have sex with men (still less between them and woman-identified women) has grave implications for AIDS education policy: Spain currently has the highest rate of infection in Europe (Esteva and Fontrodona). However, it is insufficient to dismiss such an unwillingness to identify as "closeted." Rather, as the "gay community" of the 1970s splinters into the multiple constituencies of a loosely queer alliance, Anglo-Americans have much to learn from cultures who have always lived just such a diversity, have never been in thrall to what Guy Hocquenghem called the "mirage" of a uniquely homosexual desire (Hocquenghem 36). To cite the introduction to a U.S. anthology of lesbian and gay history, "the future may be less closed than we feared, but more open than we hoped." (Duberman, Vicinus, and Chauncey 6) This volume, the first of its kind, will help all of us to embrace that openness offered when cultures collide and identities fade, to seek truly to understand the question asked by and of queer lives at the linguistic crossroads: ¿Entiendes?

Works Cited

Almaguer, Tomás. "Chicano Men: A Cartography of Homosexual Identity and Behavior." *differences: a journal of Feminist Cultural Studies* 3.2 (1991): 75–100.

Bautista, Juan Carlos. "La sonrisa de sor Juana." Texto leido en el Primer Foro sobre Derechos Humanos de las Lesbianas, UNAM, 6, 7, 8 octubre 1989. *fem* 14.95 (November 1990): 13–16.

Bellessi, Diana. "Mes de la Historia y el Orgullo Gay y Lesbiano." *Feminaria* 3.6 (November 1990): 38.

Bouger, Kathy. "Latin American and Caribbean Encuentro Survives Lesbian-baiting." *off our backs: a women's newsjournal* 24.3 (March 1994): 9, 27.

——. "Sixth Latin American *Encuentro* Faces Threats of Violence, Disunity." *off our backs* 23.10 (November 1993): 8.

Chamorro Gundin, Fernando. *Resultados obtenidos con técnicas proyectivas en una muestra de 200 delincuentes homosexuales españoles*. Madrid: Dirección general de instituciones penitenciarias (Departamento de homosexuales de la central de observación), 1970.

de Lauretis, Teresa. "Queer Theory: Lesbian and Gay Sexualities. An Introduction." *differences: a journal of Feminist Cultural Studies* 3.2 (1991): iii–xviii.

——. "Sexual Indifference and Lesbian Representation." *Performing Feminisms: Feminist Critical Theory and Theatre*. Ed. Sue-Ellen Case. Baltimore: Johns Hopkins University Press, 1990. 17–39.

Duberman, Martin, Martha Vicinus, and George Chauncey, Jr., eds. *Hidden From History: Reclaiming the Gay and Lesbian Past*. New York: Meridian, 1989.

Esteva, Jordi, and Oscar Fontrodona. "Tú sí puedes parar el SIDA." *Ajoblanco* 47 (December 1992): 25–30.

Foster, David William. *Gay and Lesbian Themes in Latin American Writing*. Austin: University of Texas Press, 1991.

Guasch, Oscar. *La sociedad rosa*. Barcelona: Anagrama, 1991.

Guílver, Lubara, and Roger de Gaimon. "Prefacio" to Jean Nicolas, *La cuestión homosexual*. Barcelona: Fontamara, 1978. 9–16.

Halperin, David. "'Homosexuality': A Cultural Construct." *One Hundred Years of Homosexuality*. New York: Routledge, 1990. 41–53.

Hiriart, Berta. "Primer Foro sobre Derechos Humanos de las Lesbianas: El apartheid homosexual." *Mujer/Fempress: Unidad de Comunicación Alternativa de la Mujer* 98 (December 1989): 4.

Hocquenghem, Guy. *Homosexual Desire*. London: Allison and Busby, 1978. Durham, N.C.: Duke University Press, 1993.

Humphreys, Laud. *Tearoom Trade: A Study of Homosexual Encounters in Public Places*. London: Duckworth, 1970.

López García, Guadalupe. "Homosexualidad: defensa de espacios." *fem* 16.114 (August 1992): 32.

López García, María Guadalupe (Grupo Patlantonalli). "Tiempo de entender: Foro sobre derechos humanos de lesbianas." *fem* 14.94 (October 1990): 31–33.

Martínez, Elena. "Conversación con Magali Alabau." *fem* 17.119 (January 1993): 22–23.

——. "Lesbian Literary Voices from Latin America." *In the Life: Newsletter of the June L. Mazer Lesbian Collection* 5 (Summer 1993): 2–3.

——. "Las 'otras' voces de mujeres: narrativa y poesía." *fem* 17.121 (March 1993): 36–37.

Montero, Rosa. "El misterio del deseo: así son y así viven las lesbianas en España." *El País*. 31 Oct. 1993: 16–28.

Moraga, Cherríe. *Loving in the War Years: Lo que nunca pasó por sus labios*. Boston: South End Press, 1983.

Nichols, Geraldine Cleary. *Escribir, espacio propio: Laforet, Matute, Moix, Tusquets, Riera y Roig por sí mismas*. Minneapolis: Institute for the Study of Ideologies and Literature, 1989.

Peri Rossi, Cristina. *La nave de los locos*. Barcelona: Seix Barral, 1984.

————. *The Ship of Fools*. Trans. Psiche Hughes. Readers International, 1986.

Randall, Margaret. "'Coming Out as a Lesbian Is What Brought Me to Social Consciousness': Rita Arauz," in *Sandino's Daughters Revisited: Feminism in Nicaragua*. New Brunswick: Rutgers University Press, 1994. 265–85.

————. "To Change Our Own Reality and the World: A Conversation with Lesbians in Nicaragua." *Signs* 18.4 (Summer 1993): 907–25.

Sabater, Antonio. *Gamberros, homosexuales, vagos y maleantes*. Barcelona: Hispano Europea, 1962.

Smith, Paul Julian. *Laws of Desire: Questions of Homosexuality in Spanish Writing and Film, 1960–90*. Oxford: Oxford University Press, 1992.

Vaughn, Jeanne. "'Hay que saber mirar': The Construction of Alternative Sexualities in Cristina Peri Rossi's *La nave de los locos*." *Monographic Review/Revista Monográfica* 7 (1991): 251–64.

ONE

Re-Loading the Canon

Mary S. Gossy

*Aldonza as Butch: Narrative and the
Play of Gender in* Don Quijote

Aldonza Lorenzo is butch. I realize while I say this that I am writing both
as a feminist theorist and as a Cervantist, as both a radical critic and as
a Hispanist. It is hard to play all those roles at once, but not impossible.
For the Hispanists and scholars of narrative in us, I would like to show the
utility of gender theory for the study of the Spanish texts at the foundation
of modern narrative and how those texts are still making contributions to
everybody's understanding of representational practices. For the feminist
theorists in us, I would like to demonstrate that new readings of old and
canonical Spanish texts can contribute to new structures of representation,
and conceptions of subjectivity, in the present. I would like to affirm that
these several perspectives can benefit from the interaction that this essay
proposes.

In some ways, the Cervantist-feminist theory tension is not unlike the
connection between butch and femme. In both cases, it is the differences
between the two terms that make the relationship exciting and that produce new meanings for text and for experience. Of course, there is no
direct analogy between the two relationships: I would not suggest that
Cervantism is "butch" and feminist theory "femme" (perhaps the opposite,
but that would be another essay). In terms of feminist theory and practice
in the twentieth century, a butch is a woman who plays a role culturally
encoded as masculine in relationship to a femme, who is a woman playing
a role culturally encoded as feminine. Their relationship is not an imitation of the behavior of heterosexual men and women in relationship to
each other. It is, rather, a displacement and reinterpretation of gender roles
whose specific values come from the relationship enacted by two female
bodies together. The interaction between Cervantism-lesbian theory is like

butch-femme in this last respect. The tension and association of the two terms produces new possibilities for meaning in each.

What I have learned from the fact that Aldonza Lorenzo is butch is that Cervantes's representation of her in the *Quijote* is part of a trajectory in narrative practice that has rarely been followed except in some very radical and recent texts. The dilemma of feminist theory about representational practices has been that when the female body is depicted, it is invariably transgressed in some way (de Lauretis 103–57) and that the only way to preserve the female body from transgression is to consign it to the realm of the unrepresentable—an equally problematic fate because it exiles women from discourse. Teresa de Lauretis discusses this economy of desire in terms of the Oedipus myth, in which the hero's story is told over the bodies of women and the feminized spaces through which he travels. The recurrence of Greek myth as metaphor in her work is a direct result of her reading of Freudian psychoanalysis, which is also one of my theoretical bases. Greek mythology also participates indirectly in the representation of Aldonza, where, as in contemporary feminist theory, Oedipus is displaced by Medusa and the question of violence and narrative is reframed. Cervantes has given us an exemplary treatment of this problem in his depiction of Aldonza Lorenzo. I do not suggest that Cervantes knew what a butch was in twentieth century terms—I do suggest that he knows what he is doing when he represents a female body that constitutes itself in "masculine" terms in relationship not to a male body, but to the idea of a woman who is constituted as ideally feminine. In the relationship between Aldonza and Dulcinea, not as real women but as gendered textual functions, butch-femme works as a figure of writing and of representation that suggests the possibility of a narrative that does not consume women's bodies.

I do not think that these are utopian suggestions, especially since the text so clearly marks the degree to which they are conditioned by existing forms. For it is Sancho Panza, the material male body par excellence, whose discourse announces the new representation. When Sancho describes Aldonza in the paragraph that follows, he may be read as the enunciator of traditional narrative itself, historically determined as male, as the continuing rehearsal of the story of Oedipus. As I will show later, Cervantes's representation of Aldonza is revolutionary precisely because it does not sidestep the dominant tradition or pretend that it does not exist, but rather transmutes it. Never one to mince words, Sancho says of Aldonza:

> Bien la conozco, . . . y sé decir que tira tan bien una barra como el
> más forzudo zagal de todo el pueblo. ¡Vive el Dador, que es moza de

chapa, hecha y derecha y de pelo en pecho, y que puede sacar la barba del lodo a cualquier caballero andante, o por andar, que la tuviere por señora! ¡Oh hideputa, qué rejo que tiene, y qué voz! Sé decir que se puso un día encima del campanario del aldea a llamar a unos zagales suyos que andaban en un barbecho de su padre, y aunque estaban de allí más de media legua, así la oyeron como si estuvieran al pie de la torre. Y lo mejor que tiene es que no es nada melindrosa, porque tiene mucho de cortesana: con todos se burla y de todo hace mueca y donaire. Ahora digo, señor Caballero de la Triste Figura, que no solamente puede y debe vuestra merced hacer locuras por ella, sino que, con justo título, puede desesperarse y ahorcarse; que nadie habrá que lo sepa que no diga que hizo demasiado de bien, puesto que le lleve el diablo. Y querría ya verme en camino, sólo por vella; que ha muchos días que no la veo, y debe de estar muy trocada; porque gasta mucho la faz de las mujeres andar siempre al campo, al sol y al aire. (1.25, 244) [1] [I know her well . . . and I can tell you that she pitches a bar as well as the strongest lad in the whole village. Praise be to God! She's a brawny girl, well-built and with hair on her chest, and she will know how to keep her beard out of the mud with any knight errant who ever has her for his mistress. Oh, son-of-a-whore, what muscles she's got, and what a voice! I can tell you that one day she went up the village belfry to call in some of their lads who were working in a fallow field of her father's, and they could hear her as plainly as if they had been at the foot of the tower, although they were nearly two miles away. And the great thing about her is that she's not a bit shy. There's a good deal of the court lady about her, too, for she jokes with everybody, and makes light and fun of everything. I tell you, Sir Knight of the Mournful Countenance, that you're not only quite right to play your mad pranks for her, but you've got reason to despair and hang yourself; anyone who knows you will say you acted better than well, even though the Devil himself should carry you off afterwards. Oh, I wish I were on the road only for the joy of seeing her. I haven't set eyes on her for ever so long. She must be changed, too, for always trudging about the fields in the sun and wind greatly spoils a woman's looks.] (209)

The first thing that Sancho says about Aldonza is that she "pitches a bar as well as the strongest lad in the whole village." On the literal level, this means that she is as good at festive games of strength as the men are. But according to Agustín Redondo, who has made a comprehensive study of this description (Redondo 19), "tirar la barra" [throwing the bar] figuratively meant, in Cervantes's time, *futuere,* that is, "to have sexual inter-course (with a woman)" (Traupman 123b). Redondo's work shows how the representation of Aldonza participates in carnivalesque structures in the *Quijote.* My aim is to demonstrate how Cervantes represents Aldonza as butch in order to push the limits of traditional narrative. While Redondo says that by this description "Aldonza se transforma de tal modo en *mujer fálica*" (Redondo 19) [Aldonza transforms herself in this way into a phallic woman], he does not take his interpretation to the conclusion suggested by the Latin dictionary. Instead, he perceives her as a *serrana,* a "mítica cazadora y salteadora, briosa y rolliza, que, en la sierra, atacaba al viajero, se lo llevaba a su cueva y saciaba en el su sanguinaria sensualidad" (Redondo 13) [a mythological huntress and highwaywoman, spunky and sturdy, who in the mountains would attack the traveler, carry him off to her cave, and satisfy in him her sanguinary sensuality]. But Aldonza lives in a town, not in the mountains, and there is no sign in her name—despite its connotations of transgressive sexuality[2]—of the kind of castrating ("sanguinary") eroticism that the *serrana* image evokes. Perhaps because she can "throw the bar," the assumption is that she has taken it from some man, and thus Redondo sees her as a carnivalesque inversion of femininity that comically matches and emphasizes the "desvirilización" (Redondo 20) of Don Quijote. But Aldonza has never met Don Quijote. She does not know, and does not care, who he is. He was in love with her, but "ella jamás lo supo ni se dio cata dello" (1.1, 40) [she never knew it or gave it a thought (35)]. The man is irrelevant to her. She has no need to castrate him—she has discovered that the *barra,* like the phallus, belongs (as much as it can) to anyone who is willing to play with it. Aldonza is thus as much a Sphinx as she is a Medusa, and the question she poses in the text is related to how she plays with the *barra.* To "tira la barra" means *futuere* [to have sex with a woman], and Aldonza does it as well as the young men of the village (who, in the absence of further evidence, I assume to be heterosexual); the not very subtle implication is that she must be doing it with women.

This knowledge surfaces, at least unconsciously, when Redondo refers to Aldonza as "un verdadero marimacho" (Redondo 12) [a real butch] citing as evidence for the appellation her height, strength, stentorian voice, the manly scent she exudes after perspiring, and her hairiness. While "mari-macho" today has acceptations that go from 'mannish' to 'lesbian,' the following citation from Lope de Vega's "La Serrana de la Vera," which the *Diccionario de Autoridades* uses to define "marimacho," may help to clarify its meaning in the Golden Age: "Lindo talle, hermosa moza,/si marimacho no fuera." (*Diccionario de Autoridades,* 500b). This quotation distinguishes gendered behavior from the gendered body. A marimacho may be a woman of "lindo talle," that is, one with a body that men find attractive, but she can never enter into the symbolic economy of "una hermosa moza" [a pretty girl] because she doesn't *act* like one. A marimacho is defined by her "aspecto y modales masculinos" [masculine aspect and affect], her "ademanes o maneras" [mien or manners] as a butch "conjunto de [. . .] gestos y actitudes habituales" [combination of habitual gestures and attitudes] (Moliner 2.352, 2.433), all of which, in Sancho's story, help to describe Aldonza's performance of gender. She is not a woman trying to castrate men or to be a man. Rather she "resignifies masculinity in a butch identity. As a result, that masculinity, if that it can be called, is always brought into relief against a culturally intelligible 'female body'" (Butler 123). No one in the story or the criticism doubts that Aldonza is female. What strikes Sancho as eminently *tellable* and at the same time destablizes the narrative is that she is not a *heterosexual* female, that is, not an object of or participant in male desire. A woman's performance of masculinity and her orientation of this performance toward another woman (figured in the *Quijote* as "tirar la barra") are not the same as, or imitations of, a man's. Aldonza "tira la barra" as well as, but not in the same way as, the manliest fellow in town. To whom does she throw it? To another woman. The bar here becomes not a sign of division, but, as in Sue-Ellen Case's formulation, the sign of connection on a narrative level between butch and femme (Case 56–57).

Where is this other woman, the one at the other end of the bar? Since Aldonza is a butch, we should be on the lookout for a femme. If, as Case suggests, "the butch-femme couple inhabit the subject position together—'you can't have one without the other,' as the song says"; if, as according to Judith Butler, "[i]n both butch and femme identities, the very notion of an original or natural identity is put into question [and] indeed, it is precisely that question as it is embodied in these identities that becomes one source of their erotic significance"; and if, finally, as in Luce Irigaray's title, "the one doesn't move without the other" (Case 56; Butler 123), then we must look for a woman whose representation is intimately linked with, but not erased by Aldonza's; a woman who is thus coupled with her and turned out in the full array of her culture's feminine drag: Dulcinea.

Dulcinea, in combination with Aldonza, works to perpetuate the writing process of the *Quijote* after its reported interruption at the end of the eighth chapter. In the midst of the action of the battle between Don Quijote and the gallant Basque, the manuscript upon which the narrator bases his version of the story comes to an abrupt end. Don Quijote and the Basque are left suspended in the narrative space, horses charging, swords

aloft, but frozen. The narrator tells in the next chapter how, in the marketplace in Toledo, he discovered another manuscript that continued the story.
An avid reader, he picks up some ancient notebooks, and seeing that they
are written in Arabic, finds a translator to tell him what they contain. The
translator opens one book up in the middle and starts to laugh. When the
narrator asks him what's so funny, he says:

> Está, como he dicho, aquí en el margen escrito esto: "Esta Dulcinea
> del Toboso, tantas veces en esta historia referida, dicen que tuvo la
> mejor mano para salar puercos que otra mujer de toda la Mancha."
> (1.9, 93)
> [This is what is written in the margin: "They say that Dulcinea del
> Toboso, so often mentioned in this history, was the best hand of any
> woman at salting pork in all La Mancha."] (76)

The lowly activity of salting pork—Aldonza has her hand in prohibited
flesh—juxtaposed with the pretty name makes the translator laugh and signals to the narrator the presence of the story's continuation. This quotation
highlights the simultaneity, but not confusion, of Aldonza as threatening
Other—she has a Moorish name, and it is her body that performed the
act of salting pork in El Toboso, a Moorish town—and Dulcinea as idealized Other. The two of them, together in the margins, inscribed in Arabic,
a foreign but intelligible language, are, through a process of translation,
integral to the production of narrative. The story can start up again after
the couple Aldonza-Dulcinea appears. They function in, but are not of,
the dominant structure. The discourse and modes of representation that
they encode differ from what comes before their mention. Their joint appearance produces a more complex text than before, one mediated by an at
times unfathomable multiplicity of narrators and points of view, in which
mastery of interpretation and unity of meaning are incessantly called into
question. The formulae of traditional narrative (in the specific example of
the romance of chivalry) are displaced, and a new kind of story is told.
Cervantes says in the prologue that "todo él es una invectiva contra los
libros de caballerías" (1. Prólogo 25) [the whole of (the book) is an invective against books of chivalry (29)]. Leaving aside the question of whether
this is an ironic or literal stance, what it signals is a direction away from
established narrative forms, a direction that specifically challenges the (not
only courtly) male-hero to female-space relationship fundamental to traditional narrative. It is important to remember here that the couple Aldonza-
Dulcinea may be related to, but is not just another of the many material-
ideal pairs in the *Quijote*. The couple butch-femme is not part of the same

ideological structures as self/other, subject/object, materiality/ideality, or reality/illusion that critics have long been able to see Cervantes's novel as deconstructing. A crucial point of this essay and other theory about butch-femme is that butch-femme is not an opposition; it is a couple, in which two female bodies are subjects in relation to each other, together. The difference between those binary *oppositions* and a butch-femme *couple* is not only structural, it is also specifically one of gender. When Aristotle first theorizes power in the *Politics,* he says that "The first point is that those which are ineffective without each other must be united in a pair. For example, the union of male and female." Immediately, the second paired example he cites is "ruler and ruled." An idea of domination and of value is implicit in binary pairs and oppositions. One term is always in control of, or needs to control, the other. These qualifications are not part of the construction of the butch-femme couple. The other important point, from the position of feminist theory, is that Aristotle's choice of examples is not arbitrary. As Monique Wittig states in her discussion of the *Politics,* "From that time on, male and female, the heterosexual relationship, has been the parameter of all hierarchical relations" (Wittig 42). *Don Quijote* is a generalized challenge to the ideological motors of any narrative not in spite of, but specifically because of the fact that it does not consume women's bodies.

But the *Quijote* only begins this project, and few if any authors have taken it up since. Like the narrator before he found the notebooks in the market in Toledo, the feminist reader does not yet have access to the new textuality in the original language. Instead, in terms of point of view, the reader's acquaintance with Aldonza and Dulcinea is mediated by the male gaze. For example, there is no "objective" or omniscient narrator to tell us what Aldonza *really* looks like. This emphatic absence of objectivity is characteristic of Cervantine perspectivism, the effect of which is to put into question the very notion of objectivity or of a single authoritative meaning. But it is also a metaphor for the position of the female body in narrative. If, as Teresa de Lauretis and many other critics suggest, narrative is oedipal, then *Don Quijote* is a story, like Sancho's description or the translator's version, conditioned by a man's point of view. But it is also a beginning of something new. In *Don Quijote,* a text where, as the title indicates, the Man and the book are indistinguishable from one another, the position of Aldonza "stress[es] the duplicity of that scenario and the specific contradiction of the female subject in it, the contradiction by which historical women must work with and against Oedipus" (de Lauretis 157). Aldonza is a woman, but masculine ("de pelo en pecho" [with hair on her chest]), strong, vociferous, not attached to any man ("con todos se burla" [fooling around with everybody]), and playfully uncontained by cultural strictures ("y de todo hace mueca y donaire" [mocking and making light of everything]). Sancho narrates her, but in the act of narrating her, he emphasizes the volume of her voice, which is the loudest one in the book. Here Aldonza functions as a figure for a representation of the female body in writing that does not participate in the objectifying structures of traditional narrative. By making Aldonza butch, Cervantes explicitly problematizes narrative's use of the female body. In his formulation, only a crazy man would idealize and fetishize a female body and narrate himself over it: the female body of oedipal narrative as told by Don Quijote is, thus, emphatically a fantasy. In contrast, Aldonza has a self-determining, autonomous textual body that exists within but is not controlled by narrative tradition: her body is represented but not transgressed. She is not coupled with Don Quijote, but rather with Dulcinea. The couple Aldonza-Dulcinea, as butch-femme as can be, destabilizes the desire that organizes oedipal narrative. Normally, this desire produces either a narrative that is predicated upon the body of a woman who has died prior to the beginning of the story, but who is somehow essential to its motivation, or a narrative that tells itself over and through the body of a woman, and often ends with her extinction. It is stunning to note that no women's bodies are sacrificed to the narration of *Don Quijote*. In this, despite the fact that it is so often called the first modern novel, the text is atypical of the Western narrative tradition. It suggests what is still a narrative innovation: a representation of women's bodies in narrative that neither destroys nor excludes them. It works because instead of locating the female body as a feminine lack to be completed or eradicated by male desire, it represents that body *as both and neither masculine and feminine,* as two different women who jointly inhabit a subject position. This is in contradistinction to the Renaissance figure of the androgyne[3] or perhaps is an example of Cervantes's development of thought on that figure. The androgyne is a patriarchal fantasy that, despite hopeful claims to the contrary, subsumes the female into the male and eradicates the integrity of the female body. Unlike it, the butch-femme couple suggested by the Aldonza-Dulcinea relationship of two female bodies enacting and exchanging masculine and feminine roles, makes possible a process in which women are represented in terms of their relation to each other, in a way that is not controlled by the objectifying practices of traditional narrative. Sancho has seen and tells of Aldonza, but as a narrative entity she and Dulcinea exceed the limits of his vision, and their narrative identities are not contained by his story.

The Aldonza-Dulcinea couple suggests possibilities for a trans-oedipal narrative strategy. But before I explain how these possibilities might work, I want to note how they have been repressed in narrative tradition since the *Quijote*. I will not trace the history of dead and used women all the way through Western narrative since 1615, but rather will just mention how oedipal narrative takes its revenge in the 1970s (and recently revived) Broadway musical *Man of La Mancha*. In this story, Aldonza is transmuted into a prostitute and, as the feminine-space-to-be-traversed par excellence, is gang-raped at an inn. In the 1992 revival, she was played by Sheena Easton, a tiny, conventionally sexy but big-voiced female pop singer. Since her character is that of a narrative use-object, her voice (unlike Aldonza's) serves only to advance the dominant story. The musical bears as little resemblance to the *Quijote* as the structures of most narrative do.

It is also important to remember that if Aldonza is not just a passive, sexualized space to be traversed, neither is she a "phallic woman." She has none of the attractions of the phallic mother because she does not enact castration. Rather, as part of the butch-femme couple, she calls castration into question. The phallic mother, on the other hand, is related to Medusa, and both figures are actively utilized by men who take pleasure in pornography, particularly in the representations of lesbians that are an integral part of most pornographic texts. To read Aldonza as a *serrana* is to read her as a lesbian in a pornographic context. A *serrana*, a big strong woman who hunts men down and then wears them out with her sexual aggressivity, is in contemporary terms comparable to a dominatrix, a phallic mother with whom the male reader can identify, knowing that despite her omnipotence he can still have sex with her and soothe his fears of castration. But she is also a Medusa, whose ugliness, as the sign of castration, terrifies him. According to de Lauretis, Freud summarizes this theory of pornography in the following comments:

> The sight of Medusa's head makes the spectator stiff with terror, turns him to stone. Observe that we have here once again the same origin from the castration complex and the same transformation of affect! For becoming stiff means an erection. Thus in the original situation it offers consolation to the spectator: he is still in possession of a penis, and the stiffening reassures him of the fact. (*SE* 18:273)

It is no coincidence that pornography should participate in the theorizing and explanation of the oedipal structures of narrative, since the relation between the reader and narrative is often analogous to that between the user of pornography and his text. Narrative, the telling through a feminine space, frequently participates in the same structures as pornography. The representation of the female body in narrative and in pornography shows the woman, castrated and dead, to the man and reassures him "that he is still in possession of a penis." That is—parenthetically but not unmentionably—precisely the effect of lesbian scenes constructed in writing and images for the male user of pornography. As others have mentioned, and as I saw for myself at the video store the other night, an "all-girl action" porn video sells itself with the slogan, printed over the picture of two naked women entwined with each other but looking at the viewer, "The only dick is you." The double horror of not one but *two* (castrated) vulvas spread across the scene *reassures* the viewer that he has not been castrated and that his is the biggest, best, and unique penis. He will be the hero who fills the feminine gap, thus bringing the story to closure. But (as in Freud's formulation) the erection is only temporary and so is the relief of castration anxiety: this might be an explanation for the proliferation, in sheer numbers, of pornographic texts for male consumption. Every erection yields to a period of flaccidity that demands more reassurance. So stories keep being told over the bodies of women.

But Cervantes was doing something different. The representation of Aldonza *and* Dulcinea, together in a subject position, displaces the thrust of oedipal narrative. In all the variety of lesbian porn made for straight male consumption, I have not yet found a single example of the representation of a butch-femme lesbian couple: the women couples shown in that kind of pornography are uniformly "feminine"—I hesitate to say "femme" because, as I have already explained, a femme identity is somewhere constituted in relationship with a butch woman's. In pornography made by lesbians for lesbians, I would suggest that only those images that show butch lesbians alone, or perhaps in leather or s/m drag, would appeal to a male viewer, precisely because in this representation the butch, without her femme, is transmuted by the male gaze into a dominatrix, the phallic woman of Redondo's formulation. But a butch is not a phallic woman. The phallic woman is a fantasy constructed within the oedipal framework: a fantasized body that, once it becomes phallic, ceases to be (again, within the oedipal formulation) female. The butch, on the other hand, is a female body that consciously represents masculinity, putting on and taking off the phallus at will. The phallic woman is invented by the oedipal gaze. The butch, in complicity with the femme, invents herself.

At the end of his description of Aldonza, Sancho says: "Y querría ya verme en camino, sólo por vella; que ha muchos días que no la veo, y debe de estar ya trocada; porque gasta mucho la faz de las mujeres andar siempre al campo, al sol y al aire" (1.25, 244) [Oh, I wish I were on the road only for the joy of seeing her. I haven't set eyes on her for ever so long. She must be changed, too, for always trudging about the fields in sun and wind greatly spoils a woman's looks (208)]. Sancho would like to see her, but he does not go back on the road to make that vision possible. The pleasure in seeing her is only imagined. She is "changed." The verb "trocar" means to exchange, to interchange, to turn from one thing into its opposite, and finally, to vomit (Moliner 2.1396). To invoke the early sexological vocabulary for homosexuality, Sancho knows that Aldonza is the inversion of what he wishes she were. She is not a woman conforming to his expectations or desires—because she moves herself, from the top of the town's steeple, through the fields surrounding it, wherever she wants. He "hasn't set eyes on her" during the time of narration—she is not determined by his gaze, or by Don Quijote's, yet she does exist in the narrative. The butch-femme subject is a space inhabited by two female bodies together that, by definition, cannot be construed of as a locus of male desire. As a coupled subject, it cannot be thought of as desiring the man; that is, because of the femme's orientation toward the butch and the butch's toward the femme, he cannot project his desire onto them. The butch-femme couple restates female subjectivity in a way that disrupts the flow of oedipal narrative precisely because it calls the primacy of the male phallus into question. The representation of butch and femme makes possible a narrative that does not ignore or dismiss Oedipus, but rather decentralizes him, forces him to reanalyze his desire, and reminds him that the road is not the only way to get around.

The couple Aldonza-Dulcinea and its relationship to butch-femme, inscribed in *Don Quijote* at the beginning of the seventeenth century, is still something new in narrative. It suggests a practice that writes and reads the female body without destroying it, objectifying it in male desire, or exiling it from the powers of discourse into the unrepresentable. In this regard, it may be useful to remember that many critics have suggested that the death of Medusa is an archetype for the structures and functions of oedipal narrative; she has to die to keep the story moving. I do not know how to keep Medusa from being slain in the service of oedipal narrative.[4] But I think that Aldonza and Dulcinea, as butch-femme couple, do not suffer her fate. If a sister Gorgon had stayed alert at Medusa's side, would Perseus still have been able to kill her, or both of them? When it comes to outwitting Oedipus, two heads are better than one.

Notes

1 The English translation is fundamentally that of J. M. Cohen, *The Adventures of Don Quixote* (Harmondsworth: Penguin, 1950). When I have altered Cohen's translation, it has been in the interest of greater literalness. The Spanish edition of the text is Miguel de Cervantes, *Don Quijote de la Mancha,* 2 vols., ed. Martín de Riquer (Barcelona: Juventud, 1971). Part and chapter numbers of the *Quijote* are followed in my text by the page numbers of this edition.

2 The name is associated with promiscuous women, prostitutes, and eroticism in general; Redondo 11–12.

3 See Diana de Armas Wilson, *Allegories of Love: Cervantes's Persiles and Sigismunda* (Princeton: Princeton University Press, 1991) for a thorough discussion of the concept of the androgyne in the Spanish Renaissance.

4 It is interesting to note the repression and persistence of the idea of Aldonza as castrating Medusa in Joan Ramón Resina's "Medusa en el laberinto: Locura y textualidad en el *Quijote*" *MLN* (March 1989): 286–303. At one point Don Quijote compares the sierra with "el laberinto de Perseo" (1.25, 249), confusing Perseus with Theseus. Resina reads this slip as a sign of Don Quijote's identification with Perseus and of his desire not only to decapitate the giant that is terrorizing the kingdom of Micomicón, but also to exterminate his own madness. Resina overlooks the fact that Medusa is a woman. Don Quijote's Medusa is the woman who stands between him and Dulcinea: Aldonza Lorenzo.

Works Cited

Butler, Judith. *Gender Trouble: Feminism and the Subversion of Identity.* New York: Routledge, 1990.

Case, Sue-Ellen. "Towards a Butch-Femme Aesthetic." *Discourse* 11.1 (1988–89): 55–73.

Castro, Américo. *Cervantes y los casticismos españoles.* Madrid: Alianza, 1974.

Cervantes, Miguel de. *Don Quijote de la Mancha.* Ed. Martín de Riquer. Barcelona: Juventud, 1971.

Cervantes, Miguel de. *The Adventures of Don Quixote.* Trans. J. M. Cohen. Harmondsworth: Penguin, 1950.

de Lauretis, Teresa. *Alice Doesn't: Feminism, Semiotics, Cinema.* Bloomington: Indiana University Press, 1984.

Freud, Sigmund. "Medusa's Head." *Standard Edition of the Complete Psychological Works of Sigmund Freud.* Vol. 18. Trans. James Strachey. London: Hogarth, 1955.

Irigaray, Luce. *Et l'une ne bouge pas sans l'autre.* Paris: Editions de Minuit, 1979.

Moliner, María. *Diccionario del uso del español.* 2 vols. Madrid: Gredos, 1987.

Real Academia Española. *Diccionario de Autoridades.* Madrid: Gredos, 1969.

Redondo, Agustín. "Del personaje de Aldonza Lorenzo al de Dulcinea del Toboso: Algunos aspectos de la invención cervantina." *Anales cervantinos* 21 (1983).

Traupman, John C. *The New Collegiate Latin and English Dictionary.* New York: Bantam, 1966.

Daniel Balderston

The "Fecal Dialectic": Homosexual Panic
and the Origin of Writing in Borges

Near the end of a 1931 essay on the defects of the Argentine character, "Nuestras imposibilidades" [Our Impossibilities], in which he discusses the Argentine penchant for taking pride in putting one over on someone else ("la viveza criolla"), Borges writes:

> Añadiré otro ejemplo curioso: el de la sodomía. En todos los países de la tierra, una invisible reprobación recae sobre los dos ejecutores del inimaginable contacto. *Abominación hicieron los dos; su sangre sobre ellos,* dice el Levítico. No así entre el malevaje de Buenos Aires, que reclama una especie de veneración para el agente activo—porque lo embromó al compañero. Entrego esa dialéctica fecal a los apologistas de la *viveza,* del *alacraneo* y de la *cachada,* que tanto infierno encubren. (*Discusión* 17–18) [1]
> [I'll add another strange example: that of sodomy. In all of the countries of the earth, an invisible reproof falls on both partners in the unimaginable contact. "Both of them committed an abomination; their blood shall be upon them," says Leviticus. Not so in the Buenos Aires underworld, which showers the active partner with a sort of veneration—because he put something over on his companion. I leave that fecal dialectic to the apologists of trickery, backbiting and mockery, who conceal so much of hell.]

But of course he does not, and cannot, leave this "fecal dialectic" alone (though he does remove the reference to the matter from subsequent editions of *Discusión* and hence from the so-called *Obras completas*). What I will examine here is his phobic treatment of a theme that evidently fascinated him.[2] I will not, for now, speculate on the enigmas of Borges's sexual nature,[3] though it is worth noting that his failed relationships with a variety of women have been the focus of literary gossip for many years in Buenos Aires, and that the recent publication of some love letters to Estela Canto, and the revelation that Borges sought psychiatric help for impotence for several years in the 1940s, show the currency of that gossip.[4] Instead, I will discuss first Borges's treatment in a series of essays of the homosexuality of two eminent nineteenth-century men of letters whose works and lives he mentions often, Oscar Wilde and Walt Whitman, and then discuss the treatment of sexual preference in a variety of stories, especially in "La intrusa" (*El informe de Brodie* [1970]) and "La secta del fénix" (1952, later included in the second edition of *Ficciones*).

First, Wilde. The Anglo-Irish writer is the subject of an early essay in *El tamaño de mi esperanza* (1926) on "The Ballad of Reading Gaol," and of the later "Sobre Oscar Wilde" in *Otras inquisiciones* (1952). In both the relation of work to life is alluded to, but only laterally. In the essay on "Reading Gaol," the simplicity and directness of the language of the poem is contrasted with the verbal ingenuity of Wilde's earlier works; this new simplicity is called "austerity," and the poem is offered as possible evidence of Wilde's religious conversion, though a limit is set to the usefulness of such speculation: "Erraría sin embargo quien arbitrase que el único interés de la famosa Balada está en el tono autobiográfico y en las inducciones que sobre el Wilde final podemos sacar de ella" (134) [Nonetheless one would err if one were to judge that the only interest of the famous Ballad is in the autobiographical tone and in the insights that we can derive from the Ballad into the final Wilde]. Before alluding to the trials and prison sentence, the discussion of Wilde's literary activities is encoded in a reference to another writer who flaunted his sexual preferences. Wilde, according to Borges, was not a great poet or dramatist, but his epigrams and wit put forth an aesthetic creed that was highly influential: "Fue un agitador de ideas ambientes. Su actividad fué comparable a la que hoy ejerce Cocteau, si bien su gesto fué más suelto y travieso que el del citado francesito" (132) [He was an agitator for fashionable ideas. His attitude was comparable to that exercised today by Cocteau, although his activity was more fluid and more mischievous than that of the aforementioned little Frenchman]. And then comes an account of the famous trial, notable for its reticences:

> Es sabido que Wilde pudo haberse zafado de la condena que el pleito Queensberry le infligió y que no lo hizo por creer que su nombradía bastaba a defenderlo de la ejecución de ese fallo. Una vez condenado, estaba satisfecha la justicia y no había interés alguno en que la senten-

cia se realizase. Le dejaron pues una noche para que huyese a Francia y Wilde no quiso aprovechar el pasadizo largo de esa noche y se dejó arrestar en la mañana siguiente. Muchas motivaciones pueden explicar su actitud: la egolatría, el fatalismo o acaso una curiosidad de apurar la vida en todas sus formas o hasta una urgencia de leyenda para su fama venidera. (133)

[It is well-known that Wilde could have escaped from the judgment in the Queensberry Case and that if he failed to do so it was because he was convinced that his fame would exempt him from the sentence being applied. They left him free for a night so that he could flee to France and Wilde refused to take advantage of the long passageway offered him by that night and let himself be arrested the following morning. Many motives might explain his attitude: egocentrism, fatalism, perhaps a curiosity to experience all that life offered him, even the desire to shape his future fame into a legend.]

Note the lack of any reference here to the content of the charges against Wilde: "the Queensberry Case" is made to stand for both the first trial in which the Marquess of Queensberry was found innocent of libel and for the second and third trials in which Wilde was tried and then found guilty of sodomy. The incident in question actually took place after the acquittal of Queensberry and the arraignment of Wilde before the second trial (Ellmann 452 and 456); it was not, then, properly part of the "Queensberry Case," but part of the Crown case against Wilde. The matter at issue, the "unimaginable contact" between Wilde and a series of boys, is completely erased from Borges's account.

The later essay takes a different tack. Once again Wilde is celebrated for his epigrams and wit, though now Borges affirms that Wilde's real achievement was his ability to tell the truth. After years of rereading Wilde, Borges says, he has discovered something other critics ignore: "el hecho comprobable y elemental de que Wilde, casi siempre, tiene razón" (692) [the verifiable and elementary fact that Wilde is almost always right]. The alleged reason why other readers have failed to discover this "fact" is said to be due to Wilde's polished prose: "su obra es tan armoniosa que puede parecer inevitable y aun baladí" (692) [his work is so harmonious that it may appear inevitable or even trifling]. A further difficulty resides in the gap between Wilde's life, for Borges an example of scandal and tragedy, and the essential happiness expressed in his work: "Una observación lateral. El nombre de Oscar Wilde está vinculado a las ciudades de la llanura; su gloria, a la condena y la cárcel. Sin embargo . . . el sabor fundamental de su obra es la felicidad" (692) [One lateral observation. Oscar Wilde's name is linked to the cities of the plain; his glory, to his conviction and imprisonment. Nonetheless . . . the fundamental flavor of his work is happiness]. Then, after contrasting Wilde with Chesterton, whose optimistic philosophy is belied by the nightmarish qualities of his work, Borges concludes that Wilde was "un hombre que guarda, pese a los hábitos del mal y de la desdicha, una invulnerable inocencia" (693) [a man who, despite the habits of evil and misfortune, retains an invulnerable innocence]. Once again, euphemisms—references to the cities of the plain, bad habits—stand for the scandalous revelation of Wilde's homosexuality, that Love which not only does not dare speak its name but of which Borges does not dare speak. In reference to the most public case of homosexuality in the nineteenth century,[5] Borges proves more Victorian than the Victorians themselves.

Though Borges contrasts Wilde to Chesterton at the close of the essay in *Otras inquisiciones,* the contrast to Whitman would be equally revealing, for in Whitman's case the relation of life to work is particularly problematic for Borges. "Who touches this book touches a man": Whitman constantly asserts the identity of the author and the speaker of the poems, yet the speaker's openly avowed homosexuality—or perhaps better, pansexuality—was not matched by any comparable admission by the man himself, as witnessed by the famous exchange with John Addington Symonds.[6] The differences between the poetic persona and the historical man are the focus of Borges's two essays on Whitman, "El otro Whitman" (originally 1929, collected in the 1932 edition of *Discusión*) and the much later "Nota sobre Walt Whitman" (included in the 1955 edition of *Discusión*). Eduardo González, in *The Monstered Self,* has discussed Borges's suppression of the homoerotic elements in Whitman's poetry in his translation of *Leaves of Grass* (50–51).[7] The same issue may be approached through a discussion of Borges's treatment of Whitman's homoeroticism in his essays on the North American poet.

In "El otro Whitman," he finds Whitman to be "poeta de un laconismo trémulo y suficiente, hombre de destino comunicado, no proclamado" (207) [a poet of a trembling and sufficient laconism, a man whose destiny is communicated, not proclaimed], a poet with a single theme, "la peculiar poesía de la arbitrariedad y la privación" (208) [the strange poetry of arbitrariness and privation]. In a note to the essay (omitted from the *Obras completas* version), Borges writes:

> Casi todo lo escrito sobre Whitman está falseado por dos interminables errores. Uno es la identificación sumaria de Whitman, hombre

caviloso de letras, con Whitman, héroe semidivino de *Leaves of Grass* como don Quijote lo es del *Quijote;* otro la insensata adopción del estilo y vocabulario de sus poemas—vale decir del mismo sorprendente fenómeno que se quiere explicar. (*Discusión* 70n.)
[Almost everything written about Whitman is rendered false by two unending errors. The first is the summary identification of Whitman, cautious man of letters, with Whitman, semi-divine hero of *Leaves of Grass* just as Don Quixote is hero of the *Quixote;* the other is the senseless adoption of the style and vocabulary of the poems—that is, of the very surprising phenomenon that the critic is trying to explain.]

The "other" Whitman of the title of the essay is Whitman the individual man, a point more fully developed in the later essay.

"Nota sobre Walt Whitman" expands on the point just mentioned, insisting that though Whitman never visited California or the Platte River, the speaker describes his experiences there; that though Whitman was a poor man of letters, the speaker of the poems was a noble savage; that though Whitman was in New York in 1859, the speaker of the poems was in Harpers Ferry, Virginia, witnessing the execution of John Brown (250). The crucial line for our argument here is the following: "Este [Whitman] fue casto, reservado y más bien taciturno; aquél [el yo de los poemas] efusivo y orgiástico" (250) [This Whitman was chaste, reserved and rather taciturn; that one was effusive and orgiastic]. Even before the more recent biographies, there were abundant grounds for doubting that Whitman the man was absolutely chaste; Borges is forcing the issue because for him the contact with other male bodies was, as he put it, unimaginable.

Not by chance, though, the essays on Whitman are key links in the chain that goes from "La nadería de la personalidad" to "Borges y yo." In Whitman the floating signifier that is the "I" escapes definition in the best poems. In "When I heard at the close of the day," for instance, the proper name is blotted out, the subject of public fame and private unhappiness, while the "I" finds a more anonymous pleasure:

When I heard at the close of the day how my name
        had been receiv'd with plaudits in the
        capitol, still it was not a happy night for
        me that follow'd, . . .
But the day when I rose at dawn from the bed of
        perfect health, refresh'd, singing, inhaling
        the ripe breath of autumn, . . .

And when I thought how my dear friend my lover was
    on his way coming, O then I was happy, . . .
And that night while all was still I heard the
    waters roll slowly continually up the shores,
I heard the hissing rustle of the liquid and sands
    as directed to me whispering to congratulate
    me,
For the one I love most lay sleeping by me under
    the same cover in the cool night,
In the stillness in the autumn moonbeam his face
    was inclined toward me,
And his arm lay lightly around my breast—and that
    night I was happy. (276–77)

Borges refers guardedly to this poem in his late story "El otro" [The Other] in *El libro de arena* (1975). In that story Borges sits, seventy years old, by the Charles River in Cambridge, to be joined by a fifteen-year-old Borges who is sitting by the Leman River in Geneva. The younger Borges recites "con fervor, ahora lo recuerdo, aquella breve pieza en que Walt Whitman rememora una compartida noche ante el mar, en que fue realmente feliz" [with fervor, now I recall, that brief piece in which Walt Whitman remembered a shared night by the sea, when he was truly happy]. The dialogue continues:

>   —Si Whitman la ha cantado—observé—es porque la deseaba y no sucedió. El poema gana si adivinamos que es la manifestación de un anhelo, no la historia de un hecho.
>   Se quedó mirándome.
>   —Usted no lo conoce—exclamó—. Whitman es incapaz de mentir. (18–19)
>   ["If Whitman has sung about it," I observed, "it is because he desired it and it never happened. The poem gains in stature if we discover that it is the expression of a desire, not the story of an event."
>   He stared at me.
>   "You don't know him," he exclaimed. "Whitman is incapable of lying."]

The importance of the poem for the older Borges would seem to be not the startlingly direct reference to a homosexual encounter, but the force of the public/private dichotomy, the opposition of "my name" and "I." And yet, reading this poem as a prototype of "Borges y yo" [Borges and I] ignores what for the younger Borges must have been its most important aspect: its testimony to an experience of intense happiness. In "La felicidad escrita" [Writing about Happiness], an essay in the 1928 collection *El idioma de los argentinos,* Borges argues that happiness is an experience that has yet to be adequately recorded in poetry (45, 53). That Whitman's expression of happiness in this poem was both intensely personal and homoerotic must be said to count, even if, as Borges suggests in "El otro," it was an expression of a happiness imagined and not experienced, something which is impossible for us to know either way.

In discussions of both Wilde and Whitman, then, Borges retreats into a facile distinction between work and life and assumes that there could be no imaginative traffic from one to the other. The two cases are opposite, though. In Wilde's case, the "black legend" of Wilde's public vice must be washed away to save the innocence and happiness of the writings; the public scandal is unavoidable, though, so Borges refers to it guardedly and euphemistically. In Whitman's case, no reference is made to the homoerotic elements in *Leaves of Grass,* and the man is turned into a kind of monk who presides over the rites of democracy as a chaste and almost disembodied celebrant. In the references to both writers, the assertion that their work was essentially happy implies by contrast (given the antithetical nature of the discussions of work and life) that their lives were essentially sad, and not in Quentin Crisp's sense of that word.

Borges's work occasionally includes suggestions of the homoerotic together with careful signs of the suppression of those elements. The clearest of these is the equivocal epigraph to "La intrusa" [The Intruder] (1025) which reads, rather laconically, "2 Reyes, I, 26." The first chapter of the second book of *Kings* does not have a twenty-sixth verse, but the second book of *Samuel,* sometimes also known as the second book of *Kings,* contains the most famous of all declarations of homosexual love: "I am distressed for thee, my brother, Jonathan: very pleasant hast thou been unto me; thy love to me was wonderful, passing the love of women."

"La intrusa" is the text in which Borges most clearly expresses what Sedgwick and others have called "homosexual panic."[8] In the story, the familiar (and often critiqued) notion in Lévi-Strauss of woman as a medium of exchange is enacted in the "love triangle" that links each of the Nilsen brothers to Juliana. Yet, as the story makes clear, woman here is the token that allows the functioning of homosexual desire, even though—in the perverse world of the story—that desire requires the death of the woman: the Nilsen brothers will only be free to desire one another when their desire is constituted not in relating to a present woman as alleged "obscure object of desire" but in relation to their shared memories of a dead woman. The woman must be "sacrificed" to the incestuous desire of the two brothers; she is the fetishized totem that makes possible their transgression of the incest taboo.

The epigraph, on David's love for Jonathan "passing the love of woman," makes credible a gay reading of the story. But note that the homosexual desire that "passes the love of woman" is for Borges constituted through violence. Here, that violence is committed by two brothers against a woman; in other stories ("La forma de la espada," "El muerto," "El Sur," "La muerte y la brújula") by man against man; once (in "Emma Zunz") by a woman against a man.[9] And, since violence is allied with representation and writing, so the scene of writing is disrupted by the experience of death. When, at the close of "La muralla y los libros," Borges defines "el hecho estético" [beauty] as the "inminencia de una revelación, que no se produce" (635) [imminence of a revelation, which is not produced], he could be describing the tantalizing movements of desire in his fiction.

In the early eighties the story was adapted for the screen by Carlos Hugo Christensen, an Argentine-born director active in Brazil since at least 1955.[10] Christensen's Portuguese-language adaptation of the story, A Intrusa, fills out the brief story with the usual excursions into gaucho culture (horse races, knife fights, songfests) but also with explicitly homoerotic elements. The Nilsen brothers are improbably cast as pretty blondes who look as though they work as models in their spare time modeling jeans for Calvin Klein. When Borges was told of one of the additions to the story, a bedroom scene in which both brothers begin kissing Juliana and end up kissing one another, his outrage was expressed in terms stronger than those he used when a good piece of fiction was turned into a terrible film.[11] Isidoro Blaisten's memory of Borges's remark is: "I said they were in love with the same woman, but not at the same time and in the same bed—or in such an uncomfortable position!" (conversation, July 1991).[12] Roberto Alifano, in turn, recalls that Borges came out in favor of censorship vis-à-vis this film, though he usually opposed it (162). No doubt Borges would add Christensen to the list of the damned mentioned in "Nuestras imposibilidades": "una invisible reprobación recae sobre los dos ejecutores del inimaginable contacto." The unimaginable, the unspeakable, the fascinating contact.

So far, I have not commented on the phobic content of the phrase from "Nuestras imposibilidades" which speaks of a "fecal dialectic." After the initial quotation from the 1931 essay on politics, Borges never has anything directly to say about gay male sex nor about the rectal area of the male body. In fact, reference to male bodies and the "unspeakable contacts" between them is suppressed in Borges's many works; even the 1931 essay was eventually omitted from Borges's "complete" works. Yet the matter does not stop there; as is often the case with what is repressed, it leaves its mark everywhere. One reader of this article has suggested that homophobia inflects the famous beginning of "Tlön, Uqbar, Orbis Tertius," where it is suggested that "los espejos y la cópula son abominables, porque multiplican el número de los hombres" (431) [mirrors and copulation are abominable because they multiply the number of men].

In a 1952 story, "La secta del Fénix" [The Sect of the Phoenix], later included in the second (1956) edition of *Ficciones*, Borges writes:

> Sin un libro sagrado que los congregue como la Escritura a Israel, sin una memoria común, sin esa otra memoria que es un idioma, desparramados por la faz de la tierra, diversos de color y de rasgos, una sola cosa—el Secreto—los une y los unirá hasta el fin de los días. . . . [P]uedo dar fe de que el cumplimiento del rito es la única práctica religiosa que observan los sectarios. El rito constituye el Secreto. Este, como ya indiqué, se trasmite de generación en generación, pero el uso no quiere que las madres lo enseñen a los hijos, ni tampoco los sacerdotes; la iniciación en el misterio es tarea de los individuos más bajos. Un esclavo, un leproso o un pordiosero hacen de mistagogos. También un niño puede adoctrinar a otro niño. El acto en sí es trivial, momentáneo y no requiere descripción. . . . El Secreto es sagrado pero no deja de ser un poco ridículo; su ejercicio es furtivo y aun clandestino y los adeptos no hablan de él. No hay palabras decentes para nombrarlo, pero se entiende que todas las palabras lo nombran o mejor dicho, que inevitablemente lo aluden, y así, en el diálogo yo he dicho una cosa cualquiera y los adeptos han sonreído o se han puesto incómodos, porque sintieron que yo había tocado el Secreto. (523)
>
> [Without a sacred book that brings them together like the Bible for the people of Israel, without a common memory, without that other memory that is a common language, scattered over the face of the earth, differing in race and aspect, only one thing—the Secret—unites them and will go on uniting them to the end of time. . . . I can testify that the performance of the rite is the only religious practice observed by the members of the sect. The rite constitutes the Secret. This Secret, as I have already indicated, is transmitted from generation to generation, but custom requires that mothers not teach it to their children, nor the priests either; the initiation in the mystery is left to the lowest individuals. A slave, a leper or a beggar serve as initiators. Also a child

can teach another child. The act in itself is trivial, brief and requires no description. . . . There are no decent words to name it, but everyone understands that all words name it or rather that inevitably they all allude to it; in conversation I have sometimes said something that made the initiated smile or grow uncomfortable, because they felt that I had referred to the Secret.]

The content of this passage is undeniably homoerotic. The secret taught by one boy to another, the secret revealed in empty spaces such as basements [13] and vacant lots (charged with frightening energy for Borges, as revealed by Estela Canto),[14] the secret which serves to unite a diverse group of people and is jealously guarded from others, the secret whose name one dare not speak: that secret, for Borges, was male homosexuality.[15]

The phoenix is the symbol of this secret because in it male creates male without the intervention of the female. The eleventh edition of the *Encyclopaedia Britannica* notes: "According to Pliny (*Nat. hist.* x. 2), there is only one phoenix at a time, and he, at the close of his long life, builds himself a nest with twigs of cassia and frankincense, on which he dies; from his corpse is generated a worm which grows into the young phoenix" (21: 457). Woscoboinik, commenting on the appearance of the phoenix in this story and in a couple of other Borges texts, comments:

La mujer se presenta en el mito sólo ligada a Venus, que de diosa de la belleza, el amor y la fecundidad, pasa a ser la de la muerte. Así, el Fénix es simultáneamente su propio padre y su propio hijo, "heredero de sí mismo", inmortal, que renace de sus cenizas y atestigua el paso del tiempo. Fantasía de autoengendramiento narcisista y tanático, que niega la paternidad, la mujer, la relación sexual y la procreación. (160) [Woman is only present in the myth linked to Venus, who instead of being goddess of beauty, love and fecundity is here goddess of death. Thus, the Phoenix is simultaneously father and son, "heir to itself," immortal, reborn from the ashes and testifying to the passage of time. A fantasy of narcissistic and deathly self-engendering, which denies paternity, woman, sexual relations and procreation.]

The "phoenix sect" of the Borges story must be constituted through that ultimate act of "male bonding," anal penetration, but that act is shrouded in secrecy.

But of course if he returned so often to this secret, once even calling it a "fecal dialectic," it must be because he was in some way implicated in that dialectic. Peter Stallybrass and Allon White find that "disgust always bears the imprint of desire" (191) and analyze the processes of "displaced abjection" through which the phobic material is negated, incorporated, and expressed. In Borges, the fear of a "fecal dialectic" manifests itself first in the suppression of references to male-male contact, whether the bodies in question be those of Wilde or Whitman or perhaps even David and Jonathan. Then, homoeroticism is coded in violent contact between men, particularly in the important leitmotiv of the knife fight. The recurrent representation of this topos places the "Borges" figure (Dahlmann in "El Sur," Fierro in "El fin," Lönnrot in "La muerte y la brújula," and so on) in the place of the "victim" or "passive partner," as in the revealing last lines of the poem "El tango," where things are as explicit as they will ever be in Borges:

> . . . El tango crea un turbio
> Pasado irreal que de algún modo es cierto,
> El recuerdo imposible de haber muerto
> Peleando, en una esquina del suburbio. (889)
> [The tango creates a confused unreal past that is in some sense true, the impossible memory of having died fighting on a suburban street-corner.]

And finally, since writing is impossible from the place of the victim, there is an insistent doubling, an appropriation of the place of the other in order for the story to be told: this is most explicit in "La forma de la espada" [The Shape of the Sword] in which John Vincent Moon pretends to be not the one marked by the sword but the one who marked him,[16] but the same process is at work in many other texts including "La muerte y la brújula" [Death and the Compass], "Los teólogos" [The Theologians], and "Abenjacán el Bojarí, muerto en su laberinto" [Abenjacán el-Bokhari, Dead in His Labyrinth]. Apropos of Kafka's "In the Penal Colony," Judith Butler has written:

> The question is not: what meaning does that inscription carry within it, but what cultural apparatus arranges this meeting between instrument and body, what interventions into this ritualistic repetition are possible? The "real" and the "sexually factic" are phantasmatic constructions—illusions of substance—that bodies are compelled to approximate, but never can. (146)[17]

Deleuze and Guattari (apropos of the same Kafka story) speak of "this cruel system of inscribed signs" (145). Writing can only be performed by a speaker who assumes simultaneously both the position of the victimizer and that of the victim, in a strange position of alienation from self. Borges describes this sense of alienation in the early essay "La nadería de la perso- nalidad" [The Nothingness of Personality], and in that essay he reveals the desire to liberate a feminine (homosexual?) soul: in conversation with his friend, "encima de cualquier alarde egoísta, voceaba en mi pecho la volun- tad de mostrar por entero mi alma al amigo. *Hubiera querido desnudarme de ella y dejarla allí palpitante*" (*Inquisiciones* 90) [beyond any sort of egotistical display, the desire to reveal my soul completely to my friend was crying out in my breast. *I would have liked to bare myself of it/her (my soul) and leave it lying there, palpitating*].[18] The feminine principle here is the excluded middle that makes possible the homosocial but that does not succeed in erasing the homosexual.

Juan Orbe, approaching the inscription of the "lower bodily strata" from a completely different angle than I do here, has noted the importance of the latrine in a key Borges text, "La biblioteca de Babel" [The Library of Babel], in which reference is made to "letrinas para el bibliotecario sen- tado" (466) [latrines for the seated librarian]. Also, in "La lotería en Babi- lonia" [The Lottery of Babylon] there is a sacred latrine named "Qaphqa" in which messages "de variable veracidad" [of varying truthfulness] are left for the all-powerful Company that runs the lottery (458). Orbe notes the association of writing to fecal "production" in Borges but does not see the presence of homoeroticism in this obsessional element. However, the fre- quent presence of an Other, almost always male, almost always locked in some sort of phallic combat with the protagonist, suggests that the "fecal dialectic" is "fecal" only because it involves (phantasmatic) anal penetra- tion. The fecal "production" that is writing (for Borges, in this account) is the result of male-male impregnation, an impossibility for human bi- ology but certainly not for the human imagination.[19] And the phobic site of writing is the rectum.

In "Crazy Jane Talks with the Bishop," Yeats[20] writes:

'A woman can be proud and stiff
When on love intent;
But Love has pitched his mansion in
The place of excrement;
For nothing can be sole or whole
That has not been rent.' (255)

Put "Borges" in the place occupied by "woman" here, and all hell would break loose.[21] His (feminine) soul would be revealed and would lie palpitating before him, before us. To hold off that revelation,[22] to cover his ass, he writes.[23]

Notes

In memory of Estela Canto

1   In the 1932 preface to *Discusión*, Borges describes the essay in these terms: "*Nuestras imposibilidades* no es el charro ejercicio de invectiva que dijeron algunos; es un informe reticente y dolido de ciertos caracteres de nuestro ser que no son tan gloriosos" (177) ["Our Impossibilities" isn't the tawdry piece of invective that some have claimed; it is the incomplete and painful report on certain features of our being that are less than glorious]. The 1955 edition (and subsequent ones, including the *Obras completas*) omits the essay, and the sentence in the preface just quoted is glossed with a note (dated 1955): "El artículo, que ahora parecería muy débil, no figura en esta reedición" (177n.) [The article, that would now seem rather weak, does not appear in this new edition]. Josefina Ludmer has already commented at length on Borges's fear of "weakness" in his treatment of the gaucho and the compadrito (221–36, esp. 224); since the essay in question deals with the defects of the Argentine national character, the admission of possible "weakness" is especially revealing. The omission is curious not only because Borges thus suppresses his most explicitly homophobic passage; the essay could also be read in relation to his later critiques of Argentine nationalism when that idea became identified with the figure of Juan Domingo Perón. The "Revolución Libertadora" against Perón of course also took place in 1955.

2   Borges is not discussed in David William Foster's *Gay and Lesbian Themes in Latin American Writing*, though his name is invoked once in the book apropos of *No país das sombras* by the Brazilian writer Aguinaldo Silva. Borges is however mentioned prominently in a bizarre story by Jorge Asís, "Los homosexules controlan todo," in which the narrator "defends" Borges against the charges made by his homophobic friend Aldo, who asks: "Che, ¿y ese Borges? . . . . —Borges, ¿también? —¿También qué? —¿Se la come?" (21) [Hey, and that Borges guy? Borges, too? What? Does he suck dick too?]. The friend goes on to insist that homosexuals occupy all positions of power in Argentina, and that Borges, by virtue of being so famous, must therefore also be homosexual.

3   For Borges's most direct assertion of his love for another man (in this case, apparently for the Mallorcan poet Jacobo Sureda, the recipient of the *Cartas de juventud*), see the odd confessional moment in "La nadería de la personalidad," in which Borges explains that he desired to bare his soul to his friend, quoted on p. 40 of this essay. What is curious about this passage is how excessive it is in its original context. In the midst of a philosophical argument derivative from Schopenhauer, Borges suddenly dramatizes his sense that the self is an empty shifter with this very personal anecdote. What's more, the "personal" quality of the anecdote contradicts the thesis of the essay that "personality" is an empty concept; even though Borges reaches this conclusion by the end of the narration of the episode, to tell the story he has had to posit or postulate the reality and presence of the notion of "personality." Later he will do much the same thing in at least two stories, "La escritura del dios" and "La busca de Averroes."

In a 1984 interview with Mirta Schmidt, Borges says that he has had various homosexual friends with whom he reached an accord ("un pacto tácito") not to discuss their homosexuality (qtd. in Stortini 112). The odd things about the conversation reported by Borges with a gay friend in Seville is that the friend insisted on coming out to him and asked whether Borges would still accept his friendship. Borges does not speak in the interview of any gay Argentine friends he had, but of course he was close for many years to José Bianco, whose homosexuality was a secret to no one.

4   The gossip has focused on the question of whether Borges was impotent. The evidence offered—the alleged testimony, usually at third or fourth hand, of the women who were the objects of his attentions—could as easily be taken as signs that Borges did not give free expression to his "true" sexual nature. Canto offers a fascinating discussion of the enigmas of Borges's sexual nature in her book; see also Julio Woscoboinik's appendix to the second edition (1991) of his 1988 psychoanalytic study of Borges, in which he comments on the points of contact between Canto's experiences with Borges and his own hypotheses based on a reading of the work (257–62).

5   Cf. Neil Bartlett on Wilde: "If a stranger asked you to name a homosexual, would you give your own name in reply? Or if you asked someone else, your sister, for instance, or your father, to name a homosexual, what would their response be? There is one, just one, whose name everyone knows. In fact he is famous above all else for being a homosexual. And since his name alone can conjure my past, it was his name I started with, the first entry I looked up in the catalogue. His words began to ghost my writing" (26). On Wilde, also see Koestenbaum ("Wilde's Hard Labor") and Sedgwick (*Epistemology of the Closet*, chap. 3). For a useful account of Wilde's period (without focusing on Wilde per se), see Dellamora; both Dellamora and Bartlett reconstruct elements of a homosexual life just prior to the "discovery" of homosexuality in the Wilde cases.

6   On the correspondence with Symonds, see Sedgwick, *Between Men* 203–4, and Moon 11–13.

7   González's point is well taken, though Borges's translation of one of Whitman's key homoerotic poems, "When I heard at the close of the day," is quite faithful to the original.

8   For Sedgwick's discussion of the concept, see *Between Men* 83–96 and *Epistemology of the Closet* 19–21, 138–39, 182–212.

9   Though he does not propose directly that Emma Zunz be read against lesbian theory, Bernard McGuirk's fascinating analysis of the story as "écriture feminine" could easily be extended in this direction ("Z/Z," unpublished manuscript). The repugnance that Emma feels during intercourse with the Swedish sailor and the laconic description of her relations with her friends the Kornfuss sisters and of their visit to the gym would certainly justify this approach.

10   Among his productions in Brazil were *Mãos sagradas* (1955) and *Alice* (1968).

11   See, for example, his review of the Spencer Tracy version of *The Strange Case of Doctor Jekyll and Mister Hyde*.

12   Roberto Alifano's recollection is less colorful, but the substance is the same. Alifano writes: "Borges se sintió absolutamente defraudado por la película; su indignación se debía a que el director presentaba a los hermanos Nilsen como homosexuales. 'En ningún momento ni remotamente pasó por mi cabeza la idea de la relación homosexual entre esos dos hombres,' me comentó Borges. Casi inmediatamente me dictó un artículo que tituló *La censura* donde a pesar de pronunciarse en contra de esa arbitrariedad tan usual de los gobiernos totalitarios, la aprobaba en el caso específico de la película basada en su cuento" (162) [Borges felt absolutely let down by the film; his indignation was due to the fact that the director presented the Nilsen brothers as homosexuals. "At no point did the

idea of a homosexual relation between those two men ever go through my head," Borges commented to me. Almost immediately he dictated to me an article he entitled "Censorship" in which he declared that although he was opposed to that frequent arbitrary measure imposed by totalitarian governments, he approved of it in the specific instance of the film based on his story].

13 The revelation of the Aleph takes place in Carlos Argentino's basement, and I have already noted elsewhere (*El precursor velado* 40) that the basement scene is charged with erotic energy, perhaps with suggestions of mutual masturbation.

14 Canto writes of Borges's fear of beaches (50) and vacant lots (52), repeatedly insinuating that as a boy Borges must have suffered some sort of rape: "Se tiene la tentación de imaginar que una experiencia extraña y aterradora acechaba al niño Georgie en uno de esos terrenos baldíos. Una experiencia que tuvo que ver con la muerte. . . . Todo esto, naturalmente, es una pura 'conjetura'" (52) [One is tempted to imagine that some strange and terrifying experience happened to young Georgie in one of these vacant lots. . . . All of this, of course, is pure "conjecture"].

15 Earlier accounts have tended to see the "Secret" in "La secta del Fénix" as sexual intercourse in general, and perhaps male-female genital intercourse in particular: in particular, see Christ 155–59. In a note on this passage, Christ clarifies that in a conversation with Borges in New York in 1968, Borges claims that the "Secret" is procreative heterosexuality, citing Whitman on what "the divine husband knows, from the work of fatherhood" (190). The exchange replays some of the misunderstandings between Whitman and Symonds and can hardly be regarded as the last word on the story.

16 In "The Mark of the Knife," I comment at length on this story, which ends with John Vincent Moon's revelation that he is the villain of his story, the one on whose face is written the mark of his infamy (495).

17 Earlier in *Gender Trouble,* Butler writes: "If the creation of values, that historical mode of signification, requires the destruction of the body, much as the instrument of torture in Kafka's *In the Penal Colony* destroys the body on which it writes, then there must be a body prior to that inscription, stable and self-identical, subject to that sacrificial destruction. In a sense, for Foucault, as for Nieztsche, cultural values emerge as the result of an inscription on the body, understood as a medium, indeed, a blank page; in order for this inscription to signify, however, that medium must itself be destroyed—that is, fully transvaluated into a sublimated domain of values. Within the metaphorics of this notion of cultural values is the figure of history as a relentless writing instrument and the body as the medium which must be destroyed and transfigured in order for 'culture' to emerge" (130).

18 I assume that the "friend" in question is the Mallorcan poet Jacobo Sureda, with whom Borges carried on a passionate epistolary relationship in 1921 and 1922, recently published by Carlos Meneses as *Cartas de juventud.* Meneses in his introduction is at pains to assert that the letters are of interest because in them Borges reveals his passion for Concepción Guerrero, a young woman he met in Argentine in the period between the two trips to Europe (47–52). Equally interesting in the letter, however, is the strength of Borges's feelings for Sureda, who would seem to be the "friend" mentioned in "La nadería de la personalidad." The epistolary romance with Concepción Guerrero and Jacobo Sureda, then, anticipates the love triangle in "La intrusa."

19 For a brief consideration of the relations between anality and *écriture,* see Sedgwick, *Epistemology of the Closet* 208n.

20 Yeats is perhaps Borges's favorite among twentieth-century English-language poets, but this poem is not one he cites, for reasons that should be obvious by now.

21 "Entrego esa dialéctica fecal a los apologistas de la *viveza,* del *alacraneo* y de la *cachada,* que tanto infierno encubren" (*Discusión* 18) [I leave that fecal dialectic to the apologists of trickery, backbiting, and mockery, who conceal so much of hell].

22 And remember: "esta inminencia de una revelación, que no se produce, es, quizá, el hecho estético" (635) [this imminence of a revelation that does not take place is, perhaps, the aesthetic fact (beauty)].

23 Cf. Roa Bastos: "Sentí por primera vez que la escritura era para mí los bordes de una cicatriz que guardaba intacta su herida secreta e indecible" (74) [I felt for the first time that writing was for me the edges of a scar that kept intact a secret and unspeakable wound]. As this essay goes to press, I have received the new Foster sourcebook on gay and lesbian themes in Latin American writing, with an interesting essay on Borges by Daniel Altamiranda.

Works Cited

Alifano, Roberto. *Borges, biografía verbal.* Barcelona: Plaza y Janés, 1988.

Altamiranda, Daniel. "Borges, Jorge Luis." *Latin American Writers on Gay and Lesbian Themes: A Bio-Critical Sourcebook.* Ed. David William Foster. Westport: Greenwood Press, 1994. 72–83.

Asís, Jorge. "Los homosexuales controlan todo." *Ultimos relatos.* Ed. Nelly Pretel. Buenos Aires: Nemont Ediciones, 1978. 17–24.

Balderston, Daniel. "The Mark of the Knife: Scars as Signs in Borges." *Modern Language Review* 83.1 (1988): 69–75.

———. *El precursor velado: R. L. Stevenson en la obra de Borges.* Buenos Aires: Editorial Sudamericana, 1985.

Bartlett, Neil. *Who Was That Man? A Present for Mr. Oscar Wilde.* London: Serpent's Tail, 1988.

Borges, Jorge Luis. *Cartas de juventud (1921–1922).* Ed. and intro. Carlos Meneses. Madrid: Editorial Orígenes, 1987.

———. *Discusión.* Buenos Aires: M. Gleizer, 1932.

———. *El idioma de los argentinos.* Buenos Aires: M. Gleizer, 1928.

———. *Inquisiciones.* Buenos Aires: Editorial Proa, 1925.

———. *Obras completas.* Buenos Aires: Emecé, 1976.

———. *El tamaño de mi esperanza.* Buenos Aires: Editorial Proa, 1926.

Butler, Judith. *Gender Trouble: Feminism and the Subversion of Identity.* New York: Routledge, 1990.

Canto, Estela. *Borges a contraluz.* Madrid: Espasa-Calpe, 1990.

Christ, Ronald. *The Narrow Act: Borges' Act of Allusion.* New York: New York University Press, 1969.

Deleuze, Gilles, and Félix Guattari. *Anti-Oedipus: Capitalism and Schizophrenia.* Trans. Robert Hurley, Mark Seem, and Helen R. Lane. Minneapolis: University of Minnesota Press, 1983.

Dellamora, Richard. *Masculine Desire: The Sexual Politics of Victorian Aestheticism.* Chapel Hill: University of North Carolina Press, 1990.

Ellmann, Richard. *Oscar Wilde*. New York: Alfred A. Knopf, 1988.

Foster, David William. *Gay and Lesbian Themes in Latin American Writing*. Austin: University of Texas Press, 1991.

González, Eduardo. *The Monstered Self: Narratives of Death and Performance in Latin American Fiction*. Durham: Duke University Press, 1992.

Koestenbaum, Wayne. "Wilde's Hard Labor and the Birth of Gay Reading." *Engendering Men: The Question of Male Feminist Criticism*. Ed. Joseph A. Boone and Michael Cadden. London: Routledge, 1990. 176–89.

Ludmer, Josefina. *El género gauchesco: Un tratado sobre la patria*. Buenos Aires: Editorial Sudamericana, 1988.

McGuirk, Bernard. "Z/Z." Unpublished manuscript.

Moon, Michael. *Disseminating Whitman: Revision and Corporeality in* Leaves of Grass. Cambridge: Harvard University Press, 1991.

Orbe, Juan. *Borges abajo: entreguerra, escritura y cuerpo boca-ano*. Buenos Aires: Corregidor, 1993.

"Phoenix." *Encyclopaedia Britannica*. 11th ed. New York: Encyclopaedia Britannica Company, 1911. 21: 457–58.

Roa Bastos, Augusto. "Algunos núcleos generadores de un texto narrativo." *L'Idéologique dans le texte (Textes hispaniques)*. Actes du IIème Colloque du Séminaire d'Etudes Littéraires de l'Université de Toulouse-Le Mirail. Toulouse: Université de Toulouse-Le Mirail, 1984. 67–95.

Sedgwick, Eve Kosofsky. *Between Men: English Literature and Male Homosocial Desire*. New York: Columbia University Press, 1985.

———. *Epistemology of the Closet*. Berkeley: University of California Press, 1990.

Stallybrass, Peter, and Allon White. *The Politics and Poetics of Transgression*. Ithaca: Cornell University Press, 1986.

Stortini, Carlos R. *El diccionario de Borges*. Buenos Aires: Editorial Sudamericana, 1986.

Watney, Simon. *Policing Desire: Pornography, AIDS and the Media*. 2d ed. Minneapolis: University of Minnesota Press, 1989.

Whitman, Walt. *Complete Poetry and Collected Prose*. Ed. Justin Kaplan. New York: Library of America, 1982.

Woscoboinik, Julio. *El secreto de Borges: indagación psicoanalítica de su obra*. 2d ed. Buenos Aires: Grupo Editor Latinoamericano, 1991.

Yeats, William Butler. *The Collected Poems*. New York: Macmillan, 1956.

TWO

(Neo)historical Retrievals

Jorge Salessi
The Argentine Dissemination of Homosexuality, 1890–1914

Introduction

A close reading of the writings of key figures in the Argentine state technocracy between 1890 and 1914 shows the consistent preoccupation of these writers with the study and definition of medicolegal categories of homosexuality, uranism, sexual inversion, and pederasty. These studies, I suggest, reflected more than a longing for stricter border controls around the definitions of nationality and class. During a period of pervasive cultural, political, and economic insecurity created by the process of immigration and modernization, these longings became especially intense regarding issues of sex and gender.

Reconstructing the historicity, conditions of emergence, and ideological contingencies of these medicolegal categories of analysis, in this essay I explore the conceptual phenomena denoted by different categories of this sexual science, noting connotations, contradictions, and incoherences. Following some of Eve Kosofsky Sedgwick's ideas about the turn-of-the-century crisis of homo/heterosexual definition, I will call this development and dissemination of a homophobic ideology *homosexual panic,* when it is directed against men.[1] I am aware of the risks of a mechanical transference of theories from one cultural context to another. However, while research on the construction of homosexuality in Latin America has been scarce, much of published research on the history of homosexuality in the United States and Europe has focused on the same historical period I examine here.[2] Thus, while reconstructing the sociopolitical conditions of emergence of the definitions of same-sex behavior in Argentina, I have found it very useful to compare the Argentine taxonomic elaboration with contemporary developments studied by George Chauncey, Jr.[3] Like Chauncey's work, this essay suggests that the homophobia disseminated by the texts I explore is a reaction to the ever-increasing access to the paid work force of women who were often the main economic support of the family, the organization of a women's movement within the new and powerful Argentine labor movement, and the glaring visibility of a rich homosexual subculture thriving in a city with a large proportion of young males without traditional family ties.

However, as we will see in the texts of the Argentine positivist technocrats, the "broad shift in conceptualization" is different from the change Chauncey notes between the conceptions and definitions of sexual inversion and homosexuality (145). The understanding of this difference is crucial, I believe, for the understanding of Argentine, and perhaps Latin American, definitions and conceptions of sexual deviance.

Let me briefly reconstruct a historical context. The 1880 declaration of Buenos Aires as the capital city and federal district of the Argentine republic marks the end of the domestic quarrels between local chieftains and the beginning of the great immigration that, between 1880 and 1914, transformed Argentina and created a new culture. Although smaller in absolute numbers than the immigration reaching the United States earlier in the century, relative to the native population the immigration to Argentina was by far larger. Most of these immigrants, unable to become small farm owners due to the latifundia structure of land tenure, established themselves in one of two coastal cities, Buenos Aires and Rosario, to work in the growing urban industries and commercial ventures. By 1900 the immigration that had been imagined by the Argentine ideologues of the mid-nineteenth century as suburban and white (preferably Anglo-Saxon) had in reality become an immigration of large and visible groups of foreigners, mainly Italians and Spaniards, many of whom were young males without traditional family ties and often from the poorest areas of their home countries.

Out of this immigration grew a new Argentine middle class that forced the redefinition and rearrangement of the previous class structure. At the same time, the concentration of most workers in Buenos Aires during the first decade of the twentieth century allowed a new Argentine labor movement to develop and challenge the hegemony of the patrician landowning class, which until then had kept a tight grip on power by fair means or, more often, foul. By the 1900s Buenos Aires had become a major port and a city of immigrants; farmers had become urban dwellers and laborers, in many cases seasoned by the class struggles of the old country. The immigration that had provided the labor necessary for the integration of Argentina into the Eurocentric blueprint of progress, modernization, and internationalism was now a foreign force living within its national borders and capable of striking against and paralyzing the meat and grain exporting economy that continued to enrich the landowning class.

At this point Argentina not only had to be imagined again—it had to be recreated. Its national icons, songs, anthems, colors, images, and guiding fictions had to be mass produced and distributed among all cultural groups and social classes. These cultural productions carefully targeted the children of the immigrant, the first generation of Argentines who, in order to be trained and inducted into the imagined national community, had to be separated from the "foreign" parents.[4] A positivist technocracy of State officials, physicians, psychiatrists, lawyers, criminologists, pedagogues, prolific writers and politicians, subservient to the patrician landowning class, took charge of this reimagination, mass production and distribution.[5] By examining their works in this context, this article is also a reflection on a specific instance of the crossings between definitions of sexualities and a pernicious brand of turn-of-the-century Argentine nationalism.

Third Sex and Feminine Uranism

Juan Bialet-Massé's 1904 study of *El estado de las clases obreras argentinas a comienzos de siglo* [The State of the Argentine Working Classes at the Beginning of the Century], undertaken by order of President Julio Roca, was a preliminary investigation into a first national labor law. With this measure the government hoped to control the new Argentine labor movement that had emerged, organized, and demanded participation in the country's political decision making. In Bialet-Massé's text, the "third sex" was the term used to characterize women who were beginning to work for wages and play an important role in the development of the Argentine labor movement.

In his study Bialet first worried that "la mujer, entre nosotros, más bien hace concurrencia al hombre en profesiones y oficios que hasta ahora estaban reservados por las costumbres a los hombres; las libres instituciones del país en nada las obstaculiza" (424) [women among us are competing too well with men in professions and offices that until now were traditionally reserved for men; the country's free institutions are not hindering them in any way].[6] Claiming that "el trabajo de la mujer no puede, pues, admitirse sino por las fatalidades del destino" [women's work must not be allowed unless fate demands it], overlooking the unpaid work they traditionally performed at home, he warned that women working for wages became

> eso que se llama el tercer sexo, que tiene en Londres solamente más de 300.000 representates y en Europa más de 3.000.000, que ha aparecido en los Estados Unidos invasor, y que felizmente no tiene todavía entre nosotros sino algún que otro individuo afiliado. Ese tercer sexo se compone de las mujeres que quedan sin hombre con quien aparejarse, por efecto de emigraciones a las colonias; [y] de las que, por efecto de una moral extraviada, han renunciado o renuncian al matrimonio. (426)
>
> [that thing called the *third sex*, which in London alone has more than 300,000 representatives, and in Europe more than 3,000,000, and which has appeared in the United States as an invasion, and which happily still has none amongst us, save some affiliated individuals. This third sex is made up of women who remain without mates due to emigration to the colonies; and who, due to deviant morals, have renounced or are renouncing marriage.]

Here, Bialet used the definition of sexual inversion—third sex, intermediate sex, or *sexuelle zwischenstufe*—proposed by Karl Ulrichs in writings published between 1860 and 1879. In Bialet-Massé's text, however, the "incorrect" sexual object choice—homosexuality as we understand it today—was not the central feature of inversion. What defined deviation, or the "immoral," was either the independence from men gained by women who worked for wages; the circumstantial absence of a man; or the voluntary and conscious rejection of the traditional marriage that established the division of labor as well as the roles and hierarchies of "feminine" women and "masculine" men.

In early twentieth-century Argentina, women who earned their own living were subversive because, making themselves economically independent from men, they refused to accept the roles of wives and prolific mothers, pillars of the project of modernization and immigration through whom the class in power sought to create the new "Argentine race." On the same page where he warned about the "invasion" of the third sex, Bialet defined the role of women:

> La misión de la mujer, en lo que a cada sexo toca en la perpetuación de la especie, es la maternidad, la crianza y educación de los hijos; en el vientre de las mujeres está la fuerza y grandeza de las naciones. . . .

Entre nosotros hay matrimonios que tiene seis y ocho hijos; y no son raros los hermosos casos de doce o más, y hasta de veinte hijos tenidos por una sola mujer, y se conocen casos de veinte y cinco hijos en un hogar. No arranquemos de la frente de la mujer argentina esa corona de gloria. (426)

[Woman's mission, as far as each sex has a part in the perpetuation of the species, is maternity, and the raising and education of children; in women's wombs lie the strength and greatness of nations. . . . Among us there are marriages that have six or eight children; twelve or more are not rare, and up to twenty children born of one mother, and cases are known of twenty-five children in one home. Let us not snatch this crown of glory from the Argentine woman's brow.]

The third sex, therefore, was the sexual category used to name—and thereby contain and control—the woman who emancipated herself economically from men.

Furthermore, in Bialet-Massé's text the third sex is said to have "invaded" Europe and the United States. In the terminology of Argentine positivist discourse, invasion was synonymous with infection; the two words were used interchangeably.[7] Thus the third sex was represented as an infection threatening the health of growing national bodies. Moreover, Bialet-Massé denoted members of the third sex as *affiliated*—by which he meant associated with the labor movement—and this, he said, posed a very specific threat: "Cuando la mujer toma parte en un movimiento general, el triunfo es incontrastable. . . . Cuando doscientas mujeres asisten a un mitin, hay dos mil que por timidez no van a él, pero que las acompañan y hacen una propaganda tan eficaz como las que salen a la calle" (151–52) [When women take part in a general movement, its triumph is assured. . . . When two hundred women go to a meeting, there are two thousand that, out of shyness, stay at home, but who accompany those who do go and their propaganda is as effective as that of those going out in the streets]. *All* women thus were part of a network whose direct or indirect involvement in labor movements threatened the very fabric of society. Bialet-Massé's study promoted a prophylaxis that would arrest the external invasion of third sex women threatening the national health; a text by Victor Mercante complemented this strategy by advocating measures to halt the spread of an infection of "feminine uranism" inside the national borders.

Victor Mercante portrayed this infection as an epidemic in an article published in 1905 in the *Archivos de Psiquitría y Criminología*[8] [Archives of Psychiatry and Criminology] entitled "El fetiquismo y el uranismo femenino en los internados educativos" [Fetishism and Feminine Uranism in Boarding Schools]. Mercante was a pedagogue and an important official of the state educational bureaucracy. He specialized in women's education and child criminology and was the director of the Escuela Normal de Mercedes, one of the most important training institutions for teachers; he was also an inspector for the Consejo Nacional de Educación; and professor of Pedagogy in the Universidad de la Plata.

As a pedagogue, Mercante described the general features of women: "El alma de la mujer es el alma inquietante del misterio, dijo un escritor genial y desconocido [most likely himself]. Flor caprichosa y turbadora, que guarda en sus pétalos y en su cáliz los gérmenes del ensueño" (22) [Woman's soul is the unsettling soul of mystery, said an outstanding and unknown writer. A capricious and disturbing flower that keeps in its petals and its calyx the germs of illusions]. Here he appropriated the tedious commonplaces of Latin American *modernismo* then in vogue to describe woman—her body transformed into objet d'art, but which might be difficult to control or might disturb a social order. In the soul of this woman-receptacle were kept, although in a latent state, the "germs" of the sickness that threatened to spread throughout society.

As the scientist confronted with the seemingly fragile and dangerous test tube, Mercante asked himself fearfully "¿Qué surgirá al romperse aquella crisálida que absorbe nuestra atención, Manón, Lucrecia o Mesalina? ¡Cuántas existencias envenenadas, cuántos destinos truncos, cuánta amargura, cuántas lágrimas, cuántas desesperaciones trágicas regará en la vida aquella existencia en flor!" (22) [What will come forth when that chrysalis that absorbs our attention breaks: Manon, Lucretia, or Messalina? How many poisoned existences, how many destinies cut short, how much bitterness, how many tears, how many tragic desperations will this nubile existence in bloom spread in life!]. Thus, Mercante, through the "objective" lens of positivist observation, began to construct an entire history within a framework of three treacherous women: Manon, the stereotypical prostitute of the nineteenth-century opera, the rebel; Lucretia, the Renaissance poisoner, the woman who competed in men's power games; and Messalina, the adulterous Roman matron, the woman who appropriates for herself the prerogatives of the double standard. The "poisoned," "tragic," or "bitter" life narratives of these women—generally created and repeated by male writers, male historians, and male teachers—were the cautionary models imagined by this educator for his adolescent pupils.[9]

As an educational bureaucrat, Mercante declared, "Pude, con sorpresa, constatar que el uranismo pasivo (acerca del impulsivo no tengo datos) constituye en los grandes internados de educación, una epidemia" [I was able to verify that in large boarding schools passive uranism (I have no data regarding the impulsive one) constitutes an epidemic]. His observations were of a single educational institution, "internado X . . . , escuela de enseñanza superior de Buenos Aires donde estudian niñas de 12 a 22 años" [boarding school X . . . a school of higher education in Buenos Aires, where girls from 12 to 22 years old study]. Assigning responsibility for spreading the disease through the whole educational system, Mercante said that his "anotaciones comprenden, además, establecimientos particulares y del estado" [findings include, moreover, both private and state schools], yet he later criticized one very specific type of private school—"de régimen conventual" [that with a conventual regimen], or the nun's school (25). This was the ideal medium for the propagation of "feminine uranism" threatening the national educational system.

Describing this specific medium, while adding a new definition to the taxonomy of homosexuality growing out of these Argentine texts, Mercante claimed that "La *homosexualidad* femenina no es por lo común impulsiva; hay una tendencia morbosa a mantenerse contemplativa y romancesca, si es posible con cierta operosidad mística. Aquí su parentesco claustral. El culto de las reclusas a María es un síndroma sicopático donde el amor ha sufrido la *inversión,* pero dentro de una actitud completamente pasiva, extática" (25, my emphasis) [Feminine *homosexuality* is not usually impulsive; rather there is a morbid predisposition toward contemplation and romanticism, if possible with a mystical leaning. Here its relationship is with the cloister. The cult of Mary's recluses is a psychopathic syndrome in which women's love has undergone an *inversion,* but within an attitude that is completely passive, ecstatic]. In Argentina in 1905, during a transition in the elaboration of a taxonomy of sexual deviations, the definition of sexual inversion coexisted with the definition of homosexuality.[10] However, in Mercante's conception, as in Bialet-Massé's, what defined sexual deviance was not so much the "incorrect" sexual object choice as the absence of a "correct" sexual object.

In Mercante's article, women who as adolescents began to reject the role defined for them and who instead associated with other women were described as "mystics" because, since the sixteenth century in Latin America, convents have provided a space in which women could develop models of lives different from that of the wife and mother, although still remaining within a patriarchal power structure.[11] Furthermore, private nun's schools, usually associated with convents, were not as easily controlled as public ones. Mercante insisted that "el fenómeno se manifiesta, es curioso, en

aquellas escuelas más claustrales y donde las maestras se entregan a fre-
cuentes disertaciones acerca del culto a las santas mujeres, con letreros alu-
sivos en los pizarrones" (25) [the phenomenon manifests itself, curiously,
in those more cloister-like schools where the women teachers give frequent
dissertations on the cult of women saints with illustrative inscriptions on
the blackboards]. These were the dangerous alternative models: oral dissertations and written inscriptions constitute what Carolyn Heilbrun calls
"narratives, or the texts, plots or examples by which women might assume
power over—take control of—their own lives" (17).

Mercante represented the vigilante male-run national educational system, and his article reflected the tensions between a state male bureaucracy and a remote, elusive private school where women lived, studied, and
worked. The persistence of gender markers in the Romance languages permits the Argentine pedagogue to stress that students, teachers, and admin-
istrators in these schools were women, and he repeatedly criticized their
incredulity and lack of vigilance, which allowed the epidemic to spread:
"suelen escapar, tras el disimulo, a las perspicaces observaciones de las di-
rectoras" (25) [through dissimulation it usually escapes the perspicacious
observation of the headmistresses]. Mercante noted that it was during
breaks between classes that the sickness became most evident. It appeared,
for example, in "furtivos besos [que] sellan los momentos de fe y de esperanza" (26) [furtive kisses that seal moments of faith and hope] and "las
profesoras, en efecto, abandonaban los patios para entregarse a quehaceres
del momento. No advertían que la quietud de aquellos seres sin trabajo
no podía ser sino ficticia" (25) [the women teachers, in effect, would leave
the courtyards in order to devote themselves to the tasks of the moment.
They were not aware that the calm of these idle beings could not be but
fictitious].

Mercante proposed measures to halt the spread of the infection: "la pro-
hibición del beso, del abrazo y de la vida quieta y dual" [the prohibition
of kissing, embracing and the quiet and dual life], but also that "dissertations" and "illustrative inscriptions" be replaced by "lecciones variadas y
confortantes y atrayentes sobre temas científicos; no herir la imaginación
narrando sucesos altisonantes y de subido color místico acerca de la vida as-
cética" (25) [various comforting and attractive lessons on scientific topics;
to not injure the imagination by narrating grandiloquent events, and ones
of a strong mystical tone on the ascetic life]. The "tone" of these lessons
"on scientific themes" can be read in Mercante's own discourse.[12]

In "feminine," "passive uranism," as defined by Mercante, we begin to
see the significance of the distinction between "passive" and "active" roles

in the Argentine taxonomy of sexual deviance. As Chauncey notes the distinction between passive and active originally pertained to notions of sex between males (127)—doctors and criminologists in the United States and in Argentina made a clear differentiation between insertive ("active") and receptive ("passive") roles—but was later applied to the conception of relationships between women. This distinction was important in Mercante's article. In spite of the feminine characterization that he gave to this homosexuality of the inverted but passive woman, he nevertheless identified an active and a passive "element" in uranistic adolescent girls. He defined the pairs of girls who meet between classes as

> novios que conversaban de sus asuntos. No obstante el carácter espiritual y femenino de aquel connubio, un elemento era el activo, otro el pasivo. . . . El apareamiento ocurre entre dos estructuras diferentes del punto de vista moral. Una, eminentemente sugestionadora, manda, vigila, cuida, ofrece, da, dispone, describe el presente, imagina el futuro, salva las dificultades y vitaliza a su compañera. Otra, obedece, acepta, se resigna, evita motivos de disgusto a su mancebo y enaltece sus afectos con palabras llenas de sentimiento y de sumisión. (26)
> [beloveds that talked about their matters. Notwithstanding the spiritual and feminine character of the connubial relationship, one element was active, and the other passive. . . . The pairing off occurs between two structures that are different from the point of view of morality. One, preeminently suggestive, commands, oversees, cares for, offers, gives, disposes, describes the present, imagines the future, resolves difficulties, and vitalizes her companion. The other obeys, accepts, resigns herself, avoids displeasing her beau and exalts her emotions with words and promises full of feeling and submission.]

In this pair, the passive adolescent was homosexual because another woman was her sexual or affective object choice, not because she had inverted the feminine role prescribed for her. The active woman was the invert, the transgressor, and the source of the infection.

Mercante stated that "la psicopatía despunta en niñas mayores de quince años y nace aislada, de una histérica" (25) [the psychopathology breaks in girls over fifteen, and appears isolated, in a hysteric], whereas the passive adolescent was the "imitative" induced to join the "cult" by the active adolescent. He alleged that "neófitas eran las que por primera vez ingresaban al establecimiento. La vacante, principio activo y sin novia, comenzaba la conquista con los ojos; luego la aproximación y por fin el ofrecimiento. . . .

El afecto va creciendo; la mujer, imitadora, se adapta, y la neófita contrae estado" (26) [the ones who came into the establishment for the first time were neophytes. The available active principle without a girlfriend would begin the conquest with her eyes, later by drawing near and finally with an offer. . . . Affections increase; the woman, imitative, adapts herself, and the neophyte changes civil status].

The anxiety over these "psychopathological," "hysterical," vitalizing young women expressed the patriarchal landowning class's fear of the activism of women who, in the first decade of the twentieth century, were highly visible in the public demonstrations of large, new labor unions.[13] These were the "suggestive" women who, when the domestic "infection" was represented as an invasion threatening the national borders from outside, were identified as foreign agents of perturbation. Their activism disturbed Bialet-Massé, who wrote "las mujeres que entran por ese camino son francamente anarquistas y anarquistas exaltadas; algunas de ellas se hacen notar por sus facultades oratorias. Hay en el Rosario una joven puntana de palábra enérgica y dominante, que arrastra a las multitudes" (435) [the women who enter this route are clearly anarchists and exalted anarchists at that; some of them are noted for their oratorical faculties. In Rosario there is a young woman *puntana* (originally from the northern area) endowed with energetic and dominating speech who sways the multitudes]. This is a good example of a turn-of-the-century Argentine fear of the power of women's discourse, and a good example, likewise, of the fear of revolt, in this case by the Argentine labor movement.

The two decades between 1890 and 1910 were foundational, and particularly violent, in the history of this movement. During the 1890s in Leopoldo Rodríguez's words, "el movimiento obrero estaba integrado y liderado por extranjeros. En esos años arribaron a Buenos Aires conocidos dirigentes anarquistas que colaboraron en la organización sindical. Era una época de notable aumento de la agitación obrera" (112) [the workers' movement was mostly made up of and led by foreigners. In those years, well-known anarchist leaders arrived in Buenos Aires and collaborated in the organization of syndicates. At the time there was a notable increase in workers' agitation]. The Argentine government reacted by delegating to employers and police officials the responsibility for containing, channeling, and derailing the demonstrations of discontent. In the next decade, however, the situation became much more serious. In 1902 Argentina saw the first general strike in its history. At this point, government reaction started to be institutionalized, and National Law 4144 was passed; known as the *Ley de residencia* [law of residency], it authorized the expulsion of any foreigner whose conduct threatened security or disturbed public order. In 1910 the *Ley de Defensa Social* [social defense law] was passed, a new measure intended to repress the leaders—the so-called external agitators—who were helping to organize and were often the visible faces of large popular movements. Between 1902 and 1910, a state of siege was imposed five times for a total of eighteen months as a preventive measure against workers' demonstrations. Rodríguez pointed out that "en esa década de violencia anti-obrera, rara era la huelga o manifestación que no terminase con la intervención policial o militar y la muerte de militantes. La culminación de la agitación tuvo lugar en los años 1909 y 1910" (86) [in that decade of antilabor violence, it was a rare strike or demonstration that did not end with police or military intervention and the death of militants. The height of the agitation took place in 1909 and 1910].

This was the "epidemic," the social "perturbation" that propagates itself. To contain it, the doctors, hygienists, criminologists, and pedagogues worked on two fronts: fighting the foreign invasion of women activists and defending society against the internal infection of feminine uranism, the passive followers. In *Las multitudes argentinas* [The Argentine Multitudes], the first sociological study of postimmigration Argentina (published in 1899), José María Ramos Mejía, an influential mentor of a generation of state technocrats, defined the characteristics of "the [feminine] multitudes" and of their "seductive" leaders and spokespersons, while he imagined and described a dynamic between the groups and their representatives.

The spokespersons of large popular groups, wrote Ramos Mejía, are "los dominadores de la multitud, los que, surgidos o no de ella, han tenido calidades de cierto órden que les ha permitido dominarlas, dirigirlas y, a veces transformarlas" (3) [the dominators of the multitudes, those that, having risen out of them or not, have qualities of a certain order that have permitted them to dominate, direct, and sometimes transform those same multitudes]. Ramos Mejía described the archetypal leader: "Tienen una aureola peculiar llena de efluvios carnales que seduce irresistiblemente la imaginación y los sentidos siempre alborotados de las mujeres. . . . Lo propio pasa con la multitud, que, punto más punto menos, tienen las mismas deficiencias y particularidades mentales de la mujer" (91–92) [They have a peculiar aura full of carnal exhalations that irresistibly seduce the imagination and the always agitated senses of women. . . . The same thing happens with the masses, who, have more or less the same deficiencies and particulars as women]. In Ramos Mejía's analysis, the Latin American predecessors of these leaders were "esa abundante pululación de hechiceros, astrólogos, judiciarios, nigrománticos, casi todos nativos . . . que a la par que hablaban de cuentos de amor y hacían sus hechizos, encantamientos y 'cercos eróticos,' en sus sortilegios mezclaban incitaciones a la desobediencia, y tendían a despertar en la plebe el sentimiento de una suficiencia profética de fuerzas" (20) [that abundant swarm of sorcerers, astrologers, judiciaries, necromancers, almost all natives . . . who while they were telling love stories were casting their spells, enchantments, and "erotic hoops," and in their charms mixed incitements to disobedience and tended to awaken in the plebeians a prophetic feeling of strength]. In the first decade of the twentieth century, however, when power relations "inverted," when the Argentine labor movement organized and met in celebrations and union demonstrations, Mercante's homophobic ideology was meant to control and prevent what Ramos Mejía called "la mujer de la plebe, [que] asociada a la turba, le imprime un aspecto terrible, porque en tales circunstancias, pierde más pronto que el hombre todos los instintos dulces y amables, que son la tónica del alma. Ellas arengan a la gente, la inflaman con sus imprecaciones inesperadas, en la plaza, en la calle, hasta en el púlpito de la iglesia" (155) [the woman of the multitude, who associated with the mob, impresses it with a terrible force, because in such circumstances, she more quickly than man loses all the sweet and kind instincts that are the tonic of her soul. These women harangue the crowd and inflame it with their unexpected imprecations, in the plaza, in the street, even in the pulpit of the church]. By likening both the crowd ("having more or less the same deficiencies as women") and the powerful, active figure who stimulates the crowd with *women,* Ramos Mejía thus instilled in the concept of a social and economic transformation an element of the "cloisterlike," uranistic "epidemic" we saw described by Mercante.

Sexual Inversion

Complementing his, and Gustave Le Bon's notion of the woman/crowd, J. M. Ramos Mejía in *Las multitudes argentinas* defined an aesthetic of the new Argentine social classes, homologizing it with the sensibility of a "sexual invert." It is important to point out that his ideas, disseminated through prolific writings and *from key positions in the state bureaucracy of the time,* became models for sociopolitical analysis and for the official and "scientific" ideology and discourse of the modern Argentine state. Ramos Mejía was the founder and first president of the Círculo Médico Argentino in 1875, founder and first director of the Asistencia Pública in 1882, founder and first professor of the nervous and mental illness chair of the Universidad de Buenos Aires in 1887, president of the Departamento Nacional de Higiene in 1892, and president of the Concejo Nacional de Educación in 1908. A hygienist, psychiatrist, sociologist, and mentor of the criminologists working for the state, Ramos Mejía, in the words of Hugo Vezzetti, represented "la encarnación moderna del moralista y un paradigma del gobernante" (14) [the modern incarnation of the moralist and a paradigm of the ruler] in postimmigration Argentina.

Central in Ramos Mejía's work was the definition of sexual inversion as the model for establishing a categorical difference between the patrician and landowning class and the new social classes and cultural groups that emerged from immigration. In *Las multitudes,* Ramos Mejía described *el guarango* [the uncouth] as one of the models—or types, characteristic of different categories of phrenology—and the most representative of the new upper, middle, and lower classes of the new society of Buenos Aires. Despite his variations, the *guarango* is always an urban dweller, a member of "the multitude" of the modern metropolis. As Manuel Bejarano explains in his study of the immigrant's patterns of settlement in Argentina at the turn of the century, "en las ciudades, en efecto, los niveles económico-sociales más altos, con exclusión del de la élite tradicional, fueron efectivamente alcanzados por los inmigrantes" (147) [in cities, in actuality, the highest socioeconomic levels, with the exception of the traditional elite, were effectively reached by immigrants]. Thus, although a city dweller in D. F. Sarmiento's mid-nineteenth-century conception represented the prototype of the "civilized man," by the end of the century, as immigrants filled the city, the urban dweller became the "degenerate." Therefore, the countryside and its inhabitants, Sarmiento's "barbarism," became the zone that defined and represented the power of the landowning class and was (re)conceived as the repository of the "real" sacred national values.

Ramos Mejía defined the patrician class by its difference: "Procede de padres cultos y de nobles abolengos ya afinados por el buen vivir y por la constante corrección . . . todo eso que ha ido lentamente llenando poco a poco el alma con el voluptuoso perfume de ideales y ambiciones *chères au coeur, que mon esprit rêvait,* y que se refugian, con cierto pudor varonil, en la modesta penumbra del hogar de abolengo" (272) [Comes from cultured fathers and noble lineages refined by good living and by constant correction . . . all that which has slowly been filling the soul with the voluptuous perfume of ideals and ambitions that are *chères au coeur, que mon esprit rêvait,* and which hides itself, with a certain virile shyness, in the modest penumbra of the ancestral home]. French, the language of one of the main

European cultural models, was used to define the traditional patrician class by association. This "virile" class was in contrast with the new society of inverted *guarangos* described on the following page:

> El guarango representa uno de esos vertebrados que en épocas remotas buscarán con curiosidad los sociologistas del porvenir, para establecer el encadenamiento de los tipos sucesivos de nuestra evolución. Es un invertido del arte, y se parece a los invertidos del instinto sexual que revelan su potencia dudosa por una manifestación atrabiliaria de los apetitos. Necesita de ese color vivísimo, de esa música chillona, como el erotómano de la carne; quiere las combinaciones bizarras y sin gusto de las cosas, como éste de las actitudes torcidas y de los procedimientos escabrosos para satisfacer especiales idiosincracias de su sensibilidad. (273, italics in original)
> [The *guarango* represents one of those vertebrates that sociologists of the future will seek with curiosity in years to come in order to establish the succession of types in our evolution. He is an invert of the arts and resembles inverts of the sexual instinct who reveal their dubious potency through an irritable manifestation of their appetites. He needs brilliant color and shrill music, as the erotomaniac needs flesh; he likes bizarre and tasteless combinations of things, like the invert of warped attitudes and obscure procedures, to satisfy the special idiosyncrasies of his sensibility.]

After describing the customs of the sexual invert *guarango*, Ramos Mejía concluded: "Lo que en materia de gusto y de arte se le ocurre a un guarango, sólo un invertido puede pensarlo" (274) [What ideas a *guarango* has in terms of taste and art, only an invert can imagine].

Ramos Mejía's identification of inversion with the aesthetic of the Buenos Aires urban dweller is similar to Chauncey's definition of inversion as "a broad range of deviant gender behavior of which homosexual desire was only a logical but indistinct aspect" (116). However, Ramos Mejía's use of inversion, in this particularly convulsive moment of Argentine social history, also denoted the "incorrect" sexual object choice: it is "an irritable manifestation of their [sexual] appetites." In this sense, therefore, inversion is also quite similar to the modern concept of homosexuality that Foucault proposes as a "certain quality of the sexual sensibility" and "a kind of interior androgyny, a hermaphroditism of the soul" (57) or the "special idiosyncrasies of sensibility." Thus, the term "inversion" in Argentine texts of the turn of the century denoted a broad range of "incorrect" social, sexual, and gender behaviors and continued to be used in conjunction with a new concept of "homosexuality" based on sexual object choice.

Pederasty

To better understand the forms of representation and connotations of the different categories of homosexuality of the Argentine sexual science we are tracing, we must first consider the historical demographic context of the times.

At the turn of the century male foreigners between the ages of twenty and forty were a large and highly visible part of the population of Buenos Aires. In 1895 two thirds of the immigrant population were men; in 1914, Carl Solberg notes, "nearly four fifths of Buenos Aires' male adults were foreigners" (96–97). But to these statistics must be added a great number of single men, seasonal laborers aged twenty or older, who did not appear in the statistics because they stayed only briefly in Buenos Aires en route to the countryside or their countries of origin.[14]

In this historical context, homosexual panic was used to control these single men who became a steady flow of "traffic," working by turns on farms or in the new industries, joining workers' protest movements or seeking ways to become small landowners themselves. Ramos Mejía, who by 1899 saw the new Argentine society as a "multitude" of "sexual inverts," earlier had regulated prostitution, as a representative of the state *higienista* bureaucracy; state-regulated heterosexual prostitution was a measure conceived as a defense against the proliferation of homosexual relations in a city with a large population of young single men, who in many cases found a place to socialize only in the brothels.

Particularly relevant at this point is a book entitled *Buenos Aires, la ribera y los prostíbulos en 1880* [Buenos Aires, the Riverside and the Brothels in 1880], written in the mid 1900s by a Buenos Aires assistant police chief, Adolfo Bátiz. This book was a memoir that covered the period approximately from 1880 to 1906. Bátiz's work focused on two important themes: first the promotion of a national heterosexual prostitution of "humble" women of "pure race," sexuality reorganized and regulated by sexual science; and, second, the danger posed by a subversive homosexuality of Italian "models," represented as sexual anarchists, "activists," who effectively proselytized among a new Argentine youth of passive pederasts, against whom prostitution was recommended as a prophylactic measure. In Bátiz's book the key category of homosexuality was pederasty: it was "la lujuria por doquier, y ahora la lujuria y la pederastía" (13) [lust everywhere, and now lust and pederasty] that impelled him to write. For Bátiz, the term "pederasty" denoted a sexual practice between two men, but did not specify the role or mode that they might adopt. Here we should note that in these texts pederasty may have denoted a sexual practice similar to some of classical Greece, but did not denote a similar institution that, as David Halperin explained, drew a clear distinction between "the roles of pederast and philerast, relegating them not only to different age-classes but virtually to different 'sexualities'" (44). In order to understand the significance of Bátiz's conception of pederasty we must first review another text published the same year (1908) by Eusebio Gómez.

Gómez was a lawyer and criminologist. As a young and important member of the Argentine positivist state bureaucracy, he was the director of the Penitenciaría Nacional and a professor of Penal Law of the Universidad de Buenos Aires. In 1908 Gómez published *La mala vida en Buenos Aires* [The Profligate Life in Buenos Aires]. In the chapter entitled *Los homosexuales* [The Homosexuals] and under the subtitles *Los invertidos sexuales— La moral de los invertidos sexuales—Invertidos aristócratas e invertidos plebeyos* [Sexual Inverts—The Morality of Sexual Inverts—Aristocratic Inverts and Plebeian Inverts], he wrote, "Es importante notar la existencia de ciertos sujetos a los que, siguiendo la terminología de la ciencia contemporanea, designamos con la denominación de invertidos sexuales" (175) [It is important to note the existence of certain subjects whom we, following the terminology of contemporary science, designate with the denomination of sexual inverts]. Here, as in Mercante's text published three years earlier, was the interchangeable use of the terms "homosexuality" (in the title of the chapter) and "sexual inversion" (in the subtitles). Notwithstanding the persistence in the use of inversion, Gómez defined a "homosexuality / sexual inversion" that denoted more than the incorrect sexual object choice, the sexual mode or role adopted in male-male sex. He explained that *un fenómeno* [a phenomenon] becomes noticeable to the observer of modern cities like Buenos Aires: "es la tendencia creciente a buscar la satisfacción de los apetitos que determina el instinto sexual con procedimientos contrarios a las leyes de la naturaleza" (175–76) [it is the growing tendency to seek satisfaction of the appetites of the sexual instinct, with procedures contrary to the laws of nature]. Here, more than sexual object choice, what was defined as deviation was a "procedure," a form of action or the enacting of sexual roles (receptive/insertive). Writing a history of what he understood to be "procedures contrary to the laws of nature," Gómez added that "el fenómeno, empero, no es moderno; la pederastía . . . en Grecia era practicada al amparo de cierta tolerancia . . . y en Roma, en tiempos del Imperio, se llegó, en este sentido, a todos los excesos" (176) [the phenomenon, however, is not modern; pederasty . . . in Greece was practiced under the shelter of a certain tolerance . . . and in Rome, in the times of the Empire, it led to all manner of excesses]. Defining homosexuality and pederasty, Gómez explained:

> Consiste la homosexualidad en la inclinación hacia las personas del mismo sexo, para el cumplimiento y satisfacción de los apetitos carnales. Cuando la inclinación indicada es de hombre a hombre, se llama uranismo o pederastía; safismo o tribadismo cuando es de mujer a mujer. La sodomía es el término que sirve para distinguir las relaciones sexuales caracterizadas por la *inmissio membri in anum,* sean esas relaciones entre personas de distinto sexo o pertenecientes ambas al mismo. La pederastía reviste formas diversas: la masturbación recíproca, el coito bucal y la *inmissio penis in os alterius* [*sic*]. (Coito bucal) (177)
>
> [Homosexuality consists in the inclination toward persons of the same sex for the fulfillment and satisfaction of the carnal appetites. When the indicated inclination is of a man for a man, it is called uranism or pederasty, sapphism when of a woman for a woman. Sodomy is the term which serves to distinguish sexual relations characterized by *inmissio membri in anum,* whether these relations be between persons of different sexes or of the same one. Pederasty takes diverse forms: reciprocal masturbation, anal coitus, and *inmissio penis in os alterius* (*sic*). (Mouth Coitus)]

Let us first note the inconsistency in the categories, which were intermingled and were confused in the texts of sociologists, psychiatrists, criminologists, and pedagogues. According to Gómez, "The indicated inclination . . . of a man for a man is called uranism;" however, Mercante's article, written four years earlier defined uranism as an epidemic among women.

At this point the Latin American taxonomical elaboration seems to differ from the one studied by Chauncey. In Gómez's book, homosexuality and sexual inversion continued to be used simultaneously. Despite Gómez's lack of differentiation, and in accordance with the development noted by Halperin, "the conceptual isolation of sexuality per se from questions of masculinity or femininity made possible a new taxonomy of sexual behaviors and psychologies based entirely on the anatomical sex of the person engaged in a sexual act (same sex vs. different sex)" (39). Indeed, Gómez above all defined homosexuality as an "inclination toward persons of the same sex." However, he defined sexual inversion as a "procedure contrary to the laws of nature," and it was in these procedures that men could *invert* their conventionally defined insertive role.

Homosexuality, like pederasty, meant incorrect sexual object choice, but did not specify the role adopted in the sexual relation. Passive pederasty denoted the inversion of the insertive role defined as correct for men. According to this conception of sexual deviation, once the man inverted his sexual role, he also inverted his dress, manners, and modes defined as correct for his biological sex. As we will see below, the sexual invert, in addition to being perceived as generally adopting a receptive, passive role, was also usually represented as a transvestite.

The definition of a receptive or insertive role was central to the definition of sexual and gender deviance in these texts. Deviance was the activism of women we have seen, and the passivity of the men we will see shortly. The distinction between "passive" and "active" homosexuals, deeply rooted in Latin American cultures, was also, in my opinion, a Mediterranean conception of sexuality revived and adapted to the turn-of-the-century sociohistorical moment. As we have seen, Gómez traces the roots of "modern" pederasty to the sexual practices of Greece and Rome.[15] This distinction in the representation of sex, in a masculine discourse that established a hierarchical relationship between insertive and receptive roles, could be reactivated in Latin America, certainly in Argentina, by the "polarization of masculine and feminine modes of behavior in Victorian thought" (Chauncey 121).

This polarization moved from defining a broad range of deviant gender behavior to defining a sexual behavior. In Gómez's formulation, the repetition of the definition in Latin—adding the "vice" of sodomy, *inmissio membri in anum,* to that of pederasty, *inmissio [penis] in os [alterus]*—reflected the masculine concept of sex that, as Halperin explains, is always *inmissio* or "penetration" (49). More than just pederasty (which, denoting only sexual object choice, was perceived, like sodomy, as a reprehensible but ideologically excusable vice) it was the inversion, passive pederasty, that particularly worried Bátiz.[16]

In the second chapter of his book, Bátiz recalled his childhood impressions of Buenos Aires: "En los primeros tiempos recorrí la parte sur . . . entrar en la Boca era decir jolgorio, sobre todo cuando llegábamos a algún prostíbulo, regenteados siempre por italianos y mujeres del bajo fondo itálico" (22–24) [In the early years I explored the southern part of the city . . . to enter into *la Boca* meant frolic, especially when we entered some brothel, always ruled by Italians and women of the italianate underworld]. Here we should remember that between 1890 and 1914, with very occasional exceptions, Italians constituted a visible majority of immigrants in Buenos Aires.[17]

Bátiz described his walks to the north: "Otro día, tomaba desde la casa Rosada por el Paseo de Julio hasta el muelle de la empresa Las Catalinas. . . . A los jardines del Paseo 9 de Julio le[s] había tomado antipatía porque era[n] el refugio de los pederastas pasivos que se juntaban alrededor de la estatua de Mazzini, el revolucionario y hombre de las libertades itálicas" (25) [Another day, I would take the Paseo 9 de Julio from the *Casa Rosada* all the way to the docks of *Las Catalinas*. . . . I had a special antipathy toward the gardens of the Paseo 9 de Julio because they were the refuge of the passive pederasts who gathered around the statue of Mazzini, the revolutionary and man of Italic liberties]. In the north, then, the other symbolic pole of the city, Bátiz inscribed a pederasty that (inside the city) was represented as "passive" and in a "refuge" around the statue of Giuseppe Mazzini. Bátiz drew a symbolic axis around which he organized a dense constellation of meanings: Italian lust and pederasty from south to north, and a national, heterosexual prostitution in the west (Buenos Aires) coming in contact with a cosmopolitan, homosexual prostitution infiltrating in from the east (Europe).

Bátiz's description was a variation on the representation of sexual deviance characterized as the relation between the activist and suggestive leader and the suggestible group, which we saw in the texts of Bialet-Massé, Mercante, and Ramos Mejía. Furthermore, in Bátiz's text the passive, suggestible, receptive mode also became "national" in contrast to the active, suggestive, insertive role of the revolutionary, or the Italian "external agitator."

Bátiz's narrative first identified the origin of a "Roman," "atavistic" pederasty. In Gómez's history it was "in Rome in the times of the Empire [that pederasty] led to all manner of excesses." In Bátiz's book this active pederasty became "traffic" between Rome and Buenos Aires designed to subvert a new group of Argentine youths. Apparently concerned about the proliferation of heterosexual prostitution, Bátiz alleged that "la prostitución ha tomado caracteres alarmantes porque tiene un crecimiento mayor que el normal y lógico, que estamos en los límites de la decadencia romana" (79) [prostitution has taken on an alarming character because it is increasing beyond the normal and logical to such a level that we are on the edge of Roman decadence]. Although he was alluding to the stereotypical decadence of imperial Rome described by Edward Gibbon, he immediately went on to identify in early-twentieth-century Rome "la existencia con vida pública de una agencia de proporcionar modelos a los pederastas pasivos, sita en Roma, calle Corso Umberto l" (79) [the existence in public life of an agency which provides models to passive pederasts, located in Rome in the Corso Umberto I]. Imperial Rome became turn-of-the-century Rome, now characterized synchronically and diachronically as a historic center of homosexuality, further represented as the source, "agency," business office and means by which male homosexual prostitutes offer sex for hire to a new Argentine youth of passive pederasts.

The police chief also recreated the representation of an invasion that we have seen in other texts. Immediately after identifying the Roman agency he warned "que existe el tráfico de modelos con caracteres internacionales desvergonzadamente" (79) [that there exists a traffic of models of a shameless international character]. The obligatory use of gender markers in Spanish gives no doubt that these were all male models. The suggestive and active invasion of a foreign pederasty, when inscribed inside the national borders, became the same infection and danger of epidemic, now of suggestible and passive national pederasty, gathering around the leader who seduced them. And Mazzini, the *carbonaro,* the organizer of secret international societies of young men, was constructed as the seductive activist around whom the new Argentine youth, lovers of "Italian liberties," congregated.

Bátiz argued that national security was threatened by external agitators who were represented as Roman models of a (homo)sexual anarchism proselytizing quite effectively among a new Argentine youth. Bátiz also warned that an already well-known group of "nuevos escandalosos de la juventud argentina" [new scandalmongers of Argentine youth] now "vienen a Nápoles y a Roma pidiendo modelos" (83) [come to Naples or Rome looking for models], thus becoming the clients of the Roman "models for passive pederasts" (79).

It is important to note that when Bátiz inscribed the Italian pederasts outside national borders, he always called them models; he never used the term "active pederasts." This representation made them dangerous agents of "perturbation," activists and foreign agitators, but from the sexual point of view these men were not stigmatized. Like the sodomites defined by Gómez, they do not invert the insertive position conceived as correct for their biological sex. What worried Bátiz was the inversion of the new Argentine youth, irremediably seduced by the Roman models.

To contain this pederasty, Bátiz promoted a national prostitution. Drawing the same distinction between Argentines and foreigners working in prostitution, Gómez asserted that "descúbrense, en la primera, ciertos rasgos de nobleza, de que la otra parece ser incapaz. La pasión del amor verdadera . . . es muy general en la prostituta criolla, la que, además, muéstrase desprovista de esa fiebre de acumular dinero que caracteriza a la meretriz importada" (132) [in the first can be discovered certain traits of nobility of which the other seems incapable. Passion for true love . . . is general in the *criolla* prostitute, the one who furthermore shows herself to be lacking that fever to accumulate money which characterizes the imported harlot]. He added "asi se explica que tales mujeres [extranjeras] llegan a sentir por el hombre un desagrado profundo y que se dediquen al amor sáfico" (134) [thus it is explained why such foreign women feel a profound dislike for men and give themselves over to sapphic love]. Bátiz advocated a national prostitution of "humildes prostíbulos de las chinas criollas de pura raza, tipo indiano" (29) [humble brothels with *criollo* women of pure race, of the Latin American indigenous type]. This was prostitution designed as a pro-phylactic measure against passive pederasty. Writing about *el culteranismo*, the public auction of women (a common practice of heterosexual prostitu-tion in Buenos Aires at the time), Bátiz described "un círculo cuyo cordón era resguardado por una hilera de muchachos y al centro se echaba la mujer más fea o más linda para rematarla" [a circle whose cordon was protected by a line of men, and the ugliest or prettiest woman was thrown into the center to be auctioned]. He added, "Yo creo que es preferible el cultera-nismo . . . que la pederastía" (82–83) [I believe that *el culteranismo* . . . is preferable to pederasty]. Two pages later, substantiating his argument for a national and humble heterosexual prostitution to protect passive young Argentines from the active homosexual models, Bátiz again warned that there exists in Rome a house "que proporciona modelos a los pederastas pasivos . . . y que hace o hacía el tráfico de los modelos" (86) [that provides models for passive pederasts . . . and does or did traffic in these models].

The Homosexual Subculture

Beyond attempting to control women and men who break the cultural, economic, and social constructions proposed as national by the official Argentine ideology, the homosexual panic disseminated by means of the texts we have seen also aimed to regulate and control a visible subculture of men, made up of homosexuals and transvestites in Buenos Aires.

This group of homosexuals was studied and described in great detail by Francisco de Veyga in a series of clinical histories published between 1902 and 1904. A medical doctor, criminologist, and specialist in the study of homosexuality, Veyga was an intimate friend of Ramos Mejía and one of his most favored disciples.

Veyga studied and documented a homosexual subculture that seemed to acquire visibility during carnival. In an article published in 1902, for example, Veyga described a heterosexual married man who began to wear female costumes during carnival, continued throughout the year, and ended up dedicated to his newly acquired fame as a star among homosexual transvestites. In the following passage, Veyga's use of theatrical imagery and vocabulary reflected his concern with the public visibility of drag culture. This concern in turn expressed the anxiety that the "truth" of gender, as Judith Butler argues, "is a fantasy instituted and inscribed on the surfaces of bodies" (136).

Finding proclivities in the past of one of his patients, Veyga wrote:

Antes de casarse, y hasta algún tiempo después, su gran afición en materia de diversiones, era el disfraz carnavalesco. Tenía un débil por la figuración en comparsas y fiestas de aparato escénico. La fotografía adjunta (fig. 3) lo representa en un traje vistoso, luciendo una buena presencia. En este teatro, donde la promiscuidad de sexos se realiza en grande escala, las relaciones homo-sexuales no resultan difíciles de trabar. En las sociedades carnavalescas hay otra cosa que un propósito estético, por lo general; la exposición de las formas, la intención de los aires musicales[18] y el caracter decididamente erótico que dan a sus reuniones, dice, a gritos, cuál es el fin directo a que tienden. Y bien, es allí, en esas fiestas, recibiendo el interesado elogio a sus dotes físicas, y rozándose con uranistas de toda especie, que empezó a recibir las primeras sugestiones en el sentido de su cambio. . . . Un día encontró un sujeto que lo abordó de lleno—el seductor de siempre, el agente inicial de estas desviaciones que parecen obras exclusivas de la naturaleza—y no titubeó en rendirse. El hombre dice que "tanto le habían hablado del asunto" y veía a su alrededor tantas escenas de esta clase, sin oír que fueran vituperables, que "le pareció su deber probar."

De allí se lanzó al público.[19] Su aparición en el mundo en que figura "fue un éxito ruidoso," como ya le habían anunciado y como él presumía. Tomó el nombre de *"Rosita de la Plata,"* celebrando a una écuyere que por aquel entonces hacía gran figura en la escena demi-mundana, no tardando en superarla en cuanto a fama. Dicha fama la conserva, aunque ya su estrella se va apagando por el desgaste del tiempo y la ruda competencia que le hacen en el mercado tantos tipos nuevos, más o menos dotados que él. ¿A qué la debe? A bien poco por cierto. A su cuidado de estar siempre en acecho de fiestas y a su actividad infatigable en el trabajo de la imitación femenina. "Rosita" sigue la moda y hace la moda entre sus congéneres. Ahí está retratado en esa fotografía con traje de *matinée,* dando envidia a muchos por su aire gracioso y la arrogancia al mismo tiempo. *Ella* ha impuesto la moda de varios trajes y de estos retratos disparatados que parecen ser una especialidad de esta gente, tan personales son. (Veyga, "Inversión adquirida" 203) [Before getting married, and for some time afterward, the diversion to which he devoted the greatest enthusiasm was dressing up for carnival. He had a weakness for performing in carnival song and dance groups and in parties with stage designs. The adjoining photograph (fig. 3) represents him in showy dress, cutting a good figure. In this theater, where promiscuity of sexes is achieved on a grand scale, homosexual relations are not difficult to start up. In carnivalesque associations in general there is a purpose other than the aesthetic: the exhibition of forms, the intentionality of the musical airs and the decidedly erotic character of their meetings, all boldly proclaim the goal to which they tend. And indeed it is there, in those parties, receiving loaded compliments on his physical endowments, and mixing with uranists of every species, that he began to perceive the first intimations of his change. One day he met a subject who approached him head on—the usual seducer, the initial agent of these deviations which seem to be exclusively the work of nature—and he did not hesitate to yield. The man says that "they had spoken to him so often of the matter," and that he saw around him so many scenes of this type, without understanding that they might be reprehensible, that "it seemed to him his duty to try it."

From there he threw himself into the public. His appearance in the world in which he figures "was a smashing success," just as it had been predicted to him, and as he himself supposed. He took the name of *"Rosita de la Plata,"* celebrating an *écuyère* who at that time cut a considerable figure in the demi-mondaine society, and took little time to surpass her in fame. He still preserves said fame, although his star is already fading from the ravages of time and the rude competition presented by so many newcomers in the market, more or less gifted than he. To what does he owe his fame? To very little, to be sure. To his care in always lying in wait for parties and to his indefatigable activity in the labor of feminine imitation. "Rosita" follows fashion and sets the fashion for his peers. Here, he is portrayed in the photograph, in a *matinée* dress, inciting envy in many for his gracious air and arrogance at the same time. *She* has imposed the fashion of several costumes and of these outrageous portraits which seem to be a speciality of these people, so idiosyncratic are they.]

The narration documenting the path out of the closet and the subsequent life of "Rosita de la Plata" followed a stereotypical pattern of the life and career of a theater diva; moved by an original "great passion for performing" she first "surrenders herself to the scene," then "throws herself to the public," "has a smashing success," and "surpasses her rivals in fame," until "her star fades from the ravages of time."

Notwithstanding the exaggeration with which he sought to implant and disseminate homosexual panic in this fragment, as well as in the rest of his articles on sexual inversion, Veyga in his articles depicted a large, visible, and well-defined subculture of homosexuals and homosexual transvestites who shared habits, dress, language, and meeting places, both during carnival and the rest of the year. Among these men were role models who jockeyed for "fame" through their "fashionable dresses," and styles, which could be "set" and which other people would "follow," and fashionable habits, such as "the fashion . . . of these outrageous portraits which seem to be a speciality of these people." Dresses, styles, fashions, and photographs circulated within this subculture in a profusion of "so many scenes of this class," in which "homosexual relations are not difficult to start up" because "mixing with uranists of every species" there was an always renewed variety of "so many newcomers." These became marginal modes of performance, functioning within and questioning the wider system of representations of gender.[20]

The creation of a new space in which these men were able to distance themselves from the humiliation they endured as sexual outcasts while creating an alternative moral order and culture in which they were in control, began with the adoption of a new naming system with which these men, by taking female names, reinvented their gender. Rosita "took the name of Rosita de la Plata," a name like " 'Aida', tal es el poético nombre con que nuestro sujeto se hacía distinguir en el mundo especial de su figuración" (Veyga, "Invertido imitando" 368) [Aida, such is the poetic name with which our subject would make himself be distinguished in the special world in which he moves]. Luis D. "ha adoptado el nombre de 'La Bella Otero,' la célebre cocota parisiense, de la que pretende ser rival" (Veyga, "Inversión adquirida profesional" 493) [has adopted the name "La bella Otero," the celebrated Parisian cocotte of whom she presumes to be the rival]; "Aurora [es un], hombre de treinta años" (Veyga, "Inversión adquirida" 195) [Aurora is a thirty-year-old man] while "Manon, que tal es su nombre de batalla, había sido un niño sano hasta la edad de 15 años" (Veyga, "Inversión congénita" 44) [Manon, for such is her *nom de guerre*, had been a healthy boy until the age of fifteen]. The selection of clothing was as telling of one's "true gender" as the selection of a name: "Un adolescente recién entrado a la inversión y que se ha adornado con el nombre 'Darclée,' no puede entregarse a la escena sin su peluca y su camisa de mujer" (Veyga, "Amor en invertidos" 337) [An adolescent who has just entered inversion and who has adorned himself with the name "Darclée," cannot give himself to the scene without his wig and a woman's blouse]. Most of these men adopted the names of fashionable characters and divas of the glittering world of the opera, the theater, the circus, or the cafe-concert: Rosita after Rosa Robba, a well-known circus horse rider of the period; Aida after Verdi's opera; Manón after Massenet's and Puccini's operas; La bella Otero after the daring Spanish actress of the music halls and cabarets of turn-of-the-century Paris; and Darclée after Hericléa Darclée, the Rumanian soprano who sang her world-famous Tosca in Buenos Aires in 1897, 1903, and 1907. Veyga, exasperated with the dramatic visibility—and pride—of the men creating these parodic repetitions, concluded: "Y al fin, hechos por entero a la vida de esta gente, con un nombre que ellos se han dado o han permitido que les den, pasan a ser personajes de escarnio o de galería pública, sin inquietarse de su triste reputación, cuando no enorgullecidos de ella" (Veyga, "Sentido moral de invertidos" 23) [Finally given entirely to the life of these people, with a new name which they have given themselves, they end up becoming despicable characters of the public and police record, without being troubled by their sad reputation, when not proud of it]. After coming out and renaming themselves "these people give themselves entirely to" a parallel, parodic reality.

Veyga described a large group of men who gathered in balls, parties, and social events all year. These gatherings fulfilled a number of social functions that strengthened the sexual identity of the members of this subculture. Emphasizing the importance that one of these reunions has in reaffirming the sexual identity of a forty-year-old man, Veyga wrote,

> La ocasión quiso que sus compañeros de entonces lo llevaran a una fiesta de maricas, hablándole con entusiasmo de las novedades que allí había de encontrar. Esa fiesta debía decidir su situación para siempre. El interés que las damas le produjeron fue immenso, a punto de "sentirse enloquecido con sus gracias y sus atractivos"; pero a decir verdad (según él), no fue un interés, de aproximación casual el que experi-

mentaba, sino de "simpatía afectiva" y de "compañerismo." . . . El hecho es que desde esa noche, ligando amistad con gran número de los asistentes, su medio y su campo de acción fueron esos que se le acababan de revelar a su vista. (Veyga, "Inversión adquirida" 203) [Chance required that his companions take him to a party of *maricas,* enthusiastically telling him about the novelties that he would encounter there. That party decided his situation forever. The interest that the "ladies" provoked in him was immense, to the point that he "felt crazed by their grace and attractions"; but to tell the truth (according to him), he was not experiencing a purely casual interest, but one of "affectionate sympathy" and "companionship." . . . The fact is that from that night, having made friends with many of the partygoers, his medium and his field of action became those that had just been revealed to him].

This feeling that it was "not . . . a purely casual interest, but one of 'affectionate sympathy' and 'companionship,'" suggests that this man was encountering a well-developed social network that encouraged the assertion of his newly found identity.

The evidence of this rich marginal world in late nineteen- and early twentieth-century Buenos Aires is an important antecedent in the history of homosexual subcultures. As Jeffrey Weeks notes, "Until comparatively recently, very few people found it either possible or desirable to incorporate sexual mores, social activities, and public identity into a full-time homosexual 'way of life'" (202). However, in the homosexual subculture of Buenos Aires we see precisely this incorporation of sexual mores, social activities, and public identity into a full-time "homosexual 'way of life.'" Some of these men came out, found their peers, and asserted their sexual identities, others were like Manon, who "con ropas femeninas; [y] así ataviado da rienda suelta a sus sentimientos de invertido, asistiendo a tertulias y bailes de invertidos, en que junto con otros congéneres desempeña el rol de gran dama" (Veyga, "Inversión congénita" 46) [in feminine clothes; and thus clad gives free rein to his inverted feelings, attending inverted soirées and dances in which, together with others, she acts out the role of grande dame]. Incorporating sexual mores with a public identity, some of these men took their parody of the "truth of gender" to the streets. La bella Otero creates "desorden y escándalo, motivados con frecuencia por su costumbre de salir a la calle vestido de mujer" (Veyga, "Inversión adquirida profesional" 493) [disorders and scandals, motivated by his habit of going out into the street dressed as a woman]. And "solo por excepción usa traje varonil, prefiriendo la indumentaria femenina que usa con desenfado y hasta con elegancia. Sale poco de su casa y, por lo general, en carruaje, para evitar incidentes callejeros molestos que le serían imposible esquivar, dada su relativa notoriedad entre los aficionados al género" (Veyga, "Inversión adquirida profesional" 494) [only exceptionally does he wear male garb, preferring feminine accoutrements, which he wears with ease and even elegance. He leaves his house seldom and generally in a carriage, to avoid tiresome street incidents which would be impossible to evade, given his relative notoriety among the aficionados of the genre].

Besides public visibility, disorder, and scandal—of dressing in drag outside in the streets or inside at parties and balls—these men flaunted ceremonies and rites that were caricatures of traditional sex/gender systems. The incredulity in Veyga's tone shows that even the exceptions reinforce the rule for him: in his article entitled "Invertido imitando la mujer honesta" [Invert Imitating the Honest Woman], Veyga described Aida, who is discreet (in male clothing) at work, imitated "an honest woman" in drag, was serially monogamous, prudish in conversation, and—the best proof that she is a *mujer honesta*—claimed to get no pleasure out of the sexual act with her "husband." Explaining that "el 'casamiento' de invertidos sexuales no es un hecho raro, por cierto, pero esta ceremonia no se realiza ordinariamente sino como acto de ostentación escandalosa" [the marriage of sexual inverts is not a rare occurrence, to be sure, but this ceremony ordinarily happens only as an act of scandalous ostentation], Veyga nevertheless seemed shocked as he described the marriage of Aida "con el aparato convencional de una boda real: ella, vestida de blanco, adornada la cabeza de azahares; él de frac y guante blanco" (Veyga, "Invertido imitando" 371) [with the conventional apparatus of a real wedding: *she* dressed in white, her head adorned with orange blossoms, he in tuxedo and white gloves]. Here the parody called into question the "naturalness" of the "conventional [heterosexual] apparatus," and thus "makes public" the "dramatic and contingent construction of meaning" that Butler calls "gender as a corporeal style, an 'act,' as it were, which is both intentional and performative" (139).

Aside from their concern with these parodic repetitions, Veyga's histories conveyed a recurrent preoccupation with the photographs of these men in drag. Along with each case history, Veyga published a series of photographs that fascinated but baffled him. At the beginning of the long fragment of Rosita's history quoted above, Veyga called special attention to "the adjoining photograph [of Rosita] in showy dress, cutting a good figure," and later he pointed out a "photograph in a matinée dress." "These outrageous portraits," the doctor proclaimed, "seem to be a speciality of these people." From the number, poses, and settings of the photographs published in different specialized and popular journals of the period, it is evident that these men made a habit of dressing in drag and having their picture taken, to be kept, copied, shown, given, or passed around and commented upon. La bella Otero wrote, knowingly, that s/he had "el honor de regalarle al Doctor Veyga algunos retratos con mi dedicatoria" (Veyga, "Inversión adquirida profesional" 496) [the honor of giving Dr. Veyga some portraits with my dedication] and did not, according to the doctor, care to "disimular mucho su deseo de figurar como caso clínico en el libro que preparamos sobre los invertidos sexuales" (Veyga, "Inversión adquirida profesional" 494) [hide very well his desire to figure as a case study in the book on sexual inversion that we are preparing].[21]

Veyga's concern with these photographs exemplifies the potential Walter Benjamin saw in photography: the mechanical reproduction of photographs had the possibility of disseminating ad infinitum the parodic repetition of drag with its challenge to the "authenticity" of gender. Furthermore, this dissemination of photographs subverted the traditional homogenizing function of the mass media. Susan Buck-Morss, writing about Benjamin's interest in photography, explains that "photography democratized the reception of visual images by bringing even art masterpieces to a mass audience" (133). But in Veyga's history, these masterpieces were images that, erasing the gap between sign (women) and referent (men), made clear that gender is a mere inscription on the surface of the body.

Pointing out the explosive potential of this erasure, Benjamin explained that photographs "acquire a hidden political significance. They demand a specific kind of approach; free floating contemplation is not appropriate to them. They stir the viewer; he feels challenged by them in a new way. . . . For the first time captions have become obligatory" (226). So, below each photograph our doctor added captions such as *Manón—Invertido sexual congénito en traje de baile* (Veyga, "Inversión congénita" 18) [Manón—Congenital Sexual Invert in Dance Costume]; *Rosita de la Plata—Invertido por sugestión* (Veyga, "Inversión adquirida" 200) [Rosita de la Plata—Inverted by Suggestion], and the like. But the tension between captions describing men (*invertido* in Spanish using the masculine adjectival ending) and the drag images of women made visible a "fluidity of identities that suggests an openness to resignification" (Butler 138). Veyga not only made obvious this fluidity in the pages of his texts; he further contributed to the reproduction and dissemination of these images of wo/men.

Of Manón's photographs Veyga wrote, "Las fotografías que publicamos bastan para dar una idea de su porte correcto y sugestivo" (Veyga, "Inversión congénita" 46) [The photographs we publish suffice to give an idea of his correct and suggestive carriage], and of a photo of Aurora that "la ilusión que debía ofrecer en aquella noche puede medirse por la actitud que tiene en la fotografía adjunta" (Veyga, "Inversión adquirida" 195) [the illusion that he must have offered that night can be measured by the demeanor in the adjoining photograph]. Challenged, Veyga then tried to reorganize, to fix the "right" construction of gender. Of course this operation was first performed on Aurora's own body. Veyga recalled that "cuando lo trajeron al Depósito [the service of the Police Department where the doctors worked with the police] estaba todavía vestido de mujer y es excusado decir las penurias que pasó para acomodarse al local. El cambio de ropa fue obra difícil" (Veyga, "Inversión adquirida" 195) [when they brought him to the Deposit he was still dressed as a woman, and we may be excused from speaking of the deprivations he underwent to become accommodated to the locale. The change of clothing was a difficult task]. Afterward the police took a mug shot of Aurora required to portray a man, which Veyga also published, next to Aurora's photo in drag, in an effort to shatter the illusion: "Puede además valorarse el arte de que dispone para arreglarse, comparando la cara que tiene en dicho retrato [in drag] con la que ofrece [portraying a man] en el que complementa la ilustración de este caso" (Veyga, "Inversión adquirida" 195) [The art which he uses to arrange himself can also be valued, comparing the face that he has in said portrait with the one that complements the illustration of this case]. Roland Barthes explains that "photography, moreover, began historically as an art of the Person, of civil status, of what we might call, in all senses of the term, the body's formality" (79). And in spite of Veyga's effort to (re)construct the gender of Aurora, Rosita, or Manón, their published photographs were indeed documentation of an "identity and civil status, . . . the body's *formality*" forever deconstructed by images of fe/males of "correct and suggestive carriage."

Photographs and captions were a visual representation of the attempt to contain the explosive possibilities of these images. In the same way that the explicatory captions tried to tame the visual images, the taxonomy of sexual inversion, which Veyga elaborated throughout six articles published between 1902 and 1904, tried to explain and control this subversive "art of the Person[a]" spreading through the city.

In his first two articles (published in 1902), Veyga specified a sexual inversion defined as "congenital." However, in his third article (1903) the doctor added the definition of an "acquired sexual inversion." Later on he further defined an "acquired-professional sexual inversion." Examining Veyga's six articles sequentially, two things become clear: the doctor's growing effort to define sexual inversion as an "acquired" form of sexual deviance and his mounting struggle with a group of men who define their condition as congenital. As we will see, the category and concept of acquired sexual inversion prevailed in Veyga's articles published after 1903 and was reaffirmed in later texts of Argentine sexual science.

Before examining the various definitions and connotations of sexual inversion—congenital, acquired, or professional—we should first note that in Veyga's conception of congenital (minoritizing) and acquired (universalizing) homosexuality we see one more instance of the "radical and irreducible incoherence" that Sedgwick observes: "It holds the minoritizing view that there is a distinct population of persons who 'really are' gay; at the same time, it holds the universalizing [view] that sexual desire is an unpredictably powerful solvent of stable identities" (85).

In Veyga's taxonomical definitions of sexual inversion, homosexuality— which denoted sexual object choice—appeared but became secondary to sexual inversion, which, going beyond sexual object choice, denoted the "pathology" of transvestites who inverted the active and insertive mode and the dress and manners considered correct for men. Acquired sexual inversion was the social evil contracted from a demographically, politically, and sexually volatile environment. Male-male sexual contacts had increased in a city with a large population of young males, both on the streets and in the "supposedly all-female bordellos" (Guy 86); Veyga used as supporting evidence the growing visibility of the homosexual subculture and homosexual prostitution. In his definition of acquired-professional sexual inversion, while reaffirming the view that sexual inversion was an acquired social evil, Veyga conflated *all* transvestites with prostitutes, whom he called "professional inverts." These "professionals" in turn he linked with *lunfardos,* the inhabitants of the marginal world of rogues, petty thieves, and unemployed immigrants. Thus Veyga criminalized all sexual inverts and disseminated the notion that all men living on the margins of society were homosexuals.

After his definition of congenital sexual inversion (in contradiction with his subsequent definition of acquired sexual inversion) Veyga defined the more discrete category of professional inverts, or men who supported themselves by homosexual prostitution. Throughout his later articles, Veyga identified these men as "pseudo-inverts," men who adopted the incorrect role, dress, and manners simply to make a cold profit, although these professionals identified themselves as *maricas* [sissies]. Weeks explains that "a number of studies have suggested that many males who prostitute themselves regard themselves as heterosexuals and devise complex strategies to neutralize the significance of their behavior" (197). But this was not the case with the professionals in Veyga's case studies. The doctor reported that Aurora feels "como si hubiera nacido marica" (Veyga, "Inversión adquirida" 198) [as though I had been born a *marica*]. La bella Otero, the other "professional sexual invert" in Veyga's histories, wrote in the first sentence of an "Autobiography," published with the clinical history: "Siempre me he creído mujer, y por eso uso vestido de mujer" ("Inversión adquirida profesional" 495) [I have always thought of myself as a woman, and therefore I wear women's clothing]. Both Aurora and La bella Otero viewed themselves as "born" or "born like" homosexuals, but in an effort to criminalize all homosexuals, Veyga defined *maricas* as passive pederasts, prostitutes, and criminals, and *lunfardos* as (active) pederasts. Thus the relationship between sexual inverts and *lunfardos* reproduced the stereotyped relationship between "passive" female prostitutes exploited by "active" male pimps.

As a means of promoting social regulation, Veyga attempted to identify the homosexual subculture with the *lunfardo* world of wayfarers, unemployed immigrants, seamstresses, petty thieves, and prostitutes. The *lunfardo* underworld of turn-of-the-century Buenos Aires (and its language of secret codes) was the core of the mythical construction of today's imagined *porteño* "identity."[22] And in its time this keystone of an imagined "Argentine identity" was defined as a community of homosexuals. Veyga alleged that "el mundo de los maricas se encuentra, además, tan íntimamente ligado con el de los lunfardos y el de la prostitución, que bien puede decirse que forma parte de ambos" (Veyga, "Sentido moral invertidos" 28) [the world of maricas, furthermore, is so intimately linked with that of lunfardos and that of prostitution, that it can be said to be part of both]. Thus, Veyga links *maricas* with *lunfardos* and with prostitution. In the same article, all *lunfardos* became pederasts and pimps: "El lunfardo es pederasta de condición y sabe explotar por las buenas o por las malas al invertido" (28) [The lunfardo is a pederast by condition who knows how to exploit, by good means or bad, the invert]. Thus all male inhabitants of the low life of turn-of-the-century Buenos Aires were represented as pederasts or stereotypical male pimps, and the inverts were, correspondingly, represented as stereotypical female prostitutes.

Veyga's articles also portrayed all homosexuals, *lunfardos,* pederasts, and inverts (whether professionals or not) as criminals. He first writes: "Es frecuente, la regla por mejor decir, que el invertido profesional sea un delincuente" (Veyga, "Inversión adquirida" 199) [It is frequent—or rather the rule, to say it better—that the professional invert is a delinquent]. Then he lumped all categories together under one term: the *cofradía* [confraternity]. Describing Aurora's first contact with other male homosexuals working in prostitution, Veyga pointed out that Aurora "estaba muy ajeno, por cierto, a suponer que en Buenos Aires había toda una 'cofradía' que ejercitaba este comercio. . . . Pero muy pronto supo que no era un privilegio suyo el medio de vida que había encontrado y que por el contrario se las tenía que ver con competidores numerosos y avezados en el oficio" (Veyga, "Inversión adquirida" 198) [Aurora was, certainly, very far from supposing that in Buenos Aires there was a whole cofradía that exercised this trade. But very quickly he learned that the mode of life that he had entered was not exclusively his, and that on the contrary, he had to contend with numerous competitors, sharp-eyed in the practice of the trade]. This term, however, was used by the members of the homosexual subculture to identify themselves. Here, a reading of a letter published by the criminologist Eusebio Gómez in *La mala vida en Buenos Aires* is illuminating. Apparently making few or no corrections, Gómez transcribed "la siguiente carta que nos dirige Mysotis, invertido congénito, joven de la clase que llamaremos 'aristócrata'" (184, quotation marks in the original) [the following letter directed to us by Mysotis, a congenital invert, a young man of the class we will call "aristocratic"]. Responding to a request for information that the criminologist sends him, Mysotis writes, "Es ridícula su exigencia de que le cuente, en la forma comprometedora de la carta, los detalles de mi vida. . . . Yo soy así porque así he nacido; y de todos modos tendría que serlo, porque, para mí, la belleza no tiene sexo. . . . Yo no hago nada de extraordinario: me gustan los hombres y por eso tengo expansiones con ellos. Los trato con exquisito *savoir faire,* como dice una de las de la cofradía, que escribe la crónica social de cierto diario" (185) [Your requiring me to send you the details of my life, in the compromising form of a letter, is ridiculous. . . . I am like this because I was born like this. Anyway, this is the way I should behave because beauty has no sex. . . . I do not do anything extraordinary: I like men and for that reason I amuse myself with them. I treat them with exquisite *savoir faire,* as one of the members of the *cofradía,* who writes the social column for a certain newspaper, says]. Further on, Gómez added that "ofrecen los homosexuales de Buenos Aires una particularidad digna de ser señalada: es la tendencia a asociarse, formando una especie de secta, designada por ellos con el pintoresco nombre de 'cofradía'" (191) [the homosexuals of Buenos Aires have a particularity worth noting: the tendency to associate, forming a kind of sect, which they designate with the picturesque name of "*cofradía*"]. This was not a *cofradía* of men who make their living from homosexual prostitution, as Veyga would have it, but a community of class-diverse homosexuals: some were "of the class we will call aristocratic," as was Mysotis and Aida, "nacido en buena cuna y criado en la holgura" (Veyga, "Invertido imitando" 370) [who was well born and grew up well off]; others were middle-class professionals, such as the journalist who "writes the social column for a certain newspaper;" some were hairdressers like Manón; still others were servants like Rosita; and some were men who sometimes worked as hairdressers but also made a living from homosexual prostitution, such as Aurora. And then there were men who, like La bella Otero, lived exclusively from homosexual prostitution. This wide social spectrum not only reflected the ordering of the social classes of the times but also disorganized it and created a group in which sexual identities were as important or more important than social class. This was particularly significant in a society such as Argentina's, remarkable for its social stratification. On the other hand, Aida and La bella Otero represented two very different positions in the diversity of intentions and uses that some of these transvestites hoped to achieve with reference to already existing identities within their society. Subversion may always be the effect, but some transvestites, such as Aida, declared by word or deed their intent to assimilate.

The Seducers

In Veyga's clinical histories, this large group of *maricas,* homosexuals, and transvestites—members of the *cofradía*—appeared to be linked to an even larger group of men, who, despite having sexual relations with men, were very seldom called pederasts or homosexuals but were defined by Veyga as "seducers." Like Bátiz's models, the seducers were not stigmatized because they did not invert the insertive role.

In the fragment of Rosita's story quoted above, Veyga mentioned "the usual seducer, the initial agent of these deviations which *seem* to be exclusively the work of nature." The seducer, although he did not reverse the "correct" role in choosing another man as a sexual object, was guilty of indulging in practices *contra natura* and of fostering the "inversion" of men *upon* whom he practiced sex. La bella Otero's first sexual partner was "el seductor [que] le invitó a dormir . . . iniciándole en la pederastía pasiva" (Veyga, "Inversión adquirida profesional" 492) [the seducer who invited him to bed . . . thus initiating him into passive pederasty]. Aida's first spouse is "el seductor [que] tiene que convertirlo en 'esposa' para poseerlo" (Veyga, "Invertido imitando" 368) [the seducer who has to make him his 'wife' to have her].

Veyga defines the "seducer" early in his investigations, in his second
article published in 1902. This definition of an "initial agent" and propaga-
tor who is a product of the environment substantiated the conception of
an acquired sexual inversion that spread in a city with a large population
of young single men. Defining the "seducer," Veyga wrote:

> Existen al lado de los invertidos, para determinar o fomentar las ten-
> dencias homosexuales, tipos previamente inclinados al goce corporal
> dentro de su sexo. . . . Por más extraviadas que sean las concepciones
> de la mente enferma, siempre hay en el medio ambiente una base que
> les sirve de pie, y en este caso, lo de "convertirse en mujeres" sea del
> tipo libertino o casto, responde a la existencia de una clase especial
> de sujetos, mas numerosos quizá que la de aquellos o por lo menos
> tanto, que buscan de satisfacer las impulsiones viriles sobre un indivi-
> duo de su mismo sexo . . . al lado del invertido se encuentra siempre
> al sodomita. (Veyga, "Invertido imitando" 373–74)
> [Besides inverts, to determine and foment homo-sexual tendencies,
> there exist types previously inclined to sexual delights with their own
> sex. . . . No matter how farfetched the conceptions of the sick mind
> are, there is always a base in the environment which serves as a foot-
> hold, and in this case the phenomenon of "turning into women" of
> the loose or chaste type responds to the existence of a special class of
> subjects, more numerous than or at least as numerous as that of the
> sexual inverts, that seeks to satisfy virile impulses upon an individual
> of their own sex. . . . Beside the invert we always find the sodomite.]

Veyga offered a good example of the form of representing sex that Halperin describes: "Sex as is constituted by this public, masculine discourse
is either act or impact: it is not knit up in a web of mutuality" (48). In
Veyga's definition this "special class of subjects . . . seeks to satisfy *virile im-
pulses upon*" another individual. This was the origin of the sexual deviance
acquired from the environment.

Notwithstanding the sexual scientists' clear tendency to define sexual deviations as acquired, Veyga also took a position with respect to the peren-
nial argument over the congenital or acquired definition of homosexuality.
In his first article on congenital sexual inversion (1902), Veyga's rhetoric
already moves within the space Sedgwick calls the unstable "gap between
long-coexisting minoritizing and universalizing [definitions]" (47). Leaning early toward the acquired definition, Veyga argued that "la educación
de las funciones sexuales, en uno u otro sentido, influye para determinar

o no la inversión en los sujetos congénitamente predispuestos, de igual manera que, en los no predispuestos, condiciones especiales de educación y ambiente pueden determinar perversiones sexuales adquiridas" (Veyga, "Inversión congénita" 47–48) [the teaching of the sexual functions, in one sense or the other, influences the determination of the inversion, or lack thereof, in congenitally predisposed subjects in the same way that special educational or environmental conditions can determine acquired sexual perversions in those not predisposed]. Here we should note the emphasis on the possibility of "the teaching." Veyga at this time still supported the possibility of "congenitally predisposed subjects," but a year later writing about acquired sexual inversion, he recognizes that "la clasificación que se basa en la naturaleza de origen de esta desviación psicorgánica es puramente artificial, no existiendo en la clínica un rasgo determinado que distinga al invertido nato del que se convierte en tal por cualquier motivo . . . hay algunas veces tal semejanza de detalles, que bien pueden identificarse unos casos con otros" (Veyga, "Inversión adquirida" 193) [the classification based on the nature of origin of this psycho-organic deviation is purely artificial, given that in the clinic there exists no determining feature that distinguishes the born invert from the one who converts for whatever reason . . . sometimes the details are so similar that the one can be identified with the other].

As social and political instability were created by the great number of transient immigrants and seasonal laborers, by women and men organizing and demanding economic and political changes, and as the homosexual subculture became more visible and male-male sex proliferated in a city replete with single men; Veyga, like the rest of the Argentine medicolegal establishment of the time, became a sexual constructivist. Thus in 1903, after identifying and defining the "seducer" a year before, the doctor argued that

> el ambiente obra de tal manera sobre la imaginación del sujeto que puede decirse que es el factor determinante del delirio y el que al mismo tiempo lo entretiene y conserva. Las tentativas contra-naturales, el ejemplo y las sugestiones indirectas que a título de broma corriente se reciben con insistencia desde el colegio hasta el cuartel y desde el cuartel hasta la vejez, es lo que decide a definir, cuando no a hacer estallar la psicosis en estos sujetos. (Veyga, "Amor en invertidos" 335) [the environment operates in such a way in the mind of these subjects that it could be said that it determines and sustains the growth of these deliria. The counter-natural tendencies, the example and the direct and indirect suggestions which, as a joke, are constantly received

from high school to the barracks and from the barracks to old age, are what determine, if not cause, the psychotic break in these subjects].

The specific "environments" and institutions that induced the "psychotic break"—that is, the spaces and institutions that required special vigilance—were the high schools of the national educational system (thus Mercante's concern with the epidemic of feminine uranism in boarding schools) and the barracks of the national army.

In 1908 Gómez, the criminologist working with a somewhat more modernized taxonomy than Veyga (replacing invert with homosexual), also defined an "homosexualidad adquirida, que puede determinarla así mismo, especialmente sobre seres con cierta predisposición, la vida en común . . . Los cuarteles y los colegios suministran copiosos ejemplos" (181) [acquired homosexuality, which can be determined by, especially in beings with a certain predisposition, life in common . . . Barracks and schools provide copious examples].

José Ingenieros (a disciple of Ramos Mejía and the closest colleague of Veyga in the police department, a very influential Argentine physician, criminologist, psychiatrist, sociologist, editor and publisher of important scientific and cultural journals, and critic of art and literature) noted the same definition of a sexual deviation and identified the same spaces and institutions as places from which the acquired sickness was spread. He published an article in 1910 on the pathology of the sexual functions, in which he classified and ordered the sexual deviations studied by different authors whose investigations were published between 1902 and 1910. In this article, Ingenieros expressly said that his ordering was based as much on studies by foreigners as on "la bibliografía nacional [que] cuenta con publicaciones aisladas de Ramos Mejía, Mercante, Eusebio Gómez . . . y principalmente con varias monografías clínicas de De Veyga" (4) [the national bibliography that includes isolated publications of Ramos Mejía, Mercante, Eusebio Gómez . . . and principally various clinical monographs by De Veyga]. Referring to inversion and feminine homosexuality, Ingenieros wrote, "La inversión instintiva se observa menos frecuentemente en las mujeres; la educación y el medio son poco propicios al desarrollo del 'tribadismo,' siendo menos raro en mujeres independientes de toda traba (artistas, intelectuales, etc.) . . . aunque la inversión sentimental o romántica es muy frecuente en los colegios e internados femeninos (Mercante), en las mujeres casadas suele ser una desviación adquirida por insuficiencia sexual o afectiva del marido" (25) [Inversion is seen less frequently in women; education and the environment are not very conducive to the development of 'tribadism,' being less rare in women free of any social tie (artists, intellectuals, etc.) . . . although sentimental or romantic inversion is quite frequent in girls' boarding schools (Mercante), in married women it is usually a deviation due to sexual or affective deficiencies of the husband]. Under the category of "instinctive parafrodisias," Ingenieros defined "la inversión del instinto sexual u homoestesia" [the inversion of the sexual instinct or sexual homoaesthesia]:

> Debe considerársela como una "tendencia congénita." . . . Suele confundirse esta "tendencia congénita" con las pseudo-inversiones adquiridas, casi siempre secundarias a las prácticas sexuales contranatura, frecuentísimas en los internados de ambos sexos, en los conventos, en los cuarteles . . . En todos estos pseudo-uranistas la tendencia sexual es primitivamente normal pero ha sido desviada por la educación. . . . *Los homosexuales militantes . . . pretenden hacer creer que son verdaderos invertidos congénitos . . . comprendiendo que su perversión adquirida es más disculpable con el disfraz de la anomalía congénita.* . . . Las explicaciones dadas por los mismos uranistas (alma de mujer en cuerpo de hombre, error de conformación sexual, equivocación de Dios, etc.) son simplemente ridículas. (23–24, my emphasis)
> [It must be considered as a "congenital tendency." . . . This "congenital tendency" usually is confused with acquired pseudo-inversions, almost always secondary to the counternatural practices, very frequent in boarding schools for both sexes, in convents, and in the barracks. . . . In all these pseudo-uranists the primitive sexual tendency is normal but has been deviated by education. . . . *Militant homosexuals want to make us believe that they are true congenital inverts . . . because they understand that, thus, their acquired perversion will be more justified under the disguise of the congenital anomaly.* . . . The uranist's explanations (a woman's soul in a man's body, errors in sexual conformation, God's mistake, etc.) are simply preposterous.]

For reasons of space I cannot explore here Ingenieros's notion of the existence of a movement of militant homosexuals in Buenos Aires in 1910. The Argentine state technocrats were very concerned with homosexual scandals within the Argentine and Prussian armies, which at the time had very close professional ties. Thus all girls' and boys' schools, convents, and especially army barracks were identified as the ideal medium for the proliferation of "counternatural practices" that give rise to the acquired inversion "secondary to counternatural practices." Two pages later, Ingenieros wrote:

"Es muy rara la inversión primitiva de las tendencias sexuales, a pesar de la exageración que en este sentido difundió Krafft-Ebing. Los invertidos son, generalmente, pederastas pasivos que se acostumbran a cohabitar con hombres" (27) [The primitive inversion of the sexual tendencies is very rare, despite the exaggerations of Krafft-Ebing. Inverts are, generally, passive pederasts who get used to living with a man].

   In response to this presumed need to take defensive measures against this acquired pseudo-inversion, represented as spreading outward from schools and army barracks, José María Ramos Mejía was named president of the Consejo Nacional de Educación in 1908, and in 1911 Veyga left the police of Buenos Aires and his teaching position to further pursue his career as army surgeon and psychiatrist. Hugo Vezzetti explains that Veyga,

> fiel discípulo de José M. Ramos Mejía, puede decirse que continúa
> su obra a la vera de ese modelo de multitud en orden que es el ejér-
> cito, y no lo hace mal, a juzgar por los resultados de una carrera en
> la que alcanza la Dirección General de Sanidad del Ejército y el grado
> de General de la Nación. Que ello lo haya llevado a dejar la cátedra de
> medicina legal, no constituye un cambio de rumbo . . . la creación del
> servicio militar obligatorio [in 1901] reunía una masa heterogénea de
> población a la que se trataba no solo de atender sanitariamente sino
> de organizar y unificar también en el orden moral subjetivo. (178)
> [faithful disciple of José María Ramos Mejía, can be said to continue
> his labor at the side of that model of multitude-in-order that is the
> army, and he does not do a bad job, to judge by his career in which he
> achieved the position of Surgeon General of the Army and the rank of
> General of the nation. That such results led him to leave his professor-
> ship of legal medicine does not constitute for him a change of direc-
> tion. . . . The creation of obligatory military service brought together
> a heterogeneous population mass who was to be not only attended in
> sanitary terms but also organized and unified into the subjective moral
> order.]

Conclusion

In comparing the Argentine taxonomic elaboration of categories of sexual deviance with the contemporary medical inquiries studied by George Chauncey, Jr., and others, I suggest that in Argentina the medicolegal category of homosexuality did not seem to replace the category of sexual inversion. It is true that to define deviance after the 1900s doctors looked mainly at the issue of sexual object choice, but while doing so they further (re)defined correct roles for the sexual behavior of men and women. The persistent distinction between an active and a passive role in male-male sex—as well as in a relationship between two passive uranist women—in my opinion was a residue of a Mediterranean concept and representation of sex. It is not by chance that the category of "pederasty" subsisted with a new emphasis on the more discrete categories of passive and active pederasty. The definition of the passive pederast coexisted with that of the sexual invert, the passive pederast who, after inverting the sexual role, inverted the dress and manners defined as correct for his biological sex.

The euphemistic references to and definitions of the pederast, the foreign model, the local seducer, and the sodomite, reflected the conception of a sexual behavior perceived as an acquired vice or a procedure *contra natura,* not unlike Foucault's view of sodomy prior to 1879, but no further stigmatized. Models or seducers did not invert the active, insertive role defined as correct for their biological sex, and therefore they were not defined as anything other than men. The Mediterranean pederast or the Latin American *bugarrón was* what we understand today as the homosexual but in the texts of an Argentine sexual science of the turn of the century, primarily the sexual invert—the passive pederast—became the stigmatized category of male sexual deviance.

The Argentine taxonomic elaboration of categories of homosexuality has to be examined within a very specific historical context. Between 1900 and 1910 the European Argentina that had been imagined a century earlier had become the reality of a sudden metropolis and above all a major port at the mouth of the Río de la Plata, which centralized the culture, wealth, and goods of a large portion of the South American continent. By 1910 many of the immigrants who had reached Argentina at the turn of the century had not been able to acquire land and had therefore established themselves in Buenos Aires, working in the new urban industries and commerce. Out of this large new urban population grew different social classes which in thirty years rearranged the power structure of colonial times. At this point Argentina had to be imagined again. In charge of this re-envisioning was a positivist scientific technocracy subservient to the traditional landowning class. These state bureaucrats produced a body of writing outlining a sexual science with explicit definitions and categories of sexual deviance, such as uranism, homosexuality, pederasty, and sexual inversion. This explication reflected their fear of an inversion of power between social classes and gender groups. While women working for wages or joining labor movements were perceived as doing jobs traditionally defined for men, men were apparently underemployed or unemployed, crowding the city, and in many cases having sex with other men. Thus activist women, feminists, socialists, and anarchists were defined as the opposite of the imagined national model of the white, prolific, submissive Argentine mother and wife, while passive men were defined as the opposite of the model of the new virile, nationalist Argentine youth.

As women started to compete with men in the industrial and commercial job markets in a city with a large population of young foreign men, male-male sexual encounters became more numerous and visible, while a subculture of homosexual transvestites flourished and mixed with groups of other homosexuals and transvestites who occasionally made their living from homosexual prostitution. This image of a city thriving on female labor and homosexual prostitution further concerned the state technocrats anxious about sexual inversion. As a defensive measure, the positivist Argentine state technocracy devised a campaign of social and moral reform and of the production and indoctrination of an ideal Argentine youth. The story of how this campaign was launched from the nation's elementary and secondary schools and from the barracks of the national army will remain to be told.

Notes

This essay was first published in the *Journal of the History of Sexuality,* Vol. 4, No. 3, January 1994. I thank the University of Chicago Press for its permission to publish it here.

1 See Sedgwick's *Epistemology of the Closet* 182–212.

2 For a discussion on notions of sexual deviance among Hispanics in the United States, see Ana María Alonso and María Teresa Koreck, "Silences: Hispanics, AIDS, and Sexual Practices."

3 See Chauncey, 114–46.

4 Here I am obviously in debt to the work of Benedict Anderson in *Imagined Communities.*

5 For a broader discussion of what positivism means in Latin American and Argentine thought and policy, the romantic, libertarian fantasies it rejects, the racism it legitimates, and the "modernization" it promises, see Leopoldo Zea's *Pensamiento positivista latinoamericano.*

6 I would like to thank Elizabeth Zayre, Patrick O'Connor, Sylvia Molloy, and Nicolas Shumway for their help with the translation of Spanish texts, as well as for their generous comments on earlier versions of this essay.

7 See, for example, *"Defensa sanitaria marítima contra las enfermedades exóticas viajeras"* 307.

8 Hereinafter this publication will be cited as *Archivos.*

9 For a discussion on the importance of new fictions and narratives in women's education see Carolyn Heilbrun 37.

10 Chauncey notes that "during the transition in medical thinking . . . some doctors, as

one would expect, used the terms [homosexuality and sexual inversion] interchangeably"
(124).

11   For a relevant discussion on the meaning of the relatively autonomous space of the convent in Latin American, and on the possible interpretations of the acts of nuns or *beatas*
resisting the *status quo* and the state, see Jean Franco, especially chap. 2, "Sor Juana
explores space" 23–54.

12   In another article, also published in the *Archivos,* this educator of women claims that
"lo que hace a las mujeres particularmente aptas para cuidar la primera infancia es que
ellas mismas continúan siendo pueriles, fútiles y limitadas de inteligencia" [what makes
women particularly apt for watching over early childhood is that they themelves continue
to be puerile, futile, and limited in intelligence]. See "La mujer moderna," in *Archivos* 8
(1909) 333.

13   For a history of women's participation in the early Argentine labor movement, see Donna
Guy's ground-breaking work, especially chaps. 2 and 3; Masiello, chaps. 2 and 3; and
Marifran Carlson, chaps. 4 to 7.

14   For a fuller treatment of the statistics, see Bejarano's article 123–38. He notes that in
Buenos Aires, toward 1910 "constantemente existía una gran masa de hombres nómadas,
sin ataduras de ninguna especie" (138) [constantly there existed a great mass of nomadic
men without ties of any kind].

15   For a discussion of the conceptions and forms of representation of male-male sex in
classical Greece, see Halperin 48–49.

16   For a highly relevant discussion of notions of sexual deviance and anal intercourse between males in Nicaragua, see Roger N. Lancaster's *Life is Hard* 234–78. In a chapter
titled "Subject Honor, Object Shame" Lancaster explained that in our day, in Nicaragua, "It is certainly not the stigma of the fully rationalized, medicalized system of sexual
meaning that elaborates a category, 'the homosexual,' to identify both practice and identity. Rather it is anal passivity alone that is stigmatized, and it is anal passivity that defines
the status identity in question" (242).

17   For statistics on Italian immigration, see Oscar Cornblit, "Inmigrantes y empresarios en
la política argentina," *Los fragmentos del poder,* ed. Tulio Halperín Donghi 399.

18   Such as the original tango with its popular, anonymous, and "obscene" lyrics. See Salessi,
"Tango, nacionalismo y sexualidad. Buenos Aires, 1880–1914" 45–51.

19   *Público* in Spanish meaning both the public and the audience.

20   For a discussion on drag and the denaturalization of essentialist gender identities, see
Butler 138.

21   To my knowledge Veyga's book on sexual inversion was never published.

22   Today *lunfardo* is the word that, changing meaning through time, denotes the *porteño*
slang (*porteño* meaning inhabitant of the port city of Buenos Aires). In our day this argot
has enriched the colloquial language of Buenos Aires.

Works Cited

Alonso, Ana María, and María Teresa Koreck. "Silences: Hispanics, AIDS, and Sexual Practices." *Differences* 1 (Winter 1989): 101–24.

Anderson, Benedict. *Imagined Communities.* London and New York: Verso, 1983.

Barthes, Roland. *Camera Lucida.* Trans. Richard Howard. New York: Hill and Wang, 1981.

Bátiz, Adolfo. *Buenos Aires, la rivera y los prostíbulos en 1880*. Buenos Aires: Aga Taura, [n.d.].

Bejarano, Manuel. "Inmigración y estructuras tradicionales en Buenos Aires (1854–1930)." *Los fragmentos del poder*. Ed. Tulio Halperín Donghi. Buenos Aires: Sudamericana, 1987. 75–150.

Benjamin, Walter. *Illuminations*. Ed. Hannah Arendt. Trans. Harry Zohn. New York: Schocken, 1981.

Bialet-Massé, Juan. *El estado de las clases obreras argentinas a comienzos de siglo*. Córdoba: Universidad Nacional de Córdoba, 1968.

Buck-Morss, Susan. *The Dialectics of Seeing: Walter Benjamin and the Arcades Project*. Cambridge, Massachusetts: M.I.T. Press, 1989.

Butler, Judith. *Gender Trouble: Feminism and the Subversion of Identity*. New York: Routledge, 1990.

Carlson, Marifran. *¡Feminismo! The Women's Movement in Argentina from its Beginnings to Eva Perón*. Chicago: Academy Chicago, 1988.

Chauncey, George. "From Sexual Inversion to Homosexuality: Medicine and the Changing Conceptualization of Sexual Deviance." *Salmagundi* 58–59 (Fall 1982–Winter 1983): 114–46.

Cornblit, Oscar. "Inmigrantes y empresarios en la política argentina." *Los fragmentos del poder*. Ed. Tulio Halperín Donghi. Buenos Aires: Sudamericana, 1987. 389–438.

De Veyga, Francisco. "El amor en los invertidos sexuales." *Archivos de Criminología y Psiquiatría* (Buenos Aires) 2 (1903): 333–41.

———. "El sentido moral y la conducta de los invertidos." *Archivos de Criminología y Psiquiatría* (Buenos Aires) 3 (1904): 22–30.

———. "Invertido sexual imitando la mujer honesta." *Archivos de Criminología y Psiquiatría* (Buenos Aires) 1 (1902): 193–208.

———. "La inversión sexual congénita." *Archivos de Criminología y Psiquiatría* (Buenos Aires) 1 (1902): 44–48.

———. "La inversión sexual adquirida." *Archivos de Criminología y Psiquiatría* (Buenos Aires) 2 (1903): 193–208.

———. "La inversión sexual adquirida. Tipo profesional." *Archivos de Criminología y Psiquiatría* (Buenos Aires) 2 (1903): 492–96.

"Defensa sanitaria marítima contra las enfermedades exóticas viajeras." *Anales del Departamento Nacional de Higiene* (Buenos Aires) 8 (1898): 307–24.

Douglas, Mary. *Purity and Danger: An Analysis of the Concepts of Pollution and Taboo*. London: Routledge, 1989.

"El cólera—Informe de la Oficina Sanitaria." *Anales del Departamento Nacional de Higiene* (Buenos Aires) 5 (1895): 85–147.

Foucault, Michel. *Historia de la sexualidad*. Vol. 1. Trans. Ulíses Guiñazú. México: Siglo Veintiuno, 1987.

Gómez, Eusebio. *La mala vida en Buenos Aires*. Buenos Aires: Juan Roldan, 1908.

Guy, Donna. *Sex and Danger in Buenos Aires: Prostitution, Family and Nation in Argentina*. Lincoln: University of Nebraska Press, 1991.

Halperin, David. "Sex Before Sexuality: Pederasty, Politics, and Power in Classical Athens." *Hidden from History: Reclaiming the Gay and Lesbian Past*. Ed. Martin Duberman, Martha Vicinus, and George Chauncey, Jr. New York: Meridian, 1989. 37–53.

Heilbrun, Carolyn. *Writing a Woman's Life*. New York: Ballantine Books, 1988.

Ingenieros, José. "Patología de las funciones sexuales—Nueva clasificación genética." *Archivos de Criminología y Psiquiatría* (Buenos Aires) 9 (1910): 3–80.

Masiello, Francine. *Between Civilization and Barbarism: Women, Nation, and Literary Cultures in Modern Argentina.* Lincoln: University of Nebraska Press, 1992.

Mercante, Victor. "El fetichismo y el uranismo femenino en los internados educativos." *Archivos de Criminología y Psiquiatría* (Buenos Aires) 4 (1905): 22–30.

———. "La mujer moderna." *Archivos de Criminología y Psiquiatría* 8 (1909): 333–94.

Ramos Mejía, José María. *Las multitudes argentinas.* Buenos Aires: Lajouane, 1912.

Rodríguez, Leopoldo. *Inmigración, nacionalismo y fuerzas armadas.* México: Editora Impresora Internacional, 1986.

Salessi, Jorge. "Tango, nacionalismo y sexualidad. Buenos Aires: 1880–1914." *Hispamérica* 60 (1991): 33–54.

Sedgwick, Eve Kosofsky. *Epistemology of the Closet.* Berkeley: University of California Press, 1990.

Solberg, Carl. *Immigration and Nationalism.* Buenos Aires: Paidós, 1985.

Vezzetti, Hugo. *La locura en la argentina.* Buenos Aires: Paidós, 1985.

Weeks, Jeffrey. "Inverts, Perverts, and Mary-Annes: Male Prostitution and the Regulation of Homosexuality in the Nineteenth and Early Twentieth Centuries." *Hidden from History: Reclaiming the Gay and Lesbian Past.* Ed. Martin Duberman, Martha Vicinus, and George Chauncey, Jr. New York: Meridian, 1989. 195–211.

Zea, Leopoldo. *Pensamiento positivista latinoamericano.* México: Porrúa, 1980.

Oscar Montero

Julián del Casal and the
Queers of Havana

By the end of the nineteenth century, the gentle reproaches of cultural patriarch Andrés Bello about the "melindrosa y femenil ternura," [affected, feminine tenderness] and the "arrebatos eróticos," [erotic raptures] of certain writers had paradoxically hardened into the ambiguous aesthetic of *Modernismo,* nurtured on the one hand by the decadent, and often implicitly homoerotic literatures of Europe and North America, and fueled on the other by the none too subtle homophobia of various discourses of national affirmation.[1] In the context of such discourses, founded and developed during the second half of the nineteenth century, the life and works of Cuban *modernista* Julián del Casal constitute a peculiar case. Casal's literary novelty and his position among the first *modernistas* are familiar; what is less clear, although it is a recurring topic among his readers, is Casal's role in the deviant side of a foundational erotics of politics, as Doris Sommer has aptly called it. The pages that follow review some of the more suggestive aspects of Casal's eroticism and tentatively frame it with the explicit evidence of a homosexual subculture flourishing in fin de siècle Havana.

Evidence of such a culture is found in two treatises dealing with prostitution and homosexuality in Havana around 1890. The first, *La prostitución en La Habana,* is a sociomedical treatise published by Dr. Benjamín Céspedes in 1888. The second treatise, an attack on Céspedes and his work, was published a year later by Pedro Giralt with the odd title of *El amor y la prostitución. Réplica a un libro del Dr. Céspedes* [Love and Prostitution. Reply to a Book by Dr. Céspedes]. The two treatises, a pseudo-scientific study and its moralizing response, very likely provoked a *crónica* published by Casal in *La Discusión* on 28 December 1889.[2] Casal's *crónica,* "A través de la ciudad. El centro de dependientes" [Throughout the City. The Center for Store Clerks] describes a visit to a residence for store clerks, one of the places of homosexual activity discussed in the treatises. The treatises in question outline a portrait of queer Havana that frames Casal's *crónica* and that may enrich, or even taint, a literary persona long frozen in aesthetic isolation.[3]

Questions concerning Casal's sexuality rose almost as soon as he began publishing, and comments about the peculiar eroticism of his work became a commonplace of literary histories; yet the relationship between the two has remained obscure, or at best oblique. Obscurity and obliqueness are not necessarily undesirable, though repeated references to the mystery surrounding Casal's sexuality have gone hand in hand with a canonization of his text as a brilliant, though marginal and unique parcel of *Modernismo*'s cultural monument. A tentative, perhaps controversial, and certainly provisional turn from that monument is in order. Suppose that the monument occupies Havana's main promenade around 1889; and in the evening, when the music plays, out come the queers, *"maricones"* and their "clients," marginal types who seem to circle the monolithic monument.

Any mention or allusion to Casal's sexuality has always carried the implication that it was not only aberrant in some way or other but radically unique. Whatever Casal was, he was the only one; it follows, or so the argument suggests, that Casal's work is at once brilliant and anomalous. Casal's secret is his alone. The founding gesture of homosexual panic, evident in the critical writings about Casal, is not really intolerance (Casal is admired for his poetic gifts etc.), but isolation: Casal is different, unique, as a poet and as an individual. The sexuality of Casal's body not only does not have a name but it is reduced to the category of the anomalous and the isolated. The psychological vocabulary used in a great deal of criticism (repression, sense of guilt, abnormality), has contributed to that isolation. Yet, independent of Casal, removed from the complex metaphoric web where illness, sexual preference, and literary production shift vertiginously to produce various readings, what was it like to be queer in Havana around 1890? If it is impossible, and perhaps unnecessary or undesirable, to out Casal (the hard evidence is certainly missing), it does seem pertinent to people the dreary isolation of his sexuality with other bodies, with some background noise as it were, provided by so-called hustlers, drag queens, pretty boys, and their bourgeois clients.

The frequent comments about the peculiarities of Casal's textual eroticism, and the sexuality that seems to nurture it, have gone hand in hand with a characteristic flight into what may be called the more readable, and more palatable, side of his "nature" and his writing, that is to say, his

"Nihilismo" and his "Neurosis," the titles of two of his best-known poems, which have been read as a rather narrow aesthetic credo, or more radically still, as the definitive expression of a vital ideology.[4] Along these same lines, Casal's tropical *mal de siècle* is somehow justified by his early death from an illness seemingly willed by the poet, a fitting ending for a morbid trinity of "isms": exoticism, eroticism, pessimism.

Whether well-intentioned or apologetic, Casal's first readers reveal a peculiar version of homosexual panic.[5] One of the most explicit versions of this panic, though not the only one, may be found in the portrait written by a contemporary of Casal, writer and polemist Manuel de la Cruz (1861– 96). In the portrait written by De la Cruz for his *Cromitos cubanos* [Cuban Sketches], the contrast between a desired virility and Casal's ambiguous interior, the place of culture but also of abnormality and neurosis, is explicit.[6] Casal's often quoted definition of the modern writer as a "neuró- tico sublime, o un nihilista, o un blasfemo, o un desesperado" [a sublime neurotic, or a nihilist, or a blasphemer, or a desperado] deliberately and forcefully inverts the terms of national virility spelled out by De la Cruz.[7] Casal's rather militant swerving from a virile national discourse is backed by European models yet remains no less nationalistic, however peculiarly so. Nevertheless, the charges of De la Cruz and others have stuck; Casal's self-sublimation of neurosis has remained isolated and anomalous and for that reason perfectly coherent with *Modernismo*'s parceling of the aesthetic and correlative professionalization of the writer.[8]

Yet such parceling, however historically justified, seems to dampen the impact of Casal's neurotic sublime version of the writer, aesthetic in the etymological sense of the word, still touching the emotions and the senses, certainly mine at any rate. In a visit to one of the Centers for Clerks, accused of sheltering explicit homosexual practices, Casal, the neurotic sublime of his own definition of the artist, brushes what was on the streets of Havana at the time he wrote, c. 1890: that is, a full-blown queer culture, violently pushed to the edge by the scientific and moralizing discourses of profes- sionals and pamphleteers, some of whom also doubled as readers of Casal and arbiters of culture in the emerging republic. Before taking it to the streets, so to speak, a brief aside on queer theory is in order.

Max Nordau, the popularizer of a homophobic version of decadence, wanted artistic representations to come into the "bright focal circle of con- sciousness" (61). By contrast, queer theory, because it flees, like Blanche at the bowling alley, from the merciless glare of such a cruel metaphor, may produce hazy results. Queer theory is "fuzzily defined, undercoded, or discursively dependent on more established forms" (Lauretis iii). Paradoxically, richly so one must add, Spanish American *modernismo* partakes of a double coincidence: on the one hand, it coincides with the development of nationalistic cultures, "ostensibly grounded in 'natural' heterosexual love" and marriage (Sommer 6); on the other hand, *Modernismo* may be said to be the founding moment of Spanish American literary queerness, inasmuch as an "against the grain," often willful marginality comes to be a part, if not the central part, of the new aesthetic, rejected by the likes of Manuel de la Cruz and embraced by Casal. The queer "revels in the discourse of the loathsome, the outcast, the idiomatically proscribed position of same-sex desire," the queer "attacks the dominant notion of the natural, is the taboo-breaker, the monstrous, the uncanny" (Case 3). At one point or another, so were most *modernistas,* but when the winds of homophobia blew their way, they lay their cards on the table and beat a hasty retreat; hence the other side of *Modernismo,* the cure, the antidote, the healing of the wound of European decadence, one of whose secrets was a newly named "perversion": homosexuality.

Casal was born in Havana in 1863, the son of a well-to-do Spanish immigrant and a Cuban woman of Irish and Spanish descent. By the time he was ten, whatever remained of what according to his biographers must have been a rather pleasant childhood was wiped out. 1868, the same year Casal's mother died, also marks the beginning of the first war for Cuban independence, ten years of battles and skirmishes that devastated the Cuban countryside; before the war ended, the father's business, and Casal's patrimony, lay in ruins. These biographical misfortunes form an anecdotal core used by generations of readers to anchor the recurring themes of physical decadence and moral defeat. Thus physical and spiritual exhaustion becomes the referent of what may be called the weariness of representation, the other side of creative desire, a commonplace of artistic modernity and certainly one of the salient characteristics of *Modernismo*.[9] The representation of the *mal de siècle* in *modernista* texts is frequently associated with the erotic, remarkably so in the work of Casal, whose erotic drift is backed by a vaguely defined sexual deviance, ambiguously though insistently named, and by illness. The pairing of sexual deviance and illness is of course common in the medicolegal systems worked out during the second half of the nineteenth century. Casal's case exemplifies the homophobic slant of discourses about sexuality and nationalism adapted to the Cuban situation: illness triumphs as a referent (Casal dies before his thirtieth birthday), while sexual deviance or uncertainty are eclipsed, though never silenced, becoming Casal's open secret.[10]

It is true that Casal's death was as dramatic as it was premature, seemingly staged like so many things about him, his room, his impoverished dandyism, the settings of his poems, and of course his elegant writing style. Having recovered from an almost deadly bout of high fevers, the result of a vaguely diagnosed lung ailment, Casal attended a soiree at a friend's house. Between puffs of his cigarette, a telling prop for a man in cigar-smoking Cuba, certainly so in 1893, he laughed at a joke, and the laughter turned into a vomit of blood that stained the white shirt front: a kind friend removed the still burning cigarette from Casal's fingers. The pose of the laughing smoker, vaguely erotic like everything about Casal, wedded to a horrible death, has become part of his literary legend: Eros meets Thanatos in the tropical night. Yet in the hands of his first critics, the force of Thanatos won out as if Casal had been meant to die, and somehow his death justified all of his poetry; he was "enamored of Thanatos," wrote Darío.[11] Whatever his sexual orientation, Casal's famous illness eclipses and in a sense excuses whatever deviance might have lurked in the lurid images of his writing. The reading of Casal's death as a predetermined aesthetic consequence of his writing is commonplace. There is no question that illness and imminent death are sources of imagery for Casal's poetry and prose, but the creative energy to bring this about must not be slighted. However, in the hands of friends and critics, the so-called morbid aspect of Casal's literary persona has been bound in the straitjacket of biographical causality, succeeding all too well in setting Casal and his work in a barren field, however exotic and attractive it might be.

Subsequent generations of critics would refer to the mystery of Casal's sexuality, ever veiled and ever suggestive of death. The tortured yet dazzling eroticism of Julián del Casal's writing is inevitably associated by an entrenched critical tradition with the mystery of that sexuality, repressed, death-driven, certainly neurotic. The evident culture-building aspect of his erotic literary representations is thus masked, and such a mask, or rather pall, enshrines Casal among the *modernistas* and at the same time robs him, and us, of an empowering legacy. A hundred years after Casal's death, the devastating reality of AIDS is made more bearable, and culturally more fruitful, when that legacy is appropriated, when its queer aspects are allowed to mirror, however speculatively, our own predicament. The web of lies generated by AIDS is countered by a rereading of Casal that would deliberately blur the traditional image of Casal as a rather marginal, however significant, *modernista*. This cultural speculation is what queer theory and, as far as I am concerned, what queer identity are about: to be permitted a cultural presence, to be subjects, however illusory that position might be, of culture rather than the objects of various attempts, old as the word "homosexuality" itself and as recent as the latest weekly rag, to find the causes of our so-called deviance.

In spite of the secret character of Casal's sexuality, references to it are plentiful; yet they are also repetitive, oscillating between the writer's biography and his work, both of which feed on and feed the secret of Casal's sexual identity, or more properly perhaps, his sexual orientation, either homosexuality or a quasi-masochistic asceticism. Max Nordau's famous definition of "degeneration" lurks in many of the comments made by Casal's early critics, not necessarily because they had read Nordau's treatise, which was published in 1892, but because they share the same sources, that is the naming and parceling of sexuality that is one of the strongest branches of scientific positivism.[12] In his biography of Casal, Emilio de Armas gives a summary of the question of sexuality in the legend about Casal. Referring to Casal's secret, Emilio de Armas writes, "sus amigos solían hablar de él en el tono de quienes comparten un secreto de iniciados" [his friends would speak about him in the hushed tones of those who share the secret of the initiates].[13] Casal's secret is "la extraña cosa / que te deje el alma helada" [the strange thing that will chill your soul] of his poem "Rondeles" [*Rondeaux*] which begins thus: "De mi vida misteriosa, / tétrica y desencantada, / oirás contar una cosa / que te deje el alma helada" [About my life, disenchanted, mysterious, and somber, you will hear something that may chill your soul].[14]

Another Casal critic, Mario Cabrera Saqui, writes apologetically that the poet was "un supertímido por la exagerada diferenciación de su instinto varonil, un tímido superior de la categoría de Amiel" (273) [a supertimid because of the exaggerated differentiation of his masculine instinct, a superior timid on the order of Amiel]. According to Carmen Poncet, Casal was "un tipo sicológicamente intersexual" [a psychologically intersexual type], one of those individuals possessing "un mecanismo sexual perfecto; pero que frecuentemente se inhiben por la falsa conciencia que experimentan de su capacidad" (35–40) [a perfect sexual mechanism, but who are inhibited by the false awareness they have of their abilities]. In other words, Casal had the right equipment but was afraid to use it, that is, afraid to use it as a heterosexual. It is certainly remarkable that Professor Poncet was able to assess the perfection of Casal's "sexual mechanism" nearly fifty years after his death. According to Argentine scholar José María Monner Sans, the issue should be closed; it is too complicated, he writes somberly, full of anecdotes and episodes. The stage is thus set for a safe, and not altogether unhasty, return to the text, to the representations of sexuality, enlightened or obscured as the case might be, by the secret in question. Thus any reading that mentions or skirts, as is often the case, the question of sexuality in Casal, or more properly the question of its textual representations, is predetermined by the ambiguous character of Casal's open secret. Certainly, its very ambiguity is one of the strands in Casal's work that still crackles and sears with the peculiar energy that went into its making. In Casal's case, temporarily turning from the text will hardly lead to the solving of a back fence riddle but rather will enrich an inexorable and desired return. So a detour is in order, a cruise around the square: it's 1889 and what's doing in Havana?

As it emerges in the writing of the day, treatises, newspaper stories, and literary texts, Havana was a busy, somewhat ragged, colonial capital, as cosmopolitan perhaps as much larger Latin American cities, but certainly limited in the geographical as well as the cultural sense of the word; it must have been, and still is, a hard city to get totally lost in. I know that Casal went by those same squares and sidewalks where men and women cruised. I cannot affirm, or deny, whether he rejected that marginal space or if he simply crossed the street, but in order to deal with what Lezama Lima called "el quitasol de un inmenso Eros" [the umbrella of a huge Eros] in his "Ode to Julián del Casal," in order to share the verses that say "Nuestro escandaloso cariño te persigue" [Our scandalous love pursues you], that transform the secret and the punishment woven around Casal's sexuality into erotic sympathy, the presence of those others must be mentioned, those who cruised the periphery of Havana's squares.

The "problem" of homosexuality in the city is discussed in a chapter on male prostitution in Benjamín Céspedes's *La prostitución en La Habana;* Pedro Giralt deals with the topic throughout his irate reply, *El amor y la prostitución.* A useful aspect of the two works is their explicit vocabulary. At the same time, a series of complex metaphoric twists run from the body and its "sexually transmitted diseases" to the city and the national question, the question of the day among Cuban intellectuals. By contrast, in Casal's *crónica,* while vaguely but almost certainly alluding to one of the treatises, the relationship among the young clerks is described exclusively in terms of friendship and fraternity not of course in sexual terms. The rather elaborate description of the main room of the residence takes up almost half of the brief article. Casal's version shows the nature of the censorship in the press where he published much of his works or perhaps the limits that the writer imposed on himself. It also shows that the sublimation at work in the *crónica,* rather than merely repressive, is also fruitfully subjective:

in other words, self-sublimation is also self-representation, a cultural practice that is subtly yet powerfully opposed to the insistent objectivity of the scientific and political treatises that deal with the clerks' deviant sexuality.

If Dr. Céspedes discusses sexuality from the point of view of a physician and sociologist, Giralt replies by condemning the moral implication of such an analysis. Both consider the body of the homosexual as the grotesque referent of a number of maladies. In his prologue to the Céspedes book, Enrique José Varona, an early Casal critic and one of the most prominent literary and political figures of the day, praises it because "nos invita a acercarnos a una mesa de disección, a contemplar al desnudo úlceras cancerosas, a descubrir los tejidos atacados por el virus" (xi) [it invites us to approach a dissecting table, to gaze at the exposed cancerous sores, to discover the tissues attacked by the virus]. Varona prefaces the doctor's sociomedical treatise by deploying the prestigious metaphor of social disorder as illness; he moves seamlessly from the tissues on the doctor's table to the city: in both cases dissection is not only useful but necessary because pointing out the locus of disease somehow marks the beginning of the healing process.

The distancing maneuvers are significant, and Dr. Céspedes uses a common device: he did not himself examine the young pederast; he is merely reporting on the examination conducted by an anonymous learned colleague. In a chapter titled "La prostitución masculina" [Male Prostitution], there is a detailed description of the city's queer underworld. The following paragraph presents a fundamental definition of homosexuality, an "aberration" that is repeatedly compared to prostitution, in other words, not the aberration of an individual or a group of individuals, but a highly socialized phenomenon that threatens the rest of the populace:

> Y aquí en la Habana, desgraciadamente, subsisten con más extensión de lo creíble y con mayor impunidad que en lugar alguno, tamañas degradaciones de la naturaleza humana; tipos de hombres que han invertido su sexo para traficar con estos gustos bestiales, abortos de la infamia que pululan libremente, asqueando a una sociedad que se pregunta indignada, ante la invasión creciente de la plaga asquerosa; si abundando tanto pederasta, habrán también aumentado los clientes de tan horrendos vicios. (190)
>
> [And unfortunately here in Havana, there subsist, more extensively than one may believe and with greater impunity than anywhere else, enormous degradations of human nature; types of men who have inverted their sex in order to traffic in bestial desires, abortions of infamy teeming freely among us, revolting our society, which facing the

growing invasion of such a disgusting plague, asks with outrage if the
abundance of so many pederasts does not also signal an increase in the
number of clients for such horrible vices.]

Dr. Céspedes comments on the relationship between homosexuals and
prostitutes, but much more disturbing is the presence of the so-called
clients, suggesting the sort of exchange that has transformed the capital
"en una de esas ciudades sodomíticas [into one of those sodomitic cities]
an insular version of decadent Rome. The doctor divides pederasts into
three groups: "el negro, el mulato y el blanco" [negroes, mulattos, and
whites]. Classifying is of course a way to insist on scientific objectivity and
to distance the observer from a supposedly marginal group that nevertheless appears to be spread throughout the entire city: "repartidos en
todos los barrios de la Habana" [spread throughout all the neighborhoods
of Havana]. Like prostitutes or vampires, "por la noche se estacionan en
los puntos más retirados del Parque y sus alrededores más solitarios" [at
night they stake out the periphery of the Square and its more isolated
surroundings]. There follows a description of the "effeminate pederast,"
also archetypical. It could apply to decadent Rome or to the New York of
tomorrow:

> Durante las noches de retreta circulan libremente confundidos con
> el público, llamando la atención, no de la policía, sino de los concu-
> rrentes indignados, las actitudes grotescamente afeminadas de estos
> tipos que van señalando cínicamente las posaderas erguidas, arquea-
> dos y ceñidos los talles, y que al andar con menudos pasos de arrastre,
> se balancean con contoneos de mujer coqueta. Llevan flequillos en la
> frente, carmín en el rostro y polvos de arroz en el semblante, ignoble
> y fatigado de los más y agraciado en algunos. El pederasta responde a
> un nombre de mujer en la jerga del oficio. (191)
> [When the band plays in the evening, they walk about freely, min-
> gling with the populace; the grotesquely effeminate gestures of these
> types call the attention, not of the police, but of the outraged gather-
> ing; they walk cynically showing off their prominent buttocks, their
> waist arched and cinched, walking with small, mincing steps, swaying
> this way and that like a flirtatious woman. They wear bangs on their
> foreheads, rouge and rice powder on their face, ignoble and worn for
> the most part yet charming among some others. In the slang of their
> trade, pederasts go by a woman's name.]

The repulsion that one is asked to feel before the archetypical stereotype of the effeminate homosexual is undermined by the mention of the charming faces among them. Dr. Céspedes goes on to say that some of them have a favorite lover and that they celebrate parties among themselves, where they "mimic" (*fingen*) births and baptisms. From the point of view of the doctor, this mimicking of heterosexuality at its most "natural," birth, and its most sacred, baptism, is particularly repellent.[15] Following the lead of nineteenth-century sociology, particularly echoing Lombroso's physiognomically typed offenders, the doctor links homosexual behavior with criminality and disease; yet because of his scientific objectivity, he avoids making an explicit moral judgment, adding that "no siempre son pasivos en sus relaciones sexuales" [they are not always passive in their sexual relations] and sometimes "se prestan a ser activos" [lend themselves to an active role]. Dr. Céspedes's description proves that the practice of homosexual acts, at least among men in late-nineteenth-century Havana, was a relatively public, fully socialized affair. The fact that such practices are never mentioned, never explicitly so at any rate, by Casal, or any of the writers grouped around the journal *La Habana Elegante,* only confirms the transgressive character of such practices and the need to keep them secret, that is to say unwritten about except in sociomedical treatises. It is important to point out that the dominant strategy of suppression is to keep homosexuality out of written texts not classified as legal or medical, which is to say to keep it out of literature. By contrast, as will be seen in the comments on Giralt's response to Dr. Céspedes, homosexuality, particularly as it affected the relationship between the urban elite and the working classes, was the talk of the town.

The "vice" described by Dr. Céspedes has another privileged location, the communal residences of young apprentices and clerks, many of them recent arrivals from Spain. The chapter on male prostitution concludes with the report of an interview with a young clerk, approximately fifteen years of age, who visits the doctor because he says he may be "dañado por dentro" [hurt inside]. The doctor tells him he has a "chancro infectante sifilítico," an [infectious, syphilitic sore] and then goes on to describe the boy: "noté lo afeminado de su rostro, tan agraciado como el de cualquier mujer, y lo redondo y mórbido de sus formas de adolescente" [I noticed his effeminate face, as charming as that of any woman, and the morbid roundness of his adolescent body], "morbid" of course in the double sense of "soft and delicate" and "diseased or causing disease." The word is one of the key adjectives of the various discourses on decadence and signals illness as well as "erotomania" and "egomania," Nordau's double-headed *bête noire*.

The interview with the boy reveals another aspect of the queer life of the period. In the residence for clerks where he lives, some of the men caress him and "hacían conmigo ciertos manejos" [they did certain things with me]. "Con casi todos" [with most of them], he admits. The boy then says that they hit him ("me pegaban") and goes on to say that the men "me besaban y me cogían de la mano y yo tenía que hacerles" [they kissed me and they took my hand and I had to do it with them or to them]. Among the faceless "all of them," there is a remarkable exception. The boy says that "Habían [*sic*] dos que dormían juntos, pero a esos se les miraba con más respeto" [There were two who slept together, and they were looked upon with more respect]. The gay boy is abused by men whose sexual identity is not in question because their sexually active role simultaneously ratifies their heterosexuality and masks the evident homosexuality of their acts. In this violent setting, the boy's mention of two men who slept together, and were thus respected as a couple, is remarkably moving. Faced with what must have been the daunting authority of the doctor, this nameless boy manages to point to a homosexual role model, as if to add its worth to the doctor's scientific diagnosis. In other words, in the interview with the doctor, quoted verbatim by Dr. Céspedes and probably conducted by him in the first place, the references to the grotesque and the sick are countered by the respect of a group of men for a gay couple who slept together. As for the person in charge of the residence, he is as indifferent as the police and "con tal de no aflojar dinero, en lo demás no se mete en esas cosas feas" (194) [as long as he didn't have to shell out any money, he didn't get mixed up in those ugly things], which suggests the relative tolerance toward the sexual practices in the residence.

Though referring only to "pederasty," Dr. Céspedes reproduces the two fundamental aspects of the original definition of homosexuality:[16] on the one hand, it is a disease with identifiable symptoms, especially when the body, as in the case of the boy in the interview, is marked by "sores" etc.; on the other hand, as the corporal metaphor broadens its scope, it is a social disease that "infects" the rest of the healthy political body, the same metaphoric slippage harrowingly at work in current AIDS phobia. The somatic metaphors have an evident source in the boy's body; but even before the interview, such anthropomorphic metaphors are applied to the city, in the same way that they are applied to the decadent aspects of Casal's work. In the description of queer life in Havana, the metaphoric web deployed by the doctor, and by Varona in his prologue, is at one with the epistemology of the period. It is in fact the common denominator of discourses dealing with illness and homosexuality, as well as with various symbolic practices, specifically literature, which is decadent when it favors "external adornment," Nordau's expression, in short when it does not signify clearly. Nordau repeatedly refers to the decadents' failure to grasp "the phenomenon of the universe" (266) and to their obsession with form and ornament, which are supposedly devoid of meaning. This is the crux of Varona's founding, extremely influential, criticism of Casal's work: too precious for its own good and certainly not good for the republic, neither the culturally sound Cuban republic of letters nor the yet-to-be-founded political republic.

Dr. Céspedes locates homosexuality between disease and symbolic practice. Pederasts are depraved beings, marked by the symptoms of disease. They also mimic the social behavior that defined "woman" at the time, particularly woman as prostitute: they wear makeup and sway as they walk.[17] The setting described by Dr. Céspedes is absolutely marginal. Homosexuals live in dens, and although they cruise the heart of the city, they confine themselves to the periphery of its square and to the late evening hours. Dr. Céspedes's pederasts are marginal not only because of their sexual preference but because of their social class, which he hastens to define by lumping together career criminals, "dirty alcoholics," and hairdressers and "maids" of prostitutes. The clerks of the guild residences are foreigners for the most part and dangerously close to the class in question; besides, the doctor asserts, their living conditions tend to foster aberrant same-sex practices. Except in the passing, though alarmed, mention of the clients, the class of intellectuals and professionals, such as the doctor himself, is beyond the reach of the marginal group, thus reified in the name of science and presented as an object of study, a monstrosity in a natural history museum. The nature of the solution finally offered by the doctor is neither moral nor psychological, but social: "mancebos célibes" [celibate young men] should not be lodged in phalansteries, where the absence of women must lead them to "incontinencia bestial entre hombres" (195) [bestial incontinence among men].

Dr. Céspedes's *La prostitución en La Habana* had an almost immediate answer. The year after the study's publication Pedro Giralt y Alemán published *El amor y la prostitución. Réplica a un libro del Dr. Céspedes* [Love and Prostitution. Reply to a Book by Dr. Céspedes]. Giralt defends the virility of the clerks and accuses Dr. Céspedes of being an anti-European charlatan. Giralt's book unwittingly broadens the scope of homosexuality in the colonial capital. He rants about the "vices" of the bourgeoisie and the professional classes, specifically the *criollo* class. According to Giralt, the doctor is "hombre vulgarísimo y completamente inepto para especular seriamente en los altos y sublimes principios de la Ciencia [a most vulgar man, totally inept for the serious study of the lofty, sublime principles of Science]. He goes on to say that the doctor has blamed an entire social group for the isolated defects of one individual, namely the young boy interviewed by the doctor (83). In his angry pamphlet, Giralt attacks the "fanaticism of *criollismo*," because he believes that the doctor has suggested that prostitution and homosexuality are European vices that have contaminated the island's national aspirations. In other words, barely five years before the second war of independence, Cuban nationalists or *criollistas* wrongly blame Europe, specifically a hated Spain, for the queering of the capital, so goes Giralt's argument. Giralt's name-calling defense merely turns the table: you Cubans, especially bourgeois professionals, are the queers, not the poor immigrant boys trying to survive in their new home, even if such survival means an occasional sexual transaction with one of the hated clients, the real villains in Giralt's diatribe.[18]

Giralt's argument has no rhyme or reason, but his vigorous mudslinging is enlightening. He drags the doctor's scientific study into the debate about nationalism that was the order of the day. Giralt turns his ire not on the pederasts but on their clients, who are not clerks but *criollo* members of the urban elite:

> ¿Cómo calificaremos, pues, a estos pederastas activos y *paganos* que van o iban a solicitar a los *maricones* para *ocuparlos* pagándoles con dinero? No obstante estos, más culpables que los *pasivos*, no han sido deportados, y se están paseando por las calles de la Habana. ¿Serán dependientes? ¡Ah, si se pudiera decir ciertas cosas que la vergüenza pública prohibe revelar; si fuera lícito contar con nombres y apellidos ciertas historias íntimas y secretas cuyos detalles se cuentan *sotto voce* por los corrillos; las confidencias de algunas mujeres a sus comadres y de éstas a sus íntimos, aparecerían a la luz del sol con toda su repugnante fealdad más de cuatro entes, al parecer bien educados, que llevan levita y ocupan señalados puestos. (emphasis in the original, 83–85)
> [How should we label these active, pagan pederasts who pursue these queers in order to pay them for their services? They are more to blame than the *passive* ones, yet they have not been deported, and they walk the streets of Havana with impunity. Are they clerks? Oh, if only one could say certain things that public decency forbids us to reveal, if it were lawful to name certain names, and certain intimate, secret stories whose details are told *sotto voce* here and there, what women whisper to their friends (*comadres*), and what these in turn whisper to others,

the repugnant ugliness of more than one apparently well-educated so-and-so, who wears coat and tie and goes to a respectable job, would be forced into the light of day.]

Giralt is up on the latest back-fence gossip in colonial Havana, and he wants nothing less than to out the professional *criollos,* whose vice is that much more repugnant because they practice it out of choice not out of need, as do some of the poor boys described by the doctor. As opposed to Dr. Céspedes's attempts to sound scientific, Giralt is refreshingly explicit in his pamphleteering: the people in question are queers, *"maricones."* His comments reveal that homosexuality was not at all marginal; what makes a homosexual marginal is his class, not his sexual preference. The less fortunate ones, those from the working classes, are deported to the Isle of Pines, but their clients stroll about freely because their good name, their education, in short their social class, the class of those who "wear a frock coat and occupy distinguished posts," protect them. Giralt's defense of "the honest, suffering class of store clerks" suggests the breadth and complexity of homosexual and homosocial practices in the Havana of 1889.[19] Moreover, if Giralt's challenge to Céspedes's scientific authority is chaotic and illogical, it also rejects the body of the boy examined by the doctor as the source of an ambiguous metaphoric web and transforms the question of homosexuality into a sociopolitical contrast between classes: on the one hand, the working classes, in this case made up for the most part of recently arrived Spanish immigrants; on the other, the local professional bourgeoisie, which controlled the local press and, as did Casal, often directed more or less veiled attacks at the colonial authorities.

Casal's *crónica,* "A través de la ciudad, El Centro de Dependientes" [Throughout the City. The Center for Store Clerks] was published under the pseudonym of Hernani on 28 December 1889; it was written after a visit to the Center, located on the top floors of the building that housed the Albizu theater. The Center was one of many *centros, liceos* and *colonias,* social and residential guilds that spread throughout the island for the purpose of housing the newly arrived work force and in many cases teaching various skills to its members. Casal describes the conditions that drove the young men to abandon their homeland, the effort of their toil and the way in which many of them are integrated into Cuban society. The Center's secretary guides the visitor through the various rooms, which compose a true phalanstery with reading halls and classrooms, where the members have free access to the curriculum of a business school.

Céspedes's book was published in 1888, and Giralt's the following year.

Casal returned from a brief stay in Madrid, his only travel outside of Cuba, during January 1889. It is highly improbable that he did not know of the two books, one of them with a prologue by the prominent Enrique José Varona, who was to write reviews of Casal's own books.[20] More than likely, Casal was given the assignment of writing a *crónica* for *La Discusión* in order to smooth over the debate between *criollos* and *peninsulares,* that is between pro-independence nationalists and supporters of Spanish rule. Giralt's attack on Dr. Céspedes had dragged the thorny issue of sexual deviance into the debate, and Casal's *crónica* must also gloss over the allegations about the clerks' sexual practices.

Casal writes that he is driven by curiosity; he wants to gather "los datos que reclamaba nuestra insaciable curiosidad" (2:18) [the facts required by our insatiable curiosity]. It is unlikely that a mere residence for clerks would have provoked much curiosity, certainly not an "insatiable curiosity." The gossip about the two pamphlets and the sexual doings of the clerks and their so-called clients must have been the topic of conversation in what is still a rather chatty, extroverted city. Significantly however, Casal's curiosity for the facts leads to silence. Unlike other *crónicas* where the subjective reaction of the writer is almost immediately present, the *crónica* about the Center reads more like a reporter's account of the scene of a crime. The Center is absolutely empty, except for the neutral presence of its secretary, a hazily outlined third party.

In order to show that the lurid details mentioned by the boy interviewed in *La prostitución en La Habana* are not the norm, Giralt refers to the "strict discipline" maintained at the Centers and to the fact that "está prohibido hablar de política" [it is forbidden to talk about politics]. Casal almost quotes Giralt when he writes that at the Center "está permitido hablar de todo menos de política" [one may speak about anything except politics], and he goes on to describe the love among the young men in terms of sympathy and friendship:

> ¿No es más agradable comunicarse sus ensueños de riqueza y sus proyectos para lo porvenir? ¿No es más bello recordar la patria lejana, donde se ha pasado la infancia y donde hay seres queridos que nos aguardan? De este modo ¿no se obtiene más pronto el fin apetecido, que es el de estrechar cada día más los lazos de cariño, simpatía y amistad entre los dependientes? (2:19)
> [Is it not more agreeable for them to share their dreams of wealth and their projects for the future? Is it not more beautiful to remember the distant homeland, the place of their childhood, where there are loved

ones awaiting us? This way, is not the cherished goal more quickly obtained, that is, to bind more strongly the ties of love, sympathy and friendship among the clerks?]

If the doctor pointed to the sores in the boy's ass, a clear sign of the activities at the Centro, Casal sentimentalizes the relationships among the men who live there. On the one hand, one may recall the respect for the couple who slept together, mentioned by the boy, and the possibility of sentimentalizing such a relationship, in other words, of placing it beyond the doctor's scientific hold; on the other hand, one should point to the strong current of sentimentality in *Modernismo,* a version of the tradition of sensibility rooted in the eighteenth century and later exemplified by Spanish poet Gustavo Adolfo Bécquer and French poet François Coppée, both admired by the *modernistas.*

Modernismo's tradition of sentimentalism retreated before its ultimately triumphant formalism, the good side of *Modernismo,* bequeathed to the various avant-gardes. Yet in the homophobic setting of fin de siècle Havana, sentimentalism, rather than just quaintly maudlin, may be a strategy of survival; oblique, sentimental appeals to the reader defer self-representation and the representation of others, and this deferral is both our loss and our gain. On the one hand, Casal's unwillingness or inability to deal frontally with his sexuality and that of the clerks robs us, queers of today, of a potentially empowering legacy; on the other, the sentimentalism and deliberate pathos that at times characterize his style must be considered in the context of other representational strategies that have fared better in the critical tradition, namely, his unquestionable formal mastery. As queer readers, our task may be to superimpose loss and gain, to find our identity not only in the affirmative proclamation of same-sex desire but also in its various disguises: in the sentimental appeals to the reader as well as in the fabulously masked, exotically draped, richly embossed *modernista* image brilliantly created by Casal, the Helen of his *museo* to linger briefly on just one: "Envuelta en veste de opalina gasa, / recamada de oro . . . indiferente a lo que en torno pasa, / mira Elena hacia el lívido horizonte, / irguiendo un lirio en la rosada mano" (1:118) [Wrapped in a vestment of opalescent gauze, / embroidered in gold . . . indifferent to what is happening around her, / Helen looks toward the livid horizon, / raising a lily in her rosy hand].

If in the poetry, the image of the draped, ambiguously sexed body triumphs, in Casal's *crónica* about the store clerks, the body of the boy in the doctor's interview, with its sores, but also with its "morbid" shape and attractive face, disappears. Yet Casal's other *crónicas,* as well as his poetry and fiction, teem with bodies, arabesque of sores at the doctor's office, flying bodies at the circus, the lapidary flesh of the heroes in the museum. At the circus, the body of an acrobat becomes a "símbolo viviente," a "living symbol" in a remarkable slippage between choreography and writing. In Casal's *museo* an ever-present erotic gaze seems to convulse the rigid statuary: Prometheus, "marmóreo, indiferente y solitario, / sin que brote el gemido de su boca" (1:116) [marmoreal, indifferent and solitary, / never a moan issuing from his mouth]; and Polyphemus, "mirando aquella piel color de rosa, / incendia la lujuria su ojo verde" (1:117) [gazing at that rosy skin, / lechery his green eye sets aflame]. By contrast, in the *crónica* about the Center, the emptiness of the place is remarkable. The clerks are lost in an abstract, bodiless plural as if the love, sympathy and friendship among them depended on their very absence, somehow compensated by an abundance of signifiers describing in detail the decorations of the interior, rather an interior within an interior, for the great hall contains "un teatrito precioso, alegre como una pajarera y reluciente como una caja de juguetes" (2:19) [a precious little theater, happy as a bird cage and shining like a toy box]. The aesthetic reduction of the large hall is breathless, almost violent, as if to close itself off from the possible entrance of a body. In the broadest sense, such a reduction glosses over the bodies that were there. The eye is fixed on the ornamentation of the walls, decorated with *panneaux,* which in turn contain Venetian mirrors, draped and tasseled. In the middle of the great hall, perhaps peopled by the very young men who are the subjects of the two pamphlets, the roving eye and the subjectivity that it signals seem to seek refuge in that "precious little theater," in turn reduced first to a "bird cage" then to a "toy box." What cannot be named in the *crónica* is not only homosexuality or pederasty; it is the erotic body, which must be aesthetically transformed, which must be moved to another register. In other words, it must be represented in a different way, in other places, by its very absence in "a precious little theater," or by its contortions at the circus, frozen in the statuary of the *museo,* deformed by disease, transformed into a vision of terrible beauty set in privileged, distant, aesthetic places, that is, represented as symbolic sublimation, where any reading must inexorably return.[21]

That return to the text, however, is now tainted by the echo of those queers, drag queens, and clients of fin de siècle Havana, transformed into objects of study and scorn by the sociologist-doctor and the moralizing pamphleteer. The morbidness of a boy's body, radically distanced by the doctor, now echoes the morbidness of Casal's style, radically distanced by a critical tradition, always thought to possess a masterful upper hand and certainly the last word when it comes to Casal. Little matter whether he so much as exchanged a greeting with the queers in Havana's main square. They inhabited his city and will lend their choral presence to any subsequent reading. Thus, though never fully open, the door to Casal's interior, to the transgressive nature of his eroticism, aesthetically distanced, deliberately veiled by the signifiers of draping and adornment, ever suggestive in its homoerotic imagery, is invitingly ajar.

Notes

1   Bello, "Juicio sobre las obras poéticas de Don Nicasio Alvarez de Cienfuegos," *Obras completas* 9:210.
2   *Prosas* 2:17–20. All subsequent references to Casal's *Prosas* will be given parenthetically. Unless otherwise noted, all translations are mine. I thank Emilie Bergmann, whose comments were so helpful during the revision and rewriting of this paper. Part of my research on Casal has been funded by a grant from the Professional Staff Congress of the City University of New York, whom I also thank.
3   Some critics, notably Cintio Vitier and Emilio de Armas, have sought to counteract the aesthetic marginality imposed on Casal: Vitier by affirming Casal's sincerity and the power of that very isolation; de Armas by reading Casal in the context of Cuba's oppressive political and cultural climate. Both approaches are illuminating, but they don't challenge the premise of isolation imposed on Casal's aestheticism, grounded on the commonplace that states that the "superficial" aspects of Casal's work and of *modernismo* inexorably lead to an aesthetic, and implicitly a moral, impasse.
4   "Read 'Nihilismo' and you will see how sincere was the poet's desire for death," writes Anderson Imbert in his influential *Historia de la literatura hispanoamericana* 206.
5   The term has been fruitfully reactivated by Sedgwick; Marjorie Garber points out that it was coined by Dr. Edward Kempf in 1920 "to describe the fear fostered by same-sex contiguity in army camps, prisons, monasteries, boarding schools" (137); and Centers for Clerks in fin de siècle Havana, one might add.
6   The contrast between Manuel de la Cruz's "virile," patriotic exterior and Casal's problematic, and implicitly deviant, interior is discussed by Agnes Lugo-Ortiz, "Patologizar el interior" 162–166. I thank Agnes for sending me a copy of her manuscript. The *modernista* interior as the autotelic place of luxury and pleasure is contrasted to the museum as the imposition of order over nature by Aníbal González 33ff.
7   Casal's definition is from his *busto* of José Fornaris (1827–90), *Prosas* 1:275–80; significantly, Fornaris was one of the founders of *Siboneísmo,* the poetry of national affirmation, thrown in the face of colonial oppression. See Vitier's "Fifth Lesson," *Lo cubano en la poesía* 131–79.
8   On the parceling of the aesthetic in *Modernismo,* see Angel Rama, *La ciudad letrada* 164–71, and "El poeta frente a la modernidad," *Literatura y clase social* 78–143.
9   Akin to what Terry Eagleton calls Schopenhauer's "death of desire."
10 On the open secret in the context of the binary oppositions of the second half of the nineteenth century, see Sedgwick 67–90.

11   From Darío's prologue to the poems of Manuel Pichardo, quoted by Monner Sans 257–58.

12   If for Bataille eroticism is always transgressive, for Foucault it operates inexorably within the "machinery of power." As Casal's case suggests, however, it is perhaps less a question of a radical polarization between transgression and the powers that defuse it than a drift, Wilde's "to drift with every passion," taken from the early Pater. See Richard Ellman's introduction to *The Artist as Critic* ix–xviii.

13   The comments by De Armas summarize most of the critical references to a "conflict [in Casal] whose origin is sexual," although Casal's erotic life remains "draped in total darkness." See 32–41 of the sensitive, well-documented biography by De Armas.

14   *Rimas, The Poetry of Julián del Casal* 1:209. All subsequent references to this edition of Casal's poetry will be given parenthetically.

15   The role of such theatrics in the building of gay and lesbian culture is discussed by Judith Butler and Marjorie Garber, respectively.

16   On the development of the term "homosexuality," see Chauncey.

17   In the *Crónica Médico-Quirúrgica de la Habana* 16 (1890): 79–81, in a section titled "Pederasty in Havana," a Dr. Montané notes, as does Dr. Céspedes, that "pederasts" wear makeup and otherwise adorn themselves; he also mentions "their strange taste for perfumes and bright objects, their monomania for photographs, in which they appear [*en las que se hacen representar*] in theatrical costumes or in women's dresses." The doctor circulated "among the members of the Congress" he is addressing "some samples he was able to procure," seemingly of photographs, perhaps still kept in some archive in Havana. I am grateful to George Chauncey for the gift of a photocopy of the pages cited. For discussion of similar photographs in Argentina, see Jorge Salessi in this volume.

18   On active-passive roles in Mexico and Latin America, see Almaguer, and Murray and Dynes. Significantly, the ubiquitous and persistent active-passive pairing seems to be threatened by Dr. Céspedes's objectivity—not all were passive who seemed so, he says. Giralt, however, insists on it, though he damns the "active" ones more than their "victims."

19   The political implications of class divisions in the gay population of 1889 Havana are no less significant today and are particularly pertinent in a Latin American and Latino context. For a suggestive discussion of homosexuality and class among Chicano men and in contemporary Mexico, see Almaguer and Blanco, respectively.

20   Varona wrote a review of Casal's first book of poems, *Hojas al viento,* for *Revista Cubana* (May 1890), and a review of his second book, *Nieve,* for the same publication (August 1892). The first is included in *Prosas,* and both are included in *The Poetry of Julián del Casal.* Casal in turn dedicated one of his "*bustos*" to the formidable *homme de lettres,* who wrote a moving eulogy after Casal's death, also in *The Poetry of Julián del Casal.*

21   On Casal's *museo ideal* and on his visit to the circus, see my *Erotismo y representación en Julián del Casal* (Amsterdam: Editions Rodopi, 1993).

Works Cited

Almaguer, Tomás. "Chicano Men: A Cartography of Homosexual Identity and Behavior." *Differences* 3.2 (1991): 75–100.

Anderson Imbert, Enrique. *Historia de la literatura hispanoamericana*. 1st ed. México: Fondo de Cultura Económica, 1954.

Armas, Emilio de. *Casal*. La Habana: Letras Cubanas, 1981.

Bataille, Marcel. *Erotism: Death and Sensuality*. Trans. Mary Dalwood. 1957; San Francisco: City Lights Books, 1986.

Bello, Andrés. "Juicio sobre las obras poéticas de Don Nicasio Alvarez de Cienfuegos." *La Biblioteca Americana* I (London, 1823): 35–50. In *Obras completas*. 22 vols. Caracas: Ministerio de Educación, 1951–1969. 1956; 9:197–213.

Blanco, José Joaquín. "Ojos que da pánico soñar." *Función de medianoche*. México: Era, 1981. 183–90.

Butler, Judith. *Gender Trouble: Feminism and the Subversion of Identity*. New York: Routledge, 1990.

Cabrera Saqui, Mario. "Julián del Casal." *Poesías*. By Julián del Casal. Edición del Centenario. La Habana: Consejo Nacional de Cultura, 1963. 265–87.

Casal, Julián del. *The Poetry of Julián del Casal*. Ed. Robert J. Glickman. 3 vols. Gainesville: University of Florida Press, 1978.

———. *Prosas*. Edición del Centenario. 4 vols. La Habana: Consejo Nacional de Cultura, 1963.

Case, Sue-Ellen. "Tracking the Vampire." *Differences* 3.2 (1991): 1–20.

Céspedes, Benjamín. *La prostitución en La Habana*. La Habana: Tipografía O'Reilly, 1888.

Chauncey, George. "From Sexual Inversion to Homosexuality." *Salmagundi* 58–59 (1982–83): 114–46.

Cruz, Manuel de la. "Julián del Casal." *Cromitos cubanos*. 1892; Madrid: Calleja, 1926. 229–43.

Eagleton, Terry. *The Ideology of the Aesthetic*. Oxford: Basil Blackwell, 1990.

Foucault, Michel. *The History of Sexuality. Volume I: An Introduction*. Trans. Robert Hurley. New York: Vintage, 1980.

Garber, Marjorie. *Vested Interests. Cross-dressing and Cultural Anxiety*. New York: Routledge, 1992.

Giralt, Pedro. *El amor y la prostitución. Réplica a un libro del Dr. Céspedes*. La Habana: La Universal, 1889.

González, Aníbal. *La crónica modernista hispanoamericana*. Madrid: José Porrúa Turranzas, 1983.

Lauretis, Teresa de. "Queer Theory: Lesbian and Gay Sexualities: An Introduction." *Differences* 3.2 (1991): iii–xviii.

Lezama Lima, José. *Poesía completa*. La Habana: Instituto del Libro, 1970.

Lugo-Ortiz, Agnes I. *Identidades imaginadas: biografía y nacionalidad en Cuba 1860–1898*. Diss. Princeton University, 1990.

Monner Sans, José María. *Julián del Casal y el modernismo hispanoamericano*. México: El Colegio de México, 1952.

Montané, Dr. (?). "La pederastia en La Habana." *Crónica Médico-Quirúrgica de la Habana* 16 (1890): 79–81.

Murray, Stephen O., and Wayne Dynes. "Hispanic Homosexuals: Spanish Lexicon." *Male Homosexuality in Central and South America*. Ed. Stephen O. Murray. Gai Saber Monograph. San Francisco: Instituto Obregón, 1987.

Nordau, Max. *Degeneration*. 1892; New York: Appleton, 1895.

Poncet, Carmen. "Dualidad de Casal." *Revista Bimestre Cubana* 53 (1944): 193–212.

Rama, Angel. *La ciudad letrada*. Hanover, N.H.: Ediciones del Norte, 1984.

———. *Literatura y clase social*. Mexico: Folios Ediciones, 1983.

Sedgwick, Eve Kosofsky. *Epistemology of the Closet*. Berkeley: University of California Press, 1990.

Sommer, Doris. *Foundational Fictions: The National Romances of Latin America*. Berkeley: University of California Press, 1991.

Varona, Enrique José. "*Hojas al viento:* Primeras poesías. Por Julián del Casal," *La Habana Elegante*, 1 June 1890. In *The Poetry of Julián del Casal* 2:421–23; and in Casal, *Prosas* 1:26–29.

———. "*Nieve*. Por Julián del Casal. Habana 1892." *Revista Cubana* 16 (August 1892): 142–46. In *The Poetry of Julián del Casal* 2:436–39.

———. "Julián del Casal." *Revista Cubana* 18 (October 1893): 340–41. In *The Poetry of Julián del Casal* 2:413.

Vitier, Cintio. *Crítica sucesiva*. La Habana: Contemporáneos, 1971.

———. *Lo cubano en la poesía*. La Habana: Instituto del Libro, 1970.

Wilde, Oscar. *The Artist as Critic: Critical Writings of Oscar Wilde*. Ed. Richard Ellman. New York: Random House, 1968.

THREE

*Nationalisms, Ethnicities,
and (Homo)sexualities*

Agnes I. Lugo-Ortiz
Community at Its Limits: Orality, Law, Silence, and the Homosexual Body in Luis Rafael Sánchez's "¡Jum!"

To the beloved memory of Ruth Anthony El Saffar,
dancing Amazon of the twenty-first century

Overture: Community and the Rhythms of Its Law

El hijo que tiene Asunción
toma vino y es un bandolero

Asunción, Asunción ese hijo
va a ser marinero (maricón)

El hijo que tiene Asunción
se acuesta en la cama
con un baby doll

El hijo que tiene Asunción
se pone la faja
de su hermana Ivonne

Asunción, Asunción ese hijo
va a ser marinero (maricón)

Song popular in Puerto Rico (c. 1960s)
[Rough translation: The son of Asunción / drinks wine and is a bandit / Asunción, that son of yours is going to be a . . . sailor (a faggot, "maricón" in Spanish, which rhymes with "Asunción") / The son of Asunción / wears a baby doll to bed / The son of Asunción wears his sister Ivonne's girdle / Asunción, that son of yours is going to be a . . . sailor (a faggot).]

The scene is a familiar one: it is a small community party. The lights are dim and alcohol flows freely. Couples approach the dance floor as the music starts. The local band is known to everybody at the party and so is the song they play. Bodies start moving as this Puerto Rican–style merengue invades the room, conquering the flow of sensations, dissolving the boundaries of the building. Music is king and master: "Asunción, Asunción / ese hijo va a ser marinero" [Asunción, that son of yours is going to be a sailor], the band interpellates, predicts, prescribes. In one of the corners of the hall male adolescents gang together—away from (afraid of?) the female bodies dispersed around the room. While rules of verbal decorum forbid the band from uttering the word, these young men, beer or rum in hand, shirts partly unbuttoned, defiantly, loudly and self-righteously affirm what the rhyme would otherwise impose: "Asunción, Asunción / ese hijo va a ser maricón" [Asunción, Asunción, that son of yours is going to be a faggot]. There is pleasure in their voices, in the disclosure of a word concealed by the impostures of verbal decorum but revealed through the demands of the rhyming pattern ("Asunción/maricón"). There is pleasure in the communal laughter that follows and supports the blatant naming, the unsubtle and cocky utterance of an "I know better"; the flaunting of presumed parental failure and shame. There is pleasure in savoring the word that now fills the mouths of the group, that tasty and juicy "maricón" (yet who among them fears being called that name?).

The scene is a familiar one. Bodies move in a synchronized fashion, so do the mouths. The members of the community sing and dance together. The community appears to become one in the act of a musical utterance: in a shared voice and in simultaneous bodily movements. Bodies talk. The linguistic order of the lyrics intersects with the nonverbal/orphic order of the rhythm inscribing itself into the flesh. Through this encounter, the community—subliminally—establishes itself and its limits, stating its unwritten laws about sex and gender. Across the border, demarcating the law, is Asunción's son and, perhaps, Asunción her/himself, for the name in Spanish, equivocally, can be either a man's or a woman's.

The 1960s: A Decade of Anxieties

"El hijo que tiene Asunción" was an extremely popular song in Puerto Rico throughout the second half of the 1960s and still is today. It is sung by high school students riding the bus on an academic trip to a museum, by "respectable" middle-class Puerto Rican tourists when traveling through México or Europe, and by drunken party-goers whenever possible. It is as if Puerto Rican society, as an illusory whole, unites its dispersed, multiple, and dissonant voices in the musical naming of a recognizable, abject figure: the abnormal and deviant body of the "maricón." He is the "other" that the national community's utterances (in a fiction of oneness) simultaneously invent, obsessively desire (through its naming), reject (through denigration), fix, and possess (through relentless definitions).

The 1960s marks an era of vertiginous cultural, political, and economical reorganizations in Puerto Rico, when established models of authority appeared to be shaken or crumbling, and dominant discourses of "identity"—sexual, gender, or national—underwent significant disturbances. The shift from a society organized primarily around agriculture to a problematically modern and industrial one (mainly based on foreign investments) was almost complete by the middle of the decade (see Dietz, Picó). This entailed a general restructuring of society, a transformation in the relations of production and in patterns of property tenure. It also implied the emergence of modern cultural institutions and modern mechanisms of subjectification, which eventually led to radical reconfigurations in the operative modes and constructions of sexuality and gender.[1]

The song about Asunción's son is not the only verbal event that signals a period full of anxieties about these rapid—and for many threatening—social transformations. In 1960, for instance, René Marqués, the most renowned and prestigious Puerto Rican writer of the period, published his influential essay "El puertorriqueño dócil" [The Docile Puerto Rican]. In this pseudo-sociopsychological text, Marqués proposed his theory about the "docility" (and, for him, increasing "effeminization") of Puerto Rican men in the face of what he perceived as the deculturalizing emergence of an "Anglo-Saxon-style matriarchy" in the country. This theory framed the ongoing redefinitions of woman's place in society in terms of a process of devirilization and denationalization. Since the 1940s, women had been entering the paid labor force in unprecedented numbers (see Azize), challenging, among other things, the power relationships embedded in traditional family structures, which for Marqués were synonymous with the most precious and deepest stronghold of Puerto Rican national identity: *machismo*.

By the late sixties and early seventies, anxieties about gender dislocation were further inscribed and thematized in numerous popular culture texts as well. These ranged from the many television shows that mockingly presented, on a daily basis, caricature-like homosexual characters and men dressed as women during prime-time hours, to several other songs similar to the one about Asunción's son. The homosexual images constructed in these popular texts can be read as symptomatic of complex cultural shifts and, in particular, of the emergence of a new field of public utterances about gender and sexuality. Throughout this decade, a multifaceted discourse on homosexuality was starting to imprint, in various ways, the shape of collective representations about sexual identities and practices.

Indicative of this process is the new penal code approved in 1974 in which homosexuality and lesbianism acquired a specific criminal status. Before this time, only sodomy (between any two human beings) was penalized, and it was included in the same article that legislated against bestialism: "Toda persona culpable del infame crimen contra natura, cometido con un ser humano o con una bestia, incurrirá en pena de reclusión en presidio por un término mínimo de cinco años"[2] [Any person guilty of the infamous crime against nature, with a human being or an animal (beast), will be condemned to jail for a minimum term of five years].

In the old law, homosexuality had lacked a specificity of its own, and lesbianism was nonexistent. In 1974 a relatively more modern notion of same-sex acts started to inflect legal taxonomies, carrying, as well, a greater number of years in jail: "Toda persona que sostuviere relaciones sexuales con una persona de su mismo sexo o cometiere el crimen contra natura con un ser humano será sancionado con pena de reclusión por un término fijo de diez (10) años"[3] [Any person engaging in same-sex sexual relations, or who commits the crime against nature with a human being, will be condemned to jail for a fixed term of ten (10) years].

In this context, what is especially remarkable and relevant about the popular culture texts alluded to above is how they also exhibit a "taxonomic drive." All of them show a preoccupation with fixing the visibility (the clear-cut "otherness") of the "maricón," of determining his identity as unequivocally identifiable and prescribable. In consequence, this simultaneously created a comfortable border on the other side of which an increasingly problematic definition of "maleness" hoped to rest undisturbed, a border with which society attempted to establish its recognizable yet fragile limits amidst a milieu of instability.[4]

Luis Rafael Sánchez: Narrating Silence and Difference

In 1966 Luis Rafael Sánchez published his first collection of short stories, *En cuerpo de camisa*.[5] By that time, Sánchez was already considered one of the most promising young writers in the country and was well respected

for his works as a playwright. Nevertheless, the book attracted little sustained attention from local literary critics, and still today (and especially
after the overwhelming editorial and critical success of *La guaracha del
Macho Camacho*, 1976) it remains practically ignored.[6] There has been a relative silence around a group of texts that, in many ways, laid out the narrative and aesthetic project carried out by Sánchez in subsequent works. The
departure from institutionalized ("proper") linguistic norms and linear
narrative conventions, the interplay of perspectives, the literary reelabora-
tion of popular culture and orality, the representation of marginal subjects
as privileged narrative material, and an aesthetics of "lo soez" (the "low"
and "vulgar") are some of the elements already present in the short stories
that comprise this book.[7]

Carlos Alonso, in a suggestive reading of *La guaracha del Macho Camacho,* has pointed out that "the novel constitutes a relentless dismantling
of the ponderous and solemn meditations on the problematics of Puerto
Rican cultural specificity that has characterized—indeed, become synonymous with—the country's intellectual and artistic endeavors" (348). This
assertion is true about a significant part of Sánchez's literary production,
including *En cuerpo de camisa.*[8] But this dismantling certainly does not mean
a departure from an obsessive entanglement with issues about the specificity of Puerto Rican national culture or from a relentless desire to think
the national community. It is rather a redefinition of the terms of this
"specificity" via the transformation of the aesthetic paradigms organizing
his narrative. Sánchez himself singles out the desire to make "the nation"
present as a kind of absolute horizon within which Puerto Rican literary
production, including his own, has been shaped:

> Y los personajes y los tonos que ella perfila y las intervenciones y las
> omisiones temáticas que en ella se citan se corresponden con las velei-
> dades y los asombros y los desconciertos y el caudal de contradicciones
> que el país gesta a diario; literatura obsesivamente fisionomista de un
> país sobrado de narcisismo, literatura obsesivamente recapituladora de
> la historia alterna que la historia oficial desanima, literatura asediada
> por la violencia y el desquicio que son retratos notables del país.[9]
> [And the characters and tones that are profiled in it (Puerto Rican lit-
> erature) and the thematic omissions that are quoted in it correspond to
> the fickleness and the wonders, and the wealth of contradictions that
> the country fosters every day; a literature which obsessively draws the
> physiognomy of an excessively narcissistic country, a literature which

obsessively recapitulates an alternative history which the official history discourages, a literature besieged by the violence and the madness that are remarkable portraits of the country.]

In this sense, literary critics have observed and celebrated Sánchez's fictional elaboration and aestheticization of orality and popular, "plebeian" culture as a means to reformulate and question the foundations of the national community (e.g., J. L. González, Gelpí, and Barradas). Sánchez has been understood as breaking away from a literary tradition grounded in and affirmative of a puritan, institutionalized, and metropolitan-oriented conception of language (*langue*). This is the language of a literature sanctioned by the laws of the dictionary, which excluded and silenced the multiplicity of voices comprising the concrete and symbolic social totality. Sánchez's vindication and incorporation of the Puerto Rican popular *parole* has been interpreted as partaking of a paradigmatic transformation in the definitions of Puerto Rican national culture, one which has entailed greater attentiveness to issues of racial and class-based marginalization and political disempowerment. While the defense of language (Spanish) has been constructed as a political arena for the preservation of national culture against United States colonialism, language itself has also become a field in which internal debates about national identity have taken place.[10] Furthermore, Sánchez's pervasive fictional inscription of black characters also aims to dismantle the presupposition of the world (read: the nation) as a "white" one. His narrative denaturalizes dominant assumptions about Puerto Rican national culture both by marking race and by fictionally deconstructing established linguistic norms.

Most recently, Julio Ortega, in a study of Sánchez's later works, has read his uses of orality as an antiauthoritarian device through which a liberating sense of community could be built. While acknowledging the anti-essentialist nuances subtly made in parts of Ortega's essay, the strongest undercurrent of his analysis is the celebration of orality—the voice of the margin—as the most effective means for cultural and political resistance.

La oralidad es también una operación relativizadora porque el habla es un flujo disolvente, que desata lo atado, y hace los códigos equivalentes al rebajarles la autoridad atribuída. *El sujeto definido* no tiene instrumento más poderoso que el habla contra la tiranía de los códigos . . . lo oral es el espacio de lo comunitario, la fuente de identidad. . . . [L]a oralidad representa en América Latina no el lenguaje de la autoridad sino el de la marginalidad . . . darle la palabra escrita a la voz popular, oralizar las formulaciones del archivo de la narración moderna, y, en fin, revalidar a los antihéroes de la oralidad marginal como los nuevos héroes culturales (comunitarios) de la respuesta (la sobrevivencia) de Puerto Rico como nuevo emblema de la historia colonial latinoamericana.[11]

[Orality is also a relativizing operation because it is a dissolving flux which unties that which is tied, and which renders all codes equivalent, diminishing the authority that has been conferred upon them. . . . Orality is the space of community, the source of identity. . . . *The defined subject* has orality as the most powerful instrument against the tyranny of codes. . . . Orality is, in Latin America, not the language of authority but of marginality . . . to give the written word to the popular voice, to oralize the formulations of the archive of modern narrative and, finally, to revalidate the antiheroes of marginal orality as the new cultural (communitarian) heroes of the response (survival) of Puerto Rico as a new emblem of Latin American colonial history.]

In privileging orality as the voice of the "margin" (a term that is inscribed here in its singular form), the passage obscures other forms of cultural marginalization which do not pass directly through ethnic and class-based definitions of the popular, nor through their particular linguistic modalities. The passage overlooks the complex set of social oppositions within which the manifold structures of cultural authority are contested and undermined (e.g., gender and sexuality[12]). Ortega's understanding of orality as a liberating source of communal identity through which a defined subject ("sujeto definido") reestablishes itself opens a wide range of questions: Who is this apparently preexistent, *defined* subject which undertakes the uses of orality? How is it defined? Doesn't the phrase "defined subject" connote, to a large degree, notions of "completion" and "fixation," which contradict the celebrated fluidity of orality? If there is a will to reaffirm a defined subject, what are the boundaries within which this subject establishes its identity? Who is the "not-I" of the community? What are the processes through which this is determined?

Among the stories that comprise *En cuerpo de camisa*, there is one that recounts a particularly bizarre event, if seen in light of the critical evaluations made by Ortega and others about the relationships between orality, antiauthoritarianism, and marginality in Luis Rafael Sánchez's works. It is a story that, in a kind of self-reflective operation, puts into question any absolute understanding of both orality and community. In "¡Jum!" Trinidad's son, a young "effeminate" black man living in a black community, is suspected of being a "fag." Murmuring and gossiping about him spread wildly, pervading every corner, occupying every second and entangling every person in town:

En cada recodo, en cada alero, en las alacenas, en los portales, en los anafres, en los garitos.

—¡Jum!

Por las madrugadas, por los amaneceres, por las mañanas, por los mediodías, por las tardes, por los atardeceres, por las noches y las medianoches.

—¡Jum!

Los hombres, ya seguros del relajo, lo esperaban por el cocal para aporrearlo a voces.

—¡Patito!

—¡Pateto!

—¡Patuleco!

—¡Loca!

—¡Maricastro!

—¡Mariquita!

Las mujeres aflojaban la risita por entre la piorrea y repetían, quedito.

—¡Madamo!

—¡Mujercita!

Hasta el eco casquivano desnudó su voz por el río con un inmenso jjj uuu mmm. (49–50)

[(The difficulties in translating Sánchez's uses of orality are immense. My translations will never do justice to the richness of his writing. When the difficulty proves insurmountable, I will paraphrase the text.)

On every street corner, under every eave, in the cupboards, in the portals, in the ovens, in the gambling dens.

—Hum!

Every dawn, every daybreak, every morning, every noon, every afternoon, every dusk, every night, every midnight.

—Hum!

Men, confident of the mockery, waited for him in the coconut grove, in order to beat him up with their voices.

(What follows in the story is a list of derogatory epithets for homosexual, something like fag, little faggot, pansy, patsy, queen, queer, butterfly, etc.)

Women released little mocking laughs, amidst a flux of pus, and quietly repeated.

—Madame! (Queen!)
—Little woman!
Even the joyful echo undressed its voice down by the river with an
immense hhh uuu mmm.]

Like the singing voices that communally warned Asunción (in the song
commented on above) that her/his son was going to be a "faggot," the community to which Trinidad's son belongs becomes unified in an increasingly
rhythmic and well-orchestrated *parole*—the utterance in which difference
is constructed and ejected. Through a single shared voice the community
of black people appears as if it were an unfractured totality. Trinidad's son,
in silence (he never utters a single word) and tired of the mockery, decides
to leave the town. In spite of having marginalized him, people are angry at
his departure, interpreting it as an aloof, racist, and self-hating attitude on
the part of the young man. Accompanied by dogs, the community follows
him to the edge of town screaming denigrating epithets. Pushed over the
bank of the river that borders the town, the son of Trinidad drowns.

The story is complex in its reflection upon and allegorical representation of an instance in a process of community formation: the relationships
between collective cohesiveness and individual difference; the role of violence in the articulation and placement of differential internal "otherness";
the interplay between *langue, parole,* and an altogether different site for
the production of meaning: *silence;* the tensions between a disembodied
collective voice and a concrete embodied silence; the reconstitution of a
center and the formation of new margins; the relativization of marginality
which suggests its potential to be recentered and to become a new locus
for the exercise of an oppressive power; and finally, the constant mobility
and transferability of the centers of power.[13]

Overall, the stories in *En cuerpo de camisa* make audible a popular speech
fictionally uttered by marginal characters and communities. But in "¡Jum!"
the play of orality can be read as more than just opposed to the linguistic
normativity of Puerto Rican literary tradition. The performance represented in the text also positions orality against (and imposed on) the silence
of the homosexual body. Just as within Puerto Rican literary historiography, the popular *parole* is rendered as a device for the deconstruction of the
power system epitomized in institutionalized language, the story also flips
this around. It unfolds the unstable character of any utterance: orality as a
force that, depending on its contexts and uses, could work as a means of
suppression. Moreover, the text seems to propose the absence of verbal language (the absence of logos?) as a catastrophic vacuum in front of which all

symbolizations (linguistic categorizations) panic and reassert their will to power. In the story, orality becomes the word of the law, of the community as law, and silence the voice of the "other." This is a literary (allegorical) strategy for rethinking the mechanisms of national self-definition and its dynamics of inclusions and exclusions by thematizing a process of communal formation vis-à-vis sexual difference. It is also a strategy to utter other disenfranchised social sectors, which have been unrecognized by discourses of national liberation.[14]

The Enactment of Orality as "Arrebato"

"¡Jum!" textualizes the agonistic encounter between a ritual order ruled by an orchestrated *parole* and an elusive one structured by silence, between a communitarian "arrebato" and the puzzling performance of the mime. The voice of the community is figured in an *in crescendo* set of repetitions. This dynamic starts with a semantically loaded interjection ("¡Jum!") that insidiously traverses the "throats" of the members of the community, permeating the totality of communal space and time. It is a totalitarian device that infiltrates, controls, and at the same time creates the basic conditions for collective existence: on "every street corner, under every eave, in the cupboards, in the portals, in the ovens, in the gambling dens; [e]very dawn, every daybreak, every morning, every noon, every afternoon, every dusk, every night, every midnight."

The homogenization of the collective voice is further intensified through a series of polyphonic verbal variations around one single meaning, a multiplicity of voices saying with different words the same thing. It is a repertoire of orality's wealth of derogatory terms for "homosexual": "Patito, patuleco, loca, mariquita, madamo, rabisalsero," etc. Finally, it culminates with the collective, simultaneous repetition of one single phrase, the final sentence of ejection: "¡Que no vuelva!" [Let him not come back!].

Similar to what Roberto González Echevarría has observed for *La guaracha del Macho Camacho*, this strategy for constructing the communal voice is affiliated to a specific Afro-Antillean musical and ritual structure: the "arrebato." Fernando Ortiz, in his *Los bailes y el teatro de los negros en el folklore de Cuba* describes it in the following terms:

> La aludida socialidad [de la música y baile africanos] se ha reflejado también, no sólo en el dialogismo del canto y la coralidad de la respuesta, sino por ese efecto, al que ya aludimos, *de imbricamiento de voces*

que suele ocurrir al final de los cantos dialogales, cuando el *akpuón* [solista] "arrebata el canto," es decir reanuda su cantar comenzando otra frase, antes que el coro haya terminado su respuesta. En esos momentos se juntan varias voces, con frecuencia a tonos distintos, produciendo impremeditadamente curiosas combinaciones de polifonía. . . . Aparte de su impresión artística, en ese efecto se da también la de una mayor intensidad en la expresión emotiva. *Las voces al unísono son como una sola; cuando se diversifican en tonalidades distintas parece que son más.* Orquestalidad de timbres orales, pluralidad de tonos y matices, que *al final de un canto intensifican también el efecto del crescendo tan buscado en la música negra.*[15]

[The already mentioned sociability (of African music and dances) is not only reflected in the dialogism of the chant and in the chorality of the response, but in the effect, alluded to before, of *entanglement of voices that usually occurs at the end of the dialogical chants,* when the *akpuón* (the soloist) violently "snatches the song," that is to say, restarts the song with a new phrase, before the choir has finished its response. In those moments, several voices come together, frequently in different tones, spontaneously producing curious polyphonic combinations. . . . Besides its artistic impression, this effect also provides a greater intensity to the emotional expression. *The many simultaneous voices are like one; when they become diversified in different tonalities, they seem as if they were more.* Orchestration of oral timbres, plurality of tones and nuances, that, *at the end of a chant, intensify the in crescendo effect that black music searches for.*]

Sánchez's story figures the violence of a ritual performance, an instance of collective cohesiveness in which communal identity is affirmed through an orphic and Dionysian hunt—the pursuit of the silent body of Trinidad's son. It is an Orphic chase marked by a discursive orality in which margins are insistently constructed and through which abject difference is ejected, a simultaneously Orphic and Apollonian sacrificial rite.

In the midst of this ritual "arrebato," Trinidad's son lies on the ground "[e]xtendidos los brazos como cruces" (54) [with his arms extended in the form of a cross]. The sacred tool of this sacrifice is the communal verbum: "se vestían las lenguas con navajas" (51) [tongues were dressed with blades]; "una sombra le asestó la palabra" (52) [a shadow hurled the word]; "el murmureo era dardo y lanza" (53) [murmur was dart and spear]; "voces hirientes" (54) [hurting voices]. The Dionysian *parole* conducts the musical and violent enactment of a law, the relentless demarcation of the limits of community. Inside ("arrebatada") is the homogeneous collective voice; pushed toward the outside, a silent and ambiguous body.[16]

The Silent Abject

> Que el hijo de Trinidad se prensaba los fondillos hasta asfixiar el nalga-torio. Que era ave rarísima asentando vacación en mar y tierra. Que el dominguero se lo ponía aunque fuera lunes y martes. Y que el chaleco lo lucía de tréboles con vivo de encajillo. (49)
> [That Trinidad's son tightened his buttocks to the point of suffocating his ass. That he was a weird bird, going on vacation on both earth and sea. That he wore his Sunday clothing on Mondays and Tuesdays as well. And that he wore a vest with laces of embroidered clover leaves.]

Excess, unintelligibility, maladjustment, dislocation: the voice of the community, mystified, reads the surfaces of the suspected homosexual body. Trinidad's son does not have his own name and, as in the song about Asunción's son, in Spanish the name "Trinidad" could be either a woman's or a man's. The general ambiguity of the character is further enhanced by a plurivalent mark in the naming of his origins. Trinidad is, as well, a word etymologically linked to the number three, suggesting the breakdown of binary categorizations.[17]

In the verbal vacuum constructed by the silence of Trinidad's son, the community inscribes its anxieties about a gender-crossing body, a visual transgression that threatens to destabilize communal norms of differentia-tion and self-understanding:

> —¡Que se perfuma con Com tu mi!
> —¡Que se pone carbón en las cejas!
> —¡Que es mariquita fiestera!
> —¡Que los negros son muy machos!
> —¡Y no se están con ñeñeñés! (50)
> [That he wears *Come to me (Com tu mi)* perfume!/That he puts make-up on his eyebrows!/That he is a partying (flaming) fag!/That black men are very macho!/And do not go around so sissy!]

"Los negros *son* muy machos" [Black men *are* very macho]. The son of Trinidad is perceived as introducing an ontological disruption, an inter-nal difference that disturbs the dynamics of identity within the community both in gender and racial terms—what makes black men *men* and *black*.

His gender-crossing, in the community's perception, is equivalent to the desire to transgress racial distinctions. In the measure that Trinidad's son is not man enough, neither is he black enough. Echoing René Marqués's anxieties about the denationalizing effects of the colonialist "effeminiza-tion" of Puerto Rican men, the young man's apparent crossing of gender boundaries is simultaneously constructed as issuing a challenge to the racial demarcations that provide cohesiveness to the community: "¡Que el hijo de Trinidad es negro reblanquiao!" (51) . . . "Que escupía el recuerdo de los negros" (52) [That Trinidad's son is a whitey-black! . . . That he spits on the memory of black people!]. The community's logic seems to work as follows: Black men are very macho; Trinidad's son is not very macho; ergo: Trinidad's son is not black . . . but the community knows he is black. The suspected "marica" triggers a chain of disruptions within a complex network of categorical equivalencies (sexuality, gender, and race). Follow-ing some of Kristeva's propositions, the son of Trinidad may be read as a figure of abjection.

> [W]hat is *abject* . . . is radically excluded and draws me toward the place where meaning collapses. . . . [It is a] "something" that I do not recognize as a thing. A weight of meaninglessness, about which there is nothing insignificant, and which crushes me. [It] is that thing that no longer matches and therefore no longer signifies anything[;] I behold the breaking down of a world that has erased its borders: fainting away. . . . It is thus not lack of cleanliness or health that causes abjection but what disturbs identity, system, order. What does not re-spect borders, positions, rules. The in-between, the ambiguous, the composite (2, 4).

The abject epitomizes a crisis of meaning, an instance in which cognitive borders seem to collapse, eroding the intelligibility of communal order. Trinidad's son is not an external "other" but, worse, the outsider inside that shakes the community's inner demarcations. Therefore, he must be ejected in order to safeguard the communal fantasy of immanence. This ejection is performed by the community by raising new frontiers:

> La Ochoteco, que le daba la fiambrera, le mandó un papelito dicién-dole que estaba enferma y que no cocinaba más. Perdolesia le trajo las camisas planchadas y se quejó de la reúma. No se llevó las sucias. Lulo el barbero le dijo que no le tocaba el pasurín. *Y Eneas Cruz compró alambre dulce para marcar la colindancia.* (51, my emphasis)
> [The Ochoteco woman, who cooked for him, sent him a note saying

that she was sick and that she was not cooking anymore. Perdolesia brought his ironed shirts and complained about her rheumatism. She did not take the dirty ones with her. Lulo, the barber, declared that he was not touching his kinky hair. *And Eneas Cruz bought barbed wire to mark the borders of his own property.*]

The ultimate construction of the frontier is achieved by pushing him over the edge of the river that bordered the town.

The crisis of meaning thematized in the story is further enacted by the abject's deep silence, which contrasts markedly with the verbal richness through which the community becomes one.

The (Dis)Order of the Mime

[T]he mime does not imitate any actual thing or action, any reality that is already given in the world, existing before and outside his own sphere; he doesn't have to conform, with an eye toward verisimilitude, to some real or external order, to some *nature*. . . . But the relation of imitation and the value of adequation remain intact since it *is still necessary to imitate, represent, or "illustrate" the idea, . . . the representation of the thing through thought, the ideality—for a subject—of what is. . . .* There is no imitation. The Mime imitates nothing. . . . His movements form a figure that no speech anticipates or accompanies. They are not linked with *logos* in any order of consequence. . . . The act always plays out a difference without reference, or rather without a referent, without any absolute exteriority, and hence without any inside. The Mime mimes reference. He is not an imitator; he mimes imitation. (Derrida 194, 195 and 219, my emphasis)

Trinidad's son shares with the mime its imitative performance and its silence—imitation in the sense proposed by Derrida: imitation of the idea, not of a supposedly "true" nature of the thing imitated.[18] Trinidad's son dislocates the system of objects which signifies "gender" and in so doing discloses its mobility as an artificial system of signs instead of a naturalized embodied referent. What he *is* does not evoke any clearly preexistent order; he himself founds a new (dis)order of things. When leaving the town he carries in his bag: "el traje de hilo, el petrolatum, el polvo *Sueño de mayo,* la esencia *Com tu mi,* la peinilla, la sortija" [the linen suit, hair-gel, *Sueño de mayo* face powder, *Come to me* perfume, the comb, the ring]—a mélange of objects conventionally pertaining to men (the suit, the hair-gel) and to women (the face powder, the perfume), whose juxtaposition and mobility produce an unclear image of the owner's gender. By mutual cancellation, these objects empty the possibility of a clearly defined, gendered subject and, in consequence, of any stable subject at all.

His mimicry is all act, all surface, all movement, exteriority and body. It is a silent performance. The (dis)order represented by Trinidad's son takes place outside of the realm of verbal language, in sharp contrast to the linguistic (almost baroque) excess through which the community is figured. It is as if Trinidad's son is perceived to disrupt not only the logic of established categories (masculine/feminine, black/white) but also to retreat from the very same instrument for the construction of this logic: verbal language— the instrument on which the community has established its foundations (and the nation, Puerto Rico, its identity).

The silence of Trinidad's son suggests a refusal to submit to the logic of any symbolization. Against the community's ritual repetition of terms which strive to define and fix his identity ("patito, pateto" etc.), he responds with a deep silence—an uncomfortable abyss that could be filled with everything and/or nothing.

On Deep Silence

At a superficial level Trinidad's son could be read as an intensely homographic figure, in the sense formulated by Lee Edelman: a stereotypical image that plays into the idea of the unequivocal legibility of homosexuality (275). In front of the "visible" marks signifying "homosexual," heterosexuality could assert the absolute exteriority and "otherness" of homoerotic desire. Some may argue, as well, that the story also recycles the myth of silence and isolation as the essential characteristics of gay life. But what seems most remarkable about this story is how this presumed "otherness" is not a preexistent condition. It only comes into being through the utterance of the community. What the story thematizes is the presence of difference *within* and the process through which it is made into an *outside:* violent verbal marginalization and deadly suppression. The son of Trinidad is not a stranger to the group, even the way in which he is referred to in the story suggests a sense of familiarity. He is the child of someone that everybody knows, Trinidad. He is, fundamentally, a *son* of the community.

As suggested at the beginning of this essay, Sánchez's early literary production must be read within a juncture in which discursive paradigms about identity were undergoing significant changes in Puerto Rico. Throughout the sixties and seventies, established notions of nationality started to be questioned and challenged, especially by Marxist historians, who progressively proposed the disenfranchised elements of society as the main protagonists of national history. These revisions of the terms of nationality, nevertheless, acquire a deeper, self-critical perspective in a story that takes issue with the structural ways through which notions of "self" and "other" come to be, with the inner violence that this could entail. Sánchez's text can be read as an instance in which the subtle discursive relocations of sexuality, prevalent through the decade, and an incisive reflection on the presuppositions of the phenomenon of being-in-common are articulated. Its critical stance is unequivocal:

> La voz subió ronca y fue a explotar, justamente, en sus oídos. Lo esperaron. Satos sarnosos, satos tucos, satos cojos, satos con el guau en el hocico, en el lomo, en las patas. La jauría lo empujaba techo abajo. Era una procesión. El y los satos. Después, el pueblo. O mejor, el pueblo, después él, después los satos y al final, otra vez y siempre, el pueblo. Más sangre, más dolor, más risa, más voces, más sombras, más sombras negras de negros, más caras negras de negros, más lenguas negras de negros.
> —¡Que no vuelva!
> —¡Que no vuelva!
> —¡Que no vuelva! (53)

[The voice harshly rose and exploded right in his ears. They waited for him. Mangy mongrels, tailless mongrels, limping mongrels, mongrels with the woof in their muzzles, in their backs, in their legs. The pack of dogs pushed him downhill. It was a procession. He and the mongrels. Afterward, the people. Or better, the people, afterward him, afterward the mongrels, and at the end, once again and always, the people. More blood, more pain, more laughter, more voices, more shadows, more black shadows of black people, more black faces of black people, more black tongues of black people.
—Let him not come back!
—Let him not come back!
—Let him not come back!]

"El pueblo" [the people], a pivotal concept in nineteenth-century bourgeois theories of the nation-state, which has been reappropriated by left- and right-wing populist rhetorics alike in Latin America, is inscribed as a problematic—not heroic—agent. What is at stake in the story is, on the one hand, a critical dislocation of any essentialist understanding of "the people" and of popular orality as unproblematic instruments of subversion and, on the other, an inscription of the notion of difference. Through orality (language) a community that aspires to a totalizing self-definition exercises its law and its violence. Silence, in this case, may then be read as a radical deconstructive proposition against any pretense to political absolutes. It also implies a complex network of power struggles that comprise yet surpass the specificity of sexual politics. Or rather, in the thematization of the problem of sexual marginalization are ciphered the conflictive and manifold issues of the processes through which (national) communities are formed: the configuration of borders, the construction of differences vis-à-vis a collective subject, and the oppressive potential (but not inevitability, I might add) of any politics of identity.

At the end of the story, the reader is made a witness to the community's crime. He or she is left in front of the blank page, after literally contemplating the typographical representation of the drowning young man.

> La sangre y el agua se gustaron. Menos voces, que, menos guau, no, menos sombras, vuelva. El agua era tibia, más tibia, más tibia. Las voces débiles, más débiles, más débiles. El agua hizo glu. Entonces que no vuel-va, que no vuel-va, que no vuel-va, el hijo de Trinidad.
> glu . . .
> que
> glu . . .
> no
> glu . . .
> vuelva
> glu . . .
> se
> glu . . .
> hundió. (54–55)
> [Blood and water tasted and liked each other. Less voices, let, less woof, him not, less shadows, come back. The water was warm, warmer, warmer. The voices weak, weaker, weaker. Water said glu. (What follows is an onomatopoeic representation of the sound of the water through the Spanish word for "come back," "vuelva"; "vuel-va")
> the son of Trinidad
> glu
> let
> glu
> him
> glu
> not

glu
come
glu
back
glu
drowned.]

"¡Jum!" speaks a silence; it utters a vacuum. In a strict sense, the text opens a "deep silence" in Puerto Rican (and Latin American) political and literary imagination. A "deep silence" as it has been partly conceptualized by Bernard Dauenhauer: "the silence of the to-be-said . . . that silence beyond all saying, the silence of what-ought-to-be-said," a silence that does not predetermine the nature of the utterances to follow, but which opens the space for the act of uttering itself (19). "¡Jum!" opened not just a space for saying homosexual, but also for saying the many silences dwelling within the multiple "arrebatos" of the (national) community.

Notes

I would like to acknowledge the continuous and generous critical advice offered by Diane Miliotes and Laurie Milner. They read several versions of this paper and provided crucial support throughout the project's development. Arcadio Díaz-Quiñones, Ivette Hernández, Irma Lloréns, Oscar Montero, and Antonio Vera-León were also generous with their time, carefully reading a later draft of the paper and making important critical suggestions. I am also grateful to Johanna Emanuelly Huertas for her legal advice on the criminal history of homosexuality in Puerto Rico. The writing of this paper was partially supported by a Ford Foundation Research Fellowship. Unless otherwise noted, all translations are mine.

1   We still lack a study of the multiple processes through which modern forms of subjectification emerged in Puerto Rico. This paper aims to contribute to a much-needed reflection on the role of literary discourses in the configuration and problematization of established conceptions of the "Puerto Rican cultural being."

2   Article 278, *Código Penal de Puerto Rico,* in effect from 1902 to 1974.

3   Article 103, *Código Penal de Puerto Rico,* in effect from 1974 to the present.

4   The history of gay and lesbian liberation movements in Puerto Rico—which emerged alongside these discourses of sexual anxiety—has still to be written. Frances Negrón-Muntaner has taken important steps in that direction. See her essay "Echoing Stonewall and Other Dilemmas: The Organizational Beginnings of a Gay and Lesbian Agenda in Puerto Rico, 1972–1977."

5   *En cuerpo de camisa* [1st ed.] (San Juan: Ediciones Lugar, 1966). This first edition included: "Que sabe a paraíso," "La maroma," "Tiene la noche una raíz," "Aleluya negra," "Memoria de un eclipse," "La muerte minúscula, la muerte mayúscula," "¡Jum!," "La recién nacida sangre," "El ejemplo del muerto que se murió sin anunciar que se moría," "La par-

entela," and "Etc." The second edition (Río Piedras: Editorial Antillana, 1971) includes a new story, "La malamañosa." There have been five reeditions of this collection. The most recent one (Río Piedras: Editorial Cultural, 1990) has been expanded to include three new stories: "Los negros pararon el caballo," "Responso para un bolitero de la 15," and "Los desquites." It also includes an introduction by Mariano Feliciano. I will be quoting from the third edition (Río Piedras: Editorial Antillana, 1975). The story "¡Jum!" was also reprinted in *La gran enciclopedia de Puerto Rico* ("El cuento en Puerto Rico," vol. 4 [Madrid: Ediciones R, 1976] 252–55).

6   Early reviews of the book were written by Luce López-Baralt, "De Luis Rafael Sánchez *En cuerpo de camisa*"; Juan Martínez Capó, "La Escena Literaria"; and José Emilio González, "El primer libro de cuentos de Luis Rafael Sánchez."

7   Cf. Luis Rafael Sánchez, "Apuntación mínima de lo soez."

8   Part of Sánchez's own writing also partakes in the "solemnity" that is dismantled in texts such as *La guaracha* and *En cuerpo de camisa*. For example, in his essay "La generación o sea" Sánchez takes an explicitly magisterial and almost scolding position against the uses of linguistic/speaking crutches among young Puerto Ricans. This is a normative essay in which the voice of a linguistic/grammatical (and grammatological) authority claims to regulate the uses of orality. An analysis of Sánchez's cultural proposals which reduces them to a common denominator (e.g., his "plebeian" project) overlooks the contradictions that make him a more complex and interesting writer. Cf. Barradas, "Jangueando con el o sea."

9   Luis Rafael Sánchez, "Nuevas canciones festivas para ser lloradas" 19.

10   During the 1970s, in the pro-independence newspaper *Claridad*, Sánchez published a series of articles under the title *Escritos en puertorriqueño*. This title underlined (despite the contradictory features of many of the essays) that not only a Spanish of metropolitan affiliation was proposed as a defense mechanism for the protection of Puerto Rican culture but also *Puerto Rican Spanish*, with its many idiomatic variations and the linguistic richness of its popular modalities.

11   Julio Ortega, *Reapropiaciones* 15, 18, 19, and 26. My emphasis.

12   For an enlightening discussion of the slippery distinctions between sexuality and gender, see Eve Kosofsky Sedgwick's *Epistemology of the Closet* 27–35.

13   The fact that the repressive community in this story is a black one could be interpreted by some readers as a stereotyping gesture on the part of Sánchez. I would like to argue differently. Sánchez's fictional universe, since his early writings, shows a desire to deconstruct a vision of the world as white. In this regard, most of his characters are blacks, underlining the Afro-Antillean character of his invented world. This feature, nevertheless, does not entail a heroic vision of those elements marginalized by Eurocentric interpretations of Puerto Rican nationality. Rather than a bipolarized conception of power, Sánchez proposes a more complex and many-sided one, as I will show later in this essay. The "margin" is not an essence, but an unstable and problematic site which is also crossed and informed by inner conflicts and hierarchies.

14   It is significant that in one of the few early reviews of *En cuerpo de camisa*, José Emilio González, rather than asserting the communal killing of Trinidad's son, reads his death as an act of suicide: "acosado por la condena social, el hijo de Trinidad—homosexual— se suicida" [besieged by social condemnation, Trinidad's son—homosexual—commits suicide]. It is as if the critic refused to read the "criminal" dimension of the community's (the nation's?) act. Cf. "El primer libro de cuentos de Luis Rafael Sánchez" 7.

15   Quoted by González Echevarría in "La vida es una cosa 'phenomenal': *La guaracha del Macho Camacho* y la estética de la novela actual" 101. My emphasis.
16   Some may argue that Sánchez's allegory of community as "totality" is problematic, that it reduces the many contradictions and inconsistencies through which collectivities are structured. I partly agree with this proposition, although it seems to me that this critique overlooks the specific poetic (not realist) aesthetics of the story—aesthetics affiliated to recognizable forms of Afro-Caribbean poetry (most notably that of Luis Palés Matos and Nicolás Guillén). As if in a nutshell, the story produces an *effect of totality,* inscribing a moment in which the laws of the community crystallize, synthesizing processes of inclusion and exclusion, interiority and ejection, discursiveness and silence. Rather than formulating community as totality, the story is indeed a critique of discourses which conceptualize community invariably as such.
17   Also obvious are the religious connotations of the name and their relation to Christian mythology, with its ideas of victimization and sacrifice.
18   For an important reflection on Derrida's notion of "imitation," see Judith Butler's works, especially her essay "Imitation and Gender Insubordination," which I follow in my own analysis.

Works Cited

Alonso, Carlos. "*La guaracha del Macho Camacho:* The Novel as Dirge." *Modern Language Notes* 100.2 (March 1985): 348–60.

Azize, Yamila. *La mujer en la lucha.* Río Piedras: Editorial Cultural, 1985.

———, ed. *La mujer en Puerto Rico.* Río Piedras: Ediciones Huracán, 1987.

Barradas, Efraín. "El machismo existencial de René Marqués." *Sin nombre* 8.3 (1977): 69–81.

———. "Jangueando con el o sea: Luis Rafael Sánchez y el español puertorriqueño." *La Torre* 6.22 (1992): 185–97.

———. *Para Leer en puertorriqueño: acercamiento a la obra de Luis Rafael Sánchez.* Río Piedras: Editorial Cultural, 1981.

Butler, Judith. *Gender Trouble: Feminism and the Subversion of Identity.* New York & London: Routledge, 1990.

———. "Imitation and Gender Insubordination." *Inside/Out: Lesbian Theories, Gay Theories.* Ed. Diana Fuss. New York & London: Routledge, 1991. 13–31.

Cachán, Manuel. "*En cuerpo de camisa* de Luis Rafael Sánchez: la literatura alegórica de otro puertorriqueño." *Revista Iberoamericana* 5.162–63 (1993): 177–86.

Cohen, Anthony P. *The Symbolic Construction of Community.* London & New York: Ellis Horwood Ltd./Tavistock Publications/Methuen, 1985.

Colón Zayas, Eliseo. "La problemática del ser puertorriqueño en los cuentos de Luis Rafael Sánchez." *Pensamiento crítico* 4.26 (1981): 21–25.

Dauenhauer, Bernard P. *Silence: The Phenomenon and Its Ontological Significance.* Bloomington: Indiana University Press, 1980.

Derrida, Jacques. "The Double Session." *Dissemination.* Trans. Barbara Johnson. Chicago: University of Chicago Press, 1981. 173–286.

D'Emilio, John. "Capitalism and Gay Identity." *Powers of Desire: The Politics of Sexuality.* Ed. Ann Snitow, Christine Stansell, and Sharon Thompson. New York: Monthly Review Press, 1983. 100–13.

———. *Sexual Politics, Sexual Communities: The Making of a Homosexual Minority in the United States, 1940–1970*. Chicago & London: University of Chicago Press, 1983.

Díaz-Quiñones, Arcadio. *El almuerzo en la hierba (Lloréns Torres, Palés Matos, René Marqués)*. Río Piedras: Ediciones Huracán, 1982.

———. "El oficio de la memoria." *Sin nombre* 12.1 (1981): 27–38.

Dietz, James. *Economic History of Puerto Rico: Institutional Change and Capitalist Development*. Princeton: Princeton University Press, 1986.

Edelman, Lee. "Tearooms and Sympathy, or, the Epistemology of the Water Closet." *Nationalisms and Sexualities*. Ed. Andrew Parker et al. 263–84.

Emanuelly Huertas, Johanna. "*Quíntuples:* Las máscaras de la representación." *Revista de Estudios Hispáncos*. Universidad de Puerto Rico. Año XVII–XVIII (1990–1991). 339–51.

Feliciano, Mariano. "Luis Rafael Sánchez y sus cuentos de seres marginados." *Luis Rafael Sánchez: Crítica y bibliografía*. Ed. Nélida Hernández and Daisy Caraballo. 49–61.

Fernández-Olmos, Margarite. "Luis Rafael Sánchez and Rosario Ferré: Sexual Politics and Contemporary Puerto Rican Narrative." *Hispania* 70.1 (1987): 40–46.

Foucault, Michel. *Historia de la sexualidad, vol. I. La voluntad de saber*. Trans. Ulises Guiñazú. México: Siglo XXI, 1977.

Fuss, Diana, ed. *Inside/Out: Lesbian Theories, Gay Theories*. New York & London: Routledge, 1991.

García, Gervasio, and Angel G. Quintero. *Desafío y solidaridad: Breve historia del movimiento obrero puertorriqueño*. Río Piedras: Ediciones Huracán, 1982.

Gay Left Collective, ed. *Homosexuality: Power and Politics*. London: Allison & Busby, 1980.

Gelpí, Juan. "Desorden frente a purismo: La nueva narrativa frente a René Marqués." *Literatures in Transition: The Many Voices of the Caribbean Area*. Ed. Rose Minc. Gaithersburg, Md.: Montclair State College/Ediciones Hispamérica, 1982.

———. "La cuentística antipatriarcal de Luis Rafael Sánchez." *Hispamérica* 1.43 (1986): 113–20.

Girard, René. *Violence and the Sacred*. Trans. Patrick Gregory. Baltimore: Johns Hopkins University Press, 1979.

González, Aníbal. "*La guaracha del Macho Camacho* de Luis Rafael Sánchez." *Revista Interamerica de Bibliografía/Interamerican Review of Bibliography* 34.3–4 (1984): 419–23.

González, José Emilio. "El primer libro de cuentos de Luis Rafael Sánchez." *Revista del Instituto de Cultura Puertorriqueña* 12.44 (July–September 1969): 7–15.

González, José Luis González. *El país de cuatro pisos y otros ensayos*. Río Piedras: Ediciones Huracán, 1980.

González Echevarría, Roberto. "La vida es una cosa 'phenomenal': *La guaracha del Macho Camacho* y la estética de la novela actual." *Isla a su vuelo fugitiva*. Madrid: José Porrúa Turanzas, S.A., 1983. 91–102.

Hernández, Nélida, and Daisy Caraballo, eds. *Luis Rafael Sánchez: Crítica y bibliografía*. Río Piedras: Editorial de la Universidad de Puerto Rico, 1985.

Kristeva, Julia. *Powers of Horror: An Essay on Abjection*. Trans. Leon S. Roudiez. New York: Columbia University Press, 1982.

López-Baralt, Luce. "De Luis Rafael Sánchez, *En cuerpo de camisa*." *El Mundo* 5 August 1967: 30.

———. "*La guaracha del Macho Camacho,* saga nacional de la *guachafita* puertorriqueña." *Revista Iberoamericana* 51.130–131 (1985): 103–23.

Marqués, René. "El puertorriqueño dócil." *Ensayos (1953–1971)*. Río Piedras: Editorial Antillana, 1972. 153–215.

Martínez Capó, Juan. "La Escena Literaria." *El Mundo* 9 March 1968: 24.

Meléndez, Concha. *Obras completas*. Vol. 4. San Juan: Instituto de Cultura Puertorriqueña, 1972.

Morán, Carlos Roberto. "Los lenguajes, la dependencia, el intento liberador." *Sin nombre* 7.1 (1977): 57–61.

Mosse, George L. *Nationalism and Sexualities: Middle-Class Morality and Sexual Norms in Modern Europe*. Madison: University of Wisconsin Press, 1985.

Nancy, Jean-Luc. "Of Being-in-Common." *Community at Loose Ends*. Ed. Miami Theory Collective. Minneapolis/Oxford: University of Minnesota Press, 1991. 1–12.

——. *The Inoperative Community*. Ed. Peter O'Connor. Trans. Peter O'Connor, Lisa Garbus, Michael Holland, and Simona Sawhney. Minneapolis & Oxford: University of Minnesota Press, 1991.

Negrón-Muntaner, Frances. "Echoing Stonewall and Other Dilemmas: The Organizational Beginnings of a Gay and Lesbian Agenda in Puerto Rico, 1972–1977." 2 parts. *Centro* 4.1 and 2 (1992): 77–95 and 98–115.

Ortega, Julio. *Reapropiaciones. (Cultura y nueva escritura en Puerto Rico.)* Río Piedras: Editorial de la Universidad de Puerto Rico, 1991.

Parker, Andrew, Mary Russo, Doris Sommer, and Patricia Yaeger, eds. *Nationalisms and Sexualities*. New York & London: Routledge, 1991.

Picó, Fernando. *Historia general de Puerto Rico*. Río Piedras: Ediciones Huracán, 1988.

Quintero Rivera, Angel, et al. *Puerto Rico: Identidad nacional y clases sociales*. Río Piedras: Ediciones Huracán, 1979.

Ramos, Julio. "*La guaracha del Macho Camacho:* Texto de la cultura puertorriqueña." *Texto crítico* 8.24–25 (1982).

Ríos, Rubén. "Puertorriqueños: Album de la sagrada familia literaria." *El Mundo* 14 January 1990: 34–36.

Sánchez, Luis Rafael. "Apuntación mínima de lo soez." *Literature and Popular Culture*. Ed. Rose Minc. Montclair, N.J.: Hispamérica, 1981. 9–14.

——. *En cuerpo de camisa*. 3d. ed. Río Piedras: Editorial Antillana, 1975. 5th ed. Río Piedras: Editorial Cultural, 1990.

——. "Escrito en puertorriqueño: la generación o sea." *En Rojo/Claridad*. 23 January 1972: 22.

——. *La guaracha del Macho Camacho*. Buenos Aires: Ediciones La Flor, 1976.

——. "Nuevas canciones festivas para ser lloradas." *Literatures in Transition: The Many Voices of the Caribbean Area*. Ed. Rose Minc. Gaithersburg, Md.: Montclair State College/ Ediciones Hispamérica, 1982. 17–20.

——. "Prólogo." Emilio S. Belaval. *Problemas de la cultura puertorriqueña*. Río Piedras: Editorial Cultural, 1977. 7–21.

Sedgwick, Eve Kosofsky. *Epistemology of the Closet*. Berkeley: University of California Press, 1990.

Weeks, Jeffrey. *Against Nature: Essays on History, Sexuality and Identity*. London: Rivers Oram Press, 1991.

Arnaldo Cruz-Malavé
Toward an Art of Transvestism: Colonialism and Homosexuality in Puerto Rican Literature

The inferiority complex that overwhelms us nowadays originates in geographic, historical and political limitations, suitable in any case for fusing censure with enervation. Not to speak of the contempt that that abundant number of effeminates puts into circulation all on its own.—Antonio S. Pedreira [1]

There is a zone of nonbeing, an extraordinarily sterile and arid region, an utterly naked declivity where an authentic upheaval can be born.—Frantz Fanon [2]

Carlos Rodríguez Matos, a gay Puerto Rican poet, has reminded us that from the publication of Carlos Alberto Fonseca's 1942 love poem to an "ephebe," "En voz baja . . . Para un efebo" [Softly . . . For an Ephebe] to that of Víctor Fragoso's *El reino de la espiga* in 1973, there was a lapse of thirty-one years in which there was no mention of lesbian or gay themes in Puerto Rican poetry ("Actos de amor" 23–24).[3] The reasons that he gives for this lapse are well known, for they are part and parcel of a process of national formation that in Puerto Rico, as elsewhere,[4] has not only silenced lesbian and gay desire in writing but lesbian and gay reality. Rodríguez Matos's assertion could be extended to the rest of Puerto Rican literature, and it would essentially be true. But it would be true not so much because there are no lesbian or gay representations in Puerto Rican literature prior to the 1970s—Luis Rafael Sánchez's 1966 short story "¡Jum!" comes to mind. It would rather be true because there are no literary examples of the tradition that the love poem by Fonseca—the only one by him that we know of—seems to invoke. That is, there is prior to the 1970s no poetic persona or writing subject for whom homosexuality is seen as the key factor that determines his or her being, as the source (or one of the sources) of his or her identity. There is no lesbian or gay writing subject.

The expression of a lesbian and gay identity is a recent development in Puerto Rican literature. It is the creation of poets such as Víctor Fragoso, Alfredo Villanueva Collado, Luz María Umpierre, and Carlos Rodríguez Matos himself.[5] Exiled in the United States since the 1970s, most of these writers have drawn inspiration from figures by now canonical in North American lesbian and gay literature, such as Whitman, Rich, and Lorde, in order to construct—or better yet, to "uncover"—a specifically Puerto Rican lesbian and gay subjectivity. However, following the example of Puerto Rico's most influential female poet, Julia de Burgos, they have also conceived this uncovering of their sexual self as a search for a free and authentic national space. Conflating their self with the colonial body of the island of Puerto Rico, or as the critic Rubén Ríos Avila has put it, the "I-Land" ("Gaiety Burlesque"), they have set out to liberate both the sexual and national geography of their identity: "Hay un pueblo isleño / esclavo en el Caribe / pero una isla amazónica libre / en el exilio / aquí en mi cuerpo" [There's an island people / enslaved in the Caribbean / but a free amazon island / in exile / here in my body] is the affirmation with which Umpierre brings to a close her discovery of sexual and national identity in *The Margarita Poems* (38).

Yet, if it is true that the emergence of a lesbian- and gay-identified literature in Puerto Rico has been repressed, and that this literature constitutes consequently a limited corpus, shifting our focus of attention from the question of "repression" and "lesbian and gay identity," would allow us, I believe, to ask questions that would shed light on the status of homosexuality in Puerto Rican literature and that may, in the end, reveal the centrality of the lesbian and gay experience to this literature: What is the expression of homosexuality in Puerto Rican literature prior to the emergence of this homosexually identified literature of the '70s and '80s? Why does a literature like this come into being in the '70s? Is this literature of lesbian and gay identity the only mode of expression of Puerto Rican lesbian and gay writers? And if it is not, what other forms do lesbian and gay consciousness take in recent Puerto Rican writing?

The Paternal Abject

Certainly the most significant work on Puerto Rican culture in the past two decades has been the unpacking of the concept of *a* Puerto Rican national identity. Caught between what had been traditionally seen as the overriding polarity of Puerto Rican cultural life—the competing claims of North American "cultural imperialism" and of a suppressed indigenous culture—"progressive" historians and critics had not dared turn a critical eye "home," lest they debilitate and disrupt the unified resistence of our *gran familia puertorriqueña*.[6] It is not until the early '70s when, as a result of the crisis of Puerto Rico's model of economic development, the unitary concept of *a* Puerto Rican national culture, which had underwritten it, began to appear as a more restricted (and restrictive) term, as a class construct. Once the "Pandora's box" of a national culture had been opened and its "papers" disseminated, to quote from the title of a well-known book of the times,[7] it seemed incredible that we Puerto Ricans had for so long lived within the paradoxical confines of the *casa solariega,* or patrician home, of our colonial modernity.

Everything then seemed new—new history, new literature, new criticism—and we would walk around dazed, not recognizing ourselves, or recognizing ourselves in the difference of our multiple identities. It is then that Manuel Ramos Otero publishes his first collection of homoerotic tales (1971); A. G. Quintero Rivera edits important documents in the history of the working class (1971); Isabelo Zenón Cruz reexamines Puerto Rican culture from an Afro-American perspective (1974); Miguel Algarín and Miguel Piñero edit the first anthology of U.S. Puerto Rican or *nuyorican* poetry (1975); and Rosario Ferré, among others, sets out to deconstruct, in her poems and short stories, the constitution of "woman" (1976). The words of the day are confrontation and rupture, and one progressive critic is heard saying that we are just emerging from the primitive[8] while another bemoans our tribal fall.[9] At any rate, wherever our judgment might fall, on the side of celebration or regret, the truth is that all of the tribes with which we Puerto Ricans live nowadays, and which we are, seemed then to make their first appearance.

What "new" historians like Quintero Rivera and cultural critics like Juan Flores, José Luis González, and Arcadio Díaz Quiñones were discovering—or better yet rediscovering—[10] was something that the polarity colonial domination/national culture had obfuscated—a Gramscian sense of culture in which "national culture" had played the part of "sovereignty," of a hegemonic discourse.[11] Unable to build a separate nation and unwilling to eschew participation in the world's most powerful market, the Puerto Rican bourgeoisie projected sovereignty onto the terrain of national culture: we Puerto Ricans could, the ideologues of the bourgeoisie claimed,[12] be, as in the official Spanish title of the "Commonwealth" of Puerto Rico,[13] free and dependent. We could, that is, be (culturally) free within (political and economic) dependency; defeat the *gringos,* as it were, by other means: Puerto Rican means. "National culture" became then the discourse by which the Puerto Rican bourgeoisie, heirs to the nineteenth-century *hacendado,* or planter, class, sought and gained hegemony for its model of capitalist modernization within dependency. Writing from the margins of this modernization, either from the perspective of those that had been marginalized within the "nation" or from the vantage point of those that had literally been excised from it (a third of all Puerto Ricans had by then migrated to the United States), the new Puerto Rican historians, writers, and critics traced the outlines of this hegemonic discourse.[14]

Canonized by the works of Antonio S. Pedreira and René Marqués, the hegemonic discourse that underwrote Puerto Rico's modernization paradoxically harked back to the paternalistic rhetoric of the nineteenth-century *hacendados.*[15] As has been rigorously demonstrated in a recent book by Juan Gelpí,[16] its master trope was that of the nation conceived of as a family, a monstrous sort of family—racially miscegenated, pathological, infantilized—over which a father-teacher presided with his disciplining voice. Assuming this paternal-magisterial voice,[17] Pedreira and Marqués sought to constrain and to give shape to the polymorphous perversity of the nation-child. To become a nation was to become a man, and to become a man was, as has been lucidly expressed by María Elena Rodríguez Castro, to fit into the mold of the "national home": a seigneurial abode constructed with equal parts Hispanicity, Eurocentrism, sexism, and whiteness.

What guaranteed the solidity of this edifice was the author's paternal-magisterial voice, what Díaz Quiñones has called his "oracular" voice (29) and Luis Rafael Sánchez his "divine words" ("Las divinas palabras de René Marqués")—his words beyond discussion, his silencing words. But what if the author's paternal voice were more conflicted? What if the otherness that he seeks to contain and to exclude were already inscribed in his voice? To attack the father would only follow then the path of his exclusionary logic, would only end up securing his place. What if in a colonial "nation" like Puerto Rico—in that queer state of freedom within dependency, of nation without nationhood—[18] impotence and lack were the only weapon, the ultimate ruse? It is my contention that, in a brilliant Nietzschean-like reversal,[19] Puerto Rican canonical texts have not ruled through potency but through impotence; that unlike those Latin American foundational texts that Doris Sommer has so passionately analyzed,[20] Puerto Rican canonical texts have rallied us and bound us through failure and impotence. It has been an exhibited impotence, such as the protagonist's self-castration in

Marqués's well-known story, "En la popa hay un cuerpo reclinado." An impotence that has cunningly incited us to close ranks around the father, with righteous indignation or with rage.[21] At the center of the author's paternal voice there's not a subject but an *abject*:[22] the monstrously mangled body of a nation-child that cannot accede to man/nationhood,[23] the castrated body of a "feminized" man[24] that bears, like all figures of gender-crossing, the marks of a "category crisis,"[25] of the impossibility of sustaining paternal hierarchies that the discourse of national identity both spectacularizes and condemns.

The Eve of Man

In order to understand the centrality of homosexuality in Puerto Rican literature and culture even prior to the emergence of a lesbian and gay literature of identity, in order to understand, that is, how the specter of homosexuality haunts Puerto Rico's hegemonic discourse of national identity, how homosexuality is not only its excluded other but its abjected self, one must first know that one of the most important Puerto Rican writers of the twentieth century, a writer who is generally cited as the Puerto Rican classic, René Marqués, was a homosexual. An immensely controversial figure who never identified himself as a "gay" writer and whose comments on what he saw as a North American phenomenon, the gay movement, were quite disparaging, Marqués was not only a homosexual but one of the most coherent proponents of Puerto Rican nationalism in literature, and needless to say, one of the most ardent advocates of Puerto Rican independence. Work by Efraín Barradas, María Solá, Arcadio Díaz Quiñones, and Juan Gelpí has identified his ideological positioning in Puerto Rican society as a kind of left-wing conservatism—of a paternalistic sort. If it is true that Marqués was a proponent of independence and an unrelenting critic of North American imperialism, it is equally true that, as an admirer of Tennessee Williams, he also suffered from what for the sake of time—and understanding the relative untranslatability of all cultural terms—we may call the "Blanche Dubois complex."

He produced an overwhelmingly beautiful and passionate literature in which there was a constant longing for a more orderly, more harmonious, and indeed more genteel and aristocratic past disrupted by North American colonialism, or by what he used to call in a manner that will forever endear him to all camp sensibilities, *los bárbaros* [the barbarians, the brutes] (see, for example, *Los soles truncos* [1958]). What one may fail to grasp, caught up as one may be in the lyricism of his dramas, is that this idealized past evoked, or rather invoked, by Marqués, paradisaical as it may seem, is also the differentiated realm where women assume their "naturally" subordinate position relative to men, blacks before whites, and servants before their masters. Colonialism represents then in Marqués's texts a fall from a world of paternal order, hierarchy, and grace—a fall which his texts diligently reproduce in order to purge. In Marqués's parable—a parable which he told over and over again—Puerto Rico was often a male child who had to come to terms with his fallen national past before achieving manhood and independence.

This parable reveals all its latent homosexual symbolism in a coming-of-age story published by Marqués shortly before his death, La mirada [The Gaze]. Here homosexuality is the "flaw" that the male protagonist must purge in order to achieve manhood. Yet if it is true that homosexuality in La mirada is an individual condition, it is also true that, through its identification with colonialism and the "barbarian invasion," homosexuality becomes in La mirada the collective condition of all Puerto Ricans, indeed of all colonials. Homosexuality becomes then in Marqués's text the central myth of the Puerto Rican nation—the myth that attempts to explain our inability to achieve nationhood as the story of the growing pains of a pato or maricón [faggot]. Constantly besieged by martirio and locura [martyrdom and madness], that is, by the possibility of being clavado [nailed/fucked] or becoming a loca [madwoman/drag queen], Marqués's protagonist must reproduce that which he seeks to erase. He must minutely detail the geography of homosexuality in order to make it vanish.

It is the decade of the '70s, and most of Puerto Rico has been invaded by the "unisex" sect, a (homo)sexual or same-sex hippie movement that is an emblem for the leveling effects of Puerto Rico's North American–style modernity. In an attempt to recover difference, the protagonist withdraws from the University of Puerto Rico (practically the headquarters of the sect) for the paternal home in Alto del Monte [Top of the Mountain], a space inscribed, in Puerto Rican literature and in Marqués's own writing, as the locus classicus of paternal hacendado culture. The protagonist's search for a pure space of hierarchical differentiation finds him constantly fleeing and, like a deconstructionist, discovering that that space has "always already" been contaminated. The novel's plot turns when the hippie band of unisex levelers invades and, as it were, opens up the most sacred of spaces: a small stretch of beach overlooked by Alto del Monte's paternal gaze—an overdetermined space where, as children, the protagonist and his friend Julito were caught by his father masturbating.

Were this a movie, a siren would go off at this point, and the camera would begin to zigzag with foreboding. For in what could only be called a manifestation of "homosexual panic,"[26] the protagonist, aided by an LSD-spiked brown ball or cookie, decapitates one of the band's members and castrates another. Perversely, however, this does not solve his problem of difference but rather defers it, for as a result, he is ominously incarcerated with the rest of the unisex gang. There, in the *recinto cerrado* [enclosed precinct] of the jail, he desperately attempts to maintain a separate identity from the unisex inmates by constructing himself another closet; he immerses himself in the prison's library. He becomes a volunteer librarian, but his overzealousness in ordering the disarray of the library and updating its collection causes this endeavor to fail. He then organizes scholarly panels on Puerto Rican history, but the inmates's lack of "culture" reduces these lectures to jiving and jesting or *relajo*. He even volunteers as a Spanish teacher, but the book he orders for class, predictably Marqués's other novel *La víspera del hombre* [The Eve of Man] (1958), is deemed subversive, and he is humiliatingly reassigned to the prison's shoe shop. Finally, having exhausted all other escapes, he submits to gang rape.

But unexpectedly, at this very point in which the protagonist submits to (homo)sexuality, to sameness, in which "indifference," or the collapse of binary oppositions, takes over his body, the narrator assumes an allegorical language. Playing on the double meaning of *clavar* [to nail/to fuck], the narrator rewrites the rape scene as crucifixion:

> Y sintió el dolor punzante. Y su mano izquierda fue llevada a agarrar el clavo del guitarrista bueno y la mano derecha a agarrar el clavo del guitarrista malo. Y el jovenzuelo, en tarea frenética, clavaba su pequeña y puntiaguda lanza entre su tetilla y costado derechos con intención de herir, pero sin lograrlo, mientras los dos guardas o sumos sacerdotes, con los calzones a media pierna se masturbaban o parecían masturbarse a un ritmo unísono desde la puerta de entrada.
>
> Entre el dolor y el placer él supo que era sólo una máquina de sexo y que respondía a cada pieza en movimiento como respondían ellos a él, pieza a pieza, hasta que el dolor desapareció o se hizo imperceptible y sólo el placer triunfó en todo su cuerpo, en toda su epidermis y sus entrañas con quejidos y gritos sincronizados por todos ellos, y movimientos rítmicos también sincronizados hasta llegar al paroxismo de coro trágico en un ¡ay! gozosamente triunfal y, simultáneamente, el semen en su boca y en todo su cuerpo, bautizado con el líquido sagrado, como un llanto también trágico y final, definitivo.
>
> Y en la angustia agónica y postrera del rito gritó, o creyó gritar:

"¡Padre mío! ¿Por qué me has abandonado?" Y se desmayó. (65)
[And he felt the piercing pain. And his left hand was made to grab
the nail of the good guitarist and the right hand the nail of the bad
guitarist. And the youth was frantically nailing his small and pointed
spear between his right nipple and his right side trying to wound him,
but not succeeding, while the two guards or high priests, with their
pants down to the middle of their legs, were masturbating, or seemed
to masturbate, in unison from the entrance door.

Between the pain and the pleasure he knew that he was only a sex
machine and that he reacted to each part in motion as they reacted
to him, a part to a part, until the pain disappeared or became imper-
ceptible and only pleasure triumphed in his entire body, in his entire
skin, and in his insides with moans and screams synchronized by all of
the others, and rhythmic movements also synchronized by them, until
they all reached the paroxysm of a tragic chorus in a joyfully triumphal
oh! and simultaneously the semen in his mouth and in his entire body,
baptized with the sacred liquid, as with tears, also tragic and final,
definitive.

And in the dying anguish of the rite he screamed, or thought he
screamed, "My father! Why have you forsaken me?" And he fainted.]

Carlos Hortas has enumerated the symmetries between this "sexual nailing" and Christ's crucifixion: the thieves on the right and left sides of
the crucified Christ become, in Marqués's novel, hippie guitarists whose
penises are nails; the Roman soldiers double up as penis-wielding prison
guards; and like Christ, the protagonist laments being "forsaken" by God
the father, has his side pierced, and ends his "passion" in ritual death.

Yet there is a distance here between the words and actions of the characters, on the one hand, and the allegorical interpretation that the protagonist and the narrator attempt to impose on these words and actions, on the
other. The passage just quoted is the culmination of a rape scene in which
the protagonist is forced at knife point to fellate a black man whom he
has just befriended, an archetypal black man with an archetypically huge
penis. Apologetically, the black man advises: "No hay remedio. Perdona.
Pero debes hacerlo. Tu salvación" (64) [Nothing we can do about it. Sorry.
But you've got to do it. It's your salvation]. Further on, as the black man
himself becomes a victim of rape, he exclaims: "¡Por Cristo! Usa saliva!"
(64) [For Christ sake! Use saliva!]. It is this character's words, "salvación"
and "Cristo," whose meaning we have just seen is rather material, that become springboards for the narrator's allegorical impulse that rewrites rape

as crucifixion. Here, as throughout the novel, the characters' words are one of the indicators of a separation, of a fault line between the diegesis and the allegorizing interpretation—a separation that forces us as readers to adopt a double vision: the double vision of camp.

Traditionally allegory has been conceived of not just as a comparison, or as an extended metaphor, in Quintilian's sense, but as a transformation, such that a literal level of meaning is recuperated and subsumed into a more generic or universal structure, as in Dante's well-known four-part formulation in his *Epistle* to Can Grande.[27] Specifically one could argue that, for an allegorical interpretation of the scene quoted above to obtain, rape would have to be transformed, or rather transfigured, through the religious language of crucifixion, that through it the menacing sameness of the protagonist's body, his (homo)sexuality, would have to be folded in and contained within the hierarchical paternal structure of Christian redemption. But, instead, the body and the paternal language of the scene remain separate and proliferate, displaying the irreducible incongruity of a body that cannot be spoken and of a language that cannot refer. And it's not an incongruity that could be reduced to parodic intentionality, for certainly many of Marqués's other texts corroborate the earnestness of his attempt to "transfigure" the colonial condition of the Puerto Rican "man," not the least of which is his *Vía crucis del hombre puertorriqueño* [Calvary of the Puerto Rican Man]. Nor could it be attributed to a modern (or postmodern) deferral of teleology, as in Kafka's nontotalizable allegories (see Clifford). The body and the language simply separate, and in their separateness foreground the intractability of a (homo)sexual body and the predictability of a paternal language that circles in upon itself—a language whose proliferation is not a sign of its playful provisionality but of its obsessiveness, whose very appeal—and repulsion—is that it is thoroughly totalizable, ineffective, obsolete.

Andrew Ross has argued that the "camp effect" is generated when "the products . . . of a much earlier mode of production, which has lost its power to dominate cultural meanings, become available, in the present, for redefinition according to contemporary codes of taste" (139). And in this sense we could say that the incongruity of a modern body and an obsolete language in Marqués's discourse of national identity was always on the verge of degenerating into a "camp effect." Much has been said of Marqués's nostalgia of a nineteenth-century *hacendado* past. What has been broached much less, and what Díaz Quiñones correctly underscores ("Los desastres de la guerra: Para leer a René Marqués" 36–44), is his longing for modernity. For Marqués was after all the most technically innovative playwright of his time, the most up-to-date, and his fondness for nineteenth-century interiors was not unlike the new industrial bourgeoisie's restoration of "Old San Juan." It was a backward glance that, like the bourgeoisie's recourse to nineteenth-century paternalistic rhetoric, was terribly modern— a way of "nationalizing" North American–style modernity, of imposing his authority in the midst of its "democratizing whirlwind," [28] of mooring himself. [29] The tension between the body of modernity and the language of paternalism was always there threateningly lurking amidst the optimism of the bourgeoisie's modernizing discourse, but Marqués—less pragmatic, more faithful—attempts to resolve this tension by aesthetic means. And it's this aesthetization which ultimately frees his paternalism and makes it available for camp. [30]

At the end of the novel, not only has the protagonist's body not been transfigured through crucifixion, has he not attained paternal identification, but his "sexual nailing" has led instead to "feminization" and castration. Once out of the "enclosed precinct" of the jail, the protagonist returns to the small stretch of beach overlooked by *Alto del Monte*'s paternal gaze, the paternal space of prohibition whose invasion by the gender-leveling hippies provoked his "homosexual panic." Now he himself invades and, as it were, re-homosexualizes this paternal space by having sex with his childhood friend Julito and thus completing the masturbation scene interrupted by his father at the beginning of the novel. The fear of castration and gender-crossing which originally provoked his panic is still evident in this reprise, and crucifixion is once again invoked. But now there is no attempt to transfigure the "sexual nailing" of the protagonist through the paternal language of Christian redemption. Instead, the protagonist's "sexual nailing" is displaced onto a hallucinatory scene in which his friend Julito, dressed as a woman in black, carries around the protagonist's severed testicles in a matching black bag or *bolso* (*bolsa* being Spanish slang for testicles).

Mock allusions to the "last of the Atridae" during this hallucinatory scene relate castration to another of the novel's thematic axes: matricide. In the hallucinatory dream, the cross-dressed Julito delivers the protagonist's severed testicles to his mother causing her to reel back in horror and fall from a balcony to her death. The protagonist's castration causes thus, in the hallucinatory projection, the mother's death. In the meantime, perversely, while the son is being "nailed," his "real life" mother lies on her death bed. Earlier in the novel, his father had warned him that his "mad" talk of the unisex gang was killing his mother: "Y cada vez que hablas como un loco, matas a tu madre" (63) [And each time you talk like a madman, you kill your mother]. This warning recalls in addition the injunction with which the father interrupted the son's homosexual masturbation scene at the beginning of the novel: "Oye bien lo que te digo. Eso te lo dio Dios para las mujeres, no para que lo uses solo y mucho menos con otro mucha-cho. Si llegas a caer en eso te volverías loco" (12) [Listen to me! God gave you that for women, not to use it alone and much less with another boy. If you fall into that, you'll go crazy]. Significantly now that the son has transgressed the father's injunction, now that he has completed the very act that the father had proscribed, he has both become a *loco,* or rather a *loca,* and caused his mother's death.

In Freud's Oedipus complex, it is the father's threat of castration that forces the male child to relinquish his desire for the mother and to ulti-mately accede to paternal identification (see "The Dissolution of the Oedi-pus Complex"). In Lacan's linguistic reading of the Oedipus complex, cas-tration plays an analogous role. It severs the child from the specular order of the Imaginary—an order where the child finds his identity in other ob-jects, of which the mother's body is a primary source—and thrusts him into the paternal and linguistic order of the Symbolic. And it is with this entry into the Symbolic that the child gains access to the "Name-of-the-Father," or "phallus," which for Lacan signifies "the cultural privileges and positive values [that] define male subjectivity within patriarchal society" (Silver-man 183). Castration then functions in Marqués's *La mirada* in a similar way; it severs the protagonist from the maternal world—a severance which is here underscored by her death. But unlike in Freud and Lacan, the pro-tagonist's castration in *La mirada* does not lead to paternal identification. It does not propitiate the constitution of a phallocentric male subject, but registers instead a fall into abjection, into an in-between state that is not a "third"[31] but a gap, a neither-nor.

It is true that there is a certain pathos at the heart of the Lacanian male subject, that he can never quite correspond to the ideal "paternal function" that speaks through him, and that his identity, if it is to be functional, needs therefore institutional support. But what *La mirada* spectacularizes is not pathos but pathology, or rather *pato*logy: a falling of the would-be male national subject not outside paternal logic but inside of it, where it can neither be represented nor institutionally shored up—a falling, that is, as the protagonist's father had warned, into a madness or *locura* where paternal binarism implodes, where the would-be national subject is always already, as in the title of Marqués's other coming-of-age story, in the "Eve of Man."

As the novel closes, the protagonist, condemned like the tragically transgressive figures of Orestes and Oedipus to perpetual exile, prepares to leave the paternal *Alto del Monte*. He has not been transfigured, but he has been transformed. He now bears the mark of the castrated. He is now indistinguishable from the (homo)sexual members of the unisex gang: his beard is overgrown and his hair is long. Like the cross-dressed Julito, he now picks up his—empty—black bag and steps out into a world without order or meaning, without stable differences. If at the end of *La víspera del hombre* the protagonist recognizes his position as transitional (he has left the maternal world of childhood, but has not yet attained the "realm of Man" [262]), in *La mirada* that transitional position is inscribed in the protagonist's own body: he is the *loca* that must forever navigate toward paternity—a monstrously hybrid figure carrying around an empty bag.

Much has been made of the rupture that recent Puerto Rican writing represents with respect to Marqués—a discontinuity emblematized for some by Luis Rafael Sánchez's *La guaracha del Macho Camacho* [Macho Camacho's Beat], which appeared a year after *La mirada*, in 1976.[32] I want to suggest here that much of recent Puerto Rican writing can be said to begin instead where Marqués's protagonist leaves off, that much of it begins, as it were, when the author puts on heels and clutches an empty bag in order to enter a world without meaning, a world of "indifference." But before I do let me retrace my steps.

National Identity as Patology

Reading back from Marqués, one encounters the text that en(gender)ed his reading of Puerto Rico's colonial status as failed bildungsroman. It is the book that has been credited with founding Puerto Rican letters in the twentieth century: Antonio S. Pedreira's 1934 social, historical, and literary interpretation of Puerto Rico, *Insularismo*.

The very title of Marqués's coming-of-age story, *La víspera del hombre*, is a quote from the final chapter of *Insularismo*, "Juventud, divino tesoro" [Youth, divine treasure], itself a quote of the Nicaraguan *modernista* poet, Rubén Darío's "Canción de Otoño en Primavera" (88). As Pedreira, following in the tradition of Latin American writers such as Sarmiento, Rodó, and Vasconcelos, sets out to define and diagnose the Puerto Rican national character, youth or adolescence appears as the most appropriate emblem for the Island's colonial condition. According to Pedreira, Puerto Rico, and especially the generation of the 1930s to which he belongs, are in a state of transition—no longer Spanish and not yet North American. Using an organic metaphor, he divides the history of Puerto Rico into three major stages: the first, which begins with the Spanish conquest in 1493 and ends with the coming of the nineteenth century, is a sort of preconscious state of "formation and passive accumulation" (27); the second, covering all of the nineteenth century until the Spanish-Cuban–North American war of 1898, is a period of "waking and initiation" (27); and the third, encompassing the subsequent decades of North American occupation, is the present moment of "indecision and transition" (27). Translating this organic periodization into a failed bildungsroman, Pedreira claims that Puerto Rico had a birth, a childhood, and an adolescence, but that at the point in which adolescence was to turn into full manhood and independence, the North American occupation thwarted it. Consistent with the bildungsroman, he also tells this tale in the not uncommon form of a seafaring voyage of discovery:

> Tres siglos de callada y lenta navegación no fueron suficientes para en-
> contrar la ruta de El Dorado. En el siglo XIX empezamos a vislumbrar,
> entre la bruma, las costas de nuestra conciencia colectiva y cuando nos
> preparábamos para el grito jubiloso de ¡Patria a la vista!, una mano
> guerrera nos quebrantó el timón, quedando nuestra nave al garete.
> (133–34)
> [Three centuries of quiet and slow navigation were not sufficient to
> find the route of El Dorado. In the nineteenth century we began to
> glimpse, through the mist, the coasts of our collective conscience, and
> when we were getting ready for the jubilant cry of Fatherland in view!,
> a warring hand broke our helm, leaving our ship adrift.]

Ironically youth has not been for Puerto Rico what Darío's verse ("Youth, divine treasure") seems to evoke: an infinite state of possibilities. It has been instead a state of impossibility and stagnation, an aimless drift-ing between coasts without a helmsman or master to lead to port. Puerto Rico's fundamental problem is, he insists, "the problem of man" (109). Drifting between coasts, Puerto Rico as youth faces before him an empti-ness—an emptiness where, as Pedreira states, "the man awaits" (166). It is this emptiness, this in-between state, this ambiguous and dangerous space of stagnation and repetition where, as with Marqués's protagonist, there is rupture but no rebirth, where an undying corpse perpetually awaits, that Pedreira tries to conjure up and to transcend.

Most of what he considers the *taras,* or defects, of the Puerto Rican personality may be traced to this "mixed and equivocal" state (36). Puerto Ricans are "docile" because a "biological civil war" rages within them: the African and the European, the master and the servant in them lead them to contrary dispositions and thus to indecision (35–36). Or they are "insular" and self-centered, not as an affirmation of self but as a defensive reaction to external manipulation and aggression. Puerto Rican self-centeredness is an exoticism. Or they oscillate between rhetorical flourish and skepticism. They either believe in everything, or believe in nothing at all. Either way they empty words of their "proper" and "virile" meaning. Puerto Ricans are superfluous. Faced with the weight of imperial powers, Puerto Ricans are, like chess players, strategic. Constantly besieged, they are constantly mobilized, leaving no stable identity behind them. Puerto Ricans live in the realm of the paradoxical.

Puerto Ricans' equivocalness, superfluity, and mobilization are finally emblematized in *Insularismo*'s closing chapter in the figure of the "effeminate" (167). Dissecting what he considers the Puerto Ricans' "inferiority complex," Pedreira finds in the Island's "tupida cantidad de afeminados" [abundant number of effeminates] a visible sign of the geographical, historical, and political limitations that hamper Puerto Ricans' ability to create and thus to constitute the nation (167). It is against this background of Puerto Rico's "transitional" state of adolescence, conceived of as effeminacy and impotence, or what he also terms the Island's "medio patológico," both its pathological and *pato*logical milieu of depressed and unproductive men, "castrated of the most fundamental virtues" (167), that he calls on Puerto Ricans to transcend their youth.

Yet Pedreira's final call is itself pathological, or *pato*logical. For unlike the visions with which his Latin American predecessors Sarmiento, Rodó, and Vasconcelos end their essays on the character of the nation or of the continent, Pedreira's call, in what could be termed, consistent with his analysis, a very Puerto Rican turn of phrase, slips back into the paradoxical. At the end of *Facundo* (1845), the Argentinian Sarmiento invokes, as a counterpart to his authorial voice, the providential figure of general Paz, a figure around which the nation is already beginning to galvanize (287). In concluding *Ariel* (1900), the Uruguayan Rodó's author surrogate, Próspero inscribes, and even brands, the image of his "magisterial voice," or *voz magistral,* on the consciousness of his youthful listeners, literally shaping them thus into a "band of brothers" which will henceforth promote his version of Latin-Americanness (58). And in closing *La raza cósmica* (1925), the Mexican Vasconcelos prophetically reveals the very "biological" evidence of Latin America's future as the cradle of a new "cosmic race" (49 and ff.). The queerness of Pedreira's discourse of national identity stands out then against this canon. For at the end of *Insularismo,* Pedreira does not so much have an authorial voice as a figure for the nation to bequeath, inscribe, or reveal but an emptiness—a conspicuously displayed emptiness which is the task of Puerto Rico's youth to fill. But youth is itself in Pedreira's rhetorical stock a paradoxical figure. It is as much a sign of Puerto Rico's *patology* as it is its possible cure. Thus Pedreira's final words ("Atended al *divino tesoro,* pues el título más alto se puede convertir en mote" [174] [Pay attention to youth's *divine treasure,* for the highest title can also become an epithet]) give no grounding to youth's task—no assurance. They are as much an inspirational call as a curse.

At the beginning of this essay I said that the crisis of Puerto Rico's hege-monic discourse of national identity in the early '70s created the possibility of new subjectivities, of which the emergence of a lesbian and gay literature of identity is an expression. But it also made possible a different relation-ship to the canon—one that may not be simply characterized as the oppo-sitional creation of an alternative identity with a concomitant alternative canon, as necessary and as valorous as that is.[33] It also ushered in the appro-priation by lesbian and gay artists of the figure of paternal abjection and of the centrality which the hegemonic canon—even if under the ambivalent sign of spectacularization and condemnation—has accorded it.[34]

In a sense, we could say that Pedreira's warning about the creative pos-sibilities of youth degenerating into an onerous condition, or "epithet," seems to have come true in contemporary Puerto Rican writing. Ungrate-fully, contemporary Puerto Rican writers have decided to speak not from the space of a stable, "virile," and "mature" identity but from that *"patologi-cal* milieu" of castration and gender-crossing, superfluity and equivocalness that both Pedreira and Marqués display and condemn. If in the latter's texts, Puerto Rico is imagined as a torturously closeted young man end-lessly sliding toward the "normality" of heterosexuality and the recovery of a paternal order, in contemporary Puerto Rican writing this ambiva-lent *pato* opts instead for his *locura* and blossoms into a self-conscious drag queen. Perhaps no image is more powerfully representative of this cultural moment than Arnaldo Roche Rabell's 1990 painting "For the Record: The Eleventh Commandment." In it Roche has substituted his own mother's rubbed-in body for the figure of Moses presenting the tablets of the Law, and over her torso he has traced his own severed face. "I'm trying to create mirrors where people can go and see themselves," Roche has said (Alba-nese 35). And sternly his face seems to order us to look and to recognize ourselves not in the tablets of paternal law but in the tablet-shaped mirrors of his castrated, cross-gendered self.

But in assuming this abject condition, this "epithet," Puerto Rican writ-ers have not simply celebrated nonidentical being, or hybridity,[35] and the cultural practices that, classed under the rubric of *relajo,* are in Puerto Rican

Arnaldo Roche Rabell, "For the Record: The Eleventh Commandment," 1990. Oil on canvas, 96 × 96 inches. Used with permission of the Frumkin/Adams Gallery.

culture associated with it.[36] They have not simply embraced the centrality of the abject's nonessentialist, cross-gendered identity while inverting its negative valuation. They have also redeployed the figure of the abject in the service of new strategies and new contexts. Specifically, in the works of writers like Luis Rafael Sánchez and Manuel Ramos Otero cross-gendered abjection has been respectively redeployed as pedagogy and subversion. It is these redeployments that I will now briefly sketch.

Magisterial Drag

At the center of Luis Rafael Sánchez's 1976 novel *La guaracha del Macho Camacho* is the *loca* as a figure for the author's voice and the burlesque drag show as an emblem for the novel's procedures.

Undoubtedly alluding to *Insularismo,* Sánchez's hybrid text jests about Puerto Ricans' aptitude for impasse ("la capacidad criolla para el atolladero" [27]), and as in Pedreira's text, the novel's central images cluster around the concepts of stagnation and repetition. Pedreira's nautical metaphor of Puerto Rico as a ship adrift however has changed. In an inescapably modern world, Sánchez's characters seem to be weighed down not so much by a colonial legacy that distorts their personalities, turning them indecisive and abject, as by an external condition. Their world is now an objective, even grotesque, image of indecision. And all of the novel's characters are now caught in the grip of a paradoxically noncirculating urban flow whose very concrete figure of deadlock is a massive traffic jam, as "phenomenal as life itself, *made in Puerto Rico*" (27).

Sánchez's *La guaracha* recounts the lives of six main characters during the five o'clock traffic jam: a pro–North American senator caught in the traffic jam on his way to an assignation with his mulatto mistress; his right-wing terrorist son also caught in the traffic jam on his way to racing his new car; his mistress furiously waiting for him at their usual rendezvous; his aristocratic wife waiting her turn at the psychoanalyst's couch; the mistress's idiot son waiting to be picked up in a park where he is being taunted by other children; and doña Chon, the mistress's neighbor, on her way to pick him up. All of the inchoate intentions of these characters, frozen in time and in space by the five o'clock traffic jam, finally coalesce—Pedreira-like— in an image of stunted youth. For in an ironic reference to García Lorca's exalted elegy, "Llanto por Ignacio Sánchez Mejías," all of their conflicting intentions clash and end, as in Lorca's refrain, in the mistress's son's death "a las cinco de la tarde," or "at five o'clock." But Sánchez's character does not face here, as in Lorca's poem, a heroic death. Instead, he is run over by the senator's son who accelerates through a side street at the very moment that he escapes into the street in order to avoid the other children's taunts—a final grotesque image of crossed intentions.

Even if displaced onto the new terrain of the modern city's infrastructure and onto mass culture—the traffic jam is ironically punctuated by the refrain of Macho Camacho's *guaracha:* "Life's a phenomenal thing"— Pedreira's configuration of Puerto Rico as failed bildungsroman is clearly visible here.[37] The difference however is distance. Writing after what we have called the crisis of the hegemonic discourse of modernity, Sánchez's rewriting of Pedreira's plot reads rather as caricature than as national "interpretation." For in what I would call, consistent with by now standard definitions of postmodernism,[38] Sánchez's postmodern fiction, there is not, as in *Insularismo,* an examination of the national psyche or ontology, but "merely" a simulation of social discourses. In Sánchez's *La guaracha,* as I have argued elsewhere,[39] all of the characters are quotes, and Pedreira's plot is just that—a plot. The massive traffic jam then is not just a metaphor for Puerto Ricans' spiritual enervation and indecision but a locus like Bakhtin's marketplace where all social discourses converge and are carnivalized.

But is *La guaracha* simply a carnivalesque collection of voices? Is there no overriding authorial voice? No, there is certainly here an overriding authorial voice whose manipulation of the carnival of voices is the sign of a pedagogic intent. And this pedagogic intent is nowhere more evident than in one of the sections devoted to the senator's right-wing son, Benny. In the midst of this character's "monologue," the author's voice interrupts and, assuming a stance not unlike that of his essay, "La generación 'O sea'" [The "You know" Generation], addresses the readers, as national audience, directly ("Créame, yo lo conozco" [127] [Believe me, I know him]) in order to critique what Benny's syntactically broken Spanish represents: his stunted youth (126–27). And as in *Insularismo*'s final chapter, Sánchez's condemnation of Benny's arrested youth is here a way of invoking the possibility of another youth—a youth that may finally transcend Puerto Rico's condition of stag(nation): "Sueño vivo . . . agazapado en la mirada de los muchachos y las muchachas que altisonan y venden *Claridad* . . . deslumbrados porque la historia los invita a hacer el viaje . . . porque en las manos les conversa la construcción de la libertad" (128) [A living dream . . . lurking in the eyes of the boys and girls who shout and sell *Claridad* . . . dazzled because history is inviting them to take that trip . . . because the building of freedom is talking to them through their hands].

Yet if there is in Sánchez's novel, as in Pedreira's text, a pedagogic intent, what are the forms that this pedagogic intent takes? In *La guaracha,* the place of pedagogic instruction is not a classroom but a theatrical scene. Casting us, as readers, in the role of audience, the narrator consistently addresses us and forces us to move from the "referential" frame of the traffic jam to what I would call the novel's privileged frame—a theatricalized scene where he, the narrator, is performing, as in a one-man show, the very novel that we are reading: "Descansen, permitido el cigarrillo, el aliento a tutti frutti que comercia el chiclet Adams permitido, una cervecita, un cafetito, el cansado estire las piernas, el remolón marque la página y siga leyendo otro día y el que quiera más novedad véala y escúchela ahora" (79–80) [You may take a break. Smoking is permitted. The tutti-frutti breath Adams' Chiclets trades in, a little beer, a spot of coffee are also allowed. The tired may stretch their legs. The lazy may mark the page and continue another day. But whoever wants more news may see it now and hear it here]. Assuming the social and cultural differences that intersect and collide in the traffic jam as discursive differences, the narrator displaces our attention from the novel's very real social characters to his simulation of their sociolects. Like the impersonators studied by Esther Newton in *Mother Camp: Female Impersonators in America,* he does not so much copy his models as "enact" the very structure of their linguistic identity. Constantly moving between referential and theatrical frames, insistently foregrounding the quotable nature of the novel's characters, the narrator forces us as readers to recognize what Judith Butler has called their (and his) "performative" identity.

If the revealing moment of burlesque is, in Rubén Ríos Avila's apt description, the "mock-reversal of our expectations . . . when the can-can dancer turns around, lifts the skirt and gives us a glimpse of ass" ("Gaiety Burlesque"), and if according to Severo Sarduy, one of Sánchez's most significant intertexts, transvestite "simulation" produces an "excess" whose effect is to underscore the structure, the body, the "support," then *La guaracha* could best be described as a burlesque drag show. Indeed in one of the novel's passages this identification becomes manifest. Describing the senator's lecherous advances toward a schoolgirl caught in the traffic jam, the narrator switches from this "referential" frame to the scene of his theatrical performance, and addressing us as audience, places us in the senator's voyeuristic gaze. Raising our libidinal expectations, he then makes us, like the senator, pursue the schoolgirl. But at the moment of climactic revelation when we are about to "see her emerge like Venus from the foam" (219) on an isolated beach, the narrator mocks our expectations and reveals instead his and the schoolgirl's artifice:

> Visión dantesca consumirá, visión merecedora de un Canto de Maldoror, una vida imaginaria de Marcel Schwob, un nuevo informe de Brodie: la peluca de la estudiante, pongamos que se llama Lola, colgará de un uvero, las tetas del burlesco *Mother of eight* colgarán de un arbusto de hicacos. ¡Extraordinario, colosal, asombroso!: Lola no es Lola, Lola no es Lolo, Lola es Lole: un mariconazo hormónico y depilado. Cámara rápida, movimiento adulterado por la rapidez

funambulesca, chaplinesca, tatiesca, totoesca, cantinflesca, agrelotesca,
correrá y correrá y correrá. (219)
[A Dantesque vision the senator will consume. A vision worthy of a
Song by Maldoror. One of Marcel Schwob's imaginary lives. A new
report by Brodie. The schoolgirl's wig—let's say her name is Lola—
will hang from a grapevine. Her tits, like those in the burlesque *Mother
of Eight,* will hang from a cocoplum bush. Extraordinary, colossal, astounding! Lola isn't Lola. Lola isn't Lolo. Lola is Lole: a hormonal
and depilated screaming queen. Rapid camera movement. Movement
adulterated with acrobatic, Chaplinesque, Tatiesque, twatesque, Can-
tinflaesque, Agrelotesque rapidity. He'll run. And he'll run. And he'll
run.]

Like this transvestite, the narrator-performer of *La guaracha* seduces us
and the senator only to reveal in the end the very techniques that constitute
his writing, the very languages that are his many drags.

Significantly the paradigmatic figure of seduction and mock-reversal
here is the senator—a figure whose ultimate authority seems to reside in
his self-identity as a *macho,* as male. And in *La guaracha del Macho Camacho,*
as in Sánchez's other "novel," *La importancia de llamarse Daniel Santos,* the
eponymous *macho*'s self-presence is both the object of desire and repudiation. Whether Sánchez lures the macho in *La guaracha* or spies his beau-
tifully sweating body in *Daniel Santos* (4), his writing—a writing which
aspires to magisterial status, which claims a national space—aims to de-
bunk the *macho*'s authority, to usurp his place. *La guaracha* may thus be
read as the story of this usurpation. Insistently announced by the voice of a
disc-jockey, Macho Camacho's *guaracha* does not appear in the text of the
novel, and it is only finally furnished in an appendix. In its place is this other
guaracha, Sánchez's *guaracha*—a *guaracha* whose authority is underwritten
not by the *macho*'s self-presence but by the author's ambivalent transvestite
voice.

Bend-over Bolero

No other Puerto Rican writer has cultivated abjection as fiercely and as un-
compromisingly as Manuel Ramos Otero (1948–90), recently lost to AIDS.
Whether in his readings where he would appear in good *modernista* fashion decked out in a *geisha*'s kimono or in his fiction, Ramos Otero's most
frequently assumed authorial persona was that of a drag queen. Psycho-

analysts have defined transvestism as a fetishistic practice whose object is to "disavow," in Freud's term (see "Fetishism"), the male child's traumatic sight of the woman's lack of penis, interpreted as castration, through a phallic substitute.[40] By wearing the woman as fetish, the transvestite secures, psychoanalysts have claimed, the "wholeness" of his own masculine identity. But Ramos Otero's transvestism was not a compensatory plenitude; it was not a way to become whole. It was instead a way of displaying castration, of provoking by exhibiting lack—a way, as in the Spanish proverb, of showing off the noose in the hanged man's home.[41]

Certainly in Ramos Otero's stories dresses and makeup as well as writing and tattoos are phallic substitutes. But instead of securing a male identity by completing a "castrated" "effeminate" body, these phallic instruments split open, dismember, slash. "Behind every story," says the narrator of one of Ramos Otero's most "exemplary" tales, "Inventario mitológico del cuento," ". . . there is a perfumed corpse" (*El cuento de la mujer del mar* 79). And it is this body waiting to be tortured by makeup, to be tattooed by the phallic pen that is the primal scene of Ramos Otero's writing. A body rots under our very eyes, and Ramos Otero perversely refuses to make it disappear, to transfigure it under the violent weight of abstraction, to turn it into a compensatory image of male and national identity.

"Rien ne tue un homme comme d'être obligé de représenter un pays" reads the famous epigraph to Cortázar's novel *Hopscotch*.[42] And like Cortázar and Borges, two of his most frequent intertextual references, Ramos Otero dramatizes writing and representation as death. But while Cortázar's and Borges's characters are either surprised by the surreal or caught in what Doris Sommer has called "dead-end plots" or "no-win [linguistic] games" ("A Nowhere for Us: The Promising Pronouns in Cortázar's 'Utopian' Stories" 66, 75) that disperse their identity and inevitably lead them to death (consider here Borges's "The South" and "Death and the Compass," and Cortázar's "Continuity of Parks," "The Night Face Up," "Secret Weapons," "Instructions for John Howell," "The Island at Noon," and "Axolotl"), Ramos Otero's characters actively plot their own entrapment and insistently summon their own death.

It is a beautiful body, a seductive corpse. A body whose cancerous breast implants are identified, as in "Inventario mitológico del cuento," with the topography of Puerto Rico—with the *Tetas de Cayey,* or Cayey's twin peaks. An island-body all cut open, seasoned, and adorned. An island-body all prettied-up, singing love ballads or *boleros*—abjection's songs: "usted me desespera, me mata, me enloquece" (*El cuento de la mujer del mar* 73) [you make me despair, you kill me, you drive me mad]. An enticing body laid out on a table for the macho's phallic writing, for his penetrating gaze. A body dressed for consumption. A body poised for death.

And yet surrender and abjection are not here the languages of passivity. Nor are Ramos Otero's stories merely about the "death of the author" or of the unitary self. His stories are decidedly more interested in power and certainly more perverse. They are surely not about renouncing power from the top or about undermining one's own privilege for the sake of *jouissance*. His stories are told from the bottom—literally from the bottom. From abjection's cuts and bruises, from its "poppy asshole in raw flesh" ("Vida ejemplar del esclavo y el señor" 176, my translation). They are masochistic fantasies in which, consonant with Deleuze's definition, "the victim speaks the language of the torturer" (17)—the language of degradation, the language most accessible to him. But when the victim speaks this language he wields it not as a tribute but as a weapon. He uses it to install himself.

"[H]azlo como te digo o no lo hagas . . . méteme el puño entero o no me lo metas" (*Cuentos de buena tinta* 175–76) [Do it to me the way I tell you to or don't do it at all . . . put your whole fist inside me or don't put it in at all]. So orders the "slave" in Ramos Otero's "Vida ejemplar del esclavo y el señor," and the imperative used here ends up inverting the power relation between the master and the slave. Through it the slave transforms his marginal position into a new center of (author)ity and his abjection into a new means of affirming himself.

In one of Ramos Otero's most emblematic tales, "Loca la de la locura," the narrator, a transvestite cabaret singer, assumes the abject role assigned to women by the *bolero* in order to seduce the macho, the penetrating male, the *bugarrón*, to whom the *bolero* gives, as s/he states, a certain "authority" (235). Framed by "the frayed crepe paper leaves of a palm tree backdrop [that] sketch shivering knife stabs" on her skin, she writhes and sings: "hay en tus labios en flor un veneno mortal" (234) [your budding lips hold a fatal venom]. Seduced by this vision of martyrdom, of a "suffering Madonna who knows that she has nevertheless given birth to Christ" (234), Nene Lindo, the *bugarrón*, assumes his position as wielder of the phallic "machete" (234), as torturer. But in her overzealousness to carry out his orders, to be faithful to her own degradation, Queen of Madness, the cabaret *bolero* singer "dives into a brown kiss like a cement-wall-tearing ivy" (236) bending him over and fucking him. Attempting to regain his "top" positionality, Nene Lindo then pulls out a gun, and s/he ends up—however regrettably—decapitating him. Kneeling in front of Nene Lindo's tomb, Queen of Madness now waxes epiphanic: "Presentía que el mundo ya no sería el mismo. Ahora estoy sin máscaras. Con un puñal de huesos para unirme a la revolución" (240) [I felt the world would no longer be the same. Now I am without masks. And armed with a dagger of bones to go join the revolution].

A national allegory of sorts, the day of Nene Lindo's decapitation is November 19th, Puerto Rico Discovery Day. And as in Ramos Otero's other stories,[43] there is here both the invocation of a national identity and its short-circuiting. In the end, his stories narrate the triumph of the *loca*'s castrated and castrating body, of h/er "dagger of bones." They represent that moment when the homosexual body's refusal to be transfigured into a phallic national image paradoxically becomes the ultimate and only image, when the spectral installs itself as an image—an image of a nonimage—in order to preempt the recovery of the body for a national discourse.

If from the perspective of a lesbian and gay identity Puerto Rican lesbian and gay literature has been repressed, from the perspective of transvestite abjection Puerto Rican homosexuality has been both spectacularized and condemned. It is this transvestism that Luis Rafael Sánchez and Manuel Ramos Otero reclaim—one in order to gather the nation under the pedagogic sign of *relajo;* the other to free the body from the phallic representations of a national discourse. Instead of rejecting the canon and staring at repression's blank page, their appropriations speak to us of a literature that is much queerer, much more perverse. They restore for us a *patology,* or a *mariconería,* that is both a rupture and a continuity, that is both in Puerto Rico's future and in Puerto Rico's past—both a debunking and a faith.

Notes

1 Antonio S. Pedreira, *Insularismo* 167: "El complejo de inferioridad que hoy nos agobia proviene de las limitaciones geográficas, históricas y políticas, propicias en todo caso para fundir el vituperio con el apocamiento. Ni que mentar hay el menosprecio que por su cuenta pone en circulación esa tupida cantidad de afeminados." My translation.

2 *Black Skin, White Masks* 8.

3 Rodríguez Matos acknowledges the researcher José Olmo Olmo for identifying Fonseca's poem.

4 Andrew Parker, Mary Russo, Doris Sommer, and Patricia Yaeger argue in *Nationalisms and Sexualities* that the nation, "[t]ypically represented as a passionate brotherhood, . . . finds itself compelled to distinguished its 'proper' homosociality from more explicitly sexualized male-male relations, a compulsion that requires the identification, isolation, and containment of male homosexuality" (6). Further, they suggest that the "idealization of motherhood by th[is] virile fraternity would seem to entail the exclusion

of all nonreproductively-oriented sexualities from the discourse of the nation. Indeed, certain sexual identities [such as lesbianism] and practices are less represented and representable in nationalism" (6–7).

5 I do not discuss here the works of Manuel Ramos Otero, whose *Concierto de metal para un recuerdo y otras orgías de soledad* (1971) may be said to be the first book of Puerto Rican literature written by a openly homosexual writer. I reserve discussion of Ramos Otero for a later section because, as I will argue, his literary project is not to conflate gay and national identity, but to radically undermine all claims of identity.

6 In *Conflictos de clase y política en Puerto Rico* and in "Clases sociales e identidad nacional; notas sobre el desarrollo nacional puertorriqueño," A. G. Quintero Rivera has traced the concept of a *gran familia puertorriqueña* to the hegemonic aspirations of Puerto Rico's nineteenth-century *hacendado,* or planter, class.

7 I am referring to Rosario Ferré's *Papeles de Pandora.*

8 Angel Rama as quoted by Arcadio Díaz Quiñones, "Recordando el futuro imaginario: la escritura histórica en la década del treinta" 35. The word Rama uses to refer to the Puerto Rican society in crisis is "arcaica" [archaic]. See his "Crisis y transformación de la literatura puertorriqueña" 5–9.

9 For an ambivalent take on this "tribalism," see Edgardo Rodríguez Juliá's urban chronicles: *Las tribulaciones de Jonás* and *El entierro de Cortijo.*

10 These historians and critics revive a rich Puerto Rican socialist and anarchist tradition in which "national culture" is critiqued as the culture specific to the bourgeoisie. See A. G. Quintero Rivera, *La lucha obrera; Conflictos de clase y política en Puerto Rico,* and *Patricios y plebeyos: burgueses, hacendados, artesanos y obreros;* G. García and A. G. Quintero Rivera, *Desafío y solidaridad;* R. Campos and J. Flores, "Migración y cultura nacional puertorriqueñas: Perspectivas proletarias"; C. Andreu Iglesias, ed., *Memorias de Bernardo Vega.* More recently, see Julio Ramos's introduction to his anthology of the works of the anarchist organizer and intellectual, Luisa Capetillo, *Amor y anarquía.*

11 A Gramscian understanding of "national culture" is certainly explicit in two of the key texts of this "new" critique: J. L. González's *El país de cuatro pisos,* which starts with a quote from Gramsci's *Prison Notebooks,* and A. G. Quintero Rivera's "Clases sociales e identidad nacional; notas sobre el desarrollo nacional puertorriqueño." It is also implicit in A. Díaz Quiñones's "Recordando el futuro imaginario: la escritura histórica en la década del treinta."

12 In *La historia del Partido Popular Democrático,* Luis Muñoz Marín, the patriarch of the party that launched, in 1940, Puerto Rico's process of modernization, discusses his strategy of deferring the issue of Puerto Rico's political status and of focusing instead on the creation of a democratic culture. In this history *cum* autobiography, Muñoz, son of one of the ruling patrician families "defeated" by the U.S. occupation, comes across as defiant. In an observation that is as brilliant as it is arrogant, he compares himself with his "contemporary," U.S. imperial expansion (both were born in 1898), and judges himself superior: "Creo que yo he podido aprender más que mi contemporáneo, por una razón sencilla . . . : yo he podido dedicarme bastante a observar su crecimiento, mientras él . . . escasamente ha tenido tiempo o interés para observarse a sí mismo" (73, my translation) [I believe that I have been able to learn more than my contemporary, for a simple reason . . . : I have been able to devote sufficient time to observing its growth, while it . . . has hardly had the time or the interest to observe itself]. Vigilance and astuteness appear here as the marks of his combativeness.

13 In Spanish the Commonwealth of Puerto Rico is known as the *Estado Libre Asociado*, or the Free Associated State, a brilliant (and/or astute) amalgam of the three status options presently available to Puerto Ricans.

14 See in addition to the work of A. G. Quintero Rivera, J. Flores, J. L. González, and A. Díaz Quiñones, the recent work of Juan Gelpí and María Elena Rodríguez.

15 Another way of describing this hegemonic discourse of modernization is to say that it is populist. The paradox of a modernizing project and a precapitalist rhetoric is of course typical of populism. For a discussion of populism, see Juan José Baldrich's doctoral dissertation, "Class and the State: The Origins of Populism in Puerto Rico, 1934–1952," and Doris Sommer, *One Master for Another: Populism as Patriarchal Rhetoric in Dominican Novels.*

16 See his *Literatura y paternalismo en Puerto Rico.*

17 In *The Voice of the Masters,* Roberto González Echevarría deconstructs what he terms, following José Enrique Rodó's canonical essay, *Ariel* (1900), the Latin American essays's "magisterial voice." It is my contention that, unlike the texts studied by González Echevarría, Puerto Rican canonical texts *exhibit* their failure to assume that "magisterial voice."

18 In addition, Puerto Rico's status, in U.S. jurisprudence, is that of an aberrant "unincorporated territory," a territory which "belongs to but is not a part of" the United States. See Manuel del Valle y Colón, "Puerto Rico Before the United States Supreme Court," 13–91.

19 I am thinking here of Nietzsche's reading, in *The Genealogy of Morals,* of the Judeo-Christian morality of weakness, what he calls "slave morality," as a ruse to conquer and overcome the aristocratic, the strong.

20 In *Foundational Fictions: The National Romances of Latin America,* Sommer demonstrates how in the emerging Latin American republics of the nineteenth century "erotic passion" was an "opportunity (rhetorical and otherwise) to bind together heterodox constituencies" (14).

21 We could thus read Edgardo Rodríguez Juliá's chronicle on Luis Muñoz Marín's funeral, *Las tribulaciones de Jonás,* as the power of the patriarch to rally the nation through impotence and death, and in his text, Muñoz is indeed portrayed, shortly before his death, as an aphasic or defective model of paternal authority. Finally, using a very Puerto Rican turn of phrase, Rodríguez Juliá reminds us that in the funeral the leadership of Muñoz's party must "cargar el muerto" (60), that is, literally carry (the coffin of) the deceased and to figuratively submit to his authority. See Rubén Ríos Avila's brilliant discussion of defective authority in Rodríguez Juliá's texts, "La invención de un autor: escritura y poder en Edgardo Rodríguez Juliá."

22 In her introduction to *Inside/Out: Lesbian Theories, Gay Theories,* Diana Fuss notes that "the homosexual" is often culturally represented as "specter and phantom, as spirit and revenant, as abject and undead. Those inhabiting the inside . . . can only comprehend the outside through the incorporation of a negative image. This process of negative interiorization involves turning homosexuality inside out, exposing not the homosexual's abjected insides but the homosexual as the abject, as the contaminated and expurgated insides of the heterosexual subject" (3).

23 The nation as castrated figure—impotent father and/or dead or deformed child—dates back to the Puerto Rican nineteenth century. Pictorially, it is inscribed in what is emblematically the most important Puerto Rican painting of the nineteenth century, a real

foundational "text" if there is one, Francisco Oller's *El velorio* (1893). See Jorge Soto's pictorial reworking of this image in *El velorio de Oller en Nueva York* and Rafael Trelles's recent installation *Visitas al Velorio* (1991). For a textual reworking of this figure, see Edgardo Rodríguez Juliá's ambitious novel, *La noche oscura del Niño Avilés* (1984).

24 I certainly do not mean to equate castration with "femininity." On the contrary, I mean to underscore the fact that such an equation is a fundamental presupposition of patriarchy. In this sense, see Luce Irigaray, *Ce sexe qui n'est pas un*.

25 In *Vested Interests: Cross-Dressing and Cultural Anxiety*, Marjorie Garber argues that the figure of the transvestite in a text is the overdetermined sign of "a *category crisis elsewhere*, an irresolvable conflict or epistemological crux that destabilizes comfortable binarity, and displaces the resulting discomfort onto a figure that already inhabits, indeed incarnates, the margin" (17). In what follows I will be arguing, along these lines, that the figure of the transvestite and the "effeminate" in Marqués and Pedreira are an overdetermined sign for the crisis of the hierarchical binaries that sustain their paternalistic national discourse.

26 For a relevant discussion of "homosexual panic" and the "closet," see Eve Kosofsky Sedgwick, "The Beast in the Closet," *Epistemology of the Closet* 182–212.

27 In his *Tenth Epistle* to Can Grande, Dante formulates a four-part allegorical interpretative scheme which rises from the literal to the allegorical meaning proper, then to the moral, and finally to the anagogical.

28 His words are "vendaval democratizador," "El cuento puertorriqueño en la promoción del cuarenta," *Ensayos (1953–1971)* 93.

29 A clear emblem of this attempt to "nationalize" modernity by appealing to a nineteenth-century paternalistic rhetoric is the figure of the father in Marqués's novel, *La víspera del hombre*, don Rafa, who paradoxically stands in both for the old *hacendado* values of his inland farm of San Isidro and for capitalism's displacement of the protagonist Pirulo toward the more modern coastal farm of Carrizal and ultimately toward the city, which is, in the end, the father's home. Don Rafa, it can be argued, teaches Pirulo to assume the displacement of modernity while retaining paternalism's centering values. In this sense, Marqués's novel is faithful to the traditional bildungsroman (for example, Goethe's *Wilhelm Meister*), where capitalism's dislocations, represented by youth, can still be recuperated by a premodern ideological structure. See Franco Moretti, "The Comfort of Civilization," *The Way of the World*.

30 On camp as an aesthetization of life, see Susan Sontag's classic "Notes on Camp."

31 It is not, that is, another ontological category such as Magnus Hirschfeld's "third sex." It is, however, a "third" in the sense employed by Garber in *Vested Interests:* "The third is that which questions binary thinking and introduces a crisis" (11).

32 See, for instance, Díaz Quiñones, "Los desastres de la guerra: Para leer a René Marqués" 21; and José Luis González, "Plebeyismo y arte en el Puerto Rico de hoy," *El país de cuatro pisos* 102–4. For a reading of Sánchez's text not simply as a "text of rupture" but as a "hybrid" text, see Gelpí's *Literatura y paternalismo en Puerto Rico*.

33 Although my focus here is not a Puerto Rican lesbian and gay literature of identity, I certainly do not mean to either devalue it or dismiss it. My intention is instead to widen the register for a possible Puerto Rican homosexual criticism by exploring the varied—and central—nonidentity-based forms that homosexual desire and consciousness have taken in Puerto Rican culture. In this sense, a Puerto Rican lesbian and gay literature of identity may be seen as one more expression or mode of lesbian and gay desire and consciousness in Puerto Rican culture.

34 I certainly do not mean to claim here that the appropriation of the figure of paternal abjection is the only way in which homosexual desire has expressed itself in Puerto Rican literature or culture. It is just *one* of the many nonidentity-based ways in which lesbian and gay desire has asserted itself in Puerto Rican culture. Furthermore, although Magali García Ramis's bildungsroman *Felices días, tío Sergio,* whose "impotent" protagonist represents an alternative rallying point for the nation, could be convincingly read as an appropriation of paternal abjection, it seems that by and large this sort of appropriation is more available to male than female writers. For an important discussion of García Ramis's text as bildungsroman, see Gelpí.

35 By "hybridity" I do not mean here a positive ontology but that negative, abject state of neither-nor that the hegemonic discourse both displays and condemns. I do not mean, that is, the traditional developmentalist view of Puerto Rican culture as a *"puente entre dos culturas,"* or a harmonic "bridging" of Latin American and North American cultures—a view presupposed by both the liberal endorsement of Puerto Rican culture and the left's disparaging evaluation of it.

36 *Relajo,* literally relaxation, designates the set of cultural practices through which Puerto Ricans carnivalize all solemn and unitary forms. Because *relajo* seems to have no other function than this carnivalization, it has often been the target of criticism by Puerto Rican and Caribbean intellectuals. For an important statement on the relationship of *relajo* to Latino identity politics in the United States, see Juan Flores and George Yúdice, "Living Borders/Buscando América: Languages of Latino Self-Formation."

37 For a perceptive reading of *La guaracha* as a rewriting of *Insularismo,* see Gelpí, *Literatura y paternalismo en Puerto Rico* 17–45.

38 For postmodernism as the crisis of "master narratives," such as the hegemonic discourse of modernity of which we speak, see Jean-François Lyotard, *The Postmodern Condition: A Report on Knowledge,* Fredric Jameson, "Postmodernism and Consumer Society," and Jean Baudrillard, "The Ecstasy of Communication."

39 For a detailed analysis of *La guaracha,* see my "Repetition and the Language of the Mass Media in Luis Rafael Sánchez's *La guaracha del Macho Camacho.*"

40 See, for example, Otto Fenichel's classic psychoanalytic essay on transvestism, "The Psychology of Transvestism." For a review of the literature on transvestism as fetishism, see Carole-Ann Tyler, "Boys Will Be Girls: The Politics of Gay Drag."

41 For a reading of Ramos Otero's writing as provocation, see Rubén Ríos Avila, "La escritura como provocación."

42 "Rien ne tue un homme comme d'être obligé de représenter un pays" [Nothing kills a man like being obligated to represent a country] is Jacques Vaché's comment to André Breton, quoted in *Rayuela* 14.

43 For a detailed analysis of Ramos Otero's fiction, see my "Para virar al macho: La autobiografía como subversión en la cuentística de Manuel Ramos Otero."

Works Cited

Albanese, Lorelei. "Arnaldo Roche's Wounded Puerto Rico." *The San Juan Star* (San Juan, Puerto Rico) 12 June 1986: 35.

Algarín, M., and M. Piñero. *Nuyorican Poetry.* New York: William Morrow, 1975.

Andreu Iglesias, César, ed. *Memorias de Bernardo Vega.* Río Piedras: Huracán, 1980.

Bakhtin, Mikhail. *Rabelais and His World.* Cambridge, Mass.: Harvard University Press, 1968.

Baldrich, Juan José. "Class and the State: The Origins of Populism in Puerto Rico, 1934–1952." Ph.D. Diss., Yale University, 1981.

Barradas, Efraín. "El machismo existencialista de René Marqués," *Sin Nombre* 8.3 (1977): 69–81.

Baudrillard, Jean. "The Ecstasy of Communication." *The Anti-Aesthetic.* Ed. Hal Foster. Port Townsend, Wash.: Bay Press, 1983.

Butler, Judith. "Imitation and Gender Insubordination." *Inside/Out: Lesbian Theories, Gay Theories.* Ed. Diana Fuss. 13–31.

———. *Gender Trouble: Feminism and the Subversion of Identity.* New York, London: Routledge, 1990.

Campos, Ricardo, and Juan Flores. "Migración y cultura nacional puertorriqueñas: Perspectivas proletarias." *Puerto Rico: Identidad nacional y clases sociales (Coloquio de Princeton).* Río Piedras: Ediciones Huracán, 1979.

Clifford, Gay. *The Transformations of Allegory.* London, Boston: Routledge & Kegan Paul, 1974.

Cortázar, Julio *Rayuela.* Buenos Aires: Sudamericana, 1975.

Cruz-Malavé, Arnaldo. "Para virar al macho: La autobiografía como subversión en la cuentística de Manuel Ramos Otero." *Revista Iberoamericana* 59.162–63 (Jan.–June 1993): 239–63.

———. "Repetition and the Language of the Mass Media in Luis Rafael Sánchez's *La guaracha del Macho Camacho.*" *Latin American Literary Review* 13 (July–Dec. 1985): 35–48.

Darío, Rubén. *Cantos de vida y esperanza.* Madrid: Austral, 1980.

del Valle y Colón, Manuel. "Puerto Rico Before the United States Supreme Court." *Revista Jurídica de la Universidad Interamericana* 19 (1984): 13–91.

Deleuze, Gilles. *Masochism: Coldness and Cruelty.* New York: Zone Books, 1989.

Díaz Quiñones, Arcadio. "Los desastres de la guerra: Para leer a René Marqués." *Sin Nombre* 10.3 (Oct.–Dec. 1979): 15–44.

———. "Recordando el futuro imaginario: la escritura histórica en la década del treinta." *Sin Nombre* 14.3 (April–June 1984): 35.

Fanon, Frantz. *Black Skin, White Masks.* New York: Grove Weidenfeld, 1968.

Fenichel, Otto. "The Psychology of Transvestism." *Psychoanalysis and Male Sexuality.* Ed. Hendrik M. Ruitenbeek. 1930; rpt. New Haven: College and University Press, 1966. 203–10.

Ferré, Rosario. *Papeles de Pandora.* Mexico City: Joaquín Mortiz, 1976.

Flores, Juan. *Insularismo e ideología burguesa (Nueva lectura de A. S. Pedreira).* Río Piedras: Huracán, 1979.

———, and George Yúdice. "Living Borders/Buscando América: Languages of Latino Self-Formation." *Social Text* 24 (1990): 57–84.

Fragoso, Víctor. *El reino de la espiga.* New York: Nueva Sangre, 1973.

———. *Ser islas/Being Islands.* New York: El Libro Viaje, 1976.

Freud, Sigmund. "The Dissolution of the Oedipus Complex." *The Freud Reader.* Ed. Peter Gay. New York, London: W. W. Norton, 1989. 661–66.

———. "Fetishism." *The Complete Psychological Works of Sigmund Freud.* Vol. 20 (1927–31). Trans. James Strachey in collaboration with Anna Freud. London: Hogarth Press and the Institute of Psycho-Analysis, 1961. 149–57.

Fuss, Diana. *Essentially Speaking.* New York and London: Routledge, 1989.

———, ed. *Inside/Out: Lesbian Theories, Gay Theories.* New York, London: Routledge, 1991.

Garber, Marjorie. *Vested Interests: Cross-Dressing and Cultural Anxiety*. New York, London: Routledge, 1992.

García, Gervasio L., and A. G. Quintero Rivera. *Desafío y solidaridad*. Río Piedras: Huracán, 1982.

García Lorca, Federico. "Llanto por Ignacio Sánchez Mejías." 1935. *Antología poética*. Ed. Guillermo de Torre and Rafael Alberti. Buenos Aires: Losada, S. A., 1971. 163–68.

García Ramis, Magali. *Felices días, tío Sergio*. Río Piedras: Cultural, 1986.

Gelpí, Juan. "La cuentística antipatriarcal de Luis Rafael Sánchez." *Hispamérica* 15.43 (1986): 113–20.

———. *Literatura y paternalismo en Puerto Rico: Estudio del canon*. Río Piedras: University of Puerto Rico Press, 1993.

González, José Luis. *El país de cuatro pisos*. Río Piedras: Huracán, 1980.

González Echevarría, Roberto. *The Voice of the Masters*. Austin: University of Texas Press, 1985.

Hortas, Carlos. "René Marqués's *La mirada*: A Closer Look." *Latin American Literary Review* 8.16 (1980): 201–4.

Irigaray, Luce. *Ce sexe qui n'est pas un*. Paris: Minuit, 1977.

Jameson, Fredric. "Postmodernism and Consumer Society." *The Anti-Aesthetic*. Ed. Hal Foster. Port Townsend, Wash.: Bay Press, 1983.

Lacan, Jacques. *Ecrits*. Trans. Alan Sheridan. New York, London: W. W. Norton, 1977.

Lyotard, Jean-François. *The Postmodern Condition: A Report on Knowledge*. Minneapolis: University of Minnesota Press, 1984.

Marqués, René. *En una ciudad llamada San Juan*. Río Piedras: Editorial Cultural, 1970.

———. *Ensayos (1953–1971)*. Río Piedras: Antillana, 1972.

———. *La mirada*. Río Piedras: Antillana, 1975.

———. *Vía crucis del hombre puertorriqueño*. Río Piedras: Antillana, 1971.

———. *La víspera del hombre*. Río Piedras: Cultural, 1985.

Moretti, Franco. "The Comfort of Civilization." *The Way of the World*. London: Verso, 1987.

Muñoz Marín, Luis. *La historia del Partido Popular Democrático*. San Juan: Editorial El Batey, 1984.

Newton, Esther. *Mother Camp: Female Impersonators in America*. Chicago: University of Chicago Press, 1972.

Parker, Andrew, Mary Russo, Doris Sommer, and Patricia Yaeger. *Nationalisms and Sexualities*. New York, London: Routledge, 1991.

Pedreira, Antonio S. *Insularismo*. Río Piedras: Edil, 1969.

Quintero Rivera, A. G. "Clases sociales e identidad nacional; notas sobre el desarrollo nacional puertorriqueño." *Puerto Rico: Identidad nacional y clases sociales (Coloquio de Princeton)*. Río Piedras: Ediciones Huracán, 1979.

———. *Conflictos de clase y política en Puerto Rico*. Río Piedras: Ediciones Huracán, 1976.

——— and Gervasio L. García. *Desafío y solidaridad*. Río Piedras: Ediciones Huracán, 1982.

———, ed. *La lucha obrera en Puerto Rico*. San Juan: CEREP, 1971.

———. *Patricios y plebeyos: burgueses, hacendados, artesanos y obreros*. Río Piedras: Huracán, 1988.

Rama, Angel. "Crisis y transformación de la literatura puertorriqueña." *Zona de carga y descarga* (Sept.–Oct. 1972): 5–9.

Ramos, Julio, ed. *Amor y anarquía: Los escritos de Luisa Capetillo*. Río Piedras: Huracán, 1992.

Ramos Otero, Manuel. *Concierto de metal para un recuerdo y otras orgías de soledad*. Río Piedras: Cultural, 1971.

————. *El cuento de la mujer del mar*. Río Piedras: Huracán, 1979.

————. *Cuentos de buena tinta*. San Juan: Instituto de Cultura Puertorriqueña, 1992.

————. *Invitación al polvo*. Río Piedras: Plaza Mayor, 1991.

————. *El libro de la muerte*. Río Piedras, New York: Cultural and Waterfront Press, 1985.

————. *La novelabingo*. New York: El Libro Viaje, 1976.

————. *Página en blanco y stacatto*. Madrid: Playor, 1987.

Ríos Avila, Rubén. "La escritura como provocación." *El Mundo* (San Juan, Puerto Rico) 6 March 1988.

————. "Gaiety Burlesque: Homosexual Desire in Puerto Rican Literature." *Piso 13* 2.3 (Sept.–Dec. 1993): 8–9. Originally read at the Third Annual Lesbian and Gay Studies Conference at Yale University, 1989.

————. "La invención de un autor: escritura y poder en Edgardo Rodríguez Juliá." *Revista Iberoamericana* 59.162–63 (Jan.–June 1993): 203–19.

Rodó, José Enrique. *Ariel*. Mexico City: Porrúa, 1983.

Rodríguez Castro, María Elena. "Las casas del porvenir: Nación y narración en el ensayo puertorriqueño." *Revista Iberoamericana* 59.162–63 (Jan.–June 1993): 33–54.

————. "La escritura de lo nacional y los intelectuales puertorriqueños." Ph.D. Diss., Princeton University, 1988.

Rodríguez Juliá, Edgardo. *El entierro de Cortijo*. Río Piedras: Huracán, 1982.

————. *La noche oscura del Niño Avilés*. Río Piedras: Huracán, 1984.

————. *Las tribulaciones de Jonás*. Río Piedras: Ediciones Huracán, 1981.

Rodríguez Matos, Carlos. "Actos de Amor: Introducción al estudio de la poesía puertorriqueña homosexual y lesbiana." *Desde Este Lado/From This Side* 1.2 (Fall 1990): 23–24.

————. *Matacán*. Madrid: Playor, 1982.

————. *Llama de amor vivita: Jarchas*. South Orange, N.J.: Ichali, 1988.

Ross, Andrew. "Uses of Camp." *No Respect: Intellectuals and Popular Culture*. London: Routledge, 1989.

Sánchez, Luis Rafael. "Las divinas palabras de René Marqués." *Sin Nombre* 10.3 (Oct.–Dec. 1979): 11–14.

————. *En cuerpo de camisa*. San Juan: Ediciones Lugar, 1966.

————. "La generación 'O sea'." *Claridad* (San Juan, Puerto Rico) 23 January 1972:22.

————. *La guaracha del Macho Camacho*. Buenos Aires: Ediciones de La Flor, 1976.

————. *La importancia de llamarse Daniel Santos*. Hanover, N.H.: Ediciones del Norte, 1988.

Sandoval Sánchez, Alberto. "La identidad especular del allá y del acá." *Boletín del Centro de Estudios Puertorriqueños* 4.2 (Spring 1992): 29–43.

Sarduy, Severo. *La simulación*. Caracas: Monte Avila, 1982.

Sarmiento, Domingo. *Facundo: Civilización y barbarie*. Madrid: Alianza Editorial, 1970.

Sedgwick, Eve Kosofsky. "The Beast in the Closet." *Epistemology of the Closet*. Berkeley: University of California Press, 1990. 182–212.

Silverman, Kaja. *The Subject of Semiotics*. New York, London: Oxford University Press, 1983.

Solá, María. "René Marqués ¿escritor misógino?" *Sin Nombre* 10.3 (Oct.–Dec. 1979): 83–97.

Sommer, Doris. *Foundational Fictions: The National Romances of Latin America*. Berkeley: University of California Press, 1991.

————. "A Nowhere for Us: The Promising Pronouns in Cortázar's 'Utopian' Stories." *Dispositio* 9.24–26 (1984): 66, 75.

————. *One Master for Another: Populism as Patriarchal Rhetoric in Dominican Novels*. Lanham, Md.: University Press of America, 1983.

Sontag, Susan. "Notes on Camp." *A Susan Sontag Reader*. Intro. Elizabeth Hardwick. New York: Vintage Books, 1983. 105–19.

Tyler, Carole-Ann. "Boys Will Be Girls: The Politics of Gay Drag." *Inside/Out: Lesbian Theories, Gay Theories*. Ed. Diana Fuss. 32–70.

Umpierre, Luz María. *The Margarita Poems*. Bloomington: Third Woman, 1987.

Vasconcelos, José. *La raza cósmica*. Mexico City: Colección Austral, 1976.

Villanueva Collado, Alfredo. *Grimorio*. Barcelona: Murmurios, 1986.

———. *En el imperio de la papa frita*. Santo Domingo: Colmena, 1989.

———. *La voz de la mujer que llevo dentro*. New York: Arca, 1990.

———. *Pato salvaje*. New York: Arcas, 1991.

Zenón Cruz, I. *Narciso descubre su trasero*. Vol. I. Humacao: Furidi, 1974. Vol. II (1975).

José Quiroga

Fleshing Out Virgilio Piñera
from the Cuban Closet

Si pregunta por mí, traza en el suelo
una cruz de silencio y de cenizas
sobre el impuro nombre que padezco.
—Emilio Ballagas

Silence, Secret and Sex

"What he wrote" said Guillermo Cabrera Infante of Virgilio Piñera "are only the notes in the margin of his marginal life." And he adds: "Few people like him could say my life is an open book and then say in the same breath that his book is an open life."[1] But is the life truly an open book? And is the book truly the perfect imitation of life? Cabrera Infante can only conceive of one secret in Piñera's life/book, and this secret is, of course, the fact that Piñera liked men. But is this truly the only secret? Seen from a certain kind of angle this is certainly not a secret at all—for if we actually think that this is the most private inner sanctum of a life, then we are playing into Cabrera's heterosexist reading of a gay writer (of any gay writer) as one who is defined by his "condition." I'd rather use a different anecdote in order to illuminate Piñera's situation within Cuban literary discourse. The place is Algiers, and the time is 1964. According to the Spanish writer Juan Goytisolo, and as recounted by Guillermo Cabrera Infante, when Ernesto "Ché" Guevara saw a volume of Virgilio Piñera's *Teatro completo* in the Cuban embassy, he hurled it against a wall: "How dare you have in our embassy a book by this foul faggot!" he shouted, to an astonished and at that time, fairly closeted, Goytisolo.[2]

Why did El Ché react with such venom toward such an insignificant vol-

ume of plays? Let us pause and consider what is it that El Ché considers
truly indecent, in order to trace an arc around the complicities involved in
"gayness" and subversion: the fact that Piñera's book is found in an embassy (that this representative Cuban space outside of Cuba contains this
book as an embodiment of *letras patrias*) and that the book in some way
may be misconstrued as a model of what revolutionary Cuban literature
is. The sin is also compounded by having such a book by such a foul faggot in another revolutionary situation (Algiers), for according to El Ché,
the space of the faggot is diametrically opposed to the very hygiene of the
revolution. I will have more to say on what is it that bothers El Ché so
much, not only about Piñera but precisely about this book, but for the
moment I want to place this scene in an emblematic space, as a perverse
response to Cabrera Infante's notion of Piñera's life "as a book." Piñera's
book, I think, is not only a book without secrets but an object that, presumably, everybody kicks around. It may be that it is precisely because
of the lack of a secret that *Teatro completo* is thrown about, from one corner of the room to the other—but this is also a gesture that the passive
silence of the book seems to allow. For, rather than a book of life that has
only one secret insistently proclaimed as a nonsecret, Piñera's volume is
marked by reticence, and the "secret" is constructed and deconstructed by
other people's voices and in other people's memoirs. In this sense, Piñera's
death in Havana in 1979 not only mobilizes Cabrera Infante's recollection
of Piñera's books and of Piñera's life, but is the prelude to a dispute, on
Piñera and on the relative tolerance of the revolution toward homosexuals.
What I would argue is that the main topic of this dispute is not secret, but
silence—certainly an element that forces us to qualify the idea of life as an
open book.

Some facts of Virgilio Piñera's "life" can be read in a volume. The son
of a working-class family, Piñera was born in Cárdenas in 1912 and, before the Revolution of 1959, left Cuba three times for Argentina (1946–
47, 1950–54, 1955–58), where he met Borges and his circle, published in
Anales de Buenos Aires, and established a friendship with Witold Gombrowicz, another expatriate living in Buenos Aires, whose novel *Ferdidurke,*
Piñera, among others, translated.[3] Piñera had already written a considerable body of work before the Revolution of 1959: his novel *René's Flesh,*
a collection of stories (*Cuentos fríos*) and plays like *Electra Garrigó, Jesús,*
and *Aire frío.* After 1959, Piñera wrote for the journal *Revolución* and the
literary supplement *Lunes.* He was arrested on 11 October 1961, and spent a
brief period in jail. Although he was not sent to the notorious UMAP camps
("Unidades Militares de Ayuda a la Producción," active from 1965 to 1967)

where the Revolution imprisoned homosexuals and other "antisocial" elements, Piñera was, according to most accounts, internally ostracized, a writer who was seldom published, and whose immense output trickles out of Havana in piecemeal fashion after his death.[4] It is this silence during the more or less ten years before his death that I would like to examine at this point.[5] Depending on your political point of view, this was the silence of fear, of repression, of inner exile, the silence of the literary closet and of the refusal to come out of that closet or, perhaps, this was the silence of the heroic. For me, it completes the arc of the book that is thrown from one corner of the room to the other in Algeria by El Ché. Silence suspends the book in midair, in midflight, in a perfect seesawing motion: in one corner of the room, the book signifies total outness, in the other corner, the book is consigned to the realm of the totally closeted. In one corner Cuba, in the other corner Algeria, in one corner the hero, and then, in the other, the coward. Leaving aside for the moment the very implications of this opposition (and the notions of masculinity deployed by that very opposition), I want to leave this book flying in the air, *volando;* I want to arrest the motion of this flying object and read Piñera's silence as a kind of cypher that becomes, over time, an intricate weapon.

What kind of a weapon can silence ever be—especially when a society as a whole is bent on a theatrical demonstration of what it means to defy all possible odds for the sake of revolutionary social justice? Before the paradox can be explored, consider this scene from Piñera's best novel, *René's Flesh,* an erotic tale of masculine desire, a tropical version of Witold Gombrowicz's *Ferdidurke,* an account of the nightmares of masculinity that climax in a school scene where the attentive pupils of Dr. Márblo patiently lick René's flesh in order to initiate it into a bizarre cult of the flesh. "It's necessary that René's flesh be licked systematically. What I mean is, licked from the top of his head to the tip of his toes," says Swyne, one of the instructors:

> Just as we test the point of a pen once or twice and, assured of its quality, move it from left to right over the sheet of paper, and now and then the hand pauses as the brain vacillates between one thought and another, so too Roger stuck out his tongue to it once or twice to assure himself of the quality of its point. Without a doubt, it would only have occurred to a master in such an art to have chosen that part of the body for his test. Roger resembled one of those calligraphers who makes a few strokes in the margin of the page with his pen. He let go of the toe and moved over to the face. He slipped one hand

under René's head and leaned the other on his chest. Then he looked
at Swyne.

He was indicating the tongues that were to second Roger's. One for
each part of the body: two legs, two arms. As for the thoracic cage
and the stomach, they were considered one single section.

"Roger, please open the session," he said.

Roger licked René's forehead profoundly. He shook his head in
doubt. He passed his tongue over the rebel's lips. He shook his head
again.

"What's wrong, Roger?" Swyne asked.

"Hard as a rock," was all he said. (104)

[Igual que probamos una y otra vez el punto de la pluma y una vez
cerciorados de su bondad lo hacemos correr a izquierda y derecha del
papel, y a veces la mano se detiene porque el cerebro vacila entre un
pensamiento u otro, así también Roger sacó su lengua y tomando un
dedo del pie de René, la aplicó una y otra vez a fin de cerciorarse de
la bondad de su punta. . . . Roger se asemejaba a esos calígrafos que
pasan su pluma por los bordes del papel. Soltó el dedo y se trasladó
a la cara. Pasó una mano por debajo de la cabeza de René y apoyó la
otra en su pecho. Entonces, miró a Cochón.

Este fue señalando las lenguas que debían secundar la de Roger. Una
por cada parte del cuerpo: dos piernas, dos brazos . . .

—Roger, abra usted la sesión—dijo.

Roger lamió profundamente la frente de René. Movió la cabeza con
aire de duda. Pasó la lengua por los labios del rebelde. Volvió a mover
la cabeza.

—¿Qué pasa, Roger?—preguntó Cochón.

—Pétrea—se limitó a decir Roger.][6]

This has to be one of the more erotically charged moments in Cuban literature. The equation between Roger's tongue and a pen, and René's flesh
and the surface of paper, is the most transparent exposition of the erotics of
writing itself. The contact between tongue and flesh doubles the charged
eroticism of a writing inscribed as licking the hardened flesh of the allegorical René. Why is René's flesh so hard? This is the question that haunts
Piñera in his novel. As part of the school's program of instruction, students initiated in the cult of the flesh are subjected to contemplate strange
pictures of themselves as gleefully suffering, crucified Christs. The subjects
realize the weakness of the flesh so that in turn those same students can
be recruited for a political cause, which in Piñera's novel is centered on

chocolate. Flesh and politics are the two foci of Piñera's allegory which the loyal reader is treated to lick in order to soften its deliberate hardness. Within this allegory, Piñera is a voyeur—inscribing, examining the fissures within heterosexuality, as he denies himself the inner gaze that fathers and teachers demand of René.

Ramón, René's father, opens *René's Flesh* with a demand for self-observation: "Mira, tu cuerpo, el mío, el de tu madre, el de todo el mundo está hecho de carne. Esto es muy importante, y por olvidarlo con frecuencia, muchos caen víctima del cuchillo" (24) [Look: your body, mine, your mother's body—everyone's body is made of meat. This is very important, and because it is often forgotten, many people fall victim to the knife] (14). The father's demand is in itself a critique of Piñera's literature, for Piñera's stories and novels are outbursts of energy, twisted and convoluted tales that are written with no attention to style—as a matter of fact, with a deliberate flatness of style. Piñera is not the careful writer inscribed in the Neo-Baroque Cuban tradition of Lezama or Carpentier; he does not allow the reader to stop and look, he turns readers away from themselves. Indeed, one can say that the point of *René's Flesh* and of much of Piñera's works is to prevent the inner gaze—all of Piñera's plots are elaborate, masturbatory foils for something that the reader must not stop to contemplate. Our eyes are fixed on the shape and contours of reflections that try to overcome a certain kind of heaviness, against which all of the characters complain. This avoidance of the self, of observation, that gives the reader no respite, is what leads to Piñera's collapsing of text into flesh. But in this complex textual realm, the flesh does not reveal the true essence of a self. Flesh is, rather, a shield that avoids the readers' gaze into the self.

Piñera's story "El enemigo," for example, starts with a man asking his shoe shiner whether he is not afraid of himself. The man responds that he does not know what fear is, which then prompts the narrator to explain how the prime mover of *his* life is precisely fear. But this is not a fear that originates from the outside, or that goes outside, but a fear that is constantly inside: "Mi miedo es mi propio ser y ninguna revolución, ningún golpe de fortuna adversa podría derrocarle" (190) [My fear is my own self and no revolution, no stroke of adverse luck would be able to defeat it]. The narrator knows that the origin of this fear is guilt, but he does not know what it is that he feels guilty about (in fact he feels guilty for not knowing the origins of this guilt). The narrator understands that the only shield that he has left in terms of this guilt is literature, since authors do not only write about what they live, but also write about what they do not live. But literature is furthermore, as the narrator says, a shield that is perforated, traversed by the wounds of a battle. And, in Piñera's own words: "la tremenda perforación que él nos muestra es nada menos que la obra" [the immense perforation that it shows is none other than the work]. So Piñera collapses text into flesh in order to show a certain kind of wound: the flesh is the shield that the author puts up in order to cover himself, in order to engage in the battle against fear. The work, "la obra" is the perforation of that shield. Piñera's flesh is not just any flesh, but one that exists in order to be wounded, one that demands sacrifice as the site of observation. The book that we have been trying to read is one that Piñera writes on flesh in order to expose the wounds of the flesh, the work that allows the flesh itself to be wounded. The writer avoids the wounds, but the wounds are inevitably there, a result of the very kind of avoidance that the author seeks by means of writing. In this constantly moving universe of resistance and repression, readers are not necessarily asked to perforate the flesh, but to uncover a common space, as readers and writers, where pain and humiliation coexist. This is to be accomplished, once again, without looking at the self, without the inner gaze that literature seems to demand.

No critic should violate the space where the writer avoids self-observation without understanding, first of all, the subtleties of the system. My intention then is not to have Piñera look at himself, but to fill in the gaps to be found within his silence, and at the same time try not to betray its profoundly conflictive gesture. In order to uncover what Piñera's silence may mean, I want to read the introduction of the book that El Ché has thrown from one side of the room to the other. My aim is not to explain or examine Piñera's silence within the context of the cultural politics of the Cuban Revolution, but rather to complicate and nuance this silence from within. For gay writers need not be seen in terms of the context of their lives, their lives themselves provide the context of how they dangerously intersect with the state.

Montage for a Future Text

Any text on Virgilio Piñera should be ideally a kind of montage that aims to situate the intersection of this particular gay writer within the Cuban revolutionary situation, at least between 1959 and 1965. Piñera's subtle readings of sex, gender, and society within the context of silence, exile, and cunning demand precisely this kind of juxtaposition of different modes, with camera angles from Dziga Vertov, cinematic montages by Eisenstein, and the rapid narrative of revolutionary Cuban newsreels produced during the first years of the revolution. Since I cannot do justice to such an approach at this point, I will say that Piñera's silence demands at least a cursory reading of the issues *Bohemia* published in 1959, precisely the period in which he writes the introduction to the *Teatro completo* ignominiously thrown about by El Ché. A weekly compendium of news, information, cultural life, and social mores, *Bohemia* intersects, joins, and juxtaposes Eros and Thanatos in completely unabashed terms, by giving voice to a particularly important dialectics within the time: that of the pen and the sword. These two phallic objects (pen and sword) appear all over the pages of *Bohemia:* capitalists and revolutionaries, schoolteachers and farmers, the dead and mangled bodies of a revolution inscribed on the page. The context of the first years of the revolution is in itself a kind of montage of desires for the sword and fantasies of the pen. All these cultural scraps of a capitalism on its way out and of a hypermasculine and nationalist socialism on its way in, actually intersect in Piñera's notion of theater, as he explains it in his introduction to the collected edition of his theatrical works.

This is where we turn to *Teatro completo* and its preface, "Piñera teatral," which Virgilio writes as a kind of unveiling for a volume of masks—not a literary text but a text *of* literature, in other words, an essay presented as a deconstruction, but one that seems to avoid its own deconstructive turn, even as it constantly proclaims its self-awareness. Piñera, the man who avoids looking at himself, can only do so in this text as a character, and the character we find in "Piñera teatral" performs within a society engaged in a mass theatrical endeavor. Literature, as Piñera says in the introduction, has confined him to a cell [una prisión]. Unable to perform in life, the writer creates performances, and even, he adds, performs while writing. The passive act of writing entails the active art of performing, and these are joined in what Piñera calls "una salida"—a word that can only be poorly translated as a kind of verbal "sally." "Una salida," for Piñera, is a physical or verbal strike, it is what joins and translates words and actions. What the salida exposes is the particularly fictive condition of reality. As if to excuse himself for the opposition, he states, "Pero con todo, y a pesar de todo, soy teatral. . . . Es por ello que no he podido resistir al título de efecto, Piñera teatral y, lo que es de mayor importancia, hablar de mi teatro (perdón, de mi casi teatro, ya volveremos sobre esto) un poco a lo clown." [But after all and in spite of it all, I am theatrical. . . . This is why I have not been able to resist this title, theatrical Piñera, and what is even more important, to speak of my theater (I am sorry, of my quasi-theater, we will get back to this), like a clown.][7]

This seems like a deliberate cover-up for the central statement that follows, whose echoes have been surely understood by Ernesto Ché Guevara in the Cuban embassy in Algiers: "Siempre pensé asombrar al mundo con una salida teatral. Envidio al hombre que salió desnudo por la calle, envidio a ese otro que asombró a La Habana con sus bigotes de gato, envidio al que se hizo el muerto para burlar al sacerdote, y por supuesto, a Fidel Castro entrando en La Habana. Es la eterna historia de los literatos. . . . El marqués de Sade,—un libertino de poca monta—se vió reducido al triste papel de escribiente de su propia sexualidad" (8). [I always thought of surprising the world with a theatrical sally (salida). I envy the man that went out to the streets naked, I envy that other one that suprised Havana with his cat whiskers, I envy the one who feigned being dead in order to play a joke on the priest, and of course I envy Fidel Castro, entering Havana. It is the eternal story of literary men. . . . The Marquis de Sade—a petty libertine—saw himself reduced to the sad part of being the writer of his own sexuality.] The very simplicity of these words is deceptive, the mechanisms of avoidance extremely complex. Piñera does not pursue the image of himself as a modern-day Sade.[8] What he does, however, is substitute sadism for envy. The connections between envy and sadism, joined by the homoerotic desire for Fidel, allow for a network of dizzying rhetorical strategies.

Envy undoes the dichotomy between passive (writer) and active (hero), it mobilizes the scene of writing as sadistic perversion. The sadistic game (the crying game) that the writer will play consists in a kind of subtle tease whose immediate effects can be seen when Piñera explains the argument of his play *Jesús,* the story of a barber who discovers he has the ability to perform miracles, but decides not to act like the biblical Jesus, not to perform. It is because of Jesús's refusal to perform like his original in the biblical story, that he is condemned to death, forced to eat a Last Supper, etc. The key element that structures this play is Piñera's favorite: inversion—a word whose rhetorical deployment is in itself fraught with deliberately sexual overtones. Once again, Piñera brings Fidel into the equation: "¿Qué representa el personaje Jesús en mi obra? Pues el anti-Fidel. Y pesar de ser el anti-Fidel siente la nostalgia de no haber podido ser Fidel" (17) [What is represented by the character of Jesús in my work? Well, the anti-Fidel. And in spite of being the anti-Fidel he feels the nostalgia of not having been Fidel].

The very theatrical framework of these comments implies their masking a much more subversive reading of a sexual kind. For they immobilize Fidel as an actor who plays a part on a stage that the writer records, and they obscure, at the very least, the facile dichotomy between passive/active by framing it in the theater of words and actions. This mimetic play corresponds to Piñera's strategic take on the erotics of power and can be seen as a deliberate rhetorical ploy: the construction of a text that works by means of a series of veils, one that employs all of the usual dichotomies deployed in nationalist discourse while at the same time angling them toward a sexual reading. The intersections between the writer and the man of action are transformed into a meditation on the passive observer of reality, (the one who can only act by performing and by recognizing himself as a performer), and, on the character of the play who inverts the real acts of Jesús and at the same time stands in opposition to Fidel, the man of action who frames Virgilio Piñera's self-awareness within the rhetoric of envy.

Although all of these categories are fluid and mobile, these statements in themselves do not amount to an explanation for Virgilio Piñera's silence in subsequent years. There is no cause and effect in the difficult relationships between faggot and revolution but actually a series of complications that can be perceived in the baroque manner in which the system unfolds. It is not only the tone in which all of this is being said (as a seemingly careless construction of mirrors upon mirrors, of complications upon complications) but actually the very kind of neutrality and fluidity that these statements imply. Piñera does not provide the standard context for his self reading, but actually reads himself into a context. At the same time, the context that he has created for himself is predicated on his own powerlessness—a kind of identity of the meek that is fully aware of its own subversive power. The rhetorical play in "Piñera teatral" reveals an individual fully aware of his power within society, but it also reveals Piñera's lack of desire for the sexual status quo to change. What he desires is precisely to be at the space where this fluid construction is mobilized, where desire itself lies in being or not being passive or active, in constant doubt as to performance and frankness. What Piñera got in return is precisely the very construction of rigidity as national official discourse. Like René's flesh, official culture hardened into untenably fixed categories that have no basis in actual fact: homo and heterosexuality were *voiced* as mutually untenable contradictions that only silence could reveal as fiction.

Piñera's silence during the last decade of his life has to do with a secret exposed, but not necessarily exposed by him. The unquestionable power of the queer in this ontology is based on allowing the representation to continue, forcing the hetero to avoid self-reflexion and also forcing him to act all the time. Piñera says (but he does not say—his silence says it for him) that this is the only power that faggots may have, what allows them to subvert and at the same time reaffirm the blindness of masculinity. It is, moreover, a silence that is an assertion of passivity as power, the presentation of the pharmakon that actively refuses to come out in script. This power is affirmed as a silence: it cannot be named, for it is powerful as long as it reaffirms a fictional weakness, as long as it does not come out as power. There is no inside to this performance, but only successive masks that reproduce some level of theatricality. In this way, Piñera implicitly situates himself at the border where men are always playing the role of men, while the homosexual voyeur paradoxically reminds them that they should forget how artificial their own artifice may be. In this sense, El Ché's throwing of the book testifies that Piñera has already sexualized the revolutionary hero, he has turned him into a representation, has furnished that representation with a (homo)erotics.

What is true for Piñera is also valid, in a sense, for the work of other gay writers operating within the space of revolution, and here I should mention the paradoxical voice of Reinaldo Arenas within his recently published memoirs, *Before Night Falls*. In the midst of what seems like a phallic paradise of sorts (Cuba after the Revolution, the scene where compulsory heterosexuality is affirmed while it is at the same time denied) Arenas states his preference for the anonymity and fluidity of a sexual mode, and laments the Anglo definition of "gayness" that accompanies the assertion of homosexual identity, one that polarizes that same fluidity which is framed as somehow "edenic." A seemingly insignificant comment by Arenas, this is actually one of the more poignant moments in his book, the site of an ambivalence where homosexuality leads to the acceptance of silence as an ethical choice. Not to constitute a visibly "gay" minority allows the secretive members of that group (Piñera, Arenas, and others) to participate in delectable erotic scenes with otherwise straight but willing sexual partners. Arenas decries the vocal and separate community of the queer, where that paradisaical fluidity ends, where the nomadic search for bodies yields to the rigid parameters of the tribe.[9] Comments such as these shed light on Piñera's work and force us to understand what may be, for a North American audience, its more regressive modes.

The difficult conclusion to Piñera's manipulation of silence is that we should allow the blindness of heterosexuality to remain. And this nuances the very nature of the secret, of homosexuality, of sex and gender within revolution. That the most radically gay writer of his generation, the one who publicly opened the closet on Emilio Ballagas and homosexuality in 1955; the one who constantly criticized the official prerevolutionary attempts at veiling the "gay sensibility" of most Cuban art, chose silence and not contestation during the sixties and after definitely should make us pause. As Piñera himself says in his essay on Ballagas: "Tal dialéctica idiota produce tales mitos idiotas."[10] It is simply not enough to say, as Lourdes

Arguelles and B. Ruby Rich argue, that "the absence of any . . . public gay countercritique and resistance in this period [late sixties]" lies in the lack of a tradition of feminist discourse that would have situated the personal and the political in its proper context, or in the "contemporary conception of homosexuality . . . as a legacy of the prerevolutionary period . . . as something performed in the dark with little or no nonsexual implications."[11] Piñera's silence is born out of the insistence on his own nomadic sense of liberty, one that refuses the hygienized identities of a fictional self and that sought, as in his essay on Ballagas, to understand how and in what ways homosexuality was a "fatal," but also a liberatory, exception to the social norm. He openly reveals by his mere presence and absence that gender is not constituted according to a code of conduct but is, on the other hand, performatively constituted by the very "expressions" that are said to be its results. For Piñera, to turn that performance into a conscious gesture, to isolate its participants into a political tribe, goes against the grain of his erotic pleasure, one that depends precisely on the uncontrolled flux of desires.

It is important at this point in the growing internationalization of the gay movement to understand Piñera's silence as the theatrical embodiment of an impasse that many Cuban homosexuals felt and continue to feel within the repression of a masculinist order that condemns them to support either the capitalist or the socialist version of a nightmare. It was in order not to come out of this impasse that I feel compelled, as a reader (as a passive reader) to rehearse the modes of a confession that Piñera would never allow for himself in the text, playing off the passive and active modes of the confession with a melancholic tone diametrically opposed to the (repressed) desires that charge Piñera's mechanical plots. Back to Emilio Ballagas's lines quoted at the beginning of this essay, lines that Piñera took out of the closet in his famous 1955 defense of Ballagas as a homosexual writer: "Si pregunta por mí / traza una cruz de silencio sobre el impuro nombre que padezco." If Piñera gives us the true perversion of the master, if he situates us in the space where out of the closet, the individual steps onto the stage, then it is high time not to delineate a cross made of ashes and silence, but to tell him what Piñera didn't say: that I love El Ché, that the schizophrenic juxtaposition of his modes leaves me aphasic, that I move conscious only of my link (my subjection) to the whims of his power, while remaining in the space created by his sadism. And in the operatic demonologies created at this time, there's nothing lost by seducing this matador into a room full of smoke, where the smoke might confuse the roles, for us to fulfill what El Ché's burning cigar has held as a promise, with a smoke that has a particular color—green and cobalt—and a voice that must have a texture like the skin of ripened plantains. This is now what it means to be the author of one's own sexuality.

The book is still suspended, it is fragile, it is still arrested in midflight.

Notes

A version of this paper was read at the conference on "Gender, Sexualities, and the State: A Latino / Hispanic Context" at the University of California at Berkeley, 14–16 March 1993.

1   *Cold Tales* xi. All quotes in English are from this edition; page numbers appear in parenthesis in the text.

2   The account is found in Cabrera Infante's introduction to the volume cited above.

3   For the best account of Piñera in Buenos Aires, see Carlos Espinosa Domínguez "El poder mágico de los bifes (La estancia argentina de Virgilio Piñera)." Recollections written by Piñera appear in Rita Gombrowicz's compilation of documents, *Gombrowicz en Argentine (1939–1963)*, especially 69–88. The best essay on Piñera and Gombrowicz is Daniel Balderston's "Estética de la deformación en Gombrowicz y Piñera."

4   The best essay on the relationship between Piñera and the revolution is still Reinaldo Arenas's verbal tour de force "La isla en peso con todas sus cucarachas," reprinted in *Necesidad de libertad*, 115–31. For a good account of the strained relationship between the revolution and gays, see Allen Young's *Gays under the Cuban Revolution*. Because its treatment of gays was a crucial point of discussion among leftists in the United States, the literature of gays under the revolution is quite voluminous. I prefer to leave the political issue aside at this point. The issue deserves a much more comprehensive treatment that is outside of the bounds of this essay, which concerns basically the contradictions that need to be dealt with in terms of Piñera's sexual openness.

5   According to the *Diccionario de la literatura cubana*, Piñera's last work was a volume of poems titled *La vida entera* and published in 1969.

6   The Spanish text is from *La carne de René* 113. I am using Mark Schafer's translation, *René's Flesh*. Page numbers appear in parentheses.

7   Virgilio Piñera, "Piñera teatral" *Teatro completo* 8. All quotes are from this edition. Translations are mine.

8   As editor of *Ciclón*, the Cuban literary journal founded by José Rodríguez Feo after a dispute with José Lezama Lima and *Orígenes*, Piñera had risked all kinds of official cultural propriety by publishing fragments of a translation of Sade's *Las 120 jornadas de Sodoma*. In 1955, this was a deliberate slap in the face to official culture, given the obvious sexual implications of the work. As Piñera writes in the presentation (the text appears in a section of the journal titled "Textos futuros"): "Estas ciento veinte jornadas son como la culminación paroxística de todos sus escritos sobre la vida sexual del hombre: vida sexual que, para decirlo de una vez es una de las cuatro patas sobre las que descansa la gran masa humana" and later on, as a conclusion, "Pero dejemos al lector juzgar por sí mismo. Le creemos inteligente, sin moral al uso, sabedor que si debe leerse un escritor como Kafka que expresa, a través del terror, el absurdo de la vida humana, también está en el deber de informarse sobre un escritor llamado Sade que expresa, por medio del terror, la obscura

vida sexual del hombre." See Piñera, "Textos futuros: La 120 jornadas de Sodoma" 35.

9   I can only guide the reader to Nestor Perlongher's dazzling *La prostitución masculina* for
a more detailed consideration of this. See, especially, 127–34.

10 "Ballagas en persona" is an account of Piñera's attempts to deal with the official gloss
over Ballagas, who was married and had a child but was nevertheless a tormented homosexual throughout his life. Piñera begins the essay by stating "No bien Ballagas murió,
sus amigos comenzaron esa labor de enfriamiento que consiste en poner la personalidad del artista a punto de congelación." Piñera's aim is against the veiled discourse that
constantly alludes, but never, out of "respect" openly names Ballagas's "crime": "Si los
franceses escriben sobre Gide tomando como punto de partida el homosexualismo de
ese escritor; si los ingleses hacen lo mismo con Wilde, yo no veo por qué los cubanos no
podamos hablar de Ballagas en tanto que homosexual. ¿Es que los franceses y los ingleses
tienen la exclusiva de tal tema? No por cierto, no hay temas exclusivos ni ellos lo preten-
derían, sino que franceses e ingleses nunca estarán dispuestos a hacer de sus escritores ese
lechero de la Inmortalidad que tanto seduce a nuestros críticos." The essay was not only
scandalous but amounted, as early as 1955, to what we might now term a conscious outing
of one of Cuba's most important poets. I think it leads directly, as a sort of precursor outing of homosexuality, to Lezama's famous homosexual scenes in *Paradiso*. What Piñera
does, however, is not simply *out* Ballagas but explain his poetry and his life given the
complexity of the very closet and the very silence with which he (Ballagas) surrounded
himself. See Piñera "Ballagas en persona" 41–50.

11 Lourdes Arguelles and B. Ruby Rich, "Homosexuality, Homophobia and Revolution"
691.

Works Cited

Arenas, Reinaldo. *Necesidad de libertad. Mariel: testimonios de un intelectual disidente.* México:
Kosmos, 1986.

Arguelles, Lourdes and B. Ruby Rich. "Homosexuality, Homophobia and Revolution: Notes
toward an Understanding of the Cuban Lesbian and Gay Male Experience, Part I." *Signs:
Journal of Women in Culture and Society* 9.1 (1984): 683–99, esp. 691.

Balderston, Daniel. "Estética de la deformación en Gombrowicz y Piñera." *Explicación de textos
literarios* 19.2 (1990–91): 1–7.

Diccionario de la literatura cubana. La Habana: Editorial Letras Cubanas, 1980.

Espinosa Domínguez, Carlos. "El poder mágico de los bifes (La estancia argentina de Virgilio
Piñera)." *Cuadernos hispanoamericanos* 471 (Sept. 1989): 78–88.

Gombrowicz, Rita. *Gombrowicz en Argentine (1939–1963).* Paris: Editions Denoël, 1984.

Perlongher, Néstor. *La prostitución masculina.* Buenos Aires: Ediciones de la Urraca, 1993.

Piñera, Virgilio. "Ballagas en persona." *Ciclón* (La Habana) 1.5 (1955): 41–50.

————. "Textos futuros: Las 120 jornadas de Sodoma." *Ciclón* 1.1 (1955): 35.

————. *Teatro completo.* La Habana: Ediciones R. 1960.

————. *La vida entera.* La Habana: UNEAC, 1969.

————. *Cold Tales.* Trans. Mark Schafer. Hygiene, Colo.: Eridanos Press, 1988.

————. *La carne de René.* Madrid: Alfaguara, 1985.

————. *René's Flesh.* Trans. Mark Schafer. Boston: Eridanos Press, 1989.

Young, Allen. *Gays Under the Cuban Revolution.* San Francisco: Grey Fox Press, 1981.

Yvonne Yarbro-Bejarano
The Lesbian Body in Latina Cultural Production

Elsewhere in my work on the lesbian body, I made the point that, given the pervasiveness of various historical and cultural constructions of the female body and gender roles, neither the lesbian body nor lesbian desire can exist in a vacuum free from their pressures ("De-constructing"). In *Loving In the War Years,* California Chicana Cherríe Moraga engages in a project of textual dismemberment of the female body in order to re-imagine it in the space of lesbian desire. Moraga's poetry constantly constructs, destructs, and reconstructs the entire female body in recognition of how it has been appropriated and in the attempt to reclaim it. Virtually every poem in the collection hinges around a fragment of the body, which emerges whole and intact only when reconstructed in such a way that the heart replaces the head and mouth and sex merge, both represented as organs of speech and sex: "It's as if la boca were centered on el centro del corazón, not in the head at all. The same place where the cunt beats" (142).

In this paper, I wish to focus on a specific strategy of lesbian represen- tation within this overall project of reclamation, that of working simul- taneously within and against dominant cultural codes. In the title poem "Loving in the War Years," Moraga fills the signifiers of cult stars Bogie and Bergman in the film "Casablanca" with lesbian meanings to express the potentially fatal perils of loving women in a hostile, homophobic world:

> Loving you is like living
> in the war years.
> I *do* think of Bogart & Bergman
> not clear who's who
> but still singin a long smoky
> mood into the piano bar

. . . while bombs split
outside, a broken
world.

. . . .

Loving in the war years
calls for this kind of risking
. . . Not knowing
what deaths you saw today
I've got to take you
as you come, battle bruised
refusing our enemy, fear. (30)

Latina lesbians have no corner on this strategy; the same appropriation of heterosexual codes has always been at play in drag and butch-femme.

In their recent show, "Belle Reprieve," two members of New York's Split Britches, together with England's Bloolips, offer a hilarious, brilliant, gender-bending deconstruction of "Streetcar Named Desire," in which Blanche is played by a drag queen (of course), Mitch by a faggot, Stella by ravishing femme Lois Weaver and Stanley by bodacious butch Peggy Shaw. In their version of the scene where Stanley gets Stella back after beating her because Stella is hooked by her desire for him, Stella/Weaver, resplendent in cleavage, embraces the repentant Stanley/Shaw, complete with ripped T-shirt, kneeling at her feet. The T-shirt is discarded, and Stella throws arms and legs around a Stanley with breasts who carries her off stage in a very satisfyingly hot representation of lesbian desire. One of the straight Seattle papers ran a photograph of this scene with their review of the show, providing an unlikely, inevitably transitory, yet public space for lesbian bodies and desires.

In Latina cultural production, what interests me is the cultural specificity of the lesbianization of the heterosexual icons of popular culture. Since Latinas are multicultural, this involves taking over signifiers of both Latino or Latin American as well as of the dominant culture as Moraga did with "Casablanca." For as Gloria Anzaldúa writes, "(t)o live in the Borderlands means knowing/ . . . that denying the Anglo inside you/ is as bad as having denied the Indian or Black" (194). Within Chicano/Mexican culture, the primary sites of Moraga's lesbianizing strategies are the impact of popular Mexican Catholicism on sexuality and the narrative of La Malinche. La Malinche, otherwise known as Malintzín Tenepal, Doña Marina, and La Chingada [the fucked one], was sold to the Spanish colonizer Cortés, served as his translator and tactical advisor, and bore a mestizo or mixed-race child. Signifying betrayal of the race and culture, La Malinche is the reference point for the performative gender roles of masculinity as *chingón* (active) and femininity as *chingada* (passive). Moraga's writing forces its way through the structures of heterosexuality to liberate a space for the imagining of a Chicana lesbian desire that is both damaged and erotically empowered by culturally specific sexual/religious meanings, particularly in texts such as the play *Giving Up the Ghost* and the story "La ofrenda."

Rather than examine these strategies in depth in Moraga's writing, I would like to trace some horizontal parallels among a variety of cultural activities and media. Visual artist Ester Hernández, photographer/poet Marcia Ochoa, and performer/stand-up comic Monica Palacios, together with writer Gloria Anzaldúa, also exemplify what Chicana artist and art critic Amalia Mesa-Baines defines as the "re-positioning" of cultural icons, or what European American art critic Lucy Lippard calls "turning around," the reversal of an accepted image, often with humor and irony. This strategy of filling traditional imagery with new meanings is more complex than rejection, for such strategies both critique and derive power from the image reversed or re-positioned.

What characterizes much of this work is its outrageous outness, its in-your-face claiming of public space. For example, the cover of the anthology *Chicana Lesbians* is graced by the serigraph "La ofrenda" [the offering] by California Chicana Ester Hernández. In contrast to the self-effacing plain brown paper wrapping of yore, the book cover is white, with attention-grabbing, large letters for the title and its subtitle "The Girls Our Mothers Warned Us About," turning the whispered bedroom conversations between mothers and daughters into a public performance of identity. As opposed to other traditions of performing queer identity through the closet, the cover of *Chicana Lesbians* and the other work presented here practice an aesthetic of bold display, similar to that of the home altar (Ybarra, Turner). They simultaneously affirm communal traditions of spectacle ranging from religious and secular theater to altars and *retablos* and openly appropriate them for lesbian representation.

The context of the anthology interrupts a heterosexual reading of Hernández's image. "La ofrenda" works within and against two cultural traditions, the cult of the Virgin of Guadalupe and the tattooing of religious images on the body. Within Chicano culture, the full-back tattoo depicted in "La ofrenda" is a real practice which, while working-class marked and (generally but not always) masculine-gender specific, is not necessarily seen as taboo or irreverent. Instead, it is a part of the free circulation of religious icons and devotional practices within the *barrio* (Turner), as opposed

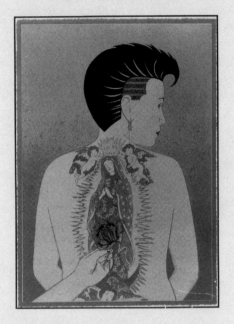

CHICANA LESBIANS
*The Girls Our Mothers
Warned Us About*

Edited by Carla Trujillo

Cover of *Chicana Lesbians: The Girls Our Mothers Warned Us About*. Ester Hernández, "La Ofrenda," 1988. Serigraph, 25⅛ × 37½ inches. Used with permission of the artist.

to the relative confinement of religious imagery to the private or sacred sphere in much of Anglo America.[1] For viewers from classes and cultures that do not practice this *particular* mode of inscribing "the force of the law on its subject . . . in order to . . . demonstrate the rule, to produce a 'copy' that makes the norm legible" (de Certeau 141), Hernández's image provides the frisson of "exotic," "primitive," "savage," or even "criminal" alterity.[2] Within the context of working-class Chicano culture, the female body merely replaces the male's as the normative site of the venerating tattoo. Together the image of the Virgin and the sheer size of the image construct the lesbian body-as-altar, while the lesbian context presses the religious icon transgressively into the representation of lesbian desire.

The feminine hand offering the rose makes the object of veneration both the image of the Virgin and the woman bearing it; that is, the woman offered the rose is not necessarily a *substitute* for the Virgin. The offering is both the rose extended in desire to the woman/Virgin as well as the lesbian body offered in desire to the lesbian viewer. The drops of blood on the offering fingers, produced by the rose's thorn, are at once erotic and a reference to the suffering occasioned by "loving [women] in the war years."

The editor of the anthology, Carla Trujillo, pointed out to me that from a distance the halo and figure of the Virgin resemble a vagina, and the rose a clitoris. (When informed of this reading, Hernández's only comment was, ". . . Interesting.") Read this way, "La ofrenda" reconstructs one lesbian body out of two, displacing and rearranging its anatomy (back/hand/sex) in a way not dissimilar to Moraga's (mouth/heart/sex), but here refiguring the organs of lesbian sex through the intensity of religious iconography and devotion. While "La ofrenda" in this context repositions the sacred image for lesbian representation, it also derives power from it, sharing in what Mesa-Baines calls "the transfigurative liberation of the icon" (137).

In reading this image, it is important to remember the semiotic richness of the Virgin of Guadalupe in Mexican/Catholic culture, productive of both religious and nationalist meanings. In her syncretic fusion of the Catholic Virgin Mother and the preconquest fertility deity Tonantzín, Guadalupe signifies the racial construction of Mexican national identity as the *mestizo* or hybrid product of the sexual union of Indian woman and male Spaniard. The intense investment in these particular meanings of the Virgin in the Mexican/Chicano imaginary is revealed by the violence of responses to contemporary artists' revisioning, such as Rolando de la Rosa's montage of Marilyn Monroe's face and bare breasts over the Virgin, itself a comment on the commercialization of sacred symbols in Mexican advertising (Lippard 43). When Chicana artist Yolanda López depicted the Virgin in the short dress and high heels of a contemporary working-class Mexican woman on the cover of the Mexican feminist magazine *fem*, its office received a bomb threat (Lippard 42). Another image of the Virgin by Hernández, titled "La Virgen de Guadalupe defendiendo los derechos de los Xicanos" [The Virgin of Guadalupe Defending the Rights of Chicanos] (1975, etching and aquatint, 19 × 15 inches), depicts her in karate attire and delivering a powerful kick. The appearance of this image on the cover of a Santa Rosa radio station's programming guide sparked fierce opposition, including the collection and burning of copies of the magazine.

At the same time that the anthology's imaging of the lesbian body in "La ofrenda" claims *mestiza* identity as an important subject position for

Marcia Ochoa, "(sometimes it's the little things that give you away)," 1991. Detail, black and white photograph and text series. Used with permission of the artist.

lesbian Chicanas, the reference to lesbian sexuality interrupts the discourse on femininity as sexless maternity in which the icon of the Virgin participates (both mother and virgin). This blending of the sensual with the spiritual, bare flesh and sexual desire with the power of religious iconography, is part of the cultural project Anzaldúa calls unlearning "the *puta/ virgen* [whore/virgin] dichotomy," of reading the pre-Columbian Mother back into Guadalupe (84). Both of Hernández' images of the Virgin disrupt dominant discourses on femininity and masculinity by transferring the codes assigned one gender to the other. The cover of *Chicana Lesbians* revisions the Chicana feminine, working within and against traditional cultural discourses to insist on the inclusion of lesbianism in the definition of both femininity and ethnicity.

Marcia Ochoa, a young Latina poet and photographer, uses the same title, "La ofrenda," for her first chapbook. As in Hernández' serigraph, there is a dual offering in the cover image of the chapbook: the heart and the lesbian body, both offered to the viewer. The rich seductiveness of the naked breasts and upturned face plays off the heart, stripped of romantic euphemism. Also offered is the display of how the signifiers of gender differentiation are manipulated. The shuffling of butch-femme codes demonstrates the willful construction of the lesbian body, in this case not the femme complemented and read as lesbian through the image of the butch, but the play of both signifiers across the same lesbian body. The butch image on the back cover, completely clothed, legs slightly spread and arms crossed in a stance of nonavailability, bespeaks the agency of touching and desiring, and completes the cover image of the same body as object of desire, alluring and slightly dangerous, offering a heart that the title poem reveals to have been ripped from that very body:

> With knowing hands
> and obsidian, I
> plunge
> through flesh, ribs, cartilege to reach
> inside.
>
> Quietly I sever
> each vein, aorta —
> bloodless I
> pull away clean.
>
> Superior vena cava sighs when I
> extricate

 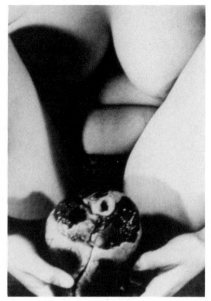

from my carcass this
mass
still undulating.

Take this, and eat it:
this is my body, which is broken for you:
do this in remembrance of me. (7)

The lesbianization (and fusion) of Aztecan blood sacrifice and Catholic Mass simultaneously replaces religious ritual with lesbian sex and the Christ/sacrificial victim figure with the lesbian body, broken and "eaten" in the enactment of a desire both dangerous and replenishing. The cover of *Chicana Lesbians* collapses two lesbian bodies in the construction of a third; in Ochoa's poem the lesbian body "knowingly" entered in a reenactment of sex/sacrifice is that of the poetic subject herself, offered in remembrance to the lover/other.

Ochoa's chapbook combines images taken from two different photographic works. In the triptych "La ofrenda," the text of the poem is placed below three images. On the left, the heart is held in the conventional place by a headless woman who offers both crotch and heart to the viewer. The central image, in which the heart is held between the subject's drawn-up legs, provides a graphic image of Moraga's reconstruction of the lesbian

Marcia Ochoa, "La ofrenda," 1991.
Black and white photograph triptych
and text. Used with permission of the
artist.

body positioning the heart in the vulva and displacing the head. In the
right-hand image, already discussed as the front cover of the chapbook, the
viewer looks down on the face and breasts of a woman who holds the heart
slightly away from her body in a gesture of offering and seduction. Like
Moraga, Ochoa restructures a colonized reality by rearranging its parts to
create a different reality, here through photographic representation.

Another piece by Ochoa, called "(sometimes it's the little things that
give you away)," measuring 30 × 40″, extends the strategy employed in
shorthand form by the chapbook, that of allowing the signifiers of butch-
femme to play across a single lesbian body. In this work, Ochoa combines
a running text with thirteen images in cinematic fashion. The photographer takes control of both visual and verbal signifiers, juxtaposing the
lesbian body with labels for lesbians in both English ("dyke") and Spanish ("tortillera," or woman who makes tortillas), and appropriating other
stereotypical phrases, for example "good with your hands," to comment on
lesbian sex. The following text is dispersed across the individual images, at
certain points positioned below a blank space:

Translated
into Spanish
and back into English

dyke
means
tortillera.
That means
you have to be good with your hands,
caress the masa
into moist passion.
My mother never finished teaching me how to
make tortillas.
No more standing by the side of the road for
you, sister.
Use the gas grill for that authentic flavor.
My mother gave up any hope that I would make tortillas
when she saw that I wore not dresses but combat boots.
(Sometimes it's the little things that give you away.)

The visual series begins with the butch image featured on the chapbook's back cover, where it appeared along with the biographical information about the poet, therefore suggestive of her authorial and sexual persona. While in the chapbook this persona is undermined and complemented by the front cover image, in the photocollage the butch figure dressed in black undergoes a gradual transformation, slowly taking on the accoutrements of a femme identity, first a necklace, then a headscarf, then an off-the-shoulder top, then a skirt (worn initially over the pants), and ending with classically "feminine" provocative poses. Ochoa sets up a dissonance between the visual and verbal texts by juxtaposing the final femme image with the following text: "My mother gave up any hope . . . when she saw that I wore not dresses but combat boots." The final phrase, "sometimes it's the little things that give you away" is not accompanied by an image.

The clichés of the verbal text take on a new resonance in this multilayered context, deconstructing binary notions of lesbian sexuality figured at times in butch-femme role-playing and arguing for a more fluid and multiple performance of lesbian identifications. In an artist's statement, Ochoa explicitly links ethnicity and gender in her revisioning of lesbian identity through photographic representation: "because if I can't be Carmen Miranda, I can't be a Nazi dyke either—I'm too boy to be Latina, but I'm too Latina to be a boy." Working from what she calls a "history of erasure," Ochoa's "exploration and explosion" of constructs require images that "haven't [been] found . . . before." Through a process of decentering that is both voluntary and involuntary she relocates herself within a new

Marcia Ochoa, "(sometimes it's the little things that give you away)," 1991. Detail, black and white photograph and text series. Used with permission of the artist.

hybrid cultural and sexual identity that is at the same time productive of an aesthetic, an aesthetic of the multiple image. Lippard has commented on the frequency of the binary image in artists who straddle two cultures (185), but Ochoa's multiple identities seem to require at least three (or thirteen).

No literary text, camera, or silkscreen mediates between Californian Monica Palacios and the consumer of the image of her body on the stage. In her act, which she calls an autobiographical trip—"part stand-up comedy, part performance art, part chihuahua"—she makes herself the spectacle, drawing the gaze to her body. She constructs various onstage personas, but the object of the gaze is always her body, which she offers for the visual pleasure of the audience, at times choosing costumes that reveal and accentuate her form, at others offering verbal aids to the imaginative recreation of what is not seen ("I took off my bra—thump, thump").

Like Moraga's appropriation of Bogart, and Hernández' takeover of masculine tattooing practices and martial arts, Palacios invades the field of stand-up comedy, which is notoriously male-dominated, racist, and homophobic. Traces of this homophobia can be found in reviews of her show. Having never interviewed a lesbian before, a Latino reporter of *The Los Angeles Times* compares their encounter to the "day E.T. met little Elliott" (26 February 1991). The extent of Palacios' "alien" monstrosity is contained in the title of her act, "demurely" titled "Latin Lezbo Comic": she is at once Latina, lesbian, and funny. She distinguishes her show from stand-up comedy: instead of a steady delivery of one-liners, Palacios performs her life story through comedy. Like Moraga's first piece for the theater, *Giving Up the Ghost,* Palacios' show places the lesbian body, lesbian existence, and lesbian desire center stage, a stage dominated by privileged men for over 2000 years. Centering the Chicana lesbian subject also means decentering the traditionally privileged spectator, and Palacios' show raises the same issues of audience reception as Moraga's work for the theater. For example, a white lesbian and gay audience in Seattle is more difficult to work than a Latina lesbian audience in Los Angeles, or a women of color/lesbians of color audience in Seattle's "Specific Passions" reading series.

One important difference from Moraga's work for the theater, of course, is that Palacios' response to minus privilege in so many categories is humor, a spoofing that extends to white gay culture ("I really wanted to live in West Hollywood so I could be a hip-happenin'-homo, but I didn't want to devote my life to—pastels") and aspects of her Chicana identity as well: "I was born of Mexican-American persuasion, then I became a Chicana, then a Latina, then a Hispanic, then a Third World member, then a woman of color. Now I'm just an Amway dealer and life is great." Like Moraga in *Ghost,* Palacios stages lesbian desire and lesbian sex, breaking some mighty taboos. Palacios declares the show's "didactic" purpose of eradicating people's misconceptions about lesbian sex—"[the word] lesbian makes people think of some yucky sexual activity that has to do with a tractor"—while miming driving a tractor, a gesture which recurs throughout the show. At another point she pulls out a diagram of a nut and screw to illustrate the "universal language" of sex, attacking the misinformation that lesbians "do not fuck but reach orgasm through giggling." Palacios complains about films that represent lesbian sex:

> artsy interpretive dance move stuff . . . swaying and twirling . . . exploring their womanhood. . . . Honey I'm horny. Get the leotards. If I'm watching lesbian sex scenes, I want to see these gals suck face! I want to see them bump, grind, insert—to name a few verbs! I want to get so hot and bothered, I have to get up to pour myself a coke! And now, there are safe sex lesbian videos . . . remember when safe sex for lesbians was just keeping your fingernails short?

Like Moraga, Hernández, and Ochoa, Palacios is principally concerned with how sexuality interrelates with culture and ethnicity, as she phrases it at the end of her show: "weaving the lesbian side of me with the Mexican side of me . . . demanding change! Will four quarters be OK?" This project involves lesbianizing the signifiers of Mexican culture, as when a microphone appears to her like the Virgin of Guadalupe, announcing her calling to comedy, or when she lusts after the mariachis' outfits . . . for herself. In her story "La Llorona Loca: The Other Side," Palacios revisions the weeping woman seeking her dead children of Mexican/Chicano folklore as a lesbian who elopes with La Stranger arriving in town one day. Or her homoerotic evocation of the two *comadres'* performance of the popular song "Cucurucucú Paloma":

> They'd be really close together, looking into each other's eyes like only Mexican women can who sing together. . . . And their lips would be really close together—quivering—full of passion and ruby red lipstick. Filling the air with music, culture, make-up, woman sweat, woman breath, and BEER!

Palacios mines the vein of humor in the borderlands between Mexican and Anglo culture, as when she remembers visiting her grandmother so she could hear the "Beverly Hillbillies" in Spanish (which she sings on stage) or in her story on the lesbian La Llorona when her eerie cries are momentarily confused with "really loud Carly Simon music."

Just as she exposes Latino homophobia, relating her coming-out experience in her own family, Palacios mexicanizes the signifiers of European-American history and popular culture to negotiate complex relations of power and race. She appropriates the game show format of "Jeopardy" to play "Mexican Denial," a syndrome that produces both the refusal to acknowledge the Mexicanness of a city like Los Angeles as well as the internalized racism of some of its Mexican inhabitants (for example, the host Hope Crane, whose name is a translation of Esperanza Garza). In another bit, Palacios refigures interracial lesbian desire in terms of Manifest Destiny, performing an encounter with a white pilgrim woman in a lesbian club. Attracted by her "alluring beauty" and her "big bulky buckle shoes," the Palacios persona recognizes that her desire for the white woman is informed by "something so hauntingly historical."

Although lesbianism is also a primary impulse in Anzaldúa's *Borderlands,* the lesbian body is not represented within the context of sexual desire as in the work of the other Latinas considered here. *Borderlands* charts the border crossings among the writing subject's multiple subject positions, and in this mapping of subjectivity, gender, the Indian or dark component of racial identity and lesbianism are privileged as factors that prevented her from feeling "at home" in the "homeland," the border between Texas and Mexico. Her "difference" forced her to confront the exclusions that operate to construct "home" in the first place: the oppression of women, the repression of "darkness," and the exclusion of gays and lesbians. The text foregrounds the *political* ramifications of "queerness": "Being lesbian and raised Catholic, indoctrinated as straight, I *made the choice to be queer*" (19). Like writing and being Chicana, queerness means "living in the borderlands," "a way of balancing, of mitigating duality" (19). All three (being Chicana, writing, and queerness) are vehicles for breaking down dualisms in the production of a third thing, or hybrid element. Anzaldúa defines this process or activity as "mestiza" or "border" consciousness.

In her essays on writing in *Borderlands,* Anzaldúa refuses the Western dichotomy between mind and body. Drawing on indigenous shamanistic traditions, she refers to the "animal soul" (or "nahual") and describes writing as a process of "carving bone" or "making face" (73). The lesbian body is the site of a writing that is a "path/state to something else" (73), a "reprogramming" of consciousness (70) to produce a "tolerance for contradictions" (79). The production of this consciousness involves the lesbian body centrally:

Suddenly, I feel like I have another set of teeth in my mouth. A tremor goes through my body from my buttocks to the roof of my mouth. Shock pulls my breath out of me. The sphincter muscle tugs itself up, up, and the heart in my cunt starts to beat. . . . Something pulsates in my body, a luminous thin thing that never leaves me. . . . That which abides: . . . my thousand sleepless serpent eyes blinking in the night, forever open. (51)

The imagery is similar to the other reconstructions of the lesbian body considered here, but Anzaldúa's intimate journey within her body is an implosion inward, a solitary journey rather than that of a body coupled or re-membered in sex.

A crucial component of Anzaldúa's lesbian subjectivity is internalized oppression, which she calls "intimate terrorism" or the Shadow-Beast. Her project involves not only recognizing how we have denied and repressed the unacceptable parts of ourselves—the female, the dark or the queer side—but also empowering ourselves through their reclamation. In *Borderlands,* the repressed dark force is symbolized by Coatlicue, Lady of the Serpent Skirt, a pre-Columbian deity similar to India's Kali in her nondualistic fusion of contradictory yet complementary opposites.

In the re-vision of Coatlicue and other Chicano/Mexican legends and myths, Anzaldúa employs a strategy similar to other Latinas' deconstruction of La Malinche, La Virgen, and La Llorona for lesbian representation. The Texan writer works within and against the legend of La Llorona, a woman who for some reason—the different versions speak of unrequited love, abandonment, or adultery—killed her children by drowning them and as punishment must forever roam creeks and riverbeds wailing and searching for her lost children. Anzaldúa counts her as one of the "three mothers" of the Chicano people, along with La Virgen and La Malinche (30), pointing to the ambiguity surrounding these three symbols: "the true identity of all three has been subverted—*Guadalupe* to make us docile and enduring, *la Chingada* to make us ashamed of our Indian side, and *la Llorona* to make us long-suffering people. This obscuring has encouraged the *virgen/puta* dichotomy" (31). She revisions La Llorona's endless wandering in terms of Chicanas' commitment to self-definition and self-representation: "she is *la Llorona,* Daughter of the Night, traveling the dark terrains of the unknown searching for the lost parts of herself" (38).

Anzaldúa incorporates and transforms La Llorona as part of her project of refusing dualistic dichotomies in the production of *mestiza* consciousness, reclaiming La Llorona as one of the aspects of Coatlicue, the repressed dark force. The poem "My Black *Angelos*" figures Anzaldúa internal border-crossings as the weeping woman/Coatlicue entering the poet's body, becoming her terrifying yet empowering muse:

> *Aiiii aiiiii aiiiiii*
> She is crying for the dead child
> the lover gone, the lover not yet come:
> . . . I hear her at the door.
>
> Taloned hand on my shoulder
> behind me putting words, worlds in my head
> turning, her hot breath
> she picks the meat stuck between my teeth
> with her snake tongue
> sucks the smoked lint from my lungs
> with her long black nails
> plucks lice from my hair.
>
> *Aiiii aiiiii aiiiiii*
> She crawls into my spine
> her eyes opening and closing,
> shining under my skin in the dark
> whirling my bones twirling
> till they're hollow reeds. (184)

In conclusion, these Latinas write, perform, and represent the lesbian body, taking it apart, traveling within it and putting it back together, through the creative appropriation and reconfiguration of received cultural signifiers, practices, and discourses traditionally embedded in heterosexual contexts. They adjust and expand the meanings of images and narratives from both dominant and Latino cultures. Generating hybrid representations in a mode of up-front performativity, they communicate their multipositional identity and reference their own shifting realities.

Notes

1 See the black and white photographs by Texan Chicana Kathy Vargas accompanying Turner's essay for Ray López Jr.'s forearm tattoos of the Virgin of Guadalupe and the Virgen de San Juan de los Lagos (47).

2 Thanks to Julio Ramos for directing my attention to de Certeau on tattoos as inscription of the law and nineteenth-century anthropology's attitudes toward tattoos as signs of otherness.

Works Cited

Anzaldúa, Gloria. *Borderlands/La frontera: The New Mestiza*. San Francisco: Spinsters/Aunt Lute, 1987.

de Certeau, Michel. *The Practice of Everyday Life*. Trans. Steven Rendall. Berkeley: University of California Press, 1984.

Lippard, Lucy R. *Mixed Blessings: New Art in a Multicultural America*. New York: Pantheon, 1990.

Mesa-Baines, Amalia. "El mundo femenino: Chicana Artists of the Movement—A Commentary on Development and Production." *Chicano Art: Resistance and Affirmation*. Los Angeles: Wight Art Gallery, UCLA, 1991. 131–40.

Moraga, Cherríe. *Giving Up the Ghost*. Los Angeles: West End Press, 1986.

———. *Loving in the War Years (lo que nunca pasó por sus labios)*. Boston: South End Press, 1983.

———. "La ofrenda." Trujillo. 3–9.

Ochoa, Marcia. *La ofrenda*. Ann Arbor: self-published, 1991.

Palacios, Monica. "Latin Lezbo Comic" (unpublished).

———. "La Llorona Loca: The Other Side." Trujillo. 49–51.

Ramos, Julio. "Faceless Tongues: Inscriptions of Subaltern Speech in Nineteenth-Century Latin America" (unpublished).

Trujillo, Carla, ed. *Chicana Lesbians: The Girls Our Mothers Warned Us About*. Berkeley: Third Woman Press, 1991.

Turner, Kay. "Home Altars and the Arts of Devotion." *Chicano Expressions: A New View in American Art*. New York: INTAR, 1987. 40–48.

Yarbro-Bejarano, Yvonne. "De-constructing the Lesbian Body: Cherríe Moraga's *Loving in the War Years*." Trujillo. 143–55.

FOUR

Biographical Constructions,
Textual Encodings

Licia Fiol-Matta

The "Schoolteacher of America": Gender,
Sexuality, and Nation in Gabriela Mistral

The Chilean poet Gabriela Mistral, 1945 Nobel Prize for Literature, is considered a canonical figure in Latin America. The recognition and status
she achieved in her day, however, derived less from an attentive reading
of her poems and prose works and more from her public persona: the
"Schoolteacher of America," a celibate, dutiful, heterosexual woman.

Although in many ways this persona was assigned to her by external
institutions, in an amplification of traditional women's roles, the case of
Mistral does not fit a neat paradigm of victimization or oppression. As I
shall discuss below, Mistral herself set the process in motion early in her
life. She invested a tremendous amount of energy and time (approximately
twenty years) in creating this persona. Even after it was no longer strictly
necessary for Mistral to adhere to its tenets, she continued to portray herself as the poor, suffering rural schoolteacher from a remote valley in Chile
who, in an act of supreme self-sacrifice and exemplary abnegation, offered
to become a spiritual mother to all the children of Latin America.

This fact has made her a troublesome figure, sometimes an embarrassing one, for feminism in Latin America. Talk of Mistral, as an author and
as an historical figure, has served remarkably antifeminist purposes. Undoubtedly homophobia has played a critical role in this, at best oversight,
at worst downright repudiation of her figure and her work.[1] Homophobia
also accounts, in part, for the distinctively hagiographic quality of most
Mistral criticism. If Gabriela Mistral entered, and if she remained in, the
canon of Latin American literature, for years it was primarily due to factors
other than a responsible (not to say sophisticated) reading of her work.

That Gabriela Mistral was a lesbian is widely acknowledged in literary
and social circles, but rarely treated in literary criticism, occupying, instead,

the space of the "open secret." Most literary criticism on Mistral has in fact frozen her into a heterosexist conception of womanhood and of the woman author in Latin America. Male and female critics alike have created an abstract heterosexuality for Mistral, even though nothing conclusive is known about her heterosexual loves. Furthermore, not only is Mistral compulsorily heterosexual for them, on top of it she is either asexual or frustrated.[2]

The dominant paradigms in most criticism on Mistral were, until recently, the repression hypothesis, according to which she sublimates sexual desire (primarily through religious imagery), and an untroubled "Latin Americanness."[3] I'm not trying to suggest that these interpretations do not bear at times a concrete relationship to the poems, but that they are noteworthy and ultimately unacceptable for what they erase or distort from a larger and more complex picture.

Fortunately, the centennial of her birth in 1989 renewed an interest in Mistral and provoked a surge of studies on various facets of her work and life.[4] Many of these readings, as was to be expected, merely recycled old commonplaces and clichés, and drew heavily on Mistral's prestige as a Nobel Prize winner and as a figure of relative importance in the continental discourse of *América*. There were, however, important manifestations of truly subversive readings, at least some of which aspired to transcend the chiefly academic domain of discourse that envelops Mistral's figure and safeguards her status as national icon (particularly in Chile). In that vein, a new feminist revision of Mistral has emerged. This feminist revaluation of Mistral has served as a much-needed corrective to the hegemonic version. Unfortunately, it, too, has been mostly silent on the question of Mistral's sexuality, still an explosive subject.

I would like to continue this focus on Mistral's use of quintessentially "female" (read minor, inferior, unimportant) languages and practices, but to different purposes. Her gender discourse is indeed a mask, meant to deceive the heterosexist, patriarchal order of her time and place (Latin America in the first half of the twentieth century). But the fact of being a "mask," one that outsmarts mechanisms of oppression on the individual level, does not automatically mean that this mask or its use was progressive. And the ways in which Mistral manipulates the available cultural representations of Woman, especially Woman as passionless, de-sexualized mother, also point to a movement by which Mistral (sort of) submerges and (sort of) articulates a lesbian identity and a lesbian desire. This would automatically exclude her from the "community" of women she appears to create and that, without a question, she eventually represents.

I want to suggest preliminary ways in which to unravel Mistral's participation in the dominant discourse, as well as in the social practices the discourse authorized. It is primarily in this aspect that my reading departs somewhat from previous feminist readings, which tend to celebrate the Mistralian construction of a "community," "family," or "audience" of women.[5] I do not regard Mistral's brand of cultural feminism as progressive; Mistral's alliances with several male-dominated establishments is an obvious fact and must be analyzed in a noncelebratory manner. I do think that, without a nuanced analysis, we could come close to an antifeminist and, even in feminist circles, a *homophobic* condemnation of Mistral. We would then be substituting one set of reductive and coercive readings for another.

I propose to regard the whole issue of "Mistral," the poet and the historical figure, as instructive of the *conditions of possibility* of female and lesbian authorship in early-twentieth-century Latin America, of its strategies and possible ironies. I will take Mistral's unique intervention in the reproduction of the national discourse as a privileged place in which to investigate these conditions.

I

Woman-identified discourse is not, in and of itself, necessarily radical, and this is proven by Mistral, who uses a conservative gender discourse to cautiously enter the public sphere. This she does through a national institution par excellence, the school.[6] From the school, she makes a case for her entrance into the affairs of the state; from the state, she launches her peculiar strain of the national discourse and so becomes a foundational subject for the mythical space of the nation.[7]

Admittedly, Mistral started working in the schools because of financial need and because the professionalization of women was taking place mostly in the arena of education. However, these facts alone do not account for Mistral's early assumption of a national imperative, the mass production of female subjects in the continental context, through a state prerogative, the education of girls. While the state of Chile was Mistral's principal employer and patron for most of her life, the nation, *América,* was Mistral's ticket to international fame and to the protection afforded by this total immersion in the conservative, state-sponsored cultural politics of the day.

Thus we can regard gender, school, and nation as "closets," primarily, but not exclusively, of sexuality. This contiguity or superimposition of closets depends on the confounding of public and private spaces, of masculine and feminine codes, of heterosexual and homosexual identities. This is illustrated by the title informally awarded Mistral throughout Latin America: *la Maestra de América*. The school and the woman, coded as domestic, private, prepolitical, are inserted, in this title, into the overarching discourse of the public good, the discourse of *Nuestra América*. The epithet is emblematic of the double movement that characterized Mistral's life. On the one hand, Mistral's public persona complied with the patriarchal demand for lesbian invisibility and for the assumption of socially acceptable "female" roles in Latin America. On the other, however, she used the protection of this same mask, of this masquerade,[8] to assemble a space from which to live and write. The masquerade of "gender," in its historically and culturally accurate form, enabled Mistral to become an author and to lead a lesbian life. In this way she managed a double subversion: first, of the male-dominated poetic canon in Latin America, notorious for its objectification of Woman, for its disdain of woman poets until very recently, as well as for its repression of homosexuality and even more of lesbianism; second, of the patriarchal-heterosexist order, as it existed at that time in Latin America.

This double subversion is guaranteed by a set of binary oppositions. These binary oppositions, like all binaries, only make sense when taken together. Not only public/private; but prosaic/poetic, displayed/hidden, major/minor, persona/person, succeed precisely because they act in concert. Indicatively, the only binary that is not securely anchored in Mistral's persona has to do with her sexual indeterminacy.

Mistral's contemporaries mistook Mistral's endless deferral of the question of her sexual identity with a stable sexual identity itself, but the two are not identical. Mistral astutely manipulated the constructions of the "private" and of the "woman's life" to simulate the speech of disclosure, while in effect never saying anything on the substance of disclosure. We can say, with Eve Kosofsky Sedgwick (1990), that the series of relations, in their repetition and their difference, between the binaries, resemble the closet as a signifying space, with its apparently discrete "inside" and "outside." School, gender, nation, as discursive units with specific effects, "hide" an indeterminacy that is mostly sexual in nature. Paradoxically enough, a shrewd positioning within the discourse of the nation, with its homophobia and its problematic (to say the least) treatment of women, allowed Mistral to elude its most punitive injunctions.

II

Mistral's masquerade served a number of practical purposes. Some of the more obvious benefits of the masquerade concern Mistral's sources of financial support. The state of Chile was always her main employer, first as a schoolteacher, then as a lifelong consul.

The masquerade enabled Mistral to leave Chile in 1922, where she was trapped in a consuming, bureaucratic existence that afforded her limited possibilities of intellectual growth and literary recognition. The trip to Mexico, undertaken as a state representative, proved crucial to Mistral's career as a writer. Upon her return from Mexico in 1924, Mistral was often away from Chile on state business, but also on engagements resulting from her ascending fame as the schoolteacher-mother-poet-model for the women of Latin America.

Once in definitive exile, as "cónsul particular de libre elección" (a post to which she was appointed in 1932), Mistral had the freedom to choose and change at will her country of residence, anywhere in Europe, Latin America, or the United States. As a means of self-support, Mistral began to contribute to the major newspapers of Latin America, a practice she would continue throughout her life. Before receiving the Nobel Prize, she had already held several visiting professorships in Latin America and the United States, and was a prestigious guest speaker in Latin America, Europe, and the United States. The prize only increased an already frenzied pace of activity.

The Nobel Prize was the culmination of a process of consecration that was slow to crystallize. It entailed the final recognition of Mistral's involvement in the conservative cultural and sexual politics of the Latin American states. Mistral's adoption of this discourse illustrates her collaboration with the state agenda. She tailored her discourse to the state's interest in recruiting women for the work force (particularly as schoolteachers). Her status as the "schoolteacher-poet" suited the continental discourse's doctrine, which upheld the redeeming power of letters, belles lettres, and aesthetics in the formation of the "good national subject."[9]

The state was not merely socially conservative because of religious and cultural reasons; it was also crucially interested in marriage and reproduction for economic reasons. Women were, as well, a source of cheap or unpaid labor, for example, in the schools. Therefore, the state had a direct stake in the persona of the schoolteacher-mother-icon. The potential of the persona lay in its ability to symbolize, strictly in the state's terms, both the continuation of restrictive social mores and the absorption of women into the labor force as *normalistas* and other service professions.[10] The entrance of women into the labor force was made in the name of progress, but only in patriarchal and heterosexist terms: it could not disturb the normative status quo of heterosexuality and reproduction. Women's productivity was thus maximized, and at a low cost for the state.

The masquerade allowed Mistral to do what men in the public sphere did but, most importantly, it allowed her to escape the two crucial demands on Latin American women: marriage and motherhood. These demands were clearly incompatible with who she was and what she wanted to do.

I should now turn to the relationship between the masquerade and the closet. It is not possible to overemphasize the punishment that a revelation of her sexuality would have brought Mistral in human terms. Anywhere from scandal to outright expulsion from community life would have en-sued. (Mistral's notorious sensitivity to scandal might be placed in this context.) Most certainly, the state would have terminated her employment, as schoolteacher or consul. To this litany of horrors I need not add that Mistral's writing career would have been over. Probably Mistral would have continued to write, but undoubtedly under very adverse conditions. In any case, her work, as we know it today, would have been of a very different nature, and its survival would have depended on a very different set of circumstances.

If her gender was an obstacle that could be overcome with the masquer-ade and incessant "networking," her sexuality was an element of danger, something that could not be spoken about, not even within the confines of the female world. The solution was to submerge her sexuality in the place where, paradoxically enough, it was the most on display: in gender. Because sexuality was naturalized through gender, and gender was depen-dent on naturalized interpretations of seemingly discrete bodies, gender discourse became, for Mistral, the ideal closet. Gender discourse would both satisfy the imperatives of the state and protect her from rejection by her community (although it is important to note just how much distance Mistral put between herself and her community, and the extent to which this community became more and more abstract, especially in her poetic works. *Poema de Chile* is the most radical instance of this depuration of the community to the barest of elements.)

For variegated reasons, of which I privilege two which seem to me the most determining (the possibility of living a lesbian life of some sort and the possibility of publication), Mistral undoubtedly aligned herself with the hegemonic discourses of her day. What has remained unnoticed is the strategic import of her actions.

Because she assumed discursively the versions of womanhood sanctioned by the state, even while never living them out herself, the hegemonic formations were able to ignore the fact that no certification or proof of Mistral's heterosexuality actually existed. But since heterosexuality is an unmarked identity, which does not need to be proven to be assumed as true, it was less important for Mistral to "be" heterosexual than to *perform* satisfactorily as one. And Mistral consistently performed the persona of heterosexual in her public identities as schoolteacher, educator, and, later, traveling writer. She permanently bracketed the question of her sexual identity through her carefully crafted persona.

Nowhere does this become as transparent as in her adoption of the discourse on the nation, in the case of Mistral especially a masquerade since she never practiced any of its prescriptions for women. What she did do, however, was to use the masquerade of womanliness and, more, to become an ideologue of this masquerade. It is nearly impossible, without further documentation, to assess the exact level of Mistral's conscious undertaking of these processes. Unwittingly or not, however, in many ways she contributed to the formulation of a discourse that would justify the confinement of women to the home, to mothering, and to the service sector of the economy.

III

By the time Mistral left Chile for Mexico in 1922, many of the elements of her particular strain of the national discourse were basically in place. These are what I take to be the salient, strategic characteristics of this discourse at the moment of its emergence:

Mistral speaks as the exception that guarantees the norm. In this way, Mistral follows a tradition of woman writers in Latin America, who present themselves as "oddities" or "freaks" that, on the individual level, give the lie to the status quo but, paradoxically enough, confirm it in a larger way by their very singularity.

Naturally, Mistral does not often call attention to this status as exception. Instead, she found an ingenious way to mask her difference from the norm: her rhetorical "spiritual motherhood" and her symbolic adoption of the children of Latin America. By becoming the spokesperson of this discourse based on these two rhetorical positions, she drew attention to herself only as a sad aberration of the normal course of things. Of course, this avowed "aberration" has sexual indeterminacy as its subtext.

Mistral speaks primarily in the official capacity of the "educator" (and not of the poet). She writes with publication in mind and advertises herself through a multiplicity of contacts that were begun when she had not yet left Chile. Mistral's later international stature only made easier the continuation of a discourse crafted much earlier. But this did not happen without considerable work on Mistral's part. Even once in exile and no longer working directly as an educator, the alignment with the "magister" figure of the nineteenth century would persist in her speeches and journalistic writings, as a permanent feature of her public persona.

I am not trying to suggest that the fact that Mistral was a poet of some renown in her native Chile had nothing to do with her ascending notoriety. It certainly enhanced her value as the schoolteacher-mother-icon: she was not only *la maestra,* but *la maestra-poeta.* However, the vision of Mistral as poet was very limited in her time. Certainly the status of a protean, creative figure of freedom, whose emergence is closely related to the development of *las vanguardias,* has historically not been extended to women poets. Until recently, Latin American women poets of the twentieth century were regarded as vastly inferior to their male counterparts. Mistral is somewhat of an anomaly, because, compared to her female contemporaries, she achieved an extraordinary measure of recognition. Despite the accolades, the recognition that Mistral achieved in her lifetime was never more than ambivalent, sometimes quite uncomfortable, and, as I have suggested, largely due to her persona and her participation in the state plan, articulated through a national agenda. To be sure, her poetic fame gave her social capital, but not enough social capital to guarantee her the stature she achieved in the continental context (and needed to achieve in order to defer the question of her sexual identity and account for her status as unmarried and childless). What made Mistral "exceptional" in this early moment, 1924, was less the poetic quality of her work and more the elevation of her person to symbol.

Mistral derives her authority from her status as the patriarchal archive. Though much is made of Mistral's pedagogic and social ideas, as if she had a system of thought properly authored by her, in the work most closely associated with the early establishment of her persona she employs, rather, commonplace clichés of love of the country, statements of admiration for an abstract geography of Latin America, typologies of its racial types, and eulogies of powerful male figures. Mistral's brand of the national discourse constitutes, not an original program of nationalist emancipation for Latin America, but, rather, an imitation of this discourse. (I am not requiring a system or program of emancipation from Mistral, but, rather, questioning the myth that she actually *had* one.) Indeed, Mistral presents herself as a compiler of sorts of the essential bibliography of the nation. This is easily seen in *Lecturas para mujeres;* she even signs the preface as "La recopiladora." Her prestigious affiliations include Bolívar, Sarmiento, Martí, and Rodó, men whom she wrote about in invariably flattering terms in her journalistic pieces or educational manifestoes. She also mentions men she knew personally and/or worked with, to whom she owed political debts, as in the case of the Mexican José Vasconcelos.

Mistral partitions the national discourse into two seemingly discrete areas: the prepolitical and the political proper, coded feminine and masculine, respectively. This is not necessarily Mistral's invention, but she does insist rather more than usual on having a separate audience, composed solely of women. When Mistral addresses the schoolteacher, it is clear that she is referring to "maestras," women. And when she invokes the student, it is generally her "alumnas," again, women, she is referring to. The national discourse, as employed by Mistral, divides the national subject along gender lines.

This device allayed any fears that Mistral would overstep her boundaries and appear as the "wrong" model for women. The division helped to insure, in the eyes of the hegemony, that this inversion or excess did not happen, but it also created a problem. The national subject's claim to a privileged epistemological standpoint is predicated on its universality, its indivisibility.[11] Although the national discourse had begun to address all national subjects in one breath, at least since Sarmiento's educational reform in the nineteenth century, it still took as natural the division of roles between the genders, thus constructing women as second-class citizens virtually excluded from the public sphere. (For example, the importance accorded to the schoolteacher and the relative permissiveness that allowed women to become schoolteachers in the first place were predicated on the notion that the primary school was an extension of the home and, as such, should provide a maternal atmosphere to the child.)

By an excessive display of this already existing feature of the national discourse (a sexual division of labor), principally through her very person, Mistral inserted that which is classified as private, minuscule, ordinary, commonplace, that is, the home, women, and children, into the public, grand, transcendental sphere of politics and the state, a male-dominated arena. Through the logic of inversion, the public, male spheres could also enter the realm of the domestic. Her moralistic tone and the discourse of "values" concealed the fact that she united what the discourse of the nation separated (namely, the public and the private, the prepolitical and the political) and separated what the discourse of the nation united (namely, women and men). Uniting the public and the private excused her existence in the public sphere, and separating the sexes surreptitiously took the issue of her (hetero)sexuality out of the discussion. Typically, there was both allegiance *and* simulation of allegiance to the national discourse. An undeniable degree of compliance "closeted" a great deal of performance.

Mistral's performativity raises the issue of her adherence to the beliefs of the discourse. Was she aware of the contradictions raised by her very person? Did she manipulate the discourse, as I have suggested, or did she actually subscribe to this ideology? If she consciously manipulated the discourse, we would have to consider her persona and the writings most closely related to this persona as practices approximating parody, although not constituting parody per se. If, on the contrary, we take Mistral to have believed in the prescriptions of her discourse, we would have to consider the persona and the writings as instances, possibly, of a "camp" sensibility. Indeed, there are many ways in which Mistral can be studied from the point of view of "drag."[12] In any case, there is a difference between a performativity that unmasks the addressee (as in Sor Juana's "Respuesta a Sor Filotea de la Cruz") and a performativity that does not unmask the addressee. It seems that Mistral's performativity would belong in the latter category.

Mistral employs the maternal body as her organizing metaphor. The national body, as a signifier of clear boundaries, of restrictions and regulations, is translated for women through the maternal body, and the civic duties of women are outlined in a didactic, strongly moralistic tone. Again, there are strong echoes of Sarmiento in this basic ingredient of Mistral's posturing.

The mapping of the national discourse onto women through the ubiquitous maternal body is fractured by Mistral's desire. Accordingly, this body will come to exceed the discourse to which it was once attached (love of country, dutiful obedience, defense of the nation, regulated knowledge of the schoolteacher, unpaid labor of housework and childcare, cheap labor in the schools), to become the object of the author's desire, as a woman's body. In other words, desire resignifies the national body. No longer utilitarian, collective, abstract, a body of maximum production and profit, it emerges as a poetic, intimate body of maximum pleasure.

However, this body of pleasure is yoked to the body of reproduction, as we shall see. I will now turn my attention to two texts written by Mistral that might illustrate both these characteristics and the excesses they gave rise to.

IV

According to Mistral, shortly before leaving Mexico in 1924, where she had been working with the Ministry of Education, José Vasconcelos, Mistral's employer and the minister of education himself, asked Mistral to compile a primer: "Recibí hace meses de la Secretaría de Educación de México el encargo de recopilar un libro de *Lecturas Escolares*" (Mistral 1924, xv) [Months ago I received a request from the Ministry of Education of México, asking me to compile a book of *School Readings*].[13] In all truth, this was not as informal a request as she would have us believe from her introduction. The understanding that Mistral would produce a primer for the girls' school that bore her name was specified in Mistral's contract before she left Chile: "escribir textos de lectura de carácter literario para las Escuelas Primarias y Superiores para niños y especialmente uno para la Escuela-Hogar que lleva su nombre" (quoted in Ibacache 144) [write schoolbooks of a literary character for the primary and secondary school levels and, especially, one for the School-Home that is named after her]. Mistral recounts that she decided to produce a reader "only" for the girls in attendance at the Gabriela Mistral School, which Vasconcelos had opened in Mexico in honor of his guest:

> Comprendí que un texto corresponde hacerlo a los maestros nacionales y no a una extranjera, y he recopilado esta obra sólo para la escuela mexicana que lleva mi nombre. Me siento dentro de ella con pequeños derechos, y tengo, además, el deber de dejarle un recuerdo tangible de mis clases. (xv)
>
> [I realized that a textbook should be written by native schoolteachers and not by a foreigner, so I have compiled this work only for the Mexican school that is named after me. I feel that I have certain rights inside it, and, in addition, I have an obligation to leave it a tangible souvenir of my lessons.]

The preface inscribes the insider/outsider tension that would plague Mistral throughout her life. It would also become a creative tension, but for the moment I will focus on its quality of "solution" (a way out of uncomfortable situations, to which she generally reacted defensively). I would like to point to the shifting, perhaps opportunistic character of the insider/outsider construction in Mistral.

Gabriela Mistral's name came to index the topic of "women's education" in Latin America. The primer, signed by the very name of the school for which it was intended, would serve as the prototype of the reader for an impossible totality: the "girls" of Latin America, Gabriela Mistral's meta-phorical "students." This book, which Mistral entitled *Lecturas para mujeres* [Readings for Women], provided a crucial vehicle for Mistral. Mistral took advantage of Vasconcelos's request in order to introduce many of her own writings and begin to establish her presence as that of an author. Its preface, "Palabras de la extranjera" [Words of the Foreigner/Foreign Woman],[14] represents a calculated effort on Mistral's part to strengthen her persona of the schoolteacher-mother-icon of the female national subject. The pref-ace is a manifesto of women's civic duties and an elaboration of the ties between the conservative family and the state, but since the book itself is an inaugural gesture in the creation of a specifically literary authority, that of Gabriela Mistral, the author, the preface is also an apology for Mistral's anomalous existence.

The preface opens with a reaffirmation of the exclusively female, same-sex world of Gabriela Mistral's portion of the nation: "Es éste el ensayo de un trabajo que realizaré algún día, en mi país, destinado a las mujeres de América. Las siento mi familia espiritual; escribo para ellas, tal vez sin preparación, pero con mucho amor" (xv) [This is the draft of an essay that I will write one day, for the women of Latin America. I feel as if they are my spiritual family. I write for them, perhaps without training, but with much love]. She twists the typical national, patriarchal metaphor of the "family;" her "family" consists solely of women. Mistral does not write for the "male" portion, so to speak, of the national subject. She reinforces the already existing separation of the spheres, and laments the lack of "ma-terials" to sustain that separation: "Siempre se sacrifica en la elección de trozos la parte destinada a la mujer, y así, ella no encuentra en su texto los motivos que deben formar a la madre" (xv) [When making our selection, we always sacrifice the excerpts most appropriate to women, and so, she does not find in the textbook the motifs that should shape the mother]. Mistral's text will purportedly address a lack (of readers for women), but it will also create a utopian, undifferentiated space (of women readers): mothers, potential mothers, or simply, spiritual mothers (such as herself): "Y sea profesionista, obrera, campesina o simple dama, su única razón de ser sobre el mundo es la maternidad, la material y la espiritual juntas, o la última en las mujeres que no tenemos hijos" (xv) [And whether she be a professional, a worker, a peasant, or simply a lady, her one reason to be in this world is motherhood, material and spiritual; or the latter in the case of those of us who do not have children]. The adjective "espiritual," so often noticed in connection to Mistral's "spiritual" motherhood or "spiritual" love, here appears as a bond or connector between women, as a demarcation or boundary, *and* as a strained explanation for Mistral's own unrealized biological motherhood and abstention from marriage.

Mistral's appropriation of the discourse to establish a feminine, "spiritual" space, through a female "readership," should not obscure the fact that she reinforces the nation's contradictory demands on women, while avoiding them herself. Mistral allows that women do work outside the home (she lists a string of professions), but she writes that this labor must never interfere with woman's "natural" disposition toward motherhood (an endorsement of the national discourse). While striving to absorb women into the work force in greater numbers, at the same time the state required women to continue their domestic duties and assume their traditional, heterosexual identities. Production and reproduction were expected simultaneously, even if, at the discursive level, they were articulated as incompatible.

Mistral admits that the "new" woman's financial independence is an advantage for women, but when she states that this entails a "loss" of the traditional values the nation so admires in women (xvi), Mistral's position is necessarily ambivalent. She, at the time, was attempting precisely to become, if not a "new woman," an increasingly independent woman, in financial and other terms. If the "new woman" may constitute a "betrayal of the race" ("*una traición a la raza*," xvi, emphasis Mistral), this indicates that there were, perhaps, professions or identities which, in the hands of large numbers of women, did not necessarily follow the national prescription for public health; professions or identities which, in the hands of large numbers of women, would be considered quite nocive.

Mistral's rhetoric denies this problematic relationship; she highlights her own profession of "schoolteacher," one which was indeed being produced en masse. Her strategy is to deflect attention from herself and her literary *profession* (as opposed to *attribute*), assuming writing as an obligation for which she claims to be unfit ("escribo . . . sin preparación" [xv]). Mistral converts her public life, so different from her own prescriptions for women, into a permutation of the life of the home and children. Her name becomes a guarantee of something that she desired most emphatically *not* to be involved in: marriage and reproductive motherhood.[15] Her name also serves as an assurance of a steady supply of schoolteachers, a profession which Mistral quite possibly wanted to leave.

When reproductive motherhood itself is identified as the goal of the education of women, we see that the idea of education or pedagogy is the equation that unites woman and state and justifies Mistral's intervention in the national discourse. The reproduction of the good female national subject (the mother), according to Mistral, is achieved through the education equation: "*Para mí, la forma del patriotismo femenino es la maternidad perfecta. La educación más patriótica que se le da a la mujer es, por lo tanto, la que acentúa el deber de familia*" (xviii, emphasis Mistral) [*In my opinion, perfect patriotism in women is perfect motherhood*. Therefore, the most patriotic education one can give a woman is one that underscores the obligation to start a family].

The rhetoric of love of country, another obvious element of nationalism, functions as a bridge to the essay's (and Mistral's) organizing metaphor, the maternal body:

> El patriotismo femenino es más sentimental que intelectual, y está formado, antes que de las descripciones de las batallas y los relatos heroicos, de las costumbres que la mujer crea y dirige de cierta forma; de la emoción del paisaje nativo, cuya visión afable o recia, ha ido cuajando en su alma la suavidad o la fortaleza. (xviii)
>
> [Feminine patriotism is more sentimental than intellectual, and it is formed less by the descriptions of battles and heroic deeds and more by the descriptions of the customs that, in a way, woman creates and directs; by the description of the emotion of the native landscape, the sight of which, be it affable or strong, has instilled in her soul softness or strength.]

The native soil and the female body are equated in one emotion, "love." The woman's abstract body functions as a compendium of the geography of Latin America. This ideal continent-body excludes all the problematic axes of difference, as well as the structural inequalities in the population, by projecting them elsewhere, beyond the felicity of the clearly demarcated borders of "la tierra de milagro" (xviii) [the land of wonder]. The land and the woman's body, spoken about as national symbols, remain hidden as state sites of production and reproduction.

What is the status, then, of Mistral's own body, a female body that does not reproduce? Immediately after the passage suggesting the equation between the maternal body and the geography of Latin America, Mistral defends her role as a spokeswoman for the nation from a vague, unnamed attack:

> La índole hispanoamericanista de mis *Lecturas* no es cosa sugerida a última hora de servir a un gobierno de estos países. Hace muchos años que la sombra de Bolívar ha alcanzado mi corazón con su doctrina. Ridiculizada ésta, deformada por el sarcasmo en muchas partes, no siendo todavía conciencia nacional en ningún país nuestro, yo la amo

así, como anhelo de unos pocos y desdén en olvido de otros. Esta vez como siempre estoy con los menos. (xviii)
[The Spanish American nature of my *Readings* is not something that I came up with at the last minute to please the government of one of these countries. The shadow of Bolívar has illuminated me with its doctrine for many years now. Ridiculed; deformed by sarcasm in many parts; not yet national consciousness in any of our countries, I love it just like that, as the hope of a few, and the disdain of oblivion in others. In this, as in everything else, I am in the minority.]

Her eccentric Bolívar operates as a mirror of herself. The threat of exclusion from the discursive "nation" produces a high level of anxiety. Gabriela Mistral posits herself as both an object of attack *and* a constitutive part of this discourse. In contrast to the abstract, felicitous, proper community she has just delineated through references to the landscape, now she claims membership in a sort of "secret society" of persecuted, misunderstood national heroes. The title of the preface, "Palabras de la extranjera," suggests that Mistral could manipulate her status as outsider, in response to real and perceived censure, while in effect accepting her universal characterization as *the* female Latin American, in her guise of mother and schoolteacher.

With strong moralistic overtones, Mistral attempts to regain control of the enunciative situation, but the national imperatives are lost amidst the repetition of its rhetoric:

Sin intención moral, con las lecturas escolares de los maestros formamos sólo retóricos y *dilettantes;* creamos ocios para las academias y los ateneos, pero no formamos lo que Nuestra América necesita con una urgencia que a veces llega a parecerme trágica: *generaciones con sentido moral, ciudadanos y mujeres puros y vigorosos e individuos en los cuales la cultura se haga militante, al vivificarse con la acción: se vuelva servicio.* (xix, emphasis Mistral)
[Lacking moral intent, with the readings that we now provide to our teachers we succeed only in forming rhetoricians and dilettantes. We supply leisure for the academies and the atheneums, but we do not form what Our America needs with an urgency that on occasion, it seems to me, verges on the tragic: *generations with a moral sense; pure and vigorous citizens and women and individuals in whom culture becomes militant when it is animated by action and turns into service.*]

The adoption of a tragic mode of speech appears almost caricaturesque; Mistral consciously posits herself as the guardian of Martí's "Nuestra América" discourse, complete with prophetic tone and a Messianic privilege of suffering that embodies the travails of an entire race. The stress on the utilitarianism and service proper of a good national subject, which women are only by imitation ("ciudadanos *y* mujeres," my emphasis), and only in the arena that precedes the political one, undermines the credibility of the discourse as enunciated by this particular subject. It also exposes some of the discourse's own anxieties about its allegedly compliant subjects. It is a curious inside/outside position, both for women in general and for Mistral in particular. The status of Mistral as a woman, as a good national subject, is in question and must be reaffirmed continually. This confirms the precarious nature of Mistral's social authority, at least in 1924. It also suggests that her literary stature did not translate into the social authority and power needed to shield her from accusation. Literary stature did not serve to correct what she herself perceived as her vulnerability and consequent instability as a public figure.

The "maestra-poeta" adopts the tragic mode to describe her own life at the end of the essay. Her strategy is to belittle herself and aggrandize the men, who, as rightful, unquestioned citizens, possess the right to this discourse (Vasconcelos, Sarmiento):

> VI. *Gratitud.* Ha sido para la pequeña maestra chilena una honra servir por un tiempo a un gobierno extranjero que se ha hecho respetable en el Continente por una labor constructiva que sólo tiene paralelo digno en la del gran Sarmiento. . . . Será en mí siempre un sereno orgullo haber recibido de la mano del licenciado señor Vasconcelos el don de una Escuela en México y la ocasión de escribir para las mujeres de mi sangre en el único período de descanso que ha tenido mi vida. (xx)
>
> [VI. *Gratitude.* It has been an honor for this insignificant Chilean schoolteacher to serve, for a while, a foreign government that has gained the respect of the Continent, thanks to a work of construction that finds its parallel only in that of the great Sarmiento. . . . I will always be proud to have received from the hand of Minister Vasconcelos the gift of a school in Mexico, as well as the opportunity to write for the women of my blood in the only rest period my life has known.]

The passage is worth examining in some detail. There is no reference to the fact that she is a poet; she calls herself "maestra" and, for greater effect, diminishes her prestige as such ("pequeña"). Once again, she emphasizes her status as outsider by referring to herself as "chilena." Though ostensibly Mistral spoke in the name of an *América* where literal national origin was secondary, she did not hesitate to refer to herself as a foreigner or as a Chilean when it served another purpose: of differentiation, of admission into a closed circle of privileged, literate figures. By equating Vasconcelos's educational reform with that of "el gran Sarmiento" in the nineteenth century, she is alluding, in fact, to her participation in this (male) society of great educators (*and* writers). The fact of "ridicule" mentioned previously in connection to Bolívar only corroborates her membership in this select group: Sarmiento, for one, endlessly defended himself from one accusation or another. In addition, calling the school a "gift" is a clever way of personalizing a bureaucratic issue. It is a shrewd way to point to her own importance as a figure of prestige: Mexico earned the respect of the "Continent," because Mexico enlisted Gabriela Mistral, heiress to Bolívar and Sarmiento, peer to Vasconcelos. The insinuation is double. First, others should follow this example and make similar invitations. Second, Mistral expects something in return for her "services."

However, Mistral is careful to conclude this preface by a reference to "las mujeres de mi sangre." Mistral wished to emphasize and retain her creation of a female readership and a female community, even if this community could not be but imaginary or textual. By stating that her stay in Mexico has been the only "rest period" she has had until then, Mistral subtly indicates that leaving Chile and her existence there as a schoolteacher brought, not only a concrete change to the circumstances of her life but, most of all, a concrete change to the circumstances of her writing (here related elliptically to "rest").

V

Through an analysis and presentation of "Palabras de la extranjera," I have been trying to elucidate the movement by which Mistral exhibited her gender discourse, tailored to the state's needs, while submerging the various "closeted" identities which ran counter to the demands of that same state.

Mistral's discourse in "Palabras," as an example of her speech in a primarily official capacity, is an authoritarian one, with no representation of women as subjects of their desire or their creativity. The maternal body is spoken about in the strictly utilitarian terms of reproduction, and education's goal is to produce more adequate national subjects by making the school an extension of the home.

The devaluation of the feminine space was a characteristic of this official discourse. Josefina Ludmer (1984) has suggested that a subjugated group will deterritorialize and resignify the marginal or subordinated space it has been compelled to embrace as its own. Thus, what may seem on the surface an acceptance of the dominant discourse on the part of the subaltern might entail a strategy of subversion. In Mistral's persona, however, I find no evidence that Mistral was involved in a project of resistance or deterritorialization. Certainly Mistral, the poet, resignified many of the symbols of the dominant discourse. Mistral the persona, however, did not exhibit an attitude of confrontation or subversion. Mistral's elevation as a public figure depended precisely on the regulation of the majority of women's lives by the state. Although Mistral was able to (painstakingly and slowly) carve out a lifestyle in which she could escape marriage and motherhood, we must remember that this option was not readily available to most Latin American women.

Poetry's status within the official discourse was ambiguous. It inhabited a zone between acceptable and unacceptable discourse. Even though *Lecturas* contains many poems and writings by Mistral, Mistral does not allude to her profession as poet in the preface to the reader. When it comes to women readers, poetry's aim is not creation per se, and much less the expression of a female lyric "I." The aim of poetry is to educate in a "feminine" manner, through beauty or aesthetics, and to instill in the woman a patriotic love of her country. In other words, poetry and by extension literature are deployed for a specific, pedagogic effect, ostensibly in the service of the "nation" and concretely for the benefit of the state. When poetry did not fulfill this utilitarian function, it was not spoken about much, as if it approximated the stuff of scandal.

The transformation of the maternal body of order and service into the maternal body of pleasure and creativity did not follow a linear progression in Mistral. Already some of her earlier writings had presented the mother as an idiosyncratic, poetic figure.[16] However, it is safe to say that it was only after having secured a degree of social authority, with her intervention in the educational reforms of the state, her assumption of the role of spokesperson, and her articulation of a conservative gender discourse, that Mistral was freer to articulate the maternal body as a body of desire. I see a direct relationship between Mistral's apparent (though always insecure) success in postponing and eventually eliminating from public discourse the troubling issue of her sexual identity and Mistral's own ability to approach subjects barred by the constraints of the national discourse she had decided to represent.

This might be illustrated by a consideration of Mistral's second book of poems, *Ternura* [Tenderness].

A few words are in order about *Ternura*. First, it is the most critically ignored and misunderstood of Mistral's poetry; partly because of *Ternura*'s subject matter, the mother-infant relationship, and partly because of *Ternura*'s poetic form, the lullaby or, more broadly conceived, "literatura infantil" [children's literature]. Latter-day critics have been too quick to skip over these poems in favor of Mistral's more "serious" books of poetry. In so doing, they have replicated an antifeminist gesture, whereby an entire category of women's expression is dismissed as ideological brainwash or as simply inferior to more "elevated" (read male) standards of poetry. A variant of this critical disdain is to view these poems as mere preparatory exercises for more worthy poetic ventures.

Ternura was, actually, the most widely read of Mistral's poetry books. According to Palma Guillén (xiii), nine or ten editions were printed during Mistral's lifetime; many more than any other of her books of poetry. This might be due to their appeal to "popular" content or to their use in the schools and educational programs underway. Parts of *Ternura* appeared originally in *Desolación*, Mistral's first collection of poems; yet other sections of *Ternura* were published as part of *Tala*, Mistral's third book. This suggests that these lullabies constitute an integral part of Mistral's poetic production, which should underscore the autonomy of many of these lullabies as full-fledged poems in their own right.

In 1945 Mistral edited all her so-called "literatura infantil" into an expanded edition of *Ternura*, which became the definitive version we know today. To this 1945 edition Mistral appended an extraordinary poetic essay, "Colofón con cara de excusa" [Colophon with the Semblance of an Excuse], ostensibly to explain the creation of these "children's poems." This essay, according to Mistral, was also requested by a male figure. This time, however, instead of the minister of education, it is her *editor* who places the request: "Ahora tengo que divagar, a pedido de mi Editor" (Mistral 1945, 106) [Now I have to digress, at the request of my Editor]. Male control is still a condition of possibility for publication, but, we will notice, the place is now writing, *literary* writing. Mistral is now firmly anchored in her position as author; so anchored indeed, that she won the Nobel Prize for *Literature* that same year.

The essay's very placement in the spatial configuration of the book is already a clue as to its nature. Instead of the authoritarian preface of *Lecturas para mujeres*, "Colofón" is an afterword, staged as a series of thoughts. Though it retains a mild defensiveness, and the self-deprecating pose of the "compiler" (although with an important shift: "la recopiladora" is now "la desvariadora;" roughly, "the delirious or nonsensical one"), the tone of the essay is intimate, and it has abandoned the stance of the schoolteacher-turned-doyenne of the subject of women's education. Even the sections that pertain to the "race," the discourse of Nuestra América that Mistral never quite abandoned, call attention to the violence, as opposed to the felicity, at the heart of Latin American nationalism: "soy de los que llevan entrañas, rostro y expresión *conturbados e irregulares,* a causa del injerto; me cuento entre los hijos de esa cosa torcida que se llama una experiencia racial, mejor dicho, *una violencia racial*" (108, emphasis Mistral) [I am one of those whose entrails, face, and expression are *turbulent and irregular,* because of the graft; I count myself among the children of that twisted thing we call a racial experience, or, better stated, *a racial violence*]. By remarking on the "monstrous" birth of the race (109), Mistral distances herself somewhat from her earlier role as the spokeswoman of the nation. She turns both her body and the abstract body of Nuestra América into a twisted, deformed creature, born of violence; a far cry from "la tierra de milagro" of the earlier essay. Instead of an appeal to the abstract homogeneity of the common good, signified in "Palabras" by the "race," allusions to the "race" in "Colofón" call attention to the troubling difference of Latin America.

In addition, Mistral no longer claims membership in the "secret society" of illustrious men: there is no mention of Rodó, Bello, Sarmiento, or Vasconcelos in this essay. Curiously enough, there is no mention of Martí, the author of *La edad de oro* and *Ismaelillo.* There is only one allusion to a nineteenth-century male figure, Rubén Darío, an interesting choice if we compare him to the above: foremost poet of Latin America, renovator of Latin American verse, and not particularly regarded as a bastion of the national discourse. And even the allusion to Darío, in the company of Homer, Shakespeare and Calderón, is discarded by Mistral when she claims that not one of them is superior to "la memoria de los niños" (109) [the memory of children], a construction which must be unpacked carefully in the case of Mistral.

After the requisitory nod toward male authority in the form of her editor, Mistral begins by stating that lullabies are sites of exclusively female language. The mother, says Mistral, speaks to herself, not to the child, since the child cannot engage in any kind of verbal conversation with its mother at the infant stage: "Conté una vez en Lima el sentido que tendría el género de la Canción de Cuna *en cuanto a cosa que la madre se regala a sí misma y no al niño que nada puede entender*" (106, emphasis Mistral) [Once I told this story in Lima, about the sense that the lullaby genre would acquire if it were regarded *as a thing that the mother gives to herself and not to the child, who cannot understand any of it*].

This striking opening sentence reverses the hegemonic interpretation of lullabies, which stresses the lullaby's primarily utilitarian function. The oral formula ("conté") downplays the significance of this reversion, in which the mother, not the child, is the object of the lullaby. The writing subject's attention is diverted from the national imperative: the problem is no longer the nation and how women might best serve it. Mistral is preoccupied with the eccentric aspects of women, the ways in which they do not conform, the ways that they find to be creative, the ways in which they can be characterized as something other than merely the reproductive vessels of the national discourse, as mothers or schoolteachers. The subject is women and poetry, even when it is ostensibly about lullabies in Latin America: "¿Por qué las mujeres nos hemos atrevido con la poesía y no con la música? ¿Por qué hemos optado por la palabra, expresión más grave de consecuencias y cargada de lo conceptual, que no es reino nuestro?" (106) [Why have we women been so daring with poetry, instead of music? Why have we chosen the word, the form of expression most loaded with consequence, charged with the conceptual, which is not our domain?].

Mistral is saying something very radical in a purportedly "humble" language. She is saying, first, that women have always used words creatively, even though they have not had access to "higher" forms of the word and literature, such as writing. ("Porque las mujeres no podemos quedar mucho tiempo pasivas, aunque se hable de nuestro sedentarismo, y menos callarnos por años. La madre buscó y encontró, pues, una manera de hablar consigo misma, meciendo al hijo, y además comadreando con él, y por añadidura con la noche, 'que es cosa viva'" [106] [For we women cannot remain passive for very long, even if we are described as sedentary; let alone be silent for years. The mother sought and found a way, then, to talk to herself, while rocking her child, and gossiping with him, and so with the night, 'a living thing'].) Women, Mistral implies, have always been preoccupied with questions of self. Selfhood is here personified by "la noche . . . persona activa y plural," [night . . . a plural, active person] and "el niño" [the child] (106), who is made into something larger than its empirical existence by "la mujer-madre-noche" ("[la noche] . . . engruesa al bulto pequeño" [106] [(night) . . . enlarges the small bundle]).

Mistral's twist to the interpretation of women's lullabies (that they are uncreative; that they are poetically inferior; that the woman is given solely to her child), shows Mistral skillfully manipulating tradition in a way that seems to empower women. This is, undoubtedly, a movement of deterritorialization, an inversion of categories, a subversion of the traditional view of women as childbearers and caretakers.

But this is only true of the beginning section of "Colofón," and this beginning is revealed to be a stage for a complicated set of maneuvers. I believe that Mistral's chief interest in the essay is strategic: to "cover," so to speak, with her intentional inclusion in the essay's "nosotras," her own existence as a woman in a male-defined world: that of published literature, that of the author. Mistral is masquerading in the guise of a mother and disguising the fact that she chose a rather different route from that of most Latin American women. Her criticism of "[la] caída lenta de la maternidad corporal" (107) [the slow decline of bodily motherhood] and "la rehusa de muchas mujeres a criar" (107) [the refusal of many women to raise children], which, according to Mistral, affects the poetic quality of the lullabies (107), is rather problematic; she admonishes women for not doing what they are "supposed" to do, while reserving the right to abstain from her very prescriptions.

At the same time that Mistral reaffirms women's creativity, she lays out her difference with respect to this tradition. The first difference between the transhistorical Latin American mother, a figure invented by patriarchal heterosexuality (whose static quality Mistral appropriates for her own purposes) and Mistral, is that Mistral does not sing: she writes. "Writing" lullabies is referred to as an unnatural way of conceiving popular literature: as an abortion (107), thus echoing Mistral's penchant to speak of herself as an aberration.

The implicit substitution of verbs is crucial. With it, Mistral invades the male-dominated arena of the written text, under the guise of "song," of "oral literature," while aligning herself with traditional concepts of "woman," as in the singing mother. The effect is that this incursion has not taken place, that she has not transgressed the limits imposed by her status as a woman. Mistral presents herself as a continuant of tradition, as a compiler of lullabies and not as an author of poems; as one more in a long line of rural women whose lives have been idealized in the discourse of patriarchal heterosexism, particularly in its national expression.

One could construct a cultural-feminist "reclaiming" of female tradition, and a vindication of neglected feminine creativity, were it not for the inescapable fact that Mistral presents herself as a loner figure that does not fit into this idealized community of women either. This is achieved, not only through her indirect reference to herself, when she states that biological motherhood is necessary to the creation of "real" lullabies (107), but more directly when she writes: "Estas canciones están harto lejos de la folklóricas que colman mi gusto, y yo me lo sé como el vicio de mis cabellos y el desmaño de mis ropas" (108) [These songs are very removed from the folkloric ones, which I like the best, and I am aware of this, in the same way I am aware of the vice of my hair and the disarray of my clothes].

By placing the aberration of writing, the abandonment of mothering and its detrimental effect, her own "lullabies," and her figurative body (here turned into an indigent body) in the same continuum, Mistral unambiguously marks her separation from the tradition of women's creativity she has just "celebrated."

In the next movement, she states that her lullabies are poor, mutilated emblems of a love that has no language, a silent love: "Nacieron, las pobres, para convidar, mostrando sus pies inválidos, a que algún músico las echase a andar, y las hice, mitad por regusto de los arrullos de mi infancia, mitad para servir la emoción de otras mujeres—el poeta es un desata-nudos y el amor sin palabras nudo es, y ahoga" (108) [The poor things were born in order to invite some musician to set them to music, even as they showed their disabled feet. I made them, half out of love for the "hums" of my childhood, half to enable the emotion of other women—poets undo knots, and a love without words is a knot, and it chokes]. Two things are important in this passage. First, she clearly refers to herself as a poet, even if somewhat indirectly. Second, it is no longer clear what kind of love she is talking about. Since she has allowed that women have always used words creatively, and that they have addressed themselves and their children for centuries, it does not follow that the "love without words" that she mentions is either one of those. Indeed, by now the child has merged with her own poetic self, and the tradition of oral lullabies has been left behind. Mistral concludes her "Colofón" with a series of self-referential, ambiguous paragraphs, in which the possibility of lesbian love might well reside in that most commonplace of phrases, "the love that dare not speak its name."

The poetic "I" retreats into her "country," her "house," her "homeland," her "planet," all metaphors of the self, of her subjectivity in a culture from which she feels alienated, exiled. The realm of dreams and sleep also escapes the economy of labor and the space of "acceptable" discourse: "En el sueño he tenido mi casa más holgada y ligera, mi patria verdadera, mi planeta dulcísimo. No hay praderas tan espaciosas, tan deslizables y tan delicadas para mí como las suyas" (108) [In sleep/dream I have had my lightest, most comfortable house; my true homeland; my sweetest planet. No plains strike me as so spacious, so slippery and so delicate, like sleep's/dream's]. These metaphors relate directly to the discourse of the nation. They are its uncanny counterparts. Instead of an idealized, abstract community, we have an obsessive retreat from the collective consciousness. The sleep or dream induced by lullabies welcomes silence (the absence of speech) and the love without words (the failure or impossibility of speech). In her official capacity, Mistral was the producer of speech, of discourse, as well as the embodiment of millions of women. In this poetic capacity, she is alone and silent; released from the body of order; a destitute repository of that which must not or will not be said.

Once again Mistral refers to her life as a "hard" one: "Tal vez a causa de que mi vida fue dura, bendije siempre el sueño y lo di por la más ancha gracia divina" [Maybe because my life was harsh, I always blessed sleep and consider it the most divine of graces]. In "Palabras" she had ended the final section with a reference to "rest" and the possibility of writing (for women). In "Colofón" she relates women to motherhood, nighttime, lullabies, poetry, sleep, and dreams, an amalgam which she names, indirectly, "mi país furtivo" [my elusive homeland] and "la escapada" [the escapade] (108). Writing these "songs" is explicitly a way to access this homeland, where the conflation of sexual love and maternal love is suggested in the complicity between the "I" and the "child":

> Algunos trechos de estas Canciones—a veces uno o dos versos logrados—me dan la salida familiar hacia mi país furtivo, me abren la hendija o trampa de la escapada. El punto de la música por donde el niño se escabulle y deja a la madre burlada y cantando inútilmente, ese último peldaño me lo conozco muy bien: en tal o cual palabra, *el niño y yo* damos vuelta la espalda y nos escapamos dando vuelta al mundo, como la capa estorbosa en el correr. (108)
>
> [Some stretches of these Songs—sometimes one or two accomplished verses—afford me that familiar exit to my elusive country, open the crack or trick of the escapade. The musical counterpoint from which the child slides off and leaves the mother, tricked, singing uselessly; this last step I know very well. In this or that word, the child and I turn our backs to the world and escape it, circling it just like the cape that hinders running.]

This "child-I" cannot, or decides not to, face the object of its desire directly, and must run away from the mother-woman. In this light, motherhood becomes allegorical, its other meaning the attraction and repulsion characteristic of repressed desire.

The abandoning of the public discourse of *América*, of Mistral's role as its spokesperson, through a conservative gender discourse and the enigmatic allusion to a love without words that "chokes" are concealed by an "acceptable" language (lullabies) and practice (mothering) that would go unpunished by the sexist, compulsorily heterosexual web of power relations Mistral was entangled in. The language of reproduction and childcare is removed from an economy of reproductive functions as they are assigned in patriarchal heterosexism.

But even an essay in which there has been such a departure from Mistral's prescriptive persona, and such an extraordinary focus on her poetic self, must regain its proper composure and return to her public capacities, albeit in a muted form. The last sections of the essay partially restore her self-deprecating stance ("artesana ardiente pero fallida" [109] [an enthusiastic but failed artisan], her persona of the "Schoolteacher of America" ("Que los maestros perdonen la barbaridad de mi hacer y rehacer" [109] [May the schoolteachers forgive me for the outrage of my doing and redoing]), and her position as the spiritual mother of (Latin America's) children, but the latter with an important caveat.

At the very end of the essay, she compares "la expresión infantil" [children's expression] to a "misterio cristalino y profundo" [crystalline and deep mystery] (110), transparent, yet unreachable and unextinguishable, simple and complex at the same time: "engaña vista y mano con su falsa superficialidad" (110) [it fools sight and hand with its false superficiality]. This section functions as a warning and compels us to look more closely at her "children's literature" with an eye to an at once hidden and obvious meaning.

Can the at once "hidden and obvious" meaning be lesbian desire? Lesbianism remained, at face value, as absent from this discourse as it had been from the more strongly prescriptive "Palabras." A (heterosexual) discourse of woman-identification can only hope to render lesbianism partially, and probably not at all. Since lesbianism is excluded from the patriarchal, heterosexist conception of motherhood in traditional Latin America, it is upon first glance wholly invisible from Mistral's poetry, especially the texts of motherhood; that is, if we read *only* at face value. If we read against the grain, however, with Mistral's sexual indeterminacy in mind, I suggest we might produce another reading.

Ternura's lullabies have been read as conservative statements on motherhood and womanhood, but, if read more carefully, at least some of these very same lullabies can emerge as erotic poems. A close reading of "Colofón" substantiates this hypothesis; in it, Mistral gives the attentive reader the clues from which to initiate this *other* reading.

I am tempted to regard "Colofón" as the essay which was heralded at the beginning of "Palabras de la extranjera": "an essay that I will write someday, in my homeland, for the women of Latin America." Exactly what, or where is this promised "homeland" of Mistral, who had referred to herself as "la extranjera" in "Palabras"? Could this homeland be located in an apparently heterosexual space, reproductive motherhood, stripped of reproduction? We may remember that in "Palabras" reproductive motherhood was a site of profit, of the maximization of female bodies, and that the emphasis was on the representation of the service sector as an extension of the home, in the case of women's labor. In "Colofón," the emphasis turns precisely to the lack of profit of the lullabies written by Mistral, to the representation of a motherhood, so to speak, without maximization and, at times, literally without the child. The "home" of "Colofón" is a narcissistic home, one which signifies only itself.

This remains slippery ground, though, since the lullabies could indeed be used for specific effects within the school and did confirm on some level the continuation of her persona, as well as the continued labor of empirical mothers and schoolteachers. Mistral never, to my knowledge, stepped outside of the discursive closets she constructed to safeguard her potentially transgressive identities and practices. But "Colofón con cara de excusa" is remarkable because of its insistence precisely on the zones that fall outside of profit: desire, narcissism, pleasure. *The stuff of scandal.*

As should be apparent from my analysis, I see only a limited theoretical value in "offering" Mistral as simply a trickster figure. Her involvement with the hegemonic formations and her closeted sexuality are problematic. Mistral, a subaltern by virtue of her gender and her sexuality, chose to represent the hegemonic discourse. The result was a divided subject, split between a unified, conservative persona and a multiple, potentially transgressive poetic self. In many ways, Mistral's poetry and poetic writings explore the nightmarish repercussions of her alliances with the powers that be. Occasionally they imagine a space where these alliances can be escaped altogether or replaced by other alliances; but Mistral's persona remained faithful to the national discourse and its conservative prescriptions for women. We cannot ignore the fact that Mistral's gender discourse, in her extremely influential, even iconic public capacity, constituted subordinated female subjects by relegating women to the household, to reproduction, and to the service sector of the economy.

As we develop new interpretations of Mistral, these contradictory aspects of her textual production will have to come under close scrutiny. In Latin America, being a woman author has historically entailed contradiction and discrimination. This inquiry into Mistral can aid us in the understanding of other high-profile women authors of Latin America, especially those with an additional discriminated or prohibited identity. I have based this study on two essays, "Palabras de la extranjera" and "Colofón con cara de excusa," that I consider not only important, but singular in the Mistralian body of writing. The essays, markedly self-conscious and bordering on self-serving, separated temporally and functionally, linked to the production of books nonetheless, illustrate the process by which Mistral crafted and secured a distinctly literary authority. This was only possible after wielding a sufficient amount of social and political authority, especially in light of her forbidden, scandalous sexuality.

I have suggested that Gabriela Mistral's public identity was aligned with a traditional woman-identified discourse in the service of the nation. Even at a great price, this persona crucially enabled her various "closeted" identities; identities which could not be made public, even if they were sometimes displayed in public, *at once hidden and obvious*. These included her existence as a woman in the public sphere; as an unmarried woman; as a childless woman; as a woman author; and, finally, as a lesbian.

Notes

1   A striking example is a story by Rosario Castellanos, "Album de familia" (1971), in which Castellanos portrays in scathing terms a famous Latin American writer, 'Matilde Casanova,' who bears a thinly veiled resemblance to Gabriela Mistral. I thank Daniel Balderston for bringing this story and its homophobic content to my attention.

2   A favorite fiction is that she remained faithful to her one true love, who committed suicide at age eighteen.

3   Mary Louise Pratt (1990) has challenged this vision of obedient nationalism in Mistral's poetry, in a study of the *Poema de Chile*.

4   See, for example, the special editions of *Acta Literaria* (1989), "La obra de Gabriela Mistral," and *Taller de Letras* (1989), "Gabriela Mistral, 1889–1989"; the special section of *Atenea: Ciencia, Arte, Literatura* (1989), "Homenaje a Gabriela Mistral," and Regina Rodríguez, ed. (1989), *Una palabra cómplice: Encuentro con Gabriela Mistral*.

5   See Horan (1990) for a different reading of this "family of women."

6   Or ISA ("ideological state apparatus") in Althusserian terms (Althusser 1970).

7   See Benedict Anderson, *Imagined Communities* (1983).

8   I use "masquerade" in a sense close to that outlined by Joan Riviere (1929) in "Womanliness as Masquerade," but without the psychoanalytic implications that are the core of Riviere's analysis: "Womanliness therefore could be assumed and worn as a mask, both to hide the possession of masculinity and to avert the reprisals expected if she was found to possess it—much as a thief will turn out his pockets and ask to be searched to prove he has not the stolen goods. The reader may now ask how I define womanliness or where I draw the line between genuine womanliness and the 'masquerade.' My suggestion is not, however, that there is any such difference; whether radical or superficial, they are the same thing." In Burgin, Donald, and Kaplan (1986): 38.

9   See Julio Ramos (1989) for an excellent overview and analysis of the changing conceptions of "letters" and the function of "literature" in Latin America.

10   This followed Sarmiento's program for educational reform, begun in the nineteenth century in Chile. It is important to note that women were recruited as schoolteachers on the basis of their "natural" disposition toward motherhood, considered "ideal" for primary education. It is equally important to note that normal education, aside from being female, was usually finished by age seventeen or eighteen, and that most *normalistas* went on to become primary and normal schoolteachers. Therefore, one must qualify the extent of educational reform in the nineteenth century, as it applied to women. While undoubtedly a reform in comparison to women's lot before, the normal system still created a sexual division of labor insofar as teaching itself was concerned and regulated the amount of education that women could receive formally. Thus, it curtailed women's advancement and, especially, conditioned this advancement to the needs of the state.

11   For recent discussions of the national subject and its claims to universality, see Homi K. Bhabha, ed., *Nation and Narration* (1990).

12   See Judith Butler (1991) for a concise elucidation of gender as a type of "drag."

13   All English paraphrases of Mistral's essays are my own.

14   Not the title generally used for this preface. Scholars refer to it as "Introducción a *Lecturas para mujeres*." I use the title "Palabras de la extranjera" for two reasons: it is the first subtitle of the preface *and* a very Mistralian title.

15   Mistral did adopt a child, her nephew, who committed suicide at age eighteen. However, she never had a biological child.

16   Some examples would be, in prose, "Recuerdos de la madre ausente" and, among her early poems, "El suplicio," "Poema del hijo," and even the "Sonetos de la muerte," a cycle for which she was awarded the prestigious *Premio de los Juegos Florales de Santiago* as early as 1914.

Works Cited

Althusser, Louis. "Ideology and Ideological State Apparatuses (Notes towards an Investigation)." *Lenin and Philosophy and Other Essays*. London: NLB, 1970, rpt. 1977. 127–86.

Anderson, Benedict. *Imagined Communities: Reflections on the Origin and Spread of Nationalism*. London: Verso, 1983.

Bhabha, Homi K., ed. *Nation and Narration*. New York and London: Routledge, 1990.

Burgin, Victor, James Donald, and Cora Kaplan, eds. *Formations of Fantasy*. London: Methuen, 1986.

Butler, Judith. "Imitation and Gender Insubordination." Ed. Diana Fuss. 13–31.

Castellanos, Rosario. "Album de familia." *Album de familia*. México: Joaquín Mortiz, 1971. 65–154.

Fuss, Diana, ed. *Inside/Out: Lesbian Theories, Gay Theories*. New York and London: Routledge, 1991.

"Gabriela Mistral, 1889–1989." Special issue. *Taller de Letras* 17 (1989).

González, Patricia Elena, and Eliana Ortega, eds. *La sartén por el mango: Encuentro de escritoras latinoamericanas*. San Juan: Huracán, 1984.

Guillén de Nicolau, Palma. "Introducción." In Mistral (1986).

"Homenaje a Gabriela Mistral." Special section. *Atenea: Ciencia, Arte, Literatura* 459–60 (Chile, 1989).

Horan, Elizabeth Rosa. "Matrilineage, Matrilanguage: Gabriela Mistral's Intimate Audience of Women." *Revista Canadiense de Estudios Hispánicos* 14.3 (Spring 1990): 447–57.

Ibacache, María Luisa. "Gabriela Mistral y el México de Vasconcelos." *Atenea: Ciencia, Arte, Literatura* 459–60 (Chile, 1989): 141–55.

Ludmer, Josefina. "Tretas del débil." Ed. González and Ortega. 47–53.

Mistral, Gabriela. "Introducción." Introduction to *Lecturas para mujeres*. México: Porrúa, 1924, rpt. 1974.

———. "Colofón con cara de excusa." *Desolación. Ternura. Tala. Lagar.* México: Porrúa, 1945, rpt. 1986.

"La obra de Gabriela Mistral." Special issue. *Acta Literaria* 14 (Chile, 1989).

Pratt, Mary Louise. "Women, Literature, and the National Brotherhood." *Women, Culture and Politics in Latin America.* Ed. Seminar on Feminism and Culture in Latin America. Berkeley: University of California Press, 1990. 48–73.

Ramos, Julio. *Desencuentros de la modernidad en América Latina. Literatura y política en el siglo XIX.* México: Fondo de Cultura Económica, 1989.

Riviere, Joan. "Womanliness as Masquerade." Ed. Burgin, Donald, and Kaplan. 35–44.

Rodríguez, Regina, ed. *Una palabra cómplice: Encuentro con Gabriela Mistral.* Santiago de Chile: Isis Internacional y Casa de La Mujer La Morada, 1989.

Sedgwick, Eve Kosofsky. "Introduction: Axiomatic; Epistemology of the Closet." *Epistemology of the Closet.* Berkeley and Los Angeles: University of California Press, 1990.

Seminar on Feminism and Culture in Latin America. *Women, Culture, and Politics in Latin America.* Berkeley: University of California Press, 1990.

Sylvia Molloy

Disappearing Acts: Reading Lesbian in Teresa de la Parra

Nunca he sabido su historia, si alguna tuvo; las historias de amor de las solteras que no murieron jóvenes y gloriosas . . . no interesan a nadie. La familia no las recuerda. Sobre el corazón pudoroso que se marchita con su secreto van cayendo los días como copos de nieve, y el secreto queda encerrado bajo la blancura del tiempo.
[I know nothing of her story, if indeed she had one. No one is interested in the love stories of unmarried women who do not die young, or famous . . . . Their families don't remember them. On the discreet heart, wasting away with its secret, days fall like snowflakes, and the secret is buried under the whiteness of time.]—Teresa de la Parra, Influencia de las mujeres en la formación del alma americana.

¿Qué me importa que digan "la pobre Teresa" si yo sé a qué atenerme?
[What do I care if they call me "poor Teresa" when I'm prepared for it?]—Teresa de la Parra, Letter to Lydia Cabrera, 12 October 1933.

They loved independence and did not love their suitors. Many things drew them together.—Jeannette Marks, Gallant Little Wales

At the end of each volume of Editorial Ayacucho's collection of Latin American classics there is a chronology divided into three columns: the one on the left is reserved for the author's life, the one in the middle for national and continental events, the one on the right for events happening in what is termed, rather naively, the "outside world" (*mundo exterior*). The column on the left is usually far less busy than the other two, obviously because more things happen in worlds "exterior" or "interior" than in the mere life of one individual. Even so, the personal column devoted to Teresa de la Parra, in Ayacucho's edition of her *Obra*, is singularly sparse. It is virtually blank from her birth till 1923, when she leaves her native Venezuela to settle

in Europe; then, from 1923 until Parra's death in Madrid in 1936, it documents her life with an economy bordering on the miserly. While so many
things were going on in Venezuela, in Latin America, and in the "outside
world," Ayacucho's skewed tripartite chronology seems to be telling us,
Teresa de la Parra was not living.

A writer's life may be uneventful, therefore striking the biographer, or
in this case the annotator, as untellable. This was not the case of Teresa de
la Parra, whose comings and goings, whose sociability, have become part
of her legend; whose illness, even while constraining her physically, led to
one of the busiest epistolary existences imaginable. Yet even a superficial
account of these *facts* is avoided, or at least not seriously engaged in, by
Ayacucho's chronologer. The untellability of Teresa de la Parra's life, I venture, resides elsewhere. To begin, then, I want to examine that untellability
to which Ayacucho's blank column so glaringly attests.

It is true that relatives of Teresa de la Parra have not been forthcoming
with specific biographical details. It is also true that Parra's life, as that of
so many Latin American women writers, was soon processed into legend,
a legend that glossed over the more disquieting gaps in her life, allowed for
the more or less satisfactory explanation of others, and thus conditioned
Parra's life into an acceptable cultural script. One of the gaps that has most
intrigued critics of Teresa de la Parra is, foreseeably, the absence of a love
relationship or, as one critic testily demands, "¿A quién amó realmente esta
mujer?" (Hiriart 61, n.1) [Whom did this woman really love?].[1] It is worthwhile to consider, if only briefly, some of the answers eagerly provided by
anxious critics. Thus Ramón Díaz Sánchez suggests of Teresa de la Parra
that "le faltó transitar caminos. Y entre estos el del amor. . . . Y en vez
del amor lo que llega es la muerte" (Díaz Sánchez 22–24) [she was unable
to explore all the roads, amongst them the road of love. . . . Instead of
love, she met with death]. Evocative of a young life cut in full flower, à la
Marie Bashkirtseff (the effusive Russian autobiographer whose early death
by consumption, in Paris, captivated so many feverish male minds), the
statement is meaningless in reference to Teresa de la Parra, who died at
age forty-seven. Another critic reads the absence of love in Parra's life as
the result of deliberate choice. Resorting to (while displacing) the conjugal
imperative, he ascribes to Parra the "married-to-her-work" cliché, so prevalent in the reading of single women whose sexuality is best ignored. "Teresa
escogió en favor de [la obra de creación] y renunció al matrimonio. Era una
opción libre y ello escogió. Por ello una vez escribió 'vivo como una monja
frente al lago Leman, escribiendo.' . . . Si Teresa se convirtió en una mística
sin fe—como ella misma decía fue por su obra literaria, para poderse en-

tregar a ella sin ataduras. Fue una forma de amor" (Lovera de Sola) [Teresa freely chose (her creative work) and renounced marriage. That is why she once wrote "I live like a nun on Lake Léman and write." If Teresa became a mystic without faith—as she herself said—it was for the sake of her literary oeuvre, so that she could devote herself to it without impediment. This was indeed a form of love]. The image of the writerly nun conjured up by this judgment—so evocative of Sor Juana Inés de la Cruz about whose presumed sexuality, or lack thereof, so much has been written—is certainly of interest here. But let us take a look at yet a third conjecture on the part of critics: Teresa de la Parra did love someone, goes this version, and that someone was the Ecuadorian essayist Gonzalo Zaldumbide. This relationship, referred to, albeit in somewhat ambiguous terms, in the correspondence between Parra and Zaldumbide, has been hailed as decisive by some critics, while considered less significant by others, including members of Parra's own family. Indeed, in a 1957 interview providing the official family version of Parra, her sister María states that "a ella no le disgustaba" (Norris, cited in Hiriart 63, n.2) [she did not dislike him], a tepid endorsement at best, and then hints at another relationship. As one critic, thwarted in his desire for precise facts, writes:

> [T]he secret existence of an unnamed admirer has been neither admitted nor denied, presenting a ghostly Pandora's box that no biographer has succeeded in opening. Teresa's feminine charms and romantic nature were indisputable, and the reticence of family and friends alike to discuss even the absence of love in her life has been pronounced. Those people wishing only to aid their comprehension of her decisions in life have been left the sole option of seeking the answer in the pages of *Ifigenia*. (Lemaître 55)

This statement is revealing on several counts. First, it tells us that it is the *absence* of love, not its *presence,* that worries critics. Second, it implies that inquiry into this life may be dangerous, even to dutiful biographers eager "to aid their comprehension." The mention of Pandora's box—so allusive to lack of control, misfortune, and, above all, female misdoing—is not, I venture, totally innocent: if Pandora's box has remained unopened it is because no one has really wanted it open. Finally, the notion that a careful perusal of *Ifigenia* is the "sole option" left to the critic as a source for the life of Teresa de la Parra brings up an immediate question (one that this essay will attempt to answer), that is: Why not look elsewhere?

This insistent effort to find out (without really wanting to find out) the details of Parra's love life is matched by what might be seen as an exercise in gender overcompensation. Even when critics cannot tell *whom* Teresa de la Parra loved, or even *if* Teresa de la Parra loved, they are all, to a man, quite certain that Parra was very *feminine*. The spirit in which this compulsory femininity is ascribed oscillates between the pornographic and the paranoid. Thus Arturo Uslar Pietri writes: "Teresa de la Parra es una de las escritoras más femeninas. Nadie le excede en este don. *Ifigenia* es un libro mujer: atractivo, oscuro, turbador. . . . En su prosa hay frases, torpezas, simples adjetivos que son como una incitadora desnudez" (Uslar Pietri 79) [Teresa de la Parra is the most feminine of writers. No one surpasses her in that gift. *Ifigenia* is a woman-book: attractive, evasive, arousing. . . . Certain of its phrases, gaucheries, even adjectives are like enticing nudities]. For his part, Carlos García Prada, in his introduction to Parra's incorrectly labeled *Obras completas,* adds a defensive twist: "Era franca y espontánea y eminentemente *femenina;* aunque conocía bien los principios técnicos y los ideales de las modernas escuelas literarias, Teresa desdeñaba la 'virilidad' de que tanto se ufanan otras escritoras contemporáneas. Su ideal era ver, sentir, obrar y escribir como mujer" (Parra, *Obras completas* 10) [She was frank and spontaneous and eminently feminine. While she was well aware of the technical principles and ideals of modern literary schools, she disdained the "virility" flaunted by other contemporary female writers. Her ideal was to see, feel, act and write like a woman].[2] This hypercorrection—not only is Teresa de la Parra feminine, she is, above all, critics tell us, *not masculine*—is already pointing to, while never naming, that part of Teresa de la Parra's life which everybody, critics and relatives alike, is either erasing or refusing to confront.

I would like to propose another reading of Teresa de la Parra here, without forcing prejudiced conventions—a necessary lover, an obligatory femininity—onto a vital *void* that is merely the result of anxiety-ridden erasure, but without overlooking, either, the precise way in which that erasure has been effected. I wish to look closely at a writer whose life has been truncated by critics (I could have done the same with Gabriela Mistral), taking into account not only her fiction but other texts, letters, and diaries expurgated by "friendly hands," as the saying goes in Spanish, and, on more than one occasion, by the hands of Parra herself.[3] Unlike the aforementioned critics, it is not my desire to read into the gaps but to read the gaps themselves, as spaces of resistance, provocation, or else—when the gaps are the work of Parra's censors—as spaces of societal shame.

Parra's work—all of it written in the first-person feminine—is riddled with gender disquiet, family dissonance, and corporeal unease.[4] Parra published three texts in her lifetime, *Diario de una caraqueña por el Lejano Ori-*

ente [Diary of a Caracas Woman in the Far East] (1920), *Ifigenia (o diario de una señorita que se fastidia* [Ifigenia, or Diary of a Young Lady Who Is Bored] (1924), and *Las memorias de Mamá Blanca* [Mama Blanca's Memoirs] (1929). In addition, there are posthumous publications: three lectures on Latin American women (*Tres conferencias inéditas* [1961]), several very partial selections of her correspondence, and an equally spotty selection of the journal she kept during the last six years of her life. I shall return to these posthumous texts and shall dwell, for a moment, on the first three texts.

Besides systematically adopting an enunciation in the first-person feminine, all three texts mimic—either as *diaries* or as *memoirs*—the autobiographical mode. However, as both the text and Parra herself, in her correspondence, make clear, this is an autobiographical *effect,* a distancing mask that cuts identification short. In *Diario,* Parra rewrites the letters sent to her by her sister María during a trip to the Far East. While keeping the sister's real name in the text, she reworks the material with a mock-naive, half-ironic *tone* that is unmistakably her own, the same tone she will go on to perfect in *Ifigenia.* Regarding *Ifigenia,* a novel that critics, not without some factual justification, have insisted on reading autobiographically, seeing Parra's condemnation of bourgeois convention reflected in that of the protagonist, the author herself has cautioned against identification:

> La verdadera autobiografía está en [el tono], no en la narración como cree casi todo el mundo. . . . Para hacer hablar en tono sincero y desenfadado a María Eugenia Alonso la hice la antítesis de mí misma, le puse los defectos y cualidades que no tenía, a fin, creía yo, de evitar que nadie pudiera confundirme con ella. Pero no calculé que el disfraz sólo serviría para los que me conocía muy de cerca y que para los demás la autobiografía (confirmada además con circunstancias exteriores de mi propia vida) iba a ser evidente. En realidad mi personaje María Eugenia Alonso era una síntesis, una copia viva de varios tipos de mujer que había visto muy de cerca sufrir en silencio, y cuyo verdadero fondo me interesaba descubrir, *hacer hablar,* como protesta contra la presión del medio ambiente. Si el caso hubiera sido en realidad el mío yo no lo habría nunca expuesto por un sentimiento de pudor muy natural. La seguridad que sentía en no creerme aludida fue lo que me hizo llevar al extremo del desenfado el tono de María Eugenia Alonso, y ese tono resultó más real que la realidad misma, nadie ha sentido la transposición, han creído en la auténtica biografía y creo que es ahí en donde está el secreto del éxito de *Ifigenia.* El público adora las confesiones. Al

principio cuando me di cuenta de esto me sentí muy *gênée* y empecé a
tomarle antipatía a *Ifigenia,* publicada dos años después de terminada
y de vivir en París. Ahora el engaño me hace gracia. (*OC* 627)
[The real autobiography is in (the tone) not in the story, as nearly
everyone believes. . . . In order to make María Eugenia Alonso speak
with both honesty and impudence, I made her the opposite of myself,
I gave her the defects and qualities that I lacked so as to avoid (or so
I hoped) being taken for her. I did not realize that the disguise would
only work with those who knew me very well, and that, to others, the
novel would inevitably appear to be an autobiography, confirmed by
certain external circumstances that matched those of my own life. In
truth, my character, María Eugenia Alonso, was an amalgam, a faithful copy of several types of women whom I had seen up close suffering
in silence and whose true depth I wanted to reveal, *to give voice to,* as a
protest against our milieu. If indeed the case had been mine, a natural
sense of modesty would have kept me from exposing it so. The certainty I felt that I would not be recognized allowed me to take María
Eugenia Alonso's impudent tone to extremes, and that tone turned
out to be more real than reality itself. No one has felt the transposition; they have taken the book to be authentically autobiographical,
and that is, I believe, the secret of *Ifigenia*'s success. The public adores
confessions. At the beginning, when I realized this, I was quite upset
and started to dislike the novel, which had come out two years after
I had finished it, when I was living in Paris. Nowadays, I find the
deception amusing.]

Memorias de Mamá Blanca is the text by Parra that most openly mimics
autobiographical enunciation and does so doubly. The tried device of the
found (or, in this case, inherited) manuscript allows for the development of
two narrative voices in the first-person feminine, that of the scribe and that
of the memorialist herself. But, as with *Ifigenia,* there is deception. More
than in the latter text, *Memorias* makes abundant use of Parra's childhood
recollections, creating for a moment a strong autobiographical illusion,
but it *transposes*—a capital concept in Parra—that personal recollection by
projecting it back to the nineteenth century, when the narrated events take
place.

These three mock autobiographies allow me to draw a few conclusions.
First, in Parra's work there is a strong tendency toward the autobiographical matched by an equally strong impulse to curb that tendency, through
strategies of displacement and transposition. For Parra, direct autobiogra-

phy is inhibited by modesty; in its stead, oblique autobiography liberates, allows for impudence. Second, the process of transposition in Parra resorts to feminine alterity, to projection onto a specular other, in an act of overt female complicity. Third and fourth, jointly, the *other* whose life or manuscript is cannibalized is related to the author through familial or quasi-familial bonding with another woman: *Diario* reinscribes a sister's letters, *Ifigenia* tells the story of women seen "up close," *Memorias* rewrites the life of a woman to whom the narrator feels tied by "mysterious spiritual affinities" (O 315).[5] But, at the same time, the specular other functions as a negative for Parra, illustrating a life model that only permits self-definition through contrast. The protagonist of *Diario* is a conventionally married middle-class woman. That of *Ifigenia* (in a particularly sadistic ending to which I will return) ends up capitulating to social pressure, marrying a stereotype of middle-class authoritarianism and conceit. The protagonist of *Memorias,* possibly the one ideologically closest to Parra, is doubly distanced from her by chronology and idealization. As in a game of charades, in which the avid reader—he or she who "adores confessions"—is defeated beforehand, Parra's text tirelessly provokes us, tempts us with resemblance only to stress difference.

Scenes of voyeurism or, better yet, of oblique vision, abound in *Memorias.* The most striking, of course, is the mirror scene of "María Moñitos," the mother striving to curl her daughter's straight hair while amusing her with fairy tales, the daughter spying on the reflection of herself she sees emerging in the mirror, a simulacrum of femininity, and demanding of the mother that she change the traditional ending of the stories she tells. There is another scene, again involving two women, the narrator and Mamá Blanca, in the introduction to *Memorias.* This other scene of voyeurism— the child, slipping into Mamá Blanca's house uninvited, calmly spying on the old woman—is fundamental to the scene of writing in *Memorias.* Bypassing direct genealogy, in an act of oblique transmission sustained by female complicity, that same child will inherit, years later, the "mysterious manuscript" that Mamá Blanca wrote in secret: "Escrito para [mis hijos y nietos], te lo legaré a ti. Léelo si quieres pero no se lo enseñes a nadie" (O 321) [It was written for (my children and grandchildren) but I leave it to you. Read it if you wish but don't show it to anyone].

Now the conspiratorial nature of this scene of transmission (the secrecy of which is reinforced by the anonymous female "you" to whom the book is dedicated) does not quite match the contents of the *Memoirs* themselves. There is a lack of proportion between the childhood recollections themselves—even when, as both Elizabeth Garrels and Doris Sommer have shown (Garrels 1–61; Sommer 290–321) they are less innocuous than they seem at first glance—and the secrecy, the clandestinity attributed to the writing, reading, and dissemination of the text. I want to argue that Parra, through one of those processes of transposition and displacement that were dear to her, is saying, of course, something *other*. By highlighting what is secret, clandestine, conspiratorial, on the threshold, as it were, of a relatively nonthreatening text, she is offering not only clues to her literary strategy but a lesson in discriminating reading, an invitation to decode an oeuvre, a life, that permanently border on the unsayable. And, by choosing a narrator who, against the author's will, publishes the text and reveals the "secret," Parra highlights, in addition, an act of necessary betrayal, so that the unsayable be named: "Lo único que considero bien escrito . . . es lo que no está escrito, lo que tracé sin palabras, para que la benevolencia del lector fuera leyendo en voz baja" (*OC* 1965) [The only thing I consider well written . . . is what isn't written, what I traced without words, so that the benevolent reader would read it in a low voice]. These words of Teresa de la Parra, referred to her *Ifigenia,* guide my own reading: what is traced without words—or what has been intentionally obliterated by others—is nonetheless there, for the complicitous reader summoned by Teresa de la Parra to discover.

Homosexualities, in Latin American literature, are not comfortable notions to contend with, and lesbianism in particular seems to give critics a hard time. For example, Gabriela Mistral's sexuality has been an open secret for years yet the image, polished to a stereotypical sheen, of the celibate pedagogue and spiritual mother of Latin America, forever mourning a (male) sweetheart who committed suicide in his twenties—an image to which Mistral herself, as is known, collaborated—still precludes the possibility of a careful, more complex and more varied reading of Mistral's life and work. If Teresa de la Parra was not subjected to a similar exercise in hagiography and reduced to a seamless legend, it may well be because, in a sense, it was not imperative to do so: unlike Mistral, Parra was not a public or even a political figure, just a "lady writer" scribbling and socializing in Paris. Still, the anxiety shown by her relatives, friends, and critics betrays a similar urge to hide. I myself knew little of Parra's personal life: the pattern emerging from the cuts to which her writing was subjected, the *residue* left behind by careless censors, have told me more than any direct declaration might have.

Brutal cuts have especially marred Parra's diary, written between 1931 and 1936, a diary whose very existence the Parra family denied until quite recently, even when a critic, Ramón Díaz Sánchez, who had managed to read

it, had extensively quoted from it in his 1954 book on Parra. Only recently
has the aforementioned Ayacucho volume of the *Obra* published scattered
entries of that journal. To give but one example of the systematic work of
deletion and revision to which the text has been subjected, I propose the
following comparison. First is the fragment of the diary corresponding to
21 January 1936, as cited by Díaz Sánchez; below it is the entry for the same
day, as cited in the Ayacucho edition:

> Pienso durante un rato en la felicidad del hedonismo y del ideal epi-
> cúreo que puedo gozar en lo que me queda de vida, sobre todo al lado
> de Lydia cuyas circunstancias como a mí se lo permiten: como yo, se
> siente mal entre la gente y encuentra su bienestar en la independencia
> y la soledad. (Díaz Sánchez 180)
> [I think for a while of the joys of hedonism and the epicurean ideal
> that I can enjoy in the time I have left to live, especially next to Lydia
> whose circumstances, like my own, permit it. Like me, she feels ill at
> ease with people and is happy with independence and solitude.]

> Pienso durante un rato en la felicidad del hedonismo y el ideal epi-
> cúreo del que puedo gozar en lo que me queda de vida sobre todo si
> las circunstancias me lo permiten: yo me siento mal entre la gente y
> encuentro bienestar con la independencia y soledad. (*O* 464)
> [I think for a while of the joys of hedonism and the epicurean ideal
> that I can enjoy in the time I have left to live, especially if circum-
> stances permit it. I feel ill at ease with people and am happy with
> independence and solitude.]

What must revert to the unsaid, in this instance, is not just the presence
of Cuban anthropologist Lydia Cabrera in Teresa de la Parra's life but the
notion that Parra would wish to share with her "the time I have left to live."
If Cabrera's presence has not been completely elided from the journal, it
has been reduced to a purely ancillary position. Díaz Sánchez observes in
his book that "Teresa hablaba escasamente de [Lydia] en sus cartas mas no
así en su Diario en el cual, sobre todo en los meses finales de su existencia,
le dedica párrafos impregnados de admiración y ternura" (Díaz Sánchez 81)
[Teresa spoke little of Lydia in her letters, not so in her journal in which,
especially in the last months of her life, she devotes passages full of admiration and love]. Yet no such passages remain in the Ayacucho edition. The
woman whom Parra, punning on her surname, called "Cabrita," little goat;
with whom she had a relationship praised by Gabriela Mistral (who knew
whereof she spoke) for its "quality of eternity";[6] who shared Parra's life

during her last five years, accompanying her from sanatorium to sanatorium in quest of an ever unattainable cure till she died in Madrid; to whom Parra left her most precious belongings; who, breaking with convention, attended Parra's burial when "the women of the family" stayed at home (Hiriart, *Más cerca* 116); who, after Parra's death, repaired to a medium to contact her friend (successfully, she claimed) (Hiriart, *Más cerca* 70); this woman is displaced, reduced, by the cuts, to a mere circumstance in Parra's life.

While not entirely absent from critics' accounts of Teresa de la Parra, Lydia Cabrera (when she is mentioned at all) has been routinely construed as a cliché, that of the loving "good friend." Indeed, the same Díaz Sánchez who quotes from Parra's journal in its unexpurgated version, comments on the importance of Cabrera in Parra's life, and observes that "unidas por esa misteriosa corriente que crean las afinidades electivas, a estas amigas sólo podía separarlas la muerte" (Díaz Sánchez 81) [united by the mysterious current of elective affinities, these two friends could only be separated by death], is the very same critic who, as I have mentioned earlier, deplored the fact that Teresa had died too young, never experiencing love. His reading is only contradictory if we don't accept the "good friends" cliché, but then how could we accept it at face value when the paranoid effort to curtail information on the part of relatives and editors, the slashes perpetrated on the texts, are telling us otherwise, revealing a very anxious agenda, making explicit the very unsayable they set out to hide?

The letters from Teresa de la Parra to Lydia Cabrera tell, of course, another story. Published only recently, in 1988, after previously unsuccessful publication attempts,[7] they document, even with their scars and their gaps, the importance of the bond. The first, slightly stiff letter, addressed to "Dear Lydia" and signed off "Very affectionately, Teresa," is from 1927; the last, from 1935, is addressed to her dear *Cabrillotica*, her tiny, weeny, goat, by a Teresa wasted by illness. Between these two dates, seventy-three letters document (onesidedly, to be sure, since Cabrera's letters were presumably destroyed by the Parra family) a complex, intense, and yes, lesbian relationship.

Some background is perhaps necessary to explain the dynamics of this correspondence and, indeed, of the relationship. Lydia Cabrera first met Teresa de la Parra in 1924, when the latter stopped in Havana en route to Venezuela, after the death of Emilia Barrios, the woman she had accompanied to Paris and possibly the greatest influence in her life. As Cabrera recalls, "Le conté que trabajaba para independizarme, tener fortuna propia e irme a París a pintar y estudiar. Como entonces parecía aún más joven de lo que era, las actividades y proyectos, el 'plante'—como se decía en Cuba—de aquella chiquilla la divirtió mucho. Me animó a realizar mis proyectos y me dio su tarjeta para que la buscase en cuanto llegase a París. Yo le di la mía y agradecida escribí 'favor de no olvidarme'" (Hiriart, *Más cerca* 52) [I told her that I was working in order to become independent, have my own money, and go to Paris to study and paint. As I then looked younger than my age, she was amused by the animation, the projects, the nerve of this child. She encouraged me to carry out my projects and gave me her card so that I could look her up as soon as I arrived in Paris. I gave her my own card, and gratefully wrote on it: "Please don't forget me"]. When Cabrera finally went to Paris, in 1927, "[Teresa] me mostró—para sorpresa mía—la tarjeta que le había dado años antes en La Habana y que decía 'favor de no olvidarme'" (Hiriart, *Más cerca* 52) [Teresa showed me, much to my surprise, the card I had given her years before with the words "Please don't forget me"]. Indeed these words will appear again in an early, particularly intense letter of Parra's as a verbal token of the beginning of their relationship. From then on the lives of these two women are very effectively intertwined. Both living in Paris, though not together, Parra writing, Cabrera studying art at the Ecole du Louvre (her work on anthropology would come later), they represent the Latin American variant of the well-to-do expatriate lesbian who chooses to leave America, North or South, in order to lead an "independent" life. (I shall return to this notion of independence, crucial in Teresa de la Parra.) Parra mentions Cabrera to other correspondents, writes for example that she is traveling to Italy "con una amiga, L.C., inteligente y muy artista, a quien quiero mucho y con quien comparto los mismos gustos (*OC* 861) [with a friend, L.C., intelligent and very artistic, whom I love dearly and with whom I share the same tastes]. The euphemism—the Cuban friend I love dearly—will reappear in other letters of Parra's. (Cabrera, for her part, refers to Parra as "esta criatura admirable que mi devoción no sabe si llamar madre o hermana" [*C* 10] [this admirable creature that my devotion does not know whether to call a mother or a friend].) When, in 1931, the first signs of Parra's tuberculosis make themselves felt, Cabrera leaves Paris to join her in Leysin, taking a room next to hers in the sanatorium. From that moment on, she will live almost constantly with Parra, save for trips in Europe with her family or brief returns to Paris. When Parra dies in Madrid in 1936, she leaves Lydia Cabrera her library (which was dispersed during the German occupation of Paris), her manuscripts (which the Parra family reclaimed), and—as a tangible example of the oblique feminine legacy so well explored in Parra's work—an emerald ring that had belonged to Emilia Barrios, her protector and benefactress, a ring that Parra wore constantly and that she had had inscribed, shortly before her death, with the words "Au revoir." Lydia Cabrera would only discover the inscription inside the ring after Parra's death (Hiriart, *Más cerca* 46–47).

The above biographical excursus seemed necessary to situate Parra and Cabrera in context. I am not interested, however, in the way the letters reproduce biographical detail, nor am I interested in determining, from what is said (or not said) in these letters, the precise emotional and sexual *forms* taken by their relationship. Rather, I look at these letters (as I look at the journal) as texts reflecting the difficulty of stating a sexual identity and, more generally, of expressing gender unease. In other words, more than in the manifestation of direct desire per se, I am interested in the way that desire sees itself, the detours to which it resorts in order to name itself, the simulation it must engage in in order to "pass," the codes it uses in order to be recognized even as it masks itself, and even the repression it exerts against itself as it internalizes conventional prejudice.

Parra's letters from the sanatoria of Leysin or Vevey, written during those periods when Cabrera was away, besides poignantly recreating the *petite histoire* of the terminally ill, often include a detailed analysis of the books she is reading and the films she goes to see in the village. References to Remy de Gourmont's *Lettres à l'amazone,* addressed to Natalie Barney, the sentimental tone of which Parra finds anachronistic (*C* 105), a long discussion of *Mädchen in Uniform* (*C* 183), comments on Colette's *Ces plaisirs,* which Parra and Cabrera read as soon as it was published (*C* 137–138), operate quite evidently within this correspondence as complicitous signs of recognition and self-expression, allowing both writer and addressee to speak a desire and reiterate a sexuality through coded references. Yet besides the impact of the coded names (Barney, Colette, *Mädchen in Uniform*), what is said about the texts or films is in itself important. If commentary of them allows Parra and Cabrera to confirm, in a sympathetic process, their own sexual identity, it also allows them to establish difference, that is, to recognize that the expression of their own sexuality need not coincide with, and indeed may diverge from, that expressed in those texts. This double process becomes very clear both in Parra's comments on *Mädchen in Uniform* and in her reading of Colette. Parra's dealings with the latter are quite complex. That she admired Colette and to a certain point considered herself influenced by her is obvious. In her journal entry for 11 September 1931, mutilated by censors but still meaningful, one reads: "Releída la 2a. Claudine de Colette que no recordaba en absoluto. Creo debió tener influencia en mí: le leí creo en 1920" (*O* 449) [Reread the second Claudine by

Colette that I didn't really remember. I think it influenced me. I must have read it around 1920]. The Claudine series, as the reader may remember and as the censor thankfully did not, devotes considerable space, in all volumes, to exploring same-sex attraction in many of its forms. A few years later, in a letter to Cabrera from Leysin, Parra mentions having read another book by Colette, probably *Ces plaisirs* (later to become *Le pur et l'impur*), which had just come out in Paris and which Parra confessed to having read in one sitting (*C* 137). Parra's reaction to Colette's *tone* is ambiguous. While indubitably attracted to its wit, she is offended (or perhaps scared?) by what she deems its impudence:

> [L]a mujer es muy simpática y conquista. . . . [E]s imposible no cederle y no reírse. Y unas cosas tan gráficas: hay algo sobre los *senos viriles* que por eso no pueden acariciarse como las mejillas y los melocotones. . . . Yo creo que Colette es una deslenguada por mal educada y vagabunda. Ha andado siempre entre gente *faisandé* y ha tenido la desgracia de tener mucho *esprit*. El horrible *esprit* brillante que mata tantas cosas y es en el fondo una escuela de vulgaridad de espíritu. Es posible que haya fibra sentimental en Colette. Yo creo que la tiene y que la esconde, es su único pudor. ¡Qué descaradita es! (*C* 137)
> [The woman is very engaging and conquers one. . . . It's impossible not to give in to her and laugh. And there are such graphic details: something about *virile breasts* that cannot be caressed like cheeks or peaches. . . . I think that Colette is loose-tongued because she has had a bad education and has drifted all over the place. She has always been around people who are *faisandé* and has been cursed with too much *esprit;* that horrible and dazzling *esprit* that kills so many things and is, ultimately, a school of vulgarity for the spirit. There may be a sentimental fiber in Colette. I think she has it and hides it; it's her only modesty. What a brazen little thing she is!]

Cabrera's judgment must have been harsher than Parra's for in her next letter Parra writes: "No me gusta nada Colette, tú tienes razón de sobra en todo lo que dices, y yo devolveré el libro" (*C* 138) [I don't like Colette at all; you are absolutely right, and I shall return the book]: a dubious statement, this, when compared to the aforementioned journal entry of 1931 in which she asserts her debt toward Colette. It is more likely that Parra (and quite obviously Cabrera) found this *particular* book by Colette unnerving, that the frank and at times ironic, though not unsympathetic descriptions of lesbians disturbed Parra and Cabrera, as an all-too-knowing mirror, more than they were able to say. I can only surmise this, of course, but one phrase in Parra's letter lends credence to the conjecture. After stating how much she dislikes Colette, Parra writes: "Lo que me gustó fueron las *ladies* que yo no conocía. No sabes cómo las *vi* y hasta que punto me conmovieron. Ella, Colette, no tiene sino los chistes" (*C* 138) [What I did like were the *ladies* I had never heard of. You can't imagine how well I *saw* them, to what point they moved me. She, Colette, only makes jokes].

Who are these *ladies*? Does Parra refer, in shorthand, to all women described by Colette? Her use of the word in English is providential, allowing the reader to guess at a more precise referent. For an important section of *Ces plaisirs,* it will be remembered, is devoted to Sarah Ponsonby and Eleanor Butler, the Ladies of Llangollen, that couple of well-to-do, late-eighteenth-century Irishwomen who eloped in men's garb, took up house in Wales, and proceeded to live together for the next fifty-three years, well respected by their small community as well as by the literary establishment at large.[8] Parra's sympathy, even more, the *emotion* she expresses toward the *ladies* is revealing, I think, of an ideological stance I will explore further. While Parra may recognize her own desire in some of Colette's other descriptions, she does not, necessarily, identify with them, or, as with her reaction to Colette herself, she identifies-while-disavowing. Instead, what draws her *emotionally* to the Ladies of Llangollen is a particular mode of relation between women that strikes closer to home, one in which she can *see* ("you can't imagine how well I *saw* them") herself, one that she can recognize *culturally.*

Before following this line of inquiry any further, however, I want to look briefly at a few other texts by Parra that will contribute to my analysis. The first is a 1933 letter from Parra to Cabrera where she describes her fellow patients' reaction to the 1931 film *Mädchen in Uniform* (a film for which, incidentally, Colette had provided the French subtitles):

> En la mesa discutieron sobre *Jeunes filles en uniforme,* apasionadamente y mucho rato. Te contaré otro día lo que me sugirió la discusión. Te hubiera divertido e interesado mucho la mentalidad de los tres: Heitor, Madriz y Cezy: "Quedó triste *de pensar* que podrían existir esas cosas" (y doblaba la cabeza hundida); Madriz intransigente, hecho una furia como ante la presencia de un monstruo misterioso. Ya se habían ido "más allá de la película." No aceptaba el beso de la maestra a Manuela. Aseguraba que cuando se besan así "otras cosas harían," y él, que ha rodado por todos los lupanares inmundos, hablaba con horror y como con asco. Me llamó la atención: 1°, que no aceptara el amor sensual pero sin realización, y 2°, la intransigencia hacia el amor

en sí, su incapacidad de comprensión. Cuánta vulgaridad me pareció que encerraba tal intransigencia en un libertino. Heitor estuvo mucho más comprensivo, pero te aseguro que era interesantísimo observarlos a los tres. Yo en la actitud *término medio,* afirmando el amor sensual que Madriz rechazaba como un absurdo: qué abismo hay entre estos hombres de nuestras tierras y uno. ¡Qué *couche* impenetrable de vulgaridad les cubre el alma y los imposibilita de sentir todo lo que está más allá de las tristes realizaciones del C . . . ! (*C* 183)

[During dinner there was a fiery discussion over *Mädchen* which went on forever. I'll tell you some other day what thoughts it suggested to me. You would have been amused and very interested in the way of thinking of all three, Heitor, Madriz, and Cezy. Cezy, bending her head as she spoke, "felt very sad *just to think* that such things might exist." Madriz, intolerant, seething with rage as if faced with a mysterious monster. He was already "beyond the film." He could not accept the teacher kissing Manuela, assuring us that when they kiss like that "they do other things, for sure." And so this man, a patron of the filthiest brothels, spoke with horror and repugnance. I was struck by: (1) the fact that he could not accept sensual love without consummation and (2) his intransigence toward that love itself, his inability to understand. How much vulgarity I found behind such intransigence, coming from a rogue. Heitor was much more understanding, but I assure you it was very interesting to observe all three. I occupied a sort of *middle ground,* defending the sensual love that Madriz rejected as absurd. What an abyss between these men from our countries and ourselves! What an impenetrable layer of vulgarity covers their souls and prevents them from feeling anything beyond the pathetic exploits of their A(rses) . . . !]

The second text I wish to take into account is a fragment of another 1933 letter, in which Parra speaks of her enthusiasm for certain sections in Keyserling's *Das Spektrum Europas* (1928), which she read in French translation:

[H]ablando de Francia, en el análisis Espectral, país que juzga Keyserling el único donde el amor no está en bancarrota, habla del *amazonismo* (etimológicamente, mujeres sin senos; *no* hombres), que se está preparando para el porvenir como reacción contra la tiranía ancestral del hombre. La tiranía y la vulgaridad, diríamos nosotras pensando en los de nuestras tierras. Opina, más o menos, que las mujeres no amorosas vivirán indiferentes al hombre, las amorosas "auront des amies." De donde saldrá la sumisión de los hombres y una especie de régi-

men matriarcal. Me hace gracia lo que cuenta de que las *doucet* [*sic*; illegible in facsimile] han declarado que el amor no es un instinto natural, sino una de las muchas invenciones funestas del capitalismo, una construcción ideológica que debe desaparecer con él. (*C* 175)[9]
[Speaking of France in *Das Spektrum*, the only country where Keyserling finds that love is not bankrupt, he speaks of *amazonism* (etymologically: women with no breasts; *not* men) that he sees coming in the future as a reaction against the ancestral tyranny of men—the tyranny of vulgarity, you and I would say, thinking of the men in our countries. He states, more or less, that nonamorous women will live indifferent to men, while the amorous ones "auront des amies," whence will come the submission of men and a sort of matriarchal system. I laughed at what he says about the *doucet* (*sic*; illegible in facsimile) declaring that love is not a natural instinct but one of capitalism's many sinister inventions, an ideological construct that will disappear when it does, and that they have founded a "League against Love."]

The fact that Parra interprets *positively* what Keyserling, with his customary murky despondency, presented as *negative* gives particular significance to this passage. So does the recourse to French—"auront des amies"—in a letter written in Spanish. Not a snobbish affectation but a verbal mask, this translated lesbianism attests as much to the difficulty of naming as to the need to name. Finally, I wish to consider a passage from a 1924 letter written by Parra, shortly after Emilia Barrios's death, to the man she was supposedly in love with, the writer Gonzalo Zaldumbide:

Siento el más profundo desprecio por esa cosa que llaman amor, que es brutal y salvaje como los toros del domingo, con los pobres caballos destrozados. No quiero sino ternura, eso que tú crees que yo no conozco y en lo cual soy maestra especialista imposible de equivocarse ni engañar. (*O* 531)
[I feel the most profound contempt for that thing called love, which is as brutal and as savage as Sunday bullfights in which the poor horses are torn to pieces. I only want tenderness, a feeling you seem to think I have never experienced but in which I am a specialist, incapable of making mistakes and impossible to deceive.]

The ambiguous reaction to Colette's depiction of lesbians; the empathy with the quaint Ladies of Llangollen; the defense of a "sensual love" not leading inevitably to physical consummation; the utopia of an all-female society where women "auront des amies"; the consideration of love as a cultural product of capitalism; the passionate rejection of the brutal physicality of love and its ensuing replacement with tenderness; and finally and most importantly, in order to provide an ideological context, the repudiation of compulsive *Latin American* heterosexuality: these are integral elements of Parra's position, one which might best be described, on the one hand (speaking in general terms), as a *resistance to lesbianism* and, on the other (speaking in particular Latin American terms), as a *lesbianism of resistance*.

I make these assessments guardedly, fully aware of the risk of anachronism incurred by retrospectively applying a sexual identity to one who did not identify herself sexually except by denial (her systematic rejection of marriage, of childbearing, of men),[10] by linguistic detour ("auront des amies"), by imperfect familial analogy (like a *second mother*, a *sister*, a *good friend*), or by euphemism (*independent, solitary, misfit*). But I am also aware that not to make these assessments, whatever their potential shortcomings, and not to follow up on them and develop them into critical tools, is, firstly, to deprive Parra's texts of the full reading they deserve and, secondly and more generally, to condone an account of Latin American cultural history in which the construction of sexualities has no role to play.

Parra's problematic relation to the physical, her insistence on the superiority of tenderness over love, her "disbelief in Freud's orgasmic theory," as Lydia Cabrera euphemistically and for all we know truthfully puts it,[11] would lead one to see Parra at first glance as an advocate of, and a participant in, romantic friendship, where the erotic stops short of the genital—what Colette (somewhat disingenuously, I find, when referring to her own lover, the Marquise de Morny) termed a "calm sentimental climate" sustained by "contained quivering"—*frémissement contenu* (Colette 594). This would indeed explain Parra's attraction for the Ladies of Llangollen, a prestigious model of female *compagnonnage* socially accredited, in addition, by class status and financial self-sufficiency. However, as Lillian Faderman has pointed out, these romantic friendships, which, with varying degrees of sexual self-awareness, had freely blossomed in the nineteenth century, had become highly suspicious by the beginning of the twentieth (Faderman, *Surpassing the Love of Men* 297–340, and "Love between Women"). Pathologized by the medical establishment, distrusted by a male-dominated society who saw the financial independence of women with increasing misgivings, these relations were surely, at the time Parra wrote, less a haven of friendship than a place of risk. Unlike Parra, the Ladies of Llangollen did not need to actively disbelieve "Freud's orgasmic theory": living at the end of the eighteenth century, they were spared the effort. That Parra gravitates

toward an outdated mode of female-female relation, even as she is aware
that it has inevitably been replaced by another, much more complex, possibly abnormal, and definitely unacceptable by society, leads of course to
resistance (her ambiguous, and ultimately negative reaction to Colette, her
need to *abject* in order to *disavow*) and to a distrust of the physical so ambitious in scope it calls attention to the very thing it would deny. Let us not
forget, after all, that this champion of the spirit over the body (*C* 182), this
contempter of Latin American men's fixation with the "pathetic exploits
of their arses," is the same person who has a good chuckle over Colette's
comments on "virile breasts" and who, in one of her early letters to Lydia
Cabrera, the first page of which has been censored, in a wonderful passage
I cannot resist quoting, resorts to fetishism to assuage the pain of absence:

> Te escribo en la cama con la ventana abierta sobre la terraza y con
> dolor en los ojos que tienen hambre. No sabes cuántos reproches
> tristes te dirigía estos días por haberme dejado sin dirección ni noti-
> cias . . . pero ya se me olvidaron. Ten presente en adelante Cabra linda
> que no estás en Jovellar 45 Vedado Habano (favor no olvidarme) me
> cantan aun los oídos y los ojos en recuerdo de la espera y la larga
> ausencia 1924–1927? Recuerda pues que andas volantona, que yo no
> soy adivina y que *si cambias de hotel y de ciudad* sin prevenirme *pierdo tu
> traza.* ¿Está entendido? ¿Has comprendido bien?
> . . . Hay una costurera haciéndome soutiens-gorge, copiado de uno
> de los tuyos. No sabes lo que conversaron conmigo antier que me los
> trajo Madame Ledemback y yo me los probé. ¡Tan petulantes, tan inú-
> tiles, tan graciosos y parecidos a ti! Que alma tienen en realidad las
> cosas y cuánto pueden decir. Yo me reí sola cuanto me pareció pues
> estaban muy graciosos. Tu tienes la ausencia graciosa y es lo que mitiga
> la tristeza. (*C* 93)

[I am writing to you in bed, my window open onto the terrace, my
eyes so hungry they hurt. You don't know how much I reproached
you these past days for having left me without an address, without
news. . . . But I've gotten over that now. Please remember, my pretty
little goat, that you no longer live in Jovellar 45, Vedado, Havana
(please don't forget me)—my ears and my eyes ring when I remember
that long wait (1924–1927!). Bear in mind, then, since you are feeling
so flighty, that I am not a clairvoyant and that *if you change hotels or
cities* without telling me, *I'll lose your trail.* Do you understand? Do you
really understand?
. . . There is a seamstress here making some bras for me, copied

from one of yours. You can't imagine the things those bras told me when Mme Ledemback brought them the day before yesterday and I tried them on. So petulant, so useless, so amusing and so very much like you! There's so much soul in things, and they can say so much. I laughed myself silly because these bras were really very funny. You have an amusing absence, and that's what makes sadness bearable.]

If, in lieu of the directly physical and more specifically genital, Parra advocates *tenderness*, I propose that this tenderness be viewed not as the watered-down sexuality so often ascribed to lesbians, but as a bonding strategy and, additionally, a strategy of group resistance. For when Parra opposes tenderness to love, it is quite clear that what she refers to by *love*, with her violent bullfighting image so emblematically Hispanic and male, is compulsory—and for men compulsive—heterosexuality, that is, a social, *reproductive* model, imperative in Latin America and synonymous with its modernity, which she shuns. In this context, tenderness—presented as a same-sex *art de vivre* instead of a heterosexual *mise à mort*—is the means of reclaiming female bodies and sexualities, liberating them from, and even allowing them to function actively against, the tyranny of a socially acceptable, obligatory model. Interestingly, both Teresa de la Parra's *Ifigenia* and her introduction to *Memorias* seriously question, even disrupt, notions of progeniture, filiation, inheritance, parenthood; the only place in Parra where such concepts are upheld, though ambiguously, are the old lady's memoirs, projected onto a nineteenth-century utopia.

I would argue that Parra's lesbianism allows her to see clearly, and critically, into a Latin American modernity whose regimentation of sexualities *and* sensualities radically excludes her. In this light, Teresa de la Parra's exile—as that of Lydia Cabrera, of Gabriela Mistral, not to mention their North American counterparts—should be read as a political gesture, signifying much more than a circumstantial decision to live abroad. Geographic displacement offered what Venezuela for Parra, Cuba for Cabrera, and Chile for Mistral could not (cannot even now) give, that is, both a place to be (sexually) different and a place to write. Or perhaps, to put it more accurately, geographic displacement provided a place to write (however obliquely) one's difference. In a letter to Cabrera, commenting on her sister's plans to take her back to Venezuela so that she might live out her life as an invalid there, Parra writes:

María me hace . . . un plan de reducirme de nuevo a menor de edad con tutela de hierro en donde llevaría ella una de las voces cantantes. ¡Buena estoy yo para semejante plan! . . . Pienso contestarle hoy mismo diciéndole que no pienso atravesar el mar hasta no poder vivir donde me da la gana haciendo lo que quiera y *sin régimen*. Yo sería capaz de matarme a disparates por espíritu de contradicción y hacerles sentir que no me dominan. (*C* 147)

[María has a plan to reduce me once again to being a minor, to a state of total dependence, with her as one of my chief guardians. As if such a plan were the thing for me! . . . I intend to write back immediately, telling her that I have no intention of crossing the ocean unless I can live wherever I wish and do as I please, *without rules*. I would be capable of doing the craziest things just to be contrary, to make them feel that they have no authority over me.]

"Without rules" and "independent" are coded words, I suggest, for a lifestyle and, yes, a sexuality over which "they"—family, institution, modern national state—have no authority. (This notion was already present, as a password, in Lydia Cabrera's own declaration of intent to Parra during their first meeting: "to become independent, have my own money, and go to Paris to study and paint.") In another letter, after telling Cabrera of a particularly unpleasant incident in the sanatorium in which she, Parra, had to defend a woman from the salacious, disparaging comments of two Latin American men, she writes: "[M]e alegro mucho de haber 'visto' el espíritu criollo ya olvidado porque me transportó de alegría al pensar que no tengo que vivir junto a él, y no sabes cómo bendigo a Emilia y te bendigo a ti por toda la independencia que tengo hoy día y ya (¡Dios lo quiera!) hasta el final de mi vida" (*C* 169) [I am delighted to have "seen" the *criollo* spirit I had forgotten, because I was overjoyed by the fact that I don't have to live with it. You don't know how immensely grateful I am to Emilia and to you for all the independence I have today and will have, God willing, till the end of my life]. That the two major female presences in Parra's life are associated with this joyous emancipation, one that is based, concretely, on the rejection of Latin American men, gives, I believe, a much more complex meaning to the word *independence,* found throughout Parra's work.

It is ironic that Parra, who achieved that independence in her own life— "Teresa was very independent" recalls Cabrera [12]—would allow the protagonist of *Ifigenia* to come very close to it and then deny it to her in the end. To read this odd, and to a point unmanageable novel as Parra bids us do, that is, as a Bovaryist Bildungsroman of the tropics, in which a rebellious young woman, foresaken by an ambitious and dashing suitor, ends up marrying a tyrannical politician and capitulating to society, is to limit the scope of that Bovarysm and impoverish its meaning. For *Ifigenia* also mirrors, provocatively, a scene out of Parra's own life, the moment in which the young woman, dazzled by the beauty and experience of an older one, accepts an invitation to leave Latin America, accompany this older woman to Paris and, under her tutelage, learn to be independent. Yet what Emilia Barrios did for Teresa de la Parra, Mercedes Galindo will not be allowed to do for María Eugenia Alonso in *Ifigenia:* Parra leaves, to live "without rules" with Emilia in Paris, never to return to the fold; María Eugenia, pressured by her family, passes up Mercedes's invitation and stays behind. What had been achieved, surely not without effort, in life, could not be repeated, at least in the Venezuela of the 1920s, in literature.

The independence Parra seeks and in good measure attains during her life must not be searched for in *Ifigenia* but elsewhere in her work. If geographic displacement insured the possibility of independence for Parra historically, temporal displacement affords a similar chance in literature. In Parra, the *colonial*, either as a concrete historical period (the world evoked in her lectures on Latin American women before independence) or as an idealized construct (the nineteenth-century paradise of *Memorias*), effects such a liberating displacement, providing, in temporal terms, the freedom that exile in Paris provided spatially.

Critics have seen Parra's recuperation of the colonial, or of the imaginary values and virtues of this "simple" time, as an eminently feminine gesture.[13] That it is, though surely not in the quaint sense those critics believe. Parra's recuperation follows gender lines, setting up a feminine world of the colony, embellished by ahistorical memory, against a masculine, regimented modern state, sanctioned by official historiography. The latter is a "banquete de hombres solos" (*O* 484) [a banquet reserved for men]; the former, a "larga vacación de los hombres y el reinado sin crónica ni cronistas de las mujeres" (*O* 490) [a long vacation for/from men and the unchronicled rule of women]. In this *unchronicled* space marked by the feminine, Parra projects the independence (in the many senses she gives the word) that modernity denies. She rescues distant precursors with whom she identifies, the unmarried *letradas* and *soñadoras,* those female intellectuals and dreamers of colonial times whose story no one remembers; who, "acorraladas por los prejuicios y por la vulgaridad ambiente" (*O* 493) [cornered by the prejudice and vulgarity of their midst], sought solace, and paradoxically found freedom, either in the convent or in self-imposed retreat, removed from society but in contact (as Parra takes pains to stress) with other women. In addition to those unmarried, *different* women left in the margins of official historiography, Parra reclaims, in a perhaps patronizing, but no less sympathetic gesture, the other marginals, the African slave and the dispossessed Indian. Identifying with the latter, she writes to Cabrera:

> Creo . . . fuertemente, en mi herencia india, en mi poco de musuché que son los de Mérida y Trujillo. Tengo también de ellos el mal de la fuga. Mi abuela contaba siempre de una india que habían comprado. La habían bautizado, instruído, hablaba español, había aprendido a leer, parecía estar adaptada enteramente a la ciudad y un día, después de muchos años, se huyó. Nunca supieron si llegaría a su tribu o se perdió. Yo siento a veces esa necesidad de huir. Soy esencialmente insociable en las tres cuartas partes de mi espíritu y todo lo arreglo con la fuga. Si no la real, la espiritual. (C 142)
> [I strongly believe in my Indian heritage, in my part of *musuché*, the Indians of Mérida and Trujillo. Like them I have the sickness of flight. My grandmother used to tell the story of an Indian woman they had bought. They had baptized her, given her instruction and taught her Spanish. She learned how to read, seemed entirely adapted to the city, till one day, after many years, she ran away. They never found out if she got back to her tribe or if she got lost. I sometimes feel the need to flee. I am essentially unsociable and resolve everything with flight, if not physical then spiritual.]

A similar recognition of the marginal, attributable in both cases, I would argue, to the personal experience of margins, that is, of sexual difference and gender unease, may be observed in Lydia Cabrera's sustained interest in Afro-Cuban lore (*Cuentos negros de Cuba* were written as a "gift" to Parra during her illness) and in the concern of Gabriela Mistral's poetry with Indians.

In one of her letters, Parra refers to a souvenir box that Cabrera, an accomplished painter before becoming an anthropologist, was decorating for her; an autobiographical box, as it were, that was to be adorned with important motifs from Parra's past. There had obviously been some discussion in the correspondence about those motifs, for Parra writes:

> Pienso que cuando tenga "mi caja" voy a declararme en mi patria: siento patria todo lo que vas a pintar en la caja, realidad idealista sintetizada. Tula, nuestro negro viejo, las martiniqueñas, los cocos de Juan Díaz y el trapiche de Tazón. He pensado hoy que soy enemiga de esa independencia que hizo nacionalidades en donde antes la gente vivía ingenuamente, sin haber tomado conciencia de ellos mismos en esa

forma tan antipática que es la nación y su derivado, el nacionalismo. (C 194)
[I believe that as soon as I have "my box" I shall declare myself in my own country. My country will be everything you'll paint on the box, an idealized synthetic reality. Tula, our old black servant, the women from Martinique, the coconut palms in Juan Díaz, the sugar-mill at Tazón. I thought today how I hated that independence which invented nationalities in places where people lived innocently, without thinking of themselves in terms as repellent as *nation* or its by-product, *nationalism.*]

This idealized synthetic reality painted by Cabrera on the box is the same idealized synthetic reality, guilelessly presented as "innocent," that Parra recreates in *Memorias* and in her lectures. It would be too simple to see this simulacrum of the colony merely as an ideological refuge (which it no doubt is) for Parra's unquestionably conservative ideology, often jarring in its class-generated thoughtlessness and its sympathy for authoritarian regimes.[14] The elaborate construction to which Parra submits the colonial, returning to it time and time again, reiterating its "synthetic" qualities while defending herself from direct identification,[15] assigning to it a value that fluctuates at each new reading (as Elizabeth Garrels has so efficiently shown in her analysis of the "closed doors" trope),[16] shows that she is guided by more than class reaction or by the phantasmagoria fostered by exile. The very paradox on which Parra's admiration for colonial times rests—she, the champion of *independence,* praising a *pre-independent* period to the point of wishing away *political independence*—points to the value of the colonial as a *figure,* "la figura que al sustraerse al flujo de la historia resiste y perdura" (Fombona xiii) [the figure that, in withdrawing from the flux of history, resists and endures].

Parra's ideological recuperation of the colonial should indeed be read as more resistant than reactionary. What is being resisted is not so much historical independence per se (Parra was researching a book on Bolívar when she died) as processes of modernization and of national state formation that, in the name of rationalism and modern progress, engage in tendentious classification and exclusion. "To organize anything rationally one has to make choices, to exclude, to resolve debates in favor of one speaker, in favor of one code of conduct," writes Doris Sommer, as she highlights, by contrast, the creative linguistic anarchy of *Memorias* (Sommer 302). To organize anything both rationally *and* nationally, nation states seem to resort to similar reductions. The same politically independent modern state that invents nationalities invents us as citizens, invents too, our bodies, our genders, our sexualities. In Parra's recreation of an all feminine, premodern utopia where women may be different and free—or free in their difference—are the unwritten unmarried women, the unwritten sexualities, the lesbian author waiting to be named.

Notes

1   Unless specifically noted, all translations from the Spanish are my own.

2   Teresa de la Parra, *Obras completas,* intro. Carlos García Prada (Caracas: Editorial Arte, 1985) 10. Subsequent references to this edition appear directly in the text preceded by *OC*.

3   Teresa de la Parra, *Obra* (Caracas: Editorial Ayacucho, 1982) 455. Subsequent references to this edition appear directly in the text preceded by *O*.

4   For astute remarks on the body in Parra's fiction, see Garrels, *Las grietas de la ternura,* especially "Los cuerpos problemáticos" 43–54. For a probing discussion on gender unease in Parra, see Sommer, "It's Wrong to Be Right: *Mamá Blanca* on Fatherly Foundations," in *Foundational Fictions* 290–321.

5   For a good discussion on female literary collaboration, see Garrels 134–36; also Sommer 312–16.

6   Rosario Hiriart, ed. *Cartas a Lydia Cabrera (Correspondencia inédita de Gabriela Mistral y Teresa de la Parra)* (Madrid: Ediciones Torremozas, 1988) 44. Subsequent references appear directly in the text preceded by *C*.

7   In her preface to *Cartas,* Hiriart describes the reticence of Cabrera and her then companion, María Teresa de Rojas, to publish Parra's letters in Hiriart's first book on Parra, *Más cerca de Teresa de la Parra.* Only after Titina Rojas's death did Cabrera relinquish and agree to publish them in memory of both Teresa and Titina (*C* 33). The letters transcribed by Hiriart have been subjected to some editing: "Nótese que hay ocasiones (en las de Teresa) en que faltan páginas; suponemos que pertenecen a contextos más amplios. El resto llega a mis manos escritas a máquina por María Teresa de Rojas, quien antes de su muerte revisó parte de este material con la colaboración de Mercedes Muriedas, secretaria de Lydia desde los años de La Habana. En éstas encontramos iniciales de nombres propios y se ve que algunos párrafos han sido suprimidos" (*C* 33). [It will be noted that in some cases in Teresa's letters (Hiriart refers to originals which she reproduces photographically) pages are missing. I imagine that they refer to more general questions. I was given the rest of the letters in a typewritten transcription done by María Teresa de Rojas, who, before her death, revised part of this material with the help of Mercedes Muriedas, Lydia's secretary back in Havana. In these, we find initials for proper names and it is obvious that some paragraphs have been deleted.]

In addition to the letters from Parra to Cabrera, Hiriart's book contains eight letters from Gabriela Mistral, the first two addressed to Parra and Cabrera together, the other six, written after Parra's death, to Cabrera. I was particularly interested in the first of those letters, which had been published twice previously, once by Lydia Cabrera (*Siete cartas de Gabriela Mistral a Lydia Cabrera*), then in Hiriart, *Más cerca de Teresa de la Parra.* In both of these publications, a paragraph has been elided from that letter; a paragraph quite explicit as to the intensity of the relationship between Cabrera and Parra, in which

Mistral chides the two for a lovers' disagreement and the ensuing temporary separation (*C* 43–44).

8   Besides Colette's account of the ladies, see Jeannette Marks, *Gallant Little Wales,* and Lillian Faderman, *Surpassing the Love of Men* 120–25. Jeannette Marks was of course herself involved in a similar relationship with Mary Woolley at Mount Holyoke. (See Wells, *Miss Marks and Miss Woolley.*)

9   The original in Spanish says *amayvorismo* for Keyserling's *amazonismo,* an obvious mistake in the transcription of the letter (see note 18). I have no explanation for the term *doucet,* which may also be the product of a faulty transcription or else a private code word. Keyserling writes that *Russians* believe that love is an invention of capitalism. (Hermann von Keyserling, *Analyse spectrale de l'Europe* [1928; Paris: Gonthier, 1965] 61.)

10 In a letter to Gonzalo Zaldumbide, dated August 1924, Parra writes: "Tengo en general, como diría María, miedo a ti y horror a los demás hombres, ¡ah si supieras quererme con alma de mujer! Me bastaría con el alma y prescindiría del cuerpo" (*O* 531) [In general, as María would say, I am frightened of you and feel horror for all other men. Ah, if only you could love me with the soul of a woman! I would be satisfied with the soul and would forego the body]. In a letter to Rafael Carías: "[C]uando Emilia decía que de tener yo un hijo algún día, todo, todo cuanto ella tuviera sería para mí sin condiciones, yo contestaba que no pensaba en casarme" (Parra, *Epistolario íntimo* 64) [When Emilia used to say that if I ever had a child everything, everything that was hers would be unconditionally mine, I used to answer that it was my intention never to marry]. In a letter to Lydia Cabrera: "Si yo hubiera buscado la *entente* completa en el matrimonio, Zaldumbide sería hoy sin duda, a los ojos de María, Seida y todo el mundo, un marido virtuoso y un hombre modelo. No habría los otros comentarios. ¿Qué me importa que digan 'la pobre Teresa' si yo sé a qué atenerme?" (*C* 191) [If I had wanted a complete *entente* through marriage, Zaldumbide would no doubt be today, in the eyes of María, Seida and the rest of the world, a virtuous husband and a model man. There wouldn't be the gossip. What do I care if they call me "poor Teresa" when I'm prepared for it?].

11 Letter to Louis Antoine Lemaître, 6 February 1980, in Lemaître 126.

12 Lydia Cabrera to Rosario Hiriart in Hiriart, *Más cerca* 62.

13 To give but one example, remarkable in its mimetic "feminine" coyness, see Anderson Imbert, *Historia de la literatura hispanoamericana* 2:100.

14 That the cultural populism of Parra and Cabrera seems to go hand in hand with sympathy for unsavory regimes is undeniable. Parra's sympathy for the "law and order" dictatorship of Juan Vicente Gómez is a fact; so are Cabrera's personal connections to the equally repressive Gerardo Machado in Cuba, whose daughter, Angela Elvira, was rumored to be Cabrera's "good friend." However, the sympathy for these regimes is far from being unqualified. In response to a 1932 letter from Cabrera detailing a political assassination commanded by Machado, Parra writes:

> Nada pongo en duda, Cabrita, todo eso es *verdad,* son los mismos cuentos horribles de Venezuela. . . . Yo digo, como decía Goethe, que "prefiero sufrir de la tiranía y de la injusticia que del desorden." Por eso soy hasta cierto punto gomista [*sic*] y hubiera sido machadista por oposición a los falsos apóstoles. Pero resulta que Machado no sabe siquiera ser tirano. Lo odioso de estos crímenes del gobierno es la cobardía, ellos tienen la fuerza por el poder, la policía, etc. y matan a indefensos por la espalda. (*C* 155–56)
>
> [I don't doubt it, little goat, all that is *true,* they're the same horrible stories one

hears from Venezuela. . . . Like Goethe, I "prefer to suffer from the tyranny of injustice than from that of disorder." That is why I'm a *gomista* to a certain extent and would have been a *machadista* to oppose false apostles. But it happens that Machado doesn't even know how to be a tyrant. What makes these government crimes so hateful is the cowardice. They have power and the police on their side and yet stab the defenseless in the back.]

Still, in a 1933 letter, Parra writes: "Hoy me asustó Glass diciéndome que había leído en el periódico "La Suiza" que Machado había hecho fusilar 200 estudiantes. He buscado en todos los periódicos y no encuentro nada. Debe ser error *o por lo menos exageración*" (*C* 162, my emphasis) [Glass frightened me today telling me that he read in *La Suisse* that Machado had 200 students shot. I have looked in every newspaper and can't find it, it must be a mistake *or an exaggeration*]. The economic nature of these dubious alliances with dictators is no less disturbing: for a time Parra received a pension from Gómez; it was a high price to pay for *independence*. There are also allusions, in the Parra-Cabrera correspondence, to an unspecified dependence between Cabrera and Machado ("Sólo él te puede sacar del atolladero" [*C* 162] [Only he can get you out of this mess]).

15 "Mi cariño por la Colonia no me llevaría nunca a decir como dicen algunos en momentos de lirismo que desearían haber nacido entonces. No. Yo me siento muy bien dentro de mi época y la admiro" (*O* 490) [My love for colonial times would never make me say, as some do, carried away by lyricism, that I wish I had been born then. No. I feel very happy in my time, which I admire].

16 "In her 1930 lectures, 'closed doors' means lack of freedom, good perhaps for the selfless women of the colonial period but bad for modern women. Modern society is one of open doors. In the 1929 novel [*Ifigenia*], the metaphorical opposition between open and closed doors is reiterated, but here it is modernity (and the masculine) that is always associated with closed doors indicating selfishness and prohibition. Instead, the 'Colonial' (that is, the feminine) is designated by open doors, representing true freedom, synomymous with generosity and forthrightness" (Garrels 21–22).

Works Cited

Anderson Imbert, Enrique. *Historia de la literatura hispanoamericana*. Vol. 2. Mexico: Fondo de Cultura Económica, 1954.

Cabrera, Lydia. *Siete cartas de Gabriela Mistral a Lydia Cabrera*. Miami: Peninsular Printing, 1980.

Colette. *Le pur et l'impur. Oeuvres*. Vol. 3. Paris: Gallimard, "Pléiade," 1991.

Díaz Sánchez, Ramón. *Teresa de la Parra, clave para una interpretación*. Caracas: Ediciones Garrido, 1954.

Faderman, Lillian. "Love between Women in 1928: Why Progressivism Is Not Always Progress." *Historical, Literary and Erotic Aspects of Lesbianism*. Ed. Monica Kehoe. New York: Hawthorn Press, 1986. 23–42.

———. *Surpassing the Love of Men: Romantic Friendship and Love between Women from the Renaissance to the Present*. New York: William Morrow, 1981.

Fombona, Julieta. "Teresa de la Parra: las voces de la palabra." In Teresa de la Parra, *Obra*. Caracas: Editorial Ayacucho, 1982. ix–xxvi.

Garrels, Elizabeth. *Las grietas de la ternura: Nueva lectura de Teresa de la Parra*. Caracas: Monte Avila, 1986.

Hiriart, Rosario, ed. *Cartas a Lydia Cabrera. (Correspondencia inédita de Gabriela Mistral y Teresa de la Parra)*. Madrid: Ediciones Torremozas, 1988.

———. *Más cerca de Teresa de la Parra (Diálogos con Lydia Cabrera*. Caracas: Monte Avila, 1980.

Keyserling, Hermann von. *Analyse spectrale de l'Europe*. 1928; Paris: Gonthier, 1965.

Lemaître, Louis Antoine. *Between Flight and Longing: The Journey of Teresa de la Parra*. New York: Vantage Press, 1986.

Lovera de Sola, R.J. "Un aspecto en la vida de Teresa de la Parra." *El Nacional,* Caracas, 4 December 1978.

Marks, Jeannette. *Gallant Little Wales*. Boston and New York: Houghton Mifflin, 1912.

Norris, Nélida Galanovic. *A Critical Appraisal of Teresa de la Parra*. Diss. UCLA, 1980.

Parra, Teresa de la. *Epistolario íntimo*. Caracas: Ediciones de la Línea Aeropostal Venezolana, 1953.

———. *Obra*. Caracas: Editorial Ayacucho, 1982.

———. *Obras completas*. Intro. Carlos García Prada. Caracas: Editorial Arte, 1985.

Sommer, Doris. *Foundational Fictions: The National Romances of Latin America*. Berkeley: University of California Press, 1991.

Uslar Pietri, Arturo. "*Ifigenia* de Teresa de la Parra." *Teresa de la Parra ante la crítica*. Ed. Velia Bosch. Caracas: Monte Avila, 1980. 77–82.

Wells, Anna Mary. *Miss Marks and Miss Woolley*. Boston: Houghton Mifflin, 1978.

John K. Walsh

A Logic in Lorca's Ode to
Walt Whitman

Federico García Lorca's *Ode to Walt Whitman* is perhaps the most significant—certainly the most complete—modern poem about homosexualities. With the poem, Lorca seemed to anticipate the multiple audiences
or vantages that would take hold of it. Indeed, it has probably been given
more misreading and misinterpretation than any other poem from his generation. Even Luis Cernuda—a part of the close subgroup of homosexualist poets of "1927" that included Lorca, Vicente Aleixandre, and Emilio
Prados (Rius 73–74)—would claim that Lorca had not gone far enough:
that the *Ode* was a grand sculpture left unfinished because Lorca had found
a flaw in the great slab of stone (449).

We may even say that the *Ode* was meant to be mistaken by anyone who
seized the tone of a few prevailing lines in it as the prime voice of the poet.
And when Lorca could not select his audience for the poem, he seems to
have arranged and presided over its misreadings. The voice that glares on
the page is a fetid and forceful one of Lorca lashing out against homosexualist types and subtypes, flinging upon them a litany of the very epithets
that had been arranged by bigots. It is only in the soft pauses—the protests
and apologies, the embers after the insults—that the poem and something
of the poet's momentous dementia can coalesce and gather intention.

The *Ode to Whitman* is often taken as the heart of Lorca's *Poet in New
York*—the piece that steers and opens so much of it. It gives perspective
to the two commanding themes of the collection: the ugliness and tangle
of the modern American city in 1929–30 (against Whitman's dream of a
hearty riverland); the rancid course urban homosexuality can take (against
Whitman's warm, pure, and soaring love). Yet Lorca may never have intended this *Ode* as part of the *Poet in New York*, at least not until the end.

The original audience Lorca allowed and the controlled circulation he felt necessary for the *Ode* should have some bearing on what we perceive as the poem's purpose.

The *Ode* was probably begun in New York before December 1929 and reworked in Havana in spring of 1930. The hiatus could be crucial, since it now seems evident that Lorca's open passage into a homosexual mien, and the acknowledgment of his proclivities as permanent, came about during his three-month stay in Havana. The manuscript of the *Ode to Whitman* is dated 15 June 1930, when Lorca was on the ship *Manuel Arnús*, traveling from Havana back to the port of New York as first stop before the return to Spain, in the company of his friend the music critic Adolfo Salazar (Eisenberg 249; see Anderson 222). The full poem was never published with any circulation in Lorca's lifetime; and Lorca never included it in his celebrated lecture-readings of *Poet in New York*.

Lorca first came into contact with Whitman's poetry—or at least with a wisp of Whitman's vision—in New York in September 1929. He had been invited for a weekend stay at the country home in Newburgh, New York, of Federico de Onís, chairman of Columbia's department of Spanish. There he met the Spanish poet León Felipe, who had been obsessed with Whitman's work and was preparing a translation of parts of it including the "Song of Myself." Felipe recalls that Lorca had only an inkling of Whitman before their encounter, when he read to Lorca two or three poems they would analyze together. In Felipe's recollection he explained Whitman to Lorca, citing verses. "Then, when I spoke to him of Whitman, there are . . . some verses there where Whitman says he wrote to love everyone, everything: children, women, men, everything. . . . When I told him these things in New York . . . he felt that Walt Whitman was not a homosexual, and then he felt wounded" (Rius 71–72, with related recollections on 161). We need not assume Lorca was or ever became an assiduous reader of Whitman or that specific poems by Whitman can fix calques and references in Lorca's *Ode*.[1] But with the samples Felipe had shown him, and the explanations of Whitman's prophecy and dilemma, Lorca seized upon a gist of Whitman. In an odd way, too, he must have thought himself something of a postfiguration of Whitman in the role of poet if not as emblem. The voice and pose Lorca puts in many of the New York poems—strutting and proclaiming or lamenting at odd and solitary hours by the edges of the city—seem a bit of Whitman in a Hispanic transfiguration.

The first printing—the only complete publication of the *Ode to Whitman* before Lorca's death—was a special edition of fifty copies, run off by a private press called Alcancía in Mexico City and released on 5 August

1933. The issue was small enough to make it immediately exclusive, but every care was taken in the reproduction. The sponsors of the "Alcancía" issue were a distinguished group of young Mexican intellectuals, led by Edmundo O'Gorman (later a renowned professor of history) and Justino Fernández (the celebrated art historian), both in their late twenties. There is reason to believe they took on the project as a kind of private anthem for a small and elitist liberal circle with strong social sympathies toward homosexuals, or even—though this would veer from Lorca's gesture— as apologia for a discreet or ennobled coterie. In this early context, the *Ode* was clearly a piece taken as justification, one that would not offend; it included for this special original audience an ethic that would elevate or redeem. Here, Lorca would be something of a spokesman—one speaking within the circle, knowing his voice would be understood exactly, and not taken as the troubled, tangled, or ranting voice that has been heard by later readers beyond the circle.

Lorca learned the publication was completed only in December 1933, during his stay in Argentina, when he met the Mexican poet Salvador Novo (Novo 201), slightly younger than Lorca and recognizably homosexual. Novo told him of the effect of the *Ode* among those in the small circle of initiates in Mexico City. Only much later did Lorca get his ration—probably under a dozen copies—from the printer. In Spain, Lorca gave the *Ode* only to circumspect and sympathetic friends: José Caballero, Luis Morales, Rafael Martínez Nadal, Carlos Morla Lynch, José Fernández Montesinos, surely young Rafael Rodríguez Rapún (Lorca's lover, apparently, from 1933 until his death). It all came to a closed and private project, not to be released beyond the fringes: fifty carefully distributed copies from a poet whose *Romancero gitano* [Gypsy Ballads] was then being run off by the thousands and would become the most familiar cycle of poems of the century in any Western literature.

By itself—without gloss and without the manuscript in which Lorca's mind can be glimpsed shifting, tearing, and contradicting itself—the *Ode to Whitman* has enough to make its purpose permanently impenetrable. But what set a purpose in the "Alcancía" edition—what dissolved forthwith the pliant ambiguity Lorca had given the voices and the rhetoric of his *Ode*—was the cover and interior drawing by Rodríguez Lozano. The printed sketch is of two naked adolescent boys, seated together presumably by the river (the East River of the poem?). The cast of the etching is homoerotic, to announce a sentiment and bring the reader by its image into a poem of sympathies. That is, the *Ode* whose lines are often taken as denunciation of homosexuality is launched (probably, without Lorca's

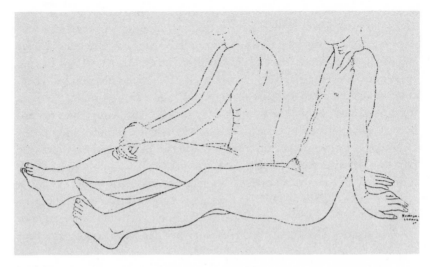

Rodríguez Lozano, cover and frontispiece sketch for García Lorca's *Oda a Walt Whitman*. Reproduction provided by Selma Margaretten and Tomás Rodríguez Rapún.

say in the matter) as a delicate, even mildly prurient hymn to the glow and innocence of it, or at least as a poem with a particular interpretation of Whitman's obsession.

Less than a year after the "Alcancía" edition, at the end of June 1934, the *Ode to Whitman*—or a part of it—*did* make its way into general printing for public distribution. It was included as one of seventeen selections by Lorca in the famous second anthology of *Poesía española*, assembled and edited by the poet Gerardo Diego: here the *Ode* was not a clandestine or private project, but a piece in the great sturdy edition from the presses of S. Aguirre, printer to the Spanish academies. Diego's anthology was an event—a gathering of Hispanic poets reaching back to Rubén Darío. But more than anything it was the banquet of the new generation, one that Lorca in a few years could refer to without blinking as the *capilla*—perhaps the finest assembly of young poets in Europe (Harris, *Cernuda* 25–26).

We might assume that word of the content of the *Ode to Whitman* had gotten about in Madrid and that its publication in *Poesía española* answered the curiosity, or was a way of quelling it. But the form of the *Ode* listed in Diego's anthology is "fragment": it lacks the first six stanzas and the last nine—some 80 lines of a total of 137. And as fragment it is essentially another poem—perhaps a neater one—with its pith and ethic removed: a safe and less troubling public version for the anthology. Let us find what remains in the truncated or dismembered *Ode* of the anthology, and what Lorca (or Lorca and his editor) thought the poem would be when it was printed outside the tolerant cadre that would be permitted to know the full printing.

The fragment begins not with the series of vile and corrupting symbols Lorca finds along the choked river (the New York of 1929–30 that betrays Whitman's robust kingdom of wheat) but with Lorca's voice (line 24 of the full poem) as it turns to address Whitman directly, confessing that Whitman was the comely angel he held as matrix amid all the spoilt dreams of a city (lines 29–33):

> Ni un solo momento, viejo hermoso Walt Whitman,
> he dejado de ver tu barba llena de mariposas
> ni tus hombros de pana gastados por la luna,
> ni tus muslos de Apolo virginal,
> ni tu voz como una columna de ceniza . . .
> [Not for a single moment, my handsome old Walt Whitman
> have I lost sight of your beard full of butterflies,
> or your shoulders of corduroy worn down by the moon,
> or your thighs of virginal Apollo,
> or your voice like a column of ashes . . .]

First incidentally, then essentially, Whitman's sexuality is brought up, not as pathogenesis but as part of the elegy. (Whitman has already been invoked as the one image of salvation within the refuse of the modern city.) Here the sexuality is defined (34–39):

> anciano hermoso como la niebla,
> que gemías igual que un pájaro
> con el sexo atravesado por una aguja,
> enemigo del sátiro,
> enemigo de la vid,
> y amante de los cuerpos bajo la burda tela.
> [old man, lovely as the mist,
> who cried out like some bird
> with its sex transversed by a needle,
> enemy of the satyr,
> enemy of the vine,
> and lover of bodies beneath the coarse cloth.][2]

After the portrait in the calming voice of one addressing the paragon, Lorca turns to make his demurrer. The voice falls out of control when it be-

262 John K. Walsh

gins to speak an outrage that threatens his own instinct of Whitman: that
the most flamboyant and squalid homosexuals of the cities should point
toward Whitman as one of their breed. For Lorca, the injustice is that a
panoptic sexual category has been manufactured to swallow Whitman as
well as those he would notice to be the slithering, loathsome subtypes of
the city. When the wretched speak at last ("That one, too! That one!" at
line 53), Lorca surely meant a rancid, emasculated voice to rise with the
lewd gesturals (45–53):

> Ni un solo momento, Adán de sangre, Macho,
> hombre solo en el mar, viejo hermoso Walt Whitman,
> porque por las azoteas,
> agrupados en los bares,
> saliendo en racimos de las alcantarillas,
> temblando entre las piernas de los chauffeurs
> o girando en las plataformas del ajenjo,
> los maricas, Walt Whitman, te señalan.
>
> "¡También ése! ¡También!" . . .
> [Not for a single moment, full-blooded Adam, virile,
> man alone in a sea, my handsome old Walt Whitman,
> because there on the rooftops,
> and packed in the bars,
> coming out in bunches from the gutters,
> trembling betwixt the legs of the drivers
> or twirling on platforms of absinthe,
> the faggots, Walt Whitman, are pointing at you:
>
> "That one, too! That one!" . . .

The fragment printed in Diego's anthology also includes the stanzas (9–
12) that define a difference between the robust sexuality of Whitman and
the fetid mores of the urban *maricas:*

> Pero tú no buscabas los ojos arañados
> ni el pantano obscurísimo donde sumergen a los niños,
> ni la saliva helada,
> ni las curvas heridas como panza de sapo
> que llevan los maricas en coches y en terrazas
> mientras la luna los azota por las esquinas del terror.
> Tú buscabas un desnudo que fuera como un río.
> Toro y sueño que junte la rueda con el alga . . .

[But you never went seeking those lacerated³ eyes
nor the dark, dark swamp where they drown the young boys,
nor the frozen saliva,
nor the cracked curves the faggots flaunt,
like the paunch of a toad, on the sidewalks, in the cars,
while the moon whips them on through the corners of terror.
You went seeking the nude who would be like a river,
bull and dream to conjoin the seaweed and the wheel . . .]

And the ending of the published fragment is a stanza in irenic Alexandrine that must be left as enigma (77–80):

Porque es justo que el hombre no busque su deleite
en la selva de sangre de la mañana próxima.
El cielo tiene playas donde evitar la vida
y hay cuerpos que no deben repetirse en la Aurora.
[It is right that a man need not seek out his joy
in the jungle of blood of the succeeding morn.
Heaven has its beaches where life can be avoided;
there are bodies that need not remake themselves at dawn.]

The meaning of the stanza is perhaps inaccessible alone in the printed poem. It appears to claim—in muted negatives—that a love that does not lean toward procreation need not be ignoble: there is a space in the heavens for those who choose another bearing. The Alexandrine came only after Lorca had discarded in the manuscript (*Autógrafos* 1:211) a wretched and garbled description of the condemned *maricas* in pursuit of adolescent prey: "in the street with a big stick like a sword. . . . Because they put to flight the boys and give them green and putrid flesh instead of soul. And the key to the world is in giving life—sons made out of soul. . . . [Y]ou go away to the shore of the river with the rat and the skeleton."

With only the fragment designed for the anthology, a reader would extract a message quite distant from that of the complete *Ode to Whitman*. The lesson would be a simple one of sexual categories that should not be swept together: that of the purist Whitman, that of the army of urban and defiled *maricas*. Lorca's [indignation] rises at the impertinence of association—by the public in making no divisions and by the *maricas* in their sacrilege of claiming the hardy Whitman for their camp. Only in the full poem will Lorca move toward an ethic of homosexualities that goes beyond these divisions and layers or boundaries, that creates a disposition that is not constrained in some vertical mold and is ultimately more tolerant. We

might say, then, that the complete *Ode* was written for a set of partisans of
a special order (as may be proved by the circumstances of its publication),
while the fragment in Diego's anthology was meant for another readership
not allowed inward beyond a rather simplistic instruction.

But what is within the full poem—what is beyond the false lead of the
published fragment—has its own labyrinth. For here the matter of homosexualist categories is regularly shattered and undone. The most forceful
voice—so acerbic it has made some readers interpret the entire poem as a
tract *against* homosexualities—is that raised in brutal condemnation in the
grotesque litany of scathing epithets:

> *Fairies* de Norteamérica,
> *Pájaros* de la Habana,
> *Jotos* de Méjico,
> *Sarasas* de Cádiz,
> *Apios* de Sevilla,
> *Cancos* de Madrid,
> *Floras* de Alicante,
> *Adelaidas* de Portugal.

The list makes the *Ode* more of a tangle: it is no longer a poem about
America, but about an internationalist—or at least Hispanic or Luso-
Hispanic and North American—blight, with a swarming Hispanic flam-
boyance in the turn of sexual epithets, at once caricature and invective.
Are we to adjust now, so that the sexualist haunts and mores in the *Ode
to Whitman* are not merely those of New York? In practical terms, the
poem now describes the two sexual underworlds Lorca knew as observer
or participant—that of New York and that of the Peninsula and Cuba.

For a moment, the ethic Lorca is leading toward seems behavioral, approaching religious dictum. He would appear to condemn those who take
the sexual as pastime, or as some ritual form of possession and collection,
and who make this sexual obsession visible or public. He would almost be
suggesting as apposite a redeemed category of celibate homosexuals. Here,
he projects the punishment, the hell, for all those who defile (116–23):

> ¡Maricas de todo el mundo, asesinos de palomas!
> Esclavos de la mujer. Perras de sus tocadores.
> Abiertos en las plazas, con fiebre de abanico
> o emboscados en yertos paisajes de cicuta.
>
> ¡No haya cuartel! La muerte
> mana de vuestros ojos

y agrupa flores grises en la orilla del cieno.
¡No haya cuartel! ¡¡Alerta!!
[Faggots of all the world, the murderers of doves!
Nothing but slaves of women, bitches in their boudoirs.
Flaunting yourselves in plazas, with the fever of a fan
or ambushed in the stagnant, silent landscapes of hemlock.

No quarter for you!
Death is oozing from your eyes
and gathering gray flowers upon the shore of slime.
No quarter for you! Beware!!]

But this preliminary identification of the physical as the measure to warrant condemnation is abruptly undone in the last breath of his warning to the *maricas* (124–26):

Que los confundidos, los puros,
los clásicos, los señalados, los suplicantes
os cierren las puertas de la bacanal.
[For the perplexed ones and the pure,
the classics, the appointed, the suplicants
will close to you the doors to the Bacchanalia.]

Here the notion of the "pure" or "classic" homosexual is raised in vague definition that will satisfy Lorca's need to cover the category he wishes to allow, even hail. Surely, it can be projected as the category in which he would wish to fix himself. The terms of the *Ode* were carried over unfortunately to Lorca's biography and played out in an absurd rationale of his death. The Baron Louis Stinglhamber, using the pseudonym Jean-Louis Schonberg, manufactured in 1956 a thesis that Lorca was killed by "impure" local homosexuals jealous of Lorca's position amid the "pure" or elitist counterparts of his Granada, and the Franco government let it flourish for a quarter century. The motive for the death would be a petty vengeance that struck at a moment when the insinuation of deviation would justify rabid execution.[4] Only in recent years has this folly been dissolved. Lorca claims the *bacanal* will be reserved for this elusive "purist" class, which will shut out the army of *maricas*. The term *bacanal* is a curious choice: it calls up physical celebration, near orgiastic, as the reward to the "pure"—which could mean that all along the gauge was not simply physical but the conditions under which the physical was sought. So that in the end it is not the sensual or sexual that defines the category Lorca seeks to impugn.

In the full poem, almost every clue Lorca issues toward settling the bounds of categories turns in the reader's eye. It is as if in writing the poem he moves from the ode of calm to rabid paroxysms whenever he approaches definition of what he wishes to condemn. But what will determine the herd Lorca's voice decries, and what is his basis in drawing what at first appear to be categories "A" and "B" among homosexuals (the first Whitmanesque or pure, the second vulgar or promiscuous and impure)?

For a moment, the poem gives a possibility that the division will be made on grounds of effeminacy or a flaunted gaudiness against a Whitmanesque masculinity. But the impulse is solemnly dismissed, as Lorca reaches to soothe the condition (92–96):

> Por eso no levanto mi voz, viejo Walt Whitman,
> contra el niño que escribe
> nombre de niña en su almohada,
> ni contra el muchacho que se viste de novia
> en la oscuridad del ropero . . .
> [Therefore, old friend Walt Whitman, I do not raise my voice
> against the boy who copies
> a girl's name on his pillow,
> nor against the lad who dresses up as missy
> in the darkness of the closet . . .]

And, of course, the simple equation of masculine homosexuality as positive and effeminacy—or Whitman's "pathic" disposition, remarked by Davenport (71)—as negative could never have been the line Lorca would draw: in the "Canción del mariquita" (from *Canciones, 1921–24* [Songs], published in 1927), he put more sympathy than derision into the figure of the local Andalusian effeminate, caught teasing his curls while a flare of scandal spreads through the back alleys and hovers above the rooftops (*OC* 316–17).

Within the genesis of the *Ode to Whitman* is the genesis of Lorca's ethical thesis about homosexualities. His early private solution seems to have been caught on the matter of procreation: the glaring proof of a cause for piaculum as inherent in the biologic bias. The conversion or "breakthrough" to another solution comes at a moment in the manuscript of the *Ode to Whitman* we described above: Lorca discards a furious stanza that would block redemption and creates the Alexandrine (lines 77–80) to find a clearing beyond procreation.

I would connect Lorca's shift in vision to the creation of his sonnet "Adam," a piece dated 1 December 1929, but not included in the canon of *Poet in New York*. The reference to Whitman as "Adán de sangre" ("full-blooded Adam" [45]) would hint that the sonnet came in tandem with the *Ode* and that Whitman as the new Adam is somewhere inscribed in the sonnet. The poem speaks of the blood of childbirth and the myth of Adam the father ("Árbol de sangre riega la mañana / por donde gime la recién parida" ["The Tree of Blood now irrigates the morn / in which the one who bore the child still groans"]) in terms of the pivotal Alexandrine in the *Ode* that spoke of the same birth blood ("porque es justo que el hombre no busque su deleite / en la selva de sangre de la mañana próxima" [77–81]). But at the end of the sonnet the poet puts another Adam or alter-Adam who is left at the edge of the myth, for whom procreation is not the mold:

> Pero otro Adán oscuro está soñando
> neutra luna de piedra sin semilla
> donde el niño de luz se irá quemando.
> [But another, hidden Adam dreams also:
> a neutral moon of stone without a seed
> in which the child of light fades and burns out.]

We may venture that "Adam" had to have been made after the start of the *Ode*—after he got beyond the impasse and uncoiled the dilemma—and date the start of the *Ode* just before December 1929.

Another Lorcan text made in the spell of *Ode to Whitman* is *El público*, the drama begun while he was in Havana and finished the following summer in Spain. This vast botch and behemoth of a play will try to fit in dramatic form all the issues he finds round homosexualities: dissimulation, persecution, genders crossing over, proclivities and "subtypes" within the spectrum, domination. In their textual history, the *Ode to Whitman* and *El público* intersect visibly, so that we can connect them in common momentum and perhaps as two poles of an obsession. In the manuscript of the *Ode*, Lorca had created in the third stanza an enigmatic image wherein "las mujeres trenzaban sus cabelleras / o llenaban de saliva los mármoles" ("the women were braiding their hair / or covering the [chunks of] marble with saliva")—an occluded reference, I think, to his unfinished notion of the women's role in the generation of homosexualist behavior. And in the last scene of *El público*, the "Prestidigitador" speaks accusingly to the "Director" (Martínez Nadal's intro. to García Lorca, *Autógrafos* xxxi): "Pero ustedes lo que querían era asesinar a la paloma y dejar en lugar suyo un pedazo de mármol lleno de pequeñas salivas habladoras" [But what you wanted was to murder a dove and leave in its place a chunk of marble covered with tiny talking [gobs of] saliva]. Apart from the image of saliva salvaged out of the *Ode* into *El público*, the accusation that a type of homosexual is "murder[er] of [the] dove" stays in both works.[5] At line 116 in the *Ode*, immediately following the scarlet string of epithets, is the condemnation: "Maricas de todo el mundo, asesinos de palomas" [Faggots of all the world, the murderers of doves]. Indirectly, the reference fits the character of "Director" in a negative homosexualist category devised in the *Ode*. The sharing of images in Havana is the sign of the obsession congealing: in one exposition (the *Ode*) it is thetic and specific (Whitman and the enemies of his image); in another (*El público*) it is symbolic, with all the crude ambition of one who surmises he has fathomed the enigma.

The matter of metric may seem minor in the *Ode to Whitman*. We have come to think that Lorca's new poetic in the New York poems included rejection or shattering of the old and regular rhythms—especially, of the mode in *Gypsy Ballads*. (Surely, part of the new system after the *Ballads* is in reaction to Salvador Dalí's stinging appraisal of them as outmoded, with "hands and feet tied to the art of the old poetry . . . now incapable of moving us" and without the requisite "dose of the irrational" [Rodrigo 262–64; see Aranda 46–47].) And Lorca in New York may have broken from the forms and let the lines spill beyond the margins partly in *response* to Whitman's format. Yet in measuring the poems of *Poet in New York* we may be unprepared to find that amid the new chaos and irregularity—the run-on lines or the screaming epithets that are shrunken or distended to the measure of his bile—Lorca kept some of the metric perfect and essential. One obvious example is "Nacimiento de Cristo" in careful Alexandrines (with assonance); it is a reaction to a gaudy replica of the Nativity set out in the snow beneath the glare of Manhattan billboards—as if in the splinters and nails of this bogus manger the slaughter were being foretold. Here he seems to be working in the system of the other *Odes* that form a transition between *Gypsy Ballads* and *Poet in New York:*

> Un pastor pide teta por la nieve que ondula
> blancos perros tendidos entre linternas sordas.
> El Cristito de barro se ha partido los dedos
> en los filos eternos de la madera rota.
> [The shepherd aims for the nipple to suckle snow that jostles
> the white dogs on their leashes among the still streetlamps.
> The little clay Christ-child got his fingers knocked off
> on the eternal splinters protruding from the wood.]

"Tu infancia de Mentón," too, has a stable meter in recollective hendecasyllables to match a verse from Jorge Guillén that will start and end Lorca's poem (see García Lorca, *Sesostris* 31). Other poems make a gambol of putting spasmodic sexual history in playful rhythms: "Fábula y rueda de los tres amigos" gives the recent bond of the poet and three confederates—all now squandered and lost amid some degeneracy—the shape of a child-like ditty; "Vals vienés" follows a homosexualist seduction amid the vapid, cymbaline beat of waltz. The *Poet in New York*, then, does keep a dose of lyric congruities amid the new temper.

In the *Ode to Whitman*, the shape we see first and last in the poem appears ametric, with long and short pronouncements in lines that would put the poetics as well as the poem in tribute to Whitman. And yet the main formal dynamic Lorca intended was one of meter against non-meter. In the descriptions of the modern city, in the vitriolic contumelies, the lines are without a count. But when Lorca looks toward Whitman in praise, or speaks of the "pure" path of the noble homosexual, the meter turns exact: it is made of perfect Alexandrines, with precise hiatus and measure, to let the voice turn stately and enamored, or hortatory. In this way, secluded within the *Ode* is the "ode"—the measured meditation in the meter he had practiced in the *Ode to Salvador Dalí* (1926) and the *Ode to the Sacrament* (1928, as homage to Manuel de Falla, but finished during late summer of 1929 in New York).

Let us find how this system works in the *Ode to Whitman*, where the counterstrophes make a kind of metric code. The first full Alexandrine follows immediately the list of rancid negatives (lines 67–72) that catch the motive of urban *maricas*: "ni la saliva helada, / ni las curvas heridas como panza de sapo / que llevan los maricas en coches y en terrazas" [nor the frozen saliva, / nor the cracked curves the faggots flaunt, / like the paunch of a toad, on the sidewalks, in the cars]. In contrast, Whitman's longing (in the Alexandrine) comes of classical, natural sentiment, with some great sway of pure forces beneath it (lines 73–76):

> Tú[6] buscabas un desnudo que fuera como un río
> Toro y sueño que junte la rueda con el alga,
> padre de tu agonía, camelia de tu muerte,
> y gimiera en las llamas de tu Ecuador oculto.
> [You went seeking the nude who would be like a river,
> bull and dream to conjoin the seaweed and the wheel,
> a father for your pain, camellia of your death,
> and would moan in the flames of your secret Equator.]

It leads into another Alexandrine (lines 77–80) we have cited as Lorca's prime plea that redemption not be denied. And set between specific excurses (on the fatal terrors of society that would make marginal the issues of homosexualities; on the numb misfortune of the effeminate and the lonely) is an Alexandrine (88–91) to ratify or bless the pursuit and to suggest the matter of passion as miniscule in a lengthening memory of the life:

> Puede el hombre, si quiere, conducir su deseo
> por vena de coral o celeste desnudo;
> mañana los amores serán rocas y el Tiempo
> una brisa que viene dormida por las ramas.
> [A man may, if he wishes, let his desire be turned
> toward the vein of the coral or a celestial nude;
> tomorrow all our passions will be but stone, and time
> a breeze that comes approaching, so slumbrous, through the
>   branches.]

The final Alexandrine is the last look at Whitman in a call for the noble to engage and protect his image (127–30):

> Y tú, bello Walt Whitman, duerme orillas del Hudson
> con la barba hacia el Polo y las manos abiertas.
> Arcilla blanda o nieve, tu lengua está llamando
> camaradas que velen tu gacela sin cuerpo.
> [And you, handsome Walt Whitman, sleep by the Hudson's shore,
> with your beard toward the Pole, your hands open to all.
> Like snow or pliant clay, your tongue is summoning
> comrades who might protect your bodiless gazelle.]

These even, calm, distended lines of the Alexandrines must be meant as crests above so many miasmic stretches wherein the rhythm changes and turns, calling as if to sick in every direction after those who defile the image.

The complete *Ode to Whitman* seems framed in a flawed syllogism that would force together two themes: one sociologic (Whitman's dream of a hearty America—his Mannahatta—against the present and tawdry, mechanical New York); one sexual (Whitman's virtuous and soaring homosexuality against the fetid and debased homosexualities of the cities). The full poem (though not the fragment in Diego's anthology) starts and finishes with a ruse that the poem is all about the societal: lines 1–34 make no mention of the sexual (which may lead us perhaps to a moment in which Lorca began with a tribute that was principally "social"). And again in the closing lines (131–37) the poem speaks simply of Whitman's dream set against the automaton of America. (There is no thought or summary of sexualities at the end, as if the matter in the middle had never come into the poem.) In fact, the transition (at the end) from lines about Whitman's homosexuality to Whitman as symbol of a fresh America could not be more abrupt: in the next-to-last stanza (a noble Alexandrine), Lorca gives the call for the "purist" or undefiled homosexuals to rally and guard the ethic or spirit of Whitman, to carry on and protect ("Y tú, bello Walt Whitman, duerme orillas del Hudson" [127–30]). Then, the final stanza opens with the same image of Whitman asleep by the Hudson, but here it is Whitman as social symbol, as if the tissue of his sexuality had never been touched inside the poem (131–37):

> Duerme: no queda nada.
> Una danza de muros agita las praderas
> y América se anega de máquinas y llanto.
> Quiero que el aire fuerte de la noche más honda
> quite flores y letras del arco donde duermes,
> y un niño negro anuncie a los blancos del oro
> la llegada del reino de la espiga.
> [Sleep on: nothing is left.
> A dance of concrete walls is threatening the meadows:
> America is drowning beneath machines and sobs.
> I wish a mighty wind from a fathomless night
> would take flowers and letters from the arch where you sleep
> and a black boy would proclaim to the gold-grubbing whites
> the coming of the kingdom of corn.] [7]

The equation or simile to connect the two strands of the poem (Whitman's robust social dream: the corroded America of 1930 = Whitman's wholesome sexuality: the abomination of urban homosexuality) holds far too many deceptions and blemishes. As poetic syllogism it is awkward and imperfect. We have seen that the category Lorca wishes to condemn is never quite defined, or the definitions are dismantled by the poet as the poem moves along. In the end one suspects that he had to condemn with ire and to divide vilely in order to find the part—any mote that might be there— and make the point that a broad category cannot stand. And yet to make any definition hold definitively would be betrayal: it would undo the empathy that reaches wherever it might. He must, therefore, signal and admit a degenerate and flaunted homosexuality and confine it vaguely in order to proclaim another, superior mode. Ultimately, we can extract the main venture as autobiographic: in order to tolerate his own homosexuality, he must disconnect it from the grotesquerie of visible categories.

Nor does the *Ode* hold firm as poem about America: in too many sections, the poem is about international or at least Hispanic forms of homosexualities as well as urban American (New York) ones. Whitman in one message is a purely American symbol, but in the sexual lesson his significance is international (or at least Anglo-Hispanic). The genesis of this Hispanic entering the American must have been Lorca's visit to Cuba and finishing the poem on the return voyage.

Yet there are a few moments in the poem when the two themes intersect, and the "social" outer frame of the poem seems to connect with the "sexual" inner frame. As example we give the opening of the poem, with its image of the boys along the East River: "los muchachos cantaban enseñando sus cinturas" [the boys were all singing, showing off their waists]. (This phrase probably generated the drawing of pubescent boys languishing on the cover of the first publication in the 1933 "Alcancía" edition.) A related or repeated image comes in lines 65–66: Whitman is beside his friend, offering him an apple, while "el sol canta por los ombligos / de los muchachos que juegan bajo los puentes" [the sun sings upon the navels / of the lads who frolic under the bridges]. The first reference is one of freedom and strength against industry; the second—in the sexual core of the poem—is one of sexual soundness or purity (the boys catch the eye of Whitman). Also, the early vision where "noventa mil mineros sacaban la plata de las rocas" [ninety thousand miners extracted silver from the stones] may have been intended to connect with the heat of the condemnation of the *maricas:* one negative moment in this later section (at line 50) describes the condemned homosexuals "temblando entre las piernas de los *mineros*" [trembling betwixt the legs of the miners]. This form in the manuscript (ed. Martínez Nadal 209) was later changed to "temblando entre las piernas de los chauffeurs," which blurred the strand of an image Lorca may have once envisioned.

Moreover, the social is interjected in the middle of the "sexual" center of the poem, when the ebbing meditation on homosexuality and procreation (lines 77–80) leads into a triptych of general societal horrors (82–87):

Los muertos se descomponen bajo el reloj de las ciudades.
La guerra pasa llorando con un millón de ratas grises,
los ricos dan a sus queridas
pequeños moribundos iluminados,
y la Vida no es noble, ni buena, ni sagrada.
[The dead are decomposing under the clocks of the cities.
War passes by weeping, trailing a million gray rats,
the rich men give to their darlings

glittering moribund newborn,
and life is never noble, nor is it good, nor sacred.]

The connection stressed in moving the poem from the celestial Alexandrine of homosexualist ethic into the secular nightmare is obvious in the last line: the nonprocreation of the noble homosexual gathers grace beside the tawdry, cheap procreation of the rich with their strumpets. It underlines the folly of a moral condemnation of homosexualities drawn on the basis of fecundation.

We have said that the *Ode to Whitman* may never have been intended as part of *Poet in New York*—at least before 1934. Yet this same *Ode,* I think, can be the wherewith to recover so much of what seems dark or ambiguous in a fleet of pieces in the collection. In the first place, the *Ode to Whitman* is specific about homosexual types and contexts, while other poems of the New York cycle that we sense as sexual are so indefinite about sexualities that they can be retrieved only with a difficult and unreliable cipher. The *Ode* may have its throes of confusion—with the poet shifting and withdrawing to confound or block out an absolute thesis—but nothing in Lorca's *Ode* is abstract: the haunts and habits of his homosexuals are explicit. Lorca speaks of "[los maricas] . . . agrupados en los bares" [the queers . . . packed in the bars], "maricas . . . abiertos en las plazas con fiebre de abanico / o emboscados en yertos paisajes de cicuta" [the queers . . . flaunting yourselves in plazas, with the fever of a fan / or ambushed in the stagnant, silent landscapes of hemlock] or even "temblando entre las piernas de los chauffeurs" [trembling betwixt the legs of the drivers] or of "los solitarios en los casinos que beben con asco el agua de la prostitución" [the lonely men in the dance-halls who swallow down with loathing the water of prostitution]. Some of the verses may have been designed out of the recent experience in Havana, where Lorca came to know a particularly flamboyant commerce of sex. A writer-friend, Luis Cardoza y Aragón (601), recalls accompanying Lorca to the exotic brothels of Havana, then to the sidestreets where male prostitutes of every shade and frame were on display: "There were also *efebos,* looking for a lover of their generous and terrible delicateness."[8]

This tangible, specific scenario of sexuality in the *Ode* (and to some extent in *El público*) suggests the true gloss to a block of incognizable poems in *Poet in New York* could be an anthropology and geography of the homosexual subculture of New York (and Cuba) in 1929–30. One could intuit that Lorca's New York in *Poeta en Nueva York* is not solely the surface of the city in the familiar geography—of Harlem, of Wall Street under the

Depression, of the slaughterhouse near Columbia, of Coney Island, of the Jewish cemetery, of Columbia University with its students scurrying frivolously through the autumn rain, of the great bridges and buildings from whose heights he could howl the horror. Lorca's New York might also circumscribe—in cautious and less overt descriptives—the edges of the city beneath the visible geography, and the rough aura of rituals in special haunts or sexual trading grounds. Certainly, New York in the 1930s had a subfusc notoriety for such dealings: a celebrated photo-guide of the time would list "homosexual headquarters" as one of the epithets of the city and could describe it as a "city in which young men linger till they are sold" (Riesenberg 207). Apparently, the nexus of such activities was discoverable to the initiates and the curious. To follow one recollection of the period (McCabe 49, writing of the year 1932), the strand that served as trading ground was along the Hudson—the river side of Riverside Drive between 96th St. and 110th St., within a few blocks of Columbia, where "hundreds of homosexuals cruised nightly." The entry to the heart of Hades (the bushes below in the park) was the stairway at 103rd St., with another hub round the Soldiers' and Sailors' Monument. There the sedulous assembled after nightfall in a kind of slow and silent prowl. Connections were made, money was demanded, and sometimes violence would flare, or a bolt of fear would clear the park.

Much of what seems a sort of scumbling around acts inexact in the *Poet in New York*—and especially in the "river" or "port" poems in the collection—can lose its blur or sense of something inchoate when it is set in this sexual geography of New York, and when the violence and disgust that loiter in many of the poems is linked to the concrete sexual sociology of New York in 1929–30. An example of an intractably opaque poem clearing in this focus is one with the odd title (which may not be Lorca's) "Navidad" or (in Bergamín's edition) "Navidad en el Hudson," dated 27 December 1929—never published in Lorca's lifetime and certainly never included in his lecture-recitals of *Poet in New York*.

In "Navidad" the conspicuous figure or phrase is *desembocadura*—river emptying out. The poet is beside the Hudson and is left with a sense of the emptiness or despair of the *desembocadura*: "Y estoy con las manos vacías en el rumor de la desembocadura" [And I am left with empty hands in the murmur of the (river) emptying out]. In the end, wherever he describes (a sentiment or a specific adventure) has as its result only: "Hueco. Mundo solo. Desembocadura" [Hollow. World alone. (River) emptying out] (line 9). Or in the absolute final frame of the poem:

Alba no. Fábula inerte.
Sólo esto: Desembocadura.
¡Oh esponja mía gris!
¡Oh cuello mío recién degollado!
¡Oh río grande mío!
¡Oh brisa mía de límites que no son míos!
¡Oh filo de amor, oh hiriente filo!
[No dawn. A fable inert.
Only this: an emptying out.
O this gray sponge of mine!
O this neck of mine recently severed!
O this great river of mine!
O this breeze of mine of limits that are mine!
O edge of love, O wounding blade![9]

I do not think this a broad emotion; nor is it a specifically social comment on a lack of spirituality in New York beside the oil-clogged Hudson
in 1929 (Harris, *Poeta* 49–50). More probably, it is a well-shadowed lament
of physical encounter that does not lead beyond, and a documentation of
the suffering or rancid numbness that is its result. The repeated word *desembocadura* was probably meant to hold an intimation of sexual experience—
of the process of river spilling empty and nothing more as sexual wake.[10]
The sense of terror or disgust in many of the river or harbor poems could
display the aftermath of some dismal sexual experience (real or imagined)
that does not last after the moment; and the riverside setting in "Navidad"
suggests reference to the haunts along the Hudson. The poet tells us he has
spent the night on the gangplanks at the edge of the city (line 1), that he
has seen "sailors wrestling with the world" (6, 9–10), and that the experience was unredeeming. Some lurid, atmospheric calque must be within the
image: "[no importa que] el parto de la víbora, desatado bajo las ramas, /
calme la sed de sangre de los que miren el desnudo" [(what does it matter
that) the birth-pangs of the snake, uncoiled beneath the branches, / calm
the thirst for blood of those who gaze at the nude]. It might evoke a kind
of skulking, gruff, and terminal courtship that the poet reviles at its end.
More speculative would be the interpretation of *marinero* in the poem.
Near the beginning is the exclamation: "¡Ese marinero recién degollado!"
[That sailor recently beheaded (killed, destroyed)!]. In the recollections of
McCabe (49)—who went to the spots with his band of righteous juveniles
to bait and batter the homosexuals—the code-phrase, the essential and uni-

versal byword for homosexual proposition in New York in the early 1930s
was: "Would you like to see the dead Marine?" (A positive response meant
a willingness to partake, and a ramble down to the bushes; one who did
not know the phrase would be eliminated as prospect.) It is entirely possible that Lorca came to know this euphemistic key (the sole vocabulary
one needed for entry) for homosexual trafficking in New York, and that
the enigmatic verses about the *marinero* are his translated reference to it.
It is surely this core of a context, here and elsewhere in *Poet in New York*,
that must be sought if meaning is to be discovered. There is no denying
that "Navidad" records a larger spiritual longing in a lingering reference to
Christmas (in the title and the date); but its effect must be in setting the
sordid and unredemptive reality in its aftermath beside this greater distress
and pursuit of purpose.

The open mode of the *Ode to Whitman,* with its identification of type
and locale, invites venture into other poems from New York—especially,
those Lorca put in obscure journals, or never published in his lifetime and
never read at the lecture-recitals. The vantage could catch a flash of the
same stirring within the thicket of obscured contexts of the poems. And
beyond the use of the *Ode* in provoking a gloss for other poems, it is plau-
sible that many poems in *Poet in New York* that seem to carry a tenuous or
disguised sexual autobiography—"Fábula y rueda," "Infancia y muerte,"
"Iglesia abandonada," etc.—came in a surge of revelation following Lorca's
education in Whitman: he now had as image the great poet, who sang of
what Lorca had thought secret in the self.

In a strict sense, the *Ode to Whitman* is the last poem of Lorca's last year
as a poet. He would write other poems in the years beyond New York, but
only as pieces for grave occasion (*Lament for the Death of Sánchez Mejías*)
or as "pastime" experiments (the pseudo-Galician poems, or the *Diwán*) or
in a burst of personal terror in the absence of his lover (the *Sonnets of Dark
Love,* which seemed to take form in a few days in November 1935). He will
not follow the program or the full obsession of poet, and for long stretches
(e.g., the period in Buenos Aires) will not write a single poem. By the
end of the year in New York and Cuba he had turned again toward drama,
perhaps with the need of commercial prospect for his return to Spain. In
Cuba, he began *El público,* transforming the fixations of the *Ode* to theater,
with the naive notion they might be put on stage; in the summer of the following year (1931), he wrote another nearly unplayable drama (*Así que pasen
cinco años*) that sought sexual definitions in a less blatant format. Then,
toward autumn of 1932—and probably while reading Antonio Machado's
"Tierra de Alvargonzález" with the plan of turning it into a play for his

Barraca—he came upon the formula for *Blood Wedding* as the first of the backcountry dramas that would flourish in the commercial theater, with roles for the great actresses who ruled the stage in his day. But in a private passion, he kept approaching the homosexualist themes and trying to redo main myths or social frames (*The Destruction of Sodom, Blackball*)—always in false starts, without finishing scripts or finding a way to hold his febrile theses in place. In the *Ode to Whitman,* with all its lunges and quandaries, something had been solved in a tentative way that Lorca would come to find definitive for himself.

Notes

1 On the other hand, Lorca's recollection of Whitman's "Song of Myself" could be reflected in the start of his *Ode*. The image of boys by the river revealing their waists, then hordes of miners taking silver from the rocks, could echo Whitman's "Twenty-eight young men bathe by the shore . . . their white bellies bulge to the sun" and the close of the same poem, "Overhead the hammers swing . . . each man hits in his place." (On the cohesion of this mood in Whitman, see Kaplan 90–93.) The obstacle in learning Whitman would be Lorca's negligible English. Even in the manuscript of the *Ode* he invariably gets the English wrong ("Eats River," "Queenboorg [Bridge]," even "Whalt Withman," etc.).

2 Martínez Nadal (*Cuatro lecciones* 102) proposes Lorca was making a specific reference to Oscar Wilde's "The Nightingale and the Rose," in which a thorn stuck into the heart makes the agonizing bird's song more beautiful.

3 [Jack Walsh's translation reads "spider-webbed eyes," a translation that preserves the image of the spider suggested in the Spanish verb *arañar*.—Billy Bussell Thompson and Emilie L. Bergmann.]

4 The gist of Schonberg's *García Lorca* first appeared in *Le Figaro littéraire* (Paris) on 29 September 1956 ("Enfin, la vérité sur la mort de Lorca"). His thesis was taken up by *Estafeta Literaria* (Madrid) in the October 1956 issue; it was debunked by the brave Dionisio Ridruejo in 1957 (258–59) and later by Gibson and Molina Fajardo.

5 ["Paloma" is, of course, a euphemism for the penis throughout the Spanish-speaking world.—BBT and ELB]

6 The first hemistich ("Tú buscabas un desnudo") would have an extra syllable in the printed text; in the manuscript the form is simply "buscabas" (ed. Martín 236).

7 [The English "corn" does not carry with it the sexual overtones of the Spanish "espiga."—BBT and ELB]

8 [For their discussions of perspectives on the homosexual demimonde, see the essays by Daniel Balderston, Oscar Montero, and Jorge Salessi in this volume.—ELB and Paul Julian Smith]

9 [Jack Walsh's translation was "O edge of love, o wounding edge!" For readers limited to the English, we have modified the translation to convey the literal sense of the original at the risk of distorting his reading of the Spanish.—BBT and ELB]

10 Ultimately, the chain of images could be derived in reference to Whitman's "From pent-up aching rivers" in the *Children of Adam*. The same image seems to irradiate other poems

in the New York cycle: in "Niña ahogada" [Girl drowned] each stanza ends with the phrase "[agua] . . . que no desemboca" [water . . . that does not empty out] that could be allegory for sexual frustration. In the "Vals vienés" the seduction-finale (with a lighter mood about it) is in images of the flow of the river, the mouth of the river, the shores (as thighs or buttocks).

[Similarly, *desembocadura* admits an association of anus with river's mouth.—BBT and ELB]

Works Cited

Anderson, Andrew A. "The Evolution of García Lorca's Poetic Projects 1929–36 and the Textual Status of *Poeta en Nueva York.*" *Bulletin of Hispanic Studies* 61 (1983): 221–46.

Aranda, Francisco. *Luis Buñuel: A Critical Biography.* Trans. David Robinson. New York: Da Capo Press, 1976.

Cardoza y Aragón, Luis. "San Mauricio." In *Poesías completas y algunas prosas.* Mexico: Tezontle, 1977. 599–602.

Cernuda, Luis. *Prosa completa.* Ed. Derek Harris and Luis Maristany. Barcelona: Barral Editores, 1975.

Davenport, Guy. "Whitman." In *The Geography of the Imagination.* San Francisco: North Point Press, 1981. 68–79.

Eisenberg, Daniel. "A Chronology of Lorca's Visit to New York and Cuba." *Kentucky Romance Quarterly* 24 (1977): 233–50.

García Lorca, Federico. *Autógrafos.* Ed. Rafael Martínez Nadal. Vol. 1. Oxford: Dolphin Book, 1975.

———. *Obras completas.* Ed. Arturo del Hoyo. Madrid: Aguilar, 1954.

———. *Oda a Walt Whitman.* México: Alcancía, 1933.

———. *Poeta en Nueva York: Tierra y luna.* Ed. Eutimio Martín. Barcelona: Ariel, 1981.

———. *El público y Comedia sin título.* Ed. R. Martínez Nadal (*Público*) and M. Laffranque (*Comedia*). Barcelona: Seix Barral, 1978.

———. *Oda y burla de Sesostris y Sardanápalo.* Ed. Miguel García-Posada. La Coruña: Esquió-Ferrol, 1985.

Gibson, Ian. *The Assassination of Federico García Lorca.* Rev. ed. Middlesex: Penguin Books, 1983.

Harris, Derek. *Federico García Lorca: Poeta en Nueva York.* London: Grant & Cutler, 1978.

———, ed. *Luis Cernuda.* Madrid: Taurus, 1977.

Kaplan, Justin. *Walt Whitman: A Life.* New York: Simon and Schuster, 1980.

Martínez Nadal, Rafael. *Cuatro lecciones sobre Federico García Lorca.* Madrid: Fundación Juan March / Cátedra, 1980.

McCabe, Charles. "Riverside Drive 1932." *San Francisco Chronicle* 7 April 1978: 47.

Molina Fajardo, Eduardo. *Los últimos días de García Lorca.* Barcelona: Plaza & Janés, 1983.

Novo, Salvador. *Continente vacío.* Madrid: Espasa-Calpe, 1935.

Ridruejo, Dionisio. *Casi unas memorias.* Barcelona: Planeta, 1976.

Riesenberg, Felix. *Portrait of New York.* Photos by Alexander Alland. New York: Macmillan, 1939.

Rius, Luis. *León Felipe, poeta de barro.* Mexico: Colección Málaga, 1968.

Rodrigo, Antonia. *García Lorca en Cataluña.* Barcelona: Planeta, 1975.

Schonberg, Jean-Louis. *Federico García Lorca: L'homme, l'oeuvre.* Paris: Plon, 1956.

FIVE

Queer Readers/Queer Texts

Suzanne Chávez Silverman

The Look that Kills: The "Unacceptable Beauty" of Alejandra Pizarnik's La condesa sangrienta

A lesbian who does not reinvent the word is a lesbian in the process of disappearing.—Nicole Brossard, THE AERIAL LETTER

Lesbians don't exist—in the eyes of the rulers or the police or the church.—Juan José Sebreli, Argentine sociologist [1]

Lesbians are absolutely invisible here.—Ilse Fuskova, Argentine lesbian-feminist (age 60) [2]

A dual masquerade—passing straight/passing lesbian enervates and contributes to speechlessness—to speak might be to reveal.—Michelle Cliff, "Notes on Speechlessness" [3]

Yo ya no existo y lo sé. . . . pierdo la razón si hablo, pierdo los años si callo. Alguna vez, tal vez, encontraremos refugio en la realidad verdadera.
[I don't exist anymore and I know it. . . . I lose my mind if I speak; I lose years if I don't. Sometime, perhaps, we will find refuge in the true reality.]—Alejandra Pizarnik,
El deseo de la palabra [DESIRE FOR THE WORD] [4]

One of the central motifs—or better, obsessions—of Alejandra Pizarnik's writing is silence. The haunting, overdetermined presence of silence is what first drew me to her work eight years ago; the confluence of this sign in Pizarnik's work and its deployment in lesbian and gay historiographic and theoretical writing are the reference points with which I will begin to plot the present essay on *La condesa sangrienta* [The Bloody Countess]. The notion of the closet, particularly in its relation to silence/silencing, must be invoked in any serious critical study of Pizarnik's work, for as Eve Kosofsky Sedgwick writes: "'Closetedness' itself is a performance initiated by the speech act of a silence—not a particular silence, but a silence that accrues particularity by fits and starts, in relation to the discourse that surrounds and differentially constitutes it" (*Epistemology of the Closet* 3). The discourse that "surround[ed] and differentially constitute[d]" Pizarnik's silence—the Buenos Aires of the 1960s and early 1970s—is described in an historical overview, significantly titled "Shrouded in Silence," which editor Stephan Likosky reproduces in his *Coming Out: An Anthology of International Gay and Lesbian Writings* (1992): "Lesbianism is shrouded in silence. . . . Not knowing what may reveal one's 'difference' to the rest of the world, Argentine lesbians must be cautious in the smallest details. . . . There have been cases where women recognized as lesbians have been fired from their jobs (under other pretexts). In a country with high unemployment, economic problems are the most severe for women, especially for those who choose independence from men" (80). Although the section of this article which deals in most detail with lesbianism is subtitled "Repression since 1976," evidence suggests that the sociopolitical climate in Argentina (as it impacted lesbians) before the military overthrow of Isabel Perón was nearly as repressive—if perhaps not as systematically so—as during the Proceso and even afterward.[5]

Traditional criticism on Pizarnik has colluded with and must therefore be implicated in the pervasiveness of the closet, in the incompleteness and the misreadings—ultimately the containment—of Pizarnik's silence. As Sylvia Molloy points out, "Homosexualities, in Latin American literature, are not comfortable notions to contend with, and lesbianism in particular seems to give critics a hard time" ("Disappearing Acts" 237). Among Pizarnik scholars the word lesbian has been invoked, to my knowledge, not at all (I mean in print, available for public consumption, in anything other than speculative or anecdotal transcontinental whispers). Thirteen years ago, in a brief introduction to an anthologized selection of Pizarnik's poetry published in Buenos Aires, Inés Malinow wrote:

> El surrealismo es un modo de buscar otros valores y otras motivaciones de conciencia: sin embargo, [Pizarnik] es una torturada. Pocas veces siente que su homosexualidad ha de aceptarse. La vive alternativamente como un dolor, como meollo de un gran misterio que la deja inerme. Es indudable que también se ha enamorado de algún hombre. (2833)
>
> [Surrealism is a way of looking for other values, other motivations of conscience: nevertheless, Pizarnik lives in torment. She seldom feels her homosexuality is to be accepted. She lives it alternately as pain and as the essence of a great mystery that leaves her defenseless. Without a doubt she has also fallen in love with a man or two.]

This quote is emblematic of Pizarnik scholarship and commentary in its emphasis on the author's (supposedly unmediated) link to surrealism in particular and to the avant garde in general. Bold though she may be in hinting at, albeit in an offhand manner, Pizarnik's difference, Malinow denies this difference its specificity, subordinating it instead to the more generic category of "homosexualidad" [homosexuality]. This difference is further undermined in Malinow's last move: recuperating Pizarnik for heterosexuality ("Without a doubt she [Pizarnik] has also fallen in love with a man or two").

In her biography *Alejandra Pizarnik,* published two years ago in Buenos Aires, Cristina Piña ventures farther into the territory of Pizarnik's sexual difference than does Malinow, whose reading of Pizarnik's "homosexuality" as "torment" and "pain," along with the unequivocable "es indudable que también se ha enamorado de algún hombre" [without a doubt she has also fallen in love with a man or two], seem destined to placate a homophobic reader. In Piña's discussion of Pizarnik's stay in Paris in the early 1960s, she mentions "la elección alternativa de compañeros de uno u otro sexo" (127) [the alternating choice of companions of either sex]. Piña's own choice of the word "compañeros" could not be more apt in terms of preserving the silence around the issue of sexuality in Pizarnik scholaship: more than a sexual relationship, "compañerismo" suggests a spiritual, emotional, and ideological bond. Piña concludes the statement I have left suspended, above, thus, "si bien el énfasis en esa época seguía recayendo en las relaciones heterosexuales" (127) [if indeed the emphasis during that period was still on heterosexual relations], clearly privileging Pizarnik's practice of heterosexuality in the 1960s. "Relaciones," like "compañeros," is a polysemous signifier, but its more common meaning—"relations"—is a sexual one. And so, Piña's biography both opens and closes the closet: open-close-open, all on one page. Pizarnik's still being mainly straight "during that time," on page 127, urges us on in the text, in her life, forward, looking for another "época," another "énfasis." We find it, finally, near the end of Piña's book, near the end of Pizarnik's life, on page 226.

In 1971, Piña informs her reader, Pizarnik "conoce a su último y gran amor, una mujer" (226) [meets her last and greatest love: a woman]. Open, wide open, at last! We learn that Pizarnik's last and greatest love was a woman. And yet, in the remaining thirteen pages of the biography, Piña does not use the word lesbian even once; she privileges the romantic friendship model over the erotic, and finally even degenders the relationship, referring time and again to "la persona tan amada" (226, 236–37) [the dearly beloved person]. The closet door once again swings to, and finally—as Piña coyly yet categorically refuses the potentially groundbreaking position of voyeuse (at least raconteuse) she seemed poised to assume just a paragraph before, "De ninguna manera me parece conducente—ni correcto—inmiscuirme en las alternativas de dicho amor" (226) [In no way does it seem conducive to me—or proper—to meddle in the choices of this love]—it slams shut. Was she or wasn't she? Only her biographer knows for sure, and she's not telling.

This brings me full circle to the annoying reticence Piña invokes in the name of "relevance" in the opening pages of her study, which ultimately, I suppose, constitutes fair warning for the hide-and-seek strategy this biographer deploys around the issue of Pizarnik's sexuality throughout her study:

> Mi enfoque biográfico de Alejandra . . . se organizará en función de su obra y de su estética, por lo cual haré "públicos" sólo aquellos aspectos de su vida que considere *relevantes* para la comprensión de su obra y la constitución de su personalidad como escritora, sin detenerme en ciertas anécdotas o episodios que pertenecen a su intimidad y cuya "publicidad" resultaría *irrelevante*. (12, emphasis added)
> [My biographical focus on Alejandra . . . will be organized around her work and aesthetics; thus I will make "public" only those aspects of her life which I find *relevant* for the understanding of her work and the constitution of her persona as a writer, without lingering on certain private anecdotes or episodes whose "publicity" would be *irrelevant*.]

Piña's insistence on the separation of "vida" ("life") and "obra" ("work"), her privileging of the latter in the name of professionalism (her criteria about what is "relevant") in a writer who was, in Pizarnik's within Piña's searingly intense words, "devorada por el desmesurado afán 'de hacer con su cuerpo el cuerpo del poema'" [devoured by the inordinately keen desire "to make with her body the body of the poem"], is an egregious example of what Sylvia Molloy has called "anxiety-ridden erasure" in reference to Venezuelan writer Teresa de la Parra's critics ("Disappearing Acts" 6). Faced with this erasure on the part of both Malinow and Piña, I long to restore the lesbian in/to the text, to replace conflations and vague, muted terms such as "homosexualidad" [homosexuality] and "la persona tan amada" [the dearly beloved person] for, as Adrienne Rich reminds us: "The word lesbian must be affirmed because to discard it is to collaborate with silence . . . with the closet game, the creation of the *unspeakable*" (*On Lies, Secrets and Silence* 202).

I see Pizarnik's sexuality not only as "relevant" but as central, to both her life and her work, especially to *La condesa sangrienta*. Piña's deliberate coyness, therefore, her knowing yet forbidding silence, leave me desiring something more—as Elizabeth Meese puts it: "The lesbian critic, 'reading as a lesbian' . . . searches for something else and finds it, there in the sometimes silent language of the look" (*[Sem]Erotics* 30).

Is *La condesa sangrienta* a lesbian text? Penelope J. Englebrecht defines "'lesbian textuality' as those texts written by women—especially lesbians—which incorporate lesbian(ism) as a principal element" (91). This definition is strategically inclusive: the all-important term(s)—"lesbian(ism)"—remain undefined. Pizarnik's *own* lesbianism, however, by Englebrecht's definition would not be a determining factor: in *La condesa sangrienta* lesbian desire is observed, described, maimed, questioned, and silenced, but it is, at some level (irredeemably, brutally, transgressively) *present* in the text. Can I call this work—unspeakably horrific, it is, nevertheless, Alejandra Pizarnik's only textual representation of lesbian desire—a lesbian's text? Unlike Teresa de la Parra, who cautions the reader against taking her novel *Ifigenia* as literal autobiography (Molloy, "Disappearing Acts" 234–235), Pizarnik offers no such caveat against identification of work with/as life. In fact, she would appear to solicit this very identification, in texts such as *El deseo de la palabra* [Desire for the Word], which Piña has quoted above, in which the poet desires to "hac[er] el cuerpo del poema con mi cuerpo, rescatando cada frase con mis días y con mis semanas, infundiéndole al poema mi soplo" (*El deseo de la palabra* 16–17) [make the body of the poem with my body, rescuing each line with my days and with my weeks, infusing the poem with my breath].

In claiming Alejandra Pizarnik as a lesbian writer, I must rely, as does Amy Kaminsky for her reading of Cristina Peri Rossi, "on a combination of textual evidence and biographical intimation" (116). Intimation is precisely (and only) what I have observed in Malinow and Piña; Sylvia Molloy's introductory remarks in the recent *Women's Writing in Latin America*, which offer a strategy for reading woman writing, are more helpful: "It is not my intention . . . to explain a writer's poetry by unmediated reference to her life. Yet if one *reads* the writer's life as another text (which it is), that is, as a social narrative whose acts, conducts, attitudes are observed, interpreted, and judged by the community of social readers, then one may find, in the life, grounds for profitable reflection on the text" (115). Reading Alejandra Pizarnik's life as a "social narrative" (for this Cristina Piña's biography—particularly in its gaps and silences, in what the biographer chooses *not* to reveal—has been invaluable) enables me, precisely, to "reflect profitably" on her texts. Reading (the lesbian in) her life enables me *not* to attribute "Pizarnik's sexual and scatological obsessions [only] to her fascination with the French poet Alfred Jarry and with surrealism in general" (Molloy, *Women's Writing* 119), as has been the overwhelming (heterosexist) trend in Pizarnik criticism, but rather to privilege an/other interpretation of "such erotic excess . . . such perversity" (Molloy, *Women's Writing* 119).

I claim Alejandra Pizarnik as a lesbian writer in part "as a feminist reader for whom the text is always contextual, [for whom] it is vital to be able to place the author" (Kaminsky 117). Also, my claim emerges from a weaving together of her life (as text) and her texts (irrevocably situated, grounded in her life, even—as the poet herself emphasizes—in her body). In this weaving, this double reading, Pizarnik's well-documented obsessions and fascination/link with surrealism—rather than singularly constitutive of an avant garde, textually transgressive poetics—emerge as effects of the closet, which efface and silence the lesbian. My claim is supported by Sylvia Molloy's unpublished talk at the 1992 Modern Language Association meeting, titled "From Sappho to Baffo: Diverting the Sexual in the Poetry of Alejandra Pizarnik." On this occasion, Molloy asserted that in *La condesa sangrienta* Pizarnik was *"telling her self* through the tale of an other, [effecting] a kind of ventriloquism and collaboration, [representing] an exclusively female erotic gaze" (emphasis added). She further characterized this book as "a *mise en abîme,* a speculation on the impossibility of lesbian desire" and called it "a philosophy of the boudoir-turned-closet . . . *Alejandra Pizarnik's most personal statement*" (emphasis added).[6]

To my knowledge, besides Molloy's talk and the present essay, there are only two other serious studies of *La condesa sangrienta.* In Cristina Piña's groundbreaking article "La palabra obscena" [The Obscene Word] (1990), the author calls attention to the singularity of her work by emphasizing "la escasez de crítica consagrada a su obra [de Pizarnik]" (24) [the scarcity of criticism devoted to Pizarnik's work]. She makes this point not only about *La condesa sangrienta* but also about Pizarnik's other prose works and her poetry:

> En el caso de Alejandra Pizarnik, quien consensualmente está considerada una de nuestras poetas más estimables . . . se percibe una especie de silencio crítico que no deja de llamar la atención pues apenas se ha escrito un libro breve sobre ella y algunos estudios, también breves, en los cuales, además, prácticamente se obvia su producción en prosa. (24)

[In the case of Alejandra Pizarnik, who is considered one of our most estimable poets . . . one perceives a sort of critical silence which is worthy of mention; only one short book has been written about her and a few essays, also short, in which, in addition, her prose is nearly obviated.]

In "La palabra obscena," an otherwise perceptive essay, *la lesbiana brilla por su ausencia* [the lesbian is conspicuous by her absence]. The only reference (and it is, as in Malinow's essay, to "homosexuality" rather than to lesbianism) is about Countess Báthory herself. Piña offers a condensed summary of Lacan's theory of the mirror:

> En este campo donde conviven y se identifican Eros y Thánatos—fascinación y hostilidad—es donde la condesa está capturada y así su placer sólo puede surgir de la agresión extrema al otro—significativamente, "la otra," pues una de las *consecuencias* de la fijación en el estadio del espejo, *además del sadismo,* es la homosexualidad—su deseo, ser el deseo del otro, pero como destrucción de ese otro. (30, emphasis added)
> [In this sphere, where Eros and Thanatos cohabit and identify with each other—fascination and hostility—is where the countess is caught and thus her pleasure can only spring forth from extreme aggression against the other—significantly, a female other, because one of the *consequences* of fixation in the mirror stage, *besides sadism,* is homosexuality: her desire, to be the other's desire, but as the destruction of that other.]

This conflation of homosexuality and pathology—Piña reading/re-writing Lacan—the insistence on the text's existence as translation and representation of the mirror stage, is elaborated in several paragraphs of Piña's lengthy study, made even more specific in lines such as these: "la captura [de la condesa], entonces . . . en el estadio especular, es la *causalidad* última de su crueldad extrema asociada al goce sexual, de su *homosexualidad,* su mutismo, su 'melancolía,' su identificación con la muerte" (31, emphasis added) [the countess's fixation, then . . . in the mirror stage, is the ultimate *causality* of her extreme cruelty associated with sexual jouissance, of her *homosexuality,* her silence, her "melancholia," her identification with death]. Piña's acceptance and reiteration of this "causal" link between specular fixation (pathology) and homosexuality-as-symptom and her refusal to name and problematize Pizarnik's textualization of lesbianism is troubling. And yet I think she has put her finger on the wound, signaling and—because she does not name it—colluding with the very reason for the critical silence around Pizarnik's work in general and, specifically, around *La condesa sangrienta:* It is the spec(tac)ular, relentlessly sadistic lesbian desire in this particular text that has silenced not only the Bloody Countess herself, but also Pizarnik and, I would argue, her critics.

Pizarnik gave herself an out, fortified her closet (just as Countess Báthory fortified the castle walls at Csejthe)—"ocultándose en el lenguaje" [hiding her self in language], as was her wont—by recognizing on the very first page of *La condesa sangrienta* her debt to an "original": "Valentine Penrose ha recopilado documentos y relaciones acerca de un personaje real e insólito: la condesa Báthory, asesina de 650 muchachas. . . . Sin alterar los datos reales penosamente obtenidos, los ha refundido en una suerte de vasto y hermoso poema en prosa" (9) [Valentine Penrose has compiled documents about a real and unusual character: Countess Báthory, murderer of 650 girls. . . . Without changing the painfully obtained true facts, she has rearranged them in a sort of vast and beautiful prose poem].[7] Penrose's 1963 "original"—*Erszébet Báthory, la comtesse sanglante* [Erszébet Báthory, the Bloody Countess]—to which Pizarnik refers in a footnote on the first page, is in fact a "refundición" [adaptation] of "real," historical information.[8] *La condesa sangrienta,* in fact, is multiply-removed: writing in Spanish in the early 1960s, Pizarnik is distanced in time, space, and language from her subject, a medieval Hungarian countess already rendered literary object, in French, by Penrose. How great is the distance, though, between Pizarnik and Erszébet Báthory, between Pizarnik and Penrose, "[quien] juega admirablemente con los valores estéticos de esta tenebrosa historia" (10) [who plays admirably with the aesthetic value of this lugubrious story] (M 71)? Language conceals and reveals. This "translated lesbianism," a term Sylvia Molloy applies to Teresa de la Parra's lapsing into French to refer to same-sex female love, "attests [in Pizarnik as in Parra] as much to the difficulty of naming as to the need to name" ("Disappearing Acts" 245).

Another serious engagement of *La condesa sangrienta* is found in David William Foster's *Gay and Lesbian Themes in Latin American Writing* (1991). Foster observes that *La condesa sangrienta* is different from *all* the other texts treated in his study, in which "the homosexual motif is developed within the context of a system of social and personal relations," in that Pizarnik's text constitutes a "mosaic of prose vignettes that are related to one another strictly by virtue of their dealing with some aspect of Báthory's indulgence of her erotic interests" (97–98). Foster then quotes the final paragraph of Pizarnik's text: "Como Sade en sus escritos, como Gilles de

Rais en sus crímenes, la condesa Báthory alcanzó, más allá de todo límite, el último fondo del desenfreno. Ella es una prueba más de que la libertad absoluta de la criatura humana es horrible" (65–66) [Like Sade in his writings and Gilles de Rais in his crimes, the Countess Bathory reached, beyond all limits, the final abyss of abandon. She is yet another proof that the absolute freedom of the human creature is horrible] (SJL 104). He calls this paragraph an "interpretive hypothesis that could have been used to develop a conventional novel" and an "unexpected coda." Although in the preceding paragraph Foster has signaled the narrative's difference from the conventional novels examined in his study by virtue of its singular focus on the erotic, he deflects this interpretation entirely and asks us to read the "coda" "in the context of the moral vision of the reconstructive dictatorships successive military tyrannies in Argentina have attempted to impose" (98). It is in this context that the book has elicited "countercultural enthusiasm . . . as a version of the . . . sadistic abuse of power permitted those protected by the agents of the established order" (98). Read in these terms, according to Foster, "the figure of Báthory speaks more to the abuse of power through the physical torment of her victims than to the issue of a legitimate homosexual erotic" (98).

If the work *can* be read—and is read, by "present generations of [Argentine] readers, who have made it a classic and Pizarnik an emblem of the poet as a marginal individual in society" (98)—by virtue of its postscript or "coda," as an allegory for the abuse of political power, why must this reading efface another, to me more obvious one: the concluding paragraph as an allegorical indictment of lesbianism, of the "evil lesbian erotic" (101) depicted in the rest of the work? It is precisely this shattering lack of legitimacy as erotic (lesbian) discourse that must not be deferred, that I must address, that I believe has silenced critics on *La condesa sangrienta*.

Foster, one (giant) step away from the critical silence around Pizarnik's lesbian writing, nonetheless relegates to the background the text's lesbian problematic, foregrounding instead the issue of abuse of power. Is it too dangerous to read Pizarnik's Báthory "as an example of sexual liberation," as other "contemporary versions of Sade which see him freeing the Western discourse on sex from its encrustations of moral hypocrisy" (98)? Foster recognizes the possibility that Pizarnik's closing paragraph may be "devastatingly ironic" if the reader sees it as belying the conventional morality that would find Báthory's actions unredeemably horrible and constituting an unacceptable program of erotic fulfillment; "devastatingly ironic" in that to accept the plausibility of the physical realization of Báthory's sexual fantasies is to go beyond Sade's "philosophy of the boudoir," to accept cold-blooded torture as a legitimate erotic (99). Yet Foster admits that the structure of Pizarnik's discourse allows just such an unthinkably, dangerously ironic reading of the final paragraph, which seems casually appended to the vignettes' noninterpretive, clinical prose (99).

The inclusion of *La condesa sangrienta* in Foster's study gains explicability only after his initial "political" reading of the work, in the proliferation of mentions of the erotic: "erotic pursuits," "calculated program of seduction," "erotic fantasies" (97), "Báthory's indulgence of her erotic interests" (98), "sexual voyeurism," "unrelenting erotic needs," "elaborate erotic tableaux" (100), "horrifying erotic needs" (101). Yet he shies away from problematizing the erotic in this text *as lesbian*. Foster affirms that "Pizarnik is associated with lesbianism . . . in specific aspects of her poetry" (98). This would appear to be a way of strengthening the rationale for the inclusion of Pizarnik in his study; however, I cannot speculate on which "specific aspects" are associated with lesbianism or by whom because, on this important point, Foster cites no sources.

He concludes that *La condesa sangrienta* provides the reader "ostensibly a cautionary access to a forbidden realm of sexuality, which *happens to be lesbian* in the case of Báthory's erotic program" (101, emphasis added). Here, Foster attributes to Báthory a "lesbian" sexuality, calls this a "forbidden realm," and yet effectively sidesteps the (silent) bond between Alejandra Pizarnik as lesbian and her lesbian character. In its very matter-of-factness, this statement decenters the text's vital link to Foster's own study, in effect, delegitimizing the work—and Pizarnik—as (a) lesbian writing.

La condesa sangrienta can only be read as marginal—as both cultural object and, more specifically, as object of study—within Foster's book. Foster distances it from "the majority of texts dealt with in this study," an inclusive study which reads these "majority texts" for their "legitimation of homosexuality in the modern world" (101). Foster argues forcefully in his introduction that: "If Latin American writing is characterized by an awareness of history and ideology, homosexuality cannot be viewed as simply the psychological complex of specific individuals, but rather . . . as an intrasubjective matter that has ultimately to do with the controlling social dynamic. . . . If this is true, the examination of homosexual topics . . . can be an integral part of a study of how Latin American fiction deals with questions of social history" (3).

In the case of his reading of *La condesa sangrienta*, Foster appears not to accept this challenge: he reads Pizarnik's text as the inscription of "Báthory's programmatic pursuit of an *evil* lesbian erotic" (101, emphasis added), yet does not submit his conclusion to the sort of "intrasubjective," historical enquiry his introduction calls for. In the end, by emphasizing *La condesa sangrienta*'s "marginal" status—"[Báthory's] sexuality resists virtually any strategy of accommodation within a scheme of 'legitimate' sexuality, heterosexual or homosexual" (101)—Foster reifies for Pizarnik's text the very liminality, the binary complementarity of center and margin, he provocatively puts into question in his preface: "I often had the sense, while composing this monograph, of engaging in something 'dirty' . . . because it sustains the framing of one constellation of sexual activities when, perhaps, what is most called for is the de-emphasis of problematized erotic practices in favor of a far-ranging project involving the re-eroticization of culture in all of the multiple dimensions such a process might imply" (viii).

Finally, Foster's very use of the word lesbian troubles me. He mentions the term five times in his essay: once to categorize the work as "lesbian pornography" (101), once to assert that Pizarnik "does not explore Báthory primarily as the locus of a lesbian matrix" (101); nevertheless, the descriptions of her "erotic fantasies" and same-sex torture constitute the pursuit of an "evil lesbian erotic" (101), again to claim that Countess Báthory is motivated by "lesbian sexuality" (101) and finally to inform his reader that the book's forbidden realm of sexuality "happens to be lesbian" (101). This seems a somewhat confusing treatment of a term which is charged, fraught with a problematic, multiple signification for many feminist critics, whether lesbian or not. Karla Jay and Joanne Glasgow, for example, in the introduction to their *Lesbian Texts and Contexts: Radical Revisions,* affirm: "Even in 1990 . . . thoughtful and concerned feminists do not, perhaps *cannot,* agree about just who *is* a lesbian. Is she a woman whose erotic desires are for other women, or is she a 'woman-identified woman'? Is she a woman at all, if *woman* is a heterosexist language construct? And if this term is so problematic, how can one hope to define or label a lesbian text?" (4).[9] These remarks remit back to the vexing tangle of issues I have been grappling with thus far in my essay—lesbian/lesbian text—issues which, despite good intentions, I believe David William Foster ultimately does not explore.

"No quiero ir nada más que hasta el fondo" [I don't want to go anywhere except to the very bottom] Alejandra Pizarnik wrote on the schoolgirl slate in her bedroom shortly before her death on 25 September 1972. The desire to touch bottom, transgress limits. And yet, that frightening, final sentence: "Ella [la condesa] es una prueba más de que la libertad absoluta de la criatura humana es horrible" [She (the countess) is yet another proof that the absolute freedom of the human creature is horrible] (SJL 104). In what follows I will try to shed some light on what is perhaps *the* crucial constant in Alejandra Pizarnik's complex subjectivity as constituted in her writing: the desire for transgression versus the desire to be silent/silenced.

In my view, a provocative point of entry for a revealing essay on Pizarnik could be: "[Báthory's] sexuality resists virtually any strategy of accommodation within a scheme of 'legitimate' sexuality, heterosexual or homosexual" (Foster 101). Just as, by analogy, the book containing the narrative of Báthory's transgressive sexuality resists any strategy of accommodation—containment—within a conventional (legitimate?) critical praxis.[10] It escapes the totalizing hermeneutical tactics of feminist, psychosexual, semiotic, or biographical criticism, yet another factor in the stubborn silence surrounding a text which first appeared well over two decades ago.[11]

La condesa sangrienta resists, but ultimately can—must—be accommodated within Pizarnik's deeply transgressive oeuvre taken as a whole. Foster does not make this move; Piña begins to, within the context of the obscene, although she avoids the question of the lesbian in/and the text. She does address directly the critical silence around Pizarnik's oeuvre, claiming that its transgressive qualities, like the writing of the "poetas malditos" and the Surrealists (especially Artaud), are the fundamental cause of this silence:

> Para los lectores y críticos que tengan una postura contraria a la transgresión generalizada que este "lugar poético" entraña, un lugar que niega la tradición, el sentido como algo dado, la lengua como un reservorio, para entenderla como un campo de experimentación, el texto como placer y erotismo, la poesía de Alejandra Pizarnik no puede sino resultar *la negación de lo poético.* . . . [T]ambién, para quienes aceptan esa suerte de "obscenidad de la represión" mallarmeana, no pueden sino resultar *incomprensibles, excéntricos, lamentables,* sus textos en prosa, pues responden a la otra articulación—más directa y subversiva—de lo obsceno. (22, emphasis added)
> [For readers and critics who may be against the generalized transgression that this "poetic space" involves—a space which denies tradition, (denies) meaning as a given, (denies) language as a reservoir, in order to understand it (language) as an experimental space, the text as pleasure and eroticism—Alejandra Pizarnik's poetry can only result in *the denial of what is poetic.* . . . Also, for those who accept Mallarmé's sort of "obscenity of repression," her prose pieces must only seem *incomprehensible, eccentric, lamentable,* for these respond to the other articulation—more direct and subversive—of the obscene.]

Piña makes one final, interesting point, also related to the critical silence which has received Pizarnik's writing:

> Queda por fin . . . un último aspecto: el de la *legitimidad* del discurso de Alejandra Pizarnik. . . . Nunca hubo textos obscenos firmados por mujeres hasta la aparición de las obras de Pizarnik. Y si lo obsceno es difícil de aceptar en general . . . resulta más revulsivo aún, dentro de una sociedad que ha restringido tan significativamente las posibilidades expresivas y vitales de la mujer, cuando es una escritora quien se atreve a articularlo. (22–23)
>
> [There is . . . one final aspect: that of the *legitimacy* of Alejandra Pizarnik's discourse. . . . There were never any obscene texts signed by women until Pizarnik's works appeared. And if the obscene is difficult to accept in general . . . it seems even more revulsive (*sic*), within a society which has so significantly restricted woman's expressive and vital possibilities, when it is a woman writer who dares to articulate it.]

Let us turn now to the text, which I will attempt to situate, to contextualize its "evil lesbian erotic" (Foster 101) within Alejandra Pizarnik's constant, overarching move toward textual liminality and—in the most literal sense as well—toward the ultimate erasure of self. The second page of *La condesa sangrienta*'s brief introductory section contains all the horror the rest of the text will position the reader to gaze upon: the nameless repetitions and variations of the motifs presented here, succinctly—Pizarnik's and the Countess's:

> La siniestra hermosura de las criaturas *nocturnas* se resume en una *silenciosa* de palidez legendaria, de ojos *dementes,* de cabellos del color suntuoso de los cuervos. . . .
>
> Sentada en su trono, la condesa *mira* torturar y oye gritar. Sus viejas y horribles sirvientas son figuras *silenciosas* que traen fuego, cuchillos, agujas, atizadores; que torturan muchachas, que luego las entierran. Como el atizador o los cuchillos, esas viejas son instrumentos de una *posesión.* Esta sombría ceremonia tiene una sola espectadora *silenciosa.* (10, emphasis added)
>
> [Here the sinister beauty of *nocturnal* creatures is summed up in this *silent lady* of legendary paleness, *mad* eyes, and hair the sumptuous colour of ravens. . . .
>
> Sitting on her throne, the countess *watches* the tortures and listens to the cries. Her old and horrible maids are *wordless* figures that bring in fire, knives, needles, irons; they torture the girls, and later bury

them. With (*sic*) their iron and knives, these two old women are themselves the instruments of a *possession*. This dark ceremony has a single
silent spectator.] (M 71, emphasis added)

What horrifies me as a reader/spectator is (for this "somber ceremony,"
as from this page, will always already have at least one other "spectator,"
although in my case, she will *not* be silent) more than what is said, *how*
it is said. The words emphasized above—night, madness, silence, and the
gaze—are well-known to readers of Pizarnik's poetry as some of her central motifs or obsessions.[12] Is this a chance identification? It surely is more
than—other than—chance that her description of Valentine Penrose on
the preceding page reads like a possible blurb for one of Pizarnik's own
slim volumes of poetry, or even for *La condesa sangrienta* itself: "Excelente
poeta (su primer libro lleva un fervoroso prefacio de Paul Eluard), no ha
separado su don poético de su minuciosa erudición" (9) [An excellent poet
(her first book bears a fervent preface by Paul Eluard), she has not separated her gift for poetry from her painstaking erudition]. Elder statesman
Octavio Paz wrote a "fervent prologue" to Pizarnik's volume of poetry
Arbol de Diana [Diana's Tree] (1962); Cristina Piña writes about *Arbol de
Diana:* "Difícilmente se encuentre otro libro—inclusive dentro de la producción de Alejandra—donde el equilibrio verbal esté tan minuciosamente
cuidado y donde, al mismo tiempo, las palabras tengan tanto aspecto de 'recién llegadas'" (*Alejandra Pizarnik* 135) [It would be difficult to find another
book—including one of Alejandra's—where the verbal equilibrium is so
painstakingly attended to and where, at the same time, the words have such
a "newly arrived" appearance].

The acts to which the countess is a silent witness—"torturan muchachas . . . las entierran" [they torture the girls, and later bury them] (M
71)—are themselves buried at the paradigmatic level in the discourse, lost,
nearly, in an enumeration which immediately afterward strikes the reader
as alarmingly casual: fire, knives, needles, irons. Torture is objectified, as
are the agents of crime, "esas viejas son instrumentos de una posesión"
(10) [these two old women are themselves the instruments of a possession]
(M 71). Agency, then, in the eyes of the narrator, rests with the countess
although in her dementia and possession, in her passivity ("la condesa *mira
torturar*") [the countess watches the tortures] (M 71), she is rendered oddly
unaccountable.

The next section, "La virgen de hierro" [The Iron Maiden], contains
the description of the iron maiden and an ostensibly objective presenta-

tion of her functioning. Again, we observe that the murder itself almost disappears. It is matter of fact, denatured, bloodless, nearly disembodied: "Muy lentamente alza [la autómata] los blancos brazos para que se cierren en perfecto abrazo sobre lo que esté cerca de ella—en este caso una muchacha" (13–14) [Very slowly (the automaton) lifts its white arms which close in a perfect embrace around whatever happens to be next to it—in this case, a girl] (M 72). The victim is female, but this is almost an afterthought; she appears, first, in the neuter pronoun and subjunctivized. In fact, much more (loving) attention to detail is found in the description of the iron maiden: "Esta dama metálica era del tamaño y del color de la criatura humana. Desnuda, maquillada, enjoyada, con rubios cabellos que llegaban al suelo" (13) [This clockwork doll was of the size and colour of a human creature. Naked, painted (*sic*), covered in jewels, with blond hair that reached down to the ground] (M 72). The narrator's gaze, falling upon the iron maiden, is erotically charged. The automaton's attributes are not only human, they are hyper-feminine: she is naked, wearing makeup, bejewelled, with excessively long blond hair. Is it chance that she is described as an "autómata," as Pizarnik's speaker presents herself in the following devastating prose poem? I quote this brief text in its entirety because of the seamless coincidence of its motifs with those of *La condesa sangrienta*:

> Días en que una palabra lejana se apodera de mí. Voy por esos días *sonámbula* y transparente. La *hermosa autómata* se canta, se encanta, se cuenta casos y cosas: nido de hilos rígidos donde me danzo y me lloro en mis numerosos funerales. (Ella es su *espejo* incendiado, su espera en *hogueras frías*, su elemento místico, su *fornicación* de nombres creciendo solos en la *noche pálida*). (*Poemas* 1982, 34; emphasis added) [Days in which a faraway word takes possession of me. I move through those days transparent, a *sleepwalker*. The *beautiful automaton* sings herself, enchants herself, she tells herself cases and things: nest of rigid threads where I dance myself and cry myself in my many funerals. (She is her *mirror* in flames, her waiting in *cold bonfires*, her mystical element, her *fornication* of names growing by themselves in the *pale night*).] [13]

The idea of madness in the poem is reflected in the notion of being overpowered by words, whereas the countess is overpowered by erotic dementia. The countess is a pale, beautiful, nocturnal creature possessed—and in possession of a beautiful automaton (the iron maiden), obsessed by fire, and mirrors, as we shall see presently. In the poem, these signifiers are extended over a somewhat broader semantic field: the night is pale, the bonfire is turned to ash, the mirror is in flames, the automaton is beautiful. Yet all of these *are* the speaker, at once *ella* and *yo*.

In "Muerte por agua" we see the fur-wrapped and bored countess riding in her carriage on a snowy road. She calls for one of her ladies-in-waiting, who remains nameless, bites her frenetically and sticks her with needles. This is the first time the reader witnesses the countess's perpetration of a crime. There are no details, there is absolutely no description of pain. The girl stands, naked in the snow and the countess asks for cold water, which is thrown on the girl by "lacayos impasibles" [impassive footmen] (M 73). The water turns to ice under the countess's protected gaze ("La condesa contempla desde el interior de la carroza," [18] [The Countess observes this from inside the coach], [M 73]). The reader is protected too, positioned inside, closer somehow to the opulently dressed countess in her carriage than to the naked, nameless, frozen girl. How is this so? Why are we closer to the murderess than to her victim? David William Foster ventures this reply: "*La condesa sangrienta* mocks an implied 'moral' reader who might nevertheless experience along with Báthory the sexual response of voyeurism through the displaced medium of the text" (101). This reader, however, must emphatically distance herself—from the sadistic countess, from the sort of shared sexual response suggested by Foster's reading. If Pizarnik's discourse solicits the complicity of my gaze, encourages my voyeurism, positions me to look with and through Báthory's eyes, my response to what I see can refuse to be as one with hers. And yet the reader—I—find myself fighting against the seduction of complicity, fighting against both the "noninterpretive, clinically expository prose" *and* the undeniable, yet "unacceptable beauty" (*La condesa sangrienta* 76) of the "sparse poetry" Foster observes in *La condesa sangrienta*, which conspire to draw the reader in, anesthetize her, defer her shock and horror.

"Torturas clásicas" [Classical Torture], on pages 23–29, is nearly at the center of this 66-page text. It is, significantly, longer than the three sections which precede it, longer, in fact, than any other section in the book. This is a coherent structural device: we learn here that the other tortures we have read about—the iron maiden, death by water, and the lethal cage (whose description I have spared my reader)—can be considered "interferencias barrocas" [baroque refinements] (M 74) and that the countess preferred to adhere to "un estilo de torturar monótonamente clásico" [a monotonously classic style of torture] (M 74) which the narrator summarizes in this section. The narrator's gaze is lascivious: the victims are "muchachas altas, bellas y resistentes . . . entre los 12 y los 18 años" (25) [tall, beautiful, strong girls . . . their ages had to be between 12 and 18] (M 74). These girls are dragged before the countess, who awaits them on her throne, dressed in white. The girls are bound and flayed, singed with pokers, cut, and, if they cry out, their mouths are sewn shut. I am shaking as I write this, even buffered as I am, multiply distanced from the original scene (I am re-writing in English Pizarnik's re-inscription in Spanish of Penrose's narration in French of a medieval Hungarian countess's blood lust). And the countess herself? When she goes to change her bloodied dress, the narrator muses parenthetically "(¿en qué pensaría durante esa breve interrupción?)" (26) [what would she think about during this brief intermission?] (M 74). This question is left unanswered.

Why does Pizarnik not probe the countess's mind? Can this silence be explained (away) by containing the text in which it occurs within a literary tradition of bad boy poets (including Sade, Lautréamont, Mallarmé and the other "poetes maudits" and even Artaud) who delighted in the representation—and living—of transgression? Does this reading not effect a dangerous metonymy, substituting the closet by the avant garde? To support my re-reading of *La condesa sangrienta,* I turn again to Sylvia Molloy, who has observed: "That sexuality must be imagined only in its most violent form—an erotic death rattle—bespeaks the magnitude of repression [in Argentina] and the resilience of Alejandra Pizarnik's closet" ("From Sappho to Baffo").

So, "what would she think about during this brief intermission?" We are never told. What we *are* told is this: "No siempre la dama permanecía ociosa en tanto los demás se afanaban y trabajaban en torno de ella. A veces colaboraba" (26) [Not always would the lady remain idle while the others busied themselves around her. Sometimes she would lend a hand (*sic*)] (M 74). With tiny silver tweezers, with needles, red-hot spoons and irons, whips, ice water, with her teeth, the countess "collaborated." But lest one read this (as the clinical vocabulary, distant tone, and the use of the word "colaborar" might persuade us to do) only or mainly as an allegory of "the horrifying inventory of persecutions and tortures that have been made . . . in the spirit of 'Nunca Más'" (Foster 98), there is the other, persistent co-text, consistently foregrounded by Pizarnik's narrator:

> Durante sus crisis eróticas, escapaban de sus labios palabras procaces destinadas a las supliciadas. Imprecaciones soeces y gritos de loba eran sus formas expresivas mientras recorría, enardecida, el tenebroso recinto. Pero nada era más espantoso que su risa. (Resumo: el castillo medieval; la sala de torturas; las tiernas muchachas; las viejas y horren-

das sirvientas; la hermosa alucinada riendo desde su maldito éxtasis provocado por el sufrimiento ajeno.) (27)
[During her erotic seizures she would hurl blasphemous insults at her victims. Blasphemous insults and cries like the baying of a she-wolf were her means of expression as she stalked, in a passion, the gloomy rooms. But nothing was more ghastly than her laugh. (I recapitulate: the medieval castle, the torture chamber, the tender young girls, the old and horrible servants, the beautiful madwoman laughing in a wicked ecstasy provoked by the suffering of others.)] (M 75)

As I pointed out earlier for the section entitled "The Iron Maiden," the coincidences between this text ("Classical Torture") and certain details of Pizarnik's other texts—and her life—are worthy of mention. For example, according to Cristina Piña: "A partir de su experiencia parisina, parecería iniciar una curva ascendente que culmina de manera exasperada en sus últimos años, cuando, infaliblemente, quienes estuvieron más cerca de ella señalan una agudización de su *procacidad verbal*" (*Alejandra Pizarnik* 126, emphasis added) [As from her Parisian experience (in the early 1960s), she would seem to begin a rising curve which culminates in exasperated fashion in her final years when, infallibly, those who were closest to her point out a worsening of her *verbal impudence*].[14]

The section entitled "El espejo de la melancolía" [The Melancholy Mirror] opens in medias res, with a distant, omniscient narrator, as if onto a fairy tale: "Vivía delante de su gran espejo sombrío, el famoso espejo cuyo modelo había diseñado ella misma" (43) [The countess would spend her days in front of her large dark mirror; a famous mirror she had designed herself] (M 79). We are told that the countess had this mirror made with special armrests, so that she was able to contemplate herself without tiring for many hours at a time. And then:

Y ahora comprendemos por qué sólo la música más arrebatadoramente triste de su orquesta de gitanos o las riesgosas partidas de caza . . . o—sobre todo—los subsuelos anegados de sangre humana, pudieron alumbrar en los ojos de su perfecta cara algo a modo de mirada viviente. Porque nadie tiene más sed de tierra, de sangre y de sexualidad feroz que estas criaturas que habitan los fríos espejos. Y a propósito de espejos: nunca pudieron aclararse los rumores acerca de la homosexualidad de la condesa, ignorándose si se trataba de una tendencia inconsciente o si, por lo contrario, la aceptó con naturalidad, como un derecho más que le correspondía. (43–44)

[And now we can understand why only the most grippingly sad music of her gypsy orchestra, or dangerous hunting parties . . . or—above all—the cellars flooded with human blood, could spark something resembling life in her perfect face. Because no one has more thirst for earth, for blood, and for ferocious sexuality than the creatures who inhabit cold mirrors. And on the subject of mirrors: the rumours concerning her alleged (*sic*) homosexuality were never confirmed. Was this allegation (*sic*) unconscious, or, on the contrary, did she accept it naturally, as simply another right to which she was entitled?] (M 79)

I have mentioned Cristina Piña's Lacanian reading of the countess's fixation in the mirror stage, with its concomitant "pathologies"—sadism, muteness, melancholy, identification with death, and homosexuality ("La palabra obscena" 31). Let me now remind the reader of Pizarnik's own celebrated fixation on mirrors, of her famous line: "He tenido muchos amores— dije—pero el más hermoso fue mi amor por los espejos" (*El deseo de la palabra* 37) [I have had many loves—I said—but the most beautiful was my love of mirrors]. Let us read what Pizarnik herself has claimed this fixation ("amor") means. In an interview with Martha I. Moia, we read the following exchange:

> M.I.M.—Vislumbro que el espejo . . . dispone en tu obra el miedo de *ser dos* . . .
> A.P.—Decís bien, es el miedo a todas las que en mí contienden . . .
> M.I.M.—¿A quién ves en [los espejos]?
> A.P.—A la otra que soy. (En verdad, tengo cierto miedo a los espejos). (*El deseo de la palabra* 250)
> [M.I.M.: I suspect that the mirror . . . configures in your work the fear of *being two* . . .
> A.P.: That's right, it's the fear of all (the women) who are arguing inside me . . .
> M.I.M.: Whom do you see in the mirror?
> A.P.: The other woman that I am. (In truth, I have a certain fear of mirrors).]

What does she fear about mirrors? Is Countess Báthory not "la otra que soy"? And *what* about her—about the countess—does Pizarnik fear? I must conclude that Pizarnik shared Piña's reading: "mirror people," of which she is one, are sexually pathological. I arrive at this conclusion weaving together "sed de tierra, de sangre *y de sexualidad feroz*" [thirst for earth, for blood, *and for ferocious sexuality*] (emphasis added) and other state-

ments, such as this: "En lo esencial, vivió sumida en un ámbito exclusiva-
mente femenino" [Essentially she lived deep within an exclusively female
world] (M 79). This brief and singular glimmer of lesbian utopia—considered as an isolated signifying fragment—immediately turns to sadistic
nightmare, followed as it is by the chilling

> No hubo sino mujeres en sus noches de crímenes. Luego, algunos
> detalles son obviamente reveladores: por ejemplo, en la sala de tortu-
> ras, en los momentos de máxima tensión, solía introducir ella misma
> un cirio ardiente en el sexo de la víctima. También hay testimonios
> que dicen de una lujuria menos solitaria. Una sirvienta aseguró en el
> proceso que una aristocrática y misteriosa dama vestida de mancebo
> visitaba a la condesa. En una ocasión las descubrió juntas, torturando
> a una muchacha. Pero se ignora si compartían otros placeres que los
> sádicos. (44–45)
> [There were only women in her nights of crime. And a few details
> are obviously revealing: for instance, in the torture chamber, during
> the moments of greatest tension, she herself used to plunge (*sic*) a
> burning candle into the sex of her victim. There are also testimonies
> which speak of less solitary pleasures (*sic*). One of the servants said
> during the trial that an aristocratic and mysterious lady dressed as a
> young man would visit the Countess. On one occasion she saw them
> together, torturing a girl. But we do not know whether they shared
> any pleasures other than the sadistic ones.] (M 79–80)

Following directly on the speculations about the countess's homosexuality, what do these "details" reveal? This "pathology" (Piña's reading)
which Pizarnik's narrator scripts as a silence, which she needs to name and
does not name ("nunca pudieron aclararse los rumores . . ."; "se ignora
si compartían otros placeres" [the rumours concerning her alleged (*sic*)
homosexuality were never confirmed; we do not know whether they shared
other pleasures]), can only be the lesbian in her self, which Pizarnik represents as an "evil lesbian erotic" in her version (a rewriting of an "adaptation") of the legendary exploits of an historical figure, Countess Erszébet
Báthory. My conclusion is supported by this harrowingly (self) revealing
paragraph:

> Si bien no se trata de *explicar* a esta siniestra figura, es preciso de-
> tenerse en el hecho de que padecía el mal del siglo XVI: la melancolía.
> Un color invariable rige al melancólico: su interior es un espacio de
> color de luto . . . [E]s una escena sin decorados donde el yo inerte

es asistido por el yo que sufre por esa inercia. Este quisiera liberar al prisionero, pero cualquier tentativa fracasa como hubiera fracasado Teseo si, además de ser él mismo, hubiera sido, también, el Minotauro; matarlo, entonces, habría exigido matarse. (45)

[Even though we are not concerned with *explaining* this sinister figure, it is necessary to dwell on the fact that she suffered from that sixteenth-century sickness: melancholia. An unchangeable colour rules over the melancholic: his dwelling is a space the colour of mourning. . . . It is a bare stage where the inert *I* is assisted by the *I* suffering from that inertia. The latter wishes to free the former, but all efforts fail, as Theseus would have failed had he been not only himself, but also the Minotaur; to kill him then, he would have had to kill himself.] (M 80)

Pizarnik's narrator warns the reader against "explaining," in an ostensibly dispassionate yet still authoritarian move, "si bien no se trata de *explicar* a esta siniestra figura" [even though we are not concerned with *explaining* this sinister figure] (somewhat weakly rendered in translation). But any reader familiar with Pizarnik's writing (poetry, diary, essays) will recognize immediately the overdetermined signs of melancholy, fragmentation of the self, and suicide.[15]

As Cristina Piña and others have observed, Pizarnik's discourse exploits and explores transgression. Pizarnik herself (she who desired to go "nada más que hasta el fondo" [nowhere except to the very bottom]) also wrote these words: "La poesía es el lugar donde todo sucede. A semejanza del amor, del humor, del suicidio y de todo acto profundamente subversivo, la poesía se desentiende de lo que no es su libertad o su verdad" (*Alejandra Pizarnik* 127) [Poetry is the place where everything occurs. Like love, humor, suicide and all profoundly subversive acts, poetry takes no part in whatever is not its freedom or its truth]. But, as Jill S. Kuhnheim notes: "Alejandra Pizarnik's production emphasizes the distance between literary activity and lived experience, for her utopic struggle against alienation and silence leads to a dystopic end: self-destruction, death (reading both life and work in this instance)" (270).

Alejandra Pizarnik's sexuality was itself resistant to accommodation in the world (culture, society, historical conjuncture) in which she lived and wrote. And in her writing she strained the established limits of literary and cultural conventions, always moving implacably toward liminality. She checks the transgressive impulse, however, closes both her text and the closet door, immediately following the text's single take on lesbianism (couched in speculations about the countess's "homosexuality"), with the narrator's identification with Theseus and Sade. These identifications are vexed, and ultimately self-defeating, for although Theseus and Sade may represent transgressive figures, they are male. Each, in his own way, strains at liminality and yet, as a model, allows only one way out: (self) castigation, in the case of Sade (the countess, like Sade, constituting "yet another proof that the absolute freedom of the human creature is horrible" [M 87]); suicide in Theseus's. For Pizarnik, unlike Theseus, *was* also the Minotaur. If her violent representation of lesbian desire in *La condesa sangrienta* attests to "the resilience of Alejandra Pizarnik's closet," the text's ultimate containment of transgression—the fact that *La condesa sangrienta* could only be "a speculation on the impossibility of lesbian desire" (Molloy, "From Sappho to Baffo")—is an equally eloquent testament to the closet's tenacity.

In closing, I should like to reflect briefly on something Teresa de Lauretis has written about Michelle Cliff: "The dual masquerade [Cliff's] writing suggests is at once the condition of speechlessness and of overcoming speechlessness, for the latter occurs by recognizing and representing the division in the self, the difference and the displacement from which any identity that needs to be claimed derives" ("Sexual Indifference" 154). The signs de Lauretis deploys around Cliff's writing coincide intriguingly; indeed, they form a concise compendium of the signs I have used to structure my own essay and have consistently foregrounded in Pizarnik's text: the transhistorical, translinguistic masquerade of Pizarnik in/as the countess, the more literal transgendered masquerade in the scene of speculative lesbianism hinted at in the description of the countess's cross-dressed aristocratic lady visitor (in "Classical Torture"); the binary speechlessness/speech, configured variously along the axis of silence/speech, or not naming/naming; finally, the divided self, an overwhelming obsession in Pizarnik's poetry, textualized here in "The Melancholy Mirror."

It seems to me that in *La condesa sangrienta* Alejandra Pizarnik comes closer, perhaps, than anywhere else in her oeuvre to overcoming speechlessness (in terms of de Lauretis's analysis), in the specular representation and even, I would argue, (self) recognition of a lesbian self divided. What she never does, however, even in this "most personal statement" (Molloy, "From Sappho to Baffo"), is to claim the identity that could derive from this representation and recognition: Pizarnik does not—and I must—name this difference as lesbian.

Notes

This essay is for Mary Docter. I would like to thank David Román, for his comments, which were helpful in the articulation of my argument. Thanks are also due Emilie Bergmann for her friendship, as well as her always insightful editorial help.

1 Sebreli is quoted in Neil Miller's *Out in the World* 195.

2 Fuskova is quoted in ibid. 214.

3 *Sinister Wisdom* 5 (1978): 7.

4 This is my translation, as are all others in this essay, unless otherwise indicated.

5 For a discussion of cultural attitudes toward and sanctions against homosexuality in Argentina, both before the 1976 coup and currently (through 1990), see Likosky 71–81 and Miller 182–217.

6 It is curious that the title of Molloy's MLA talk suggested that the topic would be sexuality (or its diversion) in Pizarnik's *poetry;* in fact, Molloy enacted another diversion, speaking exclusively about *La condesa sangrienta,* Valentine Penrose's *Erszébet Báthory, la comtesse sanglante,* and mentioning tangentially Pizarnik's other "obscene" prose texts. I do not find this at all coincidental: sexuality *is,* in great measure, diverted—suppressed—in Pizarnik's poetry, displaced, I believe, onto the text I am presently reading and which became the subject of Molloy's talk.

7 This is my translation. All other translations of *La condesa sangrienta* are from Alberto Manguel's *Other Fires,* indicated with an M and the corresponding page number, or by Suzanne Jill Levine, from *Alejandra Pizarnik: A Profile,* indicated by the initials SJL and the corresponding page number.

8 See Raymond T. McNally's *Dracula Was a Woman: In Search of the Blood Countess of Transylvania.* McNally's tome, more historical anecdote than scholarly investigation, nevertheless was invaluable in allowing me to verify how closely Pizarnik's book follows the historical facts. Yet I observed, at the same time, the great distance between her icy, aestheticizing (anaesthetizing) prose and the impossibly gruesome acts it represents. McNally's occasionally chatty, speculative book (his first chapter is a travel diary of his and his wife's trip to Czechoslovakia on the trail of the Blood Countess!) includes a useful bibliography/filmography as well as appendices which contain translated transcripts of the 1611 trial of Báthory's codefendants.

9 Many of the essays in this volume address the issues raised in Jay's and Glasgow's introductory remarks; Catharine R. Stimpson's exploration in her afterword is paradigmatic:
> Is lesbianism a metaphor? . . . "Lesbianism" might signify a critique of heterosexuality; a cry for the abolition of the binary oppositions of modern sexuality; a demand for the release of women's self-named desire; a belief that such release might itself be a sign of a rebellious, subtle, raucous textuality. "Lesbianism" might represent a space in which we shape and reshape our psychosexual identities, in which we are metamorphic creatures. (Jay and Glasgow 380)

10 *La condesa sangrienta* presents still another layer of resistance to its reader, in terms of the text's (refusal of) accommodation to any specific literary genre: is it a prose poem, as Pizarnik's first-person narrator characterizes the Penrose "refundición" *La condesa sangrienta* is ostensibly modeled on ("una suerte de vasto y hermoso poema en prosa" [a sort of vast and beautiful prose poem])? Is it a novella? An essay, as Piña claims it has been classified ("La palabra obscena" 27)? Or a "mosaic of prose vignettes" (Foster 98), as Piña

also believes, "personalmente interpreto como una sucesión de estampas" [personally I interpret it as a series of vignettes] ("La palabra obscena" 27)?

11 1971 is generally accepted as the first date of publication of *La condesa sangrienta*, in the edition of Aquarius Libros, Buenos Aires. However, as Cristina Piña points out, "*La condesa sangrienta* originariamente [fue] publicado en 1965 en la revista mexicana *Diálogos* y luego editada en forma de libro en 1971" ("La palabra obscena" 27–28) [*The Bloody Countess* originally was published in 1965 in the Mexican journal *Diálogos* and later was edited in book form in 1971]. The book was reedited by López Crespo in Buenos Aires in 1976. I use both the 1971 and 1976 editions; I have not seen the original 1965 version.

12 See my article, "The Discourse of Madness in the Poetry of Alejandra Pizarnik," *Monographic Review/Revista Monográfica* 6 (1990): 274–82.

13 This untitled poem is from *Arbol de Diana* (1962). Written only a few years before Pizarnik began working on *La condesa sangrienta* (originally published in 1965), the coincidences between the two texts are astounding.

14 Also, there are several references to the she-wolf in Pizarnik's poetic texts. Perhaps the most significant is "Los trabajos y las noches" [Labors and Nights], from the eponymous collection published in 1965:

> para reconocer en la sed mi emblema
> para significar el único sueño
> para no sustentarme nunca de nuevo en el amor
>
> he sido toda ofrenda
> un puro errar
> de *loba* en el bosque
> en la noche de los cuerpos
> para decir la palabra inocente
> (*El deseo de la palabra* 67, emphasis added)
> [to recognize in thirst my emblem
> to signify the only dream
> to never again feed on love
>
> I have been all offering
> pure roaming
> of *she-wolf* in the forest
> in the night of the body
> to say the innocent word]

What is so poignant, so ultimately tragic, is the semiotic and ontological reversal enacted in this text, in relation to the quotation from "Torturas clásicas" in *La condesa sangrienta*, around the sign "loba" [she-wolf] and the notion of the erotic. In the latter text the countess, caught up in her "crisis erótica" [erotic crisis], growls like a she-wolf and mutters curses. In "Los trabajos y las noches," on the other hand, the poetic speaker flees from the erotic ("la noche de los cuerpos" [the night of the body]), seeking solace, seeking a place safe from the hunger of love where she can speak "the innocent word": this safe, de-eroticized space is her metamorphosis as she-wolf.

15 Pizarnik herself underwent analysis and was hospitalized for depression on several occasions. She had made at least one other suicide attempt before dying of an overdose of Seconal on 25 September 1972.

Works Cited

Brossard, Nicole. *The Aerial Letter.* Trans. Marlene Wildeman. Toronto: Women's Press, 1988.

Cliff, Michelle. "Notes on Speechlessness." *Sinister Wisdom* 5 (1978).

de Lauretis, Teresa. "Sexual Indifference and Lesbian Representation." *The Lesbian and Gay Studies Reader.* New York: Routledge, 1993. 141–58.

Englebrecht, Penelope J. "'Lifting Belly is a Language': The Postmodern Lesbian Subject." *Feminist Studies* 16.1 (Spring 1990): 85–114.

Foster, David William. *Gay and Lesbian Themes in Latin American Writing.* Austin: University of Texas Press, 1991.

Graziano, Frank, ed. *Alejandra Pizarnik: A Profile.* Durango, Colo.: Logbridge-Rhodes, 1987.

Jay, Karla, and Joanne Glasgow, eds. *Lesbian Texts and Contexts: Radical Revisions.* New York: New York University Press, 1990.

Kaminsky, Amy K. *Reading the Body Politic: Feminist Criticism and Latin American Women Writers.* Minneapolis: University of Minnesota Press, 1993.

Kuhnheim, Jill S. "Unsettling Silence in the Poetry of Olga Orozco and Alejandra Pizarnik." *Monographic Review/Revista Monográfica* 6 (1990): 258–73.

Likosky, Stephan, ed. *Coming Out: An Anthology of International Gay and Lesbian Writings.* New York: Pantheon Books, 1992.

Malinow, Inés. "Juicios críticos." *Poesía argentina contemporánea.* Buenos Aires: Fundación argentina para la poesía, 1980. 2833–40.

Manguel, Alberto, trans. *The Bloody Countess.* In *Other Fires: Short Fiction by Latin American Women.* Ed. Alberto Manguel. New York: Clarkson N. Potter, 1986.

McNally, Raymond T. *Dracula Was a Woman: In Search of the Blood Countess of Transylvania.* New York: McGraw-Hill, 1983.

Meese, Elizabeth A. *(Sem)Erotics: Theorizing Lesbian : Writing.* New York: New York University Press, 1992.

Miller, Neil. *Out in the World: Gay and Lesbian Life from Buenos Aires to Bangkok.* New York: Random House, 1992.

Molloy, Sylvia. "Disappearing Acts: Reading Sexuality in Teresa de la Parra" (this volume).

———. "Female Textual Identities: The Strategies of Self-Figuration: Introduction." *Women's Writing in Latin America.* Ed. Sara Castro-Klareen, Sylvia Molloy, and Beatriz Sarlo. Boulder, Colo.: Westview Press, 1991.

———. "From Sappho to Baffo: Diverting the Sexual in the Poetry of Alejandra Pizarnik." Talk delivered at the 1992 meeting of the Modern Language Association, New York, New York.

Piña, Cristina. *Alejandra Pizarnik.* Buenos Aires: Planeta, 1991.

———. "La palabra obscena." *Cuadernos hispanoamericanos* (May 1990): 17–38.

Pizarnik, Alejandra. *El deseo de la palabra.* Barcelona: Ocnos/Barral, 1975.

———. *La condesa sangrienta.* Buenos Aires: Aquarius Libros, 1971.

———. *Poemas.* Ed. Alejandro Fontenla. Buenos Aires: Centro Editor de América Latina, 1982.

Rich, Adrienne. *On Lies, Secrets, and Silence: Selected Prose 1966–1978.* New York: W.W. Norton, 1979.

Sedgwick, Eve Kosofsky. *Epistemology of the Closet.* Berkeley and Los Angeles: University of California Press, 1990.

Luz María Umpierre

Lesbian Tantalizing in Carmen Lugo Filippi's "Milagros, Calle Mercurio"

For Lourdes and Ann,
in survival

As a reader of Puerto Rican literature, I have yet to find a narrative text written by a woman that deals with the subject of Lesbianism openly.[1] I have often thought of reasons for this absence and the main one I have come up with is the fear of the writer identifying herself as Lesbian, of being identified as one if she were to write such a narrative text and the consequences that she would have to live with in heterosexist Puerto Rican literary history and criticism and, needless to say, Puerto Rican society.

As readers, we tend to look for works that somehow validate some of the perceptions we have of life and our experiences, and for works that open new windows for our imagination and intellect. Being left in the void by the absence of narrative texts that portray Lesbian characters, situations, issues and concerns within the literature of Puerto Rico, and not being very prone to assume an "existential" posture about it—that is, "I'm alone without Lesbian texts in the World of Puerto Rican letters"—I have set out myself to fill this vacuum by reading narrative on the island, especially after 1970, from what I call a homocritical perspective. Reading from this perspective supposes bringing out of the critical closet the perceptions I have as a reader and how I approach texts, to paraphrase a television series: IN SEARCH OF. . . . This search for texts which narrate close re-lationships between women has not been totally fruitless, however, and it has turned up a few narrations which depict these relationships. Some of Rosario Ferré's short stories, for example, probably win a first prize in my Lesbian look-alike short story contest for she has produced a number of these that portray close positive relationships among women, "Pico Rico Mandorico" being the closest she has been, in my opinion, to writing a short story with Lesbian characters.

But what my reading has also produced, and now I'll refer to myself as a reader, a Lesbian, reading, is a feeling of being tantalized into an almost voyeuristic posture by texts that carry close relationships between women. The fact that these stories don't portray these relationships as Lesbian and that writers of these stories are unwilling to admit to using Lesbian themes leaves me often asking myself as a critic: Am I a female voyeur reading these texts as through a keyhole or are these texts really carrying material that tantalizes me as a Lesbian reading them into a homocritical view?

In one of the best articles I have read on Lesbians as readers, "Ourself behind Ourself: A Theory for Lesbian Readers," Jean Kennard proposes a method which she labels as "polar reading" for "lesbian readers and others whose experience is not frequently reflected in literature." "Polar reading," she adds, "permits the participation of any reader in any text. . . . It does not, however, involve the reader in denying herself. The reader redefines herself in opposition to the text; if that self definition includes lesbianism, this becomes apparent in any commentary she may make on her reading" (Kennard 77).[2] As interesting as Kennard's proposal is, her strategy stays in the realm precisely of the reader and it does not discuss the other pole: certain texts which are written as tantalizers for a Lesbian, reading.[3]

In an article on contemporary narrative written by women in Puerto Rico after 1970, Magali García Ramis mentions that what joins the works of this group of writers is the use of irony to criticize how women, in order to lead a tranquil life in Puerto Rican society, have had to adhere to archaic, unfair, unjustifiable social, political, and cultural situations (García Ramis 6, 30–31). She is referring in her article to the works of Rosario Ferré, Ana Lydia Vega, and Carmen Lugo Filippi and how some of their stories deal negatively with some female characters, which García Ramis sees as having its roots in the referential framework of Puerto Rican life. While reading her article, I was struck by the few lines which she devotes to Carmen Lugo Filippi's short story, "Milagros, Calle Mercurio." García Ramis says that the main character in the story, Milagros, apparently liberates herself from her mother and religion by becoming a prostitute and that this liberation is then bound to make her more of a slave.

I'll admit to reading these lines nervously for I had, two years before in 1985, taught that same short story to my undergraduates in a Caribbean literature course from a very different perspective. I had focused then on the obsession of the narrator, Marina, with Milagros, a teenager. From my point of view, Marina was the main character and I had read the story's ending as the fulfillment of one of Marina's fantasies with Milagros—the symbolic cutting of her hair. Granted, I had had a male Puerto Rican student in class angrily contest my reading, but several women students helped enhance my interpretation by admitting that they too had had an "interesting" experience in dealing with Marina as a narrator.

Going back to García Ramis's article, reading it made me ask myself if I had read myself into the story, done a "polar reading" as Kennard suggests, or was the story encoded with a Lesbian motif that could have tantalized me into a homocritical reading. I went back to read the story now suspicious of both García Ramis's and my readings.

I realized that one of the first things that attracted me to the story was the first-person narration and the fact that Marina, the narrator, was a dropout from the university after studying comparative literature for three years. The fact that she was now a hairdresser and was narrating this story as if telling it to a client had brought me close to the text for several reasons. My hairdresser in Puerto Rico is always telling me stories about herself and others while going about the task of doing my hair. Thus, Marina, the hairdresser, was well within my referential framework and the fact that she had studied literature closed the gap between what was being narrated and me. But while these things attracted me to the text, something in Marina herself drove me out: her "ínfulas de grandeza" [self-aggrandizement]. Marina admitted also to having set out to deflate the ego of any woman who stood before her. This "come on/push back" tension continued for me while reading the text until the appearance of Milagros. Marina had made such a case for her disdain of other women whom she had labeled as "perfectos monigotes con ínfulas de grandes damas" (Lugo Filippi 204) [perfect puppets trying to act like *grandes dames*] (a statement that seems like projection to me) that the appearance of a woman of whom she says "La recuerdo tan vivamente" (205) [I remember her so vividly], the detail with which she describes Milagros, the attention with which Marina follows her, and the obvious attraction that she has toward her appearance, all pulled me back into the story. By now, in this new homocritical reading, it was obvious to me again that Marina was the main character in the story and I had disqualified my doubts brought about by García Ramis's reading on Milagros being it. But the fact still remained in my mind that García Ramis had made a total omission of Marina and had seen the ending of the story as Milagros's embarkation into prostitution. Why, I asked myself, in her list of female characters in contemporary Puerto Rican fiction, had García Ramis chosen to disqualify, nullify Marina?

The answer to this question became clearer to me as I progressed in my rereading of the story. A woman critic of Puerto Rican literature and a writer herself, García Ramis must have safely read the story from the observance of Milagros's change from an apparently good, obedient, and observant young woman loyal to her mother and the Pentecostal church to a stripteaser in a local bar for dirty old men. I will not go into my objections of viewing Milagros's change from virgin to whore. That would take me off track from the question of reading and into characterization—that would be another essay. However, I will say that this particular reading of Milagros's change falls into a traditional pattern within the island's literary criticism and view on/of women: the dichotomy virgin/whore being so preponderant that texts seem to be reduced to this one opposition. On the other hand, in contrast to García Ramis, I was not living on the island and was separated from everyday life there. I was at a distance; I could allow myself to accept the tantalizings of Lugo Filippi's text. I could listen to Marina's story. A few examples from Marina's discourse and the use of a narrative technique will help me illustrate the story I heard from Marina.

In her description of Milagros and her first reaction to her, Marina admits that "Contemplarla suscitaba en mí un extraño fenómeno de correspondencias" (206) [Contemplating her brought up a strange phenomenon of correspondences]. Given that Marina has gone as far as to confess an attraction for Milagros, another voice now appears in the text, one that talks to Marina as "tú" [you] while describing the fantasies that Marina has of Milagros's hair. This voice, which I want to describe as the voice of fantasy, becomes then the narrator for several pages in all of which there exist the descriptions of Marina's further fantasies—imaginary conversations with Milagros and the actual following of Milagros by Marina. The fact that the story has been turned over now to this voice who is making Marina's fantasies come out of the closet was crucial for me as a reader since it glued me to the text. But I was a Lesbian, reading. What if I had been García Ramis or an island woman critic who was straight? In a partial way, some of my women students had responded to this question. They had seen these passages as a sign of "illness" in Marina, of a flaw, of something sick, statements that I had contested immediately as heterosexism. But my women students who felt this way had no doubts that Marina was the main character—they too were hundreds of miles away from the island.

Going back to the text, after these pages of second-voice revealing (Lesbian, reading) or "disturbing" (heterosexist, reading) narration, the narrative voice returns to the first person. It is no surprise then that Marina's closeted voice, the "I" who interacts in front of others, goes back at this point to making negative statements on women of the kind we saw at the beginning of the story. She now calls Milagros "madonita" and asks "¿Sería una retrasada mental con aires de modelo sanjuanera?" (209) [Was it possible that she was just slightly retarded and only had the air of a big city model?] The "come on/push back" feeling came over me again. Marina and her story were playing games. When the storyline dealing with Marina's fantasies had become revealing to me as a Lesbian, reading, but perhaps disturbing to a straight, reading, the story, as we would say in Puerto Rico: "regained *compostura*"—societal *compostura* [composure]. Thus Marina had to go back to the downplaying of women—she had to push them back.

But her *compostura* is short lived because a gossiper makes her appearance with news that Milagros has been living a double life: "aleluya" by day [virgin] / "guayanilla" by night [whore]. Milagros has been seen in a bar in Guayanilla working as a stripteaser. The second-person "fantasy" voice comes once again to displace Marina's "I." Marina is about to visualize in her mind Milagros's striptease and be aroused by it. This is a taboo. Marina is a woman character in Puerto Rican literature. How can she be allowed to eroticize Milagros in such detail? Thus, another interesting element comes into play. Marina takes on a male *persona* in her fantasy—that of Rada, the police officer called to the scene of the striptease. And at that time a true *caja china* [Chinese box] occurs before our eyes: the second voice narrates what Marina imagined she saw through Rada's eyes:

> La masa lechosa inicia su sensual contoneo, mientras el estribillo pegajoso de la melodía se impone. Esta vez la luz indiscreta persigue los convulsivos movimientos y el Rada entonces se excita viendo cómo la serpentosa figura se yergue de espaldas y muestra con estudiada morosidad dos perfectas redondeces que contrastan con la llana geografía del suave torso. . . . Los jadeos parecen haber cesado bajo el influjo de ese momento perfecto. . . . Y ahí está Milagros, ante los asombrados ojos del Rada, quien parpadea incrédulo, quien se frota los ojos para despertar y ver siempre aquellos muslos lechosos, adornados por un montoncito de pelo lleno de pizpiretos miosotis. . . . el Rada no despega sus ojos de los menudos senos que comienzan a flotar y sólo el estruendoso platillazo final lo devuelve a la realidad. (214–15)
> [That milky mass of flesh begins its sensuous gyrations while the melody sounds its refrain once more. This time the indiscreet light

pursues those convulsive movements and Rada gets excited as he watches the serpentine figure straighten itself, with her back toward them, and, with a studied slowness, display two perfect globes. Below them, the flat geography of a perfect torso. . . . The ragged breathing in the room stops for one perfect moment. . . . There, before Rada's astonished eyes, is Milagros. He blinks in disbelief and rubs his eyes, only to see those milky thighs still there before him, crowned with a small mound of hair covered with coquettish forget-me-nots. . . . Rada stares at those tiny breasts. The clashing cymbals snap him back to reality.][4]

Given the high sexual charge of the description, a double closet door has appeared to play it "safe." Within Puerto Rican society, Rada is allowed to enjoy and be aroused by the sight of Milagros's erotic dance, Marina is not. Nonetheless, the scene remains sexually charged. This playful trick by the text is crucial, in my opinion, with regard to García Ramis's "safe" reading of Milagros as turning to prostitution. After all, Rada is one who "allegedly" sees and the bar is a men's bar. In my homocritical reading Milagros stripteases for Marina, but in order to bring that about, the text has established a dual distancing via the second voice narrating what Marina fantasized that Rada saw. The story's "come on/push back" tension has continued now acquiring a greater complexity. It is obvious to me as a Lesbian, reading, that Marina was aroused by Milagros's look and body from the moment she met her. But given what I have mentioned previously in this section with regard to Puerto Rican women writers and lesbian themes, this main core of the story has to be layered with all sorts of sugar coatings to make it palatable while also leaving open a "proper" way out. The text, I thought, is playing "straight" attraction games with me as a Lesbian, reading—games of "come in and take me," read my story, Marina's story—and "push back" games—the interjection of the second voice and the further distancing using Rada's "vision," denial games.

But I'll return to the text and Marina right after the striptease. The second voice is narrating and observes that Marina cannot sleep because she is thinking of Milagros's actions: "la escena te persigue y por más que quieras abreviarla, no puedes, porque se adhiere con obstinación a tu pantalla" (216) [You try to get rid of the scene, but no matter how hard you try, it sticks to your screen]. It is obvious to me that this description is a sign of the fact that Marina has allowed herself to be aroused by Milagros sexually, and I link this to a previous passage in the story where Marina has imagined having Milagros in her life as an intelligent woman companion. Both facts are narrated in the second voice conveniently—a Lesbian, reading, could speak of Marina's fantasizing a Lesbian lifestyle; a non-Lesbian, reading, could perceive this other voice as a voice of admonishment. Through this convenient technique of second-voice narrating, the text can make of the reader a whore, if she follows Rada's vision without viewing Marina behind the observation of Milagros, or a virgin if she follows the second voice as a voice of admonishment—God, the Pentecostal church, "motherhood," and so on. The story thus plays overtly *to* the critics/readers who reduce stories written by Puerto Rican women after 1970 to the dichotomy virgin/whore. Covertly, through the use of this convenient technique, however, the text tries to make of the Lesbian, reading, a female voyeur. *Her* reading perhaps is only a product of her homocritical mind. As we would say in Puerto Rico: the writer of the text has covered all the bases in her baseball diamond.

The ending of the story is equally convenient. Milagros arrives at the beauty salon and asks Marina "maquíllame en shocking red, Marina, y córtame como te dé la gana" (216) [Make me up in shocking red, Marina, and cut my hair any way you like]. I as a Lesbian, reading, thought immediately of Marina's fantasy world becoming true, becoming real—Milagros is asking her to do whatever she pleases with her. And given the sexual attraction I have read as present in Marina toward Milagros this would be, as we would say in vulgar or earthy Puerto Rican slang, her chance to "meter mano," to get involved. However, if I have conveniently paid attention to the second voice as admonishment, if I have not wanted to see Marina looking behind Rada and have only seen a man being aroused by a woman, if I have taken Marina's inability to sleep because of the recurrent images of the striptease as signs of Marina's fear of becoming a "loose" woman like Milagros, I could say that Marina is before a temptation: she is being asked to help Milagros become more of a prostitute by acquiring the image, the "looks" of one. The second-voice narrator ends the story with the words: "Un temblequeo . . . comienza a apoderarse de tus rodillas . . . Marina ¿qué responderás?" (217) [You feel a slight trembling in your legs . . . Marina, what will you say?]. The question is not only addressed to Marina but to the reader—what kind of reading have you done? How far has your imagination's "mercurio" [mercury] gone up or down?

I'll go back to García Ramis's article, my homocritical reading, and the text. García Ramis had said that Puerto Rican women have had to adhere to archaic, unfair, unjustifiable social, political, and cultural situations in order to lead a tranquil life on the island. I would add to this that women writers of narrative fiction in Puerto Rico have had to deal with self-repression when it comes to openly writing short stories with/on Lesbian characters and themes. Therefore, they leave their texts open-ended, encoded in multiple layers, and their characters wearing multiple masks. And their texts simply act as tantalizers to a Lesbian, reading. If the homocritical reader bites the hook, the text can always conveniently close its closet door and leave the critic outside feeling like a voyeur and the characters inside as trapped stripteasers of sickly obsessive women.

In Jean Kennard's article quoted above, she gives as an example of a Lesbian reader, Adrienne Rich's "Vesuvius at Home" on the poetry of Emily Dickinson. There Rich, as a Lesbian critic/poet/reader, is left to perceive herself as an *insect* hovering against the screens of Emily Dickinson's life: "Trying to visit, to enter her mind" (Rich 158–159). But she is left, despite her brilliance and her insights, still outside; as a Lesbian, reading. I, for one, don't wish to remain the rest of my life as a female critical version of Peeping Tom or as an insect hovering. I invite women writers of fiction in Puerto Rican literature to open the doors of their minds and their pens and allow for their characters to leave the closet in a dignified way. Only then will my reading as a Lesbian not be seen as polar and my homocriticism as extremist in the history of criticism in my home country. And we would be able to generate an inclusive theory of text production and reading that allows us to express and include all of ourselves freely.

Notes

1 It is interesting that there are, however, several stories on male homosexuality written by women: Rosario Ferré's "De tu lado al paraíso" and Mayra Montero's "Halloween en Leonardo's." I am aware of the collection of poems *Primavida* by Anita Vélez that treats the subject of women bonding with women. I am also aware of a play written by a man in Puerto Rico on the subject of Lesbianism, which was performed with Lydia Echevarría in the leading role.

2 Kennard's article is by far more encompassing than the highly quoted "Zero Degree Deviancy: The Lesbian Novel in English," by Catharine R. Stimpson, *Critical Inquiry* (Winter 1981): 363–79.

3 I want to clarify here my terminology. The term "Lesbian readers" is used in my article following Kennard's concept of it. A "Lesbian, reading" is my term and I include under it a Lesbian woman reading a text looking for Lesbian clues or close relationships between women. If the "Lesbian, reading," is a critic, this may lead her to a "homocritical" posture; again, this is my copyrighted term, which means arriving at a homosexual interpretation of a given work.

4 [Translation is Diana Velez's from *Reclaiming Medusa,* with the exception of two key phrases taken from Lizabeth Paravisini-Gebert's translation in *Callaloo,* which renders

314 Luz María Umpierre

"se yergue" as "straighten itself up," and "adornados por un montoncito de pelo lleno de pizpiretos miosotis" as "crowned with a small mound of hair covered with coquettish forget-me-nots." Diana Vélez's translation reads "bends way over" and "those milky thighs still there before him, covered with strands of hair interspersed with pink and yellow forget-me-nots." These two inaccuracies, atypical of Vélez's translation, obscure the focus on Milagros's pubic hair, and substitute Milagros's abundant head of hair, which is the focus of the rest of the story. Paravisini-Gebert's translation, like the Spanish text, supports the homoerotic reading of the story.—Emilie L. Bergmann]

Works Cited

García Ramis, Magali. "Para que un día Luz María pueda comprar los zapatos que le dé la gana." *Calibán* 5–6 (1985): 6, 30–31.

Kennard, Jean E. "Ourself behind Ourself: A Theory for Lesbian Readers." *Gender and Reading: Essays on Readers, Texts and Contexts*. Ed. Elizabeth A. Flynn and Patrocinio P. Schweickart. Baltimore: Johns Hopkins University Press, 1986. 63–80.

Lugo Filippi, Carmen. "Milagros, Calle Mercurio." *Apalabramiento*. Ed. Efraín Barradas. Hanover, N.H.: Ediciones del Norte, 1983. 201–17.

——— . "Milagros, Mercurio Street." Trans. Lizabeth Paravisini-Gebert. *Callaloo* 17.3 (1994): 870–77.

——— . "Milagros, on Mercurio Street." *Reclaiming Medusa: Short Stories by Contemporary Puerto Rican Women*. Ed. and trans. Diana Vélez. San Francisco, Calif.: Spinsters/Aunt Lute, 1988. 87–100.

Rich, Adrienne. "Vesuvius at Home: The Power of Emily Dickinson." *On Lies, Secrets and Silence*. New York: W. W. Norton, 1979. 157–83.

SIX

Call to Theory/Call to Action

Brad Epps
Virtual Sexuality: Lesbianism, Loss, and Deliverance in Carme Riera's "Te deix, amor, la mar com a penyora"

Mi cuerpo anduvo, sin nadie—Rafael Alberti

I am haunted by a passage in Carme Riera's "Te deix, amor, la mar com a penyora" [I Leave You, My Love, the Sea as a Token]. In it, a young woman remembers and writes of when she was younger, when she remembered and wrote letters of love. Although the entire narrative can itself be read as a love letter, the letters here so lovingly remembered are haunting for the very reason that they cannot be read, at least not in a simply straight or graphic way. Directed to the sea, torn in a thousand pieces and scattered to the wind, or stamped with close and cryptic messages, these letters of love and remembrance spell out a strangely persistent loss of materiality that informs, in quite specific ways, the acts of writing and reading. For what is lost, and yet persists in loss, is here not merely a matter of love, but of lesbian love. Lesbianism, in Hispanic letters, does indeed seem all but lost: ghostwritten, as it were, in invisible ink.[1] Its appearance is almost always a pledge to disappearance; its presence, an artful testimony to its absence. But if the absence, loss, and disappearance of lesbianism are the established effects of literary tradition, they are also the effects of a considerable body of contemporary theory in which reality itself is represented as "always already" lost in representation. Liberating as such loss may theoretically be, it in fact often represents the wily durability of a tradition of strict secrecy and silence. Such *real* suppression may serve, in other words, to insure that some subjects are *virtually* abandoned, that they are written and read out of all actuality. It is along these lines that the letters of Riera's text point to what is at stake, both ethically and politically, in consigning the lesbian subject to a state of virtuality, where nothing can ever really be.

Set in Mallorca and Barcelona during the later years of Franco, the plot of "Te deix" is deceptively simple: an unnamed narrator writes a letter to her former lover in which she reflects on their relationship. In many ways, it is a conventional letter of love: nostalgic, lyrical, wistful, even precious. It relates the bliss of emotional and erotic encounter and the pain of a breakup largely motivated by societal and familial disapproval. Age and profession appear, at least at first, to be the principal obstacles in this love affair; but the fact that the young narrator is also her lover's student is, within the logic of the narrative, ultimately less decisive than the fact that both are female. By narrative logic I mean here nothing more, or less, than the logic of suspense. For while scenes of parental anger and communal gossip are developed in some detail, the sexual identity of the narrator—the source, as it turns out, of so much anger and gossip—is held in suspense until the final paragraph. I will have quite a bit to say about how sexual identity is finally *named* in the text, but what I want to emphasize is how they are *not* named. Such emphasis on the unnamed (and, dare I say it, the unnameable) may seem paradoxical, but only to the degree that the conventions of letter writing (and lovemaking) are assumed to be straightforward and literal-minded. For as soon as these conventions are accepted as poetic, as indirect, figurative, elusive, deferred, extraordinary, and, yes, even precious, then letters and love may indeed be written and read as other, perhaps always other, than they seem. Read thus, *poetic* conventions, embracing figurality and indirection, render an otherwise conventional love letter unconventional. My point is that not only is the theme, or content, of lesbian love "unconventional," but also the matter, or form, in which it is set forth. The suspense, silence and invisibility of the name; the subtle allusions to the "real nature" of the sexual body; and the remembrance of letters whose messages have been hidden or destroyed: all attest to the unconventional potential of poetic conventions (deferral, indirection, and occultation of meaning), to a complexity beneath the apparent simplicity of the story. What they also attest to, and what I want to explore, are the ways in which a particular reality, and its experiental contents, may be withheld, suspended, *virtualized*.

My choice of metaphor has as much to do with Riera's text as it does with the context, both critical and cultural, in which I am reading it. Virtuality is, of course, a well-established term for potentiality, for being in essence or effect though not in actual fact. But it is also an increasingly provocative concept, one whose rich philosophical significance has been expanded and recharged through modern technology.[2] Associated now with the cutting edge of scientific research and interactive information, virtuality has tended to move the mind to the machine and to remove, if not replace, the body altogether. These moves are paradoxical because at the same time that researchers and their disciples refer to such things as total computer immersion, architectural walkabouts, and experience theaters, they are also busy imagining such "non-things" as remote presence, computer generated disembodiment, and universal simulation. They seem close to touching, to feeling, an ever more vibrant reality, and yet they seem so far away. And as the body slips into something else, so, needless to say, does sex. Thus, in the imaginary age of teledildonics, "the physical commingling of genital sensations will come to be regarded as a less intimate act than the sharing of data structures of your innermost self-representations" (Rheingold 352). For all its technological and scientific underpinnings, this futuristic scenario in which bodily contact is ironically reinvented as beyond the body has already been enacted by a number of influential critical theorists for whom the body is, as Diana Fuss puts it, "never simply there" (5). In their view, the body is a cultural construct (which, *metaphorically* speaking, it is) devoid of essence; as such it cannot be grasped through such equally suspect constructs as experience, identity, and subjectivity.[3] Wary of the lure of the real, then, constructivist and anti-essentialist critics overlap, and in many respects actually outstrip, more scientifically oriented virtualists: as if by placing "reality" in quotation marks they could signify its illusive truth.

And yet, the critical uncertainty and insecurity that many of these theorists champion threaten to become the latest avatars of certainty and security when, as Fuss argues, specific terms, concepts, subjects, and *experiences,* are invalidated and set off limits.[4] Lesbian feminists are, for their part, acutely aware of problems of (in)validation and (de)limitation, especially when issues of intimacy and experience are involved. Accordingly, they are often skeptical of the strategic value of the death of the author, the disappearance of the subject, and the virtualization of reality.[5] This is not surprising, because whether as a legal class or an ontological category, lesbians and lesbianism have typically been relegated to what Ruth Robson calls "footnotes of absence" (29). Riera herself, in an interview with Lluís Racionero, finds the absence of "lesbiana" from a major Catalán dictionary full of feminist significance: further evidence that, like the letters surrendered to the sea and the wind in "Te deix, amor, la mar," lesbianism appears unreadable.[6] Of course, it is this very appearance of absence, this writing of unreadability, that is, as I hope to make apparent in my reading, one of the most notable achievements, and problems, of Riera's story.

It is in this connection that the two epigraphs to the entire collection of Riera's stories are quite revealing. The first is from Empedocles and reads:

"Jo era a la vegada arbre i ocell, / al.lot i al.lota, peix mut / dins la mar" [I was at once tree and bird, / boy and girl, and silent fish / in the sea] (my translation). Associated with the origins of rhetoric and ideas of pluralism and the transmigration of souls, Empedocles underwrites the tense (con)fusions and transformations of identity which punctuate, particularly in the realm of gender, Riera's text. The second epigraph is from Sappho, or rather a shade of Sappho. For in contrast to Empedocles, whose words are recorded by Diogenes Laertius, Sappho is set down as the author of a "never-written fragment" ("fragment mai no escrit"). Despite the classical aura surrounding both Empedocles and Sappho, his work here is clearly not of the same order as hers: it is not qualified as spurious and fragmentary, nor is it set off in ellipses and parentheses. Never mind that it too is, in reality, a fragment found only in the work of someone else, Empedocles's authority is not called into question. Sappho's authority, on the other hand, is presented as inauthentic, even ghostly; it is evoked yet altered, invoked yet subverted. As a result, Riera begins her text by reiterating, or reciting, a classical imbalance of authority.

This imbalance is not, of course, a matter of gender alone. Given the cultural resonance of Sappho's name, its affiliation with Lesbos and lesbianism, what is here recited, through Riera, is an eminently lesbian story, or history, of disauthorization and dispossession.[7] The contents of the pseudo-Sapphic fragment bear this out, for they relate the loss, or absence, of a woman beloved. In that respect, the epigraph encapsulates and anticipates a central theme of "Te deix" itself. But where the story is marked by a persistent yearning for presence, the epigraph is founded on a perpetual desire for absence: "Escolliré per sempre més la teva/ absència, donzella" [I will forever choose your absence, young woman]. More appealing than either the body or the memory of the body ("no és el teu cos, / ni el record del teu cos"), this absence is not, nevertheless, absolute. To begin with, it is the quality of a particular being, an elusive "you," apostrophized as a young woman ("donzella"), and hence intimately related to an "I" who is not just grammatically present but who speaks and desires. Presence is thus engaged with absence, as subject with object, in a mutually constitutive manner: I will always choose your absence, the absence of you; and You, in your absence, will always impress my presence, the presence of I; for such is the paradoxical condition of their, our, poetic possibility. Re-presented here as a trace or imprint ("l'empremta") in the sand, absence does indeed impress presence. More precisely, it is what the beloved impresses on the lover as her loveliest gift, her truest bequest: "el que de veritat estim / és l'empremta que has deixat / sobre l'arena" [what I truly love is the impression that you have left on the sand]. This gift is all the more impressive in that it may be taken as generating a return, or response, borne out in the very title of the story that follows: after "l'empremta que has deixat sobre l'arena," "te deix, amor, la mar" after what you have left, what I leave: after the sand, imprinted, the sea.

Even as the epigraph is born beyond itself, even as it is meta-phorized, it does not leave behind the problem of Sapphic authority. Or better yet, it does leave it behind, but in the more provocative sense of a legacy or a pledge (penyora). Much of "Te deix" is about what is left behind, be it love or letters or, as we shall see, the life of a child. But as Riera's Sapphic epigraph suggests, it is a legacy whose authority, or legitimacy, may be received and read as not merely fragmented but never-written: which is to say that it runs the risk of *not* being received or read at all. This risk is inscribed, or imprinted, in the text itself as what "happens" in the passage from "l'empremta" which "has deixat" to "la mar" which "te deix." And what happens is nothing less than the *imminence* of total erasure, the *impending* dissolution, by the sea, of the print left in the sand. There seems, in fact, to be something at once impossible and eternal in this passage from the epigraph to the story, as if erasure and dissolution could only be re-sisted by being reiterated, risked, forever. This is, as I read it, precisely what Riera effects by re-citing, and re-writing, Sappho under erasure; by signal-ing the print as the site of love; and by passing from the loving print of Sappho under erasure to the narrative proper—where; quite tellingly, the latest site, sign, and pledge of love is the sea (i.e., the site and sign of the print's erasure). What is more, all of these moves or passages or happen-ings, as I have called them, are left *forever* at risk and so also *forever* secure, by virtue of the fact that they are all apostrophic, all articulated in and as an unresolvable relation between "I" and "you," lover and beloved. As Jonathan Culler remarks, apostrophe—with its ever-present "images of in-vested passion" (138), its irreducible "strangeness" (140), and its ambivalent invocations and projections of identity (142, 148)—tends to suspend refer-ential temporality in favor of "a temporality of writing" (149). As such, it resists the narrative and "triumphs" in lyric poetry where, as Culler claims, "[n]othing need happen because the poem itself is to be the happening" (149). Culler's reading of apostrophe is important for my reading of Riera (and hers of Sappho), not only because "Te deix" is an extended, *narrative,* apostrophe in its own right, but also because the suspension of referen-tial temporality is, as I see it, one of the primary turns of virtuality.[8] It is here, indeed, that I find an additional risk, one that reaches far beyond the forever imminent erasure and impending dissolution of the print (in the sand) of the epigraph. This additional risk is, quite simply, the risk of textual entrapment, of *actually* believing that nothing need happen because the text, poetically speaking, is itself the happening. It is a risk I have been courting, perhaps at times too closely, but it is one that is motivated by the very problem of Sapphic authority, by what is, and is not, left behind in the passage from the epigraph to the story.

In the story, much is never written that was once written: the contents of letters lost, dissembled, and destroyed. This is not, to be sure, an instance of pure erasure, because it is only in and through writing that the unwritten, never-written, or erased is readable. The legacy of Sappho, of lesbian lyric, as we have seen, is also written as never-written by Riera, affirmed only to be denied.[9] It is no doubt possible to "read" such paradox as an indictment of the proper name and private property, as an intricate, if unwitting, *mise en cause* of a restricted economy of identity and meaning. But if Sappho is troubled in the citational act, that does not mean that Riera, as the ostensible author of this trouble, is in no wise implicated. Caught in the apostrophic play of presence and absence, Riera's I, the author's I, becomes as susceptible to erasure as the other authors' I, Sappho's I: problematizing authority it paradoxically (dis)authorizes itself as forever problematic. It becomes, that is, the elusive I of discourse, the poetic I, wavering between "Sappho" and "Riera," but ultimately *referring* to neither: or so a certain story goes. Another story, the one I want to read, remains suspicious of *resolving* the problem of authority by writing it out of reality altogether, "by loosing our empirical lives" (Culler 154). And among the things it most suspects is what is involved when the reality so problematized just happens to be one which has rarely known anything but problems, moral, political, economic, or otherwise. Thus, if the poetic I here chooses the absence of the woman, of the lesbian, it is also, at least in part, what the author's I, Riera's I, chooses: not necessarily in the relatively discrete sense of consciousness or intention, but in the radically indiscrete sense of something like a cultural trace which draws Riera, in subtle if problematic ways, into the virtualization of lesbianism.

I will return, toward the end of my reading, to the problem of authority, authorship, and (auto)biography as it pertains to Carme Riera herself, but for the moment I would like to expand on my metaphor of virtuality and follow some of the traces, or impressions, of writing by and about lesbians. Beyond the explicit body of the text, before, beneath, or beside it, theirs would appear to be a sort of remote presence, a virtual reality where, as Elizabeth Meese writes, "writing the lesbian means writing someone who does not yet exist" (3).[10] It is precisely the tension between being and becoming that underwrites many lesbian writers' concern with fragmentation and wholeness, recuperation and reinvention, reality and representation. Meese's lesbian : writing (the colon marks an expectant delay, a difficult promise), like Wittig's slit subjects (j/e, m/oi), are therefore attempts to move between the apparent absence and the unapparent presence of lesbians in literature: to graph an existence—in a public, published space—that has been deferred and denied, virtualized. What Wittig and Meese suggest is a mode of virtuality that does not simply doubt or deny reality, but that actually produces it, anew and with a difference. This productive virtuality, capable of generating a body from a footprint, love from a lost letter, or writing from silence and erasure, is not without its obstacles (Wittig's slashes and Meese's colons) and demurrals (Riera's Sapphic I always chooses the woman's absence, remember); but it does signify a process of cultural signification in which the imagination is itself a crucial aspect of the real. Thus, even as I read Riera's text against the specter of a dismissive, or negative, virtuality, I also bear witness to ("Jo pos per testimoni") the productivity of another virtuality which, like some rich and resistant reserve of meaning, realizes itself in writing.[11]

(Re)turning to the narrative, however, I find that the narrative itself is one of return. In other words, the narrator *returns*, as a twenty-three-year-old woman on the verge of death by childbirth, to textual activity, to letter writing; in so doing, she enables the return of other letters past, letters of youth and life and love, whose material loss nonetheless persists (the contents of these letters are not repeated or revealed). Returning in loss, these other letters function as scriptural revenants, tracing a spectral path through the body of the present letter, the one we read, the narrative. Encoded, indeed encrypted, in the actual space of the narrative, these lost letters of love guarantee a hollow—a sort of alternate, virtual space—for memory and mourning:

> No vaig oblidar-te. Cada nit t'escrivia i em guardava, curosament, les cartes en un calaix tancat amb pany i clau imaginant que un dia tu les llegiries una per una. Eren dues unces de felicitat, ja ho sé, pensar que les meves cartes formaven un caramull ben espès i podrien ocupar-te moltes hores de lectura, hores en què tornaries, inexorablement, a mi. (22)
> [I did not forget you. Every night I wrote to you and I put the letters carefully away inside a locked drawer, imagining that some day you

would read them all one by one. It was a . . . bit of happiness, I know, to think that my letters were adding up to a pretty thick pile which would keep you busy for many hours, in which you would inexorably be close to me (in which you would return, inexorably, to me)]. (64)

Measured by the thought of increasingly thick bundles of letters, happiness itself is bound up in the return, one day, of writing and reading. And yet, what is here today written or rewritten, what happily returns to us other readers, is writing as process, not as product. Contained in a safe place, this writing is, for us, without content: unreadable. But reading the unreadable, reading the imaginary return of a content absent, occult or inaccessible, of a love lived and lost, is just what this particular letter writing occasions. Carefully guarded under lock and key, these letters do not see the light of day; they are not released, one by one, and read. But they do return, inexorably, intimately, as the *desire* for a return: of the reader to the writer, of the beloved to the lover, of the woman to the woman.

The desire for a loving, literary return of one woman to another is construed, quite tellingly, as a matter of life and death. For among all the textual turns and returns, I find not just the phantasmal return of the dead to the living (of the dying lover/narrator/writer to the beloved/reader), but the uncannily real return of the living, of life, in reading, to the dead. Given my concern with the subject of lesbianism, this is a reading I do not undertake lightly; to do so may be to miss a compelling sign of deliverance. "Te deix, amor, la mar" is, after all, a story *delivered* in death. Believing her death to be imminent, the narrator/writer prepares for the delivery of her story, her letter, at the same time that she prepares for the delivery of her child. And if the coincidence of birth, death, writing, and reading were not significant enough, there is even more. Vital to the preparation for birth and death is the act of naming, a densely double act that binds the beneficiaries of both deliveries: "Pens que probablement no coneixeré la nina, perquè serà nina, n'estic segura, i no podré decidir, si no ho faig ara, el seu nom. Vull que li posin el teu, Maria, i vull, també, que llencin el meu cos a la mar, que no l'enterrin" (32) [I think perhaps I will not know the girl, because it will be a girl, I am sure, and I will not be able to decide her name if I do not do it now. I want her to be called Maria, like you, and I also want my body to be thrown into the sea, not buried] (68). Given the fact that she has withheld the name virtually until the last moment, the writer does not simply name her daughter *after* her lover; she names her *along with* her lover, in the same breath. In so doing, she fuses, at least nominally, her lover and her daughter; she delivers her daughter, with the letter that names her, to her lover, in one last loving return. Keeping in mind the title of the story, this may be indeed the finest pledge, the most loving token, imaginable.

The sea, of course, is explicitly designated as the token left, the pledge delivered, to the lover. But in the language of this letter, the sea implicitly infuses its name into others: la mar, amar, mare, Maria.[12] Given such verbal flow, rigid lines of property and propriety do not seem to hold: mother, daughter, lover are provocatively con-fused. What is more, the proper name of lover and daughter, refused until the end, is offered, albeit dimly, before: "Vaig dir el teu nom. No saps quantes vegades l'he repetit pronunciant-lo amb delectança infinita, amb el mateix gust que la primera vegada, després que em demanessis que no anteposés cap tractament a les cinc lletres que el formen, i que et parlés de tu" (26–27) [I said your name. You do not know how many times I have pronounced it with . . . infinite delight, with the same pleasure as the first time, after you had asked me to drop the formal treatment (preceding the five letters of your name and to call you, you)] (66). Counted though not recounted, the letters of the beloved's name remain here as shadowy, as virtual, as the words of the lover's other letters. Formed by five letters and freed from any potentially alienating treatment or title, rendered intimate (tu) and repeated with infinite delight, this name will later be revealed as that of the mother supreme, mare Maria. For the moment, however, the name of the mother, of Maria, is pronounced as a seemingly impossible desire. Piqued by her beloved's contrite assessment of their relationship ("Vaig ésser massa feble engrescant-me en aquella aventura de què et deus penedir" [I was weak enough to get involved in that affair you no doubt regret now]), the narrator/writer declares: "Parles com si fossis ma mare" [You talk as if you were my mother]. Far from taking offense, the beloved (Maria) quickly confesses that she certainly would have liked to have been so: "T'assegur que m'hauria agradat ser-ho" (27). This maternal exchange, articulated in a mood of (im)possibility, sets the stage for the intricate changes of position at the story's close: where the lover, as daughter, becomes a mother, and the beloved, as mother, a daughter; where Maria is the richly liquid name of lover, daughter, and mother, together. In what thus may be read as a cunning (in)version of Dante's "Vergine madre, figlia del tuo figlio," invoked in the final Canto of *Paradiso*, Riera creates a virgin mother, daughter of her daughter.[13] Maria, who has desired to be her lover's mother, is called (in) her lover's daughter. Repeated in the daughter, Maria bears the (im)possible mark of immaculate maternity, the name of the virgin, star of the sea [stella maris]. The lover, for her part, dies in the delivery of life, love, and names; unburied and dispersed into the sea, she is as much a ghost as a mother or daughter. The result of so many (con)fusions is a feminine trinity of Mother, Daughter, and Ghost, where the sign of the sea, the token of (lesbian) love, is all but essential.

In this love, the sea sweeps one woman into another, washes over time and space, and extends a mirific promise of deliverance, of salvation:

> Cada segon que passava—al rellotge de les nostres venes era la pleni-tud de migdia—, tremolava el meu cos acariciat per les teves mans, ens acostava amb fortíssims reclams a qualque misteriós, inefable lloc. Un lloc fora del temps, de l'espai (un migdia, un vaixell), fet a la nos-tra mida i on cauríem sense salvació. Sense salvació, car aquella era l'única manera de salvar-nos, perquè allà baix, al regne de l'absolut, de l'inefable, ens esperava la bellesa, que es confonia amb la teva-meva imatge quan em mirava a l'espill de la teva carn. I al recer segur, a l'escletxa més íntima del teu cos, allà, començava l'aventura, no dels sentits, de l'esperit, millor, que em portaria a conèixer el darrer batec del teu ésser, abocada, ja, per sempre més, al misteri de l'amor i de la mort. (21)
>
> [Every passing second—the clock of our veins was the fullness of noon—my trembling body caressed by your hands, brought us nearer to some mysterious, ineffable place that imperiously summoned us. A place out of time, out of space (noon, a boat), made to fit our measure, into which we would . . . fall without salvation. Without salvation, for that was the only way for us to be saved (the only way to save ourselves), because down there, in the realm of the absolute, the in-expressible, beauty was waiting for us, beauty dissolving in your-my image when I looked at myself in the mirror of your flesh. And in the safe shelter, in the most intimate cleft of your body, there the adven-ture began; an adventure not of the senses, but rather of the spirit, which would take me to knowledge of the last layer of your being, eternally destined for the mastery of love and death.] (64)

The site of this amorous encounter is the sea, or more precisely, the bodies of the lovers surrounded by the sea. Mysterious, ineffable, and absolute, it is where discrete identities collapse and bodies shimmer in a spiritual ad-venture, where the flesh is no longer opaque, but discerning. Yet what the flesh discerns is not its utter transparency or invisibility, not some dubious release through loss and disappearance. Instead, the body of the beloved retains a fleshly refuge, an intimate crevice or cleft [l'escletxa], which har-bors the secret pulse of being itself. In the fluid yet concentric movement from sea to body to crevice, lesbian desire assumes proportions at once almost mythic and divine. Nowhere is this more evident than in what I will call the eroticization of redemption. For at the moment of their first and most intensely described sexual encounter, the lovers fall without salvation. Without salvation, for that is the only way they can save themselves. This salvational trajectory is only apparently paradoxical; after all, as Hegel knows, the fall, without salvation, is the very condition of salvation. What is different is the direction and goal of this trajectory: allà baix: downward, inward, where intimate knowledge of the body is spiritual, where sexual union is a type of holy communion. Deliverance is to the desiring body, not from it.[14]

Along with deliverance, before and after it, there is reflection. As a mirroring of and on the spectacle and splendor of the flesh, it is a profoundly complex reflection.[15] It betokens, among other things, an equally complex relation between desiring subjects which, given the discursive dominance of heterosexuality, is further complicated by the fact that here the subjects and bodies of desire are lesbian. This fact, though subtly foreshadowed and suggested in various scenes, is suspensefully withheld, as I have said, until the act of naming at the narrative's close. Delivered at the moment of closure, the fact of lesbianism reopens the dilemma of desire and spurs a return to the body of the text that is itself quite revealing. And what such a return reveals, in retrospect, is the lingering concealment of the body even when it appears most naked:

> Lentament vas començar a despullar-te, t'anaves traient la roba sense mirar-me amb un gest que volia ser natural i que ara l'endevino impregnat de candor malaltís. Et cobrires el cos amb un llençol: potser tenies por de la meva por en veure'l nu, potser m'havies vist fugir rabent, espantada davant l'espectacle que, per primera vegada, s'oferia al meu davant. T'assegur que no em vaig esverar. Em bategaven els polsos amb força i dins meu anava arromangant els vels del més bell somni d'adolescent. Sempre m'havia semblat esplèndid, el teu cos; sentia en aquells moments curiositat, ganes de saciar els ulls mirant-lo tanta estrona com volgués. Per això vaig destapar-lo. I aparegué—m'en sentia creadora, car eren els meus ulls els que així el veien—, estatuari, perfecte. Els meus dits, com en un ritu, la llenegadissa dansa dels meus dits sobre la teva pell, tornaren a dibuixar els teus llavis i una per una les formes del teu cos. (20–21)

[You slowly started undressing, you took off your clothes without looking at me, assuming an air intended to seem natural but which I can now guess was pregnant with a sickly innocence. You covered up your body with a sheet: maybe you feared my fear on seeing it naked, perhaps you had imagined me running away, scared by the sight which was offered to me for the first time. I assure you I was not alarmed. My pulse was beating fast, and inside I was unveiling the most beautiful adolescent dream. I had always thought your body splendid. Now I felt curiosity and the desire to satiate my eyes looking at it for as long as I wanted to. That is why I uncovered you. And you looked—I was feeling creative, for my eyes were the ones seeing it so—statuesque, perfect. My fingers, as in a ritual, the slippery dance of my fingers on your skin outlined your lips and every one of the shapes in your body (my fingers . . . returned to outline, drew or sketched again, your lips and, one by one, the forms of your body).] (63)

Una per una: like the letters which the lover anticipates her beloved reading, one by one, here the lover recalls going back to outline or sketch [dibuixar] the forms of her beloved's body, one by one. There is an intricate temporality in Riera's story—a careful movement in time of and over and back to letters and bodies—which holds dear a specificity, unicity, and particularity within a general or generalized progression. This temporal movement may be sketched as metonymy. The form and figure of contiguity and displacement, metonymy is also, as a number of psychoanalytic critics have remarked, the form and figure of a certain femininity. Jane Gallop, for one, follows Luce Irigaray and argues that metonymy, although often figured as lack, inadequacy, insatiability, enchainment, and femininity, at once enables and maintains metaphor, itself figured as condensation, transubstantion, transcendence, liberation, and masculinity (124–29). In Riera's version, however, the metaphoric condensation of individual parts (names and identities) into a *feminine* trinity is itself implicated in a metonymic displacement of other parts (letters and bodies) that does not settle for some neo-spiritual transcendence, but that moves in the memory and desire of materiality.

Similarly, the movement of something seen and unseen, fearful and attractive, spontaneous and ritualistic, natural and artful or artificial, does not end in a synthesis in which parts and particles are overcome. Nor does the veiling and unveiling allow the body of love to be fully objectified or essentialized, totalized or mastered. Rather the lover remembers the body of the beloved in a particular process of creation and discovery, in an imaginative reinvention of something *already there,* something real: so real that it engages the lover in an intense intersubjective dynamic. If the body of the beloved is likened to a statue of the lover's making, that is not to say that it is a cold and static object under artistic control. For the lover's body is, in turn, undressed by the beloved, slowly, even morosely, "allargant amb la intenció de perpetuar-los, aquells minuts, malgrat la urgència del teu desig" (21) [(lengthening, with the intention of perpetuating them) those moments . . . in spite of the urgency of your desire] (63). Amid the urgency [urgència] and force [força] of desire, the two lovers perpetuate the body, effectively realizing it as more than a mere object in space. Extended over time, subjectivized and given to speculation, the body is a reality whose greatest guarantee is its capacity to change and to surprise. It is along similar lines that the changes, surprises, and realizations which attend the reader and the reading of Riera's text insure a return to, and a renewed reflection on, the particular complexity of relations of love, desire, and the body. This reflective (re)turn, which the "fact" of lesbianism motivates, may help to flesh out what is at stake in the fearful beauty which the lover confronts (the fear of a forbidden love, of realizing "the most beautiful adolescent dream," the fear of the fear of the other). But it goes even further, beyond the specificity of lesbianism to the (perhaps untheorizable) specificity of the myriad forms of love, forms changed and changing, imagined and invoked: one by one. This latter specificity, perpetually extended and withheld, is, furthermore, what saves and sustains the differences in *homo*sexual relations: sexual difference, as the condition of sexual communion, does not merely move between the sexes, but within them.[16]

In its depiction of sexual salvation and lesbian communion, and in its deployment of images of the sea, the body, and the mother, Riera's story bears witness to a confluence of concerns expressed in a considerable number of women's texts, theoretical as well as literary.[17] And yet, appealing as it may be, deliverance through the waters of the sea, the crevices of the female body, or the names of the mother, is here neither total nor definitive. The often painful pull of reality marks Riera's story as much as the glimpses of release. Separation, loss, and death frame the moment of erotic redemption, as do prohibition, fear, and control: this loving fusion is a memory within a memory motivated by the lovers' impending breakup.[18] This is not to deny that the fusion of bodies and the collapse of identity remain enticing notions in a world of violent divisiveness, but it is instead to point out that they too are invariably limited. As Bonnie Zimmerman puts it, "[w]e may blur the boundaries between self and other, subject and object, but there are boundaries there to be blurred" (11). However factitious they may be in the end, boundaries remain, here and now, decidedly factual. They divide and conquer, elevate and suppress, restrain and motivate. For lesbians, traditionally kept in bounds (checked and controlled) and out of bounds (marginalized and absent), the problems are particularly complex. To affirm lesbian identity is hence to affirm both the necessity and the possibility of repositioning boundaries, barriers, and limits that, for all their putative silence and invisibility, are already in position. Such affirmative action, linked to questions of agency and ability, does not however depend on the utter erasure of negativity, on the oblivion of suffering and pain. For Reina Lewis, positive images and affirmative signs are themselves limiting when they exclude the difficulties and weaknesses, the frustrations and failures, of actual existence. But the failure of certain lesbian relationships, even of lesbian identities, does not simply mean that lesbianism is virtualized once again. Better yet: failure may actually be one of the surest, slyest tokens of success.

The failure of literary lesbianism is linked to what I have called its virtualization (the idea that it is, even at its most intimately corporeal, only and forever an idea) and its virilization (the idea that it is molded and mediated through masculinity). Riera herself has elsewhere noted both the virtual absence or misrecognition of lesbian signs and the historical imperative to "masculinizar a la atrevida que osaba transgredir el rol que la sociedad patriarcal le había asignado" [masculinize the bold woman who dared to transgress the role which patriarchal society had assigned her] ("Literatura" 10).[19] A measure of just how pervasive the "failure" of lesbianism is perceived to be, may be found in what at first seems an unlikely source: recent Spanish narrative by women. Indeed, to judge by some of the most renowned works of Esther Tusquets, Ana María Moix, Montserrat Roig, and Carmen Martín Gaite, the fate of Riera's uncommon literary lovers is only all too common. In Tusquet's *El mismo mar de todos los veranos* (1978), the turbulent experience of lesbian love is broken by the return of and to the narrator's husband. In Moix's "Las virtudes peligrosas" (1982), lesbian experience is never more than intensely visual, dangerously virtual, with the two women constrained to love one another from afar. In Roig's *L'hora violeta* (1980), the constraints extend to the realm of reverie: in the midst of an erotic lesbian fantasy, Franco himself, in the form of Neptune, surges from the sea and separates the imaginary lovers. And in Carmen Martín Gaite's *El cuarto de atrás* (1978), lesbian love cannot even be imagined, let alone named: "Sólo se puede ser lesbiana cuando se concibe el término, yo esa palabra nunca la había oído" (192) [One can only be lesbian when one conceives (of) the term; I had never heard this word]. Riera's own "Jo pos per testimoni les gavines" (1977)—an intricate rewriting of "Te deix, amor, la mar"—effectively undoes the act of lesbian love through rejection, remorse, and suicide. In it, the narrator, likening herself to the beloved of the previous story, regrets *not having made lesbian love,* not merely because she leaves her own desire unfulfilled, but because she unwittingly leaves, or leads, her spurned would-be lover to suicide. As a result, lesbian love is here only retrospectively acknowledged as a desire that is at once overlaid with guilt and impossible of being realized in the flesh: as if Riera had to amend the sexual act, the lesbian fact, of the earlier text: correct it, unwrite and undo it, volatilize and virtualize it. Though virtualization may appear most resounding in "Jo pos" and *El cuarto de atrás,* all evince various degrees of virilization, of masculine control and mediation, as well. Whether it be the mysterious interlocutor and critic in Martín Gaite, the mythically clad dictator in Roig, the husbands in Tusquets and Moix, or even the editor in "Jo pos per testimoni," men are probing, prohibiting, and/or publishing presences that must, in one way or another, be reckoned with.

In "Te deix, amor, la mar," the presence of the father is, not surprisingly, central to the "failure" of the relationship. In contrast to the ultimately enabling presence of the (symbolic) mother, the father gives voice and body to a generalized, if somewhat nebulous, threat "en nom de la moral i els bons costums" (19) [in the name of morality and custom]; it is he who drives "l'escàndol públic" [public scandal] most forcefully home:

> Jo vaig haver de suportar rialletes i comentaris a mitja veu; més d'una vegada les companyes canviaven el tema de la conversa quan jo m'acostava, però ningú, tret de mon pare, no s'atreví a parlar-me a la cara, enfrontant-se amb la realitat. Tinc present encara la ganyota del seu rostre crispat, el to agre de la seva veu, però he oblidat les seves paraules, retenc tan sols dues frases que—com la tornada porfidiosa d'un anunci publicitari, que se't fica al cap, i repeteixes mentalment sense voler—m'han acompanyat tot sovint: 'Aquest és el camí de la depravació. T'enviaré a Barcelona, si això dura un dia més.' Ara puc explicar-t'ho. (19)
>
> [I had to put up with snickers and whispered comments; more than once my schoolmates changed the subject of conversation when I approached them, but nobody, except my father, dared to talk straight to me, facing reality. I still remember the grimace that contorted his face, the bitter tone in his voice, but I forget his words, I only remember two sentences, which have often echoed in my mind like the insistent slogan of a commercial that gets into your head and you unintentionally repeat over and over in your mind: "This is the way to depravity. I'll send you to Barcelona if this goes on for just another day."] (63)

The grimace of the face and the bitterness of the voice are here the troubling features of the father. They are also, by extension, the features of reality itself: repetitive, intrusive, interdictive. The father is, in effect, the bold guarantor of an ever-present principle of reality, by which pleasure is civilized, moralized, and checked. And like some cheap commercial ditty, he insidiously and unconsciously comes up again and again. If the narrator/ writer can now speak the truth about her father's role in the "failure" of the relationship, it may be for the (not so) simple reason that she is on the verge of death (and birth) and will finally be delivered from him; delivered because in recreating his image, without salvation, she can destroy it and save herself. Turning from her father, she can return—writing lovingly, consciously, and in one last act of deliverance—to her beloved. That this return, this deliverance, is achieved at the price of her life is not, of course, something that can be blissfully written off: after all, the sea is not just the loving token of triumph and endurance, but of mourning and yearning: "T'enyor, enyor la mar, la nostra" (32) [I miss (long for, yearn for) you, I miss the sea, our sea] (68). Such tension keeps every success and every failure from being definitive. Thus, if the success of amorous fusion and abiding memory fail to secure the idyll of lesbian love, failure has its own curious successes. Failure, in Riera's text, undergirds a dynamics of loss and symbolic recuperation; it contributes to an undeniably elegiac, lyrical tone; and it *succeeds,* more powerfully still, as an incisive commentary on the embattled reality of lesbian existence.

As fierce as compulsory heterosexuality is, part of what distinguishes Riera's two stories is the fact that men do bear and deliver letters of lesbian love, that they facilitate communication: correspondence runs through the husband in "Te deix" and the editor in "Jo pos." There is, however, no guarantee that these letters will be delivered or communication realized: "No sé si les circumstàncies et faran conèixer aquest escrit, ni tampoc si l'entendràs en el cas que en Toni te'l faci arribar tal com jo li he demanat" (31–32) [I do not know whether it will turn out that you ever see this piece of writing, or if you will understand it if Toni does give it to you as I asked him to] (68). Needless to say, the circumstances of delivery and communication are for me especially pressing, for they in a fashion replicate, or anticipate, those of my own written delivery, my own critical intervention. The place of men (Toni's, my own) in women's writing and in feminism, let alone lesbian feminism, is and will perhaps always be problematic; but the same holds true for the place of men outside feminism, where women's letters are typically refused, ignored, or erased. To read, write, deliver, or not, are thus never simple choices or acts of the will; instead they are highly reticular endeavors where power and subjectivity are in perpetual, often unpredictable, tension, and where complicity, in one form or another, is inevitable. There is, in short, no way to avoid the problem of these places, these letters, no way to be purely, wholly inside or outside. "Lesbianism," Zimmerman writes, "exists both inside and outside the dominant white structure" (6), at once engaged and disengaged with masculinity and heterosexuality. It is, in many respects, this persistently disjunctive overlapping of places and problems which so many feminists designate as the shape of critique. Be it a question of "double movement" (Zimmerman 6), "multiple translations and stagings" (Haraway 89), "double or multiple displacement" (Chow 103), "drift and transposition" (Meese 8), or even "the instability of all iterability" (Butler 28), the positions and strategies of critical resistance are restive and translateral. Double gestures, double voices, if not always more, figure a subject in process for whom there is no final word, no firmly set path. It is along lines such as these that I take Riera's appeal that the doublings and duplicities of women's voices be rescued and realized: "Recobremos nuestras dos voces, la que nos conecta a la razón y muestra nuestra capacidad intelectual, y la que nos une al atavismo, al mito, a la profecía. Contribuyamos a un encuentro definitivo entre Casandra y Mme. Curie" ("Literatura" 12) [Let us recapture our two voices, the one that connects us to reason and reveals our intellectual capacity, and the one that unites us to atavism, to myth, to prophecy. Let us contribute to a definitive encounter between Casandra and Mme. Curie]. Unwilling to consign myth to the dustbin of history, or to relinquish rationality to masculinity, Riera argues instead for a productive correspondence between a variety of positions, female as well as male.

Among the other positions, or transpositions, that Riera's double voices engage are those of nationality. "Te deix, amor, la mar" first appeared in a collection of short stories under the same title in May 1975, a few months before the death of Franco. In 1980, "Te entrego, amor, la mar, como una ofrenda," a considerably altered Castilian adaptation (for a considerably altered Spain), appeared in *Palabra de mujer*. Finally, in 1991, a translation from the original by Luisa Cotoner, "Te dejo, amor, en prenda el mar," was published in the well-established series Austral (Espasa-Calpe), a sure sign of commercial visibility, if not growing academic acceptance. There are, as a result, three "authorized" versions of this text, one in Catalán (or more precisely still, Mallorquín) and two in Castilian, one translated and adapted by Riera and one (translated by Cotoner) approved by her. Riera has made much of the play of boundaries and the imprint of translation on her writing. In at least two published interviews, she has underscored the connections between language, gender, sexuality, and nationality. She has done this in an exceptionally dense, deceptively simple, form: in the Catalán "nosaltres," in the pronoun "we." According to Riera, the narrative structure of "Te deix, amor, la mar" is "oriented" by the invisibility of sexual (inter)subjectivity in Catalán: "'nosaltres' sirve en catalán para los dos sexos, en castellano no lo puedo usar, perdiendo el maravilloso juego de ambigüedad que me daba el equívoco" (Racionero 15) ["nosaltres" (we) serves in Catalán for both sexes, in Castilian I cannot use it, because it loses the marvelous play of ambiguity]. Or again: "en catalán existe la posibilidad de utilizar el término en un sentido mucho más ambiguo que en castellano. 'Nosaltres' puede referirse a dos hombres, dos mujeres, o un hombre y una mujer, mientras que en castellano 'nosotras' es muy claro que son dos mujeres. Yo creo que la literatura que no tiene misterio ni ambigüedad, no interesa para nada; no hay cosa más tonta, más evidente que la verdad" (Nichols 209–10) [in Catalán it is possible to use the term in a much more ambiguous sense than in Castilian. "Nosaltres" may refer to two men, two women, or a man and a woman, while in Castilian "nosotras" clearly designates two women. I believe that literature which has neither mystery nor ambiguity is of no interest whatsoever; there is nothing more silly, more evident than truth]. These remarks illustrate not only a particular aesthetic (one that privileges mystery, ambiguity, play, suspense, and surprise), but the fact that subjects and communities see themselves and are seen by others, do not see themselves and are not seen by others, from a variety of perspectives.[20] For Riera, this aesthetics of (in)visibility and deferral translates into the ascendancy of Catalán over Castilian and sexual diversity over sexual establishment. Given the gravity of dominant social texts, continually (re)producing so-called majority perceptions, such ascendancy is difficult indeed. In the politics of translation, "we" will be intimately contested.

Along with its more obvious geopolitical implications, translation appears to operate on the level of sexual desire as well. It is, to be sure, translation of a special sort, similar, though not identical, to what Gayatri Spivak calls "the most intimate act of reading" (178). Among the range of intimate acts, translating Catalán to an ostensibly broader national public (where the Castilian subject is presumably not bilingual) is not so terribly unlike translating lesbianism to an ostensibly broader sexual public (where the reading subject is "normally" neither transsexual nor bisexual). In other words (and with translation it is always a question of other words), both the Catalonian in the Spanish system and the lesbian in the heterosexual system engage in a double movement, a translaterality, between major and minor languages, major and minor sexualities.[21] They move, that is, between spaces, some decidedly more receptive, more free and relaxed, than others. At their most assertive, they may deploy a heroic (or quasi-heroic) rhetoric of repression and resistance, silence and struggle. They may make tactical use of a varyingly intimate and (in)visible "we," "nosaltres," "we others." They, we others, may invoke the strength of an imagined community, a virtual nation, yet real in its motives and effects. Assimilationist or separatist, conciliatory or combative, they cannot help but confront, whatever their latest advances and achievements, an all too resilient and (in)visible *status quo*. Reading and writing lesbianism in Catalán is to confront, however, the ever greater translational problems that arise in the intersection of a minor language and a minor sexuality: problems of intelligibility, of visibility, to an established majority. What is more, these are also problems to (un)established minorities: the presence of Castilian speaking lesbians and homophobic Catalonians, for example, will necessarily effect the reading and writing of "nosotras" or "nosaltres," the relative (in)visibility and (un)intelligibility of lesbian existence.

Riera's reading of her writing is itself inevitably partial, more authoritative perhaps, but not for all that more true. For that matter, truth itself is, if Riera is to be truly believed, quite silly. The author's truth, silly as it may be, nevertheless lingers in some rather serious ways. The virtuality of lesbianism is such that Riera's own sexual orientation, her real experience, her true desire, itself (re)presents a problem of representation. For my part, I am decidedly less interested in the truth about Riera's desire per se than in the production and dissemination of representative truth-effects, especially as they pertain to the life and death of the author, the presence or absence of biography. The biographical bits published on Riera's life tend to ascribe, that is, a truthfulness to such textual factors in "Te deix" as age, birthplace, education, political involvement, and marital status: Riera, like the writer/narrator of "Te deix" was born and raised in Mallorca, studied in Barcelona, participated and was detained in at least one political demonstration, and met and married a male academic colleague. But if all these points of contact are true and real and authoritative, the same does not seem to hold for lesbian love; reality, yet again, would turn on the virtuality of lesbianism. "Lesbiana" may be missing from a number of dictionaries, from brief but uniform biographies, but the wistful signs of heterosexuality are everywhere to be found. On the covers, flaps, and blurbs of books, in critical introductions and annotated editions, in the directive queries of interviewers, in academic articles and journalistic reviews, biographical information continually orients the act of reading. We learn, for instance, that

Esther Tusquets has two children, that Carmen Martín Gaite was married to Rafael Sánchez Ferlosio, and that Carme Riera "no ha dejado de escribir, al principio ["Te deix" is, remember, one of Riera's first published efforts] con su hijo sentado en la falda y haciendo garabatos en el mismo papel" [has not stopped writing, at first with her son in her lap and scribbling on the same sheet of paper].[22] In fact, Luisa Cotoner's introduction for the Austral edition, *Te dejo el mar*, is positively brimming with the healthy signs of Riera's sexuality: the boyfriends she had, the man she married, even the young policeman she imaginarily seduced with "aquella cara de virgen andaluza" (16) [that face of an Andalusian virgin]. And yet, I repeat, these signs are wistfully heterosexual for the simple reason that, while they point to a sexually normative situation of matrimony and maternity, they can never fully exclude the shadow of lesbianism: lesbians may, after all, marry men and bear children: they may pass.

The ability to pass, to go undetected and to remain invisible, to *haunt* heterosexuality, together with the uncertainty, suspicion, and panic that such passing may generate, should not be underestimated.[23] Among other things, it may well motivate the (now embattled) notion of the death of the author. Traditional bio-historicism, once it has conceded the validity of an extratextual real, can exclude neither the reality of the repressed (information is not always readily available) nor its return (information may be retrieved or recreated through research). As a result, it cannot guarantee that something suspected or surmised, like lesbian experience, is wholly untrue: once points of contact have been affirmed between Riera and her text, she is, at least *virtually,* a lesbian. A more wily guarantee against the reality of lesbianism is to set reality itself off limits, to kill it. With Riera, as author, figuratively dead, the lesbian figures can have no claim to life, to reality; they can assume no correspondence, however ghostly, with those beyond. Cotoner, as Riera's translator, affirms with special authority the absolute distance of Riera from what she writes: "los personajes/'autores' de Riera responden clarísimamente a la voluntad de utilizar el modo narrativo en el que el autor/a tiene menos posibilidades de injerencia en el discurso de sus personajes, puesto que se queda completamente al margen de ellos, criaturas autónomas, con voz propia" (29) [Riera's characters/"authors" very clearly respond to the will to use the narrative mode in which the author has the least possibility for intervening in the characters' discourse, remaining completely marginal to them: autonomous creatures with their own voice]. Despite its celebratory and liberational tone, Cotoner's reading of autonomy and a voice of one's own keeps the text neatly in check. Here, authors and readers are eminently implicit, *always* inside the pages, passively receptive. Whatever the validity of such implicitness, Cotoner's narratological turn—with a reference to Baudrillard, the elusion of truth, and the disappearance of reality thrown in for good measure—is intriguing precisely because it comes on the heels of so much information about the author's life. Retreating from the world to the text, Cotoner writes as if translation between the two were no longer viable; as if, in revealing even one possible point of contact between Riera and her characters, she had already revealed too much.

Riera herself reveals a rather different position. Discussing her penchant for the epistolary form, Riera invokes a play of intimacy that always implicates the reader: "Cuando se escribe una carta se intenta explicar el punto de vista personal e intentar convencer, de la mejor manera posible, al destinatario, que siempre es el lector" (Aguado) [When one writes a letter one attempts to explain a personal point of view and to convince, in the best way possible, the addressee, who is always the reader].[24] Such personal address and engagement between writers and readers may cause some uneasiness; Guillem Frontera, for one, feels uncomfortably like an intruder, the accidental recipient of a letter intended for someone else (Introduction to *Te deix* 7). But to be addressed, engaged, is perhaps always discomforting, for it entails the responsibility of a response. This responsibility is especially acute when the reader is neither addressed nor implied in traditional terms (the ostensibly neutral reader of a great deal of narratology and reader-response theory is, as feminism shows, effectively heterosexual and male). Keeping the author apart from her characters, deadening her to their emotional signs, having her always choose the woman's absence, accordingly keeps the reader safe from any uncomfortable or risky response of her or his own, safe from responsibility. With lesbian love read (away) as a mere textual function, the reader need not respond, in any real ethical or political manner, to homophobia and heterosexism. And yet, lest such a response seem a simple yea or nay, there is always something more. Inasmuch as "Te deix" is not only a story of love between two women but of love between a student and a teacher, the reader, especially the academic reader, faces an additional responsibility: that of responding to relationships of love and sex across pedagogical positions.[25] This indeed is the dilemma written in and as Riera's story. To elude the call to responsibility by eluding reality, by virtualizing it, is to elude the text itself, to miss the ways it turns on, and returns to, the reader.

To close my reading, I want to return to the passage I evoked at the beginning, a haunting passage of letters and (en)closures, signs and seals, voices and visions, memory, mourning, and the vagaries of delivery. Disturbed by the prospect that her sense of longing and loss would itself be lost on her beloved, on her reader, the lover writes of her double-edged effort to safeguard and send it:

> la melangia, la recança i l'enyor no eren del tot perceptibles una vegada tancat el sobre i enganxat el segell. Algun cop, sota d'aquest, t'havia escrit amb lletra de puça qualque frase amorosa, per donar-te una sorpresa si et decidies a arrencar el segell sota la crida d'una veu baixa però precisa que t'indicaria el lloc del secret. (27)
> [my melancholy, my longing, and my grief were hardly perceptible once the envelope was closed and the stamp fixed on it. Occasionally, under the stamp, I would write with tiny letters (literally: with a flea's script) some love words, just to surprise you if you ever decided to take the stamp off because of a low but precise voice telling you the place of the secret.] (66)

There, below, in the space of a stamp, waits the writing of love. It is a writing, a love, sub-rosa, stamped with a certain sign of public approval but not stamped out. It may be sent, delivered, received, stamped and sent anew; it may be communally, commonly, circulated; and yet it may go, quite softly, unread, unheard. It is a writing with a voice, muffled and crying low; a writing that runs the risk both of remaining hidden and of being discovered; a writing in movement, lateral, translateral: always arriving at its destination, and yet not quite. For me, it arrives, and yet can never fully arrive, as the writing of lesbian love: arrives and yet does not, not because it is not real to me, but because I am in a sense virtual to it. It is a writing remembered and hence forever rewritten, a writing from a woman read dead (or dying: not buried, or in-terred, but scattered to the sea: mar, amar, mare, Maria) and to which the living, the life of the living, in reading, return: respond: assume responsibility. That, in reality, may be the truest delivery of all.

Notes

1 For Meese, " 'Lesbian' is a word written in invisible ink, readable when held up to a flame and self-consuming, a disappearing trick before my eyes where the letters appear and fade into the paper on which they are written, like a field which inscribes them. An unwriting goes on as quickly as the inscription takes (its) place. . . . Lesbian. This word which, like us, threatens to disappear is one we must demand, say over and over again, recalling it" (18). Within Hispanism, Amy Kaminsky's ground-breaking article on lesbianism and Latin American literature has, to my knowledge, yet to be replicated in the arena of Spanish literature. In fact, the most sustained treatment of lesbianism in Spain is found

outside of literary studies, in the sociological, legal, and historico-political work of such women as Lidia Falcón, Anabel González, Regina Bayo, and María Encarna Sanahuja Yll, and of such reviews as *Poder y Libertad: Revista Teórica del Partido Feminista de España* [Power and Freedom: Theoretical Review of the Feminist Party of Spain].

2   Woolley provides a history of the term: " 'Virtual' has a respectable pedigree as a technical term, going right back to the origins of modern science. It was used in optics at the beginning of the eighteenth century to describe the refracted or reflected image of an object. By the beginning of the nineteenth century, physicists were writing of a particle's 'virtual velocity' and 'virtual moment.' The word is still in use in atomic physics to describe the exotic behavior of subatomic particles that appear so fleetingly they cannot be detected. It has come a long way from its original use as the adjectival form of 'virtue', in the days when virtue itself meant to have the power of God" (60). Or the power of Man: for "virtual" is a term whose etymology is quite revealing. In it lies the troubling root of Western man (*vir*), his art and knowledge (virtu), his morality (virtue), perhaps indeed his reality (virility). Finding man lurking in virtuality, I find a shady truth of power, at least in its more virile (dis)embodiment as the phallus. For Lacan, "le phallus, même réel, est une ombre" (*Ornicar?* 42) [the phallus, even real, is a shadow]. The phallus casts a long shadow, true enough; but it is the shadow of a shadow, real in its effects yet ultimately without substance: forceful yet fraudulent. Virtual reality may serve as a similarly tense sign of male privilege, whose effects are technically real but whose root, ground, or foundation is implicated in unreality. The conflation of technological, textual, and sexual meaning in virtuality gives a twist to the virtualization (and virilization) of lesbian cultural production. For if the subject of lesbianism has been wrapped in invisibility, silence, negation, and loss; if it has been discounted as insignificant, reductive, utopian, romantic, essentialist, unnatural, immoral, or downright impossible; if, in short, it has been seen as more virtual than real, then to argue for both the virtuality of virility *and* the reality of lesbianism represents, I believe, an important strategy in ethico-political critique.

3   The work of Jean Baudrillard is here exemplary. But the refusal of the subject of experience runs through such thinkers as Lyotard, Derrida, Deleuze, and in a different measure, Foucault and Jameson. Paul Virilio states that "soon the only thing left will be for us to forget the specious distinction between the propagation of images or waves and that of objects or bodies" (74). Joan Scott claims that "the project of making experience visible *precludes* critical examination of the workings of the ideological system itself" (25, emphasis added). Making experience visible need not preclude critique, indeed it may be a necessary condition of it, especially for those subjects whose access to discursive legitimation has been precarious. Rather than falling into an either/or dilemma, I would argue for moving across and between experience and critique. Such double movement, which I liken to translation, would retain, as if under erasure, Scott's precluded term.

4   "[F]or skepticism that is certain of itself," writes Mark Taylor, "is insufficiently skeptical. When radicalized, skepticism becomes skeptical even of itself and thus must entertain the *possibility* of it own error" (22). And according to Fuss: "To insist that essentialism is always and everywhere reactionary is, for the constructionist, to buy into essentialism in the very act of making the charge; *it is to act as if essentialism has an essence*" (21, emphasis original).

5   To declare that the gentleman vanishes without a trace may be to underestimate his disguises. It may also be to ignore the fact that, as Donna Haraway notes, the author dies

just as "others in newly *unstably* subjugated positions" (96) set forth their own claims to authority and authorship. Or as Nancy Hartsock puts it: "Why is it, exactly at the moment when so many of us who have been silenced begin to demand the right to name ourselves, to act as subjects rather than objects of history, that just then the concept of subjecthood becomes 'problematic'?" (196).

6   The word "lesbiana" does in fact appear in recent editions of the Pompeu Fabra dictionary.

7   Here Sappho, as proper name, does not designate a property fully possessed, but one fragmented, absent, othered. As such it is curiously im-proper: a name of dispossession. On another level, Sappho's name is also linked to pedagogy (Sappho was herself a teacher): a point not entirely insignificant in a work where lesbian love occurs between a teacher and a student.

8   The lyrical quality of Riera's narrative is undeniable. Culler himself notes that, "[t]he tension between the narrative and the apostrophic can be seen as a generative force behind a whole series of lyrics" (149). It is just such tension—between the sequentiality of narrated events and the apostrophic engagement of an absent, beloved other—that constitutes the story's lyricism, its relation to the tenor of the epigraph.

9   On the significance of the counterfeited signature of Sappho, I defer to David Kurnick, a student in my class on sexuality and power in Hispanic culture. For Kurnick, "Riera includes the piece [from Sappho] not simply because it speaks of a lost lover, as does her story, but also because it engages issues of what can and cannot be represented and what will and will not be understood. The fragment addressed to a 'doncella,' appears clearly to describe a lesbian situation, especially with Sappho of Lesbos' name attached. But the piece prefigures the ensuing story not only in its female love-object, but in its condition as a 'fragmento jamás escrito.' Sappho's work is only partly extant, and only at certain historical times has been recognized as explicitly 'lesbian.' The work thus suffers doubly from a breakdown at the reception end of the process: Sappho has only been partially read, and only partially understood by those who have read her. . . . Riera displays her consciousness of the hostility language and tradition have shown to lesbian existence. Like Sappho's fragment, 'Te dejo' is a jeopardized text: at the final paragraph its narrator informs her lover (or tries to) that 'I do not know whether it will turn out that you ever see this piece of writing, or if you will understand it if Toni does give it to you as I asked him to' (68). Riera builds in a sense of contingency; the story (like Sappho's fragment) might be lost, obscured from possible readers—and if it does arrive it might (like Sappho's real, extant fragments) be misread or misunderstood."

10 Meese's writing echoes and plays with Wittig's now (in)famous statement that "les lesbiennes ne sont pas des femmes" (53), itself an echo and reconfiguration of Lacan's "il n'y a pas *La* femme." Catherine MacKinnon, for all her differences with such psychosexual theories, also points to the "virilization" and "virtualization" of lesbianism. As she puts it: "Lesbians so violate the sexuality implicit in female gender stereotypes as not to be considered women at all" (16).

11 To realize in writing is not, of course, the same as to write the real, in the sense of recording or reflecting it. To write and read lesbian experience as real, in and out of narrative fiction, is not to fix it once and for all, not to reduce it to a set of predetermined qualities and characteristics, but to loosen it from a nonspecific, or universal, virtuality which often works to keep readers, writers, and texts beyond such "unwritten" realities as homosexuality. By a nonspecific virtuality I mean something akin to what Wolfgang

Iser, conscious of the inter-activeness of reading, considers fundamental to literature: "the [literary] work . . . must inevitably be virtual in character, as it cannot be reduced to the reality of the text or to the subjectivity of the reader, and it is from this virtuality that it derives its dynamism" (106). Accepting the spirit of Iser's assessment, I would however attempt to flesh it out, render it more specific: because while all literary texts may be virtual, some seem to be more virtual than others. With the very reality of the lesbian text and the very subjectivity of the lesbian writer and reader already fraught with doubt and denial, literary work must here contend with a supplemental virtuality that threatens to undo Iser's dynamism before it can even begin. It is along these lines that Biddy Martin challenges "the only apparent basis of equality in disembodiment" (109).

12 Another possible name may well be "marica," a name which Riera herself examines: " 'marica'—'fag'—derives from 'María', assimilates and thereby degrades the subject to whom it is applied to the feminine world' ("Lenguaje" 193, my translation). Though designating male homosexuals, the word "marica," as Riera points out, is not merely homophobic; it is also misogynistic. "Marimacho," or "mannish woman," although not discussed by Riera, is similarly motivated.

13 I would like to thank my friend Linda Fleck for her suggestions here. It is interesting to note that Riera dedicates the Spanish version of the text to her daughter María (she dedicates *Palabra de mujer* to Francisco Llinás, her husband, and to Luisa Cotoner, her translator).

14 Riera explicitly links religion and sexuality: "Curiously, religion was what awoke sexual curiosity in the girls and boys of the '50's: 'blessed be the fruit of your womb' or words like 'circumcision,' 'virginity,' etc. presented us with problems of understanding which stimulated our interest. It was as if, from the beginning, religion called us to sex in order then to punish us implacably" ("Lenguaje" 187, my translation). Needless to say, punishment is rarely more implacable than when the sex in question is homosexual. On a related front, Jaume Martí Olivella reads the scene of sexual encounter as a "perfect moment of fusion, of love in the 'depth' of the sea-mirror, the flesh of the desired, non-confrontational other is . . . a beginning and an end in itself" (24). He also draws interesting connections between Riera, Tusquets, and Irigaray's *Amante marine*.

15 The vision or sight of the body is a central feature of "Te deix." The story opens with the narrator so positioned as to be incapable of seeing what she desires: "*I cannot see* the sea because it lies far away on the other side of the city. . . . I miss it only because *when I see it* I know that you are on the other side of it, and that from sea to sea, from shore to shore there is less distance than from city to city" (61, emphasis added). The problem of sight and distance recurs throughout the story, at times issuing in a close communion of vision: "My eyes, which were your eyes, for I saw the world as you looked at [saw] it, perceived nuances, colors, shapes, details that you thought surprising and new" (62). This mystical, all-consuming ability to see—"One day . . . you told me that I was staring at you . . . as if I were searching . . . your soul" (62)—reveals the body as the site (sight) of the soul: a revelation which resonates throughout the text.

16 My argument is simply for the heterogeneity of homosexuality (or homosexualities). Heteroglossia, heterogeneity, heteronymy, and other signs of contemporary discourse may invoke the seemingly same term of heterosexuality. Without disputing the value of the former, I do dispute a tendency to homogenize this series by valorizing heterosexuality (as the desire of and for difference) over homosexuality (as the desire of and for sameness): as if sexual difference were impossible between women or between men, in-

deed as if sexual difference were impossible within any *one* subject. For similar concerns, see Butler (23), Warner (206), Sedgwick (23), and Fuss (111).

17   Irigaray's "La 'mécanique' des fluides," Wittig's *Le corps lesbien,* and Kristeva's "Stabat Mater," explore the possibilities and pitfalls of liberation around the sea, the body, and the mother. Roberta Johnson sees the sea as "a metonym for the female identity of the absent lover" in Riera's fiction (154).

18   Speaking of memory, the subtitles that Riera gives to the Castilian translations of her text are interesting: "La memoria impenitente" [The Impenitent Memory] in *Te dejo el mar* and "Bajo el signo de una memoria impenitente" [Under the Sign of an Impenitent Memory] in *Palabra de mujer.*

19   In her interview with Nichols, Riera remarks that, while homosexuality was at least recognized (though not accepted) in men, "homosexual women did not exist—were not recognized as existing—at that time. Even in the Pompeu Fabra Dictionary [of Catalán], the word only appears related to homosexual men" (209, my translation). Elsewhere Riera refers to dictionaries as dictatorial and distorted ("Lenguaje" 186).

20   Perspective includes the unseen as well as the seen; by which I mean that subjects and communities are often blind and invisible to themselves. The play of blindness and insight inflects, in some quite political ways, both suspense and surprise in Riera's story. As Geraldine Nichols remarks, "[t]he regressive ending of 'Te deix' compels readers to reevaluate the whole experience: the story and their facile acceptance of the heterosexist assumptions that overdetermined their (mis)reading of it" ("Stranger" 40). Heterosexist assumptions are responsible for other misperceptions as well. In interviews with Nichols and Racionero, Riera refers to readers who read as missing, and wanted to replace, an accent over the final letter of Maria. Marià is, of course, a male marked name. The presence or absence of a diacritical sign (here a phallic marker) thus signifies the presence or absence of a certain sexuality. Readers who wanted this sign, who desired it, in the same stroke desired the "reassuring presence" of both masculinity and heterosexuality.

21   Aguado ("Suggestive Power") and McNerney comment on the dual subordination of Catalonians and women in relation to Riera's work.

22   The quote is from Cotoner's introduction to *Te dejo el mar.* On the back cover of the 1978 edition of *El mismo mar de todos los veranos,* one of the few Spanish novels with an "openly lesbian" plot, we read that Tusquets "has two children." No mention is made of the children of male authors. On the back covers of such works as *Retahílas* and *Entre visillos,* we read that Martín Gaite married Sánchez Ferlosio, though no mention is made of Martín Gaite on the back covers of Sánchez Ferlosio's *El Jarama* and *Alfanhuí,* despite the fact that they are published in the same series by Destinolibro.

23   For "homosexual panic," see Sedgwick (19–22). With "passing," I do not mean that it is always a conscious act, for the simple reason that the subject does not necessarily fix his or her sexual identity for all times and all places. Nor do I mean that there is some essential truth under a public mask: as if "coming out" were always and everywhere the same; as if a heterosexually marked past were always and everywhere a lie; as if desire itself functioned in terms of either/or oppositions. The question is thus not whether Riera is or is not lesbian, passes or not as straight, but that such "passing" is motivated in a myriad of often subtle ways (such as biographically marked and commercially marketed signs in introductions, interviews, and book jackets as well as in the connections and contrasts between the author's life and the author's work). It is in this sense that Riera— as is clear from the rather anxious beginning of the sequel to "Te deix," "Jo pos"—cannot

control how she will be imagined or perceived by her readers. Given the overwhelming predominance of heterosexual scenes and sights in society, as soon as Riera makes lesbianism visible, she makes her own sexuality, whatever it may "really" be, a not so invisible concern.

24 Akiko Tsuchiya examines the interplay of epistolary form and narrative seduction in Riera's *Qüestió d'amor propi* (1987).

25 Lesbian desire between teachers and students appears in at least two other well-known texts by Spanish women: *Julia* by Ana María Moix and *El mismo mar de todos los veranos* by Tusquets.

Works Cited

Aguado, Neus. "Carme Riera or the Suggestive Power of Words." *Catalán Writing* 6 (1991): 53–60.

————. "Epístolas de mar y de sol: Entrevista con Carme Riera." *Quimera* 105 (1991): 32–37.

Bayo Falcón, Regina. "La dictadura heterosexual." *Poder y Libertad* 1 (June 1980): 51–54.

Bright, Susie. *Susie Bright's Sexual Reality: A Virtual Sex World Reader.* Pittsburgh: Cleis Press, 1992.

Butler, Judith. "Imitation and Gender Insubordination." *Inside/Out: Lesbian Theories, Gay Theories.* Ed. Diana Fuss. New York: Routledge, 1991. 13–31.

Chow, Rey. "Postmodern Automatons." *Feminists Theorize the Political.* Ed. Judith Butler and Joan W. Scott. New York: Routledge, 1992. 101–17.

Culler, Jonathan. *The Pursuit of Signs: Semiotics, Literature, Deconstruction.* Ithaca: Cornell University Press, 1981.

Fuss, Diana. *Essentially Speaking: Feminism, Nature & Difference.* New York: Routledge, 1989.

Gallop, Jane. *Reading Lacan.* Ithaca: Cornell University Press, 1985.

Glenn, Kathleen M. "Authority and Marginality in Three Contemporary Spanish Narratives." *Romance Languages Annual* 2 (1990): 426–30.

González, Anabel. *El feminismo en España, hoy.* Bilbao: Zero, 1979.

Gould Levine, Linda. "The Censored Sex: Woman as Author and Character in Franco's Spain." *Women in Hispanic Literature: Icons and Fallen Idols.* Ed. Beth Miller. Berkeley: University of California Press, 1983. 289–315.

Haraway, Donna. "Ecce Homo, Ain't (Ar'n't) I a Woman, and Inappropriate/d Others: The Human in a Post-Humanist Landscape." *Feminists Theorize the Political.* Ed. Judith Butler & Joan W. Scott. New York: Routledge, 1992. 86–100.

Hartsock, Nancy. "Rethinking Modernism: Minority vs. Majority Theories." *Cultural Critique* 7 (1987): 187–206.

Iser, Wolfgang. "Interaction between Text and Reader." *The Reader in the Text: Essays on Audience and Interpretation.* Ed. Susan R. Suleiman & Inge Crosman. Princeton: Princeton University Press, 1980. 106–19.

Johnson, Roberta. "Voice and Intersubjectivity in Carme Riera's Narratives." *Critical Essays on the Literatures of Spain and Spanish America.* Ed. Luis T. González-del-Valle & Julio Baena. Boulder, Colo.: Society of Spanish and Spanish-American Studies, 1991. 153–59.

Kaminsky, Amy. "Lesbian Cartographies: Body, Text, and Geography." *Cultural and Historical Grounding for Hispanic and Luso-Brazilian Feminist Literary Criticism.* Ed. Hernán Vidal. Minneapolis: Institute for the Study of Ideologies and Literature, 1989.

Kurnick, David. "The Closet, Spectatorship, and the Love Object in *La ley del deseo* and 'Te dejo el mar'." Unpublished paper (January 1993).

Lacan, Jacques. "*Hamlet,* par Lacan." *Ornicar?* 26–27 (1983): 5–44.

Lewis, Reina. "The Death of the Author and the Resurrection of the Dyke." *New Lesbian Criticism: Literary and Cultural Readings.* Ed. Sally Munt. New York: Columbia University Press, 1992. 17–32.

MacKinnon, Catharine A. "Feminism, Marxism, Method, and the State: An Agenda for Theory." *Feminist Theory: A Critique of Ideology.* Ed. Keohane, Rosaldo, & Gelpi. Chicago: University of Chicago Press, 1982. 1–30.

Martí Olivella, Jaume. "Homoeroticism and Specular Transgression in Peninsular Feminine Narrative." *España Contemporánea* 5.2 (1992): 17–25.

Martin, Biddy. "Sexual Practice and Changing Lesbian Identities." *Destabilizing Theory: Contemporary Feminist Debates.* Ed. Michèle Barret and Anne Phillips. Stanford: Stanford University Press, 1992. 93–119.

Martín Gaite, Carmen. *El cuarto de atrás.* Barcelona: Destino, 1978.

McNerney, Kathleen. *On Our Own Behalf: Women's Tales from Catalonia.* Nebraska: University of Nebraska Press, 1989.

Meese, Elizabeth A. *(Sem)Erotics: Theorizing Lesbian : Writing.* New York: New York University Press, 1992.

Moix, Ana María. *Julia.* Barcelona: Seix Barral, 1969.

———. *Las virtudes peligrosas.* Barcelona: Plaza & Janés, 1985.

Nichols, Geraldine C. *Escribir, espacio propio: Laforet, Matute, Moix, Tusquets, Riera y Roig por sí mismas.* Minneapolis: Institute for the Study of Ideologies and Literature, 1989.

———. "Stranger than Fiction: Fantasy in Short Stories by Matute, Rodoreda, Riera." *Monographic Review/Revista Monográfica* 4 (1988): 33–42.

Ordóñez, Elizabeth. "Beginning to Speak: Carme Riera's *Una primavera para Domenico Guarini.*" *La CHISPA '85: Selected Proceedings.* Ed. Gilbert Paolini. New Orleans: Tulane University, 1985.

Racionero, Luis. "Entrevista con Carmen Riera: 'Cada vez tenemos menos imaginación'." *Quimera* 9–10 (1981): 14–16.

Rheingold, Howard. *Virtual Reality.* New York: Simon & Schuster, 1991.

Riera, Carme. "El lenguaje sexual." *Poder y Libertad: Revista Teórica del Partido Feminista de España* (1981): 186–93.

———. "I Leave You, My Love, the Sea as a Token." Trans. Alberto Moreiras. In *On Our Own Behalf: Women's Tales in Catalonia.* Lincoln: University of Nebraska Press, 1989.

———. *Jo pos per testimoni les gavines.* Barcelona: Editorial Planeta, 1990.

———. "Literatura femenina: ¿Un lenguaje prestado?" *Quimera* 18 (1982): 9–12.

———. *Palabra de mujer (Bajo el signo de una memoria impenitente).* Barcelona: Editorial Laia, 1980.

———. *Te deix, amor, la mar com a penyora.* Barcelona: Editorial Laia, 1975.

———. *Te dejo el mar.* Trans. Luisa Cotoner. Madrid: Espasa-Calpe, 1991.

Robson, Ruthann. *Lesbian (Out)law: Survival Under the Rule of Law.* Ithaca: Firebrand Books, 1992.

Roig, Montserrat. *L'hora violeta.* Barcelona: Edicions 62, 1980.

Sanahuja Yll, María Encarna & Lidia Falcón O'Neill. "Lesbianismo y feminismo." *Poder y Libertad: Revista Teórica del Partido Feminista de España* (1981): 98–109.

Scott, Joan W. "'Experience'." *Feminists Theorize the Political*. Ed. Judith Butler and Joan W. Scott. New York: Routledge, 1992. 22–40.

Sedgwick, Eve Kosofsky. *Epistemology of the Closet*. Berkeley: University of California Press, 1990.

Spivak, Gayatri Chakravorty. "The Politics of Translation." *Destabilizing Theory: Contemporary Feminist Debates*. Ed. Michèle Barret and Anne Phillips. Stanford: Stanford University Press, 1992. 177–200.

Taylor, Mark. *Nots*. Chicago: University of Chicago Press, 1993.

Tsuchiya, Akiko. "The Paradox of Narrative Seduction in Carmen Riera's *Cuestión de amor propio*." *Hispania* 75.2 (1992): 281–86.

Tusquets, Esther. *El mismo mar de todos los veranos*. Barcelona: Editorial Lumen, 1978.

Virilio, Paul. *The Aesthetics of Disappearance*. Trans. Philip Beitchman. New York: Semiotext(e), 1991.

Warner, Michael. "Homo-Narcissism; or, Heterosexuality." *Engendering Men: The Question of Male Feminist Criticism*. Ed. Joseph A. Boone and Michael Cadden. New York: Routledge, 1990. 190–206.

Woolley, Benjamin. *Virtual Worlds: A Journey in Hype and Hyperreality*. Oxford: Blackwell, 1992.

Zimmerman, Bonnie. "Lesbians Like This and That: Some Notes on Lesbian Criticism for the Nineties." *New Lesbian Criticism: Literary and Cultural Readings*. Ed. Sally Munt. New York: Columbia University Press, 1992. 1–15.

David Román

*Teatro Viva!: Latino Performance and
the Politics of AIDS in Los Angeles*

The patriarch of a dysfunctional Latino family living in the barrio is scandalized that his son has brought home the neighborhood's two cross-dressers. "My son's a homo!" he cries waving a pistol. The cross-dressers retaliate by biting the man's arm and announcing that they both have SIDA [AIDS]. The father, horrified of contagion, shoots. This scene appears as a segment of "Doña Flora's Family" one of the eleven skits in *S.O.S.* written, directed, and performed by Culture Clash, an immensely popular Latino comedy theatre troupe. Such a pathological, melodramatic, indeed ridiculous scene provides an entrance to an essay that will begin to locate the discourses by and about Latino gay men in contemporary U.S. theatre, discuss the ways that AIDS is imagined and/or experienced in Latino communities, and offer a cultural practice that addresses both (homo)sexuality and AIDS. My aim here is to provide a critical methodology that at once contextualizes various contemporary Latino performances that discuss AIDS and chronicles the important and often neglected work of Latino gay men in the theatre.[1]

    S.O.S. premiered in the summer of 1992 at the Japanese American Cultural and Community Center (JACCC) in the heart of Little Tokyo in downtown Los Angeles as part of the Celebrate California Series which promotes "multicultural diversity through the arts."[2] Tickets for the three-day run including an added matinee at the 800 seat capacity theatre immediately sold-out. Upon arriving at JACCC, it became clear that Culture Clash's appearance was much more than a night at the theatre for most of the Latinos in attendance. Parents brought along their children. Long-standing community leaders were present alongside Chicano youth involved in street activist politics. For all appearances, it seemed a family affair; an in-house Latino assemblage but with an open invitation addressed to all people disturbed by the recent events in Los Angeles.[3] After all, we were gathering in Little Tokyo not East Los Angeles. The idea of Culture Clash at JACCC seemed to be the type of gesture necessary to continue the "healing" of Los Angeles; a bi-cultural occasion where two communities— the Asian American and the Latino—could begin to understand each other a little better, in this case through the theatre. In the statement printed in the performance program, Culture Clash foregrounds the political nature of their work: "How can we ignore the quincentennial, the Rodney King case, AIDS, the NEA censorship and the election of yet another Republican? Time for a 'S.O.S.', a signal of distress."

Culture Clash further called attention to the political potential of the event by offering their Saturday night performance as a fundraiser for the Latino activist organization PODER, the Pro-Active Organization Dedicated to the Empowerment of Raza. "Comedy for these urgent times," the S.O.S. publicity promo promised; and "necessary funds for the needs of the Latino community of Los Angeles," PODER activists told us before the performance. Given the multitude of problems facing Latinos in Los Angeles—deportation, economic exploitation, gang warfare, inadequate health care—such an evening held the possibility of offering at least some relief for those able to afford the ten dollar tickets. In "S.O.S. Rap," an early and particularly effective scene, one of the performers catalogs a litany of these social ills repeatedly returning to the hard refrain, "todo tiene que cambiar" [everything must change]. In S.O.S., as in all of their work, Culture Clash sets out to denaturalize Anglo superiority and reclaim Latino culture and history from the perspective of La Raza. Their primary method to achieve this goal is through humor, parody, and social satire.

Throughout S.O.S., Culture Clash proceeded to critique many of the institutions and hegemonic processes that oppress Chicanos and Latinos, but as the scene in Doña Flora's family demonstrates, they fell short of imagining Latino gays and lesbians as part of the social utopia posited in their performance. Imagined gays were attacked in one scene, raped in another ("American Me Tail")[4] and lesbians, as usual, were not to be found. AIDS was presented as a threat posed by gays and women to unsettle the family and la raza. In another scene, "Angel's Flight," one of the performers positioned underneath a tapestry of La Virgen de Guadalupe explains to the men in the audience that they must use condoms to protect themselves from AIDS. But as the iconography of the scene too obviously suggests, men invoke the madonna to protect them from the whore. Women in Chicano culture, as Cherríe Moraga has argued, are continually placed within this rigid madonna/whore binary system (Moraga, Almaguer). In a gesture which immediately recalled Panamanian artist and activist Rubén Blades's appearance in the PBS video *AIDS: Changing the Rules* where Blades, talking directly to straight men, put a condom on a banana, the performer in "Angel's Flight" places a condom on an ear of corn. Douglas Crimp's complaint against the condom and the banana scene of 1987 still rings true today: "evidently condoms have now become too closely associated with gay men for straight men to talk straight about them" (Crimp 255). In their efforts to preserve *la raza* from the oppression of centuries of Anglo domination, Culture Clash imagines in *S.O.S.* a Chicano social usurpation. Their new L.A., however, fails to address the social networks—including the theatre—that oppress many Latinos outside the subject position of the straight Chicano male. If the performance, by nature of its stage venue at JACCC, is to some degree an attempt to form coalitions with other people of color, the ideal spectator is still assumed to be a heterosexual male.

In many ways, Culture Clash's performances can be best understood as participating in a long history of Chicano and Latino theatre practices and conventions originating in the United States as early as the 1840s. According to Latino theatre historian Nicolás Kanellos, this theatrical tradition has demonstrated "the ability [of Latinos] to create art even under the most trying of circumstances, social and cultural cohesiveness and national pride in the face of race and class pressures, [and] cultural continuity and adaptability in a foreign land" (Kanellos xv). Culture Clash comes out of a theatrical trajectory that recalls both the energy of the Mexican carpa [traveling circuses] of the 1890s and the political activism of El Teatro Campesino in the 1960s.

Much of the work of Culture Clash bears the influence of Luis Valdez, founder of El Teatro Campesino, who believed that the theatre should play a vital role in the awakening of the Chicano social consciousness. Like Valdez, Culture Clash insists that the theatre must remain oppositional to the exploitative practices of the dominant Anglo culture. And like El Teatro Campesino, Culture Clash posits a type of cultural nationalism with all of its inherent contradictions and problems. If, on the one hand, cultural nationalism fosters a sense of cultural pride, it also conflates all Chicano experience into a unified Chicano subject. In short, by failing to account for the differences among Latinos, Culture Clash inadvertently performs the very limits of the identity politics they invoke.[5]

Chicana feminist cultural critic Yvonne Yarbro-Bejarano has written on the female subject in Chicano theatre and the ways by which the representational systems of Chicano theatre privilege heterosexual men. Yarbro-Bejarano argues that it is precisely the operations of cultural national-ism in Chicano theatre that have led to the uncritical "reinscription of the heterosexual hierarchization of male/female relationships" (Yarbro-Bejarano, "Female Subject" 132). Yarbro-Bejarano's work on demystifying the conventions of Chicano theatre not only exposes the sexist ideology normalized in the materials of production, but also serves as a critical model to interrogate its homophobic tendencies as well.

Starting in the late 1970s, Chicanas in the theatre began organizing and networking resulting in all-women *teatros* and a series of plays that explored women's issues. Moreover, after years of struggle, Chicanas have gained entry in traditionally male-centered venues and collectives. Chicana lesbian playwright Cherríe Moraga, for example, presents the strongest critique of patriarchal and heterosexist attitudes.[6] Her plays, as Yarbro-Bejarano argues, demonstrate how female sexuality is constructed and contained within the mythical model of La Malinche, Cortés's supposed mistress and translator. La Malinche serves as a "signifier of betrayal, through which the historical experience of domination is spoken in the language of sexuality" (Yarbro-Bejarano, "Female Subject" 135). The insistence of the *chingón/ chingada* dynamic (fucker/fucked; active/passive) remains perhaps the most prevalent sociosexual system in Chicano and Latino culture. Emerging from the experience of colonization, the *chingón/chingada* dynamic locks women into subordinate roles, inscribes inflexible definitions of mascu-linity and femininity, and on a larger scale, becomes the surveillance test of true nationalism. Whoever is penetrated, in other words, is immediately interpreted by dominant Latino culture as passive. Passivity, within this system, is understood to mean open to sexual betrayal and, therefore, a threat to the nation.

The scenes in *S.O.S.* where anal rape is staged as male humiliation and punishment, for example in "American Me Tail," or where homosexu-ality—as an identity—is introduced only to be annihilated in "Doña Flora's Family," signal as much to this kind of cultural nationalism where the asser-tion of male power mitigates male anxiety regarding the loss of power in a culture of domination, as they do to the homophobic and sexist enterprise that constructs passivity as threatening and degrading. Rather than decon-structing the *chingón/chingada* polarization, Culture Clash participates in the continual reinscription of a binary sociosexual system that insists on fixed gender roles and rigid socially constructed meanings for sex acts. Chi-cano power, as staged by Culture Clash in *S.O.S.*, remains in the hands of impenetrable men who exercise their privilege in continual displays of phallic domination; a socio-masturbatory flaunting meant to eroticize these representations of power in an unending exhibition of seduction.

Despite the fact that Chicana and Latina feminists have gone to great lengths to critique the representations of women in the theatre, many plays continue to offer problematic if not degrading depictions of women. (The women actors who have appeared in Culture Clash's three productions *The Mission, Bowl of Beings,* and *S.O.S.* never speak.) And yet the fact that more plays by Latinas are included in national theatre festivals and that feminist concerns are beginning to be voiced in conventional theatre forums offers a good indication of their success.[7] While women in various areas of the theatre have slowly gained some degree of recognition, Latino gay male playwrights have historically been denied a place on the stage. One exception, as Yarbro-Bejarano notes, was Edgar Poma's play about a Chicano gay man coming out to his family. Poma's *Reunion,* produced in 1981, "broke a fifteen year silence on homosexuality within the Chicano theatre movement" (Yarbro-Bejarano, "Female Subject" 145). Yarbro-Bejarano's explanation of the play's reception is worth quoting in full:

> [*Reunion*] was performed to large community audiences at the Cultural Center in the heart of San Francisco's Mission District. Performances were followed by lengthy, lively discussions. The exclusion of a performance of this play during the TENAZ [National Teatros de Aztlán] Eleventh Festival in the Fall of 1981 revealed the depth of resistance to considering the Chicano theatre movement an appropriate vehicle for the exploration of questions of sexuality. This attitude was further demonstrated during the Festival by the virtual boycott of a workshop on *Reunion* and the heated arguments by Latin-Americans and Chicanos alike against a resolution condemning sexism and homophobia during the general assembly. Dialogue has recently been reopened within the Chicano community by a production of *Reunion* in June 1986 in Tucson Arizona by Teatro Chicano, a member group of TENAZ headed by a woman, Sylviana Wood. (145)

The problems encountered with productions of *Reunion* are typical of the resistance to gay issues in contemporary Chicano and Latino cultural discourse. Performances that foreground the perspective of gay men—as was the case with women previously—are viewed as incongruent with the larger political movement. Gay issues, as in most communities of color, are often understood by the reigning heterosexist ideology of cultural nationalism to be symptomatic of white domination. For Latinos, since

Catholicism rules as the religion of the majority and the church remains an infallible institution, homosexuality is knowable only as unnatural and therefore unacceptable. The combined rhetoric of cultural nationalism and Catholic dogma eradicates any identity based on homosexuality.

Even among straight activists and cultural theorists who work out of the Chicano movement, homosexuality is not an issue comfortably discussed. In the recent groundbreaking anthology *Criticism in the Borderlands: Studies in Chicano Literature, Culture, and Ideology,* for example, the editors—two of the leading Chicano critics in the United States—announce that their project "should offer an important cultural perspective absent to an international scholarly community" (7). Essays address a broad sampling of issues but not one of the fifteen essays is authored by a self-identified gay or lesbian. Moreover, the few essays that discuss gay and lesbian writers fail to address the ways in which sexuality informs both their work and its reception.[8] This process of neglect inevitably produces a normalized conception of heterosexuality—or heterosexism—that is never critically challenged; homosexuality remains taboo.

Current counter-hegemonic critical interventions such as *Criticism in the Borderlands,* which set forth the agenda for the issues open to discussion for cultural theorists, refuse to provide a forum for gay and lesbian concerns. AIDS, moreover, is never mentioned in the essays, an unconscionable omission given that Latinos—and heterosexual Latinos in particular—constitute one of the largest growing groups of people affected by HIV and AIDS. By the end of 1991, for example, Latinos accounted for a total of 10,276—or 28 percent—of the cumulative AIDS cases in New York City alone. Thirty-three percent of the cumulative AIDS cases in New York City among women were Latinas, 27 percent of cases among men were Latino. Injection drug use continues to be the leading mode of HIV transmission: Latino men at 54 percent, Latinas at 60 percent (Maldonado 13). Nationally, according to the Centers for Disease Control, Latinos accounted for 16.5 percent of people diagnosed with AIDS. While the majority of Latinos with AIDS continues to be gay or bisexual men, women and injection drug users represent an increasing proportion of AIDS cases.[9]

In the introduction to their anthology, Hector Calderón and José David Saldívar write: "*Criticism in the Borderlands* is an invitation, we hope, for readers—(Pan-)Americanists, cultural studies critics, feminists, historians, and anti-racists—to remap the borderlands of theory and theorists" (7). But if, as Calderón and Saldívar argue, studies of U.S. culture that fail to consider the centuries of Mexican-mestizo presence "will of necessity be incomplete," (7) they will need to recognize that studies that fail to incorporate a critical analysis of sexuality or the affects of AIDS in Chicano and/ or Latino cultures will be not merely "incomplete" but, as Eve Sedgwick succinctly states, "damaged" (Sedgwick 1).

There is no question in my mind that the work of Culture Clash and the individual and collective work of the cultural theorists in *Criticism in the Borderlands* are necessary, indeed welcome, interventions in an Anglo culture of domination and exploitation. However, these same sites of intervention—theatre and theory—must also be interrogated in such a way that denaturalizes the assumptions and destabilizes the privileges set forth in each. Cultural theorists and activists need to recognize and counter the racist and homophobic practices that oppress all Latinos. If the diverse and heterogeneous Latino populations in the United States are to successfully fight AIDS in their communities, "todo"—not just Anglo domination— "tiene que cambiar."

The groundwork for an interrogation of AIDS in the Latino population was set in February 1988, when various Latinos—gay, bisexual, and straight; health care providers, activists, and educators—met in Los Angeles for a National Strategy Symposium on Latinos and AIDS. This symposium, the first ever of its kind, was held in order to discuss and actualize a national AIDS policy and programmatic agenda specific to the needs of Latinos. As Lourdes Arguelles writes in the preface to the published proceedings of the conference, the HIV/AIDS epidemic in communities of color in the United States remained largely misunderstood, even by as late a date as 1987: "These misunderstandings, coupled with well-known historical factors having to do with the relative political powerlessness of the various communities in question, were leading to policy and programming decisions which were less than optimal in controlling the epidemic and in servicing those people of color infected" (*Latinos and AIDS* vii). AIDS challenges Latino communities already burdened with an excess of morbidity and mortality, with inadequate resources including access to education and health care, who suffer language oppression and a discriminatory U.S. legal system of deportation, and who all the while maintain stigmatizing views of sexual acts and intravenous drug use. The conference in L.A. set out to implement methods to counter these burdens but it also set out to empower community-based Latino AIDS projects, which for the most part, have not received adequate funding.

But perhaps the most significant accomplishment of the conference was the increased visibility and communal commitment of Latinos fighting AIDS—nationally and locally. Up until this time, most of the existing programs aimed at educating and informing the Latino community have had their sources outside the Latino community or have been headed by persons unfamiliar with Latino culture, its bicultural process, and the social, spiritual, and economic realities of the Latino community. The result has been inappropriate and inadequate educational materials and programs; inattentive, if not racist, disregard for indigenous or alternative health care beliefs and practices; and the exclusion of Latinos and other people of color, including women, from clinical drug trials. The leadership demonstrated at the 1988 conference was as effective at forming an AIDS coalition among Latinos as ACT UP (AIDS Coalition To Unleash Power) had proven in 1987. The proliferation of AIDS organizations specific to communities of color such as the Minority AIDS Project, Milagros, and Cara a Cara, to name only a few, have helped enormously in the fight against AIDS despite the continual struggle to maintain adequate funding for their programs and services. While many of these organizations work with clients who are gay or bisexual, services specific to gay men of color remain horrifyingly underfunded given the grave statistics of AIDS cases among gay men of color. Moreover, in Latino communities, gay or bisexual men must confront a relentlessly homophobic ideology. As Latina AIDS activist Alice Villalobos explained in 1990: "one of the most difficult and heartbreaking aspects of [Latino gay or bisexual men with HIV or AIDS] is that they are usually forced to live within the homophobic Latino/a community because of poverty and oppression. Not only are they rejected by their own people, but they also have to deal with a white, Anglo culture that categorizes them as second class citizens merely because of the color of their skin" (10). Villalobos writes as a member of ACT UP/Los Angeles in a newsletter that at the time was informing and educating primarily non-Latinos about the issues facing Latino gay men with AIDS in Los Angeles County. Such work is intense and often highly volatile. Los Angeles County includes the largest Latino population in the United States. Non-Latino AIDS activists and straight Latinos must both be educated continually about the specific experiences of gay or bisexual Latinos. Latino gay men fighting AIDS must find support from two very different and often opposing communities. "White AIDS agencies aren't sensitized about monolingual, non-documented seropositives who fear being deported," explains Juan Ledesma, former director of the East LA AIDS Hotline and now with AIDS Health Care Foundation. Arturo Olivias, former executive director of Cara a Cara Latino AIDS Project adds, "My community doesn't acknowledge that there's such a thing as a Latino man who has sex with men" (Sadownick 14). Latino gay men have realized that the fight against AIDS is interrelated with a continuing struggle against racism, classism, and homophobia, the very issues that have enabled AIDS to infiltrate communities of color so extensively in the first place.

In Los Angeles, one of the most successful areas where Latino gays and lesbians have been able to counter the pervasive ideologies that facilitate the spread of AIDS among gay male Latinos has been through performance and the arts. In part this success is due to *VIVA!* a gay and lesbian arts organization founded in 1988 that serves both as a support network for local Latino/a artists and a coalition advocating for Latino/a gay, lesbian, and AIDS visibility in other venues. Doug Sadownick reports, for example, that when Highways Performance Space in Santa Monica first opened in 1988, the inaugural events staged—a Cinco de Mayo marathon put on the Border Arts Workshop—were assailed by *VIVA!* for failing to discuss gay and lesbian issues. One month later, *VIVA!* was angered again when Highways sponsored a lesbian and gay performance festival that lacked Latino/a representation. After *VIVA!* brought attention to the issue, Latinos were added to the schedule. Highways has since proven to be one of the most visible locations for Latino/a gay and lesbian artists, thanks to its multicommunity-based structure and the intervention of *VIVA!* members. Like other gays and lesbians of color, politicized Latinos find that in order to insure that their concerns be addressed they must consciously work within and around various hegemonic systems.

Latino gays and lesbians in theatre perform their art and activism from the multiple positionalities that inform their Latino gay/lesbian identities. Their performances enact the "oppositional consciousness" that Chicana lesbian Chela Sandoval has theorized as a tactic utilized by marginalized people to resist hegemonic inscription: "The differential mode of oppositional consciousness depends upon the ability to read the current situation of power and of self-consciously choosing and adopting the ideological form best suited to push against its configurations, a survival skill well known to oppressed peoples" (Sandoval 16). Sandoval argues against a political identity reduced to a single or fixed perception by dominant culture and the identity politics engendered by such configurations. Rather, oppositional consciousness accommodates a tactical privileging of one component of identity without disturbing the notion of identity as a dynamic process. While Sandoval writes specifically within the context of U.S. Third World feminism, oppositional consciousness, as she explains, "is also a form of resistance well utilized among subordinated subjects under various conditions of domination and subordination" (16).[10] As I hope to make clear, Latino gay performers can be best understood in light of Sandoval's theory. Moreover, as Sandoval's theory begins to suggest, one of the benefits of the differential mode of oppositional consciousness is the possibility of forging links with others experiencing social marginality. With Sandoval's theory in mind, I will argue how in one localized (albeit enormous) social space—Los Angeles—counter-hegemonic coalitions based on what I identify as a "politics of affinity" are materializing through performance. I draw my examples from the performances of Latino gay and lesbian artists working in Los Angeles, in particular Luis Alfaro's solo and collaborative works. These Latino performers offer a much needed voice in the work of what Antonio Gramsci has called the "historical bloc of organic intellectuals," the counter-hegemonic practices of subordinate groups working as a coalition or "bloc" against existing power relations. In this sense, these performers participate in the process that George Lipsitz has outlined in his insightful reading of popular music in East Los Angeles. If, as Lipsitz argues, the music of Chicanos "reflects a quite conscious cultural politics that seek inclusion in the American mainstream by transforming it" (159), Latino gay performers must also work against the grain of the Latino heterosexist mainstream in order to dismantle it as well. Latino gay performers often must maneuver between Latino conventions on the one hand and dominant white gay traditions on the other. In terms of the theatre, their work may involve an interreferential allusion to the already parodic and satirical models of Culture Clash thus furthering and enhancing the intertextual dialogues within Latino theatre, or it may suggest an affinity with politicized white gay male performers in Southern California such as Tim Miller or Michael Kearns, all the while expressing the oppositional consciousness first articulated by Third World U.S. feminists.

Such a varied and deliberate tactic goes one step further than the bifocality that Lipsitz argues for popular music in East Los Angeles. Lipsitz reads the cultural performances of Chicano musicians through anthropologist Michael M. J. Fischer's concept of bifocality or reciprocity of perspectives. Bifocality, Lipsitz writes, is a process of self-respect: "prevented from defining themselves because of pervasive discrimination and prejudice, but unwilling to leave the work of definition to others [Chicano musicians], adopted a bifocal perspective that acknowledged but did not accept the majority culture's image of Chicanos" (154). Sandoval's theory of oppositional consciousness provides the basis for the explication of how Latino gay performers moreover must adjust through a *multi*focality in order to resist the stereotypes imposed by dominant heterosexist ideologies. This multifocal perspective is keenly attuned to the multiple sites of their discrimination stemming from their ethnicity, sexuality, class background, HIV status, or gender.

Luis Alfaro's performance work is a case in point. In his solo piece, *Downtown,* Alfaro—a Chicano playwright, performer, and community activist—performs various characters who live in the Pico-Union district, the heavily populated and impoverished Latino neighborhood in downtown Los Angeles where he grew up.[11] *Downtown* is a nonlinear montage of multicharacter monologue, movement, autobiography, and sound. In *Downtown,* Alfaro investigates the rhythms of his neighborhood reconfiguring Los Angeles from his working-class Latino background and his gay identity. Alfaro scrutinizes Los Angeles by laying bare the glorification of the city and the glamorization of its people fabricated by Hollywood and offered for mass consumption by the entertainment industry. He provides snapshots of his neighborhood and family—from skyscrapers and alleys, undocumented workers and the 18th Street Gang, to local junkies and his Tias Ofelia, Tita, and Romie—that suggest the formation of his politicized identity. But rather than offering a historical chronicle of his own political trajectory, Alfaro stages these stories as unrelated vignettes linked only as indelible memories of a vast urban and psychic landscape.

No comfortable claims are made for and about a Latino gay male identity in *Downtown,* instead Alfaro stages the multiple and often contradictory configurations that construct the possibility for the oppositional consciousness that emerges from a self-conscious and self-articulated Latino gay male perspective. Like Culture Clash, Alfaro draws from Latino culture, but he diffuses the centrality of his ethnicity by cultivating a deliberately gay perspective. From his marginality he offers a cultural politics that foregrounds both his ethnicity and sexuality depending on his point of emphasis and in the process destabilizes the privileged status of either.

Downtown begins with Alfaro situated against a scrim onto which drive-by film shots of downtown Los Angeles street corners are projected; Petula Clark's classic pop hymn "Downtown" provides the soundtrack. The interplay between Petula Clark's escapist view of urban life and the harsh black and white images of Downtown L.A. sets the tone for Alfaro's bittersweet relationship to the city. Alfaro first positions himself as part of this landscape by joining the nameless pedestrians projected upon the scrim. He then breaks the illusion by stepping out of the image to speak of the experience. Alfaro at once invokes the crisis of modernity—Walter Benjamin's reading of Baudelaire being "jostled by the crowd"—and the oral tradition of the epic poet composing and reciting the myths of an era. Such lofty posturing—flaneur and bard—is given a camp poignancy and a postmodern twist with Petula Clark's resounding, "you can forget all your troubles, forget all your cares, so go downtown" refrain. Alfaro's man about town—Latino, gay, and poor—can't escape the omnipresence of the pop culture that infuses the neighborhood. In his performance Alfaro will manipulate such realities by appropriation, commenting all the while on both the process of creating art and on the equally trying challenge of fashioning an identity.

With the ominous and always scrutinizing sounds and lights of a police helicopter hovering over the neighborhood in the background, Alfaro begins his first monologue "On a Street Corner" with reminiscences of formative occasions from his childhood. He offers headlines:

A woman got slugged.
A man got slapped.
A clown threw toys.
A drunk staggered.
An earthquake shook.[12]

which are then further abbreviated to simple gestures first spoken and then performed on his own body: "A Slap. A Slug. A Shove. A Kick. A Kiss." Initially sounding like non sequiturs, these masochistic gestures will be recontextualized throughout the performance and serve as the leitmotifs of the piece, physical reminders of the battles Latinos face daily. While the LAPD surveillance helicopters patrol the neighborhood, a plastic rotating Virgin Mary doll from Tijuana surveys the Alfaro household—"she would turn and bless all sides of the room." The Virgin Mary doll becomes a symbol of kinship, a token from the homeland that comforts and detracts from the urban hardships of downtown L.A., the reminder of the family mantra ingrained in the young boy's consciousness: "You see, blood is thicker than water, family is greater than friends and the Virgin Mary watches over all of us." At one point, ten-year-old Luis offers the doll to his ailing Tia Ofelia who has breast cancer in order to drive away *La Bruja Maldita* who was "slowly eating at her insides." When the boy innocently asks to see her chest, Tia Ofelia slaps him so hard on the face that even he could feel *La Bruja Maldita* eating away at his heart. Soon after his Tia dies and is buried, the Crips firebomb the 18th Street Gang living underneath her old apartment. Rummaging through the charred remains of the apartment building, he finds what's left of the rotating Virgin Mary, now useless and empty of its meaning.

Alfaro tells the story of the Virgin Mary in order to call into question the cultural belief systems of his Latino and Catholic family. This scene offers a poignant and deeply affectionate send-up of the assumptions impoverished Latinos maintain in order to endure the hardships of everyday life—inadequate health care, gang warfare, and an LAPD that essentially quarantines their neighborhoods through its aggressive surveillance. Alfaro, while critical of this system of exploitation vis-à-vis the church and the state, cannot deny the power of its influence. He ends this section with the familiar iconography of the neighborhood, expanding the connotations of his background to accommodate his emerging sexual identification:

> When I was eighteen, I met this guy with a rotating Virgin Mary. He bought it in Mexico, so, of course, I fell in love. His skin was white. He ate broccoli and spoke like actors on a T.V. series. It was my first love and like the *Bruja Maldita*, he pounded on my heart. He taught me many things; how to kiss like the French, lick an earlobe and dance in the dark. He was every Brady Bunch/Partridge Family episode rolled into one. He gave me his shirt and I told him about the fields in Delano, picking cherries one summer and my summer in Mexico. Once my grandmother sent me a crate of grapes. We took off our clothes, smashed them all over our bodies and ate them off each other. When he left, the *Bruja Maldita's* hand replaced his in my heart and she pounded on me. And she laughed like Mexican mothers at a clothes line. And I covered my tears with a smile that was like the veils at Immaculate Conception. But my sorrow was so strong that relatives near by would say *"Ay Mijo,* don't you see? Blood is thicker than water, family is greater than friends, and the Virgin Mary watches over all of us." (Blackout).

The conflicting interpretations of the signification of the iconography—for the Latino the Virgin Mary as a sign of kinship, for the white man a sign of kitsch; for nonwhites the Brady Bunch (incredibly) as a sign of normalized family structures, for whites a banal popular entertainment—sets off the imbalance that will eventually bring back the pounding of the *Bruja Maldita* against the young man's heart. In "Virgin Mary" Alfaro demonstrates the forces that shape the construction of his Latino gay male identity. The performer, over a decade later, offers this construction to his audience in order to demonstrate the tensions that give shape to his desire—"A Slap, A Shrug, A Kiss." The scene ends without resolution, only with the melancholy recognition of his desire and its problematic reception in two conflicting social fields of power; the kinship systems of his Latino family and of an imagined gay community.[13]

In subsequent scenes, Alfaro includes Eric Bogosian–like portraits of various characters from the neighborhood that extend beyond his immediate family. He inhabits the voices and movements of Latinos in the barrio, people he encounters on the street that give him a sense of himself and who inform the performance of the desperate economic conditions of the neighborhood. In these scenes, he foregrounds different aspects of the urban Latino experience and gives voice to the underrepresented thousands who populate L.A.'s downtown. While these portraits contribute to the overall social milieu of *Downtown,* their main purpose is both psychological and interreferential. Alfaro locates the soul of the persona offering it to the audience as his point of connection with the neighborhood; these are moments of both epiphany and affinity. In "Lupe," for example, Alfaro opens by describing his venture through the sweatshops where undocumented Latina women labor for less than minimum wage working twelve hour shifts on a six day week. He spots Lupe who has a face "brown like my father's" and who "paid a *coyote* $150 to smuggle her across the border." He shifts from his performance persona to the voice of Lupe. To mark the transition he puts on a dress. We meet Lupe as she's about to go out on the town on a Saturday night. Lupe's downtown—full of cumbias, *Bohemias,* and street corner lunatics—begins as a temporary refuge from the buzz of the sewing machines of the sweatshops. With her boyfriend she finds romance, but the promise of downtown—"you can forget all your troubles, forget all your cares, so go downtown"—is haunted by the distant sound of the machines "singing to me to come down to the other side of downtown and punch in, punch in, punch in." With fingers bleeding, sirens sounding, and the helicopter always overhead, Lupe fights to hang on to the romance of the city and the bargain of the border. Alfaro ends this portrait with her resounding, albeit temporary, triumph: "Tonite they can all be on fire. Because tonight there is no job. Tonite there is no stitch. No needle, no fabric, no pattern, no nothing. Because tonite is Saturday nite and my dress is too tight and my name is Lupe (blackout)."

The "Lupe" section concludes with Alfaro still in character. The identification process of the Latino gay man with the young undocumented worker suggests an intercultural affinity that recognizes both class oppression and gender specificity. Alfaro's performance of Lupe is staged neither as the omniscient privilege of the creative agent's insight which escapes the character nor as "classic" drag, where the male temporarily puts on a dress in an imagined transgression which by the end only reinforces gender binarism.[14] Instead, Alfaro's performance of Lupe reveals more about his own persona and his choices of affinity. Lupe's oppression and her defiance are interrelated to his own. Such is the tactic of performative oppositional consciousness. In "Lupe" Alfaro plays against preconceived notions of drag as gay performance in order to highlight the experiences shared by Latinos in the barrio. His performance can be interpreted as a political tactic to challenge the alienation of the oppressed by demonstrating the affinities between and among people living in the city. The multifocalities of the performer and the character—the specificity of class, gender, sexuality, and ethnicity—joined in performance enact the coalition building necessary to counter hegemonic configurations that insist on the conflation of differences.

In "Federal Building," Alfaro describes his involvement in the 1 March 1990 artist chain-gang protest regarding censorship and the crisis at the National Endowment for the Arts. Over seventy artists and their supporters marched from the County Museum of Art to the downtown Federal Building where civil disobedience turned into performance pieces staged en route. Artists dressed as criminals carried huge images of banned artists and engaged spectators read quotations about freedom of speech. Guerrilla theatre vignettes, bilingual performances and press conferences, and an extended parable involving a debate between the Spirit of Freedom of Speech and a fundamentalist from North Carolina contributed to the militant defense of artistic freedom which resulted in twenty-seven arrests.

For Alfaro the Federal Building—"the big beautiful marble structure on Los Angeles Street"—is an emblem of his relationship with the city that dates back to his early years when his father would drive the family by the halls of justice "looking for distant Mexican relatives with phony passports ready for a life in Our Lady Queen of the Angels." Like the helicopter that opens and closes *Downtown*, the Federal Building is omnipresent: always visible and always threatening to reveal its power. Like the rotating Virgin Mary doll, the building is a symbol of surveillance: "We have a long history together this *ruca* and I. She has watched me grow up and play on her steps. Watched me low ride in front of her. Watched me spit at her face at an Immigration demonstration that I don't understand but comprehend enough to know that my dad can go back anytime, just never when he wants to." The personal context of the building resurfaces for Alfaro when he returns to protest with artists and members of ACT UP/L.A. shouting in both English and Spanish such chants as "Art is not a Crime," "Alto a la Censura," and "AIDS Funding Now." Unlike some of the other protestors, Alfaro has been here before. The downtown Federal Building has always been for him a microcosmic icon of his relationship with the city, a place where the notion of home shifts to and from a sense of belonging or displacement. The specific circumstances articulated in the first half of "Federal Building," where longstanding Latino issues such as immigration and deportation were introduced as evidence of nationalist muscle, now re-surface as HIV issues with the discriminatory policies and procedures of the INS. And while the performer's ethnicity was the initial political identity foregrounded, by this point in "Federal Building" Alfaro's political tactic is to foreground his sexuality. By the end of this section, however, Alfaro demonstrates how both facets of his identity—sexuality and ethnicity—are enmeshed in his desire for, and denial by, the downtown Federal Building and the home that it has symbolically represented:

> I didn't get arrested because my government wants to control the content of art, or because a Republican congressman from Orange County thinks AIDS activists are a "dying breed." I got arrested because [former] Mayor Sam Yorty told me we were all the mayor. Because a black and white can stop you anywhere, anytime, for whatever reason. Because big marble buildings stare down with a *chale* stare. Because I've never owned anything in my life—much less a city. (blackout)

In "Federal Building" Alfaro demonstrates how AIDS issues for people of color cannot be viewed without an analysis of race and class. Although he joins the others in the spirit and mission of the protest, his personal investment in the Federal Building extends beyond the specifics of the mo-ment and involves the complex contextual history of his relation to Los Angeles as a Latino gay man. And yet, Alfaro's arrest *does* result from his protest against censorship and AIDS bigotry and not this personal back-drop. The arresting officer who "puts handcuffs on me while hundreds of people blow whistles and yell shame, shame, shame" has no idea of why Alfaro is there, only that he is "trespassing on government property." The personal agenda articulated in performance is unavailable to "the man in the helmet and plastic gloves." For the arresting officer Alfaro is only one more protestor. But for the spectator, manipulated by the performative tactics of oppositional consciousness, Alfaro's political identity as a Latino gay man is quite specific though by no means static. The oppositional consciousness model that forms the basis of this performance—the con-tinual dynamic shift in focus from Latino to gay, for example—at its most successful, unsettles the audience's own capacity to conflate differences. Instead, the operative dynamic of oppositional consciousness in Alfaro's performance suggests the possible affinities between performer and audi-ence while simultaneously forcing the spectators to consider the specificity of their own subject-positions.

Alfaro's tactic to perform the links between oppressions also points to the possible counter-hegemonic responses to oppression. In "Federal Building" Alfaro demonstrates how his multifocal identity and politics of oppositional consciousness work in the best interests of coalition movements. The demonstrators all chant various causes and concerns—anticensorship, AIDS, queer visibility and rights—in both English and Spanish. That Alfaro's performance in "Federal Building" is then about a performance, or more specifically an activist performance, suggests the deeply interdependent nature of his politics and his art. In reclaiming and recontextualizing downtown Los Angeles, Alfaro participates in the counter-hegemonic practice of both self-individualization and community formation. *Downtown* ends with Alfaro reciting (and enacting through gesture) a litany of epiphanic moments that encapsulate the characters introduced throughout the performance; each moment is prefaced by "one strong shove":

> One strong shove and the LAPD lets me know who is in charge . . .
> One strong shove and my fingers are bleeding . . .
> One strong shove and the sound of a helicopter or ambulance in the middle of the night lets me know I'm alive.
> One strong shove and a helicopter light has found me in downtown.
> (Alfaro gestures shoves in silence. Blackout.)

Caught once again in the glare of surveillance, Alfaro disappears into the darkness of the stage. The theatre then becomes the site of refuge; a place where identity can be explored or contested, created and shared.[15] His work is, as Jan Breslauer explains in describing Los Angeles performance art, "a theatre of liberation" (95).

As with other gay male playwrights or performers of color, AIDS issues in *Downtown* are thoroughly connected with the prevailing issues of class and race bias.[16] AIDS is experienced as one component in a complex system of exploitation and oppression. Through performance Alfaro stages affinities across boundaries of racial and gender difference in order to foreground the "historical bloc" necessary to intervene in the hegemonic scripts of dominant culture. While the material within Alfaro's performances displays many of Sandoval's ideas, the productions of his performance begin to materialize Sandoval's theory toward a cogent model for political praxis.

Downtown is usually produced as a solo artist evening, although Alfaro has performed it in various group shows ranging from David Schweizer's full-scale production of three solo performance pieces, *True Lies,*[17] to stripped down versions at Chicano or gay and lesbian art festivals in the Los

Angeles area. In these settings, Alfaro's work is received as either the gay piece or the Latino piece, or in the case of the LATC production, the gay and Latino piece. From this perspective, Alfaro's performance risks the appropriation of mainstream production where the work is interpreted either as an exercise in multiculturalism and thus carrying the burden of representation, or where his presence is singled out as the spectacle of difference normalizing the assumptions inherent in the other performances staged.[18] Such risks are worth taking, however, given the design of *Downtown* which allows Alfaro to contextualize difference *and* point toward a politics of affinity.

In his collaborations with other gay and lesbian performers, Alfaro continues to articulate a politics of oppositional consciousness. In *Queer Rites,* for example, Alfaro performs with two white lesbian feminists, Robin Podolsky and Sandra Golvin, and with Doug Sadownick, a Jewish gay male performer.[19] Given that it is already understood that the four performers in *Queer Rites* are queer, it is left up to the four of them to establish points of difference and points of connection. Alfaro, as the only person of color, foregrounds his ethnicity. Sadownick in turn highlights his Jewish identity and Golvin and Podolsky focus on their gender and class. Many issues are addressed throughout the performance including a woman's right to choose, coming out, censorship, AIDS, and anti-Semitism, and overall the effect here is to demonstrate how these issues are all interrelated. *Queer Rites* celebrates difference while demonstrating the effects of coalition building and dialogue between seemingly disparate communities. *Queer Rites* was performed in the summer of 1991 first at Highways and then at Celebration Theatre in West Hollywood.

The same weekend that Culture Clash premiered *S.O.S.* in downtown Los Angeles, Alfaro joined two other Los Angeles–based Latino performers, Monica Palacios and Alberto "Beto" Araiza, to premiere their collaboration *Deep in the Crotch of My Latino Psyche* at the Fourth Annual Gay and Lesbian Performance Festival at Highways. Palacios, self-described "Latin Lezbo Comic" with a solo show of the same name, is a veteran of both comedy clubs and alternative performance venues. Her work is specific to her experience as a Chicana lesbian and continually and hilariously refutes the rigid sexual scripts expected of all women in Latino culture. Araiza— a multitalented actor, playwright, and director—has toured his solo show *Meat My Beat* throughout North America and Europe. *Meat My Beat* chronicles Araiza's travels through urban gay male culture and concludes with a powerful and deeply disturbing response to his own experiences of living with HIV. Together with Alfaro in *Deep in the Crotch of My Latino Psyche* they begin to negotiate through performance a Latino gay and lesbian politics.

In scenarios that vary from stand-up, melodrama, satire, and personal testimony, the three performers set out to critique institutions in both Latino and mainstream gay communities. As "Latino homos without a home" in either community they take to the stage to carve out a niche and claim their rights. They contest a monolithic perception of the Latino gay experience by underlining the vast differences among them, from their own performance styles to their HIV status. *Deep in the Crotch of My Latino Psyche* closely resembles *S.O.S.* in style; short skits that may involve all three performers, solos, or combinations of two. But unlike Culture Clash, these performers insist on rupturing the gender binarism of the *chingón/chingada* polarity and critiquing Latino homophobia and the silence around AIDS.

Deep in the Crotch of My Latino Psyche, as its title indicates, is a humorous and sexy exploration of Latino lesbian and gay sexuality.[20] The performance, however, also seriously engages a number of political issues, most notably through Araiza's two sections on AIDS and HIV in the Latino community "HIVato" and "Safos" and Palacios's solo "Tom Boy Piece" about her coming out process. Alfaro offers a number of solos including a lyrical AIDS memorial, "Where are my heros? Where are my saints?" In "Isolation"—the most effective piece of the performance—the three actors, with only their upper torsos lit, sit on stools and face the audience as an ominous voice-over interrogates them at length about their personal lives. The performers must raise their hand in silence to answer the interviewer's questions which range in tone and intensity from "Have you ever lied about your nationality?" and "Have you lost a lover to AIDS?" to "Do you prefer flour to corn tortillas?" and "Have you ever put on make-up while driving your car?" By the end of this scene, composed of nearly fifty questions, spectators—whether Latino or non-Latino, gay or non-gay—cannot possibly consider Latino gay and lesbian sexuality within a comfortable categorization. Latino gay identities are presented as dynamic and contradictory. The material production of performance stripped down here to its most basic demystifies the performance process and facilitates the effective representation of both the silence around homosexuality in Latino culture and the real and living bodies of Latino/a queers. The interactions among these very different Latino performers in *Deep in the Crotch of My Latino Psyche* demonstrate Sandoval's idea that "self-conscious agents of differential consciousness recognize one another as allies, country women and men of the same psychic terrain" (15).

Alfaro, Araiza and Palacios, three of the driving forces behind *VIVA!*, have collaborated on various "behind the scenes" efforts to gain visibility for Latino gays and lesbians. *Deep in the Crotch of My Latino Psyche* is but one of the many tactics that demonstrate the inseparable nature of their art and activism. Perhaps their most impressive collaboration so far has been the AIDS Intervention Theatre project *Teatro VIVA!*, an AIDS outreach program that provides bilingual prevention information in both traditional (community centers and theatres) and nontraditional sites (parks, bars, community fairs and bazaars, art galleries and private homes). Funded with a $50,000 grant from the United States Conference of Mayors, *Teatro VIVA!* presents short skits on such HIV/AIDS issues as transmission, prevention, safer sex negotiation skills, popular misconceptions about AIDS, daily considerations of people with HIV and AIDS, and local community resources. The main component of the program was its bilingual mobile teatro presentations, performed in agit-prop minimalistic style, to allow for flexibility in response to the varying aspects of each venue. These performances were then followed by a question-and-answer period which allowed for more detailed discussions about AIDS. Araiza, the project director for the first grant, reports that over 5000 individuals—including nearly 2000 self-identified gay and bisexual Latinos—viewed the *Teatro VIVA!* AIDS Outreach Project. Forty presentations were given within Los Angeles County between July 1991 and April 1992. Such interventions demonstrate that Latino gay men can begin to unsettle the muscle of cultural nationalism and homophobia that have combined with other social factors to render Latino gay men powerless. Latina lesbians have already proven their power by organizing first and foremost as Latina lesbians and by forming coalitions with other women who respect the issues specific to their survival. With the supportive and reciprocal alliances between Latina lesbians and Latino gay men available through *VIVA!* the possibilities for future political work seem endless. The proven success of *Teatro VIVA!*, while localized within the confines of Los Angeles County to help combat AIDS among Latino gay and bisexual men, hints that the political landscape is changing. *Teatro VIVA!* has been refunded for 1993 by the County of Los Angeles AIDS Program Office with Palacios and Alfaro now serving as codirectors.

The theatre, of course, is only one of the many sites of contestation in the fight against AIDS and performance only one of the many means possible to counter AIDS and its insidious mystifications in dominant culture. But performance, as I have argued elsewhere, holds the capacity to articulate resistance and generate necessary social change.[21] The work of Alfaro, Palacios, and Araiza—individually and in collaboration, in the theatre and on the streets—provides one model for Latinos and our supporters to engage at once in the tactics of oppositional consciousness and in the coalition building available through an affinity politics. The name *Teatro VIVA!* translates in the most pragmatic and descriptive sense as "VIVA's theatre," the theatre component of the Latino gay and lesbian arts organization *VIVA!* However, I employ *teatro viva* here in the literal sense of "theatre" and the imperative modality of the present subjunctive of the verb "to live"; to convey quite simply, an acclamation of desire for theatre and life.

Notes

This essay was written in the summer of 1992 with support from the Graduate School at University of Washington-Seattle. I'd like to thank the many friends who helped shape my ideas throughout the writing process: Yvonne Yarbro-Bejarano, Dorinne Kondo, Luis Alfaro, Beto Araiza, Brian Freeman, Tim Miller, Susana Chávez-Silverman, Douglas Swenson and, in the final stages of revision for publication, Douglas Crimp. Thanks are also due to the two anonymous readers for Duke University Press who, along with the editors of this anthology, provided useful commentary. Versions of this paper were presented at the "Gender, Sexuality, and the State in a Hispanic/Latino Context" conference at the University of California-Berkeley and at the "AIDS Appropriations: Cultural Studies Perspectives" conference at Rice University. Questions and comments from these audiences have enabled me to clarify specific points. This essay is for my parents.

1 Readers who are unfamiliar with the extensive bibliography on AIDS and cultural representations should begin with the foundational works by Crimp, Crimp with Rolston, Patton, and Watney. I want to stress that there are necessary distinctions between AIDS-phobia, homophobia, and misogyny; that these same discrete and dynamic terms, however, are often conflated in people's understandings and responses to AIDS; and that the practice of viewing the terms as interchangeable, in this case when discussing AIDS, is itself symptomatic of the very conditions that the terms describe.

2 Press release.

3 Including not only the Rodney King verdict and the riots that resulted, but also the racist rhetoric that characterized much of the popular media's coverage of these events. For artists' responses to the L.A. riots see the special edition of *High Performance* "The Verdict and the Violence" Summer 1992.

4 "American Me Tail" is a clever take-off on *American Me,* a 1992 film about Latino prisoners and *An American Tale,* a Disney Studios animated film. The core of the skit involves the power relations within competing factions in a prison negotiated, predictably enough, through male rape.

5 Perhaps the most obvious failure of identity politics in the performance emerges from the interchangeable Chicano/Latino terminology. Chicano refers to a very specific set of political identifications among Mexican Americans; Latino, like Chicano, is a term of self-identification that differentiates from the more official and imposed term "Hispanic."

See Alonso and Koreck for a detailed account of these terms in relation to AIDS.

6   See for instance her trilogy of plays—*Giving Up the Ghost, Shadow of a Man,* and *Heroes and Saints,* along with Yarbro-Bejarano's discussion of them.

7   At the biannual Latino Festival Theatre held in the South Bronx in 1990, for example, El Teatro de la Esperanza presented one of the best received plays of the festival, Josefina Lopez's *Real Women Have Curves.* For more information on the festival see Arratia's discussion in *The Drama Review.* Also in 1990, the University of California at Irvine held "The Representation of Otherness in Chicano and Latin American Theatre and Film" conference where feminist concerns were addressed and debated. See Taylor's review of the conference in *Theatre Journal.* Not all women, of course, are able—or for that matter willing—to see their work staged in these forums. For all-women performance venues, festivals, and conferences, see Yarbro-Bejarano's essays. For discussions of more recent Latino theatre festivals, see the writings of Ed Morales. For an overview of Chicano theatre, see the invaluable work of Jorge Huerta.

8   For an insightful critique of *Criticism in the Borderlands* written from the perspective of a Chicana lesbian see González.

9   See Alonso and Koreck, "Silences: 'Hispanics,' AIDS, and Sexual Practices."

10 Yvonne Yarbro-Bejarano has already demonstrated how Sandoval's theory of oppositional consciousness provides fresh insight for critical formations in theories of difference and gay and lesbian studies, see her contribution to *Professions of Desire* and her forthcoming article on Anzaldua's *Borderlands.*

11 For an in depth discussion of Los Angeles Latinos and poverty, see Mike Davis *City of Quartz.* In "The Hammer and the Rock," a chilling chapter on inner-city social conditions, Davis explains how "poverty is increasing faster among Los Angeles Latinos, especially youth, than any other urban group in the United States" (315).

12 All quotes are from the author's unpublished performance text.

13 For an excellent discussion of kinship and conflict as it pertains to lesbians and gay men, see Kath Weston.

14 On "classic" drag, see chapter 1 of Sue-Ellen Case's *Feminism and Theatre.* But see also Marjorie Garber *Vested Interests: Cross-dressing and Cultural Anxiety* for a different reading of cross-dressing and for a more extensive bibliography.

15 On the idea of theatre and political identities as related to people of color, see Dorinne Kondo; as related to gay men in response to AIDS, see my "Performing All Our Lives."

16 See my essay *"Fierce Love* and Fierce Response" for a discussion of Pomo Afro Homos and some of these same issues.

17 Alfaro's *Downtown* was performed as *Pico-Union* on a bill with Chloe Webb's *Walkin' the Walls* and Rocco Sisto's rendition of Dario Fo's *The Tale of The Tiger. True Lies* was performed at the Los Angeles Theatre Center from 25 July–8 September 1991.

18 Most of the reviews of *True Lies* for example, while favorable of *Pico-Union,* describe in detail Alfaro's sexuality and ethnicity—some even to the extent that they talk about his physical appearance—without going into any discussion of either of the two white performers' sexuality or ethnic background, let alone their physical traits.

19 Unfortunately *Queer Rites* was not reviewed in any great detail. Rachel Kaplan writes, however, a very descriptive review of their individual performances in "A Queer Exchange" at San Francisco's 1800 Square Feet. These performances developed into the collaborative *Queer Rites.* See Kaplan for a more in depth analysis of this work.

20　Their promotional slogan: "Comedy, Drama, Pathos and Piñatas!" further accentuated the humor.
21　"Performing All Our Lives."

Works Cited

Alfaro, Luis. *Downtown.* Performed at Highways Performance Space in Santa Monica, Calif. 30 November, 1–2, 7–9 December 1990.

Alfaro, Luis, Alberto Araiza, and Monica Palacios. *Deep in the Crotch of My Latino Psyche.* Performed at Highways Performance Space, 9–11 and 14–16 July 1992.

Almaguer, Tomás. "Chicano Men: A Cartography of Homosexual Identity and Behavior." *differences* 3 (1991): 75–100.

Alonso, Ana Maria, and Maria Teresa Koreck. "Silences: 'Hispanics,' AIDS and Sexual Practices." *differences* 1 (1989): 101–24.

Arratia, Euridice. "Teatro Festival: The Latino Festival Theatre." *Drama Review* 35 (1991): 176–82.

Breslauer, Jan. "California Performance." *Performing Arts Journal* 41 (1992): 87–96.

Calderón, Héctor, and José David Saldívar. *Criticism in the Borderlands: Studies in Literature, Culture, and Ideology.* Durham: Duke University Press, 1991.

Case, Sue-Ellen. *Feminism and Theatre.* New York: Routledge, 1988.

Crimp, Douglas. "How to Have Promiscuity During an Epidemic." *AIDS: Cultural Analysis/ Cultural Activism.* Ed. Douglas Crimp. Cambridge: MIT Press, 1987.

—— with Adam Rolston. *AIDS Demographics.* Seattle: Bay Press, 1990.

Culture Clash. *S.O.S.* Performed at the Japan American Theatre, Los Angeles. 9–11 July 1992.

Davis, Mike. *City of Quartz: Excavating the Future in Los Angeles.* London: Verso, 1990.

Garber, Marjorie. *Vested Interests: Cross-dressing and Cultural Anxiety.* New York: Routledge, 1991.

González, Deena J. "Masquerades: Viewing the New Chicana Lesbian Anthologies." *Outlook* 15 (1991): 80–83.

Huerta, Jorge. "Professionalizing Teatro: An Overview of Chicano Theatre During the 'Decade of the Hispanic.'" *Theatre Forum* 3 (1993): 54–59.

Kanellos, Nicolás. *A History of Hispanic Theatre in the United States: Origins to 1940.* Austin: University of Texas Press, 1990.

Kaplan, Rachel. Review of *A Queer Exchange. The San Francisco Bay Times* March 1991: 50.

Kondo, Dorinne. "The Narrative Production of 'Home,' Community and Political Identity in Asian American Theatre." Paper delivered at the 1991 American Anthropological Association Conference.

Lipsitz, George. *Time Passages: Collective Memory and American Popular Culture.* Minneapolis: University of Minnesota Press, 1990.

Maldonado, Miguelina. "On the Out Side: Latinos and Clinical Trials." *SIDAhora* 11 (1992): 13.

Martinez-Maza, Otoniel, Diana M. Shin, and Helen E. Banks. *Latinos and AIDS: A National Strategy Symposium.* Los Angeles: Center for Interdisciplinary Research in Immunology and Disease (CIRID), 1989.

Moraga, Cherríe. *Loving in the War Years.* Boston: South End Press, 1983.

Morales, Ed. "Shadowing Valdez." *American Theatre* 9.7 (1992): 14–19.

——. "Welcome to Aztlan." *American Theatre* 10.3 (1993): 38–40.

———— "Those Who Can, Act: 'Cultural Workers' at TeatroFestival." *Village Voice* 3 August 1993: 95–6.

Patton, Cindy. *Inventing AIDS*. New York: Routledge, 1990.

Román, David. *"Fierce Love* and Fierce Response: Intervening in the Cultural Politics of Race, Sexuality, and AIDS." *Critical Essays: Gay and Lesbian Writers of Color*. Ed. Emmanuel S. Nelson. New York: Haworth Press, 1993.

———— "Performing All Our Lives: AIDS, Performance, Community." *Critical Theory and Performance*. Ed. Janelle Reinelt and Joseph Roach. Ann Arbor: University of Michigan Press, 1992.

Sadownick, Doug. "Family Among Strangers: Crossing the Borders in Gay L.A." *LA Weekly* 23–29 June 1989: 12–20.

Sandoval, Chela. "U.S. Third World Feminism: The Theory and Method of Oppositional Consciousness in the Postmodern World." *Genders* 10 (1991): 1–24.

Sedgwick, Eve Kosofsky. *Epistemology of the Closet*. Berkeley: University of California Press, 1990.

Taylor, Diana. Review of *The Representation of Otherness in Chicano and Latin American Theatre and Film Conference* at UC-Irvine, 18–20 October 1990. *Theatre Journal* 43 (1991): 377–79.

Villalobos, Alice. "AIDS and the Latino/a Community." *ACT UP/Los Angeles Newsletter* 5 (1990): 10.

Watney, Simon. *Policing Desire: Pornography, AIDS, and the Media*. 2d ed. Minneapolis: University of Minnesota Press, 1989.

Weston, Kath. *Families We Choose: Lesbians, Gays, Kinship*. New York: Columbia University Press, 1991.

Yarbro-Bejarano, Yvonne. "The Female Subject in Chicano Theatre." *Performing Feminisms: Feminist Critical Theory and Theatre*. Ed. Sue-Ellen Case. Baltimore: Johns Hopkins University Press, 1990.

———— "Expanding the Categories of Race in Lesbian and Gay Studies." *Professions of Desire: Lesbian and Gay Studies in Literature*. Ed. George E. Haggerty and Bonnie Zimmerman. New York: MLA Publications, forthcoming.

———— "Cherríe Moraga's *Shadow of a Man:* Touching the Wound in Order to Heal." *Acting Out: Feminist Performances*. Ed. Lynda Hart and Peggy Phelan. Ann Arbor: University of Michigan Press, 1993.

———— "Cherríe Moraga's *Giving Up The Ghost:* The Representation of Female Desire." *Third Woman* 3.1–2 (1986): 113–20.

———— "Gloria Anzaldua's *Borderlands/La frontera:* Cultural Studies, 'Difference,' and the Non-Unitary Subject." *Chicano Cultural Studies: New Critical Directions*. Ed. Mario Garcia and Ellen McCracken. Berkeley: University of California Press, forthcoming.

José Piedra
Nationalizing Sissies

The first part of this essay requires no academic apparatus—it is an exploration of power structures for which we all have a gut feeling if not a long-suffering experience.—A highly academic sissy friend upon reading my manuscript and who prefers to remain anonymous.

Informing Sissies

In humankind's long haul through colonial, anticolonial, and postcolonial history we have all taken turns playing a wide range of roles that define our identity and our nationality against someone else's. Some of these roles are acquired defensively and others claimed offensively. Moreover, such roles describe us as certain types, be it inherently, circumstantially, permanently, and/or transiently. Among these roles and types the sissy remains most problematic to justify, particularly to those who deem the sissy as a loser in the war and bed games of colonialism.

Colonialism could be described as a colonizing agent's "systematic" bullying and sissification of a colonized target. Bullying and sissification are one and the same colonial act viewed from two different perspectives: the victimizers' or the victims'. Upon describing colonial exchanges in terms of bullies and sissies one adds disturbing perspectives on gender and sex to the uneven circumstances that bring together the colonizer and the colonized.

Most colonialist traditions would too readily set up the sissy as a target of scorn who assumes the fake or real, but always "ultra" feminine, feminized, and/or effeminate behavior that is perceived as passive, weak, and forever ready to suit the bully's whims. Given that the paternalistic bias of colonialism prefers power to remain firmly entrenched as a man's game, it thus endorses the sissy as a man standing in for a woman—or enacting a woman's "style" of behavior. Meanwhile the bully is readily identified with the complementary "engendered" behavioral style: a "macho" man.

Libidinally speaking, machos become "someone"—that is, acquire a place in social intercourse, in the market of selfhood, and in the hierarchy of power associated with colonialism—by virtue of subjecting someone else, a sissy, to their bully behavior. In principle, this fashion of subjecting can be practiced by men, women, straights, and gays. But, in actuality, men who perceive themselves as macho models claim advantage over, and even exclusivity in, the act of sissification. These self-servingly straight men assign the state of sissyhood to other men who are henceforth lessened, taken, or "had," but not necessarily or strictly either womanized or homosexualized, at least not openly. Sissification emerges as a paradoxical form of gender and sexual assignment.

A characteristic difference between a regular macho and one acting as a bully is that the latter acts on the compulsion to test his own male powers and/or prowess on other men. He likely spends much time and effort covering up for or justifying such a compulsion. Different cultures appear predisposed to specific types of compulsions and cover-ups. However, across cultures the bias tends to benefit straight males who emerge from the bully-sissy exchange as notoriously self-effacing in matters of gender codes and sexual choices. Pressed for an explanation of his behavior the bully would not likely confess to bullying as a libidinally debasing act upon the sissified target. He is even less likely to admit to acting out a homoerotic instinct or engaging in homosexual activity.

From the heat of this most evasive battle of the genders and the sexes emerges a male bonding ritual in which "the best" wins, and the winner pretends that it matters little what gender coding or sexual activity he "inflicts" upon the loser. In his pursuit the winner has two options: (1) The bully can excuse his actions and sometimes even those of his sissy partner from homosexual overtones; (2) he can act as if he were winning over and/or inscribing himself, rhetorically and physically, on a gender-neutral and even sexually neutral tabula rasa which, in actuality, becomes "womanized" by virtue of its relatively open and, at least symbolically, dephallicized sissy receptivity. Consequently, femininity and masculinity, hetero- and homosexuality, lie at the disposal of a bullying manhood even when the man behind this act of aggression would not readily or likely recognize the gender implications and sexual specificity of his activity.

In order to preserve his "straightness" while observing the men-only quality of the bully-to-sissy colonial takeover, the bully keeps the sissy in a suspended libidinal state between maleness and femaleness, hetero-

and homosexuality, or "worse." Fantasized as androgyny, hermaphrodit-ism, virginity, or celibacy, the sissy's "inbetweenness" serves as the ultimate butt of macho rhetorical inscription, physical intervention, or both. By the same token, the process objectifies woman in her absence as she remains the hidden object of desire enacted by the sissy who operates in her stead just enough to save the bully from admitting to a gay connection. Thus a sissy becomes less of a man or a lesser man and more than a woman. In a parallel fashion, the bully becomes more of a man upon treating a lesser man as a woman. If the situation becomes too hot to handle, the bully simply represses the libidinal implications of his act.

For the bully in charge, libidinally blind bullying guarantees order be-yond gender bias and sexual preference to those who succumb to colonial circumstances beyond their control and, by implication, are subjectable to the bully's hold. From a colonialist perspective, everyone benefits from the paternalistic bully's colonial equation. According to this equation, to be sissified is to belong to the bully's colonizing order—under whose aegis, vicarious and/or submissive intercourse, belonging, and empowerment, be it sexual or just social, are better than none at all.

From the sissy's perspective, sissy behavior is not necessarily forced, imposed on him from the outside or, for that matter, of unquestionably passive character. It is more likely a matter of preference, style, taste, or "nature," some of it unavoidable, inherent, highly skilled, and successful—in short, positive qualities likely to become passionate markers of identity. Can the sissy be the real powermonger in the bully's colonial takeover?

Whether it leads or not to an actual sexual takeover, in principle, bully-ing a sissy remains a misogynist, heterosexist, and xenophobic exercise, but one that could backfire against the enforcers of such prejudices. Sissi-fication or bullying provides a libidinally tainted counterpart to colonialist takeover; it might also provide for the sissy an avenue of anticolonialist subversion and for both sissy and bully a form of postcolonial compro-mise. Although Freudian analysts might readily trace colonialism itself to a libidinal urge, the bully-sissy exchange underscores a much higher in-tensity in the manipulation of gender markers and sexual feeling and, not surprisingly, a surge in denial.

Both denial and its procedural counterpart, repression, provide a tenu-ous form of self-preserving secrecy which is forever ready to explode—that is, to run away from the control of individuals who presume to be in charge. Explosion of repressed feelings and, by extension, of people with such feelings is only an extreme case in the psychological unearthing of repressed materials and the political unearthing of oppressed beings. Such

developments should lead to a new order or a reassessment of the old one—
or at least this is the intent of psychoanalysis and liberation. If I am right,
such a new order brings into focus, if not into power, the colonized sissy,
who emerges from his position as the ultimate (oppressed/repressed) target of the (oppressing/repressing) bully. The Freudian model of the mind
and the untangling of material relegated to the subconscious serve well in
the study of the liberation of the sissy.

The bully-sissy type of exchange emerges as a type of colonialism based
on an oppressive manipulation of someone else's gender coding and sexual
behavior accompanied by a repressive attitude toward one's own—and,
by extension, toward the act itself and the gender coding and sexual behavior of the sissified target. The exchange remains tantalizingly secretive,
possibly explosive, and potentially reversible. If, politically speaking, colonialism keeps track of who is on top and who is on the bottom, libidinally
speaking who can tell top from bottom in the duet repressed by bully-sissy
duelers? At any rate, is it fun always being on top?

Willfully or not, the sissy has an important part to play in colonial exchanges. At least he appears to partake as a second-rate partner in the
macho exercise of power and not just by merely becoming a pusillanimous
target of scorn, impersonation, and/or domination. At the very least the
sissy engages in a crucial self-enhancing/self-saving activity: to (pretend
to) resist. From the perspective of the bully, this might be a theatrical act
rather than a constructive activity. The bully could argue that even a gesture of passive or active resistance or a change in relative positions at best
promotes the passivity or passionate partnering of his bullying interests.
Alpha (bully) males probably appreciate a good fight or positional shifting
from beta (sissy) males; it makes the victory that much sweeter in battle
scenes ranging from symbolic wars to real beds.

Beyond his consideration of the sissy as an overt target of domination
and a covert target of passion, the bully invests the sissy with a single-
minded activity: to provoke—leading possibly to seduction. But even
provocation or seduction provides service. If the bully has his way, these
activities shift the guilt of domination to the sissy recipient or victim who
ostensibly provoked the bullying, passionate or not. Thus the bully justifies
his domination as a guiltless response to what he perceives as the sissy's
need to be dominated.

If provocation might be a rather desperate form of empowerment, as
an act loaded with libidinal titillation, seduction remains a paradoxical act
with remarkable democratic and subversive possibilities. It could be considered a sexy show of strength—the will to dare to seduce and potentially

to entrap—even when the provoking agent is doomed to "failure": that is, bound to serve, to service, and/or to please the provoked target. Regardless of the outcome, a sissy can fight back domination by provocation and seduction, attacking the attacker, embracing the strangler, or controlling and countering an act of takeover by the will to make him want you, need you, or even be trapped in a dependency. The danger remains that such a dependency might be mutual and endlessly bonding.

Even for misogynist, homophobic, and xenophobic zealots, the sissy role and type become particularly difficult to justify not just because of their homoerotic and homosexual possibilities within a man's world, but because the sissy becomes a woman-substitute who is integral to the macho domination act. In the sissy-bully exchange it is difficult to tell who has whom, in what way, and to what extent. Whether symbolically or actually, passively or provocatively, orally, anally, or any other way, for a challenging or passionate instant or forever, the sissy bullies the bully. This type of reversible behavior relates to the theory and practice of sadomasochism, viewed as a willful alternative to the will-crushing colonial pact. The sadomasochistic implications of the bully-sissy secretive contract should serve critics to review the libidinal implications of the colonialist model, the anticolonial potential of pretended compliance, and the democratic possibilities of postcolonial compromises. And this does not just apply to the political and psychological contracts between males convinced that they are heterosexual.[1] Oppression and repression, as well as its counterpart, liberation, knows no boundaries.

At least symbolically, the bully-sissy libidinal framing of colonialism does not always succeed in enforcing its intended misogynist, heterosexist, and xenophobic bias. The exchange also plants in groups the seed for libidinal subversion. Ultimately, not just any given individual, but even an entire nation can become a sissy, if "fucked over" by another in the most symbolic or real of ways. And such sissified nations might empower themselves, more or less subversively, even if just by binding another nation to a colonial and/or libidinal commitment with sadomasochistic undertones.

Sadomasochistic or not, bully-sissy dependency is a two-way street balancing pain and pleasure. This form of embracing/strangling mutual dependency bespeaks similar relationships between colonizer and colonized, lender and debtor, consumer and commodity, subject and object, form and content, penetrator and penetrated, Self and Other. All of the above pairs ultimately connect through a pain-encased pleasure principle of exchange that matches dominating and dominated, as well as reverses or obliterates the sense of domination.[2] The parties in question tend to invest the basic colonial exchange with the urgency of a reciprocal consumerist trans-action—I have you (or bully you) because you need me to have you (to sis-sify you)/You have me (bully me) because I want you to have me (to sissify me). Transactions as such are ruled by a most emotionally loaded corollary of the laws of supply and demand, which might passionately bond the sissy and the bully to a mutual dependency until a "better offer" comes into the market. I consider this painful exercise in pleasure as endemic to a capitalist outlook in life, whereby those who supply and those who demand learn to live with each other and depend on their mutually consuming needs. In turn, such a tentative dependency is one of the last options available to the oppressed, and one of the last options a sissy gives into, gives up, or gives himself until a better, less repressive, offer comes along. In this fashion a sissy gains empowerment or, at least connects to the powers that be which readily depend on his provocation, needs, and even the timely betterment of his social contract.

I would like to explore sissy behavior as a nation-building trick: an active mediation in the exchanges between colonizers and colonized, a role or type ready to qualify, modify, taint, neutralize, and even trap—at least into an illusion of domination—whomever and whatever attempts to occupy him/her or his/her territory. This potential transforms the sissy from the perfect colonized or colonial into a model anticolonialist or postcolonial being, the ultimate internationalist nationalist being. In short, if the bully thinks of the sissy as nothing, the ground, seed, the tabula rasa for his occu-pation, inscription, insemination, and overall expression, I would think of the sissy as something else, somebody, a partner, and a rebellious agent in the colonial exchange.

My schematic study of the sissy tradition requires viewing the sissy and the sissy trick in ourselves and in our own national and international strate-gies. This takes me to what I consider the "original" sissy home trick: America's reception of Spain. This most remote sissifying experience in the ancestral history and prehistory of my Cuban being should serve me to bully my critical theories on nation building against the dominant ones—as it certainly has helped Cuban culture to survive a steady stream of outside interventions and inner manipulations.

Over the years in the Hispanic history of the Americas, transplanted and native Americans of all sorts might have learned a sissy trick or two from covertly homoerotic or overtly homosexual behavior. Spain, Colum-bus, et al. wanted lands and citizens to be had and to be put to the ser-vice of an "overseas empire." Such a rampant desire dictated some men to dominate, that is, to sissify others. Women were largely considred landless, second-class citizens, and mere receptacles of men's wants. Finally, "to have" women was indeed a problem for a culture discouraging miscegenation. For such reasons, sissies came in handy: they were capable of taking the bully without giving him back any offspring or embarrassing him with gay connections. The sissy emerged as the fertile ground on which colonialist agents symbolically planted their seed while avoiding baring the heterosexual couplings' mixed fruit or getting mixed up with homosexual "fruits" of their own imagining.

Without much stretching of our imaginations we Spanish Americans can likely count on colonizing and colonized ancestry and/or tendencies—biological, emotional, and/or cultural—to side with the colonizer and the colonized as well as with sissies, bullies, men, and women on both sides of the power seesaw. For personal as well as political reasons, I hope to prove the global participation of all of the above in a nation-building sissy trick. I am the result of a core colonial embrace between the Spanish and the Americans, and I feel that, at least symbolically, this tradition subjects the rest of the Americas to a transcontinental sissy trick against one-sided intercontinental takeovers.

Papering By and Egging On

According to legend, Christopher Columbus explained the territory, people, and culture of what was to become the Spanish New World to the royal folks back home by crumpling up a blank piece of paper. This legend rivals Columbus's alleged trick of standing an egg on its (broken) tip in order to show the feasibility of a spheric world standing on its own—with Christopher's dexterous but heavy-handed help. While the first legend rationalizes the takeover of the theoretically blank territory, people, and culture of the New World as a ground for the scripturally possessive, inscribing art of the Old, the second legend justifies the colonizers' breaking the frail, empty shell of a New World in order to strengthen Spanish scientific claims to a spherical earth materially rotating around the sun—as well as symbolically and pragmatically rotating around Spain's imperial sense of Self. In order to exert transatlantic control over the art of inscription or to prove scientifically the earth's sphericity, the nature of the world—as well as its text and shape—was thus forever Euro-altered by Columbus.

Although Columbus's blank-page-and-empty-egg-imaging of America speaks of a hypothetical "nothingness," the "discoverer" was prompt to qualify the land as "something," the people as "somebody," and both as ripe and dying to belong to somebody, arguably to Columbus. The improvised admiral and his traveling companions were virtual nobodies until they made do with the natives and their values.

Columbus never overtly revealed being disappointed about his great travel mistake—that is, his reaching the "West" Indies and Indians as opposed to India—and yet the discoverer knew he had to make do with whatever and whomever he could lay his hands on. The Indies and the Indians became Columbus's pot of gold at the far end of the transatlantic rainbow. The search for the original or any alternative overseas treasures proceeded in the name of loose categories of domination: Spain (then barely a unified nation), European Civilization (in one of its periodic rebirth crises, the Renaissance), the West's International Trade with the East (hampered by the "fall" of Constantinople, the traditional eastern route), and the Church (avid for new converts).

In the end, after what must have been (even for Columbus) some troublesome discovering, uncovering, and sampling, both symbolic and real, he decided America and the Americans were in need of reportage, remedial cover(age), and manipulation—not to mention conversion of the secular and religious, textual and sexual kinds. Even viewed from the ostensibly open-minded, historically revisionist perspective of the turn of the twentieth century, Columbus retains, at best, a paradoxical place in colonial studies: heroic voyager, genocidal trespasser, modern inventor of colonialism, but also mid-Atlantic citizen, whose success largely depended on adjusting the expectations of the colonizer to the values of the colonized.

In spite of his incredible geographical and mercantile failures and personal failings, Columbus made preliminary sense of the transatlantic connection, and henceforward I would argue that all intercontinental notions of nation in modern times are indebted to Columbus's elementary, hierarchized sense of a rainbow coalition—part colonialism, part paternalism, part collision, and part coalition. Can we invest Columbus with the honorary title of founder of the Americas' (inter)national paradigm? Not without figuring out the gender and sexual bending that this paradigm entails. The Europization of America cannot be reduced to a matter of written papers and broken eggs, in other words, of mere alien inscription and native insemination. The takeover is not as radical, one-sided, straightforward, or straight as Columbus may have wanted to show us.

Much later in the history of the Americas, Alexis de Tocqueville appears to have elaborated on Columbus's model with devastating results: America, referring now to what was to become the United States, was for him "une feuille blanche" [a white, pure, virginal, or blank leaf or page]. In the legendary memory of its colonial occupiers America became predictably crumpleable and/or fillable—that is, a readily available and/or inscribable void for all sorts of filling and fulfilling forms of colonial determinism. Immediate action was a must, including colonial nationalization and international upgrading. Even the most cursory reading of Tocqueville's slogan suggests that he contemplated filling blank America up with European things, letters, and peoples, preferably under French supervision. In other words, implicit in his proposal is the French crumpling and fulfilling of U.S. blankness, as well as breaking through the puritan shell of an emerging nation struggling to stand (up) internationally on what must have seemed from the self-aggrandizing French perspective a limited sphere of cultural possibilities.

Unlike the prevailing tendency amongst Columbus's heirs, the Anglo-American tradition of the United States, with or without Tocqueville's intervention, continues to cherish the illusion that America is not a by-product of colonization, but the creation virtually from scratch of transplanted Europeans with only the highest ideals, a will to civilize the world, and able to keep in check any muddy signs of barbarity. Americans—meaning largely European immigrants transplanted in the united states of it—remain conquerors capable of reducing others to a "feuille blanche" on which to right the wrongs in the "American" way. This attitude affects the treatment of history, architecture, wrinkles, debris, libidos, death, etc., as well as other people's sense of nation and national interests. Even compromise notions such as renewing, restoring, repairing, recycling, and regenerating tend to be largely based on the illusion of starting all over again. Residing, as it were, above it all is the American will to power, which remains the only undisposable item in the U.S. economy of international desire.

Latino-assimilation and Anglo-assimilation are two very different processes, the former overtly built on the notion of a hierarchized compromise, the latter covertly achieving a conquering amalgamation—ranging from self-righteous melting pot theories to neutralizing the Other through the advocacy rather than the reality of multiculturalism. Everyone in the States, and for that matter in the world, should attempt to be or to imitate and/or to succumb to the best, that is, America's conquering ways. What sort of influence does this diverging attitude have over gender and sexual politics, and more importantly over the treatment of the colonized, the marginal, the deviant, the objectified, the subjectable, and over the common history of the Americas?

For better or for worse, I have found no written traces of the legend of the "crumpled paper" or of the broken eggshell or, for that matter, any passages in Columbus's manuscripts rendering his occupation any worse than any other. Then or now, Hispanic texts or agents in the United States or elsewhere seem to prefer to keep only an oral, largely cynical memory of an intercontinental gesture that, no matter how nullifying it intended to be, ended up multiplying our cultural and genetic referents. In other words, we, Hispanicized citizens of the Americas—colonizing and/or colonized— have had to make peace with our war of origins and learn to live by its mixed bag of consequences. For us Columbus's Atlantic trespassing is not merely a one-sided act of occupation in which some part of us played out the passive ground and empty recipient for the other aggressive half act- ing as inscribing agent. Arguably the longest–lasting effect of the trespass war is our being forced to confront a bloody new transatlantic beginning and subsequently a colonial truce that in most European histories marks the beginning of modern times and in the United States today is gingerly celebrated as a melting pot leading to multiculturalism. Italo-Americans to this day celebrate their proud heritage on 12 October as Columbus Day; members of the Hispanidad prefer to celebrate their pride that very day as "El día de la Raza," that is, "The Day of The (Our Mixed) Race." [3]

Most non-Hispanic U.S.-based critics avoid joining the rest of the Americans in the Americas in accepting the lingering effects of a com- mon original conquest that forced/forged the togetherness of the colo- nizer and the colonized. Tocqueville's reference to America as a "feuille blanche" has been largely forgotten among the self-proclaimed heirs of Anglo-Americans who occupied American Indians and their land or con- tinue to demand that foreigners submit to Anglo-dominant molds. Indeed, from the perspective of dominant-American gatekeepers, the boundaries with the rest of the world blur over blank faces, hungry mouths, angry hands, and wishful bodies swimming toward the American bait, the green- back, the green card, the green stick, the new, green beginning.

While Hispanic Americans tend to accept as unavoidable and/or tran- scend the paradox of a two-sided colonial memory of creative bodily and soulful f(r)iction, Anglo-Americans tend to hide from it or blame Colum- bus and Hispanics for creating such a sexually charged paradox. Even when the timely pages of *Time* magazine ("Starting at Year Zero" 9 September 1991, 25.) open up the Columbus-bashing squadron to include a French- man's (referenceless) quote against American "natives," Columbus and his willing and/or reluctant Hispanic heirs remain the original models of a "nullifying" act that has generated over five hundred years of "impure" bar- barity/civilization across the Americas. Let's face it, the media—popular or academic—has Hispanics leading only in criminal records, gender hysteria, sexual deviation, and paradoxical models of maladjustment. Let me reintroduce myself as a "critical" target of such statistics.

From the perspective of the imperial and empirical Self, the caretaking urge to fulfill the Other has as much to do with the right as with the duty to fill in empty holes of bodies and souls, just as it would any other gaping hole—such as those left by lack of culture and inscription. The caretakers fantasize that their services have been solicited from abroad—in other words, as if the colonizers were responding to a fictional or factual "seduction" from the budding international bodies across the seas that are neediest for "care." The Self wants the Other to want Him/Her; and that, to my mind, can be interpreted as a position of both weakness and power. The interpretation of a libidinal want can range from a compelling need to seduce, desire to be seduced, seducing someone into seducing you, or a mutual willful seduction.[4] The nuances become dangerous when one of the parties in that game of seduction is a colonizer or a colonized, colonial, or even a postcolonial voyeur or uncritical public who has been deprived from participating in or expressing libidinal sensations or who satisfies a hunger for libidinal sensationalism.

Sissy Origins

Most "colonial subjects"—and I insist that such a definition includes virtually all of us, our ancestors, and/or heirs—fantasize the reversibility of the colonial situation, complete with sadomasochistic overtones and flying objects of desire, genital and otherwise. Deep down we have at times been sissified or bullied by internal and external circumstances ranging from guilt to adversity, from self-analysis to analysis, from our own quest to someone else's questioning of our authority, to mention but a few examples. Sometimes part of us "does in," invades, and/or evades another part. We need no outside help to be or feel subjugated. We carry with ourselves many sadomasochistic layers of exchange readily relived, relieved, or relied upon through mere examination—ranging from the most casual to the most psychoanalytically informed. Inner colonialism prepares even the most solidly domineering person to image the suffering of outer colonialism. Or vice versa, we adjust to the unbearably alien(ating) forces of colonialism, or pretend to adjust, by internalizing colonialism. Whatever our selected form of imaging the friction between Self and Other, we remain victims of that fiction. At least part of our being is sissified/bullied by our own demands, sometimes as lethally demanding as someone else's.

No matter how much we are (of) the colonizer and/or (of) the colonized, we become party to a traumatic "interpersonal" and/or "international" primal scene.[5] In hindsight, fantasizers of such a scene avoid the responsibility of facing up to colonialism; they tend to pretend that, whether inner or outer, the colonial exchange in question derives from an accidental inscription on an empty or emptied-out, filled, fulfilled, or overturned ground or an egg broken for "good cause."

It is natural that we should express ambivalence, a repressive attitude, and aversion toward historical indications that our very being, personal and social, is the result of a colonial takeover. In that regard, let us consider the world's paradoxical attitude toward Columbus as a lingering barbarically civilizing Father figure to America. Let us also consider America as a civil but barbaric Mother of all. From this perspective it is no wonder that Americans—particularly those in the United States who associate with either what Columbus did or whom Columbus did in—find it so difficult to come to terms with this continent's intercontinental primal scene. Hopefully in such matters Spanish Americans, who tend to view themselves as colonial hybrids, would have a distinct advantage.

I compare the "primal scene," the Freud-encoded individual search for origins through the interpersonal trauma of parental coupling, with a people's search for national origins through the trauma of international coupling. From such a perspective it is relatively easy for me to alternate the study of the trauma of nationals with that of nations in the symbolic and in the material arenas, and oftentimes also in the genetic and cultural spheres. Throughout such a traumatic exchange, one or more nation(al)s play the sissy role, alternatively or sequentially the in-between, go-between, mediating, and ensuing auto-defending agent. I could even venture to say that the offspring of the inter-personal/inter-national coupling is invariably born a sissy, that is, the tacit result of an exchange from which the emerging nation(al)s have to survive and build, or bully, a personal/national/international identity of their own.

According to my reading of Freud, the primal scene is problematically imaged as a painful but necessary result of the biological imperative to mingle and (pro)create—requiring an inseminating Father, an inseminated Mother, and a seminal offspring who mediates the pain and turns it into qualified pleasure and the sort of "sweet-and-sour" identity that approaches independence as a rather relative and tentative gain.

In the shifting arena of the history of the Americas, it is difficult to assign paternal, maternal, and offspring roles to anyone in particular who participates in the act or memory of the primal scene. At one point or another practically every member of the Americas has been at the bottom or on top of the domination seesaw—European countries dominating or succumbing to each other, the United States winning over or losing a battle to some other contender in the Americas or from "abroad." Although few in the present-day United States would care to keep count of the reversibility of power hierarchies, Anglo-Americans in the United States share a sissifying colonial history with other "emerging" adults and "emerging" nations: paradoxically both a reluctant and adamant need to sever their parental attachments.

In the symbolic scene of the interpersonal or the international theater, the Father tends to be the colonizing agent, the Mother the colonized, and the offspring, a colonial. At a biological level, Father breaks Mother's native egg in order to erect a common(sensical) heritage. Or, at a rhetorical level, Father attempts to inscribe himself on Mother's ground, thus rhetorically activating his target's virtual ground zero of identity by creating a "paper" image of "himself." Biologically or rhetorically this colonial perpetuation remains a bigoted, paternalistic system of partnering and/or fathering. But only in their respective roles are these fathers, mothers, and children; the individuals in question do not have to be men, women, and offspring, nor do they have to be straight, genetically, or even rhetorically connected heirs.

The act of colonial takeover viewed as a model for the primal scene suggests a libidinal dialectic and self-perpetuating, loving dependency that does not need to be procreative: a world where sissies and bullies, be they men or women, straight or gay, mingle and create anticolonialist strategies and/or negotiate postcolonial compromises that retain a sadomasochistic, atavistic attachment to an original act of colonial takeover. In fact, at least in principle, few colonizing powers want to mix in their genes with those of the colonized—colonially speaking, mixed procreation remains a taboo. By default, colonizers and colonized are liberated to engage in alternative sexual creativity.

A sissy or s/he who acts in this role presents a surprising advantage as a "passive" recipient of colonial "defaults." The sissy presumes little responsibility over an attitude or act over which s/he appears to have no actual control; the bully and society prefer not to allow or to admit to it. Within the restrictions of a colonial situation the sissy type or role opens up the active will, or the tacit agreement, of the participants to a communal, liberating, libidinal experience. But is this reality, fantasy, fair game, or beneficial strategy, and from whose perspective?

Born or bred, passive or active, unconscious or willful, permanent or transitory in its role, the sissy emerges as a paradoxical figure of identity and nationality. On the one hand, sissies might become, by default, the symbolic crumpled paper, broken egg, or "feuille blanche," the catchall for singular and social definitions of alien-imposed notions of collectivity. On the other hand, sissies might cast themselves into the colonial net of the powers that be—determined to represent a collective identity/nation emerging from a parenting situation with unsuspected bullying vigor. I deem that such a double typecasting can have devastating results for the dominant modes. Through thick and thin, the sissy attains an unavoidable and singular level of flexibility, mediation, and entrapment in the definition of selfhood and nationhood. In terms of sexual prowess, the sissy comes into his or her own by embracing, coupling, and strangling, and ultimately by merely provoking a symbiotic relationship with an obliging bully.

Primal American Scene

The same colonial shifting of responsibilities that I have outlined at the level of libidinal exchange occurs at other levels (political, aesthetic, ethical, etc.); arguably in those realms it is easier to admit. It is indeed difficult for anyone to admit to being even partly a colonizer by force or will of one's heritage. It is even more difficult for the colonized to admit sexual attraction or love toward the colonizer, even when both sides live within the same person or his/her history. I am not sure it is that much easier for the colonizer to admit such feelings to the colonized. In both cases, admittance of libidinal bipartisanship justifies, but also opens to question, the terms of what appears to be an unavoidable exchange. That is, sexuality and love bring to the surface the mutual responsibility and hence the possibility of rejecting colonialism or merely repressing colonial urges—at least at heart, if not at war.

The potential for a heartfelt rejection of colonialism is as good a reason as any for the colonial apologist or the anticolonialist critic to disguise libidinal implications behind a puritanical veil. Gender and sex stand as the induced results, rather than a driving force, of the mechanics of colonial exchange. Most colonial and postcolonial assessments of the exchanges between the colonizers and the colonized tend to be puritanically inhibited— some, like the critical establishment of the United States, more than others.

The puritanical restrictions placed on colonial sex predispose some critics to interpret, at best, the union of the sissy and the bully as a procreative model of union. And yet, unavoidably, sissies and bullies pass on the baton of power to each other in a rather creative relay race of libidos which largely remains at the margin of heterosexual or even phallic-invasive activity. Moreover, the annals of colonial, anticolonial, and postcolonial history barely record such unions, or do so under cover and duress. The exchange between bullies and sissies is colonially everywhere and textually practically "nowhere" except for those who read between transatlantic lines and sheets.

Even if colonial histories assign the ruling baton, the inscribing pen, and the germinating penis to the colonizer and passive receptivity, ground zero, or broken eggs to the colonized, this sort of activity is marred by circumstances that colonizers like Columbus claim to be beyond their control—including many a nongenerative sexual activity. In fact the colonized sissies throw bully tantrums that overwhelm the colonizers' control. Does this constitute a reverse form of sissification? Is this reversal true to the will of the colonized or are colonizers merely giving the colonized "sissies" permission to bully them?

Spanish colonizers of the Americas often give examples in their texts of incidents of overeager sexuality, bisexuality, androgyny, and hermaphroditism among the colonized as biological excuses to succumb to the charms of the native territories of the libido—that is, to rationalize being, or pretending to be, overwhelmed by locals. Notice that, whether actual or projected, the colonizer records such acts of the colonized. There is always a textual opportunity to transform the economy of libidinal desire in colonial exchanges into the colonizers' rhetorical gain. This avenue of pleasure without guilt assumes every human being to be a sissy subjectable to the bullying of sin. Is this rhetorical management of the sissy-bully libidinal exchange attributable to the Catholic undertones of Spanish American colonialism?

I have already outlined a few puritanical attitudes lingering even today in the critical approaches of a largely Protestant-controlled Anglo-American historical and literary establishment. In the critical field, I propose that the covert tendency in Anglo-Americans is to sexualize power while the overt tendency in Spanish Americans is to empower sexuality. Both of them justify their covert or overt libidinal choices in empowerment through the exorcism of guilt. Anything goes in "America" that suits the Anglo handlers. Anything goes in "America," for she made the Spanish "do it." Such an admittedly simplistic bipolar generalization is necessary to begin to ground the specificity of the Spanish powers' assignment of relative levels of sexuality, guilt, and engenderment in the Americas.

One would expect Spanish America to defend "herself" in whatever way she can against the macho attempt to do her in, to pacify and to make her a piece of the Spanish Fatherland—in Spanish paradoxically called *Madre*

Patria, the "Mother Fatherland." This passive-aggressive, not to mention gender-transgressive, situation is compounded by Columbus's symbolic and factual transatlantic insemination and birthing of America. At once he attempts to occupy and to deliver Others in the name of Spain, the Vatican, and the International Market, while the national, religious, and economic integrity of the above-mentioned entities barely qualify them as transatlantic occupying Selves. So what if the people Columbus met on this side of the Atlantic were largely oversexed, bisexuals, androgynous, hermaphroditic, gay, or mere sissies able to act out the pansexual colonizers' fantasy of occupation? In the transatlantic zeal to occupy everyone at will the sissy only seems less threatening a target of occupation than the rest.

By the fact of occupation, compensation, conversion, and apprenticeship, everything American is doomed to be—or be sissified by and bullied into becoming—Spanish. This includes the latent bisexuality of Amazons and cannibals, androgynous sirens and hermaphroditic gods encountered by a chronicler such as Christopher Columbus.[6] Such libidinal attitudes could be taken as the Spanish "misinterpretation" of the Carib peoples' aggressive nature, extendable to the rest of the Caribbean. Perhaps cannibal men eat every foreign man and a few women in sight, while Amazon women pierce with arrows every foreign woman and a few men in sight to defend themselves. The same goes for every beckoning siren and rival who plays "ugly" games of transgenderment.

In Columbus's and other colonial pages of the early Caribbean, the climate and other circumstances of certain islands lead to sissifying anatomical, physiological, and behavioral excesses. Presumably the colonizers' continued exposure might also render them vulnerable to the effect of such sissifying conditions. This might work in favor of both colonizers and colonized, for, according to the unwritten libidinal rules of colonialism, if it takes a bully to take a sissy, it certainly makes it more sexually challenging for the sissy to bully back—or at least to resist and then to yield to the act of sissification.

For the male transatlantic explorer with sex in mind, to experience is to know, to know is to meet, to meet is to join, to join is to own, regardless of the gender, sexual, genital, and genetic consequences for himself or for Others. But the Others are bound to bounce back. In their need for libidinal challenge, colonizers begin to relish the feminized sissy's not-too-easy goods, perhaps without the relishing agent's realizing the full potential and danger of the sissy's alternating roles as bait, prick teaser, and backbiting or entrapping lure.

Let me summarize the situation. In the rhetorical Spanish, and I suspect also in the other European, takeovers of the Americas—to different degrees, in varying fashions, and with diverse effects—the colonizer and the colonized meet through sissifying and bullying actions that do not necessarily respect the borders of strict gender coding, sexual behavior, or the opposite colonial conditions. Moreover, in the colonial scene there is sissy power as much as bully power among the colonizers and the colonized. Both types of power emerge in the implicitly or explicitly sadomasochistic ritual of sex among enemies—extendable to friendly sexual acts among consenting partners.

In order to redeem "sissy power" from the sissy trick it is imperative to distinguish voluntary sissy action and encounters from forced, be it faked or real, passivity. Allow me to disqualify from the sissy trick any instances in which the sissy action smacks of being merely a powerless reaction, and not even a cynical accommodation, to invasive bullying techniques—such as slanderous labeling, sexual harassment, genital altering, and rape.

Sissy Closet

In my reading of the intercontinental partnership between the colonizing bully and the colonized sissy, neither of them is frozen into the sort of activity and passivity which dooms them to one another in a one-sided fashion. Such a rationalization of dependency emerged as a backhanded compliment "active" males allot to "passive" women and gays across cultures and centuries in order to justify a second-rate form of existence in the margins of alpha male heterosexuality.

In Spanish America this sort of hairsplitting complementarity becomes more problematic to the powers that be. Receptive women (passive temptress and/or Virgin-Mary-types, rather than active and demanding "bitches") join men (*maricones,* the Mary-like, buggered or holed-out ones) in the process of "validating"—sexually, politically, even linguistically—the incoming males, who are straight machos or *bugarrones* [buggerers or holemakers], whom they presumably serve and service.[7] Male, female, straight or gay, the hole and the holed one are doomed to a womanizing brand of sissification. Meanwhile the bully, who can be from any of the above gender and sexual categories, remains a macho above suspicion of homosexual behavior. In other words, in the Spanish context, a long tradition favors active sexual performance over passive definitions of gender in determining the form of power manipulation available to the gender- and/or sexually marked underclasses. This contrast in Spanish and Anglo–American attitudes toward the impact of performance in claiming prowess informs the development of libidinal theories of marginal power across the Americas. In both the Spanish and the Anglo camps women and gays share many elements of a common predicament—as bitchy, queer, and weak receptors of societal whims.

Members of the Anglo-American feminist and gay movements have reclaimed labels and defended attitudes such as those of the "bitch" and "queer" abused by the empowering members of the "male" and "straight" world. I am thinking of the by-now-commonplace feminist and gay rights of "auto-bitchification" and Queer Nation's "auto-queerification."[8] Likewise, members of the Spanish American feminist movements have reclaimed the term "Malinche" and "weak," to empower those who mediate power. I am thinking of Gloria Anzaldúa's empowerment of Hernán Cortés's main native courtesan and translator during the Spanish takeover of Mexican history as a *malinchista* attitude of defiance, as well as Josefina Ludmer's rendering of the weak peoples' demise into "la treta del débil" [the trick of the weak]. The strategies of "pro-bitch" feminism, Queer Nation, Gloria Anzaldúa, and Josefina Ludmer converge in upgrading the notion of the receptive agent of colonialism, presumably passive females and males, into a subversive force capable of transforming libidinal traps into political trenches with a touch of nationalism. All of the above promised at least an actual conditional truce and/or symbolic unconditional liberation to both women and gays. The strategies in question make nations out of ostensibly desperate and disparate nationals who propose to break singly or together through traditionally subjugated, critically secondhand, and/or second-class identities built from within, against, and beyond the borders of dominant nations and national paradigms.

The sissy trick embraces that of the bitches, the queers, the malinchistas, and the weaklings in their proposed linguistic, political, symbolic, and material takeover of the sex act that is traditionally committed against all of the above. In this sense, none of these tricks implicitly defy Freudian theorization on the primal scene, but they indeed challenge what I consider Freud's *malgré-lui* phallocentrism. It remains difficult to think of investing the sissy in Freudian theorization without erecting him or her into a floating signifier and a floating phallus—anybody's to have, parody, or parade, albeit a second-rate or artificially concocted one. And yet, I am willing to try Freud on for size in the empowerment of the sissy as well as in the sissification of power.

Phallicizing, dephallicizing, or even dildoizing the sissy's trick indeed would be a shame, but so would shunning Freud's systematization of an individual's coming to terms with a primal scene which is so invested in a prick's painful colonial infliction. For me, the recording, remembering, and even re-membering of the imminently colonial primal scene holds the key for the ex-colonizer and the ex-colonized to model their respective identities on a common historical strategy of libidinal exchange. Prick or no prick, pricking or pricked, accepting that our colonial ancestors succumbed to each other, we postcolonials could learn to cope, survive, and triumph over the repressive phantom of colonialism.

The individual friction and fiction of the primal scene inform the sort of sissy trick that every individual develops against parental joining and upbringing to which he or she is a long-standing "passive" element and "weak" link. People out their individuality from its dependence on such a sissy closet. The same goes for nations. A bringing to consciousness of their own colonial trauma becomes the first step in forging a postcolonial collective unconsious.

Sissy Fetish

When in the midst of the first Spanish American consenting colonial exchanges, the phallus raises its head—ugly or pretty, puny or awesome, real or plastic—colonial sissies give it a parodic blow. Let me bring to your attention a late-sixteenth-century transatlantic passage that has become for me an important sissy fetish of revenge, or at least a two-headed sword. The empowering instrument is found in the hands of Botello, Cortés's fortune-telling page—but presumably it was also communally shared in the colonizer's camp:

> tenía otras como cifras y a manera de suertes que hablaban unas letras contra otras en aquellos papeles que era como libro chico. Y también se halló en la petaca una natura como de hombre, de obra de un geme, hecha de baldrés, ni más ni menos, al parecer de natura de hombre, y tenía dentro como una barra de lana de tundidor. (Díaz del Castillo 276)
>
> [he had other "figures" apparently for fortune-telling, and contradictory statements fashioned into a sort of booklet. Found in the box was also an object four inches long in the shape of a man's genitals, handcrafted in leather, no more, no less like a man's genitals. The resemblance was remarkable, and it was stuffed with a stiff bar made of flock.][9]

These are the words Bernal Díaz del Castillo uses to comment on the fallacies or "phallacies" of colonial inscription in a chapter (CXXVIII) dedicated to describing Cortés's men's retreat from Mexico City. This chapter follows the summary of Montezuma's death. Fortune-telling, contradictory statements, the small book, and the handy dildo stand erect to console the Spanish troops in their failed colonizing attempts. But does this self-serving instrument render Cortés's men and/or Bernal's buddies into sissies? And if so, can these budding colonial citizens transform their newly found sissifying ground into an alternative platform of power?

The chapter in question rationalizes a retreat which occurred in spite of the Spaniards having fought like machos ("peleábamos como varones" 272) against the native "perros" [dogs]. The same seems true of the Spanish instruments of inscription, pen and penis, which were simply not good enough to transact a fair exchange, much less to guarantee the colonizers' power against the beastly circumstances.

Think of dog behavior according to the traditional European debasement of women as "bitches." Let us also remember that the notion of dog-like behavior appears from the beginning of the Spanish rebirth of the Americas by way of the Latin-derived term "cannibal" suggesting, among other things, "dog-like" man-eating men.[10] Whether through bitchification or through queerification, natives provide a ground zero for the conqueror.

Implicit erotic bestialization of natives is not the only problematic sign of international transaction. Beyond war, sex, and sexual wars, the quest for power extends to Spain's original favorite currency of self-empowering exchange with the other: gold. Throughout the chapter in question gold becomes a problematic fetish for the Cortesian camp, at least as viewed by Bernal, a retired soldier living on a fixed income in inflationary sixteenth-century Spain. The transatlantic quest for gold proved not to be what was expected. This valued metal was not only more scarce and difficult to obtain, but also more of a symbolic commodity and problematic standard of value than expected. Finally, as Cortés's men retreat from battle, gold became a rather heavy and useless item. The desperate men make do with an icon of validation which no longer suits the original colonizing urge, much less the macho daring gold fever spurred them into.

As quoted, Bernal brings to the fore the impact of a fake, parodic, and/or homoerotic pen(is) as instrument of fate in the hands of the lonesome and desperate envoys of the Spanish Empire, who were by then sissified by adversity within an alien environment of war, ethics, and rhetoric. As always, conquering, textual, and sexual politics go hand in hand in the colonial making of a penis, and the same goes for the sissy ground on which this penis intended to inscribe itself. The problem, if any, for the colonizers was that they were pretty close to ground zero of conquering, that indeed the colonized had struck back and made them retreat from the native power and left them to their own devices without much phallic power to draw upon. The astrologer's all-knowing dildo offered a chance for not just the defeated army, but for anyone, to become an inscribing agent, or to gain/regain a position of superiority. Dildo in hand, one could even play at will a solitary game of sissy and bully, and ultimately to inscribe oneself.

Although I am still trying to figure out how to use a dildo to orient myself—or console myself while disoriented—this added instrument of pleasure/assertion does not seem to have harmed the sissy in his/her empowerment, and thus it should not hamper my own critical prowess. Spanish and American converging interests enticed Spaniards in America to resort to the astrologically adept dildo when a real pen, a penis, or any other instrument of transaction would not suffice in the task of inscribing the right inner course within Mexico, or for that matter outside of Mexico. It is then befitting to frame the textual illustrations of the birth of the sissy trick during the first two centuries of Spanish America with Bernal Díaz del Castillo's belated sarcastic comment and plastic instrumental handling of such a period. The phallic spoof of this retired soldier's reminiscences of a youth spent in Cortés's Mexican campaigns is not a mere *recherche du penis perdu*. Consciously or not, Bernal's somewhat flaccid memories of the Spanish empire's strike on Mesoamerica undermine the conservative, one-sided colonialist notions of macho power.

During the first century of the New World recent Spanish immigrants and creoles produced dildo-like, artificial transatlantic tools of colonial inscription, such as: Fray Ramón Pané's late-fifteenth-century Caribbean-written text *Relación acerca de las antigüedades de los Indios* [Account of the Antiquities of the Indians], the mid-sixteenth-century *Historia general de las cosas de la Nueva España* [General History of Things from New Spain] written in Mexico by the Spanish missionary Fray Bernardino de Sahagún, and the late-sixteenth-century text by the Mexican-born chronicler Juan Suárez de Peralta *Tratado del descubrimiento de las Yndias y su conquista* [Treaty of the Discovery of the Indies and Its Conquest]. Unfortunately there are no known comparable contemporary texts written by native or creole women. Only fragments of native women's texts or manipulated women's voices have remained. And women are often represented as usurping the male role or acting like effeminate males, although in some cases this should not be read as demeaning to either gender.

Sissy Outing

> "Dejad a vuestros maridos, y vámonos a otras tierras y llevemos mucho güeyo." (Pané 23) [11] [Leave your spouses behind and let's go to other lands carrying off much 'loot'.]
> —According to Pané's view of the Arawak myth of origin, this is the revenge of the disgruntled spouses (women, sissies?) under the command of Guacanaona [Being of the Yucca; the Sea; The-One-Without-Male-Ancestry.]
> Hay algunos hombres que practican entre ellos, y se les dice behiques. (Pané 33) [There are some men who practice among themselves and are called *behiques*.]
> —According to Pané's view of the Arawak myth of origin, these are the Arawak keepers of tradition, tellers of tales, medicine men, appeasers of the spirits.

Around the turn of the fifteenth century Columbus commissioned Father Raymond Pané to study Arawak mores, keeping in mind that the Church should discreetly reserve the biggest phallus and the sturdiest cross for the colonizer and render into powerless sissies and/or into hysterical bullies all native bearers of that cross. What emerged instead was a text that not only revealed a very tentatively gendered Caribbean Eden, but which essentially diagnosed and empathized with the sissified nature of the colonized.

According to Pané's rendering of the Arawak myth of genesis, men's and women's existence was not genetically complete or their meeting and mating arranged until they discovered a form of ethically sanitized mediation, an excuse for genital "exchanges" between them. As we shall see, what happened was a less-than-ethically sanitized and a more-than-unexpected form of genital exchange. At any rate it is likely that Spaniards and their texts radically changed the "native" situation as an anthropologist would, and indeed Pané has been labeled as the first in the Americas (Pané ni, 1–2).

Let us also keep in mind that although Arawak myths and/or their Spanish renderings still bow to the phallus, it is reduced to a borrowable and floating object of communication and an ambivalent subject of desire— as later corroborated by the aging soldier Bernal. Even the genital power of the supervising deity of carnal exchange remains "improvisationally" phallic and even parodically antiphallic.

To begin with, according to historical and present Hispano-Caribbean language and lore, Guacanaona is associated with several transgendered fantasies. First, this entity is the Being of the Yucca, a "female" root fetishized as the penis—and more specifically, a penis engaged in a male self-satisfying, masturbatory action. Second s/he is the Sea, a female power that once held the transatlantic male voyagers in the palm of her hand. Third, s/he is "The-One-Without-Male-Ancestry," an originating force with no male models or need for phallic instruction or introduction—a less-than-traditional phallic "resolution." "The One . . ." is the first in a long male-dominated generational line which undoubtedly uses, abuses, and/or fuses with matriarchal powers.

I am interested in two libidinally pregnant moments in Pané's account of the Arawak myth of origin that transform overt genital suspension, transmutability, and/or hermaphroditism into covert sissification, as they indeed affect the Hispano-American textual reconstruction of the Caribbean nations' primal scene. In both textual moments, the Spanish missionary plays with colonial fires. The very textual heritage of such a scene is enriched and complicated by the fact that, the original Spanish having been lost, it is best known through its insertion in Ferdinand Columbus's biography of his father—which is itself a reconstruction of the primal scene of this controversial heir to the Father of the Americas.

The first passage of interest in our study of the sissification of nationhood opens up the notion of repressed sexual guilt, as well as relative escape, resolution, and the new challenges implicit in a hermaphroditic ritual of engenderment:

> Dicen que un día fueron a lavarse los hombres, y estando en el agua, llovía mucho, que estaban deseosos de tener mujeres; y que muchas veces, cuando llovía, habían ido a buscar las huellas de sus mujeres; más no pudieron encontrar alguna nueva de ellas. Pero aquel día, laván-dose, dicen que vieron caer de algunos árboles, bajándose por entre las ramas, una cierta forma de personas, que no eran hombres ni muje-res, ni tenían sexo de varón ni de hembra, las cuales fueron a cogerlas; pero huyeron como si fuesen anguilas. Por lo cual llamaron a dos o tres hombres por mandato de su cacique, puesto que ellos no podían cogerlas, para que viesen cuantas eran, y buscasen para cada una un hombre que fuese caracaracol, porque tenían las manos ásperas, y que así estrechamente las sujetasen. Dijeron al cacique que eran cuatro; y así llevaron cuatro hombres, que eran caracaracoles. El cual caracara-col es una enfermedad como sarna, que hace al cuerpo muy áspero. Después que las hubieron cogido, tuvieron consejo sobre cómo podía hacer que fuesen mujeres, puesto que no tenían sexo de varón ni de hembra. . . . Buscaron un pájaro que se llama inriri, antiguamente

llamado inriri cahubabayael, el cual agujerea los árboles, y en nuestra lengua llámase pico. E igualmente tomaron a aquellas mujeres sin sexo de varón ni de hembra, y les ataron los pies y las manos, y trajeron el pájaro mencionado, y se lo ataron al cuerpo. Y éste creyendo que eran maderos, comenzó la obra que acostumbra, picando y agujereando en el lugar donde ordinariamente suele estar el sexo de las mujeres. Y de este modo dicen los indios que tuvieron mujeres, según cuentan los más viejos. (26–28)

[It is said that one day men went to wash themselves, and while in the water, it was raining a lot, and they wanted very much to have women; and that oftentimes, when it rained, they had gone in search of traces of their women, but they could find no news about them. That day, while washing up, the natives say they saw, lowering themselves among the branches of certain trees, some kind of beings who were neither men nor women, nor had they male or female genitalia, which they attempted to take, but they fled like eels. Since the natives could not take them, their chieftain commanded them to count these ungrabbable sissies and for each to call in a sore-covered male with hands rough enough to grab them tightly. The natives told their chieftain that the beings in question were four, and four sore-covered men were brought in. The sores of these men are like those from scabies, which makes the skin very uneven. After grabbing these beings, they wondered how it had been possible for the grabbers to know that these beings were women since they had neither male nor female genitalia. The men searched for the *inriri* bird . . . which perforates trees, and which we call in Spanish pecker. And indiscriminately they took all of these women without male or female genitalia, they tied up their feet and hands, brought in the above-mentioned bird, and they bound it against their bodies. And the bird, thinking they were logs, began its habitual job, pecking and hollowing out the very spot where women ordinarily have their genitalia. And thus the Indians had women, according to the elders' tales.]

In my own words: While washing up to purify themselves of evil thought, while immersed in a double female principle of water (below and above), native males and, in turn, their alien counterparts observed slimy and ambivalent but phallically eel-like beings, seductively falling off the trees. Apparently pusillanimous and sissified, but decidedly beyond the predatory, or bullying, reach of the observers, these four beings required extraordinary measures: such as the grabbing by a quartet of rough types who are experienced in the contagiously wicked art of sexual penetration. But the rough types' sickly art requires help from phallic artifice, which they find in the dildo-bird held to mediate between predator and prey—be they attached to one, the other, or both. In fact, the Italian and Spanish manuscripts of this myth of origin make it difficult to figure out the mechanics of attachment of the dildo-bird: the slimy hermaphroditic females or the rough-skinned males. At any rate, the slimy creatures with eel-like qualities implicitly demand to become females by subliminally summoning and/ or creatively seducing the rough-edged and lovesick males into action. At least rhetorically, this arbitrary penetration remains under female control. The females give as much as they take—albeit in terms contaminated with phallic penetration. Improvised or not, the females penetrate the phallically enhanced male libido, while giving the impression to men, native or alien, that they "had" women.

My second chosen passage of the Hispano-Arawaks attempts to get away from a faithful rendering of an idolatrous system that condemned native beings to a condition of bigendered bombshells ready to explode into rather arbitrary, mechanical, and sissified/sissifying sexual acts. Instead of the newcomers reveling in an Arawak myth that evokes for the Europeans a "Golden Age" for ripe-off-the-trees values, including sex without guilt, Pané records a golden shower ritual that ensures Spanish males becoming pals with their Arawak counterparts or at least guaranteed mutual understanding or even fusing of their respective male-centered myths:

> Salidos aquéllos del adoratorio, tiraron las imágenes al suelo y las cubrieron de tierra y después orinaron encima, diciendo: "Ahora serán buenos y grandes tus frutos." Y esto porque las enterraron en un campo de labranza, diciendo que sería bueno el fruto que allí se había plantado; y todo esto por vituperio. (53)
> [After leaving the (Christian) chapel those men threw the images to the ground, heaped earth on them, and pissed on top, saying "Now you will yield good and abundant fruit." And thus they buried the images in fertile ground, prognosticating a good crop from the fruit planted there; and all of this was done in the spirit of slander.]

The first passage threatens with the possibility of guilt: as bigendered women ready themselves to please (or to please themselves at will with what at first sight might seem) crafty and discriminating heterosexual males. The second passage threatens with the possibility of redemption: homosocial men piss together to "yield good and abundant fruit" on command. At least from the Spanish perspective recorded and seeded by Pané, both myths exploit the native sexual "openness" as a potential target of their transatlantic conquerors.

Spaniards first recall an Arawak myth of origin in which sexual desire, sheer will, and technical ingenuity of the phallo-prosthetic kind transforms asexual beings into targets of penetration. Updating this ritual the new-comers should be able to awaken asexual beings to alien sex while rendering intrinsically hermaphroditic beings—female "by (overt organ/functional phallic) default" into male or female "targets" of their conquering. This is an excuse for the Spaniards to "have" whomever they want.

The counterpart urinary myth revisited can be interpreted as a pissing ritual in which Spanish images—symbols of a male-dominated bond sanc-tioned by "higher" powers imposed from abroad—spur the natives' com-petitive urge. That is, upon confronting alien men's idols native believers experience a sacred and secular identity crisis overwhelmingly framed as a homosexual panic. In short, Spanish idols show themselves as threatening: "bigger," "better," and more powerful than native ones. The native re-action is to subject to a golden shower such outsize objects of rival venera-tion and alien assault. This reaction is ostensibly geared to rechoreograph mutual desire into a pas de deux of aggression and counter-aggression. Whatever the intentions and results of this exchange might have been, be they covertly militant or overtly military, the matter leads to a transatlantic male-bonding effort that still evokes panic in many a postcolonial macho.

But why would Christopher himself, Pané, as his anthropological envoy, Ferdinand in his father's biography, and so many other European mas-ters, witnesses, chroniclers, translators, and heirs inspire and be inspired by such male-bonding moments? Beyond endorsing a frankly homosexual interpretation, there are at least three possible rationales for the European rendering of Arawak male-bonding rituals. (1) The possibility of opening up the scene to a transatlantic male-bonding ritual that would lead to a peacemaking strategy. (2) The symbolic rendering of the genital gesture which becomes able to produce a male-engendered heritage through a urinary rite of fertility in which Spanish seeds are mythically rather than genetically inseminated. (3) The act justifies revenge—that is, symbolic and physical takeover—for the Spanish creators of the images upon which natives pissed.

Whether the phallus is borrowed from a bird or squandered in urinary births, the telling of both of these myths underscores a troubling trans-atlantic grafting of male supremacy. However, in either case, the Span-ish telling of the Arawak myth of origin challenges traditional European notions of macho "domination" as it encounters a Caribbean Eden of hermaphroditic women and homosocial men. How real, then, is the threat of the transatlantic phallus? Can we, the American children of the colonizers and the colonized, find in Pané's text a mythical interpretation of our origin based on a dephallicizing sissy strategy?

In the forever–golden age encountered by Spaniards in the Caribbean, golden boys, local or imported, have to learn to love female hermaphrodites with the help of a rear-admiral of a pecker joker—as *inriri,* the pig-Latin name for the bird, begins to suggest. This is the sort of legendary tale that transforms every bully of a male into a plastic receptacle of imminent sissification.

For the sake of regeneration, rather than power, everyone in Pané's Arawak legend of origins bows to a master phallus, or the transatlantic idea of such, which ultimately belongs to no one in particular—or at least to no one most people get to know. Native women and men—straight, gay, bisexual, hermaphroditic, androgynous, transgendered, or transsexual—join together to prime their improvised instrument of exchange—the borrowing of and burrowing with a floating phallus. The act is carried out with a high level of theater and pretense. This befits the behavior of good sissy nationalists, who forge their primal scene with a parodic strength that rubs against the grain of native or alien phallocentrism. Whether parodied phallocentrism is or is not a homage to real phallocentrism, the scene in question suggests a communal act of auto-sissification that serves to induct intruders into a mode of behavior that mocks, and even neutralizes, dominant models of colonial empowerment.

In the end, Pané gives some glimmer of hope for surviving Western culture's virtually inescapable phallic empowerment. Even the most straight, alien, macho colonizer suffers the weight of the phallus and makes a living from avoiding becoming a victim of its deadly responsibility. The sissy turns such avoidance into an art of entrapment. Moreover, in assessing the sissy values of this scene, think of the alternatives available to Columbus's men within Pané's textual possibilities. The incoming men would have to learn with their native counterparts to "piss on ashes" in the sort of ritual that transforms males from latent sissies into bullying buddies.

The Freudian basis for the Mongolian ritual of "pissing on ashes," as well as Pané's much earlier rendering of the Arawaks' own golden ritual, is that it established manhood by way of men pissing together or otherwise learning to play with fire.[12] This test stands as the proof that they would not become erect together—at least at the same time and to a maximum, due to a near physiological impossibility among males.

If Freud placed great importance on the basic human confict of admitting that we all come out of a mating struggle that begins with the invasion of the penis into the vagina, which is dangerously connected with penile dueling, the Arawaks—at least as viewed by some Spaniards—are ready to place that struggle under a different light. Upon recognizing the need to consummate their encounter with an invasive embrace and that in so doing a penis and a vagina come in rather handy, they concentrate on the artificiality of the instrument of invasion (a transient woodpecker at the level of male genitalia) and of the invaded space (a hollow hole at the level of women's genitalia). Power, will, and desire of the "invasive" instrument and the invaded "space," not to mention the very creative meaning of the procreative act, remain up for grabs. It does not matter what you begin your life with—only how you choose to use the available equipment. Pané's version of Arawak gender and sexual power is not derived from a notion of a person's own genital equipment, but from the highly theatrical performance of borrowed genitalia—a fleeting bird, a communal pissing penis.

Pané's and Columbus's Arawaks transform the genital struggle of man over woman, as well as that of man over man, into the colonial struggle of natives against alien forces who transgender and transmute themselves, creatively and procreatively, practically at will. The same sort of colonially shared sissification is further developed into biologically procreative, sexually creative, and rhetorically subversive nation-formation drives in the texts that follow.

Creolized Sissy

In the first quarter of the sixteenth century—as proselytizing Spaniards begin to promote Mesoamerica as a transatlantic, hybrid culture—sodomy, another hypothetical and controversial form of hole-making, becomes a way of keeping the sissy syndrome both alive and at bay. Paradoxically, early Spanish accounts would repudiate anal intercourse as the "wrong" form of mediation for both the hole-makers and the holed ones. And yet, many chroniclers believed that this was the predominant form of sexual expression between natives and a privilege of the upper classes. After reading account after account of the "fear" of sodomy, I also suspect that the practice was tantalizing and threatening on both sides of the Atlantic. As I have previously suggested, many Spaniards secretly adopted sodomy to provide human contact and sexual release while skirting the dangers of miscegenation. Add to this equation sodomy as a form of domination provoked by elite natives who desperately needed to be brought under control.

In the end, sodomy and homosexuality become transatlantic forms of birth control as well as metonymic expressions of male-centered elitism and imperialism on both sides of the Atlantic, as well as a unifying macho-saving feature of transatlantic colonialism.

Some transatlantic Christians rushed to suggest pardons upon repentance and ethically acrobatic exceptions to the rule of sodomy, for those who either do not know better—sometimes an entire native group or "class," such as the *berdache*—and those who derived momentary power from it—such as the "penetrating" agent.[13] Thereby we can deduce that the insertive role in sodomy—ostensibly the function of macho-acting sissies/gays—, could become an elitist if devious form of male empowerment over a hole that did not have to belong to a female. The penetrating penis, in fact, would be virtually depersonalized as a finger of power, semi-detached as a lively dildo or deadly bird of a certain "pecking order" which domesticating agents grabbed from the American wild in order to subject an Other to his self-righteous and guiltless will.

Worldwide colonial frameworks, such as those lingering in the Americas, attempt to subsume issues of sexual taste and libidinal performance under the terms of domination. This attitude is merely more evident and honest in the Hispanic part of the Americas. In the exchange between the *bugarrón* [buggerer] and the *maricón* [buggered], as in that between the bully and the sissy, the "dominators" rationalize their position as necessary control. At best, such a control benefits both partners by developing a sadomasochistic dependency. At worst, the underdogs' desire to be dominated bring them to "submit" to a symbolically macho or factually phallic demonstration of fill-in power.

Father Bernardino de Sahagún is one of these subliminal prescribers of a penis in every household. He provides homosexual males with an extra organic, perhaps orgasmic, quality that allows a natural tendency to want to be sodomized. Gay males are diagnosed as "sométicos," that is, prone to "subjectability" (Sahagún 557).[14] The Spanish original also suggests "somatic," loosely someone with a compromised body or bodily symptoms or injury, perhaps physically ill. And yet, in spite of Sahagún's misconceptions, we might have to thank this missionary for taking a giant step, second only to Pané, in the anthropological discussion of transatlantic gender perception and sexual exchanges.

One can make a further claim for Sahagún's text: he addresses homosexuality as a "condition," rather than exclusively as a practice of choice, not reducible to sodomy or even defined by it. The homosexual condition might be tempting, but it is certainly not contagious, in our priest's words.

And yet, this functional condition assigns a womanly role to both the "sub-jectable" and the "hermaphoditic" among the colonized (557 and 563). This is not to say that there are no macho-types among the natives. Sahagún defines him according to the Aztec category of *quáchic,* who is "el hombre varón fuerte . . . furioso y rabioso contra sus enemigos, valentazo por ser membrudo" (552) [the strong male type . . . full of fury and wrath against his enemies, a daredevil because of his well-endowed anatomy]. Everyone else is: "afeminado y de un no nada se espanta; apto más para huir que para seguir a los enemigos, muy delicado, espantadizo y medroso, porque en todo se muestra cobarde y mujeril" (552) [effeminate and intimidated by everything, he is prepared to flee rather than to pursue his enemies; being very delicate, easily scared and fainthearted, he invariably reacts in a cow-ardly and womanish fashion]. Given the fact that the Spaniards conquered with the sword and the cross—and presumably with their penises—of the two categories of people in question, Sahagún would undoubtedly pre-fer the cowardly and womanish type. Such native sissies are more easily Christianized, Hispanicized, or otherwise both warringly and lovingly ma-nipulated. But in colonial war, as in colonial faith and love, the roles of male and bully or female and sissy go together. In the end, for Sahagún, bullies and sissies are not born as such, but made—through the colonial process of war, faith, and love—and capable of reinventing the phallus and the vagina if need be, but we both should be burned at the stake anyway.

At the birth of the creole conscience, which is practically equivalent in Spanish America to a nation-forming mechanism, there must have been some creole empathy toward the "subjectable" and "hermaphroditic" citi-zens of Spain, including women, sissies, and the like—perhaps the same sort of theoretical or practical empathy that at that time became patent toward blacks and other groups perceived as dangerously contagious mi-norities. Indeed Europeans attribute syphilis, a condition iconized by Pané as the source of itchy male-like genitalia and para-libidinal urges, as alter-natively a New World or an African illness—while more nationalistic Euro-peans simply blame each other for the syphilitic scourge that mars the freedom to have sex. In the end, let's face it, white or not, practicing homo-sexuals or liberal straights, women or women-like, adamant sissies or sen-sitive itchy machos, sodomizers or sodomized, colonial creoles felt royally screwed by imperial Spain.

As the transplanted Spaniards vied with Peninsular Spain for power and the right to a transatlantically Hispanic national culture, the bully-ing power of conquering and the sissy weakness of being conquered were deemed as two aspects of a single uncivilized activity that was theoretically available to anyone willing to Hispanicize. A newfound transgendered softness took its place. To be willfully effeminate, a woman part-way (if not necessarily conditionally subjectable or hermaphroditic) was no longer a crime; on the contrary, it was a European-like mark of distinction, albeit a problematic parodic stance for male and female creoles alike. Thus the notion of creole refinement takes an interesting turn in the history of gender, sexual, and national liberation: it is oh so suave and European to be a sissy. It is a question of the right climate inspiring one "to go native." As Sahagún would put it himself: "Y no me maravillo tanto de las tachas y dislates de los naturales de esta tierra, porque los españoles que en el habitan, y mucho más los que en ella nacen, cobran estas malas inclinaciones . . . se hacen otros" (579) [I do not marvel at the flaws and nonsense of the natives of these lands, for the Spaniards who live there, and even more those who are born there, acquire the same bad inclinations . . . they themselves become others (or different)]. It is no surprise, then, that America's very nature sissifies generation after generation of natives. The process extends to creolized outsiders: "los padres y las madres no se pueden apoderar con sus hijos e hijas para apartarlos de los vicios y sensualidades que esta tierra cría" (580) [fathers and mothers cannot take command of their sons and daughters in order to keep them away from the vices and sensualities that this land generates].

Birth of a Nation of Sissies

> . . . era muy lindo hombre de a caballo. (Suárez de Peralta xiii–xiv).
> [. . . he was a pretty man of the horseback–riding sort.]—Juan Suárez
> de Peralta on his viceroy Luis de Velasco.[15]

The earliest example I could find of an open sissy form of empowerment is the work of the Mexican creole Juan Suárez de Peralta, from the late sixteenth century. Rather conventionally for the time of its writing, the work has an impossibly descriptive page-long title beginning with *Treaty of the Discovery of the Indies and its Conquest* . . . and ending with . . . *the Breaking [rompimiento] of the Englishmen, and of Francis Drake's Input That Led Him to Be Declared an Enemy.*[16] This type of "narrative" title is relatively common to the period, but I also read a paradoxical stance in Suárez de Peralta's intent. After all, the titular narration begins with the willingly one-sided Spanish conquest of the New World and ends with the equally hyperbolic English assault on Spain iconized by Francis Drake, who captained the Armadas' defeat and now poses a semi-official threat to the Spanish Americas. The title sets the action between the time Spain inscribed itself onto the New World and the time that other European nations challenged Spanish transatlantic domination. Let me set up the sequence of events the title announces in view of what I consider to be the creole author's deliberate desire to fall short not just of the title, but of the official historical program of the conquest, from which, after all, he emerges as a partial victim and perhaps a sissy hero—or at least a sissy hero-worshiper.

The title suggests yet another view of the history of the Spanish Americans in general and of New Spain, that is, colonial Mexico, in particular, as a barbarian body ostensibly awaiting the Imperial finger, pointed at, appointed, and anointed as a target of civilized conquering. This discreetly ironic view of Mexico's rebirth as a transatlantic colony is not surprising for a Euro-Mexican creole forced to rethink his position vis-à-vis the undying power struggle between the Aztec and the Spanish empires and cultures. Moreover, this man's perspective is colored by several personal and social circumstances. Chief among them is the transition from a creole pedigree to a nationalist stance that compels the author to confront the traumatic primal scene of his mixed heritage.[17]

Suárez de Peralta is also deeply concerned about the development of identity from the Hispano-Mexican primal scene to its full development as a hybrid nation. To that end, the author considers the multiple balance between action and passion, maleness and femaleness, civilization and barbarity, ad hoc authenticity and superimposed refinement, but not in terms that readily fall into a Mexican-European polarity. The failures of such a balance create abuses of power against which Suárez de Peralta both bitterly complains and offers solutions, both mediatory and subversive. I am particularly interested in this creole author's "sissy trick" in undermining ironically macho displays of power, already iconized by his "prettification" (read sissification) underlying the viceroy's "horse(man) power"—as exemplified by the epigraph to this section.

The ironic handling of power starts with the book's opening sentence, which echoes the title's opening phrase. This paradoxical setting enhances a rhetorical tradition of transatlantic chronicles that invests the lands and peoples to be called America with a travel-brochure patina. Come visit the wilds of America! Suárez de Peralta, writing (like Bernal) many decades after the fact, upgrades such a tone to one of nostalgia for the original Spanish impetus to bully everything and body in the "New World." American nature/human bounty awaits those willing to jump over the Atlantic puddle and their own inhibitions. This is reason enough for European voyages, profiting, and conquering. Let us look at this opening sentence:

"Las Yndias son tierra la más fertilísima que debe aber oy descubierta en el mundo, y más llena de todas aquellas cosas que en él son menester para el servicio del hombre y aprovechamiento dél" (3) [The Indian women/lands must be the most fertile ground/land uncovered to date in the world, and the most plentiful in the things man needs for his service and exploitation].

Going beyond the innuendos of previous chroniclers, Suárez de Peralta's hindsight account of his struggling nation's origin readily lists the potential disappointment of those expecting more than a fertile land and a great lay. In fact the Spanish model makers transplanted to Mexico hang on to their misguided expectations and utopic dreams, concentrating on rampant macho attitudes while missing the opportunity to relish and to share the Mexican bounty. Suárez de Peralta paints a picture of despotic mismanagement disguised as Euro- and phallocentrically "civilized" despotism.

In the first pages of his book the author makes a summary allusion to the failures of the Spanish gold and silver fever now substituted by equally chaotic cow and mare herding, as hardly anyone knows whose cow or whose mare is whose. Neither native metals nor imported animals become worthwhile Spanish possessions, much less icons or sources of true Mexican worth. A plethora of native and imported American products and values provide problematic justification for an irrational government and a tyrannical administration. This is still the case approximately seventy-five years after the initial transatlantic takeover.

For Suárez de Peralta machismo is at the root of senseless exploitation. Mind you, for him, exploitation is always senseless, particularly when it is done for the sake of iconic rather than practical value. For instance, the author laments that bovine skins and suet [cuero y sebo (4)] become a commodity while the meat is left to rot, eaten by wild dogs and vultures. Furthermore, the text's reference to the senseless macho quartering of cows and taming of wild mares suggests the exploitation of women—or of beta males in their stead.

If for Suárez America is feminine ground resenting macho takeover, he finds victims, martyrs, and, ultimately, heroines to counterbalance such a state of affairs. The author introduces a herd of semi-domestic cows and near-wild mares as questionable, but also questioning, icons of womanhood who are randomly and illegally skinned and quartered by creole men who do not know how to appreciate their true value. Appreciation for the womanized Other begins only when the wild dogs and vultures (the outlaw creole males we hear about later on in the text) begin to consume a female prey which Spanish creoles had reserved for themselves.

Through listing the flaws of the transatlantic system beta Spanish creole males face up to the excesses of the alpha Spanish machos. The creole coming to grips with the Spanish abuses of power, property, and propriety bring to the surface a creole conscience in cahoots with the true native values of America and of the Americans. Such a conscientization also promotes mixed transatlantic exchanges at both the human and cultural level.

Suárez de Peralta's text renders the gendered allegory of the rampant and disorderly exploitation of the New World by Spanish males, while he and his creole class stand by like sissies who identify with the feminized image of the exploited Americas and the Americans. In a more concrete fashion, the ill-fated nature of the early gold and silver fevers gives way to the equally senseless slaughter of meek cows or the haphazard domestication of rebellious mares.

Through the awareness of all of these mismanaged imperial projects and transatlantic projections, sissified Americas/Americans come into their own by way of a creole-led reassessment of their traditionally bully-to-sissy exchange. Perhaps both culturally and economically speaking, there is more merit in the products and means of production of the "New World" than first met the Spanish eye. In Suárez de Peralta's case such a reassessment early on takes the form of a revisionist retelling of Hispano-Mexican history as misguided appropriation. The alliance between creole evaluation and native values corresponds to an economic strategy capable of countering old-fashioned colonialist appropriation with a nationalist outlook on international free trade. For instance, the proper exploitation of domesticated animals will ease the burden placed on human labor and thus free transatlantic citizens for more "civilized pursuits"—perhaps including each other (xiv).

As announced by the title, next in the text is a section concerning Indian "rites and habits" which Suárez de Peralta compares with the worst records in the world, including "el pecado contra natura" (18) [the sin against nature, that is, sodomy], but he places squarely on the shoulders of the colonized the responsibility for correction or for sharing the shame of such a record. The author signals the similarities between the Aztecs and other "primitive" cultures, such as the tribes of Israel and of Guinea. The Biblical comparison in itself must have been highly problematic for the Spanish Christians of the time, not to mention the allusion to Guinea, an African enclave enslaved by Spaniards who were at least as cruel as the Aztecs were viewed to be. But nothing prepared the creoles for the tacit comparisons made by the author to the sixteenth-century "rites" enacted by the Peninsular authorities against their creole charges. In order to prepare his audience for the sissy nationalist trick, the author selects the Cortés

legacy of exploitation, iconized in the title and the text as the return of
Martín Cortés. This "case" of exploitation is investigated, endorsed, and/or
rejected by equally incompetent creoles who act like sissies—with positive
and negative results. I will illustrate this with a synopsis of several passages.

1. On the one hand Moctezuma emerges as the bad sissy: betrayer of his
own people—the text calls him "pusillanimous, chicken, whore, [whose]
cowardice and fear made you sell your kingdom and power to the Spaniards" (116). On the other hand, Marina or La Malinche, Hernán Cortés's confidante, translator, and presumably her people's traitor, becomes
a curious icon of compromise—secret holder of power within pretended
submissiveness, in short, a good sissy. Creoles will mimic her strategy as
confidants, translators, and presumably betrayers of the Spanish ways.

2. The text alludes to the possibility that Martín Cortés, a descendant of
the original colonizer, has killed his wife in a Mexican port, right before
the viceroy of New Spain, Luis de Velasco, comes to greet this illustrious
representative of Spain. In spite of being sick Velasco "went on to the port
to greet him [Cortés], carrying a banner all the way into the reception
room, where they asked for each other's hands and they embraced, arguing who would take the right side [the traditional leading or male side],
which finally went to the viceroy, who was too well educated not to yield"
(191–92).

3. With the excuse of celebrating Martín Cortés's arrival, a number of creoles transform Mexico City into a place of unspecified sexual and financial
debauchery. In spite of the attempts at cowboy-like games, the preferred
form of expression was a new form of carnival in which women are kept
at a safe distance; they remain spectators, prevented by their own mothers
from joining in these "libertades" (194) [liberties]. In the midst of these fes-
tivities creoles begin to call themselves "chicks" or "chickens" [Cuerpos de
Dios! Nosotros somos gallinas], thus symbolically acquiring, at the same
time, a consciousness of their sissiness and of the possibilities of pleasure
and restrictions on their freedom (195).

4. The creoles finally realize Martín Cortés's betrayal. They dress up,
rather ineffectually, to rebel against him. At the crucial moment they put a
poem inside Cortés's pants. The poem reads:

Por Marina, soy testigo,
ganó esta tierra un buen hombre,
y por otra deste nombre
la perderá quien yo digo (200)
[For Marina's sake, I serve as witness,

that a good man won this land,
and for another by the name Marina
what's his name will lose it.]

The original treachery by Marina repeats itself with Martín Cortés. Essentially Marina becomes "Martina" (a "Marinization," or feminization, of Martín) and the poem literarily and literally displaces his genitalia with a paper fetish pregnant with femininity. The nationalist creoles take revenge on the imperialistic creole Martín by transforming him into a bad sissy.

5. Two of the investigators of this presumed betrayal hide together under a bed in an all-male club in order to uncover the conspiracy to name Martín Cortés as viceroy. The individuals spied upon are two "brothers" who in fact have different last names: Alonso de Avila and Gil González.

6. What follows in the text is the trial and execution of the so-called brothers. I will give you a mere taste of the portrayal of Alonso de Avila's demise, which ranges from the punctilious description of his fashionable attire to the moment in which the executioner does him in, "atravesando los sesos y carne delicada" (218) [piercing his delicate brains and flesh]. The sentence having been read:

> empeçáronle á destilar las lágrimas de los ojos por el rostro abajo, que le tenía muy lindo, y él, que le curaba con mucho cuydado, era muy blanco y muy jentil hombre, y muy galán, tanto que le llamaban *dama*, porque ninguna por mucho que lo fuese tenía tanta cuenta de pulirse y andar en órden. (215)
> [the tears began to drip down his face, the very pretty face he had, and he, who took such good care of it, was such a white and gentle man, and so dashing, that they called him *lady*, because no lady, no matter how real, could rival him in the polish and care he lavished upon himself.]

The text completes the picture with the fact that this ladylike man could afford such a sissified activity, because of his money and class.[18] His brother's deportment before death is summarily dispatched by the author as markedly more contrived and predictably masculine, less theatrical and less interesting a show of cowardice. I sensed no condescension toward the presumably passive sissy; in fact, his feelings are simply less repressed, and thus more understandable, than those of his counterpart in life. The town, and I suspect the writer himself, is outraged by the death of the sissy as much or more than by the death of the sissy's macho-acting brother.

Nation in Suárez de Peralta's text, and more covertly in those of his contemporaries, is in the hands of the apparently submissive, ladylike martyrs of European civilization. For the sixteenth-century creole, more or less aware of the phallocentric imperial allure of power that he himself endured, the identification with a sissy mediator, be it the allegedly treacherous native Marina, that is, Malinche or La Chingada, or the cowardly Alonso de Avila, that is, El Chingado, is an understandable and welcome one. Fucker and fucked become one in the essentially colonial history of this continent.

The text ends with Spain's own ladylike courting and cavalier submission to England, iconized as the macho-buccaneer, Sir Francis Drake. In Suárez de Peralta's text, monarchist Spaniards enact the same passive sissy strategy of pretended submission that was previously reserved for natives and creoles: pretend to be a lady, even if you have to lay down and be laid, cry and scratch, pull hairs, seduce, and betray—whatever the sissy has to do to win in the end.

Embodying Fin de Siglo Sissy

The aftershocks of the genitally/genetically "(mis)engineered" trauma of colonialism persist beyond the colonial and into the postcolonial era. Take, for instance, the overall 1992 construct of the counter-celebration of 1492. Conservative and liberal critics in the United States joined hands/brains/bodies/souls in order to project postcolonially displaced colonial guilt onto old Spanish colonialism—especially abundant in sadomasochistically titillating images of genocide and unruly and unplaceable performances of polyvalent libidinality. Only in such a narrow libidinal terrain have Spain, Spaniards, Spanish American, and U. S. Hispanics gained an upper hand. The Anglo-American-led exorcism of the quincentennial spirit has served mostly to emphasize Columbus's transatlantic guilt as a foreign sinner and an alien signifier, both of which represent backhanded compliments from the theoretical altars of purity to which the Anglo-puritan establishment remains married.

The critical gringo manipulation of other people's gender and sex continues to occur while sweeping their own under the blank rug of criticism. This reminds me of colonial times in which Spain manipulated, engendered, and sexualized to taste the transatlantic egg in equally discreet and auto-empowering fashion. Both my critical and my national primal scene suffer from the same unearthing vagaries. But I do not wish to become a victim of silence, any more than of objectivity, alienation, engenderment, or sexualization. I rather adopt a sissy lit-espick to bully my transnational identity as a U. S.-bred Latin American cultural critic into American national mainstream and theoretical platforms. Moreover, I intend to continue displaying scandalous contradictions—seemingly transgendered and transexual, in my handling of power.

Notes

I read a preliminary version of this paper under the same title at the 1992 Entralogos Conference at Cornell University. I also read an expanded version of section 6 of this paper under the title "A Spanish Fly in the American Naval Force" at the 1993 meeting of the Renaissance Society of America. I am grateful to Kate Bloodgood and Alejandra Molina for their most helpful comments on the present manuscript.

1   At some point in our lives some bully deems us a sissy, whether we are gay or straight men. Women appear less susceptible to this label, probably because according to the bullies every woman is inherently a sissy. I could also argue that "femme" (female/feminine/effeminate acting) lesbians might be automatically considered as "sissies" by some—particularly by machos who feel these women are afraid, but dying, to be "had." These are likely the same machos who find or manufacture sissy men "dying to be had." Naturally all of the above sorts of individuals could potentially become bullies—"even" straight women.

2   For me this pleasure principle owes as much to Sigmund Freud as to Karl Marx, as it fetishizes our sense of identity and value market but not according to the laws of supply and demand that enshrine the domination of the supplying of peoples or nations. The ruling pattern is one of a mutual dependency between the Self and the Others, one that is deeply rooted in our respective personal and national heritages. I am speaking chiefly of Freud's primal scene and Marx's dictatorship of the masses, both of which empower through shifting from a sense of domination—in Freud's case: Daddy's of Mommy's; in Marx's case: demands over supply—into a sense of belonging—in Freud's case: to a world of give and take; in Marx's case: to a world in which goods are evenly shared among all.

3   For background information on the paradoxical meaning of this celebration, see my "Literary Whiteness and the Afro-Hispanic Difference."

4   For a parallel strategy among straight women, see my "Poetics for the Hip."

5   According to my interpretation of this Freudian principle, in the process of confronting or fantasizing the "primal scene," a person unavoidably finds out about the lovemaking between a father figure and a mother figure which produced them; psychoanalytically speaking, it is the individual task to work through the traumatic birth of self as a colonial agent of a couple's traumatic encounter. What is true of the individual is also true of nations.

6   I discuss the sexual lives of Amazons and cannibals in "Loving Columbus."

7   To this date, the Spanish American tendency is to excuse sodomy in those who do not know better, want to do better, and/or are too far from the norm for either reform or contaminating the general public. The Hispanic fantasy of sodomy is so strong that the rule is to nominally attribute homosexuality to sodomy and to distinguish between the two sodomitic roles: *bugarrón* being the hole-making buggerer—a dubious form of mas-

culinity, but a form, nonetheless—and *maricón* being the anally "pierced" "Mary Ann." Largely only the *maricón* is sissified by his homosexuality; in many cases the *bugarrón* is not even considered a homosexual at all. Women are "naturally" excluded from this see-saw of power and desire, which is ostensibly why Spanish observers of the New World prescribe that lesbians must be hermaphroditic if they are to have "real" sex with one another. For a further discussion of this subjects, see my "Loving Columbus."

8   See *The Queer Nation Manifesto* 1989, and the Women's Liberation Movement pamphlet, *The Bitch Manifesto* 1972. I am grateful to Gema Pérez for locating these texts.

9   Translation is mine. For another English version, see *The Conquest of New Spain*. Trans. J. M. Cohen. Harmondsworth, Middlesex: Penguin, 1963. 297.

10 The Caribs' association with cannibalism may have been enhanced by their aggressive, warlike behavior or it may simply be a matter of linguistic coincidence between the names. Furthermore, Carib means "aggressive" or "warlike" in Arawak. Likewise, the association of Caribs with "doglike" homosexual sodomitic behavior may have been prompted by the practice of cranial flattening which elongated their faces, producing what Spaniards might have perceived as doglike features.

11 My translation, as are all others from this text. There is an earlier translation: Edward Gaylor Bourne, *Columbus, Ramon Pané and the Beginnings of American Anthropology* (Worcester, 1906). In the Italian manuscript (a transcription from the lost Spanish original), it reads *gioie*, "jewels," which also suggests "joys." José Juan Arrom insists that this is a misreading of *güeyo*, which he translates as "grass," perhaps implying "tobacco." Whether we accept the connotation jewels, joys, or grass, the sentence refers to spouses, traditional "passive" agents (women or sissies) who take a/the joy out of macho life. Indeed Amerigo Vespucci and others suggest that tobacco was used by women to control pleasure, including topical genital stimulation and/or punishment. See Arrom n. 3, 57.

12 For the background on this subject, see Sigmund Freud, "On the Transformation of Instincts with Special Reference to Anal Eroticism," and "The Acquisition of Power over Fire"—the second of which expands on the (in)famous footnote on the subject in Freud's own "Civilization and Its Discontents," 90.

13 Refer to Walter L. Williams's study of the remarkably parallel role of the berdache in North American Indian societies.

14 My translation, as are all others from this text.

15 My translation, as are all others from this text. Pages will be given parenthetically in the text, unless they come from the introduction as these do.

16 *Tratado del descubrimiento de las Yndias y su conquista, y los ritos y sacrifiçios, y costumbres de los yndios; y de los virreyes y gobernadores, que las han gobernado, espeçialmente en la Nueva España, y del suçeso del Marqués del Valle, segundo, Don Martin Cortés: del rebelion que se le ymputó y de las justiçias y muertes que hizieron en Mexico los Juezes comisarios que para ello fueron por su magestad; y del rompimiento de los yngleses, y del prinçipio que tuvo Francisco Draque para ser declarado enemigo.*

17 Not to mention that the author's father was likely Cortés's close friend and ally, who did not receive his proper "dues" from the conquest of New Spain. See Suárez de Peralta ix–x.

Works Cited

Anzaldúa, Gloria. *Borderlands/La Frontera. The New Mestiza*. San Francisco: Aunt Lute Books, 1987.

Columbus, Ferdinand. *Ferdinand Columbus: The Life of the Admiral Christopher Columbus*. Trans. Benjamin Keen. New Brunswick: Rutgers University Press, 1992.

Díaz del Castillo, Bernal. *Verdadera historia de la conquista de la Nueva España*. Madrid: Austral, 1976.

Freud, Sigmund. *The Standard Edition of the Complete Psychological Works of Sigmund Freud*. Trans. James Strachey. 23 vols. London: Hogarth Press and the Institute of Psychoanalysis, 1981. "From the History of an Infantile Neurosis" 17:7–103. "On Transformation of Instinct as Exemplified in Anal Eroticism" 17:127–33. "Civilization and Its Discontents" 21:59–145. "The Acquisition and Control of Fire" 22:185–93.

Ludmer, Josefina. "Tricks of the Weak." *Feminist Perspectives on Sor Juana Inés de la Cruz*. Detroit: Wayne University Press, 1990. 86–93.

Pané, Fray Ramón. *Relación acerca de las antigüedades de los Indios*. Ed. José Juan Arrom. Mexico: Siglo XXI, 1974.

Piedra, José. "Poetics for the Hip" *New Literary History* 22 (Summer 1991): 633–75.

———. "Literary Whiteness and the Afro-Hispanic Difference." *The Bounds of Race: Perspectives on Hegemony and Resistance*. Ed. Dominick La Capra. Ithaca: Cornell University Press, 1991. 278–310.

———. "Loving Columbus." *Amerindian Images and the Legacy of Columbus*. Ed. René Jara and Nicholas Spadaccini. Minneapolis and London: University of Minnesota, 1992. 230–65.

Sahagún, Fray Bernardino de. *Historia general de las cosas de la Nueva España*. Mexico: Porrúa, 1989.

Suárez de Peralta, Juan. *Noticias históricas de la Nueva España*. Madrid: M. G. Hernández, 1878.

Williams, Walter L. *The Spirit and the Flesh: Sexual Diversity in American Indian Culture*. Boston: Beacon Press, 1986.

Index

List of Contributors

Daniel Balderston is Professor of Spanish at Tulane University. His most recent books are *The Latin American Short Story: An Annotated Guide* (Greenwood Press, 1992) and *Out of Context: Historical Reference and the Representation of Reality in Borges* (Duke University Press, 1993). He is also the translator of Ricardo Piglia's *Artificial Respiration* (Duke University Press, 1994).

Arnaldo Cruz-Malavé is Associate Professor of Spanish at Fordham University in New York City. He is the author of *El primitivo implorante: El "sistema poético del mundo" de José Lezama Lima* (Amsterdam: Rodopi, 1994) and of numerous articles on Caribbean and U.S. Latino literature and culture. He is currently working on the construction of masculinity in Puerto Rican and U.S. Latino texts.

Brad Epps is Assistant Professor in Romance Languages and Literatures at Harvard University. Among his articles are studies of Ramón del Valle-Inclán, Juan Goytisolo, Carmen Martín Gaite, Juan Benet, Pedro Almodóvar, Jean Genet, Reinaldo Arenas, Augusto Monterroso, Witold Gombrowicz, and Hervé Guibert. His book, *Significant Violence: Oppression and Resistance in the Narrative of Juan Goytisolo*, is forthcoming from Oxford University Press. He is also preparing a study of melancholy and memory in contemporary Spanish literature.

Licia Fiol-Matta is Assistant Professor of Spanish and Latin American Cultures at Barnard College. Her current project is a book-length study of women and experimental texts in Latin America.

Mary S. Gossy is Associate Professor of Spanish and Comparative Literatures and Women's Studies at Rutgers University. She is author of *The Untold Story: Women and Theory in Golden Age Texts* (University of Michigan Press, 1989), *Freudian Slips: Woman, Writing, the Foreign Tongue* (forthcoming from Michigan, 1995), and articles on feminist theory, lesbian theory, psychoanalysis, and narrative.

Agnes I. Lugo-Ortiz is Assistant Professor of Spanish and Portuguese at Dartmouth College. She is the author of *Identidades imaginadas: Biografía y nacionalidad en Cuba* (forthcoming, University of Puerto Rico Press, 1996) and essays on Victoria Ocampo, Julian del Casal, José Marti, and René Marqués, among others.

Sylvia Molloy holds the Albert Schweitzer Chair of Humanities at New York University. Her most recent books are *At Face Value: Autobiographical Writing in Spanish America* (Cambridge University Press, 1991) and *Signs of Borges* (Duke University Press, 1994). She is coeditor of *Women's Writing in Latin America* (Westview Press, 1991) and author of the novel *En breve cárcel* [Certificate of Absence] (Seix Barral, 1981).

Oscar Montero is Professor of Spanish at Lehman College (CUNY) and the Graduate Center, and is a member of the board of the Center for Lesbian and Gay Studies at CUNY. He is author of *The Name Game: Writing/Fading Writer in "De donde son los cantantes"* (University of North Carolina Press, 1988) and *Erotismo y representación en Julian del Casal* (Rodopi, 1993).

José Piedra is Associate Professor in Romance Studies at Cornell University. He has written on race in Latin American culture, including "Literary Whiteness and the Afro-Hispanic Difference" in *The Bounds of Race* (Cornell University Press, 1991) and *Revelaciones/Revelations: Hispanic Art of Evanescence* (Cornell, 1994).

José Quiroga is Associate Professor of Spanish at George Washington University. His publications in Latin American literature include essays on Vicente Huidobro and Octavio Paz. He is currently working on Latin American Avant-Garde and Postmodern Poetry. The essay in this volume is based on a longer project tentatively titled *Sexualities in the Tropics of Revolution*.

David Román is Assistant Professor of English at the University of Washington in Seattle. His writings on theatre and performance have been published in *Theatre Journal, Genders,* and various anthologies. His book, *Acts of Invention: U.S. Theatre and Performance, Gay Men, and AIDS* is forthcoming from Indiana University Press. He serves on the editorial board of *GLQ: A Journal of Lesbian and Gay Studies.*

Jorge Salessi is Assistant Professor of Latin American Literature at the University of Pennsylvania and editor of *Hispanic Review.* He has published articles on immigration and nationalism, popular culture, transvestism, photography, and performance. He is currently finishing a book on Argentine notions of hygiene, criminology, and homosexuality entitled *Medics, Crooks, and Tango Queens.*

Suzanne Chávez Silverman is Assistant Professor at Pomona College. She has published articles on Latin American literature and U.S. Latino cultural studies. She is coeditor of *Tropicalizations: Transforming "Latinidad": Beyond Self and Other* (forthcoming from University of California Press).

Luz María Umpierre is a poet and author of critical studies of Puerto Rican literature, including *Ideología y novela en Puerto Rico: Un estudio de la narrativa de Zeno, Laguerre y Soto* (1983) and *Nuevas aproximaciones críticas a la literatura puertorriqueña contemporánea* (University of Puerto Rico, 1983). Her books of poetry, published by Third Woman Press, include *En el país de las maravillas* (1987), *—y otras desgracias* (1985), and *The Margarita Poems* (1987).

John K. Walsh was Professor of Spanish at the University of California, Berkeley, until his death from AIDS in 1990. As a Medievalist, he was known for his work in hagiography and the *Libro de buen amor.* With Billy Bussell Thompson, he published on homosexuality in the picaresque in "The Mercedarian's Shoes: Perambulations on the Fourth *Tratado* of *Lazarillo de Tormes*" *MLN* (1988). In addition to his articles on García Lorca's poetry and theatre, he completed a translation of the *Sonetos de amor oscuro.*

Yvonne Yarbro-Bejarano is Associate Professor of Spanish and Portuguese at Stanford University. She is the author of *Feminism and the Honor Plays of Lope de Vega* (Purdue University Press, 1994), has published numerous articles on Chicana/o literature, and is currently working on a book on Chicana/Latina cultural production.

Library of Congress Cataloging-in-Publication Data
Entiendes? : Queer Readings, Hispanic Writings / edited by
Emilie L. Bergmann and Paul Julian Smith.
p.   cm. — (Series Q)
Includes index.
ISBN 0-8223-1600-5 (cloth). — ISBN 0-8223-1615-3 (pbk.)
1. Spanish American literature—History and criticism.   2. Spanish literature
—History and criticism.   3. Homosexuality in literature.   4. Homosexuality
and literature—Latin America.   5. Homosexuality and literature—Spain.
I. Smith, Paul Julian.   II. Bergmann, Emilie L., 1949–   .   III. Series.
PQ7081.A1E59   1995
860.9′353—dc20   94-40313   CIP